Politics in the Republic of Ireland

While Ireland was once perceived as being characterised by conservatism, Catholicism and cultural isolation, by the first decades of the twenty-first century it had become a country of cultural vitality, economic dynamism, and rapid social change. Its politics reflected this new air of liveliness. New patterns of government formation, challenges to the established political parties, ever-deepening if sometimes ambivalent involvement in the process of European integration, and sustained discussion of gender issues were among these developments – along with evidence, revealed by several tribunals of inquiry, that Irish politics was not so free of corruption as many had assumed.

The Celtic Tiger phenomenon in the first years of the new century suggested that Ireland had found a miraculous recipe for rapid and unending economic growth, but the illusory nature of much of that supposed economic expansion was exposed by the crash that occurred in 2008 and the subsequent recession. This prompted a certain amount of questioning of the architecture of the political system: the phrase 'political reform' was widely employed in political debate, and even the recovery in the economy from 2014 onwards did not quell the discussion.

The fully revised sixth edition of *Politics in the Republic of Ireland* examines and explores all aspects of Irish politics in these interesting times. It builds on the reputation that the book has established following the publication of the first edition in 1992; since then it has become the standard textbook used for the teaching of Irish politics in universities in Ireland and further afield.

Politics in the Republic of Ireland combines real substance with a highly readable style. It is aimed particularly at undergraduates studying Irish politics, but will meet the needs of all those who are interested in knowing how politics and government operate in Ireland.

John Coakley is a Professor of Politics at Queen's University Belfast and Fellow of the Geary Institute for Public Policy at University College Dublin.

Michael Gallagher is Head of the Department of Political Science at Trinity College, University of Dublin.

'Quite simply this is the best introduction to modern Irish politics that has ever been produced. The editors have assembled an impressive cast of the relevant experts on all the expected themes. Now in its sixth edition this book just keeps getting better and better.'

Paul Mitchell, *London School of Economics, UK*

'*Politics in the Republic of Ireland* is the place to start for an understanding of Irish politics. This lively new up-to-date sixth edition confirms the book's place at the top of any reading list.'

R. Kenneth Carty, *University of British Columbia, Canada*

'This is the most comprehensive, authoritative and insightful guide to the Irish political system and the forces which shape it. There is, quite simply, no better textbook on Irish politics. No student or scholar of contemporary Ireland should be without a copy.'

Mary C. Murphy, *University College Cork, Ireland*

Politics in the Republic of Ireland

Sixth Edition

**Edited by John Coakley and
Michael Gallagher**

LONDON AND NEW YORK

Sixth edition published 2018
by Routledge
2 Park Square, Milton Park, Abingdon, Oxon OX14 4RN

and by Routledge
711 Third Avenue, New York, NY 10017

Routledge is an imprint of the Taylor & Francis Group, an informa business

First edition published by PSAI Press 1992
Fifth edition published by Routledge in association with PSAI Press 2010

British Library Cataloguing in Publication Data
A catalogue record for this book is available from the British Library

Library of Congress Cataloging in Publication Data
Names: Coakley, John, editor. | Gallagher, Michael, 1951- editor.
Title: Politics in the Republic of Ireland / edited by John Coakley and
Michael Gallagher.
Description: Sixth Edition. | New York : Routledge, 2018. | "First edition
published by PSAI Press 1992"–T.p. verso. | "Fifth edition published by Routledge
in association with PSAI Press 2010"–T.p. verso. | Includes bibliographical
references and index.
Identifiers: LCCN 2017028447| ISBN 9781138119444 (hardback) | ISBN
9781138119451 (paperback) | ISBN 9781315652313 (ebook)
Subjects: LCSH: Ireland–Politics and government–1949-
Classification: LCC JN1415 .P65 2018 | DDC 320.9417–dc23
LC record available at https://lccn.loc.gov/2017028447

ISBN: 978-1-138-11944-4 (hbk)
ISBN: 978-1-138-11945-1 (pbk)
ISBN: 978-1-315-65231-3 (ebk)

Typeset in Times New Roman
by Deanta Global Publishing Services, Chennai, India

Contents

Figures

Tables

Boxes

Contributors

Fiona Buckley is a lecturer in the Department of Government and Politics, University College Cork, where she specialises in gender politics and Irish politics. Her gender and politics research focuses on women in cabinet government, executive leadership, gender quotas and candidate selection. She is co-editor of *Politics and Gender in Ireland: The Quest for Political Agency* (London, 2015).

John Coakley, MRIA, is a Professor of Politics at Queen's University Belfast and Fellow of the Geary Institute for Public Policy at University College Dublin. His research interests include nationalism, ethnic conflict and Irish and Northern Irish politics. Recent publications include *Nationalism, Ethnicity and the State: Making and Breaking Nations* (London, 2012), *Reforming Political Institutions: Ireland in Comparative Perspective* (Dublin, 2013), *Breaking Patterns of Conflict: Britain, Ireland and the Northern Ireland Question* (co-edited, London, 2015) and *Non-Territorial Autonomy in Divided Societies: Comparative Perspectives* (edited, London, 2017).

Kevin Cunningham is a lecturer in statistics at Dublin Institute of Technology. He has written a number of articles published in peer-reviewed journals and contributed to a number of academic titles on voting behaviour, electoral campaigns and public policy. He has also worked for political parties in the UK, Ireland and Australia in a strategic capacity and runs his own political polling company, 'Ireland Thinks', which regularly features in broadcast, radio and newspapers in Ireland.

David M. Farrell, MRIA, holds the Chair of Politics at University College Dublin, where he is the Head of the School of Politics and International Relations. His recent books include *Political Parties and Democratic Linkage: How Parties Organise Democracy* (co-author, Oxford, 2011), *The Act of Voting: Identities, Institutions and Locale* (co-editor, London, 2016) and *A Conservative Revolution? Electoral Change in Twenty-First-Century Ireland* (co-editor, Oxford, 2017). He is currently completing a co-edited book-length study of the 2016 Irish general election.

Michael Gallagher, MRIA, is Head of the Department of Political Science and Professor of Comparative Politics at Trinity College, University of Dublin. He is co-author or co-editor of *Representative Government in Modern Europe* (5th ed., New York, 2011), *The Politics of Electoral Systems* (Oxford, 2008), *Days of Blue Loyalty: The Politics of Membership of the Fine Gael Party* (Dublin, 2002) and a number of books in the *How Ireland Voted* series. In 1989 he devised the least squares index, the standard measure of electoral system disproportionality.

Yvonne Galligan is Professor of Comparative Politics and Director of the Centre for Advancement of Women in Politics at Queens University, Belfast. Her recent books include

States of Democracy: Gender and Politics in the European Union (editor, London, 2015) and *Women and Politics in Ireland: The Quest for Political Agency* (co-editor, London, 2015). She co-authored the report *Gender equality in power and decision-making* (EIGE, 2015) and authored the *Markievicz Report on implementation of candidate gender quotas in the Fianna Fáil Party* (Fianna Fáil, 2014).

Lee Komito is Associate Professor in the School of Information and Communication Studies at University College Dublin. He is author of *The Information Revolution and Ireland: Prospects and Challenges* (Dublin, 2004). He publishes on clientelism and information networks; e-participation, inclusion and social movements; and migration and transnational communities. His current research examines new social media, migration and identity.

Brigid Laffan is Director and Professor at the Robert Schuman Centre for Advanced Studies and Director of the Global Governance Programme, European University Institute (EUI), Florence.

Michael Marsh, MRIA, is an Emeritus Professor of Political Science at Trinity College Dublin. The author of a wide variety of articles on electoral behaviour, he has co-edited each of the last five books in the *How Ireland Voted* series, and has been a principal investigator for the Irish National Election Study since its foundation. He was co-author or co-editor of several books arising out of those studies: *The Irish Voter* (Manchester, 2008), *A Conservative Revolution?* (Oxford, 2017) and *The Post-Crisis Irish Voter* (Manchester, 2018).

Shane Martin is Reader in Comparative Politics in the Department of Government, University of Essex. His research focuses on how electoral incentives shape representatives' preferences, legislative organisation, and executive oversight. Recent research by him has appeared in *Comparative Political Studies*, the *British Journal of Political Science*, *Electoral Studies*, *Irish Political Studies*, *Legislative Studies Quarterly* and *Political Research Quarterly*. He is co-editor of the *Oxford Handbook of Legislative Studies* (Oxford, 2014) and *Parliaments and Government Formation: Unpacking Investiture Rules* (Oxford, 2015).

Gary Murphy is Professor of Politics and Head of the School of Law and Government at Dublin City University. He has published extensively on Irish politics and on the regulation of lobbying. He has held visiting professorships at the University of North Carolina, Chapel Hill, and at the University of Notre Dame. His latest book is *Electoral Competition in Ireland since 1987: The Politics of Triumph and Despair* (Manchester, 2016).

Eoin O'Malley is a Senior Lecturer in the School of Law and Government, Dublin City University, where he is also Director of the MSc in Public Policy. He has written over 30 articles published in peer-reviewed journals, and is co-editor of three books on Irish politics. These are *Irish Political Studies Reader* (London, 2008), *Governing Ireland* (Dublin, 2012) and *One Party Dominance: Fianna Fáil and Irish Politics, 1926–2016* (London, 2017). Eoin is also the author of a textbook, *Contemporary Ireland* (Basingstoke, 2011).

Kevin Rafter is Professor of Political Communication and Head of the School of Communications at Dublin City University. He is Chairperson of the Compliance Committee of the Broadcasting Authority of Ireland and was the independent rapporteur to the talks that led to the formation of Ireland's minority coalition in 2016. He is co-editor of *Political Advertising in the 2014 European Parliament Elections* (London, 2017). Prior to 2008, he worked as a senior political journalist with the *Irish Times, Sunday Times* and *Sunday Tribune*, and presented RTÉ's *This Week* radio programme.

Richard Sinnott, MRIA, is Professor Emeritus in the School of Politics and International Relations at University College Dublin. His publications include *Irish Voters Decide: Voting Behaviour in Elections and Referendums since 1918* (1995), *People and Parliament in the European Union: Participation, Democracy and Legitimacy* (co-author, 1998), *Public Opinion and Internationalized Governance* (co-editor, 1995) and *The Irish Voter: The Nature of Electoral Competition in the Republic of Ireland* (co-author, 2008).

Ben Tonra is Full Professor of International Relations at the University College Dublin School of Politics and International Relations. From UCD he teaches, researches and publishes in European foreign, security and defence policy, Irish foreign and security policy and international relations theory. He has most recently been co-editor of, and contributor to, *The International Relations and Foreign Policy of the European Union* (London, 2017), *The Handbook of European Union Foreign Policy* (London, 2015) and *Irish Foreign Policy* (Dublin, 2012).

Liam Weeks is a lecturer in the Department of Government and Politics, University College Cork. His research interests include elections and electoral systems. He is co-author of *All Politics is Local: A Guide to Local Elections in Ireland* (Cork, 2009), co-editor of *Radical or Redundant? Minor Parties in Irish Political Life* (Dublin, 2012) and author of *Independents in Irish Party Democracy* (Manchester, 2017).

Preface to the sixth edition

The first edition of *Politics in the Republic of Ireland* was published in 1992, and since that time the book has been extensively used as a textbook on Irish Politics courses in universities and colleges in Ireland and elsewhere. It is worth quoting from the preface to the first edition to remind new readers of the thinking behind the original venture:

> The aim throughout has been to produce a book that combined real substance and a readable style. It is aimed particularly at undergraduates at third-level institutions, but we hope that it will also meet the needs of the wider public interested in the politics and government of Ireland. In addition, since no country's politics can be understood in isolation, the authors have written their chapters with a comparative (especially a western European) dimension very much in mind. The venerable generalisation that 'Ireland is different', so there is no need to make the effort to compare its politics with those of other countries, is no longer adequate. It is a well-worn observation that Ireland has become a more outward-looking country since the 1950s, and its academic community has not been unaffected by this development. *Politics in the Republic of Ireland* is among the fruits of these broader horizons.

Evidently, this formula found favour with readers, so a second edition was produced in 1993, a third followed in 1999, a fourth in 2005, a fifth in 2010, and the appearance of the current edition reflects continued demand for a comprehensive textbook on Irish politics.

When a book runs into a sixth edition, it is tempting to reflect that it has proved itself to be a successful product and to conclude that it requires only minor tinkering to retain its position in the market. However, authors and editors have resisted any such temptation, and we have been determined to ensure that this 2018 edition of *Politics in the Republic of Ireland* is as fresh as the first edition was in 1992. Multi-edition textbooks run the risk of acquiring a patchwork character, with up-to-date facts and figures slotted somewhat uncomfortably into a framework that was appropriate a decade or two ago. We have been determined not to see *Politics in the Republic of Ireland* suffer this fate of death by a thousand updates, and any reader who chooses to compare the sixth edition with its precursors will immediately notice the extent of the changes. The many recent upheavals in the political party system, voting behaviour, patterns of public policy making, constitutional development and political culture require, and receive, due analysis.

Needless to say, each of the chapters has been thoroughly revised, not merely by being updated but, where appropriate, by being reorganised and generally refreshed. A number of new contributors have been recruited as authors or co-authors, and they have been as patient and cooperative as the *in situ* contributors in dealing with the editors' many requests. In response to suggestions from users of the book, a new chapter on the media and politics has been added.

As with previous editions, a number of people have helped by giving their comments on individual chapters or in other ways, and we would like to thank them all. Feedback from student users at a variety of institutions has been helpful in suggesting ideas to strengthen the book.

We would also like to thank Routledge's editorial team of Andrew Taylor and Sophie Iddamalgoda for their expeditious shepherding of the typescript towards publication. Our hope is that this sixth edition of *Politics in the Republic of Ireland* will contribute to a fuller understanding of the endlessly fascinating Irish political process.

John Coakley and Michael Gallagher
Dublin, July 2017

Glossary

Áras an Uachtaráin (*aw*-rus un *ook*-ta-rawn) – residence of the president

ard-fheis (ord-*esh*) – national convention [of a political party]

Bunreacht na hÉireann (*bun*-rokt ne *hay*run) – constitution of Ireland

Cathaoirleach (ka-*heer*-luck) – chairperson (of the Senate)

Ceann Comhairle (kyon *kohr*-le) – speaker or chairperson (of the Dáil)

Clann na Poblachta (clon ne *pub*-lak-ta) – 'party of the republic' (party name, 1946–65)

Clann na Talmhan (clon ne *tal*-oon) – 'party of the land' (party name, 1939–65)

comhairle ceantair (*koh*-er-le *kyon*-ter) – district council (in Fianna Fáil)

comhairle dáilcheantair (*koh*-er-le *dawl*-kyon-ter) – constituency council (in Fianna Fáil)

cumann (*kum*-man) – branch [of a political party or other organisation]; plural **cumainn** (*kum*-min)

Cumann na nGaedheal (*kum*-man ne *ngale*) – 'party of the Irish' (party name, 1923–33)

Dáil Éireann (dawl *ay*-run) – national assembly of Ireland; plural **Dála** (*daw*-la)

Éire (*ay*-reh) – Ireland

Fianna Fáil (*fee*-an-a *fawl*) – 'soldiers of Ireland' (party name)

Fine Gael (*fin*-a *gale*) – 'Irish race' (party name)

Gaeltacht (*gale*-tuckt) – Irish-speaking districts

garda [síochána] (*gawr*-da shee-*kaw*-ne) – (civic) guard, policeman; plural **gardaí** (*gawr*-dee)

Leinster House – seat of parliament

Oireachtas (*ih*-rock-tus) – parliament

Saorstát Éireann (*sayr*-stawt *ay*-run) – Irish Free State

Seanad Éireann (*sha*-nad *ay*-run) – senate of Ireland

Sinn Féin (shin *fayn*) – 'ourselves' (party name)

Tánaiste (*taw*-nish-deh) – deputy prime minister

Taoiseach (*tee*-shuck) – prime minister; plural **Taoisigh** (*tee*-she)

Teachta Dála (*tak*-tuh *dawl*-uh) – Dáil deputy, TD; plural **Teachtaí Dála** (tak-tuh daw-la)

Uachtarán (*ook*-ta-rawn) – president

Note: A number of the party names above have a range of alternative translations; see John Coakley, 'The significance of names: the evolution of Irish party labels', *Études Irlandaises*, 5, 1980, pp. 171–81. The pronunciation system indicated above is approximate only, and follows in part that in Howard Penniman and Brian Farrell (eds), *Ireland at the Polls: A Study of Four General Elections* (Durham, NC: Duke University Press, 1987), pp. 265–6. Italics indicate stressed syllables.

Acronyms

AAA	Anti-Austerity Alliance
BAI	Broadcasting Authority of Ireland
BBC	British Broadcasting Corporation
C&AG	Comptroller and Auditor General
CIC	Citizens Information Centre
CRG	Constitution Review Group
DUP	Democratic Unionist Party
ECB	European Central Bank
ESB	Electricity Supply Board
EU	European Union
FF	Fianna Fáil
FG	Fine Gael
GDP	Gross Domestic Product
IBEC	Irish Business and Employers Confederation
ICTU	Irish Congress of Trade Unions
IFA	Irish Farmers Association
IMF	International Monetary Fund
INES	Irish National Election Study
IRA	Irish Republican Army
IRB	Irish Republican Brotherhood
JAAB	Judicial Appointments Advisory Board
MP	Member of Parliament
NATO	North Atlantic Treaty Organisation
NESC	National Economic and Social Council
OECD	Organisation for Economic Cooperation and Development
PBP	People Before Profit
PDs	Progressive Democrats
PPG	parliamentary party group
PR	proportional representation
RTÉ	Raidió Teilefís Éireann
SC	Supreme Court
SDLP	Social Democratic and Labour Party (Northern Ireland)
SF	Sinn Féin
STV	single transferable vote
TD	Teachta Dála (member of the Dáil)
UN	United Nations

Part I
The context of Irish politics

1   The foundations of statehood

John Coakley

Most states recognise a dramatic landmark event as a formative moment in their history. For the United States, it is Independence Day (4 July), commemorating the declaration of independence in 1776; for France, Bastille Day (14 July), recalling the storming of a notorious prison in Paris, a crucial event of the Revolution in 1789; for Norway, Constitution Day (17 May), marking the adoption of Norway's first constitution in 1814, following separation from Denmark. While a number of dates could be selected in the Irish case, one has a particular resonance: Easter 1916.

In early 2016, to mark the centenary of the Easter Rising, the government organised a lavish set of public events and ceremonies, forming part of a *de facto* assertion of ownership of the heritage of 1916 (White and Marnane, 2016). This commemoration highlighted the birth of the state, and draws attention to the starting point of this introductory chapter, and a recurring theme in the rest of this book: to what extent has contemporary Irish politics been conditioned by history, and, more specifically, by the relationship with Great Britain? Although political histories of Ireland often start at 1922, and conventional wisdom stresses the 'new era' that then began, it is clear that centuries of British rule left a deep imprint. Significant elements of continuity underlay the sharp political break that took place at the time that the state was founded. Before looking at the establishment of the state itself and at subsequent developments, then, the first section of this chapter examines the legacy of the old regime (for accessible general histories, see Moody and Martin, 2011; Cronin and O'Callaghan, 2015; for the contemporary period, Bew, 2007; Jackson, 2010). The second section discusses the political background to the establishment of the independent Irish state. The third section analyses the political themes of the post-independence period, linking them with earlier developments.

The legacy of British rule

The emergence of the modern state in Ireland was shaped by intervention from the neighbouring island in medieval times. Prior to this, Gaelic Irish society, though attaining a high degree of cultural, artistic and literary development in the early medieval period, had shown few signs of following the path of early European state formation. The Norman invasions that began in 1169, and the establishment of the Lordship of Ireland that followed (with the Norman King of England exercising the functions of Lord of Ireland), marked the beginning of rudimentary statehood. Although Norman or English control was little more than nominal for several centuries, the vigorous Tudor dynasty subjugated the island in the sixteenth century, a process whose beginning was marked by the promotion in 1541 of the Lord of Ireland to the status of King. The Kingdom of Ireland continued thereafter to have its own political institutions, though a much more profound degree of British influence followed the passing of the Act of Union in 1800, which created a new state, the United Kingdom of Great Britain and Ireland (UK).

The story of Irish resistance to these processes is well known (see English, 2007). The rebellion spearheaded by the Ulster Gaelic leaders O'Neill and O'Donnell in 1594–1603, the resistance of an alliance of Gaelic and Anglo–Norman forces to Cromwellian government in 1641–50, under the umbrella of the 'Confederation of Kilkenny', and the military alliance of (mainly Catholic) Irish supporters of the deposed King James II in 1689–92, each ended in defeat. After each of these episodes, the position of the Gaelic Irish population and its allies of Norman origin was worse than before, as the victors colonised increasingly large swathes of native land. Penal laws directed against Catholics completed the process of marginalising this formerly rebellious population: its leaders either conformed to the established Protestant church, fled to the continent or risked sinking into social and political obscurity in Ireland. The main legacy of this collective experience was a fusion of religious and political interests that was of huge importance when it resurfaced again in the form of Irish nationalism in the nineteenth century. A nationalist interpretation of Irish history was able to make full use of these events in constructing an image of unrelenting resistance to English rule, with the United Irish rebellion of 1798 (notwithstanding its very different character, and roots in the ideology of the French revolution) added to the list.

The primary focus in this chapter is, however, not on Irish resistance but on the relatively neglected issue of pre-1922 state building. In looking at the legacy of the old system of government to independent Ireland, we may identify three areas in which spillover effects were important. First, at the *constitutional* level, certain roles and offices that had evolved over the centuries provided an important stepping stone for the builders of the new state. Second, at the *administrative* level, the development of a large civil service bequeathed to the new state a body of trained professional staff. Third, at the *political* level, a set of traditions and practices had been established in the decades before 1922 that greatly reduced the learning curve for those involved in the making of independent Ireland.

The constitution of the old regime

In an era when travel was slow, difficult and dangerous, it was neither sensible nor practical for expanding dynasties to seek to govern all of their territories directly. In common with the peripheral areas of other medieval monarchies, then, Norman Ireland acquired a set of political institutions that gradually evolved into modern ones. The hub around which political life revolved, at least in theory, was the King's personal representative in Ireland, an officer to whom the term 'Lord Lieutenant' was eventually applied. The Lord Lieutenant was advised on everyday affairs of government by a 'Privy Council' made up of his chief officials, and on longer-term matters, by a 'Great Council' or parliament that met irregularly.

The evolution of the Irish Parliament followed a path similar to that of the English Parliament (see Johnston-Liik, 2002). It first met in Castledermot, Co Kildare, in 1264, and for the next four centuries, it continued to assemble from time to time in various Irish towns, with Dublin increasingly becoming dominant. By 1692, it had acquired the shape that it was to retain up to 1800, resembling closely its English counterpart. Its House of Commons consisted of 300 members (two each from 32 counties, from 117 cities, towns or boroughs, and from Trinity College, Dublin), and its House of Lords of a small but variable number: archbishops and bishops of the established (Protestant) Church of Ireland and lay members of the Irish peerage. The Act of Union of 1800 abolished this parliament, creating instead a merged or 'united' parliament for all of Great Britain and Ireland. In the new House of Commons, there were to be 100 Irish MPs (about 15 per cent of the total), while the House of Lords would receive 32 additional members: the Irish peerage would elect 28 of its number for life, and four Irish Protestant bishops would sit in the House of Lords in rotation.

Although the legislative branch of government thus disappeared completely from Ireland, the executive branch did not. Throughout the entire period of the union (1800–1922), the existence of a 'Government of Ireland' was recognised – a critical weakness in the scheme for Irish integration with Britain (Ward, 1994: 30–8). The Lord Lieutenant, as representative of the sovereign, was formal head of this government (see Gray and Purdue, 2012). This post was always filled by a leading nobleman who, in addition to his governmental functions, was 'the embodiment of the "dignified" aspects of the state, the official leader of Irish social life' (McDowell, 1964: 52). He left the day-to-day running of the process of government, however, to his principal assistant, the Chief Secretary. This official had responsibility for the management of Irish affairs in the House of Commons and, although he was not always a member of the cabinet, he was at least a prominent member of the governing party. Between the late eighteenth and early twentieth centuries, effective power gradually passed from the Lord Lieutenant to the Chief Secretary, following the pattern of a similar shift in power in Britain from the King to the Prime Minister. The Lord Lieutenant's official residence, the Viceregal Lodge in the Phoenix Park, Dublin, has now become the President's residence, Áras an Uachtaráin, while the Chief Secretary's Office in Dublin Castle went on to become the core of the Department of the Taoiseach.

Even after the union, Ireland remained constitutionally distinct from the rest of the UK. Although all legislation was now enacted through the UK parliament, in many policy areas (including education, agriculture, land reform, policing, health and local government) separate legislation was enacted for the different components of the United Kingdom (Hoppen, 2016). For example, the parliament of 1880–85 passed 71 acts whose application was exclusively Irish (out of a total of 422 acts, the rest being 'English', 'Scottish', 'United Kingdom' or other). Electoral reforms illustrate the extent to which Ireland was treated in a distinctive way, even in the matter of representation at Westminster: it was only in 1884 that a uniform electoral law was adopted for all parts of the UK. But Ireland was not just constitutionally distinct within the United Kingdom. It was governed in practice in a quasi-colonial manner, under a British-dominated elite in Dublin Castle; Irish-born Catholics were perceived as 'second-class (and potentially disloyal) citizens', even into the twentieth century (Campbell, 2009: 305).

The question of electoral reform has a central place in the process of constitutional evolution. It has been assumed, since the late nineteenth century, that democratic elections to parliamentary chambers designed to represent the people have four characteristics, and these are frequently written into modern constitutions: voting is *direct*, the process is *secret*, all votes are of *equal* weight and suffrage is *universal*. Elections to the old Irish House of Commons, and to its post-union successor, always operated on the basis of direct voting: electors selected their members of parliament without the intervention of any intermediate electoral college, so the first of the four conditions was not an issue.

The second condition was met rather later. Traditionally, voting was open: a public poll was conducted at a central place in the constituency, and voters declared publicly the names of the candidates for whom they wished their votes to be recorded. This obviously permitted intimidation by opinion leaders such as landlords and clergy, but the Ballot Act (1872) abruptly and permanently changed these practices: in future, voting was to be carried out by secret ballot, except in the case of illiterates and other incapacitated persons.

Third, in the old Irish House of Commons, voters' voices were of unequal weight; large counties (such as Cork) and small boroughs (such as Tulsk, Bannow and Ardfert) were represented by two MPs each, with complete disregard for their greatly varying populations. This position was rectified in three principal stages. In 1800, the smaller boroughs were abolished at the time of the Act of Union; in 1885, all seats were redistributed to conform more closely to the distribution of the population; and in 1922, the new constitution guaranteed that all votes would be equal.

Fourth, although in many countries extension of the right to vote was characterised by a number of major reforms and the proportion enfranchised increased in stages, the process in Ireland was more complex. This may be seen in Box 1.1. The most sweeping early changes were the extension of the right to vote to Catholics (1793) and the abolition of the county 'forty-shilling freehold' (1829), one greatly extending, the other greatly reducing the electorate (the 1829 change coincided with Catholic emancipation, a legal change that permitted Catholics to sit in the House of Commons, following a vigorous campaign led by Daniel O'Connell). The reforms of 1832, 1850 and 1868 (unlike the English reforms of 1832 and 1867) were rather less far-reaching. The major reforms were those of 1884, associated with the birth of modern politics in Ireland; 1918, linked to another episode of electoral revolution; and 1923, which completed the process (for an illustration of the impact of these reforms on the proportion of the population entitled to vote, see Figure 1.1 and discussion below).

Box 1.1 Extension of voting rights, 1793–1973

Act	Major effect
Catholic Relief Act, 1793	Extension of right to vote to Catholics
Parliamentary Elections (Ireland) Act, 1829	Restriction of right to vote in counties to those with a valuation of £10 (increased from £2)
Representation of the People (Ireland) Act, 1832	Minor extension of right to vote
Representation of the People (Ireland) Act, 1850	Significant extension of right to vote in counties
Representation of the People (Ireland) Act, 1868	Extension of right to vote in boroughs
Representation of the People Act, 1884	Extension of right to vote in counties and boroughs to male householders and lodgers
Representation of the People Act, 1918	Universal male and limited female suffrage
Electoral Act, 1923	Universal suffrage
Electoral (Amendment) Act, 1973	Reduction of voting age from 21 to 18

Emergence of state bureaucracy

Underneath the political superstructure of the Irish government, the modern Irish civil service developed slowly but steadily (for the classic study, see McDowell, 1964). It consisted of a number of departments, offices and other agencies employing considerable numbers of officials and established from time to time as the need was seen to arise. Formal control of these bodies was normally collegial rather than individual: they were directed by 'boards' or 'commissions', generally overseen by the Chief Secretary. There were 29 of these bodies by 1911, employing a staff of several thousand (see Box 1.2).

Box 1.2 Civil service continuity, 1914–24

Board/agency in 1914	Location in 1924 (department)
United Kingdom government departments in Ireland:	
Revenue Commissioners	Department of Finance
Registrar of Friendly Societies	
Ordnance Survey	
Ministry of Transport	Department of Industry and Commerce
Board of Trade	
Post Office	Department of Posts and Telegraphs
Irish government departments:	
General Prisons Board (1877)	Department of Justice
Public Record Office (1867)	
Registry of Deeds (1708)	
Commissioners of National Education (1831)	Department of Education
Board of Intermediate Education (1878)	
Local Government Board (1872)	Department of Local Government and
Registrar General's Office (1844)	Public Health
Department of Agriculture and Technical Instruction (1899)	Department of Lands and Agriculture
Land Commission (1881)	
Congested Districts Board (1891)	
Fisheries branches of Department of Agriculture and Congested Districts Board	Department of Fisheries

Note: A considerable number of additional boards and agencies have been omitted from this list. Two new departments, Defence and External Affairs, were formed *ab initio*. The Attorney General's Office was based on the offices of the former Attorney-General and Solicitor-General of Ireland, and incorporated also other offices. The Department of the President of the Executive Council was, in effect, based on the office of the Chief Secretary of Ireland.

In addition to these 'Irish' departments, answerable to the Chief Secretary, a number of departments of the London-based 'Imperial' civil service also had branches in Ireland. These were controlled ultimately by the relevant British cabinet ministers, and in some cases employed very large staffs in Ireland. They included the Irish Treasury, merged with its British counterpart in 1817, but re-appearing as a branch of the latter in 1870 (Fanning, 1978: 1–13). On the same post-Union integrationist logic, the old Irish revenue boards that survived the union were merged with their British counterparts following the Anglo–Irish customs amalgamation of 1823; they also acquired a considerable staff (McDowell 1964: 78–103). The post-Union Post Office (1785) was similarly merged with its British counterpart in 1831, and underwent rapid expansion in the late nineteenth century (Ferguson, 2016: 203–14). By 1911, these bodies, 11 in all, had about 24,000 employees in Ireland, of whom 20,000 worked in the Post Office.

By the beginning of the twentieth century, then, Ireland already had a very sizeable civil service, with about 27,000 employees spread over 29 Irish and 11 UK departments. In addition, there were large field staffs in certain other areas: two police forces, the Dublin Metropolitan Police (1787) with about 1,200 members and the Royal Irish Constabulary (1836) with about

10,700, and the body of national teachers, numbering some 15,600. Together, these amounted in 1911–13 to about 55,000 workers in what would now be described as the public sector, not including the large numbers of army and naval personnel stationed in Ireland (there were about 30,000 of these in 1911).

Notwithstanding its traditional domination by Protestants, a kind of 'greening' of the Irish civil service had been taking place steadily since the advent of open competition for recruitment to lower ranks in 1876, and a deliberate policy of appointing or promoting nationalist-oriented civil servants to senior ranks from 1892 onwards, at least under Liberal administrations (McBride, 1991; see also O'Halpin, 1987). But the upper ranks of the service continued to be disproportionately Protestant, with Catholics largely excluded from the more powerful positions by a kind of 'glass ceiling'. Thus, while the proportion of Catholics had risen to 61 per cent in the lower ranks of the civil service by 1911, Catholics accounted for only 37 per cent of the upper ranks; within the Royal Irish Constabulary at the same time, 70 per cent of lower ranks were Catholic, but among senior ranks, the proportion was only 9 per cent (Campbell, 2009: 298–300).

The system of local government was comprehensively overhauled in the nineteenth century (see Potter, 2011). Many of the smaller boroughs disappeared under the Act of Union, since their only effective function had been to return MPs to the Irish House of Commons. A report in 1835 showed that most of the 68 boroughs that survived were run by corporations which were oligarchic and self-perpetuating, that almost all were exclusively Protestant and that only one (Tuam) had a Catholic majority. In 1840, however, these bodies were swept away, and were replaced in the 10 largest cities by corporations elected on a limited franchise (some smaller towns were given elected 'commissioners' with minor powers). In rural areas, the principal authority was the county grand jury, made up of large property owners selected by the county sheriff (an official appointed, in turn, by the Lord Lieutenant) and responsible for most of the activities that we associate with county councils today. In a major reform in 1898, however, their administrative functions were transferred to new, elected, county councils. A lower tier of local government was also created at the same time. This built on a network of 'poor law unions' created in 1838, initially to provide help for the poor but later also to provide health care, and took the form of a set of rural and urban district councils. The only significant change in this system before independence was the introduction of proportional representation for council elections in 1920 (see Daly, 1997: 1–92).

The birth of modern party politics

Although the impression is sometimes given that modern forms of politics began in Ireland in 1922, or at the earliest with the foundation of Sinn Féin a few years before that, this is misleading. Modern party politics began in the 1880s, and had earlier roots. The growth of party politics in nineteenth century Ireland indeed follows closely a pattern of evolution identified elsewhere (Sartori, 1976: 18–24). Three phases in this growth may be identified; the transition between them was marked by significant changes in levels of electoral mobilisation.

In the first phase, political life was dominated by *parliamentary parties* (sometimes called cadre parties), groups of MPs without any kind of regular electoral organisation to provide support at election time. Insofar as parties existed before the 1830s, they fell into this category. These were not parties in any recognisably modern sense; instead, Irish MPs were linked to one or other of the two great English groupings, the Tories and the Whigs. Already during this period, however, the connection between the Tory party and the Protestant establishment was beginning to find expression in geographical terms, as Tories achieved a much stronger position in the north than in the south. This may be seen in Appendix 2a, which summarises the results of the 31 elections that took place under the Act of Union (because of the large number of uncontested elections, we have to rely on distribution of seats rather than of votes for an indication of party strengths). This point emerges even more clearly from Table 1.1, which is based on this appendix: in the ten elections before 1832, Tories already controlled 74 per cent of the seats in the present territory of Northern Ireland, but only 45 per cent of those in the south.

In the second phase, we see the appearance of *electoral parties*, consisting no longer of loosely linked sets of MPs but rather of groups standing for some more or less coherent policy positions and supported by constituency organisations that enjoyed a degree of continuity over time (see Hoppen, 1984). This phase began around 1830 and lasted for approximately five decades. It was characterised by the metamorphosis of the Whigs into the Liberal Party, which increasingly became the party of Catholic Ireland, and of the Tories into the Conservative Party, which quickly became the party of Protestants. The MPs of these parties were supported by organisations at constituency level, commonly labelled 'Independent Clubs' on the Liberal side and 'Constitutional Clubs' on the Conservative side. From a comparative perspective, this was unusual in two respects. First, constituency organisations developed at a remarkably early stage in the Irish case. Second, the content of the liberal–conservative polarisation, with its sectarian overtones, contrasted sharply with the issues at stake behind similarly named instances of polarisation elsewhere in Europe, where such issues as church–state conflict and constitutional modernisation were to the fore. In particular, the association between Catholicism and liberalism appears anomalous in a European context, where liberalism was associated with anticlericalism.

Given the fact that the electorate was restricted to the wealthy (who were disproportionately Protestant), Irish Conservatives, though reduced from their position of overall dominance (especially in the south, where they now controlled only 24 per cent of the seats), enjoyed solid support throughout most of this period. The relationship between the Liberals and the Catholic vote was, however, much less secure, and was open to challenge from parties representing specifically Irish interests. The most significant of these were O'Connell's Repeal Party in the 1830s and 1840s, the Independent Irish Party in the 1850s, the rather amorphous National Association in the 1860s and, most importantly, the Home Rule Party from the 1870s onwards.

The third phase was marked by the birth of modern *mass parties*. These were tightly disciplined parliamentary groups resting on the support of a permanent party secretariat and a well-oiled party machine: thousands of members were organised into branches at local level, with provision for constituency conventions to select candidates and for an annual conference to elect an executive and, at least in theory, to determine policy. This development took place first on the Catholic side, with the formation of the Irish National League (1882) as constituency organisation of the Home Rule or Nationalist Party. This was modelled on an earlier agrarian organisation, the Land League (1879); another organisational predecessor, the Home Rule League, founded in 1873, had followed the model of the electoral party. On the Protestant side, a similar development took place in 1885 with the formation of the Irish Loyal Patriotic Union (from 1891, the Irish Unionist Alliance) to represent southern unionists, and a range of similar organisations, eventually brought together under the Ulster Unionist Council in 1905, to represent northern unionists. These parties were prototypes of the party organisations that appeared after 1922 in the south (see Chapter 5), and, indeed, the Ulster Unionist Council continues to the present to constitute the organisational apex of the Ulster Unionist Party in Northern Ireland.

The 1885 election marked the birth of modern Irish party politics. It resulted in a strict polarisation between Protestant and Catholic Ireland, in which the Liberals were completely eliminated, being decisively defeated by the Nationalist Party in competing for Catholic votes. In the territory that was to become the Republic of Ireland, nationalists won virtually all of the seats. In the north, a geographical balance between nationalists and unionists was established that was to persist until 1969 (and even later, but in more fragmented form) – a phenomenon of electoral continuity without parallel in Europe.

Nationalist domination of the south lasted for more than 30 years, for most of this period in single-party form; it extended also to local government level after the 1898 reforms. Where significant electoral competition arose, this was not a consequence of a challenge from outside, but reflected deep divisions within the party, as in 1890, when most MPs left in protest at the leadership of Charles Stewart Parnell, following his involvement in a divorce scandal. The Irish National League also fractured as a consequence of this split; the more electorally successful anti-Parnellites set up the rival Irish National Federation. When the two wings of the party reunited in 1900, they adopted a new body, the United Irish League, as their grassroots organisation.

Two important points need to be made about the background to the emerging Irish party system. The first is the relationship between electoral reform and political mobilisation. The appearance of significant new political forces has often been associated with major waves of franchise extension; indeed, it is obvious that parties that target disenfranchised sections of the population can win their electoral support only if these excluded people are actually given the vote. Franchise extension alone, however, does not necessarily bring about electoral mobilisation, as the Irish experience vividly illustrates. The first major change, the enormous expansion of voting strength that followed from the Catholic Relief Act of 1793, had a negligible political effect; instead, landowners simply had more voters to manage at election time. Subsequent changes in the proportion of the population entitled to vote are summarised in Figure 1.1. The first appearance of modern electoral parties began in 1830, *after* the huge disenfranchisement of 1829 and before the modest reform of 1832. Again, the wave of electoral rebellion that began in the late 1870s, and that marked the birth of modern mass politics, took place a few years *before* the 1884 reform. The major reforms of 1884

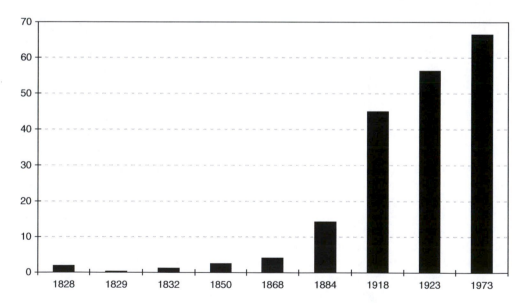

Figure 1.1 Electorate as percentage of population, 1828–1973

Source: Data taken from Coakley, 1986.

Note: The data refer to all of Ireland up to 1918, but only to the south in 1923 and 1973.

Table 1.1 Irish parliamentary representation, 1801–1918

Group (Number of elections)	1801–31 (10)	1832–80 (12)	1885–1910 (8)	1918 (1)
North:				
Tories/Unionists	73.6	78.6	69.5	76.7
Whigs/Liberals	14.1	18.5	2.5	0.0
Nationalists, etc.	–	0.0	28.0	13.3
Others	12.3	2.9	0.0	10.0
(Number)	(220)	(276)	(200)	(30)
South:				
Tories/Unionists	44.5	24.4	3.7	4.0
Whigs/Liberals	41.4	39.6	0.0	0.0
Nationalists, etc.	–	35.3	96.3	2.7
Others	14.1	0.7	0.0	93.3
(Number)	(780)	(980)	(624)	(75)
All Ireland:				
Tories/Unionists	50.9	36.3	19.7	24.8
Whigs/Liberals	35.4	35.0	0.6	0.0
Nationalists, etc.	-	27.5	79.7	5.7
Others	13.7	1.2	0.0	69.5
(Number)	(1,000)	(1,256)	(824)	(105)

Source: Calculated from Appendix 2a.

Note: Party strengths are indicated as percentages of seats won. Before 1832, party affiliations are approximate only. 'Tories/Unionists' includes Liberal Unionists; 'Nationalists, etc.' includes independent nationalists; in 1918, 'others' refers to Sinn Féin MPs. The north is defined as the present area of Northern Ireland, the south as the Republic. The number of MPs returned by constituencies in the north was 22, 23 and 25 in the first three periods; in the south it was 78 in the first and third periods and 82 in the second period, except for the last two elections, in 1874 and 1880, when the number was 80.

and 1918 may, in fact, be seen as permitting the consummation of new voter–party alliances rather than as making the match in the first place. This mobilisation was not confined to the electoral level; it extended also to the formation of new organisations with mass membership in the economic, cultural, sporting and other domains, and to the growth of a more radical press (see Legg, 1998).

Second, divisions between the main Irish parties corresponded closely to social divisions. Irish political life was dominated by three principal relationships in the 120 years after the Act of Union came into effect: between Ireland and Great Britain, between Catholics and Protestants and between tenants and landlords. By the 1880s, the two major parties had adopted fairly unambiguous positions on these issues. The Nationalist Party stood for Home Rule for Ireland, for defence of Catholic rights and for the principle of state intervention to promote the interests of tenant farmers; the Unionist Party adopted a contrary position on each of these issues. The two parties were supported by two clearly defined communities, the line of division coinciding with the religious cleavage. As an instance of early electoral mobilisation behind monolithic ethnic blocs, this development was without parallel in the Europe of the time (see Coakley, 2004).

The transition to independence

The deep divisions in Irish party political life had profound consequences for future constitutional arrangements. Election results made it clear that most voters endorsed the policy of

'Home Rule' or devolved government for Ireland. But the outcome of the struggle between supporters and opponents of Home Rule was the partition of Ireland into two states, each of which was itself deeply divided (though the Protestant minority in the South was much smaller than the Catholic minority in the North). This development may be traced from the failure of the Home Rule campaign, through the turmoil of the 1916 Rising and the subsequent war of independence, to the creation of two new Irish states (for overviews of developments in this period, see Augusteijn, 2002; Costello, 2003).

The rise of militant nationalism

Notwithstanding the strength of Irish support for Home Rule, the Nationalist Party was able to claim little success. Nevertheless, on occasions when it held the balance of power in the House of Commons, it was in a position to persuade British governments to bring forward Home Rule bills (O'Day, 1998; Jackson, 2003). The first such bill proposed to create an autonomous parliament in Dublin that would be responsible for a wide range of devolved powers, but was defeated in the House of Commons in 1886. A second similar bill was passed by the House of Commons but was blocked by the House of Lords in 1893. The third Home Rule Bill, introduced in 1912, eventually became law in 1914, facilitated by the transformation of the Lords' veto in 1911 from an absolute into a suspensory one. This bill proposed to establish a bicameral parliament in Dublin that would legislate in areas of domestic concern (essentially, those covered by the 'Irish' government departments described earlier), with a separate Irish executive or cabinet. Ireland would continue to send MPs to Westminster, but their numbers would be greatly reduced.

Implementation of Home Rule was, however, postponed because of the outbreak of war and powerful opposition in Ulster. The Protestant population of Ireland, for the most part, saw itself as being connected by a wide range of historical ties to Britain, from where the ancestors of many Irish Protestants had come as colonists in the seventeenth century. In addition to feeling British and seeing the British link as a guarantee of civil and religious liberties in a Catholic island, many Protestants, especially in the north east, regarded the Act of Union as having brought significant economic benefits and as having assisted the industrialisation of Belfast and its hinterland; these benefits, they believed, would be threatened by Irish self-rule (see Laffan, 1983; Fitzpatrick, 1998).

Stalemate on the implementation of Home Rule opened the door to a more militant alternative. This rested on a radical nationalist interpretation of Irish history that shared certain features with nationalist ideology elsewhere (Coakley, 2012: 94–115). In this view, the British presence in Ireland was based on military conquest; the lands of Irish Catholics had been confiscated and the Catholic religion had been suppressed; British trade policy had sought to stifle nascent Irish industrialisation in the eighteenth century; and the Act of Union had been procured by bribery and corruption. The catastrophic famine of 1845–49, in the course of which a million people died and a million emigrated, was later cited by nationalist ideologists as highlighting Britain's indifference to the terrible problems of Irish poverty. This version of history was widely shared among Irish Catholics. It projected British rule as damaging, and largely ignored the material benefits that it had brought. This ideological package was disseminated in the oral tradition and in popular literature and, to some extent, even through the state primary school system in the last two decades before 1922.

While Irish Catholic opinion in general drew the conclusion from this version of history that some form of self-government for Ireland was a necessary antidote, a more radical strand went further. Since British rule in Ireland had been achieved by military force, the argument ran, it could be reversed only by the same means: by armed rebellion, not by parliamentary or constitutional means. Furthermore, the delegitimisation of British rule implied a complete break and the establishment of a separate Irish republic as the ultimate goal. This perspective was reinforced by powerful cultural arguments: among other organisations, the Gaelic Athletic Association (1884) and the Gaelic League (1893) emphasised, respectively, the distinctiveness of Ireland's sporting traditions and its language, and sought to cultivate these to combat English influence (Hutchinson, 1987: 114–150).

The most obvious representative of political separatism was the Irish Republican Brotherhood (IRB), established in 1858, and committed to setting up an independent republic by force of arms (McGee, 2007). Although the IRB's attempted insurrection in 1867 was a failure, it had sympathisers in prominent places: many members and supporters of the parliamentary Nationalist Party may well have seen Home Rule as a half-way house to complete separation of Ireland from Great Britain, and a number of nationalist MPs had IRB associations. Nevertheless, extreme nationalist organisations were unable to challenge the electoral machine of the Nationalist Party. This is clear from the experience of Sinn Féin, a radical nationalist group founded in 1905 by a journalist, Arthur Griffith, whose object was to establish a separate Irish state, linked to Great Britain only through a shared head of state, the King. The limited appeal of this policy was reflected at electoral level: Sinn Féin was unable to mount a serious challenge to the Nationalist Party at parliamentary elections, and its few successes were at local level, notably in Dublin Corporation.

A spiral of paramilitary-style developments began in the years immediately before the First World War (1914–18). This was kicked off by the formation in January 1913 of the Ulster Volunteers, an armed force organised by the political leaders of Ulster unionism and committed to opposing Home Rule for Ireland. In reaction to this, the Irish Volunteers were founded later in the same year to support Home Rule. But most of the latter abandoned the organisation on the outbreak of the First World War, forming a separate body and enlisting in large numbers in the British army, in line with Nationalist Party policy. The remaining core group continued, and engaged in rebellion in April 1916 (the Easter Rising) under IRB leadership, taking over a number of prominent buildings in Dublin, including the General Post Office, and declaring Ireland to be an independent republic (McGarry, 2010; Townshend, 2015).

The 1916 Rising lasted less than a week. The rebels, led by Patrick Pearse, were reinforced by a Citizens' Army under the socialist leader, James Connolly, but were hopelessly outgunned by the British Army. The British reaction, following the rebels' surrender, was immediate and harsh. Many rebels and suspected rebels were interned, and 16 leaders, including Pearse and Connolly, were executed. Irish public opinion, initially largely unsympathetic to the rebels, shifted steadily as the relentless calendar of executions was announced. The rebel leaders came ultimately to be seen as heroes, and public alienation from the government was reinforced by a threat to introduce conscription in 1918 and by a pan-European climate of political radicalism in the closing months of the war. The main beneficiary was Sinn Féin, reconstituted in 1917 as a broad nationalist front under the leadership of Éamon de Valera, the senior surviving commander of the 1916 rebels. As Table 1.1 shows, Sinn Féin gained an overwhelming electoral victory in the 1918 general election, when it won 73 of Ireland's 105 seats, crushing the Nationalist Party, which was left with only six seats, four of them in the north.

Hardly surprisingly, Sinn Féin took this result as a mandate to pursue its separatist policy (see Laffan, 1999). Its members refused to take their seats in the British Parliament, and instead established their own revolutionary assembly, Dáil Éireann, in January 1919 (see Farrell, 1994). The Dáil ratified the 1916 rebels' proclamation of Ireland as an independent republic, set up its own government under de Valera, and in 1919–21 accepted responsibility for a guerrilla war against the security forces fought by the Irish Republican Army (IRA), reconstituted from the Irish Volunteers (Hopkinson, 2002; Kostick, 2009; Townshend, 2013; for the British response, Fanning, 2013). These efforts were reinforced by an attempt, which inevitably had strictly limited success, to set up a separate state and to obtain international recognition for it, especially by bringing American pressure to bear on the British. The Dáil could not hope to control the official Irish government agencies, and itself had only a small civil service, which operated in difficult circumstances. Nevertheless, after the local elections of 1920, it was able to detach the loyalty of most local authorities from the Local Government Board, and it enjoyed some success in establishing a network of local courts (see Mitchell, 1995; Garvin, 1996: 63–91).

The partition of Ireland

The result of the conflict between two radically different approaches to the government of Ireland was a decision by the British government to partition the island. This was given effect through the Government of Ireland Act (1920), based on the principles of the 1914 Act. But instead of concentrating power in a single capital, it made provision for two new Irish states, with parallel institutions in Belfast (to govern six north-eastern counties that contained 71 per cent of the Irish Protestant population) and Dublin (to govern the remaining 26 counties). The Act came into effect in 1921, and was successfully implemented, if in contested form, in Northern Ireland, where it formed the basic constitutional document until 1972 (see Chapter 13; Walker, 2012).

Although the Act proved largely ineffective in the south, its provisions for the government of 'Southern Ireland' formed an important precedent for constitutional development, and indeed defined the framework for the pattern of parliamentary democracy that was to become so deeply ingrained in the new Irish state. Alongside the Irish government, there was to be a parliament of two houses. The House of Commons was to consist of 128 members elected by proportional representation by means of the single transferable vote. The Senate was to consist of 64 members, of whom three were *ex officio* members (the Lord Chancellor and the Lord Mayors of Dublin and Cork), 17 were to be nominated by the Lord Lieutenant to represent commerce, labour and the scientific and learned professions, and 44 were to be elected by five other groups (the Catholic bishops were to elect four of their number, the Protestant bishops two, southern Irish peers 16, privy councillors eight and county councillors 14). In the first election to the House of Commons in 1921, Sinn Féin won 124 seats, all uncontested, and interpreted this election and that to the Northern Ireland House of Commons as elections to the 'second Dáil'. Since only four MPs turned up for the first meeting of the legally constituted Southern Ireland House of Commons (all from Trinity College, Dublin) and two for the second, it adjourned, never to meet again. Although attendance at the Senate was better (18 senators attended at least one of its two meetings), it suffered the same fate, and, in the absence of support from any significant group, the act ceased to have real effect in the south.

In any case, the provisions of the Government of Ireland Act for Southern Ireland were replaced by the provisions of the Anglo–Irish Treaty of December 1921. Drawn up by representatives of the Dáil government (led by Arthur Griffith and Michael Collins) and of the British government (led by Prime Minister David Lloyd George), this went much further than conceding Home Rule, but stopped well short of permitting complete separation. Instead, a state would be established that would be almost fully independent, but it would be a member of the British Commonwealth and would recognise the King as its head. There would be a representative of the crown to stand in for the King in Ireland on the model of the Governor-General in other dominions, and constitutional provision would be made for a parliamentary oath of allegiance to the constitution and fidelity to the King. The British would also retain naval facilities in certain seaports. Partition would remain, but the location of the boundary line would be determined by an intergovernmental commission. Since two of the six counties of Northern Ireland and other border areas had Catholic majorities, the Irish negotiators believed that this would result in a major revision of the line of the border, and that this in turn might undermine the viability of the northern state.

Although the Treaty was narrowly ratified by the Dáil in January 1922, by a majority of 64 to 57, the division that it generated was bitter and saw the resignation of de Valera as head of government and the departure of his anti-Treaty supporters from the Dáil. The constitutional position that followed was complex, and it required the pro-Treaty government to ride two horses, the Irish revolutionary experience and the British constitutional heritage.[1] First, the second Dáil continued to exist, though only pro-Treaty Sinn Féin members now attended. On 10 January 1922, Arthur Griffith was elected President of the Dáil government in succession to de Valera and a new Dáil government was appointed; on Griffith's death on 12 August 1922, he was succeeded as President by William T. Cosgrave. Second, the Treaty made provision for a meeting of 'members of parliament elected for constituencies in Southern Ireland', who duly came together on 14 January for their one and only meeting; at this they formally approved the Treaty and elected a provisional government with Michael Collins, guiding force of the IRA campaign and head of the IRB, as its Chairman. On Collins's death, on 22 August 1922, he was succeeded as Chairman by Cosgrave. Although Cosgrave's succession to both of these posts helped to disguise the anomalous existence of two governments, both pro-Treaty, with overlapping membership, this overlap was not complete. A general election took place in June 1922, and when the new (third) Dáil eventually met on 9 September 1922, again in the absence of the anti-Treaty deputies, it removed this anomaly by electing Cosgrave to the single post of President. Notwithstanding enormous political pressures, a new constitution was speedily drafted (Cahillane, 2016). The Dáil approved it on 25 October 1922, and it was enacted by the British Parliament on 5 December. When it came into force the following day, Cosgrave became President of the Executive Council (yet another title for the prime minister).

The consolidation of statehood

The new state, then, did not have a particularly easy birth. The remaining chapters in this volume look at the kinds of political structures and patterns of behaviour that have evolved in Ireland since independence (for the post-1922 political system, see also Chubb, 1992; O'Toole and Dooney, 2009; Adshead and Tonge, 2009; MacCarthaigh, 2009; Kissane, 2011; O'Malley and MacCarthaigh, 2012). Since the authors have, where appropriate, set their examinations of contemporary politics in historical context, a detailed overview of post-1922 politics is not needed here (for general historical accounts, see Lee, 1989; Keogh, 1994; Harkness, 1996; Ferriter, 2004; for the early decades of the new state, Cronin and Regan, 2000).

It is nevertheless necessary to review a number of themes that link contemporary politics with the events and institutions already discussed. First, the outcome of the independence struggle left the new state with a series of challenges to its legitimacy that took several decades to resolve. Second, the administrative structures inherited by the new state provided an important bedrock of stability. Third, the party system acquired a momentum of its own, but was marked by surprising continuity, notwithstanding the emergence of new issues. Fourth, particular challenges faced the political system in the early twenty-first century, in the aftermath of economic crisis and party political fragmentation.

Problems of legitimacy

The new Irish state was faced with a formidable challenge to its legitimacy (Garvin, 1996; MacMillan, 1993: 165–85; Prager, 1986; Regan, 1999; Kissane, 2002). At one extreme, its birth upset those who remained loyal to the United Kingdom: the sizeable unionist population, which had wished to maintain the political integrity of the British Isles, and the significant population that had supported the Nationalist Party in the 1918 election, and that would have been happy with devolved government for Ireland within the United Kingdom. Since the union appeared irretrievably dissolved, however, and the spectre of de Valera and the Republicans appeared to be the main alternative to the Free State, many former supporters of the unionist and nationalist parties switched to a position of neutrality towards (or even support for) the new regime.

At the other extreme, and with weightier political consequences, the new political order was anathema to those Republicans who took the view that the proclamation of a republic in 1916 and its confirmation by the Dáil in 1919 were irreversible. They regarded the Irish Free State as a deformed alternative to 'the Republic', deficient not only because it represented a truncation of the 'national territory', but also because it retained important links of subordination to the United Kingdom, at least at a symbolic level. This issue split the IRA, whose pro-Treaty wing became the core of the new national army; it eventually spilled over into armed conflict, during a civil war that lasted from June 1922 to May 1923 (see Foster, 2015; Purdon, 2000; Kissane, 2005). In the course of this, many people – probably more than two thousand – died as a consequence of armed clashes, executions and assassinations.[2] In the early stages of the civil war, the anti-Treaty Sinn Féin members sought to undermine the constitutional position of the pro-Treaty side. They asserted that the 1922 general election was not legitimate since the second Dáil (elected in 1921) had not dissolved itself, declared themselves to be the 'second Dáil' and met on 25 October 1922 to elect de Valera once more as 'President of the Republic'. Even after the civil war, this group (now known simply as Sinn Féin) continued to abstain from the Dáil. This fundamental challenge to a new state was not unique to Ireland: in the emerging postwar states of Finland, Estonia, Latvia and Lithuania, similar civil wars were fought, though these had a more obviously social content, pitting communists against conservatives (see Coakley, 1987).

In between these extremes, the new government gradually consolidated its position. The core of the new political elite was made up of pro-Treaty members of Sinn Féin, who reorganised under the label Cumann na nGaedheal in 1923 (this had been the name of a precursor of the old Sinn Féin, organised by Arthur Griffith in 1900; see Glossary). Led by Cosgrave, its character was shaped by other strong political figures of a broadly conservative disposition, a conservatism that was reflected in a new, close relationship with the Catholic church (see Meehan, 2010). Although the 1922 constitution was an entirely secular document, the new government quickly moved to show its deference to Catholic moral values. Thus, divorce was prohibited, restrictions were placed on the sale of alcohol, and censorship of films and publications was greatly intensified. But other policy areas showed a willingness to innovate: the government intervened in the energy production sector by creating the Shannon hydroelectric scheme in 1925, for instance, and, in a rather different area, the new government sought vigorously to promote the Irish language.

Cumann na nGaedheal struggled with some success to protect the autonomy of the new state and even to extend it within the Commonwealth. But its increasingly unreserved defence of the Treaty had two kinds of consequence for political realignment in the 1920s. On the one hand, those who had accepted Collins's argument that the Treaty represented 'freedom to achieve freedom' became disillusioned, and broke with the party, notably following two incidents in 1924–25. The first of these was the 'Army Mutiny' of 1924, when a group of senior officers demanded action from the government to end partition (though other motivations arising from army demobilisation probably took precedence over this; see Lee, 1989: 96–105; Regan, 1999: 163–97). The second was a division following the leaking of the report of the Boundary Commission in 1925 (set up under the terms of the Treaty, the commission recommended that only marginal changes be made to the line of the border). On the other hand, ex-supporters of the now-defunct nationalist and unionist parties increasingly came to identify with Cumann na nGaedheal, especially after 1927. Many former nationalist voters had briefly given their support to a short-lived party, the National League, in 1927; unionists had either remained detached, voted for independent candidates, or, in the 1920s, supported two smaller parties, the Farmers' Party and the Business Men's Party.

Three formative events marked the gradual absorption of the anti-Treaty side into the political establishment. First, in response to declining support for Sinn Féin, de Valera proposed to end the policy of abstention. When this proposal was rejected at the party's 1926 *ard-fheis* (convention), he and his supporters withdrew from Sinn Féin, and shortly afterwards founded an alternative republican party, Fianna Fáil. The popularity of this move became obvious in June 1927, when a general election gave Fianna Fáil 44 seats, to Sinn Féin's five. Second, on 10 July 1927, a leading minister, Kevin O'Higgins, was assassinated in Dublin. Among the measures adopted in response by the government was a bill requiring all future parliamentary candidates to declare that, if elected, they would take the oath of allegiance. This left abstentionist parties with a difficult choice: either to enter parliament or to accept the political marginalisation that abstention implied. Fianna Fáil decided on the former course, and de Valera and his supporters entered the Dáil in August 1927, describing their formal acceptance of the oath as an empty gesture. Ironically, by thus forcing Fianna Fáil into the Dáil, the government changed the balance of political forces there and, facing defeat, called a second general election in 1927, at which both Cumann na nGaedheal and Fianna Fáil gained, at the expense of smaller parties (see Appendices 2b and 2c). Third, in 1932, Fianna Fáil became the largest party and, although it did not have an overall majority, it was able to form a government with Labour Party support. This peaceful transfer of power from the victors in the civil war to the vanquished was an important milestone in the consolidation of democracy in Ireland. Within a year, a new general election gave Fianna Fáil an overall majority, and it was to remain in power without interruption until 1948 (see Dunphy, 1995; Whelan, 2011).

The constitution of 1922 formed a central battlefield in the early years of the life of the new state. Throughout its lifetime it could be amended by simple act of parliament (see Chapter 3). Some significant changes were made in the 1920s; and the early years of the new Fianna Fáil government were characterised, not surprisingly, by vigorous moves to dismantle some of those elements in the constitution that republicans found objectionable. Thus, the oath of allegiance, the right of appeal to the Privy Council in London (a limited but symbolically important restriction on the sovereignty of the Irish judicial system) and the Governor-General's right to veto legislation were abolished in 1933. Although these amendments were strongly opposed by the British on the grounds that they violated certain provisions of the Treaty, the context within which they took place had changed considerably since 1922. Imperial conferences that brought Commonwealth leaders together in 1926 and 1930 pushed for greater independence from London, culminating in the Statute of Westminster (1931), which authorised any Commonwealth state to amend or repeal British legislation that affected it.

The character of the constitution was even more fundamentally altered in 1936, when the Senate was abolished and the sudden abdication of King Edward VIII was used as an opportunity to bring the office of Governor-General to an end. This left the way open for a new constitution, shaped in line with de Valera's thinking, which was adopted by referendum in 1937. This stopped short of declaring Ireland a republic, made no mention of the Commonwealth and was intended to symbolise the completion of the process of Irish independence, at least for part of Ireland (see Chapter 3). The new constitution might be seen as the ultimate assertion of national sovereignty; the social values it sought to enshrine were distinctively Catholic (Murray, 2016: 115).

Opposition to a British role in Ireland also extended to the issue of 'land annuities', payments due to the British exchequer from Irish farmers as a consequence of loans taken by them to purchase their holdings under the provisions of the Land Acts of the pre-1922 period. On coming to power in 1932, de Valera simply retained these repayments for the Irish exchequer. An Anglo–Irish 'trade war' followed, with each side imposing import duties on selected goods from the other; it was concluded by a trade agreement in 1938 and British acceptance of a once-off lump sum payment. Another issue was that of the naval facilities that the British had retained under the terms of the Treaty. This was settled more amicably, also as part of the 1938 settlement: the British ceded control of the ports, thus laying the ground for the policy of neutrality that the Irish government was able to follow during the Second World War.

As these changes proceeded, the original pro-Treaty forces found themselves increasingly impotent. The spectre of extreme republicanism, raised by the Fianna Fáil victory in 1932, and the polarised climate of the 1930s, formed the background for the formation of a fascist-type movement in Ireland. This was born as the Army Comrades' Association (1931), and was transformed in 1933 into the National Guard (commonly known as the Blueshirts), led by the former head of the Garda Síochána, General Eoin O'Duffy. The parallels with continental European fascist movements were close: the fascist salute, the wearing of a distinctive shirt as a uniform, anti-communist rhetoric and, most importantly, an authoritarian nationalist ideology that was critical of parliamentary government and sympathetic towards a reorganisation of the state along corporatist lines, where conflict between parties would be replaced by cooperation between different socio-economic segments, such as agriculture, industry and the professions (see Manning, 1987; Bew *et al.*, 1989: 48–67; Cronin, 1997). This development was followed by a further realignment of anti-Fianna Fáil forces. In 1933, a demoralised Cumann na nGaedheal merged with the Blueshirts and a small new party, the National Centre Party, to form the United Ireland Party, which quickly became better known by its Irish name, Fine Gael. Led initially by O'Duffy, the party came increasingly to resemble the old Cumann na nGaedheal party, especially after William T. Cosgrave replaced O'Duffy as leader in 1934. Fine Gael, however, was no match for Fianna Fáil in electoral terms, and its share of the vote dropped until 1948. Then, in an ironic development, its worst ever electoral performance was followed by its entry into a coalition government. Even more ironically, this government moved to break the last remaining links between Ireland and the Commonwealth, with the decision in 1948 to bring the role of the King to an end and to declare the state a republic (on Fine Gael's subsequent evolution, see Gallagher and Marsh, 2002; Meehan, 2013).

Even though this convergence of the pro- and anti-Treaty sides helped to confirm the legitimacy of the state, this was not unchallenged. The rump of Sinn Féin and the IRA that survived after 1926 remained adamant in their hostility to the state, which they continued to reject as an illegitimate, British-imposed entity (English, 2012). Instead, they continued to give their allegiance to the 'Second Dáil', and then to the Army Council of the IRA, to which the remnants of the 'Second Dáil' transferred their authority in 1938. While this might appear to be of importance only in the world of myth, myths can be of powerful political significance. This historical interpretation was used to legitimate the reborn IRA and Sinn Féin after 1970.

The administrative infrastructure

If the pattern of politics in post-1922 Ireland shows strands of continuity beneath seemingly dramatic political changes, stability is even more strikingly a characteristic of the administrative system that has lain underneath. As we have seen, the old regime had built up a formidable administrative infrastructure already before 1922, and this was to be adapted to serve the new state, greatly assisting its stability and even survival (McColgan, 1983: 132–7). The fact that a considerable transformation had taken place in the civil service in the last decades of British rule, with the admission of many more Catholics, greatly facilitated this process. This is not to say that regime transition in 1922 left the old system intact: notwithstanding its role as a model for British decolonisation elsewhere, many senior officials were purged or chose retirement, leaving the civil service open to be moulded by the political elite of the new state (Maguire, 2008: 227).

The new civil service, which for many years consisted of about 20,000 employees, was made up overwhelmingly of existing staff, to which were added 131 members of the old Dáil civil service. Its character changed only slowly as new staff were recruited. Thus, in 1922, 99 per cent of civil servants had been recruited under the old regime; by 1927–28 this figure had dropped to 64 per cent and as late as 1934 a majority (50 per cent) of civil servants had been recruited to the pre-1922 service (calculated from Commission of Inquiry into the Civil Service, 1935: 3, 9, 138).

The external staff associated with certain departments posed particular problems. Surprisingly, the Department of Education had little difficulty with its body of teachers and inspectors, even though these had been recruited and trained under the old regime. The shift towards ideals of Irish nationalism was not difficult for teachers, since they had allegedly been associated with such ideas even before 1922; the main problem lay in raising their proficiency in the Irish language to a level that would allow them to become effective agents in the state's language revival policy. Matters were different in the area of security. Although the Dublin Metropolitan Police continued until 1925, the more politicised, paramilitary Royal Irish Constabulary was disbanded in the south and renamed the Royal Ulster Constabulary in the north. The new Civic Guard (Garda Síochána) was launched as a freshly recruited force in 1922, though it used the administrative structures, buildings and other property of the Royal Irish Constabulary; the fact that it was unarmed and clearly a civilian force underlined the contrast with its predecessor, helping to win it popular acceptance. By 1926 it had settled into a force of a little over 7,000.

As to its structure, the new civil service was a rationalisation of the old one. Most of the 29 'Irish' departments were reorganised into five new departments; but in areas associated with 'imperial' departments the new state had to create new structures. Thus, a new Department of Finance was created out of the Irish branch of the Treasury (Fanning, 1978: 30–80). The new Department of Posts and Telegraphs amounted to a reconstitution of the Irish Post Office, whose huge workforce it inherited (Ferguson, 2016: 359–64). But in other areas there was nothing to inherit. A Department of External Affairs had to be built from scratch (Kennedy,

2012). There was, similarly, a complete break in the military domain: the withdrawing British Army was replaced by an Irish Army built up around a nucleus of the pro-Treaty members of the IRA (Duggan, 1991: 121–4). It expanded rapidly in response to civil war needs and by the end of March 1923 had some 50,000 soldiers. This number had dropped to 16,000 by the following year, and after 1926 further rapid reduction brought this figure to 6,700 by 1932. Apart from temporary expansion during the second world war, the army was to remain at this size until the end of the 1960s. Then, following the outbreak of the Northern Ireland troubles and with increased crime in the south, the size of both the defence forces and the police was increased by about 50 per cent in the 1970s (see O'Halpin, 1996). By 2016, the defence forces numbered a little more than 9,000 and the Gardaí almost 13,000.

The formal organisation of the new system was defined in the Ministers and Secretaries Act, 1924; subsequent changes (such as the transfer of areas from one department to another, or the creation of new departments) were on a smaller scale, but their cumulative effect was to increase the number of departments under the control of individual ministers from 10 in 1922 to 15 by the end of the century. Of these, six core departments have continued with little change other than in name: those of the President of the Executive Council (renamed Taoiseach, 1937), Finance, External Affairs (Foreign Affairs and Trade in 2017), Home Affairs (Justice and Equality in 2017), Defence, and Education (Education and Skills in 2017). The other four core departments of the early service (Local Government, Industry and Commerce, Posts and Telegraphs and Agriculture) had been replaced by the end of the century by nine departments with rather unstable boundaries. These cover various areas of economic development and planning, management of the public sector, health and welfare, and culture and recreation (see listing of government departments in Appendix 4; for general evaluations of the public policy process, see Chapters 10 and 11).

The evolution of the Irish civil service has been marked by a number of distinctive developments. First, there has been a casual, politically-driven reorganisation of government departments after each general election, as functions are transferred and departments are renamed, at not inconsiderable cost (1997 and 2011 were particularly striking years, when most departments were reshuffled and renamed). Second, a 'decentralisation' programme was announced by the government in December 2003. Apparently based on little planning or forethought, this was designed to move about 10,000 public servants from Dublin to approximately 53 locations around the country, with obvious implications for the coherence of the civil service. The programme was, however, only partly implemented, due to a general reluctance of civil servants to move, and to the considerable costs involved. Third, the crisis in public finance that began in 2008 had important consequences for the civil service, with substantial salary cuts accompanied by a recruitment embargo and a retirement package that stripped the civil service of a great deal of expertise.

At the level of local government, continuity with the pre-1922 period was even more obvious. The old system continued after 1922, with only incremental change. The most significant changes were the abolition of poor law unions (1923) and of rural district councils (1925), and the transfer of their functions to county councils. This left the state with a system of local government sharply different from the European norm, where it has traditionally been two-tiered: an upper level consisting of a small number of counties or provinces, modelled on the French *départements* and traditionally acting largely as agencies of the central government, and a lower level consisting of a very large number of communes or municipalities of greatly varying sizes, each with a local council and significant administrative powers. After 1925, the latter level was largely missing from Ireland; the main focus of local representative government was at county level, but even there the influence of the central state was overpowering (Potter, 2011: 396–7).

The centralised control that post-independence governments have exercised was reflected in suspensions of local authorities in the early years of the state, and frequent deferrals of the dates of local elections. A constitutional change in 1999, however, ensured that deferrals of this kind would be much more difficult in future (see Weeks and Quinlivan, 2009), and local elections have taken place subsequently at five-year intervals, coinciding with elections to the European Parliament (see Appendices 2e and 2f). The ultimate stage in the centralisation of the Irish local government system was brought in by the Local Government Reform Act of 2014. This abolished the existing urban (town) councils and merged certain existing administrative counties (such ancient cities as Limerick and Waterford disappeared as autonomous entities), though their councils were given additional powers.[3] Most councils are divided into municipal district committees, of which there are 95, formally intended to reflect the interests of local residents.

One of the most significant changes in the area of state intervention lay in the creation of 'state-sponsored bodies' to carry out a range of functions, many of them connected to economic development (MacCarthaigh, 2009: 86–97). The number of such bodies, over which government control has been only indirect, increased steadily from an initial four in 1927 to well over 100 by 1990. In part under the impact of European Union legislation designed to encourage competition, though, the partial dismantling of this semi-state sector commenced in the 1990s, as major public sector organisations began to be sold off to private investors. Part of the Department of Posts and Telegraphs, for instance, was hived off in 1984 as a state-sponsored body, Telecom Éireann; in 1999 this was floated on the stock exchange and passed into private ownership. The national airline, Aer Lingus (1936), followed suit in 2006, and in 2015 was acquired by a large airline group dominated by British Airways. Other large civil service institutions have moved halfway in this direction; the postal services part of the Department of Posts and Telegraphs, for example, was also given the status of a state-sponsored body in 1984 as An Post, and the forestry service, Coillte, was detached from the Department of Energy in 1989. These and other state-sponsored bodies, such as the national airports authority Aer Rianta (1937) and the Electricity Supply Board (1927), remain in state ownership, but the possibility of privatisation remains.

Following a wave of agency creation in the 1990s, driven more by *ad hoc* considerations than by conscious planning, the total number of non-commercial bodies had increased to 249 by 2010 (MacCarthaigh, 2010: 8). These agencies came under particular pressure following the economic crash that began in 2008, but have proven to be highly resilient. Before the general election of 2011, Fine Gael promised to abolish 145 public agencies of this kind, but by 2014 only 45 were on the path towards abolition, while a further 33 agencies were being created (McGee, 2014). One of the most controversial of the new bodies was Irish Water, established in 2013 to centralise and modernise Ireland's fresh and waste water systems. But allegations of reckless expenditure, doubts about its charging policy, suspicions that it was a step towards privatisation and other political objections rendered the body ineffective from an early stage; its future remains to be determined.

Political issues in the new Ireland

Before considering the nature of political exchange in the Republic of Ireland, it should be pointed out that many significant policy shifts in the second half of the twentieth century took place without much public debate. Examples include the abandonment of reliance on traditional Sinn Féin-type policies of encouragement of indigenous industry in favour of the pursuit of foreign investment (see Garvin, 2004), reflected in the adoption of the first Programme for Economic Expansion (1958) and the signing of the Anglo–Irish Free Trade Agreement (1965). These matters contrasted with the debates of the 1920s and the 1930s, which focused largely on matters pertaining to Anglo–Irish relations. On these earlier issues, the principal line of division was between the pro- and anti-Treaty splinters from Sinn Féin. Other political interests also sought, however, to force alternative issues onto the political agenda, and the proportional representation electoral system permitted them to gain significant Dáil representation (see Chapters 4 and 5; for an overview of the parties' electoral strengths, see Appendix 2b).

The most significant challenge to the 'national question' was the classic source of division in western democracies in the twentieth century: the clash of class interests. This was reflected in the appearance of a small Labour Party, conceived by the Irish Trades Union Congress in 1912, and finally born in 1922 as a party committed to a moderate policy of defence of workers' rights. The party was marginalised by debates on the national question, on which it was unable to adopt a distinctive position, and moved quickly into the role that it retained until 2016: that of third party in a three-party system (see Gallagher, 1982; Puirséil, 2007; Daly *et al.*, 2012). In the absence also of a significant classical revolutionary left, the consistent weakness of Labour has been remarkable in a European context (see Chapter 5).

A second important issue was that of agriculture. In 1922, a Farmers' Party appeared, drawing its strength from the large farmers of the south and east. The Farmers' Party found it difficult to maintain an identity separate from that of Cumann na nGaedheal, and it faded away after 1927. A successor party with a similar support base, the National Centre Party (founded in 1932 as the National Farmers' and Ratepayers' League), was one of the parties that, as we have seen, merged to form Fine Gael. In 1939, a farmers' party of a rather different kind appeared. This was Clann na Talmhan, originating among the small farmers of the west. This party won significant support in the elections of the 1940s and even participated in two governments, but it was unable to prevent its voters from drifting back to the two large parties subsequently (Varley, 2010).

Three other types of political force also fought for Dáil seats. First, especially in the 1920s and the 1930s, a considerable number of independent deputies represented diverse opinions, including those of former unionists and nationalists. Increasingly, however, the support base of deputies of this kind was mopped up by the larger parties. Second, former nationalists made a more determined attempt to regroup through the National League, which won eight seats in the June 1927 general election. In fact, following Fianna Fáil's entry to the Dáil, the prospect of a minority Labour–National League coalition government, with Fianna Fáil support, appeared to be a realistic possibility.[4] The calling of a snap second election in 1927 put paid to the prospects of this party, however; it lost all but two of its seats. Third, there have been dissident republican parties caused by divisions within Cumann na nGaedheal in the 1920s (the National Group in 1924 and Clann Éireann in 1925) and within Fianna Fáil in the 1970s (Aontacht Éireann in 1971 and Independent Fianna Fáil in Donegal from 1973 to 2006). By contrast to these small groups, another republican party, Clann na Poblachta, founded in 1946 by Seán MacBride, a former IRA chief of staff, appeared destined for greater things (Rafter, 1996; McDermott, 1998). This party was able to capitalise on postwar disillusion with Fianna Fáil and win ten seats in the 1948 election. But following bitter internal disputes, most notably over the 'Mother and Child' scheme for the provision of comprehensive postnatal care in the social welfare system (on which the party's health minister, Noel Browne, had clashed with the church), its support collapsed in the 1951 election and never subsequently recovered (for minor parties generally, see Gallagher, 1985: 93–120; Weeks and Clark, 2012).

It was, indeed, precisely the intervention of Clann na Poblachta in the 1948 general election that ushered in a new era in Irish politics. Fianna Fáil was unable to form a government after the election, and was replaced in office by a five-party coalition supported also by independent deputies, the first 'inter-party' government (McCullagh, 1998). In this, Clann na Poblachta sat alongside Fine Gael, together with Clann na Talmhan, Labour and the National Labour Party (a group of deputies that had broken with Labour and maintained a separate party in the years 1944–50). Headed by Fine Gael's John A. Costello, this coalition broke up in disarray in 1951, to be replaced by a Fianna Fáil government. Costello was nevertheless back in 1954, this time heading a three-party coalition of Fine Gael, Labour and Clann na Talmhan. Following the 1957 election, though, Fianna Fáil returned for a second 16-year period in office.

The fact that a single party was in power for this lengthy period disguises the extent of change that took place between 1957 and 1973. The period began under de Valera's leadership with a cabinet still made up largely of activists of the 1919–23 period. After a transition under Seán Lemass (1959–66), one of the youngest of those involved in the independence movement, it ended with a still younger cabinet led by Jack Lynch and consisting of ministers without direct experience of the civil war (Garvin, 2004; Girvin and Murphy, 2005). The ghosts of the civil war were, however, disturbed by the outbreak of the Northern Ireland 'troubles' in 1969. In a dramatic incident in May 1970 that became known as the 'arms crisis', Lynch dismissed two ministers, Neil Blaney and Charles Haughey, for alleged involvement in the illegal purchase and supply of arms to Northern Ireland nationalists, and, in related developments, he accepted the resignations of two more. Together with the ensuing trial, this incident was to haunt Fianna Fáil for over two decades (see O'Brien, 2000), though Haughey managed to displace Lynch as party leader and Taoiseach in 1979. One belated consequence was the appearance of a new party, the Progressive Democrats, in 1985. Although the trigger for the formation of the party was a deep division within Fianna Fáil on Northern Ireland policy and on Charles Haughey's leadership, the new party managed quickly to establish a distinctive niche for itself: conservative on economic policy, liberal on social policy and moderate on Northern Ireland.

The 16 unbroken years of Fianna Fáil rule that ended in 1973 were succeeded by 16 years of alternation between Fine Gael–Labour coalitions and single-party Fianna Fáil governments; the pattern was broken in 1989, when Fianna Fáil entered a coalition for the first time (for a list of governments, see Appendix 3c; see also McGraw, 2015; Murphy, 2016). Thereafter, coalition was the norm, typically under Fianna Fáil leaders (Albert Reynolds, 1992–94, Bertie Ahern, 1997–2008 and Brian Cowen, 2008–11), but with important episodes of Fine Gael-led governments, as in 1994–97 (John Bruton) and beginning in 2011 (Enda Kenny, followed by Leo Varadkar).

From 1932 to 2011, the Irish party system was stable and predictable, dominated by three parties: Fianna Fáil, which won 49 per cent of all Dáil seats at general elections over the period 1932–2007, Fine Gael, which won 31 per cent and Labour, with 10 per cent. Behind this stability, though, lurked a big shift in issues of concern to voters, from constitutional matters to economic and social ones (see Garvin, 2010; Daly, 2016; Ferriter, 2012). Protests over high rates of unemployment and inflation in the 1950s forced these issues into the political arena, though without translating them into votes for the left. To these were added in the 1980s and 1990s conflicts over moral issues, such as divorce, abortion and homosexuality (see Crotty and Schmitt, 1998). Increasingly, too, the issue of women's rights and women's representation in the political domain acquired greater salience (see Chapter 9; Galligan, 1998; Galligan *et al.*, 1999).

Contemporary challenges

Around the turn of the century, constitutional-type issues once again acquired prominence: the negotiation of a deal to resolve the Northern Ireland problem, for instance (resulting in the Belfast agreement of 1998), and the extension of the jurisdiction of the EU (with Irish voters generally endorsing this, but initially voting against the Nice Treaty in 2001 and against the Lisbon Treaty in 2008). But a much bigger crisis was to disrupt Irish public life: a major economic crash. This followed a period of rapid economic growth, with high rates of employment and personal wealth (the so-called 'Celtic Tiger' period, from about the mid-1990s to 2008). This era was associated with a boom in construction and in other forms of investment. Since this was fuelled by favourable interest rates and ill-considered lending policies by banks and other financial institutions, the economy was left highly vulnerable to the global financial crisis of 2008. The major banks suffered severely, but they were rescued by a government decision on 30 September 2008 to underwrite their loans.

The bank rescue, however, placed an unbearable burden on the state: as property prices began to fall, leading to a full-scale crash, the government was forced to recapitalise the banks on a massive scale. The position was aggravated by rapid deterioration in the general government deficit as a consequence mainly of reduced revenues from the property sector and increased public spending. In response, the government created a 'bad bank', the National Asset Management Agency, to take over most of the large debts of the banks at discounted value, with a view ultimately to disposing of them, and it took vigorous measures to bring public sector spending under control by introducing a harsh austerity programme, cutting public sector pay, seeking to encourage early retirement and placing an embargo on recruitment. But this was insufficient, and on 28 November 2010 Ireland followed Greece into a rescue package funded by the 'troika' of the EU, the European Central Bank (ECB) and the International Monetary Fund (IMF), amounting to 67.5 billion euros.

Not surprisingly, the economic crisis had major political consequences (see Kirby and Murphy, 2011; Coakley, 2013: 1–43; Hardiman, 2012; Girvin and Murphy, 2010; Murphy, 2016; Marsh *et al.*, 2017). The opposition was able to lay the blame on successive Fianna Fáil governments, and an historic election in 2011 fundamentally transformed the party system. Fianna Fáil's unrivalled position as the largest party was brought to an end; its share of the vote dropped from 42 per cent at the 2007 general election to 17 per cent. At the same time, its rivals, Fine Gael and Labour, saw their combined share of the vote increase from 37 per cent to 55 per cent, allowing them to form a stable government with a big parliamentary majority. The new government reinforced the existing austerity programme, and promised additional structural reforms; in reality, though, its hands were tied, and it was forced to stick to reform principles imposed by the 'troika'. Ireland was finally able to leave the bailout programme after three years, on 15 December 2013. Although this experience left the state with huge debts that will be carried over for years, the economy once again began to pick up, with accelerating growth in GDP. But major challenges remain. The economy is highly dependent on large, mainly American-based corporations that moved their headquarters to Ireland in part to avail of its low corporation tax rate, but Ireland's competitive advantage in this respect depends on policies pursued by other states, notably the USA. Even more seriously, the prospect of the UK's departure from the EU will have an unpredictable impact on trade, investment, employment, economic growth and standards of living generally (see Chapter 14).

The impact of the crisis on the party system was not confined to the three traditional parties, whose support dropped further in 2016, resulting in the emergence of a minority Fine Gael–independent coalition with support from other independents and Fianna Fáil (Gallagher and Marsh, 2016). The traditional party system was shaken up by three new developments. The first was the rise of Sinn Féin. The remnants of the Sinn Féin movement that had survived after 1926 had split again in 1970, with a more activist 'provisional' wing breaking away and becoming a major political force in Northern Ireland in the 1980s. The remaining 'official' Sinn Féin was gradually transformed into a radical left group that became the Workers' Party in 1982, but most of whose TDs broke away in 1992 to form a new party, Democratic Left, which merged with Labour in 1999 (Rafter, 2011). The other wing of the movement, now known simply as 'Sinn Féin', has gradually been growing in strength, comfortably beating Labour into third position in 2016. Second, a new radical left has emerged, its origins lying in the socialist tradition and taking shape as the Anti-Austerity Alliance (since 2017, Solidarity) and People Before Profit. Third, there has been a mushrooming of support for independent deputies, whose appeal is sometimes purely local, but sometimes more ideological (see Chapter 5). In combination, these new forces have made the process of coalition building more challenging.

Conclusion

It is obvious that the birth of the new Irish state marked a decisive shift in Irish political development, but we should not ignore the extent to which its political institutions built on pre-1922 roots. Although there was a sharp break, both in constitutional theory and at the level of the political elite, narrowly defined, there was little change in much of the administrative infrastructure. The civil service, the judicial system and the educational system were merely overhauled, and continued to be staffed by much the same personnel after 1922 as before. The local government system was radically restructured in the early 1920s, but this affected only its lower tier; the county councils continued on as before, if under different political leadership.

In this, the Irish experience is not greatly different from that in other post-revolutionary societies. Radical though some strands in the independence movement may have been, it was the more cautious, conservative wing that ultimately won power in the new state and shaped its character during the early, formative years. While it is true that the context of politics was redefined with the advent of independence in 1922, and that Fianna Fáil's victory in 1932 led to further far-reaching developments, it is likely that the most profound changes in the character of Irish politics will be incremental, as the freedom of action of the Irish political system is compromised by its incorporation in a larger political entity, the EU, and by global economic realities. But these changes will also be conditioned by the changing nature of Irish political culture, the subject of the next chapter.

Notes

1   In an interesting survival of the claim of continuity with the pre-1922 independence movement, each Dáil to the present is numbered on the basis of a recognition of the Dáil of 1919 as the first one (the Dáil elected in 2016, for instance, was designated the 32nd Dáil, even in official circles, though it was only the 30th since the state came into existence in 1922).
2   Strangely, no reliable estimate of the number of deaths in the Irish civil war has ever been produced.
3   Traditionally, Ireland is said to have had 32 counties (of which six are in Northern Ireland), an image maintained by such organisations as the Gaelic Athletic Association and generally illustrated on maps, though the administrative counties have never numbered 32. While the Northern Ireland counties lost almost all administrative significance in 1973, those in the Republic increased in

number. Tipperary had for long been divided into a North Riding and a South Riding, and four cities (Dublin, Cork, Limerick and Waterford) were entirely separate from the counties whose names they shared, resulting in a total of 31. Galway City was given separate status in 1986, and County Dublin was divided into three in 1994, so the total number of county-level units was increased to 34. With the merger of the two Tipperary ridings, and the abolition of the separate status of Limerick and Waterford cities in 2014, the number fell again to 31.

4   One National League TD, Alderman John Jinks from Sligo, was famously absent for the vote of no confidence in the Cumann na nGaedheal government that could have led to this outcome; the result was a tie, and the government was saved on the casting vote of the Ceann Comhairle. A prominent Labour TD was out of the country for the vote.

References and further reading

Adshead, Maura and Jonathan Tonge, 2009. *Politics in Ireland: Convergence and Divergence in a Two-Polity Island*. Basingstoke: Palgrave Macmillan.

Augusteijn, Joost (ed.), 2002. *The Irish Revolution, 1913–1923*. Basingstoke: Palgrave.

Bew, Paul, 2007. *Ireland: the Politics of Enmity, 1789–2006*. Oxford: Oxford University Press.

Bew, Paul, Ellen Hazelkorn and Henry Patterson, 1989. *The Dynamics of Irish Politics*. London: Lawrence and Wishart.

Cahillane, Laura, 2016. *Drafting the Irish Free State Constitution*. Manchester: Manchester University Press.

Campbell, Fergus, 2009. *The Irish Establishment 1879–1914*. Oxford: Oxford University Press.

Chubb, Basil, 1992. *The Government and Politics of Ireland*, 3rd ed. London: Longman.

Coakley, John, 1986. 'The evolution of Irish party politics', in Brian Girvin and Roland Sturm (eds), *Politics and Society in Contemporary Ireland*. London: Gower, pp. 29–54.

Coakley, John, 1987. 'Political succession during the transition to independence: evidence from Europe', in Peter Calvert (ed.), *The Process of Political Succession*. London: Macmillan, pp. 161–70.

Coakley, John, 2004. 'Critical elections and the prehistory of the Irish party system', in Tom Garvin, Maurice Manning and Richard Sinnott (eds), *Dissecting Irish Democracy: Essays in Honour of Brian Farrell*. Dublin: UCD Press, pp. 134–59.

Coakley, John, 2012. *Nationalism, Ethnicity and the State: Making and Breaking Nations*. London: Sage.

Coakley, John, 2013. *Reforming Political Institutions: Ireland in Comparative Perspective*. Dublin: Institute of Public Administration.

Commission of Inquiry into the Civil Service, 1935. *Final Report with Appendices*. Dublin: Stationery Office.

Costello, Francis J., 2003. *The Irish Revolution and its Aftermath, 1916–1923: Years of Revolt*. Dublin: Irish Academic Press.

Cronin, Mike, 1997. *The Blueshirts and Irish Politics*. Dublin: Four Courts Press.

Cronin, Mike and John M. Regan (eds), 2000. *Ireland: The Politics of Independence, 1922–49*. Basingstoke: Macmillan.

Cronin, Mike and Liam O'Callaghan, 2015. *A History of Ireland*. 2nd ed. Basingstoke: Palgrave Macmillan.

Crotty, William and David E. Schmitt (eds), 1998. *Ireland and the Politics of Change*. London: Longman.

Daly, Mary E., 1997. *The Buffer State: The Historical Roots of the Department of the Environment*. Dublin: Institute of Public Administration.

Daly, Mary E., 2016. *Sixties Ireland: Reshaping the Economy, State and Society, 1957–1973*. Cambridge: Cambridge University Press.

Daly, Paul, Rónán O'Brien and Paul Rouse (eds), 2012. *Making the Difference: The Irish Labour Party, 1912–2012*. Dublin: Collins Press.

Duggan, John P., 1991. *A History of the Irish Army*. Dublin: Gill and Macmillan.

Dunphy, Richard, 1995. *The Making of Fianna Fail Power in Ireland, 1923–1948*. Oxford: Oxford University Press.

English, Richard, 2007. *Irish Freedom: A History of Irish Nationalism*. London: Macmillan.

English, Richard, 2012. *Armed Struggle: The History of the IRA*, revised ed. London: Pan.

Fanning, Ronan, 1978. *The Irish Department of Finance, 1922–58*. Dublin: Institute of Public Administration.

Fanning, Ronan, 2013. *Fatal Path: British Government and Irish Revolution 1910–1922*. London: Faber and Faber.

Farrell, Brian (ed.), 1994. *The Creation of the Dáil*. Dublin: Blackwater Press.

Ferguson, Stephen, 2016. *The Post Office in Ireland: An Illustrated History*. Dublin: Irish Academic Press.

Ferriter, Diarmaid, 2004. *The Transformation of Ireland 1900–2000*. London: Profile Books.

Ferriter, Diarmaid, 2012. *Ambiguous Republic: Ireland in the 1970s*. London: Profile Books.

Fitzpatrick, David, 1998. *The Two Irelands 1912–1939*. Oxford: Oxford University Press.

Foster, Gavin M., 2015. *The Irish Civil War and Society: Politics, Class and Conflict*. London: Palgrave Macmillan.

Gallagher, Michael, 1982. *The Irish Labour Party in Transition 1957–82*. Manchester: Manchester University Press.

Gallagher, Michael, 1985. *Political Parties in the Republic of Ireland*. Dublin: Gill and Macmillan.

Gallagher, Michael and Michael Marsh, 2002. *Days of Blue Loyalty: The Politics of Membership of the Fine Gael Party*. Dublin: PSAI Press.

Gallagher, Michael and Michael Marsh (eds), 2016. *How Ireland Voted 2016: The Election that Nobody Won*. Basingstoke: Palgrave Macmillan.

Galligan, Yvonne, 1998. *Women and Politics in Contemporary Ireland: From the Margins to the Mainstream*. London: Pinter.

Galligan, Yvonne, Eilís Ward and Rick Wilford (eds), 1999. *Contesting Politics: Women in Ireland North and South*. Boulder, CO: Westview; Limerick: PSAI Press.

Garvin, Tom, 1996. *1922: The Birth of Irish Democracy*. Dublin: Gill and Macmillan.

Garvin, Tom, 2004. *Preventing the Future: Politics, Education and Development in Ireland, 1937–1967*. Dublin: Gill and Macmillan.

Garvin, Tom, 2010. *News from a New Republic: Ireland in the 1950s*. Dublin: Gill and Macmillan.

Girvin, Brian and Gary Murphy (eds), 2005. *The Lemass Era: Politics and Society in the Ireland of Seán Lemass*. Dublin: UCD Press.

Girvin, Brian and Gary Murphy (eds), 2010. *Continuity, Change and Crisis in Contemporary Ireland*. London: Routledge.

Gray, Peter and Olwen Purdue (eds), 2012. *The Irish Lord Lieutenancy c. 1541–1922*. Dublin: UCD Press.

Hardiman, Niamh, 2012. *Irish Governance in Crisis*. Manchester: Manchester University Press.

Harkness, D. W., 1996. *Ireland in the Twentieth Century: Divided Island*. Basingstoke: Macmillan.

Hopkinson, Michael, 2002. *The Irish War of Independence*. Dublin: Gill and Macmillan.

Hoppen, K. Theodore, 1984. *Elections, Politics and Society in Ireland 1832–1885*. Oxford: Clarendon Press.

Hoppen, K. Theodore, 2016. *Governing Hibernia: British Politicians and Ireland 1800–1921*. Oxford: Oxford University Press.

Hutchinson, John, 1987. *The Dynamics of Cultural Nationalism: The Gaelic Revival and the Creation of the Irish Nation State*. London: Allen and Unwin.

Jackson, Alvin, 2003. *Home Rule:An Irish History, 1800–2000*. London: Weidenfeld and Nicolson.

Jackson, Alvin, 2010. *Ireland 1798–1998: War, Peace and Beyond*, 2nd ed. Oxford: Wiley Blackwell.

Johnston-Liik, Edith Mary, 2002. *History of the Irish Parliament 1692–1800: Commons, Constituencies and Statutes*. 6 vols. Belfast: Ulster Historical Foundation.

Kennedy, Michael, 2012. 'The foundation and consolidation of Irish foreign policy: 1919–45', in Ben Tonra, Michael Kennedy, John Doyle and Noel Dorr (eds), *Irish Foreign Policy*. Dublin: Gill and Macmillan, pp. 20–35.

Keogh, Dermot, 1994. *Twentieth Century Ireland: Nation and State*. Dublin: Gill and Macmillan.

Kirby, Peadar and Mary P. Murphy, 2011. *Towards a Second Republic: Irish Politics after the Celtic Tiger*. London: Pluto Press.

Kissane, Bill, 2002. *Explaining Irish Democracy*. Dublin: UCD Press.

Kissane, Bill, 2005. *The Politics of the Irish Civil War*. Oxford: Oxford University Press.

Kissane, Bill, 2011. *New Beginnings: Constitutionalism and Democracy in Modern Ireland*. Dublin: UCD Press.

Kostick, Conor, 2009. *Revolution in Ireland: Popular Militancy 1917–1923*. Rev. ed. Cork: Cork University Press.

Laffan, Michael, 1983. *The Partition of Ireland, 1911–25*. Dundalk: Dundalgan Press, for the Dublin Historical Association.

Laffan, Michael, 1999. *The Resurrection of Ireland: The Sinn Féin Party, 1916–1923*. Cambridge: Cambridge University Press.

Lee, J. J., 1989. *Ireland 1912–1985: Politics and Society*. Cambridge: Cambridge University Press.

Legg, Marie-Louise, 1998. *Newspapers and Nationalism: The Irish Provincial Press, 1850–1892*. Dublin: Four Courts Press.

McBride, Lawrence W., 1991. *The Greening of Dublin Castle: The Transformation of Bureaucratic and Judicial Personnel in Ireland, 1892–1922*. Washington, DC: Catholic University of America Press.

MacCarthaigh, Muiris, 2009. *Government in Modern Ireland*. Dublin: Institute of Public Administration.

MacCarthaigh, Muiris, 2010. *National Non-Commercial State Agencies in Ireland* [Research Paper no. 1]. Dublin: Institute of Public Administration.

McColgan, John, 1983. *British Policy and the Irish Administration 1920–22*. London: George Allen and Unwin.

McCullagh, David, 1998. *A Makeshift Majority: The First Inter-Party Government 1948–51*. Dublin: Institute of Public Administration.

McDermott, Eithne, 1998. *Clann na Poblachta*. Cork: Cork University Press.

McDowell, R. B., 1964. *The Irish Administration 1801–1914*. London: Routledge and Kegan Paul.

McGarry, Fearghal, 2010. *The Rising: Easter 1916*. Oxford: Oxford University Press.

McGee, Eoin, 2007. *The IRB: The Irish Republican Brotherhood, from the Land League to Sinn Fein*, 2nd ed. Dublin: Four Courts Press.

McGee, Harry, 2014. 'Coalition's "quango cull" falls well short of promises', *Irish Times*, 21 April.

McGraw, Sean D., 2015. *How Parties Win: Shaping the Irish Political Arena*. Ann Arbor: University of Michigan Press.

MacMillan, Gretchen, 1993. *State, Society and Authority in Ireland: The Foundation of the Modern State*. Dublin: Gill and Macmillan.

Maguire, Martin, 2008. *The Civil Service and the Revolution in Ireland, 1912–38: 'Shaking the Blood-Stained Hand of Mr Collins'*. Manchester: Manchester University Press.

Manning, Maurice, 1987. *The Blueshirts*, new ed. Dublin: Gill and Macmillan.

Marsh, Michael, David M. Farrell and Gail McElroy (eds), 2017. *A Conservative Revolution? Electoral Change in Twenty-First-Century Ireland*. Oxford: Oxford University Press.

Meehan, Ciara, 2010. *The Cosgrave Party: A History of Cumann na nGaedheal, 1923–33*. Dublin: Royal Irish Academy.

Meehan, Ciara, 2013. *A Just Society for Ireland? 1964–1987*. Basingstoke: Palgrave Macmillan.

Mitchell, Arthur, 1995. *Revolutionary Government in Ireland: Dáil Éireann, 1919–22*. Dublin: Gill and Macmillan.

Moody, T.W. and F.X. Martin (eds), 2011. *The Course of Irish History*. New ed. Cork: Mercier.

Murphy, Gary, 2016. *Electoral Competition in Ireland since 1987: The Politics of Triumph and Despair*. Manchester: Manchester University Press.

Murray, Thomas, 2016. *Contesting Economic and Social Rights in Ireland: Constitution, State and Society, 1848–2016*. Cambridge: Cambridge University Press.

O'Brien, Justin, 2000. *The Arms Trial*. Dublin: Gill and Macmillan.

O'Day, Alan, 1998. *Irish Home Rule 1867–1921*. Manchester: Manchester University Press.

O'Halpin, Eunan, 1987. *The Decline of the Union: British Government in Ireland 1892–1920*. Dublin: Gill and Macmillan.

O'Halpin, Eunan, 1996. 'The army in independent Ireland', in Thomas Bartlett and Keith Jeffery (eds), *A Military History of Ireland*. Cambridge: Cambridge University Press, pp. 407–30.

O'Malley, Eoin and Muiris MacCarthaigh (eds), 2012. *Governing Ireland: From Cabinet Government to Delegated Governance*. Dublin: Institute of Public Administration.

O'Toole, John and Sean Dooney, 2009. *Irish Government Today*, 3rd ed. Dublin: Gill and Macmillan.

Potter, Matthew, 2011. *The Municipal Revolution in Ireland: A Handbook of Urban Government in Ireland since 1800*. Dublin: Irish Academic Press.

Prager, Jeffrey, 1986. *Building Democracy in Ireland: Political Order and Cultural Integration in a Newly Independent Nation*. Cambridge: Cambridge University Press.

Puirséil, Niamh, 2007. *The Irish Labour Party, 1922–1973*. Dublin: UCD Press.

Purdon, Edward, 2000. *The Irish Civil War 1922–23*. Cork: Mercier Press.

Rafter, Kevin, 1996. *The Clann: The Story of Clann na Poblachta*. Cork: Mercier.

Rafter, Kevin, 2011. *Democratic Left: The Life and Death of an Irish Political Party*. Dublin: Irish Academic Press.

Regan, John Martin, 1999. *The Irish Counter-Revolution 1921–1936: Treatyite Politics and Settlement in Independent Ireland*. Dublin: Gill and Macmillan.

Sartori, Giovanni, 1976. *Parties and Party Systems: A Framework for Analysis*. Cambridge: Cambridge University Press.

Townshend, Charles, 2013. *The Republic: The Fight for Irish Independence, 1918–1923*. London: Allen Lane.

Townshend, Charles, 2015. *Easter 1916: The Irish Rebellion*, 2nd ed. London: Penguin.

Varley, Tony, 2010. 'On the road to extinction: agrarian parties in twentieth-century Ireland', *Irish Political Studies* 25:4, pp. 581–601.

Walker, Brian M., 2012. *A Political History of the Two Irelands: From Partition to Peace*. Basingstoke: Palgrave Macmillan.

Ward, Alan J, 1994. *The Irish Constitutional Tradition: Representative Government and Modern Ireland, 1782–1992*. Dublin: Irish Academic Press.

Weeks, Liam and Aodh Quinlivan, 2009. *All Politics is Local: A Guide to Local Elections in Ireland*. Cork: Collins Press.

Weeks, Liam and Alistair Clark (eds), 2012. *Radical or Redundant? Minor Parties in Irish Politics*. Dublin: History Press.

Whelan, Noel, 2011. *Fianna Fáil: A Biography of the Party*. Dublin: Gill and Macmillan.

White, Timothy J. and Denis Marnane, 2016. 'The politics of remembrance: commemorating 1916', *Irish Political Studies* 31:1, pp. 29–43.

Websites

politicalreform.ie
Contemporary issues, by Political Studies Association of Ireland

electionsireland.org
Invaluable collection of election results from 1918 onwards

historyhub.ie/
Papers and links from the School of History, UCD

ucc.ie/celt/
CELT: Corpus of Electronic Texts (collection of older historical texts)

irishstatutebook.ie
Texts of constitutions, laws and statutory instruments, including pre-1922 material

politics.ie
Current affairs discussion forum

2   Society and political culture

John Coakley

No matter how cleverly designed any system of government is, it will function well only if it is broadly acceptable, or at least not too unacceptable, to the population whose affairs it regulates. For this reason, before going on to look at the formal framework of government, or the constitution, in Chapter 3, we look in this chapter at the pattern of deep-seated popular values and attitudes to which the label 'political culture' is conventionally applied: fundamental, strongly held views on the state itself, on the rules of the political process and on the kind of principles that should underlie political decision making.

This chapter begins with a discussion of the concept of 'political culture' and an examination of its importance in political life. This will show that political cultural values do not exist in isolation; they are influenced by the social backgrounds and life experiences of those who hold them. We continue, therefore, by looking at the context within which Irish political cultural values have been acquired through an examination of the evolution of certain aspects of Irish society. We go on to consider the extent to which this pattern of evolution has generated a characteristic set of values. Finally, it is clear that no cultural pattern of this kind is homogeneous; we need, therefore, to consider divisions within Irish society and Irish political culture, and the impact of the rapid pace of social evolution over recent decades.

Political culture and its importance

The importance of political culture for political stability is now taken for granted: the way in which a society is governed must not deviate too far from the expectations of the politically conscious public, unless the state relies on coercion. The political culture of a particular society need not, of course, be supportive of democratic institutions. Well-meaning attempts to impose liberal democratic constitutions in societies that do not share the kind of thinking that underlies them may well end in failure. This happened in many of the new states that appeared in central and eastern Europe after the First World War, in areas outside Europe (for instance, in the British Commonwealth), after the Second World War, in certain post-communist societies after 1989, and in a number of war-torn countries such as Afghanistan and Iraq in the early years of the twenty-first century. As these cases illustrate, political institutions of a particular type cannot easily be imposed on a society unwilling to accept them; even authoritarian government is assisted by a supportive political culture.

The nature of political culture

The widespread use of the term 'political culture' and the creation of a systematic theory arguing its central importance in the political process date from the publication in 1963 of

The Civic Culture by two American scholars, Gabriel Almond and Sidney Verba (see Almond and Verba, 1989). Their central argument was that 'democracy is stable or consolidated when specifically democratic attitudes and practices combine and function in equilibrium with certain non-democratic ones' (Almond, 2015: 190). The view that stable democracy requires not just supportive values but also a general public that is in large measure relatively uninformed and indifferent may be surprising, but it rests on an assumption that democracy requires a balance between individuals keen to be involved in decision making and a large population that is happy to be led by the decisions of others. Research from the 1970s onwards, however, suggested that democracy was also compatible with patterns of rapid value change and the emergence of more critical citizens (see Almond and Verba, 1980). Ultimately, the notion that political stability in democracies relies on an 'allegiant' political culture was displaced by the view that democracy was increasingly characterised by an 'assertive' citizenry – one not deferring to the ruling elites, but demanding change and reform (Dalton and Welzel, 2015). This suggests that liberal democracies are populated by people subject to two types of orientation, and that comparative survey data may be used to measure them. The first type comprises 'allegiant orientations', referring to people's confidence in public institutions, their trust in others, their belief in democracy, their interest in politics and their disposition to comply with laws and other norms. The second type consists of 'assertive orientations', rooted in libertarian, egalitarian and expressive views, as measured by commitment to individual liberties, to equal opportunities and to the right of people to have a voice in collective decisions (Welzel and Dalton, 2015: 291–3).

A useful framework for applying this approach in an Irish context starts by identifying three levels (Powell *et al.*, 2015: 64–8). These three levels correspond approximately to three layers of values that a person acquires through the process of political socialisation – through the influence of family, school or peers, for instance.

- The *system* level refers to the state itself as a geopolitical structure and to people's attitudes towards it. This touches on a person's *core* values, absorbed during childhood and early adolescence; these relate to such matters as national identity, and tend to be stable and resistant to change in later life.
- The *process* level refers to the rules of the political game – the basic constitutional principles that determine how decisions are taken – and the public's view of these. Attitudes to these typically constitute a deep, *inner layer* of values, acquired during adolescence and early adulthood; these relate to fundamental principles of government, and may change, but not easily (this is the level on which the analysis of political culture mainly focuses).
- The *policy* level refers to the actual outcomes of the decision-making process – the pattern of public policy that is followed by the state and the extent to which it matches citizens' expectations. This corresponds to an *outer layer* of values, acquired for the most part in adult life; these relate to day-to-day political issues and tend to be consistent over time, but are more susceptible to change than the deeper ones discussed earlier.

Determinants of political culture

As well as describing Ireland's political culture by reference to this framework, it is important to remember that no political cultural pattern comes about simply by accident; its roots matter. The same kinds of structural forces help to shape it as those that influence political life more generally. These fall into three broad but distinct areas that interact with and influence each other. First, the shape of a country's path of *socio-economic development* is of great importance: the extent to which society has industrialised or even passed through to a post-industrial phase, the nature of this process and its effects on social structure. The second dimension is the pattern of *cultural evolution*: the degree to which particular norms and values (such as religious ones) have come to be dominant and the extent to which these are challenged by alternative values (such as loyalty to distinctive ethnic or linguistic groups). Third, a country's long-term *political experience* needs to be considered: geopolitical evolution, external influences, internal developments, patterns of past domination by distinctive groups and other consequences of the course of history may be of great significance in shaping people's contemporary political values.

This chapter rests on the assumption, then, that the pattern of political activity in any society is in large measure a product of the political culture of that society; and that political culture is, in turn, a product of a complex interplay of more fundamental societal factors. In other words, we would expect that such factors as level of socio-economic development, underlying cultural make-up (including such features as religious composition) and long-term political experience would each have an impact on people's political values at all levels, from the most profound and immutable to the most immediate and superficial.

But the causal chain need not be entirely in one direction. It is true that political culture gives substance to the institutions of state; but the direction of causation may also be reversed. Few states are merely passive victims of their political cultures; most attempt – some with exceptional vigour – also to shape their citizens' political values, and challenging elites (such as nationalist leaders) may also seek to do so, though they have fewer resources. The mechanisms for exerting influence of this kind may be direct: through speeches and other direct cues from political leaders, through central control or manipulation of the mass media or, most powerfully of all, through the education system. The teaching of such subjects as history and civics, in particular, may be a very effective mechanism for attempting to influence or even remould a political culture. But the mechanisms may also be indirect: a state may in the long term seek to transform its own socio-economic infrastructure, to convert its citizens from one religion to another or to transform patterns of linguistic usage – all with a view to promoting ultimate value change. The Irish experience is an interesting case study of the interplay between political culture and democratic institutions. It shared many structural and historical characteristics with certain short-lived democracies in central and eastern Europe that also came into existence after the First World War; it is, then, important to ask why democracy seems to have survived in Ireland while collapsing elsewhere (see Kissane, 2002, 2011).

Stability and change in Irish society

When the first systematic attempts to examine aspects of Irish political culture got under way in the early 1970s, it was still possible to describe Ireland as 'an agricultural country of small, scattered family farms'; the Irish people as being strongly attached to the Catholic church and as adhering to a religion of 'an austere and puritanical variety that is somewhat cold and authoritarian'; and Irish society as being insulated from Europe by an all-pervasive British influence (Chubb, 1970: 51, 53, 46–7; see also Farrell, 1971: ix–xx; Schmitt, 1973). These characteristics, authors suggested, combined to produce a distinctive political culture that was marked by such features as nationalism, authoritarianism, anti-intellectualism and personalism. Before going on to speculate in the next section about the extent to which such features arise in contemporary Ireland, we examine in the present section the background characteristics in Irish society that are likely to have had an impact on political values. The pattern that we encounter is one of relative stability, perhaps masking slow change, until the 1970s, but of accelerating change since then in each of the three domains that we have already discussed: economic transformation, cultural secularisation and geopolitical reorientation (on long-term Irish economic development, see Ó Gráda, 1997; McCann, 2011; on aspects of economic development, O'Hagan and O'Toole, 2017; Donovan and Murphy, 2013; and for perspectives on Irish society, Bartley and Kitchin, 2007; Kirby and Murphy, 2011; O'Malley, 2011; Inglis, 2014; Roche *et al.*, 2017).

Socio-economic development

The outstanding characteristic of socio-economic development in Ireland, viewed over the long term, has been a fundamental shift in the nature of the economy and a radical change in social structure. In this, Ireland has not been unique; researchers from different disciplines and ideological perspectives have pointed to the central importance of the revolutionary socio-economic transition through which all western societies have progressed, whether this is described as a transition from agrarian (or preindustrial) to industrial society, from feudal (or precapitalist) to capitalist society, or from traditional to modern society. This change may best be appreciated by considering 'ideal types' (theoretical descriptions that do not necessarily exist in reality) of the two kinds of society. It should be noted that these types refer to more or less integrated packages of characteristics spanning a wide range of areas, rather than being confined exclusively to economic change as implied in the narrow sense of the word 'industrial'. Many western societies have indeed progressed beyond this, into a later 'postindustrial' phase, whose implications for political culture need also to be borne in mind; but our present focus is on the great historical transition from agrarian to industrial society, which had a lasting impact on socio-political attitudes in twentieth-century Ireland.

Agrarian society has been typified as that in which the population, by definition, is overwhelmingly involved in the primary sector of the economy (with peasants relying on mixed subsistence agriculture and the industrial sector confined to small-scale cottage industries and crafts); with predominantly rural settlement patterns; mainly illiterate, and with an oral tradition dominated by village-based or regional dialects; with only a restricted transport network; and with poorly developed communications media. In stereotypical industrial society these characteristics are reversed. The population is overwhelmingly involved in the industrial or services sectors (with large-scale, machine dependent industry and a small, surviving agricultural sector of specialised commercial farmers); with predominantly urban settlement patterns; mainly or even universally literate in a modern, standardised language; and with a high degree of mobility – of people and goods, and of ideas.

A profound difference between the two types of society arises in the area of social relations. In agrarian society, the individual is born into a particular rank, kinship group and village, and faces a fixed set of occupational options. Mobility prospects are restricted not just by society itself but also by the individual's own acceptance of his or her existing role as inevitable and natural. In industrial society, by contrast, regardless of the position into which an individual is born, the prospects for spatial and occupational mobility are much greater, not just because society is open to this, but because the individual's own perspective allows him or her freely to contemplate such roles. By contrast to agrarian society, where the existing order and the individual's role within it are accepted, in industrial society the typical individual has a capacity to envisage himself or herself occupying an unlimited range of roles. In reality, the class structure of industrial society tends to be self-reproducing, and the formal entitlement to social mobility may not be realised in practice; but its more open and nominally egalitarian basis raises prospects for new forms of political mobilisation, electoral participation and ideological formation.

Where does Ireland fit between the poles of agrarian and industrial society defined earlier – or might it even have developed so far that it is better described as postindustrial? The data on occupational structure and urbanisation in Appendix 1a are summarised in Figure 2.1, which also considers two other variables, language and literacy. If economic development was relatively slow, with Irish society long remaining rural and agrarian, the pace of other aspects of social change was relatively rapid. Although secondary education, in Ireland as elsewhere, was left to private interests or to the churches until the late twentieth century, and third-level education had negligible impact on the public until around the same time, the state intervened at an early stage in primary education. After 1831 an ambitious network of 'national schools' was established throughout the country, and by the end of the nineteenth century, the great bulk of children of school-going age were attending these schools. The impact of this system and of the efforts of other agencies on levels of literacy was dramatic, as Figure 2.1 shows. By 1911, literacy levels had reached 86 per cent (the question on literacy was discontinued in subsequent censuses); and virtually all (99.7 per cent) were able to speak English. Furthermore, between the 1880s and 1920s, the stark cleavage between landlords and tenants (a common feature of agrarian societies) was overcome as the process of state-sponsored land purchase established and consolidated the principle of peasant proprietorship and led to the disappearance of traditional landlords as a class.

The level of educational development in Ireland and the growth of literacy, then, proceeded much more quickly than the more retarded pace of economic development would have suggested. This anomaly draws attention to one of the hazards of viewing socio-economic development in isolation from external relationships and influences, especially those of dependence. Although Ireland (or at least the south) was an economically backward periphery, it formed, until 1922, part of one of the world's most advanced industrial states.

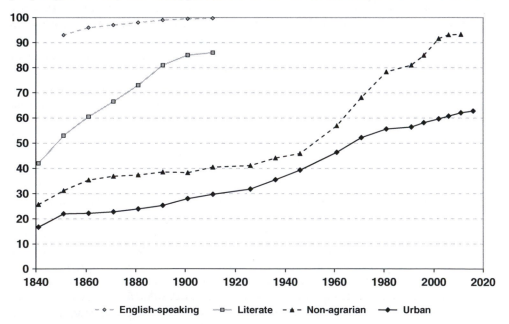

Figure 2.1 Urban population, non-agrarian population, literacy and language, 1841–2016

Source: *Census of Ireland*, various years, 1841–2016.

Note: Data are percentages.

The British government was prepared to promote a separate agenda for Ireland, overseeing the establishment there of an advanced primary education system and of a developed transport infrastructure that included thousands of miles of roads and railways.

British educational policy in Ireland was not disinterested: it also contributed to the anglicisation of the country. The earliest reliable information on the linguistic structure of the population shows that already in 1851 almost all of the population (94 per cent of those in the present territory of the Republic) were able to speak English, and that a considerable majority (61 per cent) were able to speak English only. As the nineteenth century progressed the trend of anglicisation continued, with the result that by the beginning of the twentieth century virtually the entire adult population was familiar with a single language of wider communication, English.

The right-hand side of Figure 2.1 points to a more recent and particularly striking phenomenon: it shows clearly that, after many decades of relative stability, the period since 1960 has been characterised by economic and social change that is almost revolutionary in scope. The proportion of the workforce engaged in agriculture has been plummeting and the urban population has expanded. The character of the non-agricultural workforce has been changing rapidly, with a move from traditional industry to high technology manufacturing, and a big expansion in the insurance, financial, information technology and business services sectors.

All of this has been associated with yet another development that is likely to have a considerable social effect: the growing wealth of Irish society. For most of the twentieth century, Ireland coexisted with the United Kingdom (UK) as a poorer, trade-dependent neighbour. But towards the end of the twentieth century, this began to change: GDP per capita rose more rapidly in Ireland than in the United Kingdom, which it had overtaken by 1998.[1] The associated high employment levels and living standards transformed the long-standing character of the Irish economy (Coakley, 2013: 22–6). The economic recession that began in 2008, of course, left its mark on these trends, as unemployment and emigration rates began to rise. But the economy recovered in the 2010s with surprising speed. The remarkable trade dependence on the UK, similarly, had been changing gradually since the 1970s; by 2015, the proportion of Irish goods exports to the UK (by value) had dropped to 14 per cent and of imports to 26 per cent (Central Statistics Office, 2016a: 7).

Overall, then, the Ireland of the early twenty-first century is fundamentally different from that of the early twentieth century. Aside from the areas discussed earlier, there have been dramatic improvements in infant mortality and life expectancy (for a fascinating statistical comparison of life in 1916 and a century later, see Central Statistics Office, 2016b). Dramatic though the statistics may be, they do not tell the full story: qualitative changes have also been taking place. The decline in the agricultural sector of the population, for example, does not mean simply that there are fewer farmers; the character of farming has been transformed from a way of life into just another enterprise, as small family farms have been replaced by larger agribusinesses. Indeed, rural Ireland as it was traditionally conceived is disappearing as villages in the hinterland of larger urban settlements become dormitory towns. By the end of the 1990s, the national rail and bus service interpreted the Dublin commuter area as being enclosed in a semicircle whose circumference was defined by the towns of Dundalk, Carrickmacross, Mullingar, Tullamore, Portlaoise, Carlow and Gorey (towns ranging from 80 to 100 kilometres from Dublin). By 2011, almost 10 per cent of workers spent at least an hour commuting to work, a commitment that would have been unimaginable to their grandparents.

But the very nature of work has also changed, as traditional communication mechanisms have given way to new technology. The powerful impact of the internet is the most obvious expression of this. When it was in its infancy in 1998, only 5 per cent of households in

Ireland had a connection; but that figure had risen to 85 per cent by 2015, 2 per cent above the overall EU level (Central Statistics Office, 2017). Combined with increased availability of mobile telephones, this has facilitated new forms of social networking, transforming not just individuals' private relationships but also their working environment. Indeed, the labour force itself has changed fundamentally, not just in its size and diversity, but also in respect of its level of education. Traditionally the preserve of the elite, the proportion availing of third-level education increased dramatically in the late twentieth century; by 2015 the proportion of persons aged 25–34 with a third-level education had increased to 49 per cent, well above the overall EU figure of 37 per cent.

Religion and cultural change

Given its traditional role in society and public life, the changing significance of religion is of great importance, and there, too, change has been dramatic. As regards religious affiliation, a great majority of the population belongs to the Catholic church (see Appendix 1a). Protestants, who in the nineteenth century constituted 25 per cent of the population of the island, amounted to a minority of only 10 per cent in the south immediately after partition. Furthermore, many male members of this community had been killed in the First World War; many had been associated with the old regime, and left after 1922; and many were landlords who lost their estates or who were subjected to intimidation at around the same period, and who also left. The remaining Protestant population shrank to a low of 3 per cent in 1991, but since then it has increased again, largely as a consequence of immigration. By 2016, the proportion of Catholics in the population had fallen to 78 per cent, with Protestants accounting for 5 per cent, non-Christian religions for another 5 per cent, those with no religion for 10 per cent and the balance not stating their religion.

From a comparative point of view, the position of the Catholic religion within Irish society has been rather remarkable. Unlike the position in central and eastern Europe (the most obvious part of the continent in which to look for comparable societies in an historical perspective), it was along religious denominational, rather than linguistic, lines that political mobilisation took place in the nineteenth century. Rather in the manner of the Balkans, then, a strong bond between religion and ethnonational identity developed, with Catholics tending to identify with the Gaelic cultural tradition and Protestants with the British heritage. This had implications for attitudes towards public symbols, myths of the past and perspectives on the relationship between Ireland and Great Britain. The strong association between religion and identity was reinforced by the fact that the institutional Catholic church in Ireland, up to the nineteenth century, was not a major landowner, was not linked to the old regime, and was neutral or sympathetic on the issues of democratisation and nationalism, rather than being suspicious or hostile, as in continental Europe. Already before the new state was founded, then, Ireland was noted for the remarkable loyalty of Catholics to the church and for the absence of a tradition of anticlericalism (Whyte, 1980: 3–8). This relationship was cemented through the educational system, in which the Catholic church for a long time had an unchallenged role.

It is clear that until the 1970s the level of commitment to traditional Irish Catholicism was extremely high. This was reflected not just in the character of public debate but also in objective indicators such as church attendance, participation in church activities and clerical vocations. Those attending church at least once weekly amounted to more than 90 per cent throughout the 1970s, as Figure 2.2 shows. This figure dropped a little in the 1980s and much more dramatically in the late 1990s. By 2014, only 34 per cent were weekly churchgoers. Behind these figures lies an even more stark development. Until about 1980, weekly church

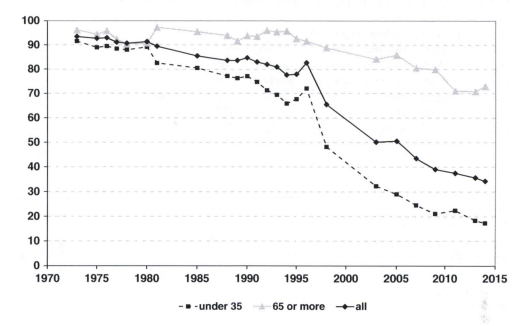

Figure 2.2 Weekly church attendance, Ireland, 1973–2014

Source: Derived from Eurobarometer trend file, 1973–99, and European Social Survey, 2002–14.

Note: The data are percentages and refer to those stating that they attend church at least once a week.

attendance was the norm among all age groups; but these then began to diverge. The decline in church attendance was quite slow among those aged 65 or more, but accelerated among the young; by 2014, only 17 per cent of those aged under 35 were weekly churchgoers, as opposed to 73 per cent of those over 65.

These changes were accompanied by a sharp decline in the moral authority of the leadership of the Catholic church, driven both by increased secularisation (as levels of worship declined) and clerical child sex abuse scandals, which shocked even the most loyal Catholics (see Fuller, 2002: 237–68). They were also matched by the erosion of other forms of religious practice, such as pilgrimages and private prayer (Inglis, 1998: 24–30). A catastrophic decline in clerical recruitment has left the Catholic church without the personnel needed to staff its schools, and raises questions about its capacity to service even its churches (Coakley, 2013: 32–5, 241–2). Increased secularisation is also reflected in a move away from traditional religious solemnisation of major life events. By 2015, 38 per cent of all marriages were civil or non-religious, but the significance of marriage itself was diminishing; in the same year, 36 per cent of all births were registered as outside marriage.

These changing patterns of religious belief and practice were, in part, a consequence of social change, but they were also driven by shifting migration patterns. For the duration of the twentieth century, the share of the population born outside the Republic of Ireland was accounted for overwhelmingly by persons born in the UK (mainly in England and Wales, but with substantial portions from Northern Ireland and Scotland). Already by the end of the century, though, a trickle of immigrants from outside Europe began (see Figure 2.3). In the early twenty-first century this expanded greatly, and was joined by substantial immigration from the new EU member states, following their accession in 2004 (see Fanning, 2009, 2011; Gilmartin, 2015). In 2016, when the proportion of the population born outside the

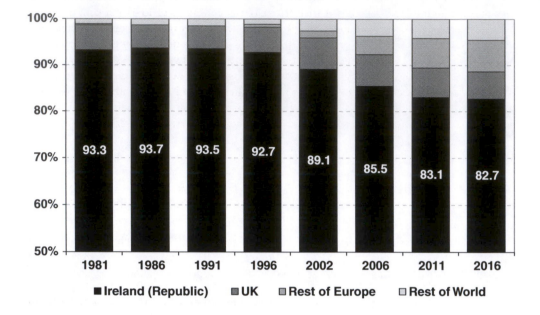

Figure 2.3 Place of birth of Irish population, census years, 1981–2016

Source: Census of Ireland, relevant years.

Republic amounted to 17 per cent, by far the most important contributor was the UK (212,000 Irish residents were born in England and Wales, 58,000 in Northern Ireland and 18,000 in Scotland), followed by Poland (115,000), Lithuania (35,000), USA (28,000), Latvia (20,000) and Nigeria (20,000).

Political experience

Given the centuries-long British presence on the island, it is not surprising that British rule has left a lasting imprint on the Irish political mentality. Whether or not Ireland was a willing recipient, Britain bequeathed to its neighbouring island its dominant language, much of its culture, many of its social practices and, most importantly for present purposes, its political vocabulary, concepts, institutions and patterns of behaviour. A large volume of Irish emigration to (and a smaller volume of reverse migration from) Britain has been characteristic of Irish population movement patterns. For long after independence, a close economic relationship also remained, with the two countries sharing a common currency until 1979 and with a remarkably high degree of Irish trade dependence on the British market: for several decades after 1922 the greater part of Ireland's imports came from Great Britain, and approximately three quarters of Irish exports were destined for Britain.

One of the most obvious aspects of the British legacy has been in the domain of language, as we have already noted. The British may have failed to assimilate the Irish to their religion; but where religious proselytism failed, anglicisation succeeded. The Irish language was in a very weak position by 1922, notwithstanding the energetic activities of revivalists. Little effort was made by the new state to halt its decline in Gaeltacht areas, though enormous resources were devoted to providing children in English-speaking Ireland with a rudimentary knowledge of Irish. While official statistics, for a long time, showed a steady rise in the proportion claiming a knowledge of Irish (from 18 per cent in 1911 to 41 per cent in 2011), this fell back to 40 per cent in 2016. The precarious position of the language is much graver than this small drop would suggest. The 2016 census reported only a tiny proportion of the population speaking Irish on a daily basis outside the education system (less than 2 per cent); in the *Gaeltacht* (Irish-speaking districts, a set of dispersed pockets mainly in the western seaboard counties), the corresponding proportion had fallen to 32 per cent. But the position of Irish as a living language in these areas was already critical, with a real possibility of its complete disappearance as a first language within decades (Ó Giollagáin *et al.*, 2007).

From a comparative point of view, the position of Irish has been unique and extraordinary. It has been given a powerful constitutional and legal position because of its status as the perceived ancestral language, yet most of the population fail to understand it and very few speak it on a daily basis. Although the language issue was used by the early nationalist movement, it was important as a symbol of Irish identity, rather than as a medium of communication. The language revival movement was, strangely, made up overwhelmingly of people whose home language was English, and, by sharp contrast to the position in central and eastern Europe, the language boundary in Ireland did not separate two ethnonational groups – speakers of the two languages felt equally Irish.

Geographical proximity and a shared language thus continued to promote British influence in Ireland even after 1922. It was not only goods and people that travelled freely to Ireland from the neighbouring island; ideas could also do so. British newspapers have always circulated widely in Ireland. They accounted for at least 10 per cent of daily newspaper circulation in Ireland in 1968, and 21 per cent in 1992; and this expansion continued into the twenty-first century, alongside growing penetration of the Irish market by British-based television stations (see Chapter 12). Given this close relationship, the decision of the UK to leave the EU has incalculable consequences, not just for British–Irish relations, but also for the North–South relationship on the island of Ireland, and the new challenges facing the border area (see Chapters 13 and 14).

Ireland's changing political culture

The long-term economic and social processes discussed earlier have produced a society in which particular patterns of political cultural values are likely to flourish. We consider these at the three levels outlined at the beginning of this chapter:

- The issue of national identity, typically a core value with implications for the geopolitical status of the state (we will examine the extent to which *nationalism* is a key component in Irish political culture);
- The question of attitudes towards democracy and decision making processes, which are typically deeply embedded in the political psychological makeup of the citizen (we will assess the extent to which a commitment to *democratic values* is characteristic of the Irish); and
- The domain of policy preferences, where people's values are more flexible (we will consider three areas, though rather more briefly than in the case of the more deeply embedded values discussed earlier: *conservatism*, a disposition to support economically non-interventionist policies, *clericalism*, a tendency to defer to the political leadership of the Catholic church, and *neutralism*, a preference for a strategy of non-alignment in the area of foreign policy).

Discussion of Irish political culture cannot be reduced simply to analysis of these five features; indeed, this list is far from exhaustive. But these features may be used as a framework for discussing Irish political cultural values, illustrating the extent to which change appears to have taken place over time in each one. In each case, the discussion begins with an examination of the meaning of the term and of its general implications, and continues with an assessment of such empirical evidence as is available – historical material of various kinds, electoral evidence and survey data (for survey-based approaches, see Fahey *et al.*, 2005; Garry *et al.*, 2006; Hilliard and Nic Ghiolla Phádraig, 2007; Lyons, 2008; Marsh *et al.*, 2008; Elkink and Farrell, 2016; Marsh *et al.*, 2017).

Nationalism?

Although the term is elastic, *nationalism* implies at a minimum a sense of loyalty to one's nation (Coakley, 2012: 4–14). The political implications of this loyalty depend on how the 'nation' is understood. If the nation with which people identify does not coincide with the state, then loyalty to it is likely to conflict with loyalty to the state (the collapse of the Soviet Union and of Yugoslavia were among the more drastic consequences of this form of conflict). Furthermore, when taken to excess, national loyalty can threaten other forms of human affiliation and can conflict with other ethical and political values (the ethnonational 'purification' of Nazi Germany through the extermination of national minorities is an example).

It is clear that as Irish people mobilised politically in the nineteenth century, the idea of an 'Irish nation' based on those who were of Catholic, Gaelic background became a central ideological ingredient, linked to the notion of autonomy (or possibly even independence) for the island of Ireland. Irish nationalism became essentially *separatist*, and increasingly rejected the legitimacy of the United Kingdom government. The ultimate expression of this attitude followed Sinn Féin's victory in the 1918 general election, when a majority of Irish MPs refused to attend the House of Commons and succeeded eventually in establishing a separate state. Had the goals of Irish nationalism been fully achieved, it is possible that nationalist sentiment in this form would have faded away or been transformed. As we saw in Chapter 1, however, full formal independence arrived only in 1949, and even then this did not extend over the whole island.

Irish nationalism after 1922, while continuing to be separatist, also became in large measure *irredentist*: achieving territorial unification through annexation of Northern Ireland was a central aim. This was written into the constitution in 1937 in the form of a definition of the national territory as comprising 'the whole island of Ireland, its islands and the territorial seas', and the irredentist policy was vigorously pursued at the rhetorical level, apparently with significant popular support, in the 1940s and the 1950s. The growing violence in Northern Ireland in the 1970s appears to have convinced policy makers that this form of nationalism was actually subversive of the state; through their efforts, but also as a consequence of other social changes, the intensity of irredentism gradually diminished in the last quarter of the century (Coakley, 2017). Furthermore, a progressive redefinition of the community appears to have taken place: identification with the population of the Republic of Ireland appears to be gradually replacing a form of identification that once extended to people living north of the border (Coakley, 2009).

Electoral evidence broadly supports this interpretation. Even in the turbulent 1920s, support for parties that rejected the legitimacy of the new state never significantly exceeded 25 per cent, and the main anti-treaty party's growing electoral success in the later 1920s and in the 1930s coincided with its increasingly moderate stance on the national question. Since then, the mainstream parties have appeared to be increasingly content with the status quo of partition. By the end of the 1990s, the decision by Sinn Féin to abide by the terms of the Good Friday agreement of 1998 (see Chapter 13), to accept the right of Northern Ireland to determine its own future, and to grant full recognition to the institutions of government there, marginalised fundamentalist nationalism; the party succeeded in bringing the great bulk of its electorate with it in this remarkable shift. The results of the May 1998 referendums in Northern Ireland and the Republic (in which respectively 71 per cent and 94 per cent voted in favour of the agreement) not only provided a popular mandate for the settlement but could also be presented as symbolically revoking what fundamentalist republicans had regarded as the irrevocable decision of the Irish people in 1918 in favour of an independent, united Irish republic.

Survey evidence suggests that, at its most basic, national identity in Ireland is not now greatly different from that in other European societies. But there are some respects in which Ireland stands out. When asked 'In the near future do you see yourself as Irish only, Irish and European, European and Irish, or European only', the Irish are much more likely to opt for 'Irish only' than the corresponding nationality in most other European countries; and over time there is relatively little evidence of change in this position (Heath and Spreckelsen, 2016: 14, 30–32). But survey evidence also permits us to explore further the character of contemporary Irish nationalism. We may use this, and supplementary information from other sources, to address a number of further questions:

- *Irredentism*: to what extent is the demand for territorial unity a continuing feature of Irish nationalism?
- *Patriotism*: in what respects is Irish nationalism a force that is supportive of the state?
- *Ethnocentrism*: to what extent are external groups regarded with hostility?

Perhaps inevitably, one legacy of partition has been increased differentiation between people on either side of the border. Especially after the outbreak of communal conflict in Northern Ireland, the attitudinal gap between the two parts of the island appears to have grown. In a survey conducted in the Republic in 1988–89, large numbers felt that Northern Ireland and the Republic were two separate nations (49 per cent agreed, 42 per cent disagreed) and that 'Northerners on all sides tend to be extreme and unreasonable' (35 per cent agreed, though 46 per cent disagreed) (Mac Gréil, 1996: 225, 234). There is evidence, however, that following the declaration of the IRA ceasefire in 1994, the psychological distance that separated southerners from the north has lessened, even if years of censorship of militant nationalist perspectives 'left huge gaps in understanding and many unrealistic expectations' (Ruane and Todd, 1996: 255).

Yet, territorial nationalism has not necessarily disappeared, though it is hard to measure. No standard question on attitudes towards Northern Ireland has been asked consistently in surveys, and polls have come up with different answers on attitudes towards unity (Coakley, 2009: 86). Broadly speaking, though, respondents favour Irish unity as a long-term goal, but typically not as an immediate solution. The findings of a 2015 poll summarise what has been the pattern since the late twentieth century. When respondents were asked if, in the context of the long-term policy for Northern Ireland, they would like to see a united Ireland, 82 per cent said they would; but if the respondent would have to pay more tax the proportion would drop to 42 per cent.[2]

When we turn to examine the extent to which Irish nationalism may be supportive of the state, it is true that we uncover patterns of patriotism that are in some respects stronger than those elsewhere in western Europe (though some counter-evidence may be found). In surveys in 1981 and 1990, the Irish were significantly more likely than other Europeans to claim that they would be willing to fight for their country in the event of war, and a much higher proportion (76 per cent in 1990) declared themselves to be 'very proud' of their nationality; the average for other European countries was 37 per cent (Ashford and Timms, 1992: 90). Irish people tend to report stronger levels of identification with their country than the European average; thus, in autumn 2016, for example, 71 per cent of Irish respondents said they were 'very attached' to their country; the overall response in EU member states was 56 per cent (Eurobarometer no. 86).[3]

In Ireland, as elsewhere, there is a darker side to nationalism: it can easily lead to intolerance and racism (see Fanning, 2012). Survey evidence from the late twentieth century identified a significant level of 'dormant' racism and ethnocentrism (Mac Gréil, 1977: 530; 1996: 128–32), and this continued into the early twenty-first century (see O'Connell, 2003; Watson *et al.*, 2007: 239). When viewed in comparative perspective, attitudes towards immigrants are not greatly different from those elsewhere in Europe. Indeed, surveys in the early twenty-first century showed Irish respondents as much more open to immigrants than those in other countries. Thus, in autumn 2016, 81 percent of Irish respondents indicated that they had a 'positive' feeling about immigration of people from other EU member states, and 57 per cent were positive about immigration from outside the EU; the corresponding figures for the EU overall were 20 percentage points lower – 61 per cent and 37 per cent respectively (Eurobarometer no. 86).

It seems that Ireland's slow pace of economic and social development, set alongside a much more developed Britain in a relationship of dependence, provided the raw material for the growth of Irish nationalism in the nineteenth century. This was reinforced by Catholic resentment at a heritage of oppression, and the church could see in self-government for Ireland a buttress against 'godless' ideas from across the Irish Sea. Britain did not help matters, arguably governing Ireland with insufficient wisdom to secure Irish loyalty to the united state established in 1800 (see Chapter 1). While nationalist sentiment may have been substantially purged by independence after 1922, at least in the south, and by increasing self-confidence arising from the Republic's undisputed statehood and economic success (as reflected in its capacity to see off the recession that followed the Celtic tiger period), an unfamiliar new pattern of immigration may well encourage the growth of a new wave of ethnocentric or even racist attitudes, a development compatible with certain structural and other conditions in contemporary Irish society (Garner, 2004: 28–34). It is striking that, notwithstanding anecdotal reports and documented evidence of casual racism (Michael, 2016), racist sentiment has not so far been mobilised politically in the manner of other west European societies.

Democratic values?

The existence of a political culture in which *democratic values* are dominant is clearly of central importance for the maintenance of democracy. This is important from a historical perspective (given the survival of aristocratic rule well into the nineteenth century, and threats from fascism and authoritarian communism in the twentieth). But it is also of continuing contemporary relevance in the light of emerging challenges to democratic norms and freedoms, reflected in the rise of the authoritarian right recorded in election results in several countries in the early twenty-first century. While observers of Irish political culture are agreed that a basic commitment to democratic values is a central feature (in that those who are involved politically are reasonably well informed about politics and broadly supportive of democratic institutions), they disagree on the extent to which this is modified by other values of a more traditional character.

Early research on Irish political culture suggested that it was marked by two apparently contradictory features. The first was deference to decisions from above, and an intolerance of those who depart from consensual political views, characterised by *authoritarianism* (or disposition to accept guidance from leaders; Schmitt, 1973: 43–54), political *conformism* (Gallagher, 1982: 19–20), and *loyalty* to state and church leaders combined with *anti-intellectualism* (Chubb, 1992: 18–20). Set in tension against these collectivist values, however, is another set of features: *personalism* (or preference for personal links rather than objective norms; Schmitt, 1973: 55–64) and *individualism* (reliance on individual action rather than cooperation; Gallagher, 1982: 16–20).

Neither of these features seems ideally suited to support democratic cultural norms. But one of the most convincing pieces of historical evidence cited in support of the apparently strong Irish commitment to democracy has been the very survival of the liberal democratic institutions that were created in 1922. The prospects for democracy in the new states that appeared in Europe after the First World War were not bright: collapse was more common than survival (see Coakley, 1986). In Ireland, objective indicators (such as socio-economic ones) were not promising. The very fact that the state and its constitutional system managed to survive so difficult a birth is attributable to the pattern of existing political cultural values, even if this provides only a partial explanation (see Kissane, 2002). Irish voters adopted the country's democratic basic law, the constitution, in 1937, at a time when democracy was collapsing elsewhere in Europe. No major political figure has spoken out against democratic institutions and practices, though certain fringe groups and personalities in the 1930s and the 1940s did advocate alternative forms of political organisation incompatible with democracy as we know it.

Electoral evidence relating to the character of Irish democratic values is also positive. Support for anti-democratic parties of the right and left has been negligible, and although individual deputies within the established parties may have wavered at times, the parties themselves have remained firmly within the liberal democratic framework. The picture changes when we move to the level of local representative institutions; observers have commented on the high degree of public acquiescence in decisions by governments to postpone local elections, or even to suspend local councils and replace them by appointed commissioners; indeed, the public appears to have little concern for local democracy (Collins, 1987: 51).

Survey evidence in general bears out the view that the Irish are relatively supportive of liberal democratic government, as may be seen in polls that set Ireland in comparative context. These allow us to test some of the generalisations made in the past about the profile of Irish political culture, notably the following:

- *Civic competence*: belief in one's capacity to influence the political process
- *Democratic norms*: acceptance of conventional principles of collective decision making
- *Political tolerance*: acknowledgement of rights of minorities
- *Trust in institutions*: positive evaluation of state and other institutions.

The first major survey of Irish political culture, dating from 1970, replicated questions from Almond and Verba's classic study described earlier, and found that in general Ireland was to be grouped with countries that had a political culture said to be conducive to democracy (Great Britain, the USA and, to a lesser extent, Germany), though in a comparative context the Irish level of 'subjective competence' (sense of having the capacity to influence the political process) was low (Raven and Whelan, 1976: 22–6, 46). More than four decades later, this continues broadly to be the pattern. Data from a cross-national survey in 2014 show Irish respondents relatively close to those in other European countries when asked a series of questions about their capacity to influence the political system: whether the system in Ireland 'allows people like you to have a say in what the government does', whether it 'allows people like you to have an influence on politics', and whether politicians 'care what people like you think'. In each of these cases, though, the Irish level was a little *below* the European average.[4] This reserve about the efficacy of conventional political behaviour suggests that there may be a vacuum that may be filled by 'personalistic' values.

One of the most historically significant challenges to democratic principles in Ireland has been the cult of political violence – the notion that on some matters, such as those pertaining to Irish independence, the majority 'has no right to do wrong'. In this view, some principles (such as that of Irish nationhood) are so important that they persist regardless of voting decisions. A 1970 survey showed that while a majority clearly opposed the use of force, a large minority (20 per cent) agreed that the use of force was at least sometimes the only way to advance an ideal (Raven and Whelan, 1976: 49), while a survey carried out in 1978 suggested that 21 per cent supported IRA activities (Davis and Sinnott, 1979: 97–9). On the other hand, despite the long tradition of revolutionary violence in Ireland, regular surveys since 1976 have shown that Irish people's attitudes to political change are not greatly different from those in other parts of the EC/EU: only tiny minorities are prepared to endorse attempts to change society by revolutionary means (Eurobarometer trends 1974–1993, May 1994: 43, 48–9). The most recent major survey on public attitudes towards the use of violence (though now rather dated) concluded with a warning that, notwithstanding a transition to exclusive reliance on parliamentary politics in the Republic, 'significant numbers of the population continue to remain sympathetic to not only the aims of the republican movement but also their use of violence to achieve them' (Hayes and McAllister, 2005: 614).

We have already raised the question of the level of political tolerance that is characteristic of the Irish. A survey in 1970 found that 61 per cent believed that they would be justified in imposing on others 'something which one believes to be good and right' and 78 per cent agreed that 'certain political groups must be curbed when they abuse freedom of speech' (Raven and Whelan, 1976: 47–8). Though this is not unambiguous evidence of low levels of political tolerance, a large survey in Dublin in 1972–73 led to the conclusion that there was 'a moderately high degree of intolerance against political and social outgroups', as well as 'a considerable degree of general intolerance and authoritarianism' (Mac Gréil, 1977: 530). Such attitudes were even more common in rural Ireland, as a later survey showed (Mac Gréil, 1996: 390–1). This is, however, an aspect of Irish political culture that seems to have changed by the early twenty-first century. In a 2014 survey in which people were asked whether they agreed that 'it is better for a country if almost everyone shares the same customs and traditions', 41 per cent agreed (of whom 9 per cent agreed strongly); the corresponding percentages for the EU overall were 45 per cent and 13 per cent – though, again, this question taps sentiments other than political tolerance.[5]

In important respects, the complex set of political cultural values in respect of democracy is summed up by levels of trust in major institutions. Here, the Irish experience is rather positive from a comparative perspective, as illustrated in survey data over the years, from 1981 (Fogarty *et al.*, 1984: 179, 243), 1990 (Ashford and Timms, 1992: 16, 98) and 1999 (Fahey *et al.*, 2005: 216). But Irish levels of trust are uneven. As Table 2.1 shows, Irish respondents trust such media as radio and television, and such public institutions as the civil service, the police and, especially, the army. But they do not trust the internet or online social networks, and they have a particular mistrust of parliament, the government and, especially, the

Table 2.1 Trust in selected institutions, Ireland and EU, 2016

Area	Ireland			EU			Irish–EU
	Trust	Mistrust	Difference	Trust	Mistrust	Difference	Difference
Radio	66	31	35	59	34	25	7
Television	58	38	20	50	46	4	8
The written press	46	49	−3	46	48	−2	0
The internet	36	52	−16	36	48	−12	0
Online social networks	21	64	−43	21	59	−38	0
The army	84	10	74	74	19	55	10
The police	78	19	59	71	25	46	7
Justice / the legal system	63	32	31	51	44	7	12
Public administration	59	35	24	48	46	2	11
Regional/local authorities	53	42	11	47	47	0	6
The government	40	56	−16	31	64	−33	9
The parliament	40	54	−14	32	62	−30	8
Political parties	22	73	−51	16	78	−62	6
The United Nations	59	30	29	45	41	4	14
The European Union	49	42	7	36	54	−18	13

Source: Derived from Eurobarometer no. 86, autumn 2016.

Note: All figures are percentages. 'Irish–EU difference' refers to the level of trust in Ireland minus the level of trust in the EU overall.

political parties, a finding that is alarming in its implications for faith in democracy. These conclusions, however, need to be seen in context: the corresponding overall levels of trust in these institutions in other EU member states are the same, or even lower. Nevertheless, this seems not to translate into an overall suspicion of democracy: 15 per cent of Irish respondents said they were 'very satisfied' with the way democracy works in Ireland, and 58 per cent were 'fairly satisfied' (a total of 73 per cent); the EU average was well below this, with 8 per cent very satisfied and 45 per cent fairly satisfied (a total of 53 per cent; Eurobarometer no. 86, autumn 2016).

Trust in public institutions also implies reliance on these institutions to resolve relevant problems. But Irish people have had a distinctive attitude towards official channels for getting things done; they often prefer to rely on personal contact with office holders (see Chapter 8). This 'personalism' in Irish political culture appears to have survived the enormous socio-economic and cultural changes of the late twentieth and early twenty-first centuries, and has potentially subversive consequences for democratic institutions. Thus, voters continue to reward politicians who are good constituency workers, even if they are in breach of approved procedures and norms. Examples have been cited in respect of Dáil deputies who have been investigated for suspected wrong-doing, often of a financial nature, but who, nevertheless, retain their local popularity. Rather than being disowned by the electorate, as might happen in countries with a stronger rule-bound political culture, their popularity may even increase, especially if they are seen as defenders of their local communities. The enormous popularity of former Fine Gael minister Michael Lowry in Tipperary has been cited as an example: he has topped the poll at every election since 1997, notwithstanding the fact that over the years he has been in the headlines for being investigated by two tribunals of enquiry and by several state agencies (Keena, 2016).

The old debate about the quality of Irish democratic values is now largely obsolete; it is clear that the overall pattern is similar to that in other liberal democracies, even if the Irish experience has distinctive features, such as personalistic values. This may well be attributable to certain aspects of the Irish historical experience, including a relatively high level of socio-economic development, at least in the latter part of the twentieth century, and the powerful attraction of British models, strong enough to counteract the influence of earlier patterns of agrarian society and of authoritarian models associated with the structures of the Catholic church. The imperfect emergence of a society with principle-driven values, and the survival of 'personalistic' values, may be attributed precisely to this historical configuration of social patterns, perhaps with the addition of colonial-type pressures that undermined the status of rule-driven political norms (Hourigan, 2015: 14–22). Of course, in many respects Irish society is now postindustrial and it is increasingly secular. To a growing extent, it is a 'typical' west European society, and, while survey evidence may point to certain respects in which the Irish deviate from other west Europeans in their attitudes towards democracy, these exceptions must be seen in the context of the overwhelming reality that the broad thrust of Irish attitudes in this area is typically European.

Conservatism?

By *conservatism* we mean a leaning in the direction of support for traditional values and a preference for low levels of state regulation, especially in economic matters. Conservatives generally support the existing social and political order, favour low taxation and prefer free enterprise to state involvement in the economy.

The historical balance sheet is rather mixed on the question of Irish conservatism. In the nineteenth and early twentieth centuries the major political forces in Irish society were radical by European standards: they stood for a dismantling of the existing system of land ownership and for the pursuit of redistributionist policies. Radical egalitarian ideology was reflected in the 1916 proclamation and in the 'democratic programme' of the first Dáil, adopted in 1919. This was widely shared in the new state, especially on the anti-Treaty side. But it is one thing to call for redistribution of wealth when the privileged group can be portrayed as an alien minority whose riches were gained by conquest; it is quite another to continue this call when members of the former underclass have enriched themselves through their own efforts.[6] Egalitarian or socialist rhetoric has been notably muted in Irish society since the new state consolidated its position. On the other hand, conservative ideology has not been vehemently and coherently articulated either; instead, policy makers experimented pragmatically with far-reaching policies of state intervention, and public opinion appears, in general, to have accepted this.

Electoral evidence indeed points towards conservative tendencies in Irish society – or, at least, towards the relatively underdeveloped state of radicalism. Over the 20 elections from 1948 to 2016, the two largest parties – both relatively conservative in orientation – have won on average 72 per cent of the first preference vote, compared to 12 per cent for the Labour Party (the rest of the left was insignificant until 2011). It might be more accurate to interpret this as evidence of the weakness of the left, rather than of the strength of the right. It is true that Fianna Fáil and Fine Gael associate themselves at European level with parties of the right or centre-right, but both span a wide range of ideological positions, and neither can be seen as an archetypal conservative party.

In the past, surveys provided little evidence of commitment to ideologies of the extreme right. Data from 1990 positioned the Irish somewhere in the middle of a group of 10 western democracies in their attitude towards heavier taxation of the wealthy (supported by 83 per cent) and provision of jobs by the government for all who want them (71 per cent), though Ireland was close to the top when it came to the view that the government has too much power (51 per cent; Johnston, 1993: 13). There is some evidence of a convergence between Ireland and the rest of Europe in respect of the correlation between left–right self-placement and other values classically associated with being on the 'left' or the 'right' (Hardiman and Whelan, 1994: 162–3), and by the second decade of the twenty-first century there were signs of the emergence of class divisions in voting behaviour. Survey evidence from 2011 suggested an increase in class-based voting (Tilley and Garry, 2017: 24) and in respondents' capacity to rank parties along the conventional left–right continuum, even if such rankings appeared not to be closely related to perceptions of party policy (McElroy, 2017: 79). This was confirmed in the 2016 election, especially in Dublin (Marsh and McElroy, 2016: 181). There appears also to be considerable (at least passive) support for the kind of interventionist policies that have created so large a public sector in Ireland. While there is some evidence that political conservatism is, then, a feature of Irish political culture, this coexists ambiguously with a rather pragmatic attitude towards economic development and an egalitarian attitude towards the distribution of resources.

In an obvious sense, this complex mixture of values may be related to the Irish path of socio-economic evolution, with the early disappearance of the traditional landed class, the installation of a strong farming class, late industrialisation and retarded development of class consciousness. It is also undoubtedly the case that the Catholic church, with its traditional horror of communism and suspicion of socialism, reinforced conservatism in the twentieth century; in this context the re-orientation of leading members of the church from the late twentieth century in the direction of support for more egalitarian educational and social welfare systems has probably come too late to have much impact on deeply ingrained popular values. For its part, rapid economic growth appears to have led, predictably enough, not to an erosion in wealth inequalities but to a growing disposition to tolerate these, rooted in a new form of conservative individualism (O'Connell, 2001: 181–8).

Clericalism?

By *clericalism* we mean acceptance of the view that religious teaching (more specifically, that of the Catholic church) possesses such authority that it should be reflected in state legislation. It is argued that the political views of the clergy should be heeded, that the laws should reflect Catholic moral principles and social teaching, and sometimes that the church itself should be given a special place in the constitution. In continental Europe, clericalism was a political force in Catholic societies opposed to the great liberal movement that dated from the time of the French revolution, a movement that stood for the complete separation of church and state and protection of the individual against both.

Historical evidence of the significance of clericalism in Irish political life and its impact on social policy is so well documented that it needs little further comment (see Gallagher, 1982: 12–16 and Girvin, 1996, for short discussions, and Whyte, 1980, for a more extended analysis). For many decades into the life of the new state, public policy was firmly guided by Roman Catholic principles. The Labour Party dropped the expression 'Workers' Republic' from its constitution in 1940 and the government refused to support Noel Browne, Minister for Health, in his ambitious welfare programme in the so-called 'Mother and Child' controversy in 1951, in response to pressure from the Catholic bishops. More significant than the effect of episcopal intervention, however, is the fact that its use was so rare. Public and elite opinion was sufficiently supportive of the Catholic position to make clerical intervention unnecessary, and when the bishops did intervene in the two cases mentioned their position was compatible with dominant lay opinion.

As the twenty-first century began, however, Catholic clerical leadership was progressively undermined. Although the 1983 and 1986 referendums on abortion and divorce respectively resulted in conservative decisions, the very fact that these matters were subjected to a constitutional poll and the size of the minority vote were themselves indicators of change, and pointers to the ultimate narrow majority in favour of permitting divorce at a 1995 referendum. The liberalisation in 1993 of the laws relating to the sale of contraceptives and to homosexuality would have been scarcely imaginable in 1973, or, perhaps, even in 1983, and the idea that same-sex marriage would be endorsed by referendum in 2015 would have been inconceivable. The authority of the Catholic bishops in speaking on matters of public morality was undermined by growing secularisation and by a series of scandals involving Catholic clergy. An official report in 2009 into reformatories and industrial schools run by Catholic religious orders (the Ryan report), revealed patterns of physical and sexual abuse of children stretching back decades, further compromising clerical authority and the standing of the Catholic church (Commission to Inquire into Child Abuse, 2009). This is likely to be a significant factor in future decision making, since it reduces the church's capacity to mount an effective campaign in such areas as abortion, where proposals for liberalisation of the constitutional and legal position have acquired a central place in public debate.

Electoral data offer indirect but convincing evidence of clericalism in Irish society. In the past, the only parties that were avowedly anti-clerical, such as the Communist Party, were electorally insignificant. Almost all votes were cast for parties that were essentially clericalist; and to the extent that change has taken place, it has occurred *within* these parties, as first Labour, then Fine Gael and finally Fianna Fáil began to adopt positions that could be seen as being in conflict with official church views. Rather strikingly, and despite the significant minority opposition at liberalising referendums, no fundamentalist Catholic parties have been able to make inroads into the space vacated by the secularising major parties since the 1990s.

We scarcely need survey evidence as to the intensity of Irish clericalism in the past. Even in the late 1980s, although the authority of the church to express its views in political areas began to be questioned, there remained significant differences between the perceptions of Irish people and of other Europeans on areas in which it was appropriate for the church to speak out: the Irish were much more favourably disposed towards church views (Ashford and Timms, 1992: 34–5). Opinion polls make it clear that a gulf has opened up between church teaching and people's views on issues of public morality. Given the declining significance of religion in people's lives, as discussed earlier, it is likely that this gap will widen further, though there are also signs that those close to traditional Catholic values and practices are developing a more distinct electoral profile, with support for Fianna Fáil as a key component in this (see Chapter 6). This may be due, in large measure, to the effects of economic growth and new wealth on individual psychological makeup, but it probably also reflects the greater exposure of Irish society to external influences. The conditions in which the Catholic church could offer spiritual consolation to a poor but happy Irish nation, and provide moral guidance in its struggles in an often hostile world, have been changed out of all recognition (see Garvin, 2004).

Neutralism?

We use *neutralism* here to refer, for want of a better word, to a predisposition to support a neutral position in the domain of foreign policy (see also Chapter 14). This feature, in Ireland as elsewhere, is derived from more profound values, such as nationalism.

Although the new state was anxious after 1922 to maximise international recognition by extending its external involvement in such bodies as the League of Nations and the United

Nations, it always stopped short of any hint of participation in an external military alliance. While the justification for this (as expressed in rejection, for example, of NATO membership) was rooted in specific hostility to Britain because of its role in maintaining the partition of Ireland, in time the policy of military neutrality became valued in its own right, and it appears to have been transformed into a canon of Irish public opinion. Much of the evidence relating to Irish feelings on this subject is indirect. It is notable that political parties have been reticent in tackling the issue of security cooperation, though this is an inevitable concomitant of deepening European integration. The dominant parties have been moving to a more accommodating position on the issue of pan-European military alliances, while those (radical left) parties that adopt an uncompromising policy on neutrality are weak in electoral support, even if they are rather vocal on the issue.

This 'neutralist' perspective seems to have survived: survey evidence in the late twentieth century consistently showed that Irish respondents supported maintaining neutrality by large majorities (Devine, 2011: 342–5); an opinion poll in 2013 showed 78 per cent agreeing that 'Ireland should have a policy of neutrality', with 15 per cent against (RedC, 2013); and a poll three years later showed that 57 per cent believed that the constitution should be amended to enshrine the principle of neutrality, with 39 per cent against (RedC, 2016). Alongside this apparently strong support for neutrality, though, was an apparently incompatible decline in the proportion of those wanting decision making in the sensitive areas of security and defence to remain at national level. A clear majority of Irish respondents in a 1993 survey (71 per cent) supported this (compared only 42 per cent of Europeans; Eurobarometer no. 39, spring 1993), and this for a long time continued to be the position. There was, however, a sharp drop in this level in 2005, and by autumn 2010 only a minority wished to see defence policy remain as a national responsibility (28 per cent in Ireland, as against 64 per cent preferring to see this as an EU responsibility; Eurobarometer no. 74). Correspondingly, support for a common EU defence and security policy had increased to 66 per cent in autumn 2016, and support for a common EU foreign policy stood at 70 percent (the former a good deal lower than the overall EU level, the latter slightly higher; Eurobarometer no. 86).

In practice, increased European integration is incompatible with Irish neutrality, and this has generated a tension between elite and mass opinion. The government promoted the insertion of an apparent commitment to military neutrality in the constitution at the time of the second referendum on the Lisbon Treaty in 2009 (see Sinnott *et al.*, 2009). But even before this, the Irish defence forces had contributed contingents to EU- or NATO-led operations in Bosnia and Herzegovina (1997), Kosovo (1999) and Afghanistan (2001). Indeed, it has been argued that Ireland's engagement with the European Security and Defence Policy was 'wholehearted and wide-ranging', and that, in relation to the size and extent of its resources, Ireland was 'a well above-average contributor to EU military operations' (Tonra, 2012: 232). This has been made possible in part by a progressive narrowing, to the point of tokenism, of the definition of 'neutrality' (Devine, 2011: 359–61). It is not, of course, unusual for public opinion to endorse a general principle without necessarily accepting all of its implications, and this may be a feature of this policy area in Ireland too. Opinion polls show very positive perceptions of the EU in Ireland (see Chapter 14; Coakley, 2013: 246–53), and Irish support for developments at EU level, in such domains as military cooperation, is likely to take precedence over reservations about imprecisely defined understandings of neutrality.

It is probable that this rather complex feature of Irish political culture arises from the country's distinctive 'colonial' and 'post-colonial' experience. But, as this experience recedes into the more distant recesses of the collective memory, and as the full geopolitical implications of membership of an increasingly integrated European Union become clear, the depth of Irish commitment to traditional values of neutrality will be put to the test. At elite level, it appears that there is a much greater willingness than in the past to contemplate participation in military alliances; it remains to be seen how long it takes for these ideas to achieve mass support, or at least acceptance. The United Kingdom's departure from the EU is likely to add further complexity to this question. It must be stressed that attachment to neutrality as a general principle does not imply that Irish political culture is in any way isolationist; on the contrary, high levels of cross-national mobility of students, workers and ideas appear to have promoted the emergence of a cosmopolitan political culture.

A divided political culture?

The discussion up to now has focused on the 'typical' Irish person's political cultural profile. Society, of course, is made up of individuals holding a great range of values; while we have drawn attention to areas where certain values are dominant or where the Irish adopt distinctive positions, we need to turn now to look at those who do not subscribe to these values, and examine the extent of *fragmentation* in Irish society and in its political culture.

Social cleavages

Clearly, economic and social development did not proceed at a uniform pace in Ireland or in any other society. As elsewhere in Europe, there was a clash between rural and urban (or agrarian and industrial) interests, and also divisions within these sectors. On the agrarian side, although agricultural labourers, small subsistence farmers and large, commercially oriented farmers have conflicting interests, these are now rarely mobilised separately, due to the shrinking size of the sector. On the industrial side, an urban proletariat developed slowly, but levels of politicised class conflict remained low by European standards (though the level of industrial disputes was high). Inevitably, some groups always lagged behind others, and the early years of the twenty-first century were marked by continuing problems of inequality and poverty (Coakley, 2013: 26–7).

In the religious domain, the most obvious historical division was that between Catholics and Protestants, and this survives, even though the Protestant minority is now very small. Within the Catholic community, recent decades have seen the growth of secular values; although there is nothing corresponding to the secular subcultures of continental Catholic Europe, tensions between traditional Catholics and those with more liberal beliefs have grown rapidly.

Contrasting perceptions of the past were also strongly held by different groups, with unionist, moderate nationalist and republican versions of history competing. Similarly, the degree of exposure to British, European and other influences tends to vary with region, class, occupation and level of education. We might expect these features, like the ones discussed in the last two paragraphs, to promote conflicting currents within Irish political culture; to what extent is there evidence of this?

Political cultural cleavages

The most fundamental political cultural cleavage faced by the new state related to the question of *nationalism*. In the early years, a strong 'republican' subculture struggled against the dominant values of the ruling group but, as we have seen, these two sets of values were largely accommodated to each other by 1948 at the latest. On the other hand, it could be argued that as mainstream Irish nationalist values became less strident, a fundamentalist nationalist subculture, comprising those loyal to the old ideals, was increasingly clearly defined. The core beliefs of this subculture included rejection of the institutions of government of Northern Ireland, since partition was seen as illegitimate, but also of the institutions of the south, for the same reason. This ideology rested on the assumption that the Irish people had made an irreversible decision in 1918 in favour of independent statehood, and that armed resistance to anyone who opposed this decision was justified. Many held to this set of beliefs with passionate commitment, extending to a willingness to engage in an armed struggle or to die on hunger strike.

If the most appropriate yardstick to measure the strength of this subculture is electoral support for the party most obviously associated with it, Sinn Féin, we would be struck by the weakness of this tradition, at least in the south. Sinn Féin's Dáil presence as an enduring political force dates only from 1997; but by this time the movement had itself been transformed, and no longer identified with the fundamentalist values described earlier. It is likely that its subsequent electoral success derived from an identification of the party with social radicalism rather than with fundamentalist nationalism. The party's acceptance of the Good Friday Agreement of 1998 is likely to have further marginalised those who still adhere to the traditional ideology. In any case, as the example of Northern Ireland shows, the cleavage between constitutional nationalism and Irish republicanism pales into insignificance beside the Catholic–Protestant cleavage over national identity.

Democratic values appear now to be deeply embedded in Irish political culture, and challenges from groups adhering to sources of authority other than 'the people's will' have been few and weak. Nationalist authoritarianism – the belief that 'the nation' has a collective destiny that must be protected by an elite, if necessary against the wishes of a majority – largely disappeared in the south after the early decades of the state, as discussed earlier. There is now little evidence that any kind of religious authoritarianism may emerge. Indeed, up to the early 1990s Catholic activists relied on public opinion and referendum results to defend their position, whereas their more 'progressive' rivals sought to bypass these and to use the courts and parliament to bring about change.

As regards attitudes towards *public policy*, there are predictable divisions within Irish society. First, there is clearly a gap between left and right, one side supporting interventionist economic policies, the other advocating private enterprise and the free market. While the boundary between the two sides is not very precise, and does not correspond entirely with social class or with party political divisions, the two tendencies are nonetheless real. Second, a deep division has opened up between secular and clerical forces, with the balance of advantage swinging from the latter to the former in the early twenty-first century. Third, there are elements of a division between those opposing and supporting a policy of neutrality in international affairs, the former arguing for a redefinition of Ireland's relationship with Europe and a reassessment of its policy of military neutrality, the latter defending the traditional position in these respects.

Conclusion

While political culture is an elusive concept and our instruments for measuring it are of limited value, the survey evidence reported in this chapter is sufficiently compatible with other evidence and with the perceptions of observers to allow us to make some generalisations about the nature of Irish political culture. First, there appears to be a consensus among the population in relation to core values in the area of national identity: there is virtually universal agreement on one of the cardinal principles of Irish *nationalism* (the need for a separate Irish state), and the legitimacy of the Republic of Ireland is now clearly established. The most serious challenge to this, in the near future, is likely to arise from the deepening of the European integration project, as identities linked to current nation-states coexist with broader emerging European forms of identity.

Second, commitment to *democratic values* appears to be solidly rooted within people's inner values, as in other western societies. The challenge from *authoritarianism* is weak – nationalist authoritarianism has receded in recent decades, and religious authoritarianism was never articulated in such a way as to constitute a serious challenge to democratic princi-ples. Irish political culture may be marked by a characteristic preference for a 'personalistic' approach to problem solving, but its democratic roots run deep.

Third, in respect of people's values relating to principles of public policy, we can detect elements both of stability and of conflict. On socio-economic issues, *conservatism* appears to be dominant, even if it is implicit and even centrist (supporting extensive state interven-tion), rather than articulated as a developed ideology; until the early twenty-first century, the challenge from the left was very weak. On foreign policy issues, there seems to be an emerging tension in respect of attitudes towards military neutrality, given a particular focus in the context of closer integration within the European Union. Most obviously of all, how-ever, on social and moral issues, conflict between *clericalism* and *secularism* emerged as a characteristic phenomenon of Irish life in the late twentieth century; and a country that had once fairly fully accepted the moral leadership of the Catholic clergy has given way to one in which secular elites and opinion leaders are dominant.

Political culture in Ireland, then, resembles that in other west European states rather closely, despite a significant lag in socio-economic development in this country. While the legacy of history and preoccupation with British dominance may have been a particular influence in the past, it is probably the pattern of underlying religious values in a slowly secularising society that will be responsible for the most distinctive elements in Irish politi-cal culture in the future. It is too early yet to assess the probable impact of high levels of social and economic equality, cultural diversity, an emerging European identity and the chal-lenge of Brexit.

Notes

1   Note that GDP per capita tends to overestimate Ireland's relative position as it includes the profits of foreign-owned multinational corporations, which have a distorting effect because of their great size. Except where otherwise noted, the statistics here and in the rest of this section are derived from three series of publications produced by the Central Statistics Office (www.cso.ie): the *Census of Population of Ireland* (2016 and earlier years); the *Statistical Yearbook of Ireland* (annual; earlier, *Statistical Abstract of Ireland*); and *Measuring Ireland's Progress* (annual since 2003).
2   These figures exclude 'don't knows'; derived from BBC–RTÉ survey, October 2015, by kind per-mission of BBC and RTÉ.
3   The data in this Eurobarometer and those cited later in this chapter are available as individual reports and as part of an interactive database at ec.europa.eu/COMMFrontOffice/publicopinion/index.cfm.
4   Derived from European Social Survey, round 7 (2014–15). Data file edition 2.1. NSD – Norwegian Centre for Research Data, Norway – Data Archive and distributor of ESS data for ESS ERIC. Data available from www.europeansocialsurvey.org/.

5   Derived from European Social Survey, round 7 (2014–15); see note 4.
6   For example, a 'New Land League' founded in 2013 claimed the mantle of its radical predecessor in the 1870s, but its elitist perspective was revealed in one of its earliest actions, resisting the repossession of a €8.5m house in Dublin whose owner, a former billionaire, was a casualty of the property crash.

References and further reading

Almond, Gabriel A., 2015. 'Attitudes, political and civic culture', in James D. Wright (ed.), *International Encyclopedia of the Social and Behavioral Sciences*, 2nd ed., Vol. 2. Amsterdam: Elsevier, pp. 190–92.

Almond, Gabriel and Sidney Verba (eds), 1980. *The Civic Culture Revisited: An Analytic Study*. Boston, MA: Little, Brown.

Almond, Gabriel A. and Sidney Verba, 1989. *The Civic Culture: Political Attitudes and Democracy in Five Nations*, new ed. London: Sage.

Ashford, Sheena and Noel Timms, 1992. *What Europe Thinks: A Study of West European Values*. Aldershot: Dartmouth.

Bartley, Brendan and Rob Kitchin (eds), 2007. *Understanding Contemporary Ireland*. London: Pluto.

Central Statistics Office, 2016a. *Brexit: Ireland and the UK in Numbers*. Cork: Central Statistics Office.

Central Statistics Office, 2016b. *Life in 1916 Ireland: Stories from Statistics*. Cork: Central Statistics Office.

Central Statistics Office, 2017. *Measuring Ireland's Progress, 2015*. Cork: Central Statistics Office. www.cso.ie/en/releasesandpublications/ep/p-mip/mip2015/

Chubb, Basil, 1970. *The Government and Politics of Ireland*. Stanford: Stanford University Press.

Chubb, Basil, 1992. *The Government and Politics of Ireland*, 3rd ed. London: Longman.

Coakley, John, 1986. 'Political succession and regime change in new states in interwar Europe: Ireland, Finland, Czechoslovakia and the Baltic republics', *European Journal of Political Research* 14:1/2, pp. 187–206.

Coakley, John, 2009. 'Voting for unity or union? The complexities of public opinion on the border issue', *Journal of Cross Border Studies in Ireland* 4, pp. 79–90.

Coakley, John, 2012. *Nationalism, Ethnicity and the State: Making and Breaking Nations*. London: Sage.

Coakley, John, 2013. *Reforming Political Institutions: Ireland in Comparative Perspective*. Dublin: Institute of Public Administration.

Coakley, John, 2017. 'Adjusting to partition: from irredentism to "consent" in twentieth-century Ireland', *Irish Studies Review* 25:2, pp. 193–214.

Collins, Neil, 1987. *Local Government Managers at Work: The City and County Management System of Local Government in the Republic of Ireland*. Dublin: Institute of Public Administration.

Commission to Inquire into Child Abuse, 2009. *Final Report*, 5 vols. Dublin: Stationery Office.

Dalton, Russell J. and Christian Welzel, 2015. 'Political culture and value change', in Russell J. Dalton and Christian Welzel (eds), *The Civic Culture Transformed: From Allegiant to Assertive Citizens*. Cambridge: Cambridge University Press, pp. 1–16.

Davis, E. E. and Richard Sinnott, 1979. *Attitudes in the Republic of Ireland Relevant to the Northern Ireland Problem*. Dublin: Economic and Social Research Institute.

Devine, Karen M., 2011. 'Neutrality and the development of the European Union's common security and defence policy: compatible or competing?', *Cooperation and Conflict* 46:3, pp. 334–69.

Donovan, Donal and Antoin E. Murphy, 2013. *The Fall of the Celtic Tiger: Ireland and the Euro Debt Crisis*. Oxford: Oxford University Press.

Elkink, Johan A. and David M. Farrell (eds), 2016. *The Act of Voting: Identities, Institutions and Locale*. London: Routledge.

Fahey, Tony, Bernadette C. Hayes and Richard Sinnott, 2005. *Conflict and Consensus: A Study of Value and Attitudes in the Republic of Ireland and Northern Ireland*. Dublin: Institute of Public Administration.

Fanning, Bryan, 2009. *New Guests of the Irish Nation*. Dublin: Irish Academic Press.

Fanning, Bryan, 2011. *Immigration and Social Cohesion in the Republic of Ireland*. Manchester: Manchester University Press.

Fanning, Bryan, 2012. *Racism and Social Change in the Republic of Ireland*, 2nd ed. Manchester: Manchester University Press.

Farrell, Brian, 1971. *The Founding of Dáil Éireann: Parliament and Nation-Building*. Dublin: Gill and Macmillan.

Fogarty, Michael, Liam Ryan and Joseph Lee, 1984. *Irish Values and Attitudes: The Irish Report of the European Value Systems Study*. Dublin: Dominican Publications.

Fuller, Louise, 2002. *Irish Catholicism since 1950: The Undoing of a Culture*. Dublin: Gill and Macmillan.

Gallagher, Michael, 1982. *The Irish Labour Party in Transition, 1957–82*. Dublin: Gill and Macmillan, and Manchester: Manchester University Press.

Garner, Steve, 2004. *Racism in the Irish Experience*. London: Pluto Press.

Garry, John, Niamh Hardiman and Diane Payne (eds), 2006. *Irish Social and Political Attitudes*. Liverpool: Liverpool University Press.

Garvin, Tom, 2004. *Preventing the Future: Politics, Education and Development in Ireland, 1937–1967*. Dublin: Gill and Macmillan.

Gilmartin, Mary, 2015. *Ireland and Migration in the 21st Century*. Manchester: Manchester University Press.

Girvin, Brian, 1996. 'Church, state and the Irish constitution', *Parliamentary Affairs* 49:4, pp. 599–615.

Hardiman, Niamh and Christopher Whelan, 1994. 'Values and political partisanship', in Christopher T. Whelan (ed.), *Values and Social Change in Ireland*. Dublin: Gill and Macmillan, pp. 136–86.

Hayes, Bernadette C. and Ian McAllister, 2005. 'Public support for political violence and paramilitarism in Northern Ireland and the Republic of Ireland', *Terrorism and Political Violence* 17:4, pp. 599–617.

Heath, Anthony F. and Thees Spreckelsen, 2016. 'European identities in comparative perspective', in Johan A. Elkink and David M. Farrell (eds), *The Act of Voting: Identities, Institutions and Locale*. London: Routledge, pp. 11–34.

Hilliard, Betty and Máire Nic Ghiolla Phádraig (eds), 2007. *Changing Ireland in International Comparison*. Dublin: Liffey Press.

Hourigan, Niamh, 2015. *Rule-Breakers: Why 'Being There' Trumps 'Being Fair' in Ireland*. Dublin: Gill and Macmillan.

Inglis, Tom, 1998. *Moral Monopoly: The Catholic Church in Modern Irish Society*, 2nd ed. Dublin: UCD Press.

Inglis, Tom (ed.), 2014. *Are the Irish Different?* Manchester: Manchester University Press.

Johnston, Michael, 1993. 'Disengaging from democracy', in Roger Jowell, Lindsay Brook and Lizanne Dowds with Daphne Arendt (eds), *International Social Attitudes: The 10th BSA Report*. Aldershot: Dartmouth, pp. 1–22.

Keena, Colm, 2016. 'Refusal to rule out Lowry sends wrong message', *Irish Times*, 26 January.

Kirby, Peadar and Mary P. Murphy, 2011. *Towards a Second Republic: Irish Politics after the Celtic Tiger*. London: Pluto.

Kissane, Bill, 2002. *Explaining Irish Democracy*. Dublin: UCD Press.

Kissane, Bill, 2011. *New Beginnings: Constitutionalism and Democracy in Ireland*. Dublin: UCD Press.

Lyons, Pat, 2008. *Public Opinion, Politics and Society in Contemporary Ireland*. Dublin: Irish Academic Press.

McCann, Gerard, 2011. *Ireland's Economic History: Crisis and Development in the North and South*. London: Pluto Press.

McElroy, Gail, 2017. 'Party competition in Ireland: the emergence of a left–right dimension', in Michael Marsh, David M. Farrell and Gail McElroy (eds), *A Conservative Revolution? Electoral Change in Twenty-First-Century Ireland*. Oxford: Oxford University Press, pp. 61–82.

Mac Gréil, Mícheál, 1977. *Prejudice and Tolerance in Ireland*. Dublin: Research Section, College of Industrial Relations.

Mac Gréil, Mícheál, 1996. *Prejudice in Ireland Revisited.* Maynooth: Survey and Research Unit, St Patrick's College.

Marsh, Michael and Gail McElroy, 2016. 'Voting behaviour: continuing dealignment', in Michael Gallagher and Michael Marsh (eds), *How Ireland Voted 2016: The Election That Nobody Won.* Basingstoke: Palgrave Macmillan, pp. 159–84.

Marsh, Michael, Richard Sinnott, John Garry and Fiachra Kennedy, 2008. *The Irish Voter: The Nature of Electoral Competition in the Republic of Ireland.* Manchester: Manchester University Press.

Marsh, Michael, David M. Farrell and Gail McElroy (eds), 2017. *A Conservative Revolution? Electoral Change in Twenty-First-Century Ireland.* Oxford: Oxford University Press.

Michael, Lucy, 2016. *Reports of Racism in Ireland July–December 2015.* Dublin: European Network against Racism Ireland. Available www.ireport.ie.

O'Connell, Michael, 2001. *Changed Utterly: Ireland and the New Irish Psyche.* Dublin: Liffey Press.

O'Connell, Michael, 2003. *Right Wing Ireland? The Rise of Populism in Ireland and Europe.* Dublin: Liffey Press.

Ó Giollagáin, Conchúr, Seosamh Mac Donnacha, Fiona Ní Chualáin, Aoife Ní Shéaghdha and Mary O'Brien, 2007. *Comprehensive Linguistic Study of the Use of Irish in the Gaeltacht: Principal Findings and Recommendations.* Dublin: Department of Community, Rural and Gaeltacht Affairs.

Ó Gráda, Cormac, 1997. *A Rocky Road: The Irish Economy since the 1920s.* Manchester: Manchester University Press.

O'Hagan, John, and Francis O'Toole (eds), 2017. *The Economy of Ireland: Policy Making in a Global Context*, 13th ed. London: Palgrave.

O'Malley, Eoin, 2011. *Contemporary Ireland.* Basingstoke: Palgrave Macmillan.

Powell, G. Bingham, Russell J. Dalton and Kaare Strøm, 2015. *Comparative Politics Today: A World View*, global ed., 11th ed. Harlow: Pearson Education.

Raven, John and C. T. Whelan; with Paul A. Pfretzschner and Donald M. Borock, 1976. *Political Culture in Ireland: The Views of Two Generations.* Dublin: Institute of Public Administration.

Red C, 2013. PANA – neutrality poll. August 2013. Dublin: Red C.

Red C, 2016. Neutrality in Ireland. February 2016. Dublin: Red C.

Roche, William K., Philip J. O'Connell and Andrea Prothero (eds), 2017. *Austerity and Recovery in Ireland: Europe's Poster Child and the Great Recession.* Oxford: Oxford University Press.

Ruane, Joseph, and Jennifer Todd, 1996. *The Dynamics of Conflict in Northern Ireland: Power, Conflict and Emancipation.* Cambridge: Cambridge University Press.

Schmitt, David E., 1973. *The Irony of Irish Democracy: The Impact of Political Culture on Administrative and Democratic Political Development in Ireland.* Lexington: Lexington Books.

Sinnott, Richard, Johan A. Elkink, Kevin O'Rourke and James McBride, 2009. *Attitudes and Behaviour in the Referendum on the Treaty of Lisbon: Report prepared for the Department of Foreign Affairs.* Dublin: Geary Institute, UCD.

Tilley, James and John Garry, 2017. 'Class politics in Ireland: how economic catastrophe realigned Irish politics', in Michael Marsh, David M. Farrell and Gail McElroy (eds), *A Conservative Revolution? Electoral Change in Twenty-First-Century Ireland.* Oxford: Oxford University Press, pp. 11–27.

Tonra, Ben. 2012. 'Security, defence and neutrality: the Irish dilemma', in Ben Tonra, Michael Kennedy, John Doyle and Noel Dorr (eds), *Irish Foreign Policy.* Dublin: Gill and Macmillan, pp. 221–41.

Watson, Iarfhlaith, Máire Nic Ghiolla Phádraig, Fiachra Kennedy and Bernadette Rock-Huspatel, 2007. 'National identity and anti-immigrant attitudes', in Betty Hilliard and Máire Nic Ghiolla Phádraig (eds), *Changing Ireland in International Comparison.* Dublin: Liffey Press, pp. 217–42.

Welzel, Christian and Russell J. Dalton, 2015. 'From allegiant to assertive citizens', in Russell J. Dalton and Christian Welzel (eds), *The Civic Culture Transformed: From Allegiant to Assertive Citizens.* Cambridge: Cambridge University Press, pp. 282–306.

Whyte, J. H., 1980. *Church and State in Modern Ireland 1923–1979*, 2nd ed. Dublin: Gill and Macmillan.

Websites

www.cso.ie
Central Statistics Office (wide range of census and other data)

www.ucd.ie/issda
Irish Social Science Data Archive (collection of survey and other data)

www.europeansocialsurvey.org/
European Social Survey (cross-national survey data since 2002)

ec.europa.eu/commfrontoffice/publicopinion/index.cfm
European Commission: Public Opinion (Eurobarometer data since 1973)

3 Politics, the constitution and the judiciary

Michael Gallagher

Constitutions are important in liberal democracies. They lay down the ground rules about how political power is attained and how it can be exercised, about what governments can and cannot do, and about the rights of citizens. Every country's constitution contains both a written and an unwritten component. That is, there are aspects of a country's political system that, perhaps through precedent and convention, have acquired the status of firm rules, even though they are not explicitly contained in the document called 'The Constitution'. We might regard these unwritten aspects as important elements in the country's political culture (see Chapter 2). For this reason, we cannot expect to get a full picture of the way in which a country's politics operates just by studying its written constitution. Constitutions might not explicitly acknowledge the existence of central features of modern politics such as large and disciplined political parties. In this chapter, we shall not examine those features of the constitution that regulate, for example, relations between government and parliament, or the rules governing the election of parliament – these are covered in other chapters – but will concentrate on the evolution of the constitution. Having examined its origins, we will outline the record of amendment, discuss the role of the judiciary in interpreting and developing the constitution, and consider whether further amendment would be desirable.

Constitutionalism – that is, the idea that the rulers are bound by rules that are not easy to change, that the power of government is subject to defined limits and that certain fundamental rights of the citizens are protected absolutely, or almost absolutely – is an integral feature of contemporary liberal democracies; yet some have argued that there is an inherent tension between constitutionalism and democracy (Murphy, 1993: 3–6; Holmes, 1988: 196–8; Loughlin, 2010). Constitutionalism prevents the people, or their elected representatives, from carrying out certain policies that might have majority support, and can be criticised as 'rule by the dead', since the values embodied by a constitution are typically those of a previous generation. Or, given that constitutions are usually interpreted by a body of judges, constitutionalism might mean rule by a 'black-robed junta' (the phrase of Jeremy Waldron, quoted in Hilbink, 2008: 229). Critics of constitutionalism, such as Martin Shapiro (quoted in Holmes, 1988: 197), argue that when we examine a law we should ask not 'is it constitutional?' but 'do we want it to be constitutional?'; we should not be guided by 'certain dead gentlemen who could not possibly have envisaged our current circumstances', but instead should rely on our collective decision about what sort of community we want to become. Defenders of the principle, in contrast, argue that there are certain rights that are so fundamental that they should be protected even against the wishes of a majority that wants them set aside. Although most liberal democracies feel that they have established a reasonable balance between constitutionalism and democracy, the tension undoubtedly exists, and has at times clearly manifested itself in Ireland.

The background: the Irish Free State constitution

Ireland's constitution (Bunreacht na hÉireann) dates from 1937 and, despite significant innovations, marked a development of previous constitutional experience rather than a complete break with it. The 1937 constitution's precursor, the 1922 Irish Free State constitution, was drawn up subject to the terms of the Anglo–Irish Treaty, so the British government was able to insist on modifications to the version produced by the Provisional Government, with a view to ensuring that it contained nothing that conflicted with the Treaty (for the Irish Free State constitution, see Ward, 1994: 167–238). As a result, the final document was rather different from what the Irish government would have wanted (for an overview, see Farrell, 1988a; Mohr, 2008). This British pressure manifested itself particularly in those articles that provided for a Governor-General, who represented the Crown and, in Article 17, for the terms of an oath that all members of the Oireachtas (parliament) had to take, swearing to 'be faithful to HM King George V, his heirs and successors' (see Chapter 1, p. 15). The Free State was declared to be a member of the British Commonwealth. Moreover, the introductory section of the Act establishing the constitution stated that if any provision of the constitution was, even after the British government's legal officers had scrutinised the document with a fine-tooth comb, in conflict with the Anglo–Irish Treaty, that provision was 'absolutely void and inoperative'.

Apart from these articles representing the result of pressure by the British, the broad outlines of the governmental system also showed a strong British influence, as the constitution provided for government by a cabinet (the Executive Council), chaired by a prime minister (the President of the Executive Council). Unlike the 1937 constitution, the Irish Free State constitution was explicitly neutral as between religious denominations and, despite pressure from some quarters to make it so, could not have been described as a 'Catholic constitution'.

The 1922 constitution did not, though, represent a slavish acceptance of the Westminster model of government. Mainly due to a desire to avoid an over-centralisation of power in the cabinet, the constitution contained some features designed to make the parliament more accountable to the people, and the government more accountable to the parliament, than was the case in the United Kingdom.

One of these was a proportional representation (PR) electoral system (the background to its adoption in Ireland is outlined in Chapter 4). There was also provision for judicial review of the constitution, for referendums on both laws and constitutional amendments, and for the legislative initiative – under which, if enough voters signed a petition calling for a particular change in the law, the Oireachtas would have either to make the change or to submit the issue to a referendum (Ruane, 2014). In addition, the constitution allowed for the appointment of ministers who were not required to be members of the Dáil, an option that, had it been availed of, would have brought Ireland into line with the mainstream in western Europe (Coakley 2013: 217–38). These 'extern ministers', as they were termed, would be appointed by the Dáil and answerable directly to it. However, apart from PR, most of these devices proved to be of little significance. No extern ministers were appointed after 1927, and even those who were appointed before then were all members of the Dáil. In 1928, when Fianna Fáil took the first steps towards forcing a popular vote on the oath of allegiance, the government promptly used its parliamentary majority to abolish both the legislative referendum and the initiative (Gallagher, 1996: 87).

The provision for judicial review did not prove much of a check on the government. For one thing, the Oireachtas itself could amend the constitution at will. The original version allowed it to do this (provided that any amendment came within the terms of the Treaty) for a period of eight years after 1922, with amendments after that period requiring a referendum.

But since this article itself could be amended, a simple extension of the period from eight to 16 years in 1929 ensured that the document was open to amendment by the Oireachtas throughout its unhappy life. Once the Supreme Court had ruled, in an important case in 1934 (see Box 3.3), that this amendment had been valid, the constitution was drained of all potential to constrain government and parliament. Moreover, although constitutions are usually more powerful than ordinary legislation, so that if the two conflict it is the constitution that prevails, the Irish Free State constitution was a weak document. Laws that contradicted the constitution, far from being thereby invalid, could simply incorporate a declaration that they amended the constitution to the extent necessary to render them constitutional (Casey, 2000: 14; Hogan and Whyte, 2003: 2161–2).

When Fianna Fáil came to power in 1932, it moved rapidly to remove those parts of the constitution that offended it most. In 1932 the Dáil passed legislation to abolish the oath (the change was not implemented until May 1933 because the Seanad exercised its power of delay), and in 1936 the Seanad and the office of Governor-General went the same way (Sexton, 1989: 165–6). It might be imagined that by now the resulting document was to Fianna Fáil's liking. Instead, it satisfied no-one. Fianna Fáil members had always viewed it with distaste because of its origins in the Treaty settlement that they had opposed, while even those who had clung so faithfully to it during the 1920s could not have felt much affection for it by 1937. Apart from the substance of the changes made by Fianna Fáil, the very fact that the document had been amended so many times (41 of the 83 articles had been changed) gave it a patchwork appearance. De Valera initiated the process of constitutional reform in 1934, seemingly still undecided as to whether something could be salvaged from the wreckage of the 1922 constitution or whether a completely new constitution was needed, but by the following year he had decided on the latter course (Coffey, 2012). For Fianna Fáil the Irish Free State constitution was inherently illegitimate no matter how it read.

The process of drafting the new constitution took around two years, from 1935 to 1937 (Hogan, 2012, 2014; Keogh and McCarthy, 2007; Kissane, 2011: 57–89). The resulting document was debated and finally passed by the Dáil, by 62 votes to 48, in June 1937. Although legally and constitutionally this new constitution could have been enacted by the Oireachtas as one long amendment to the existing constitution, that would have defeated the whole point of the exercise – it was vital symbolically to make a fresh start, and to have the Irish people confer the new constitution on themselves. Accordingly, it was put to the people in a referendum on 1 July 1937, the same day as a general election. It was passed by 57 per cent to 43 per cent and came into effect on 29 December 1937 (see Appendix 2h on results of referendums). It was drafted primarily in English and an Irish-language version was produced only at a relatively late stage (Hogan, 2012: 356–9), though Article 25.5.4 states that in the case of any conflicts between the two versions, the Irish-language version shall prevail. Inevitably, there are many points at which the two texts, if not in direct conflict, display nuanced differences (Ó Cearúil, 1999).

The constitution has been the subject of two major reviews since it came into being. The first systematic assessment was made in 1966–67, when an all-party Oireachtas committee, which included former Taoiseach Seán Lemass, examined it article by article and issued a report recommending certain changes and assessing the merits of other possible amendments. The bipartisan approach adopted by this committee was brought to an abrupt end when Fianna Fáil went ahead the following year with its second attempt to change the electoral system, and little came of its work. In 1995–96, a root-and-branch assessment of the constitution was conducted by an expert committee, the Constitution Review Group (CRG), whose 350,000-word report can be read as an informed analysis of the constitution, as well as an assessment of the arguments for change (CRG, 1996; for a critique of its work see Butler and O'Connell,

1998). The report of the CRG went to a parliamentary committee on the constitution, which was set up in 1996 and re-established after the 1997, 2002 and 2007 elections, with the brief of undertaking a full review of the constitution and recommending specific steps.

The main features of the constitution

The promulgation of a new constitution was by no means purely symbolic, for despite a high degree of continuity, the 1937 constitution differed significantly in some respects from its predecessor. We shall examine some of its main features, without going in any depth into areas, especially those concerning the operation of government and parliament, that are covered in other chapters of this book.

Nation and state

Articles 1–3 relate to 'The Nation' and Articles 4–11 to 'The State'. These articles emphasise the importance attached to the constitution's role as an assertion of the independence of the Irish state. Articles 1 and 5 both contain affirmations of sovereignty, and Article 6 says that all powers of government derive from the Irish people, emphasising that the institutions of the state should not be seen as having been in any way 'bestowed' on the people by the British in 1922. Among this group of articles, Articles 2 and 3 came to cause most controversy. Article 2 defined 'the national territory' as 'the whole island of Ireland, its islands and the territorial seas'. Article 3 declared that, notwithstanding this, the laws enacted by the state would, 'pending the re-integration of the national territory', apply only to the 26 counties, but by referring to the 'right' of the state's parliament and government to exercise jurisdiction over the whole of the national territory it affirmed a clear claim to Northern Ireland. Changes to these articles were demanded by northern unionists, as part of the 1998 Northern Ireland agreement, and, in a referendum in May of that year, the people voted overwhelmingly to replace them by new articles. The changes came into effect when the Northern Ireland executive finally took office in December 1999 (see Chapter 13). Article 2 now declares it the entitlement of everyone born in Ireland to be part of the Irish nation, while Article 3 states that it is 'the firm will of the Irish nation, in harmony and friendship, to unite all the people who share the territory of the island of Ireland, in all the diversity of their traditions, recognising that a united Ireland shall be brought about only by peaceful means with the consent of a majority of the people, democratically expressed, in both jurisdictions in the island'.

The name of the state offers some scope for discussion. Article 4 reads 'The name of the State is Éire, or in the English language, Ireland'. The 1948 Republic of Ireland Act could not change the name of the state, as that would conflict with this article; instead, it adopted the formulation that 'the description of the State shall be the Republic of Ireland' (Casey, 2000: 29–32). In different contexts, the state is now known as 'Éire', 'Ireland', 'the Republic of Ireland', and even 'the Irish Republic', a confusion that the constitution does not entirely resolve (see Coakley, 2009, and p. 323 below).

Political institutions

Articles 12–33 deal with political institutions. As far as the operation of government was concerned, there was no great change from the Irish Free State constitution. There was to be an Oireachtas, consisting of a president and two houses (see Chapter 7). The office of the president was a major innovation and is discussed further in Chapter 7. The lower house of parliament, Dáil Éireann, was to be directly elected by proportional representation, using the single transferable vote (see Chapter 4), as before. The re-emergence of the upper house, the Seanad, which de Valera had abolished only a year earlier, was surprising; given the nominally vocational basis of the Seanad (see Box 7.3), this may have been an adroit move to make a token concession to the transient clamour for the introduction of a vocationalist system of government (Lee, 1989: 272). The prime minister was now termed the Taoiseach (see Glossary), and his or her dominance within the government was strengthened in a number of ways – for example, the power to call a general election belonged now to the Taoiseach alone rather than to the government as a whole as before (see Chapter 10). It is clear, though, that for the most part the constitution merely reflected and summarised what had become existing practice, rather than enforcing a change in that practice.

Constitutions are often more framework, setting the parameters within which the institutions must operate, than code, specifying the details of precisely what must occur at every step (Elazar, 1985). In that spirit, the Irish constitution does not spell out, for example, exactly how the Taoiseach comes to be Taoiseach, or make any mention of the existence of coalition governments. This inevitably means that the constitution is silent on some matters. For example, when a Taoiseach is defeated in a vote of confidence, and the Dáil is unable to elect anyone else as Taoiseach, the Taoiseach is required to resign unless the president grants a dissolution (Article 28.10), yet continues in office until a successor is appointed (Article 28.11), leaving it unclear just what powers a caretaker government and Taoiseach have. The 1996 Constitution Review Group recommended that in such situations the outgoing government should conduct the state's business on a 'care and good management basis' only, for example refraining from making any non-essential appointments (CRG, 1996: 98–9).

The rights of citizens

The articles of the 1937 constitution that deal with citizens' rights (40–45) differed significantly from those of its predecessor. Like the earlier document, the new constitution guaranteed the usual liberal-democratic rights – habeas corpus, free association, free speech, inviolability of dwellings and so on – though (as is the case in most constitutions, and in the European Convention on Human Rights) almost invariably, the ringing enunciation of a right is followed by a qualifying clause or paragraph asserting the power of the state to curtail it if, for example, 'public order and morality' or 'the exigencies of the common good' justify that. The main difference was that the 1937 constitution also included rights articles that were strongly influenced by Catholic social thought (Hogan, 2012: 210–56; Keogh and McCarthy, 2007: 106–23, 150–73; Whyte, 1980: 51–6), and indeed 'the longer the drafting went on, the more the Catholic influence' (Kissane, 2011: 83). Two clauses of Article 44 gave Roman Catholicism a unique status. Article 44.1.2 read 'The State recognises the special position of the Holy Catholic Apostolic and Roman Church as the guardian of the Faith professed by the great majority of the citizens', while, in Article 44.1.3, the State merely 'recognised' a list of other and presumably less significant religions. Moreover, Article 41.3.2 prohibited the legalisation of divorce. These articles apart, admittedly, in many cases there is nothing visibly Catholic about the phraseology to the uninformed eye – only those familiar with Catholic social thought of the period would be able to identify the origins of the expressions used. Moreover, a number of additional rights not attributable to Catholic thought were enumerated.

The impact of Catholic thought on the constitution has led to its sometimes being branded narrowly confessional, and Hogan (2005) quotes many historians who have pronounced such a verdict. However, this is to judge one era by the standards of another. The final formulation of Article 44 met with the approval of all the other religions, while many in the Catholic church, including the pope, were clearly disappointed, since they had hoped that theirs would be recognised as 'the one true church' and were reluctant even to accept that the word 'church' could validly be claimed by other religions (Keogh and McCarthy, 2007: 150–73). Hogan points out that even those rights articles that were informed partly by Catholic social thought find parallels in documents such as the German and American constitutions and the UN International Covenant on Human Rights and, besides, that the express special recognition of one particular religion was common in European constitutions of the time and indeed later (Hogan, 2005: 298–307). The first large-scale protests against the religious articles came, 12 years later, not from non-Catholics but from the ultra-Catholic Maria Duce group, which wanted Article 44 amended to recognise the Catholic church as the one true church (Whyte, 1980: 163–5). De Valera, far from imposing a sectarian constitution on a pluralistic society, was steering a middle course between non-Catholics on the one hand and supremacist Catholics on the other, and he displeased the latter more than the former. Moreover, as Lee (1989: 203) observes, the explicit recognition given to the Jewish congregations was 'a gesture not without dignity in the Europe of 1937'.

Since 1937, the constitution has evolved in two ways. First, it has been amended, initially by parliament and then by the people. Second, it has been developed by judicial interpretation.

Amendment of the constitution

The Irish constitution, like most constitutions, is more rigid – that is, less easily amended – than ordinary legislation. The constitution was amendable by parliament for a short period, but since then any amendment has required the consent of the people.

Amendment by parliament

The constitution contained, in Articles 51–63, transitory provisions to cover an interim period. These articles are no longer included in official texts of the constitution (they can be found in Hogan and Whyte, 2003: 2159–76) but continue to have the force of law. Article 51 permitted the Oireachtas to amend the constitution for a period of three years after the first president entered office, which meant up to 25 June 1941 – though during that time the president had the right, if he chose, to refer any such amendment to the people for them to decide the matter by referendum. Any subsequent amendment would require the consent of the people.

Two packages of amendments were made in this way (Casey, 2000: 24–5; Hogan, 2012: 628–835). The first, made in September 1939, altered only one article (28.3.3, the 'emergency' article), while the second, in May 1941, amended 16 different articles simultaneously. The second amendment included some minor 'housekeeping' changes, merely ironing out defects that had been detected in the articles affected. Others were more significant (though the president chose not to put the package to a referendum), such as those relating to Articles 26 and 34, and especially to Article 28.3.3, which now looked quite different from the version approved by the people in 1937 (Greene, 2012).

Article 28.3.3 was designed to protect emergency legislation from scrutiny by the courts. In its original form, the article had stated that nothing in the constitution could be invoked to invalidate legislation designed to secure public safety and the preservation of the state in time of war or armed rebellion. The two amendments weakened the constraints on the Oireachtas in this regard. They widened the scope of the article in circumstances where each House of the Oireachtas passes a resolution declaring that 'a national emergency exists affecting the vital interests of the State'. After amendment, the article now says that 'time of war or armed rebellion' can include a time when an armed conflict is taking place that affects the vital interests of the state, even if the state is not directly involved, and a time after the war or armed rebellion has ceased but during which the Oireachtas takes the view that the emergency created by the conflict still exists. The Oireachtas declared a state of emergency after the outbreak of the Second World War in 1939, and this emergency remained in existence up to 1976, being lifted only by a resolution that simultaneously declared a fresh emergency arising 'out of the armed conflict now taking place in Northern Ireland', an emergency that was finally lifted in February 1995. In theory, Article 28.3.3 seems to give parliament a free hand to introduce draconian legislation, such as banning all opposition parties or outlawing elections, provided the right procedure is followed, though in 1976 the Supreme Court laid down a marker, stating that it 'expressly reserves for future consideration' the question of whether it would really have no jurisdiction to review the actions of government and parliament (Chubb 1991: 61). No case has arisen subsequently to test the way in which the courts' thinking on this issue has developed, but the warning shot sounded in 1976 may have counterbalanced to some extent the action of the Oireachtas in 1939 and 1941 in widening the scope of Article 28.3.3. Both constitutional review committees recommended that the declaration of an emergency should have effect for three years only and should require annual renewal thereafter (Committee on the Constitution, 1967: 37–9; CRG, 1996: 94).

Amendment by the people

Ireland is one of the few countries where every constitutional amendment requires the consent of the people. Article 46 states that a proposal to amend the constitution must be passed by the houses of the Oireachtas and then be put to a referendum (for the regulation of referendums see Ruane, 2012). Up to June 2017, 38 proposed amendments had been put to the people, of which 27 had been approved and 11 rejected (see Box 3.1 and table in Appendix 2h, p. 380). Of the 38, nine related to moral or religious issues, nine to the European Union, seven to voting, and four to various aspects of the political, governmental and judicial framework. In addition, there was one on Northern Ireland and one on citizenship, while the other seven (in 1979, 1996, 1997, 2012, 2015 and two in 2001) were on relatively minor or technical matters that did not engender strong passions.

Box 3.1 Major changes made to the Irish constitution since it was adopted in 1937

Changes to the constitution have been made to allow:

- Ireland to take a full part in the process of European integration (1972, 1987, 1992, 1998, 2002, 2009 and 2012);
- Recognition of the 'special position' of the Roman Catholic church to be removed (1972);
- Divorce to be legalised (1995);
- Ireland to fulfil its part of the Northern Ireland agreement (1998);
- Legalisation of same-sex marriage (2015).

Of the nine referendums on moral or religious issues, the first proposal was passed comfortably in 1972, with the backing of all the parties and the opposition only of conservative Catholic groups. It removed from Article 44.1 the two subsections, already referred to, that recognised the 'special position' of the Catholic church and the mere existence of a number of other churches. The two referendums of the 1980s were much more heated affairs, with deep divisions apparent within, as well as between, the parties. The first, in 1983, was aimed at preventing any legalisation of abortion. It inserted what its proponents termed a 'pro-life' amendment (it subsequently became known more neutrally as 'the eighth amendment'), to the effect that the state 'acknowledges the right to life of the unborn' and undertakes 'by its laws to defend and vindicate that right' (Article 40.3.3). The second, in 1986, would have made it possible for the Oireachtas to legalise divorce in restricted circumstances, but was decisively rejected by the voters.

The next three 'moral issue' referendums were held in November 1992 in response to the Supreme Court decision in the 'X' case (see Box 3.2). Two amendments stating that Article 40.3.3 does not limit either freedom to travel outside the state or freedom to obtain information about services lawfully available in another state were passed. They had the support of both 'liberal' and 'centrist' voters and of all the political parties (for the complex background to these issues see Kennelly and Ward, 1993). A third proposal, which would have permitted abortions only in cases where a continued pregnancy would have meant a risk to 'the life, as distinct from the health, of the mother' (except where the risk to life arose from the possibility of suicide), was defeated, as both liberal and conservative voters opposed it. Liberals opposed it because it would have restricted the availability of abortion, and conservatives opposed it because it would not have outlawed abortion completely. All the political parties except Fianna Fáil also opposed it. In 1995, there was a second vote

---

Box 3.2 The 'X' case of 1992

The 'X' case, which arose early in 1992, concerned a 14-year-old girl who had become pregnant, allegedly as a result of being raped. She intended to travel to Britain to obtain an abortion, but the Attorney General, the legal adviser to the government, obtained a High Court injunction to prevent her travelling out of the country, on the ground that she intended to terminate the life of her unborn child, which he believed would be contrary to Article 40.3.3 of the constitution (the 'pro-life amendment' inserted by referendum in 1983). This decision caused an uproar in Ireland and earned the country wide and unfavourable international publicity.

In March 1992, the Supreme Court overturned this injunction. It declared that Article 40.3.3 did in fact confer a right to an abortion on a woman whose life would be threatened by continuing with a pregnancy – including cases where this risk arose from the possibility of suicide by the mother.

This decision was welcomed by pro-choice groups and liberals in general, though there was concern that the Supreme Court had not explicitly affirmed that a woman had the right to travel out of the country, no matter what her reasons for wanting to do so. It was bitterly criticised by anti-abortion groups, who complained that when the Irish people voted in 1983 to add the 'pro-life' amendment, they had intended this to have the effect of completely outlawing abortion. The judges, in their view, had undemocratically imposed their own idiosyncratic interpretation of the article in question. However, in the words of Charles Evans Hughes, quoted on p. 67, 'The Constitution is what the judges say it is'.

on divorce, and this time the decision was, albeit very narrowly, in favour of legalisation (Girvin, 1996). In 2002, the government proposed an amendment along the same lines as the third of the November 1992 proposals, which would have restricted, without completely eliminating, the right to an abortion. It was narrowly defeated by a combination of relative liberals and a small purist section of conservative opinion, which rejected it on the ground that abortion should be completely prohibited rather than merely restricted (Kennedy, 2002). Finally, in 2015, same-sex marriage was legalised by a comfortable majority on the highest referendum turnout since 1995 (Elkink *et al.*, 2017; Murphy, 2016). The pattern of voting was very similar at each of these referendums, with a great deal of consistency as to which constituencies were the most liberal and which were the most conservative. These moral issue referendums all brought to the fore the liberal–conservative cleavage in Irish society, as discussed in Chapter 2.

Accession to, and further extension of Ireland's relationship with, the European Union (EU) has been responsible for nine referendums (these are discussed further in Chapter 14, pp. 358–60; see also Barrett, 2012; Svensson, 2016). Joining the EU required a referendum because the obligations of membership would otherwise have been in conflict with the constitution. Upon EU membership, the Union's institutions would have the power to make laws for the state and the EU's Court of Justice would be superior to Ireland's Supreme Court, thus creating an apparent conflict with at least two articles of the constitution: 15.2.1, affirming the legislative monopoly of the Oireachtas, and 34.4.6 (as it then was), affirming the finality of all judgments of the Supreme Court. However, the decision was taken in 1972 not to amend those specific articles over which EU membership might cast a shadow, but instead to introduce a catchall amendment, by adding a new subsection (Article 29.4.3) allowing the state to join the EU and adding that 'No provision of this constitution invalidates laws enacted, acts done or measures adopted by the State necessitated by the obligations of membership of the Communities' (Nicol, 2001: 117–47).

The 1987 amendment allowed the state to ratify the Single European Act, and further amendments in 1992 and 1998 allowed it to ratify the Maastricht and Amsterdam agreements respectively. The Nice Treaty caused difficulty, when, for the first time, an EU treaty was rejected at a referendum in June 2001; eventually, the treaty was put to a referendum a second time and, in October 2002, it was passed comfortably on a higher turnout (see Chapter 14). This routine occurred again with the Lisbon Treaty, which was rejected by the people in June 2008, leading the government, after a pause for reflection, to decide to ask the people to vote a second time late in 2009, at which stage it was passed with a large majority. Finally, in 2012, voters passed an amendment allowing the state to sign the EU's fiscal compact.

Of the seven proposals concerning voting, two, in 1959 and 1968, were unsuccessful attempts by Fianna Fáil to replace the PR-STV electoral system by the single-member plurality system (these referendums are described on pp. 91–2). On the second occasion, this proposal was coupled with one that was designed to permit rural voters to be over-represented at the expense of urban voters. The other four referendums caused little controversy between the parties. In 1972, there was all-party backing for lowering the voting age, and in 1979, an amendment to allow the university seats in Seanad Éireann to be reorganised got strong support among those sufficiently motivated to vote on the issue (even four decades later, none of the changes to which this amendment opened the door had been made). In 1984, a proposal to permit the Oireachtas to extend the vote to non-citizens received general endorsement, and in 1999, voters agreed to an amendment that gave constitutional recognition to local government and stipulated that local elections must take place at intervals of no more than five years.

Four referendums concerned the main institutions of the state. Two of these were rejected: in 2011, the people refused to change the constitution to give greater powers to Oireachtas committees, and in 2013, they voted down a government proposal to abolish the upper house of parliament, Seanad Éireann (see Chapter 7). In 2011, they amended the constitution to permit the salaries of judges to be reduced in line with those of other public officials (O'Dowd, 2012), and in 2013, they approved the establishment of a third superior court, the Court of Appeal.

The 1998 Belfast or Good Friday Agreement (for which, see pp. 331–8) was approved overwhelmingly by southern voters. One aspect of this was that it conferred an automatic right to Irish citizenship upon anyone born on the island; within a few years this had come to be branded by the government as an unintended 'loophole' and an inducement to 'citizenship tourism', and in June 2004 a proposal to remove this automatic right, via the addition of a new section to Article 9, was approved by almost 80 per cent of voters (see Appendix 2h). The seven less important proposals have all been passed, apart from the 2015 proposal to reduce the minimum age for candidates at presidential elections from 35 to 21, which in fact received the lowest Yes vote of any proposal, only 27 per cent.

The referendum requirement in Article 46 has been a powerful check on governments wanting to make changes that do not have broad support across the political spectrum. On only one occasion (the referendum to approve the constitution in 1937) have the people approved a proposal not backed by the major opposition party – and even then, the second opposition party, Labour, adopted a neutral position. Since 1937, whenever governments have put forward proposals not supported by the main opposition party – Fianna Fáil's attempts in 1959 and 1968 to change the electoral system, and in 1992 and 2002 to restrict the circumstances under which abortion could be made legal, along with the Fine Gael–Labour coalition's proposed legalisation of divorce in 1986, and its attempt to abolish the Seanad in 2013 – the people have rejected them.

The requirement that no changes can be made without a referendum may well enhance the status of the constitution, whose contents remain under the control of the people. The referendum requirement also means that such changes as are made, however controversial – for example, on divorce, Northern Ireland or the EU – have a legitimacy that they would not have if the decision was made by politicians alone. However, it does have some possible drawbacks. One is that the expense involved in holding a referendum to make even the most insignificant and uncontentious amendment inhibits the process of change. A second, at least according to proponents of deeper European integration, is that the referendum requirement results in the people sometimes being asked to vote on questions whose complexity means that they would be better decided by parliament – though others maintain that since European integration affects sovereignty it is right that the people have the decisive voice.

Judicial development of the constitution

Given that a constitution lays down rules about what government and parliament can and cannot do, someone is required to decide authoritatively whether they are obeying the rules, and this role is commonly performed by a judicial body. Judicial review can be defined as the power of a court to declare any law, any official action based on a law or any other action by a public official, to be in conflict with the constitution and hence invalid (Abraham, 1996: 70). In most European countries, such as Austria, Germany, Poland and Spain, there is a special constitutional court, but in common law countries, such as Ireland and the USA, this function tends to be carried out by the regular courts.[1] The importance of judicial review in

Ireland marks the country's divergence from British practice, for whereas judicial review is significant in many countries, it played little part in the governance of the United Kingdom before the 1980s.

The judges cannot alter the text of the constitution, but they decide what the text means. This power to interpret the constitution is considerable, since judges can, if they are so minded, 'discover' meanings that were never envisaged or intended by anyone initially; in the USA Charles Evans Hughes, who later became Chief Justice, bluntly declared in 1916 that 'the constitution is what the judges say it is' (Abraham, 1998: 356). Similarly, in an important Irish constitutional case in 1993, Mr Justice McCarthy observed that 'It is peculiarly within the jurisdiction of the courts to declare what the Constitution means' (Morgan, 1997: 32). In a number of European countries, the significance of judicial review is such that the judges could be counted among the policy makers (Gallagher *et al.*, 2011: 95–110). In Ireland, judicial review has proved to be the main method by which the constitution has been developed.

Constitutional cases can reach the courts by one of two routes. First, the constitution makes provision for a priori *abstract* review; that is, the constitutionality of a bill can be considered before it has become law, and without reference to any specific case. Such review can be brought about only by a presidential referral of the bill to the Supreme Court. Second, there is provision for *concrete* review: it is open to anyone affected by a law to challenge its constitutionality before the High Court, with the possibility of appeal to the Court of Appeal and the Supreme Court. The court decides whether the law is valid or must be struck down. In addition, any other act of the government (such as the signing of an agreement with another government) may be challenged in the courts as a violation of the constitution. In order to take a constitutional case, citizens must show that they have *locus standi* – that is, that they are in some way affected by the action or statute they are complaining about and are not merely busybodies.

Presidential referrals

The president of Ireland usually signs bills into law, but she or he has the power, under Article 26 of the constitution, instead to refer a bill to the Supreme Court for a decision on its constitutionality. Governments cannot directly request the president to refer a piece of legislation, but a former minister has revealed that ministers are made aware of a 'code', a form of words that, if used in the Dáil or Seanad, conveys the appropriate signal to Áras an Uachtaráin (Quinn, 2005: 204). When a bill is referred, the Supreme Court hears arguments from lawyers assigned to put the case for and against the constitutionality of the bill, and delivers its judgment. If it decides that the bill is 'repugnant to the constitution', the president may not sign it into law.

This presidential power was employed on 15 occasions up to September 2017; on eight occasions the Supreme Court found the bill constitutional, and on the other seven it found the bill, or sections of it, to be unconstitutional. The merit of this procedure is that the constitutionality of bills about which doubts have been raised can be definitively established before they become law; it prevents an unconstitutional law being in force until successfully challenged, a situation that could have consequences difficult ever to put right (CRG, 1996: 75).

However, there are two difficulties with the procedure. One is that Article 34.3.3 gives a dreadful finality to a positive verdict of the Supreme Court in such cases: it states that the validity of a bill (or any part thereof) that is cleared by the Supreme Court after referral by the president may never again be questioned by any court. Even if the views of Supreme Court judges change over time, as of course they do,[2] or if operation of the legislation reveals aspects that no-one had detected when the bill was argued about in abstract form, the legislation is immune from all further challenge. The CRG thus recommended that Article 34.3.3 should be deleted and the all-party committee endorsed this (CRG, 1996: 76–80; All-Party Oireachtas Committee, 1999: 48, 112–13). The other difficulty is the opposite; it is that a bill may be struck down too readily, because the Supreme Court is not confined to the facts of any particular case. Whereas in the normal course of events the constitutionality of a law can be challenged only by an individual with a specific case to argue, in an Article 26 referral hypothetical suppositions can be conjured up and a bill could be found unconstitutional because of a possibility that might never arise in practice (Hogan, 1997).

Judicial review

Once a bill is on the statute books, it is open to challenge by anyone whom it affects, and the courts are responsible for delivering an authoritative decision on the constitutionality of legislation or the actions of public bodies (Articles 34.3, 34.4 and 34.5). Between 1937 and 2015, the courts made 93 declarations of unconstitutionality (Hogan *et al.*, 2015). Judicial review has become more significant since the mid-1960s. Before then, the courts tended to interpret the constitution in a 'positivist' or literal manner, sticking closely to the letter of the document and taking the view that there was no more to it than the words it contained. The position then began to change, reflecting what has been seen as a virtually worldwide pattern of courts coming to play 'an unprecedented role in the policymaking process' (Hilbink, 2008: 227). Writers have spoken of 'the global expansion of judicial power', the growing 'judicialisation' or 'juridification' of politics, the transfer of 'an unprecedented amount of power from representative institutions to judiciaries', and the transformation of democracy into 'juristocracy' (Tate and Vallinder, 1995; Hirschl, 2004: 1; Hirschl, 2008). Who becomes a superior court judge may matter as much as who gets elected to parliament, or even who is appointed to government. While once it was assumed that the significant political role of the judges in the USA had no European counterpart, the political role of European courts and judges is now recognised (Dyevre, 2010).

The Irish judiciary began to adopt a more 'creative' approach during the 1960s, due partly to the accession of a new generation of judges and partly to the general changes taking place in society and political culture (see Casey, 2000: 332–85; Mac Cormaic, 2016: 72–110). Worldwide judicial activism has been facilitated by cross-national networks and annual conferences, socialising their members 'as participants in a common global judicial enterprise' (Slaughter, 2004: 99). Two newly-appointed Supreme Court judges, Cearbhall Ó Dálaigh and Brian Walsh, both regularly read law reports from the USA, and Walsh entered into a lengthy personal correspondence with US Supreme Court judge William Brennan, involving many exchanges of ideas (Mac Cormaic, 2016: 95; for international influences generally see Gallagher, 2010). Judges began to speak of the general tenor or spirit of the constitution and of the rights that those living under such a constitution must by definition, in their view, enjoy.

Article 40.3.1 proved very important in this process: 'The State guarantees in its laws to respect, and, as far as practicable, by its laws to defend and vindicate the personal rights of the citizen.' Although this may appear to be merely a pious declaration without much substance (as may, indeed, have been the intention), it has proved to be of great significance. Until the 1960s, it was assumed that the 'rights' referred to in Article 40.3.1 were only those specifically listed in Articles 40–44, but a landmark judgment in 1963 changed that. The plaintiff in the case of Ryan v Attorney General argued that the fluoridation of water violated her right to bodily integrity, a right not mentioned anywhere in the constitution. In his judgment,

Mr Justice Kenny accepted her contention that she – and by extension every other citizen – did indeed have such a right (though, unfortunately for her, he did not accept that putting fluoride in the water violated it). His judgment stated: 'The personal rights which may be invoked to invalidate legislation are not confined to those specified in Article 40 but include all those rights which result from the Christian and democratic nature of the State'. This, incidentally, is an example of a practice by judiciaries in many countries that has the effect of increasing their power: they 'are past masters at awarding immediate victory in a particular case to one party while planting doctrinal seeds that will eventually favor the other' (Shapiro, 1999: 212). The government of the day is not too put out by a decision that, after all, upholds its legislation, and only over time does the potential impact of the judgment in constraining political actors become apparent.

Subsequently, as the number of constitutional cases brought to the courts increased, judges 'discovered' many more 'undisclosed human rights' in the constitution (for a list of 18 such rights, see CRG, 1996: 246; see also Hogan and Whyte, 2003: 1413–85). One of the most dramatic judgments came in 1973, when the Supreme Court (in the case of McGee v Attorney General) accepted the plaintiff's claim that she had a right to marital privacy, and accordingly struck down the 1935 legislation banning the importation of contraceptives (Mac Cormaic, 2016: 156–77). Given de Valera's strongly Catholic views, and since it was his government's legislation that was being declared unconstitutional, it was apparent to all at this stage that the constitution was not, as indeed it never really had been, 'de Valera's constitution', the name sometimes applied to it. His creation now had a life of its own, and it was for the courts, not for any politician, to decide what its words meant. It is generally believed that de Valera did not anticipate judicial review being anything like as significant or extensive as it has proved, even though he was warned about the way things might turn out (Hogan and Whyte, 2003: xvii, 1245).

Stating the existence of unenumerated rights, and using these to strike down legislation passed by the democratically-elected parliament, clearly gives considerable power to the unelected judiciary, a point to which we return later in the chapter. On the other hand, the fact that the courts have identified unenumerated rights in the past does not mean that Article 40.3.1 is a bottomless well out of which endless new rights may be extracted. The courts have exercised great restraint here since the late 1990s, and their past activism has been seen as having filled in the gaps of standard rights that had been omitted, perhaps through oversight, from the text of the constitution. With that task complete, the doctrine of unenumerated rights may have 'withered' (Doyle, 2008a: 104–8; Hogan, 2008: vii). After peaks of declarations of unconstitutionality in the periods 1970–73 and 1980–85, since 2000 there has been a 'flight to procedure', such declarations tending to base findings of unconstitutionality on procedural failings rather than on incompatibility with broad principles (Hogan *et al.*, 2015: 27).

The courts have made a number of decisions that have had major political implications (see Box 3.3). In addition to high-profile judgments such as these, there have been many less spectacular but nonetheless significant judgments in which the courts, relying on their power to interpret the constitution, have effectively changed the law. For example, in the McKinley v Minister for Defence case of 1992 the plaintiff claimed that injuries (for which she held the defendants responsible) to her husband had deprived her of certain conjugal rights. Under common law, only a husband could claim compensation for the loss of these rights, and the state argued that this common law right was unconstitutional, since it discriminated against married women, and hence had not survived the enactment of the constitution in 1937. Instead of taking this course, the Supreme Court 'developed' the rights in question so as to vest them in a wife as well (Casey, 2000: 474; Hogan and Whyte, 2003: 263,

1328–30). The cumulative effect of such judgments in invalidating old and unreformed statute and common law embodying anomalies or injustices, in effect making new law, should not be underestimated.

Box 3.3 Major judicial decisions with political ramifications made by the Supreme Court

Ryan v Lennon 1934. SC decides 2–1 that the 1929 decision of the Oireachtas to extend, from eight to 16 years, the period during which it could amend the Irish Free State constitution was constitutional – thus, it has been said, 'effectively herald[ing] the collapse of the 1922 Constitution', because it means that the constitution will never be able to assert supremacy over ordinary legislation (Hogan, 2000: 102).

Buckley (Sinn Féin Funds) 1947. SC finds that a bill passed by the Oireachtas that would have had the effect of determining the outcome of a case about to come before the courts was unconstitutional, as it would amount to parliamentary trespassing on the preserve of the judiciary.

Ryan 1964. In a case involving the fluoridation of the public water supply, SC upholds the High Court judgment that the constitution contains unenumerated personal rights over and above those actually listed in the text. This opens the door to the judiciary subsequently to 'discover' a number of other unenumerated rights.

Byrne 1969. SC decides 4–1 that the state can be sued by any of its citizens.

McGee 1973. SC finds 4–1 that the legislation banning the importation or sale of contraceptives violates the (unenumerated) right to marital privacy and hence is unconstitutional. This was described as 'arguably the most significant [decision] the Supreme Court has ever taken' (Mac Cormaic, 2016: 175).

McGlinchey 1982. SC decides 3–0 that the test of whether an offence is political depends not on whether it had a political motivation in the mind of its perpetrator, but on whether the activity was what 'reasonable civilised people would regard as political activity'. This brought about a significant change in the state's extradition policy.

Norris 1983. SC decides 3–2 that the nineteenth-century legislation making male homosexuality illegal is constitutional. The majority judgment 'has a strong claim to be one of the worst the Supreme Court has produced' (Mac Cormaic, 2016: 207), while the dissenting judgment of Séamus Henchy has been described as 'probably the finest judgment ever delivered in an Irish court' (Hogan, 2011: 105).

Crotty 1987. SC decides 3–2 that the government may not sign the Single European Act, on the ground that to do so would restrict the freedom of governments to conduct an independent foreign policy. As a result, every subsequent major EU treaty has required constitutional change and hence a referendum.

X 1992. In a case involving a teenager known as 'Miss X', SC decides 4–1 that the constitution confers a right to abortion on a woman in situations where her life is at risk from continuing with a pregnancy, including situations where the risk is one of suicide.

McKenna 1995. SC decides 4–1 that during a referendum campaign, public money may not be used in support of only one side.

Coughlan 2000. SC decides 4–1 that during a referendum campaign, broadcasters are obliged to allow equal airtime for both sides of the campaign.

TD 2001. SC, by a 4–1 margin, overturns a High Court judgment directing the state to provide a secure place for a disturbed child; SC declares that judgment to be inconsistent with the constitutional separation of powers between the judiciary and the political arms of government. The SC judgment quells hopes and fears that the courts might 'discover' socio-economic rights in the constitution and assert the power to direct governments to spend public money in particular ways.

Maguire v Ardagh (Abbeylara) 2002. In a case taken by gardaí against an Oireachtas committee chaired by Seán Ardagh TD, SC finds 5–2 that the Oireachtas does not have the power to conduct enquiries that could lead to adverse findings of fact against an individual, a judgment that significantly clips the wings of Oireachtas committees.

The power of judges

The power of judges to tell the people's representatives that they cannot introduce the policies that they wish to runs counter to majoritarian conceptions of democracy, in that it puts significant power into the hands of unelected individuals who are not routinely accountable or answerable to anyone (Daly and Hickey, 2015: 115–44). It has been argued that the principle of judicial supremacy is accepted surprisingly uncritically in Ireland, compared with the debate it engenders elsewhere, possibly because the popular endorsement or amendment of the constitution in the referendums of 1937 and subsequently mean that judicial review might be seen as a manifestation of popular sovereignty rather than as a fetter on it (Daly, 2017: 32–3). Judges are not completely unaccountable, of course; in practice, judicial accountability takes the form of peer assessment or public scrutiny by other judges, by the barristers in the Law Library, by academic and other commentators, and increasingly by the media (O'Brien, 2013). It is worth noting that one of the strongest criticisms of the Supreme Court in recent years came from a judge who charged that, far from being aloof and unresponsive to public opinion, the court had given a constitutionally questionable judgment in 'an attempt to curry favour with a potentially hostile media', and that it should show a greater degree of independence from 'the populist consensus'.[3]

The only other form of accountability to which judges are subject is the 'nuclear option' whereby, under Article 35.4 of the constitution, they can be dismissed by majority vote of the Dáil and Seanad for 'stated misbehaviour or incapacity'. But the possibility of invoking this provision has only very rarely been considered, and never because a government found a judge's decision politically displeasing. The 'Sheedy case' of 1999 and the 'Curtin case' of 2002–07 both concerned judges whose behaviour had created widespread concern, and in each case the judge stood down as the Oireachtas moved inexorably towards invoking the impeachment procedure (for these cases see Doyle, 2008a: 378–81; Mac Cormaic, 2016: 310–25). The idea of monitoring judges' behaviour has proved difficult to implement (Cahillane, 2015). In 1999, the all-party committee recommended amending the constitution to create a 'Judicial Council' to review judicial conduct, as opposed to judicial decisions (All-Party Oireachtas Committee, 1999: 21–4). However, a government proposal to hold a referendum on this in June 2001 was withdrawn at a late stage when the opposition parties indicated that they were unhappy about some of the details. At various times subsequently such a development has been described as 'imminent', but no tangible proposals emerged until mid-2017.

Mr Justice Kenny once said that 'judges have become legislators, and have the advantage that they do not have to face an opposition' (Hogan and Whyte, 2003: 1415n133). He might have added that neither do they have to face the people, as politicians do. Their power to interpret the constitution makes them even more powerful than judges in many other countries. All of this raises the questions of who the judges are, how they came to be judges and what values they hold.

The appointment of judges

By law, Irish judges of the superior courts (i.e. the High Court, the Court of Appeal and the Supreme Court) must be barristers – or, with certain restrictions, solicitors – of at least 12 years' standing or circuit court judges of at least four years' standing (MacNeill, 2016: 60). They are appointed by the government (Articles 13.9 and 35.1), with the key actors being the Taoiseach, the Minister for Justice and the Attorney General (together with the other party leader(s) in the case of a coalition government). The rest of the government is simply informed of the name of the chosen person. (Other ministers, though, are heavily lobbied, and in turn lobby, when it comes to appointments of judges to lower courts.) Governments want to be confident that the appointee, as well as possessing the requisite professional merit, is a person of common sense, sound judgement and understanding of the human condition and of the real world, and that there are no issues around what could be euphemistically termed their 'temperament' (Mac Cormaic, 2016: 354–9). As a result, paper qualifications are not enough; a crucial factor is being known personally by one of the key players (MacNeill, 2016: 138). Until 1996, the procedure was an informal one, under which the names of appointees reached the government by a secret process involving the taking of soundings, with political connections playing an important role.

This was, in theory, changed by the creation in 1996 of the Judicial Appointments Advisory Board (JAAB), whose members include senior judicial figures, the presidents of the professional organisations representing barristers and solicitors, the Attorney General and three 'lay' members appointed by the Minister for Justice. The JAAB receives applications and forwards a list of at least seven suitable candidates to the government. However, the government is not bound to select someone from the board's list and, moreover, the board's deliberations are bypassed whenever the government decides to promote a judge from a lower court. This hardly cramps the government's style at all, and in any case it transpires that within around five years of its establishment, the JAAB, perhaps over-cautiously, deferred to legal advice that it might be infringing on the government's constitutional right to appoint judges by doing anything more than simply forwarding the entire list of applicants to the government minus those whom it deems unsuitable (MacNeill, 2016: 33, 127–9). This 'institutional drift', as MacNeill terms it, was never disclosed publicly by the JAAB, and has turned the JAAB into little more than a means of weeding out the unappointable. Bringing the operation of the JAAB back to its original intention, or going further by requiring it to submit a ranked list of no more than three names, would represent obvious reform measures (Cahillane, 2017; Morgan, 2012: 237).

Some would like the removal of all political control over judicial appointments. This would be an example of a worldwide trend towards taking important decisions out of the hands of politicians and giving them to 'non-majoritarian institutions', a term that has come to mean bodies whose members are not directly answerable to the public. While the rationale is that such bodies can take a longer-term perspective than politicians, whose horizons may be bounded by the next election, for critics this is essentially 'non-democracy' (Mair, 2013: 5–6). For example, as an independent TD, Shane Ross warned of the risk of an 'accident' caused by a judge giving 'a political judgment' (MacNeill, 2016: 211). He carried this view into his role as a minister in the government formed in 2016, pressing for a reduction in the government's role in this area. As a result, in July 2017 the Dáil passed the second stage of a bill that would establish a Judicial Appointments Commission to replace the JAAB. The new body would have 11 members, only five of them lawyers or judges, and it would be required to recommend three names to fill any judicial vacancy, from whom the government would make its choice. The judiciary had privately communicated to the government its opposition to what it saw as the downgrading of its own role in the selection process. However, MacNeill notes (2016: 219) that among common law countries, New Zealand's judiciary has been ranked the most independent globally, even though the government has greater power to choose its preferred candidates than its Irish counterpart. She also observes that, given the importance of being personally known to someone in the small circle of decision makers, if the importance of political networks is reduced, other geographic or professional networks may simply become more important (MacNeill, 2016: 113). In addition, concern has been expressed that if the role of political actors in the appointments process is reduced, this will not necessarily result in greater weight being accorded to 'merit', but may result in either a self-perpetuating judicial caste or in a process in which lobby groups supply some of the 'lay' members of the JAAB and seek to have like-minded individuals appointed to the judiciary (Keena, 2017; Kenny, 2017). It is also worth bearing in mind that perhaps Europe's most politicised judiciary is to be found in Italy, where government has no power over judicial appointments or promotions (Volcansek, 2006).

As we might expect, judges of the superior courts are not exactly a microcosm of society; a study (Carroll, 2005: 168–72) found that 40 per cent were from legal families, and around 80 per cent attended University College Dublin (UCD), though the judiciary is much less gender-unbalanced than it used to be (see Table 9.1). Most features of Irish judges' backgrounds are characteristic of judges almost everywhere. Across western Europe generally, judges tend to come from relatively privileged backgrounds, and appointment of judges is highly politicised. Irish practice is unusual in that the government alone appoints judges; the more common approach, used by most countries for their constitutional courts, is that cross-party agreement is needed for appointments, which means, in effect, that the process becomes a carve-up among the main political parties (Gallagher *et al.*, 2011: 92–5). The result of the judicial appointment process seems to be broadly similar everywhere: 'the men and women selected to judgeships almost always hold safe, sound, middle-of-the-road opinions', and are characterised by 'moderation and attachment to regime norms' (Jacob, 1996: 390–1). Irish governments have traditionally appointed barristers of their own stripe to the bench, though the Fianna Fáil-dominated administrations from 1997 onwards nominated a number of Fine Gael-associated lawyers to the superior courts.

While governments generally look for appointees of the right political background, this does not mean that they expect their appointees to act as party agents while on the bench. The appointment by governments of judges from their own political 'gene pool' is motivated not so much by a desire to influence judicial decision making in a partisan direction as to incentivise barristers to assist the party in various ways, such as research and speech writing, with the prospect of a possible reward in the form of elevation to the bench; in other words, 'patronage as reward', rather than 'patronage as control' (Elgie *et al.*, 2017; O'Malley *et al.*, 2012). As Mac Cormaic (2016: 134) puts it: 'appointments may have been party political but decisions were not'.

Judicial decision making

That said, judges' political backgrounds or their broader values could potentially inform the decisions they make. Judges could, in theory, use the constitution simply to legitimise their own preferences when reaching a decision; as trained barristers, they are well able to make a plausible case for whatever argument they wish to make. Some judges, says Mac Cormaic (2016: 11), incline towards giving the judgment that seems to follow logically from the law, whatever the consequences; others are more inclined to decide first what they believe to be 'the just outcome and then search for a legally permissible way to bring it about'. Reviewing the decisions made by the judiciary in constitutional cases, Hogan (writing as a legal academic, and subsequently a superior court judge) points to the absence of any consistent approach on the part of the judges, with a strong suspicion that they utilise 'whatever method might seem to be most convenient or to offer adventitious support for conclusions they had already reached' (Hogan, 1988: 187; see also Morgan, 2001 and Chubb, 1991: 71–3). As examples of a possible relationship between backgrounds and judgments, in cases in the 1980s involving extradition of alleged members of republican paramilitary groups to Northern Ireland, judges with a background in Fine Gael tended to be less sympathetic to a 'political offence' line of defence than did those whose background was in Fianna Fáil (Mac Cormaic, 2016: 228). More broadly, the prosperous middle-class background of most judges might lead them instinctively to be 'in favour of the individual rather than the community or the State', or, argues Morgan, there could be an inability to see that a strengthening preference for individual human rights 'inevitably has an effect in reducing the often more deserving rights of that disregarded body, the community' (Morgan, 2001: 108).

If judges do not simply interpret the constitution to accord with their own preferences, on what basis should they interpret it? The 'originalist' perspective, according to which the constitution should be interpreted in line with the intentions of the Irish people when they accepted the constitution in 1937, has obvious pitfalls: how can we know whether the people of 1937 would have felt that a law should or should not be constitutional, and, if we could know, why should the Irish people of the twenty-first century be bound by their views? Such an approach really would be akin to 'rule by the dead'. Yet, without such a constraint on the judges, the danger is that their judgments will not be grounded in anything more substantial than the values and policy preferences of the judges of the day, or some vague notion of what constitutes the public good or the prevailing public attitude.

As we noted at the start of the chapter, there is an inherent tension between constitutionalism and democracy (at least, if the latter is equated simply with majority rule). The dilemma of judicial review is inherently unresolvable. It places great power in the hands of a non-elected and unrepresentative elite, answerable to no-one. But if judges were somehow made genuinely accountable to the government or parliament, they would cease to be an independent judiciary, one of the checks and balances of a liberal democracy. Judicial review has allowed judges to make important quasi-political decisions in areas such as extradition or abortion without reference to the people or their elected representatives. However, Irish judges have not come in for the type of criticism sometimes levelled against their counterparts elsewhere. This is partly because, on the liberal–conservative spectrum discussed in Chapter 2, the judiciary often seemed, during its activist years in the 1960s and 1970s, to be somewhat closer than the Oireachtas to the liberal end of the spectrum; given that public opinion has been becoming more liberal, the judiciary has been a few years ahead of, but not wildly out of line with, public opinion. For example, governments had shown no inclination to grasp the nettle of reforming the restrictive contraception laws until the courts forced their hand in the McGee judgment of 1973.

Regardless of the policy content of judicial decisions, though, the merits of the 'creative' approach taken by the courts in the 1960s, and subsequently, have been increasingly questioned. The landmark decision of Mr Justice Kenny in the 1963 Ryan case, in which the judge spoke of the unenumerated personal rights that 'result from the Christian and democratic nature of the state', and quoted a recent papal encyclical in support of his argument, is open to many criticisms (for a detailed analysis of this judgment see Hogan, 1994; for general discussion, see Clarke, 2011). Reviewing the unenumerated rights discovered by the courts over the years, Hogan concludes:

> While the protection of such various unenumerated rights – such as the right to privacy, the right to earn a livelihood and the right of an unwed mother to custody and care of her child – may well be beneficial and salutary, it is often difficult to take this jurisprudence completely at face value, since there is nothing whatever in the actual text of the Constitution to show that these rights were intended to enjoy constitutional protection.
>
> (Hogan, 1994: 114)

The search for one 'correct' standard to apply in determining which approach the judges should employ when interpreting the constitution is likely to be elusive (Kavanagh, 1997; Doyle, 2008a: 455–68). In practice, attitudes to the judiciary often depend on 'whose ox is being gored', in the words of the American Governor Al Smith, and, significantly, the strongest objections were voiced after the Supreme Court delivered its verdict in the 'X' case in March 1992 (see Box 3.2), when anti-abortionists criticised both the specific judgments delivered (arguing that the judges had 'lost their way') and, it seemed, the principle of judicial review. Fianna Fáil Senator Des Hanafin, chairman of the Pro-Life Trust, declared that 'it is wholly unacceptable and indeed a deep affront to the people of Ireland that four judges who are preserved by the constitution from accountability can radically alter the constitution and place in peril the most vulnerable section of our society' (*Irish Times*, 6 March 1992). However, this seems to be a minority viewpoint. Calls for fundamental reform of the system of judicial appointment, for example by the introduction of US-style parliamentary assessments of proposed appointees, have up to now been voices in the wilderness. The tension between democracy and constitutionalism cannot in any case be eliminated by such devices; it can only be managed, with greater or less success.

The debate on constitutional change

Constitutional change was quite high on the political agenda at some times in the past, especially the 1970s and 1980s, but most of the issues with a constitutional dimension were largely resolved by the end of the 1990s. Prior to 2011, the initiative in proposing ideas for constitutional change lay primarily with the All-Party Oireachtas Committee on the Constitution that we mentioned earlier, which issued a number of reports assessing the merits of specific changes (Coakley, 2013: 11–12). After the 2011 election, the government instead established a Constitutional Convention. This consisted of 66 'ordinary' citizens drawn at random from the population, 33 members of parliament from both north and south of the border and an independent chair. Its terms of reference laid out a rather esoteric list of topics to examine (Coakley, 2013: 14) and empowered it to go on to propose 'such other constitutional amendments' as it saw fit; the government would consider these and decide whether or not to put them to the people. It made a large number of recommendations during its two-year lifespan; perhaps taken aback by the sheer number of these, the government put only two of them to referendums, namely the legalisation of same-sex marriage, and the reduction of the minimum age for presidential candidates. The government rejected some of the others and simply did not react to the remainder (for the Constitutional Convention see Suiter *et al.*, 2016; Suteu, 2015; and, for a sceptical assessment, Carolan, 2015). After the 2016 election, a similar body, though this time consisting only of ordinary citizens (hence it was termed a 'citizens' assembly'), was established, with a remit in particular to consider how, if at all, constitutional restrictions regarding abortion should be amended. As with the constitutional convention, critics suggested that this was at least in part a delaying tactic that would enable the government to postpone having to make a decision on a contentious subject.

In recent years, there has been considerable discussion, more among legal scholars than in the political arena, about the idea of giving constitutional status to socio-economic rights. We will discuss the latter after an overview of other aspects of the constitution's suitability for the twenty-first century.

General assessment

Attitudes to the constitution have undergone a number of changes over the years. Until the mid-1960s there was remarkably little criticism of the constitution and, perhaps, limited awareness of how important it could be as the basic law in a functioning liberal democratic society. As societal attitudes began to change from the 1960s onwards, the constitution was increasingly seen as a symbol of the past and an obstacle to progress. For many, it was regarded as a product of de Valera's Ireland, a narrow Catholic and nationalist document that sought to impose the mores of the 1930s political elite upon a changing and modernising country. Numerous demands for 'a new constitution', free of the baggage of the past, were heard. Yet, at the same time, there was a growing awareness of the merits of the constitution and of the richness of the jurisprudence that was being constructed around it. When the fiftieth anniversary of the constitution was marked in the late 1980s by a spate of assessments, the tone was celebratory and appreciative rather than critical. Brian Farrell seemed to sum up the mood: '[Since 1937,] that Constitution, Bunreacht na hÉireann, has been amended, interpreted, re-shaped by judges, politicians, civil servants and the people. One man's document has become a political community's common charter – a living and effective guarantee of broadly based and expanding liberties' (Farrell, 1988b: viii). In its ninth decade, the standing of the constitution remains high.

This change in attitudes has resulted from the development of the constitution by the judiciary and from alterations to the wording of the constitution effected by referendum. The constitution was long accused of posing an impediment to the 'liberal agenda', but with the insertion in 2015 of Article 41.4 providing for same-sex marriage this has been pretty much completed, apart from the difficult issue of abortion, where there is strong public pressure for amendment or removal of Article 40.3.3, the 'eighth amendment' (see Chapter 9, pp. 231–2). The rephrasing of Articles 2 and 3 for which the people voted overwhelmingly in 1998, i.e. the replacement of a claim over Northern Ireland by an aspiration to a peacefully united Ireland, similarly defused much of the criticism of the constitution as expressing old-style nationalism. This is not to say that there are no further political battles to be fought over the wording of the constitution (see Box 3.4). Article 41.2, incorporating the view that women's place is in the home, would find few defenders (see Chapter 9, especially p. 217, Connelly, 1999, and Dooley, 1998, for a fuller discussion), and the whole constitution contains innumerable examples of gender-specific language that the CRG (1996: xi) recommended be replaced by wording based on 'the principle of gender-inclusiveness'. The preamble to the constitution still conveys a very nationalist view of history in which unionists could not recognise themselves and, along with many other areas of the constitution, has a broadly Christian, often specifically Catholic, tone that does not match the political culture of the state as well as it did in 1937. More broadly, whereas in the past the articles on religion were criticised first for being insufficiently Catholic and then for being too 'pro-Catholic', in the twenty-first century they are more likely to be criticised for privileging the religious generally over the non-religious (Doyle, 2008b).

Box 3.4 Possible changes to the Irish constitution

Among the changes that have been suggested, apart from the addition of socio-economic rights, are:

- Remove all examples of gender-specific language and ensure that the constitution contains only wording based on the principle of gender-inclusiveness;
- Amend or remove article 40.3.3 (the 'pro-life', or more neutrally the 'eighth', amendment) in order to facilitate the introduction of a more liberal abortion regime;
- Insert a comprehensive list of fundamental rights and seek to prevent the courts discovering further unenumerated fundamental rights;
- Qualify the right to private property, so as to tilt the balance in favour of society as a whole;
- Enshrine the principle of Irish neutrality in international affairs;
- Continue to allow the parliament to declare a state of emergency, but stipulate that any such state of emergency shall automatically lapse after a period of 3 years;
- Give constitutional recognition to the office of the Ombudsman (for which, see Chapters 8 and 10);
- Give explicit recognition to the centrality of political parties to political life, and enunciate principles regulating parties' roles, rights and responsibilities.

Those sections of the constitution that deal with the institutions of government are not generally seen as in pressing need of change. The CRG recommended the introduction of the 'constructive vote of no confidence', which would prevent the Dáil voting out a Taoiseach unless it was able simultaneously to vote in a replacement, and it advocated giving constitutional recognition to both local government (this was effected in 1999) and the Ombudsman. It considered the arguments for change in the role and composition of the Seanad, and in the electoral system, but rather than making firm recommendations it called for further consideration of both questions. Many of these subjects are discussed in the other chapters of this book. The CRG also considered possible changes of a less politically controversial and more narrowly constitutional nature. We have outlined many of these areas in this chapter already, such as the character of the 'emergency' article (28.3.3) and the freezing for all time of the initial clearance of a bill following a presidential referral (34.3.3). We turn now to the issue of whether socio-economic rights should be stated in the constitution.

Socio-economic rights

The limited scope of the constitutionally affirmed rights (both enumerated and unenumerated) has been criticised by those who believe that the constitution should actively promote equality of outcome and not merely equality of opportunity. Why, it is asked, should a right to adequate food, clothing, shelter, rest and medical care not be affirmed (Murphy, 1998: 167–81; Hughes *et al.*, 2007: 136–41; Murray, 2016)? A number of academic commentators and others have argued that the constitution should be amended to provide explicit recognition of the state's obligation to ensure that all of its citizens enjoy socio-economic rights, pointing in particular to the South African constitution of 1996 as a model to be emulated (Bacik, 2008; Langwallner, 2008; O'Connell, 2008; Quinn, 2001; Whyte 2006). O'Connell argues that the courts should intervene in cases where government policies 'impact unevenly and unfavourably on the weaker sections of the community', while Quinn envisages the courts intervening on behalf of the poor and marginalised (O'Connell, 2008: 345; Quinn, 2001: 45). The Constitutional Convention considered the matter over the course of a day in February 2014, hearing arguments from both sides, at the end of which 85 per cent of its members voted in favour of strengthening the protection of such rights.

On the whole, the courts have not sought to enforce socio-economic rights, usually citing the separation of powers doctrine, under which the courts co-exist with government and parliament, each with its own remit and none being superior to the other two, as in the TD case of 2001 (see Box 3.3). The courts, in this view, do not have the role of directing, or the power to direct, the government to make specific policy choices, and prominent voices have been raised against the idea.

In 2003, the Minister for Justice Michael McDowell argued that the exercise of rights to housing, health care and higher education had to be rationed by some mechanism, and decisions on how to do this 'are, in my view, the stuff of politics, and not at all appropriate to be decided by the courts ... differences within societies concerning economic and social values and ends should, in the normal course of things, be resolved by the democratic political process' (*Irish Times*, 15 April 2003). A year later the Attorney General, Rory Brady, asked rhetorically 'What happens when you have a series of rights all of which are competing for the limited financial resources of the state?' Such decisions, he said, were for politicians, who were answerable to the people, and not for the courts (*Irish Times*, 30 June 2004). A majority of the CRG, too, was opposed to the inclusion of specific personal economic rights. It took the view that matters such as freedom from poverty are essentially political questions, so it 'would be a distortion of democracy to transfer decisions on major issues of policy and practicality from the Government and the Oireachtas, elected to represent the people and do their will, to an unelected judiciary'. There was also the danger that the state would find itself compelled by the courts to pursue certain policies regardless of whether the necessary resources were available (CRG, 1996: 234–6).

Proponents of the declaration and protection of socio-economic rights maintain that the political process cannot be guaranteed to produce acceptable outcomes, and so 'judicial intervention on behalf of marginalised groups whose pressing needs are studiously avoided by the political process can be defended as both constitutionally and politically legitimate' (Whyte, 2002: 57; O'Connell, 2008: 346). Given that the least well-off are the least likely to vote, it would hardly be surprising if the political system deprioritises the needs of the marginalised and concentrates on satisfying the well-heeled, articulate swing voter (Whyte, 2002: 35–6). Most supporters of justiciable socio-economic rights feel that the courts should act in this area only 'circumspectly' and 'as a last resort' (Langwallner, 2008: 218; Whyte, 2002: 54). Quinn goes further, though, arguing that the rationality of a government decision to close a hospital in a poor part of a city 'should therefore become the legitimate object of judicial scrutiny' and that 'the biggest benefit would be to expose the rationality of socio-economic programmes to objective analysis' (Quinn, 2001: 45). Clearly, this runs the risk that the judges would be called upon to become the ultimate arbiters of the wisdom of policy choices and carry out something akin to the 'value for money' audits conducted by the Comptroller and Auditor General (see p. 263). Whether judges are equipped to play such a role, and whether the process of government would be sustainable if they attempted to perform it, is open to debate.

The Irish constitution, it must be said, is very much in the European mainstream in guaranteeing the standard liberal rights while refraining from asserting that those under its jurisdiction possess justiciable economic rights. A general objection to constitutionalising rights

Box 3.5 Should the constitution explicitly protect socio-economic rights?

In recent years, there has been debate as to whether the constitution should be amended to declare explicitly that everyone has socio-economic rights, such as the right to food, shelter and adequate health care. There are many arguments on each side.

Those in support say that:

- Socio-economic rights are as essential to a life of fulfilment as are civil–political rights, and should be protected in the same way.
- Those who are marginalised, for example the homeless or the very poor, are, realistically, in no position to exercise their civil–political rights fully.
- The political system is responsive primarily to those who have resources such as wealth, education and access, and therefore it cannot be relied on to produce outcomes that take account of those without such resources.
- If a majority of the population votes for political programmes that leave an impoverished minority on the margins of society, the constitution and the courts have a responsibility to protect the rights of that minority.
- There would be no breach of principle in enshrining rights that commit the state to public expenditure, given that the constitution already guarantees the right to free primary education.
- If the people were to vote in a referendum to add protection of socio-economic rights to the constitution in the form of new articles, it could hardly be a distortion of democracy for the courts then to give effect to those articles.
- Constitutions exist precisely to ensure that the majority is unable to ride roughshod over the rights of minorities.

Those against argue that:

- The courts, in interpreting the constitution, have the role of ensuring that the political process is conducted fairly and freely, but decisions on policies must be made by the elected representatives of the people.
- It would be wrong for the constitution to purport to protect 'rights' such as adequate health care that in reality no-one can honestly guarantee to deliver; adding a constitutional 'right' to adequate health care will not magically bring about an improvement in the quality of the health service.
- Democracy would be undermined if a government trying to implement its manifesto was compelled by the courts to raise taxes against its wishes, or to switch spending from one area of activity in order to spend more in another area.
- Government resources are limited, and the courts would be faced with decisions as to which policy goals should take priority – decisions that should properly be made through the political process.
- Elections and voting would be devalued if the courts could set aside decisions of the democratically elected parliament in the interests of those who had not taken the trouble to vote.
- Some of those advocating justiciable socio-economic rights may be making an attempt to implement, through the constitution and judiciary, a programme for which they cannot secure support at the ballot box.
- Governments can usually be assumed to be doing their best to achieve the fulfilment of socio-economic goals, and enshrining such goals as 'rights' in the constitution would drag the judiciary into evaluating the wisdom of the policies that the government is pursuing, a task for which the judiciary is not qualified.

and policy positions in this way is that it takes the issue out of 'normal' politics, renders it immune from public debate and, moreover, resolves it favourably to one or other side – so, has been suggested, 'a system that immunized from collective control the issues that produce the most conflict would hardly be democratic' (Sunstein, 1988: 339–40). Bacik acknowledges that some 'may argue that to implement this fundamental re-writing process would be to enshrine a very particular left-wing ideology within the document' (Bacik, 2008: 142).

In the eyes of critics of the inclusion of justiciable socio-economic rights in the constitution, this drive, were it to succeed, would diminish the value of elections and of the democratic process generally by constraining the behaviour of elected representatives. In the eyes of proponents, there are certain rights, belonging to everyone, that are fundamental and must be upheld, even if a majority were to wish to disregard or override them. This principle is already universally accepted with regard to the standard liberal or civil–political rights, such as free speech, equality before the law and the right to vote, and it should be extended to no less important socio-economic rights such as food, shelter and access to health care. The debate is alive in many jurisdictions and, given the strong normative component that it contains, it will never be definitively resolved. For the moment, the courts have shown little appetite to become active in this territory, and there is little political will to amend the constitution in such a way as to guarantee additional specific socio-economic rights. Despite the strong feelings on both sides, comparative analysis suggests that constitutionalising such rights may have little or no impact on policy outcomes (Hirschl and Rosevear, 2011: 221). Were such an amendment made, this would undoubtedly increase, for better or for worse, both the role of the courts in the policy-making process and the power of the judiciary to determine public policy choices.

Conclusion

The Irish constitution is one of the oldest constitutions in Europe, having been promulgated in 1937. It has proved important in constraining policy-makers, given the requirement that it cannot be amended without the approval of the people in a referendum. The constitution is interpreted by the Supreme Court, not by a dedicated constitutional court as in most European countries, and this results in the judiciary's wielding significant power. This is a matter of concern to those who hold that all power-holders should be democratically accountable, but is unavoidable if the judiciary is to be genuinely independent of the government and parliament. While the issue of possible constitutional reform does not generate as much passion as it did in earlier decades, there is an animated debate on the question of whether socio-economic rights should be constitutionally guaranteed.

Calls for a new constitution are now rarely heard. To scrap the existing constitution would risk losing the rights and liberties 'discovered' in it by judges; most of these have had the effect of enhancing the civic rights of citizens. Despite some past accusations that the constitution is excessively long and should be replaced by one that is confined to basics, like the American constitution, in fact the Irish constitution is by no means verbose by worldwide standards; its length of about 14,000 words (in each of the two languages) compares with an estimated average length of 15,900 words in 142 national constitutions examined by van Maarseveen and van der Tang (1978: 177). No political party advocates the drafting of a new constitution, and there is no evidence that this is a priority for the electorate as a whole. Especially at a time of economic difficulties, no government would be thanked for announcing that it intended to devote a lot of time to constitutional revision. The constitution as a whole possesses the kind of widespread acceptance and legitimacy that the Irish Free State constitution never attracted, and is likely to remain the fundamental law of the state for some time to come.

Notes

1   Judges have traditionally been regarded as having more discretion in common law systems, where a decision made by a judge in a case seemingly not covered by a written statute in effect becomes the law and can be cited as a precedent in later cases. In civil law countries, judges are in theory not bound by previous judicial decisions; instead, the written law, based on a comprehensive legal code, provides the basis for an unambiguously correct judicial decision in every case, with judges being little more than legal technicians. In practice, differences between the two types of legal system are now far smaller than used to be the case (Gallagher *et al.*, 2011: 96). The constitutional court model was favoured by some of those drawing up the 1937 constitution but in the end was not chosen (Hogan, 2012: 274–5, 340–2).
2   Under the principle of *stare decisis* (let the decision stand), the Supreme Court, regardless of the views of its current personnel, would be bound by past Supreme Court decisions but, while the court will not lightly overturn a previous decision, it declared in 1964 that it was no longer bound by the doctrine (Hogan and Whyte, 2003: 977–81).
3   This was a charge levelled by High Court judge Seán O'Leary in a document he wrote when he knew he was close to death, published in *Irish Times*, 3 January 2007 ('Supreme Court judges must show "spirit of independence"'). The case concerned an individual who had committed what was universally agreed to be morally repugnant behaviour, but who was not released from jail even after the law under which he had been convicted was struck down as unconstitutional (see Doyle, 2008a: 445–54). The case caused considerable unease among the judiciary (Mac Cormaic, 2016: 1–13).

References and further reading

Abraham, Henry J., 1996. *The Judiciary: The Supreme Court in the Governmental Process*, 10th ed. New York and London: New York University Press.

Abraham, Henry J., 1998. *The Judicial Process: An Introductory Analysis of the Courts of the United States, England and France*, 7th ed. New York and Oxford: Oxford University Press.

All-Party Oireachtas Committee on the Constitution, 1999. *Fourth Progress Report: The Courts and the Judiciary* (Pn 7831). Dublin: Stationery Office.

Bacik, Ivana, 2008. 'Future directions for the constitution', in Oran Doyle and Eoin Carolan (eds), *The Irish Constitution: Governance and Values*. Dublin: Thomson Round Hall, pp. 135–43.

Barrett, Gavin, 2012. 'The evolving door to Europe: reflections on an eventful forty years for Article 29.4 of the Irish constitution', *Irish Jurist* 48, pp. 132–72.

Butler, Andrew and Rory O'Connell, 1998. 'A critical analysis of Ireland's Constitutional Review Group report', *Irish Jurist* 33, pp. 237–65.

Cahillane, Laura, 2015. 'Ireland's system for disciplining and removing judges', *Dublin University Law Journal* 38:1, pp. 55–83.

Cahillane, Laura, 2017. 'Judicial appointments in Ireland: the potential for reform', in Laura Cahillane, James Gallen and Tom Hickey (eds), *Judges, Politics and the Irish Constitution*. Manchester: Manchester University Press, pp. 123–35.

Carolan, Eoin, 2015. 'Ireland's constitutional convention: behind the hype about citizen-led constitutional change', *Icon (International Journal of Constitutional Law)* 13:3, pp. 733–48.

Carroll, Jennifer, 2005. 'You be the judge', *Bar Review* 10:5, pp. 15–34 and 167–72, and 10:6, pp. 182–8.

Casey, James, 2000. *Constitutional Law in Ireland*, 3rd ed. Dublin: Round Hall, Sweet and Maxwell.

Chubb, Basil, 1991. *The Politics of the Irish Constitution*. Dublin: Institute of Public Administration.

Clarke, Desmond M., 2011. 'Judicial reasoning: logic, authority and the rule of law in Irish courts', *Irish Jurist* 46, pp. 152–79.

Coakley, John, 2009. ' "Irish Republic", "Éire" or "Ireland"? The contested name of John Bull's other island', *Political Quarterly* 80:1, pp. 49–58.

Coakley, John, 2013. *Reforming Political Institutions: Ireland in Comparative Perspective*. Dublin: Institute of Public Administration.

Coffey, Donal K., 2012. 'The need for a new constitution: Irish constitutional change 1932–1935', *Irish Jurist* 48, pp. 275–302.

Committee on the Constitution, 1967. *Report* (Pr. 9817). Dublin: Stationery Office.

Connelly, Alpha, 1999. 'Women and the constitution of Ireland', in Yvonne Galligan, Eilís Ward and Rick Wilford (eds), *Contesting Politics: Women in Ireland, North and South*. Boulder CO: Westview and PSAI Press, pp. 18–37.

CRG (Constitution Review Group), 1996. *Report* (Pn 2632). Dublin: Stationery Office.

Daly, Eoin, 2017. 'Reappraising judicial supremacy in the Irish constitutional tradition', in Laura Cahillane, James Gallen and Tom Hickey (eds), *Judges, Politics and the Irish Constitution*. Manchester: Manchester University Press, pp. 29–48.

Daly, Eoin and Tom Hickey, 2015. *The Political Theory of the Irish Constitution: Republicanism and the Basic Law*. Manchester: Manchester University Press.

Dooley, Dolores, 1998. 'Gendered citizenship in the Irish constitution', in Tim Murphy and Patrick Twomey (eds), *Ireland's Evolving Constitution, 1937–97: Collected Essays*. Oxford: Hart, pp. 121–33.

Doyle, Oran, 2008a. *Constitutional Law: Texts, Cases and Materials*. Dublin: Clarus Press.

Doyle, Oran, 2008b. 'Article 44: privileging the rights of the religious', in Oran Doyle and Eoin Carolan (eds), *The Irish Constitution: Governance and Values*. Dublin: Thomson Round Hall, pp. 476–89.

Dyevre, Arthur, 2010. 'Unifying the field of comparative judicial politics: towards a general theory of judicial behaviour', *European Political Science Review* 2:2, pp. 297–327.

Elazar, Daniel J., 1985. 'Constitution-making: the pre-eminently political act', in Keith G. Banting and Richard Simeon (eds), *The Politics of Constitutional Change in Industrial Nations: Redesigning the State*. London: Macmillan, pp. 232–48.

Elgie, Robert, Adam McAuley and Eoin O'Malley, 2017. 'The (not-so-surprising) non-partisanship of the Irish Supreme Court', *Irish Political Studies*, doi:10.1080/07907184.2017.1318851

Elkink, Johan, David M. Farrell, Theresa Reidy and Jane Suiter, 2017. 'Understanding the 2015 marriage referendum in Ireland: context, campaign, and conservative Ireland', *Irish Political Studies* 32:3, pp. 361–81.

Farrell, Brian, 1988a. 'From first Dáil through Irish Free State', in Brian Farrell (ed.), *De Valera's Constitution and Ours*. Dublin: Gill and Macmillan, pp. 18–32.

Farrell, Brian, 1988b. 'Preface', in Brian Farrell (ed.), *De Valera's Constitution and Ours*. Dublin: Gill and Macmillan, pp. vii–ix.

Gallagher, Michael, 1996. 'Ireland: the referendum as a conservative device?', in Michael Gallagher and Pier Vincenzo Uleri (eds), *The Referendum Experience in Europe*. Basingstoke: Macmillan, pp. 86–105.

Gallagher, Michael, Michael Laver and Peter Mair, 2011. *Representative Government in Modern Europe*, 5th ed. Maidenhead: McGraw-Hill.

Gallagher, Paul, 2010. 'The Irish constitution – its unique nature and the relevance of international jurisprudence', *Irish Jurist* 45, pp. 22–50.

Girvin, Brian, 1996. 'The Irish divorce referendum, November 1995', *Irish Political Studies* 11, pp. 174–81.

Greene, Alan, 2012. 'The historical evolution of Article 28.3.3 of the Irish constitution', *Irish Jurist* 47, pp. 117–42.

Hilbink, Lisa, 2008. 'Assessing the new constitutionalism', *Comparative Politics* 40:2, pp. 227–45.

Hirschl, Ran, 2004. *Towards Juristocracy: The Origins and Consequences of the New Constitutionalism.* Cambridge, Mass.: Harvard University Press.

Hirschl, Ran, 2008. 'The judicialization of mega-politics and the rise of political courts', *Annual Review of Political Science* 11, pp. 93–118.

Hirschl, Ran and Evan Rosevear, 2011. 'Constitutional law meets comparative politics: socio-economic rights and political realities', in Tom Campbell, K. D. Ewing and Adam Tomkins (eds), *The Legal Protection of Human Rights: Sceptical Essays.* Oxford: Oxford University Press, pp. 207–28.

Hogan, Gerard, 1988. 'Constitutional interpretation', in Frank Litton (ed.), *The Constitution of Ireland 1937–1987.* Dublin: Institute of Public Administration, pp. 173–91.

Hogan, Gerard, 1994. 'Unenumerated personal rights: Ryan's case re-evaluated', *Irish Jurist* 25–27, pp. 95–116.

Hogan, Gerard, 1997. 'Ceremonial role most important for President', *Irish Times* 21 October.

Hogan, Gerard, 2000. 'A desert island case set in the silver sea: The State (Ryan) v. Lennon (1934)', in Eoin O'Dell (ed.), *Leading Cases of the Twentieth Century.* Dublin: Round Hall Sweet and Maxwell, pp. 80–103.

Hogan, Gerard, 2005. 'De Valera, the constitution and the historians', *Irish Jurist* 40, pp. 293–320.

Hogan, Gerard, 2008. 'Foreword', in Oran Doyle and Eoin Carolan (eds), *The Irish Constitution: Governance and Values.* Dublin: Thomson Round Hall, pp. vii–ix.

Hogan, Gerard, 2011. 'The judicial thought and prose of Mr Justice Séamus Henchy', *Irish Jurist* 46, pp. 96–116.

Hogan, Gerard, 2012. *The Origins of the Irish Constitution, 1928–1941.* Dublin: Royal Irish Academy.

Hogan, Gerard, 2014. 'The influence of the continental constitutional tradition on the drafting of the Constitution', in Bláthna Ruane, Jim O'Callaghan and David Barniville (eds), *Law and Government: A Tribute to Rory Brady.* Dublin: Round Hall Thomson Reuters, pp. 155–84.

Hogan, Gerard and Gerry Whyte, 2003. *J. M. Kelly: The Irish Constitution*, 4th ed. Dublin: LexisNexis Butterworths.

Hogan, Gerard, David Kenny and Rachael Walsh, 2015. 'An anthology of declarations of unconstitutionality', *Irish Jurist* 54, pp. 1–30.

Holmes, Stephen, 1988. 'Pre-commitment and the paradox of democracy', in Jon Elster and Rune Slagstad (eds), *Constitutionalism and Democracy.* Cambridge: Cambridge University Press, pp. 195–240.

Hughes, Ian, Paula Clancy, Clodagh Harris and David Beetham, 2007. *Power to the People? Assessing Democracy in Ireland.* Dublin: Tasc at New Island.

Jacob, Herbert, 1996. 'Conclusion', in Herbert Jacob, Erhard Blankenburg, Herbert M. Kritzer, Doris Marie Provine and Joseph Sanders, *Courts, Law and Politics in Comparative Perspective.* New Haven and London: Yale University Press, pp. 389–400.

Kavanagh, Aileen, 1997. 'The quest for legitimacy in constitutional interpretation', *Irish Jurist* 32, pp. 195–216.

Keena, Colm, 2017. 'Judges fear appointments will be further politicised: judiciary concerned that lay members of a planned new appointments body will pursue their own agendas', *Irish Times* 27 January.

Kennedy, Fiachra, 2002. 'Abortion referendum 2002', *Irish Political Studies* 17:1, pp. 114–28.

Kennelly, Brendan and Eilís Ward, 1993. 'The abortion referendums', in Michael Gallagher and Michael Laver (eds), *How Ireland Voted 1992.* Dublin: Folens and Limerick: PSAI Press, pp. 115–34.

Kenny, David, 2017. 'Merit, diversity and interpretative communities: the (non-party) politics of judicial appointments and constitutional adjudication', in Laura Cahillane, James Gallen and Tom Hickey (eds), *Judges, Politics and the Irish Constitution.* Manchester: Manchester University Press, pp. 136–52.

Keogh, Dermot and Andrew J. McCarthy, 2007. *The Making of the Irish Constitution 1937: Bunreacht na hÉireann.* Cork: Mercier Press.

Kissane, Bill, 2011. *New Beginnings: Constitutionalism and Democracy in Modern Ireland.* Dublin: UCD Press.

Langwallner, David, 2008. 'Separation of powers, judicial deference and the failure to protect the rights of the individual', in Oran Doyle and Eoin Carolan (eds), *The Irish Constitution: Governance and Values*. Dublin: Thomson Round Hall, pp. 256–76.

Lee, J. J., 1989. *Ireland 1912–1985: Politics and Society*. Cambridge: Cambridge University Press.

Loughlin, Martin, 2010. 'What is constitutionalism?', in Petra Dobner and Martin Loughlin (eds), *The Twilight of Constitutionalism?* Oxford: Oxford University Press, pp. 47–69.

Maarseveen, Henc van and Ger van der Tang, 1978. *Written Constitutions: A Computerized Comparative Study*. Dobbs Ferry, NY: Oceana Publications.

Mac Cormaic, Ruadhán, 2016. *The Supreme Court*. Dublin: Penguin Ireland.

MacNeill, Jennifer Carroll, 2016. *The Politics of Judicial Selection in Ireland*. Dublin: Four Courts Press.

Mair, Peter, 2013. *Ruling the Void: The Hollowing of Western Democracy*. London: Verso.

Mohr, Thomas, 2008. 'British involvement in the creation of the first Irish constitution', *Dublin University Law Journal* 30, pp. 166–86.

Morgan, David Gwynn, 1997. *The Separation of Powers in the Irish Constitution*. Dublin: Round Hall, Sweet and Maxwell.

Morgan, David Gwynn, 2001. *A Judgment too Far? Judicial Activism and the Constitution*. Cork: Cork University Press.

Morgan, David Gwynn, 2012. 'Government and the courts', in Eoin O'Malley and Muiris MacCarthaigh (eds), *Governing Ireland: From Cabinet Government to Delegated Governance*. Dublin: Institute of Public Administration, pp. 215–37.

Murphy, Tim, 1998. 'Economic inequality and the constitution', in Tim Murphy and Patrick Twomey (eds), *Ireland's Evolving Constitution, 1937–97: Collected Essays*. Oxford: Hart, pp. 163–81.

Murphy, Walter, 1993. 'Constitutions, constitutionalism, and democracy', in Douglas Greenberg, Stanley N. Katz, Melanie Beth Oliviero and Steven C. Wheatley (eds), *Constitutionalism and Democracy: Transitions in the Contemporary World*. New York and Oxford: Oxford University Press, pp. 3–25.

Murphy, Yvonne, 2016. 'The marriage equality referendum 2015', *Irish Political Studies* 31:2, pp. 315–30.

Murray, Thomas, 2016. *Contesting Economic and Social Rights in Ireland: Constitution, State and Society, 1848–2016*. Cambridge: Cambridge University Press.

Nicol, Danny, 2001. *EC Membership and the Judicialization of British Politics*. Oxford: Oxford University Press.

O'Brien, Carl, 2013. 'Judges no longer immune to glare of public scrutiny', *Irish Times* 25 January.

Ó Cearúil, Micheál, 1999. *Bunreacht na hÉireann: A Study of the Irish Text*. Dublin: Stationery Office.

O'Connell, Rory, 2008. 'From equality before the law to the equal benefit of the law: social and economic rights in the Irish constitution', in Oran Doyle and Eoin Carolan (eds), *The Irish Constitution: Governance and Values*. Dublin: Thomson Round Hall, pp. 327–46.

O'Dowd, John, 2012. 'Judges in whose cause? The Irish bench after the judges' pay referendum', *Irish Jurist* 48, pp. 102–31.

O'Malley, Eoin, Stephen Quinlan and Peter Mair, 2012. 'Party patronage in Ireland: changing parameters', in Petr Kopecký, Peter Mair and Maria Spirova (eds), *Party Patronage and Party Government in European Democracies*. Oxford: Oxford University Press, pp. 206–28.

Quinn, Gerard, 2001. 'Rethinking the nature of economic, social and cultural rights in the Irish legal order', in Cathryn Costello (ed.), *Fundamental Social Rights: Current European Legal Protection and the Challenge of the EU Charter on Fundamental Rights*. Dublin: Irish Centre for European Law, pp. 35–54.

Quinn, Ruairí, 2005. *Straight Left: A Journey in Politics*. Castleknock: Hodder Headline Ireland.

Ruane, Bláthna, 2012. 'Reflections on procedural rights in constitutional referenda', *Irish Jurist* 48, pp. 1–42.

Ruane, Bláthna, 2014. 'Democratic control and constitutional referenda – the failure of the popular initiative mechanism for constitutional referenda under the Irish Free State Constitution', in Bláthna

Ruane, Jim O'Callaghan and David Barniville (eds), *Law and Government: A Tribute to Rory Brady*. Dublin: Round Hall Thomson Reuters, pp. 185–213.

Sexton, Brendan, 1989. *Ireland and the Crown, 1922–1936: The Governor-Generalship of the Irish Free State*. Dublin: Irish Academic Press.

Shapiro, Martin, 1999. 'The success of judicial review', in Sally J. Kenney, William M. Reisinger and John C. Reitz (eds), *Constitutional Dialogues in Comparative Perspective*. Basingstoke: Macmillan, pp. 193–219.

Slaughter, Anne-Marie, 2004. *A New World Order*. Princeton and Oxford: Princeton University Press.

Suiter, Jane, David M. Farrell and Clodagh Harris, 2016. 'The Irish Constitutional Convention: a case of "high legitimacy"?', in Min Reuchamps and Jane Suiter (eds), *Constitutional Deliberative Democracy in Europe*. Colchester: ECPR Press, pp. 33–52.

Sunstein, Cass R., 1988. 'Constitutions and democracies: an epilogue', in Jon Elster and Rune Slagstad (eds), *Constitutionalism and Democracy*. Cambridge: Cambridge University Press, pp. 327–56.

Suteu, Silvia, 2015. 'Constitutional conventions in the digital era: lessons from Iceland and Ireland', *Boston College International and Comparative Law Review* 38, pp. 251–76.

Svensson, Palle, 2016. 'EU treaty referendums in Ireland and Denmark: a comparative analysis of different conceptions of sovereignty and their democratic implications', in Johan A. Elkink and David M. Farrell (eds), *The Act of Voting: Identities, Institutions and Locale*. London: Routledge, pp. 101–15.

Tate, C. Neal and Torbjörn Vallinder (eds), 1995. *The Global Expansion of Judicial Power*. New York: New York University Press.

Volcansek, Mary L., 2006. 'Judicial selection in Italy: a civil service model with partisan results', in Kate Malleson and Peter H. Russell (eds), *Appointing Judges in an Age of Judicial Power*. Toronto: University of Toronto Press, pp. 159–75.

Ward, Alan J., 1994. *The Irish Constitutional Tradition: Responsible Government and Modern Ireland, 1782–1992*. Blackrock: Irish Academic Press.

Whyte, Gerry, 2002. *Social Inclusion and the Legal System: Public Interest Law in Ireland*. Dublin: Institute of Public Administration.

Whyte, Gerry, 2006. 'The role of the Supreme Court in our democracy: a response to Mr Justice Hardiman', *Dublin University Law Journal* 28, pp. 2–26.

Whyte, J. H., 1980. *Church and State in Modern Ireland 1923–1979*. Dublin: Gill and Macmillan.

Websites

www.taoiseach.gov.ie/DOT/eng/Historical_Information/The_Constitution/Constitution_of_Ireland_-_Bunreacht_na_hÉireann.html
Current version of the full text of the constitution.

www.citizensassembly.ie/en/
Site of the Citizens' Assembly established in 2016.

www.constitution.ie
Website of the Constitutional Convention 2012–14.

constitutionproject.ie
Has posts on various aspects of the law and constitution.

www.courts.ie
Information on the courts and judicial system.

www.irishstatutebook.ie
The complete text of all legislation passed since the founding of the state.

Part II

Representative democracy at work

4   The electoral system

David M. Farrell and Richard Sinnott

The electoral system determines the format according to which votes are cast in an election and the process by which seats are allocated on the basis of those votes. The allocation of seats determines who governs. Electoral systems are matters of institutional design: they have more or less identifiable effects on the functioning of the political system, and an electoral system can be selected or rejected with a view to achieving or avoiding certain consequences (though whether the intended impacts happen is another matter; see Bowler and Donovan, 2013). Ireland's electoral system is not in common use around the world, and given that some observers, rightly or wrongly, attribute a number of features of Irish politics to this electoral system, we need to examine it in some depth.

This chapter begins by examining the way in which proportional representation by means of the single transferable vote (PR-STV) came to be adopted as the Irish electoral system and discusses the two referendums at which PR-STV was endorsed by the people contrary to the wishes of the government that initiated each referendum. The chapter then explains how the PR-STV system works, going step-by-step through a full constituency count to illustrate the process. It concludes with an analysis and evaluation of the effects of the system, looking in particular at the proportionality between votes and seats, at government stability and party cohesion, and at the roles adopted by members of the Dáil.

Proportional representation in Ireland

Electoral system options

Proportional representation, in one or other of its many incarnations, is the most frequently used electoral system because the main alternative – dividing the country up into single-member constituencies and giving the seat in each constituency to the candidate with the most votes – can lead to egregiously unfair outcomes at national level. This latter system, generally known as single-member plurality or, colloquially, as 'first past the post', is used for elections to the House of Commons in the United Kingdom (it is also used in Canada, India and the United States). The 2015 British general election illustrates its potential for bringing about an 'unfair' outcome. In that election, the Conservative Party won 37 per cent of the vote and 51 per cent of the seats, whereas the Liberal Democrats won 8 per cent of the vote and only 1 per cent of the seats. Such an outcome (which often can be even more extreme in its treatment of the larger and smaller parties) can occur because, within each constituency, the winning party takes 100 per cent of the representation (i.e. the one and only seat) while all the other parties or candidates receive zero representation. The constituency-level winner-takes-all effect tends to be cumulative across constituencies and to give an advantage to the larger parties. The result is that a party with considerably less than a majority of the votes can obtain a clear majority of the seats in parliament.

Arguments in defence of this system stress the notion of elections as 'devices to choose viable governments and give them legitimacy' (Butler, 1981: 22) and maintain that the bonus accruing to the largest party is still the best way of doing that. However, since the middle of the nineteenth century and in tandem with the extension of the franchise, alternatives have been sought. Proponents of proportional representation (PR) have come up with a wide range of ideas and systems, the main distinction being between list systems on the one hand and PR-STV on the other. The former have been generally favoured in continental Europe, while PR-STV was for a long time the preferred alternative of electoral reformers in Britain.

In a list system of proportional representation, each party presents a list of candidates in each multi-member constituency and the voter chooses between the various lists. Thus, the primary decision to be made by the voter is the choice of party. Seats are then allocated to parties on the basis of their share of the vote. In theory, a party obtaining, say, 35 per cent of the votes is entitled to 35 per cent of the seats, though how closely the outcome approaches this varies from system to system (for overviews see Farrell, 2011: 67–87; Gallagher, 2014). List systems vary in the methods they use to award seats to individual candidates within parties: in some, the matter is decided by the party organisation and is determined by the position of the candidates on a fixed list, while in others, the voters can express preferences for specific candidates on their chosen party's list. Even in the latter systems, however, the vote cast is primarily a vote for the party and may end up assisting the election of a candidate to whom the voter is actually opposed (Renwick and Pilet, 2016).

In contrast, the primary focus of PR-STV is on the choice of individual representatives. Indeed, the originators of PR-STV in Britain were highly critical of political parties and of the role they played (Carstairs, 1980: 194). Reservations about the role of parties were also quite widespread in Ireland when PR-STV was adopted, and the party affiliations of candidates were not listed on ballot papers until the 1965 general election. PR-STV does not, therefore, guarantee a close relationship between party vote shares and party seat shares in the way that list systems do, although in practice the relationship is just as close, as we shall see later in the chapter.

PR-STV is not widely used, Malta being the only other country that employs it to elect the lower house of the national parliament. It is, or has also been, used to elect upper houses or regional assemblies in a number of countries that have been influenced by Britain, including Australia, India, Nepal, Northern Ireland, Pakistan, South Africa and Sri Lanka, and is used for local elections in Scotland and in parts of the USA (Farrell and McAllister, 2006; Gallagher, 2008: 511).

PR-STV in Ireland

How did this relatively uncommon system come to be adopted in Ireland? Developed simultaneously by Carl Andrae in Denmark and by Thomas Hare in England in the late 1850s, PR-STV was strongly advocated by electoral system reformers in Britain. In the early years of the twentieth century, the problem of minority representation in the event of Home Rule seemed to make PR particularly relevant in Ireland. A Proportional Representation Society of Ireland was formed, with Arthur Griffith, founder of Sinn Féin, among its first members. Inevitably, the views of electoral reformers in Ireland were substantially influenced by thinking in Britain (Coakley, 2013: 148–50; Gallagher, 2008: 512–14). An element of PR-STV was inserted in the abortive Home Rule Bill of 1912. In 1918, PR-STV was enacted for a single local council (Sligo

Corporation) and an election was held there under the new provisions in January 1919. The next step was the decision by the British government to introduce PR-STV for the 1920 local elections in Ireland and then for the 1921 election to be held under the Government of Ireland Act.

Thus, by 1921, PR-STV had not only been endorsed by a significant section of the nationalist movement but had actually reached the statute book. It is not surprising, therefore, that when independence negotiations were under way and the issue of representation of minorities was being considered, the desirability of PR was common ground. The result was that PR was included in the 1922 Irish Free State constitution. The constitution did not specify the precise form of PR to be used, but it was assumed that this would be PR-STV, and this was the system specified in the Electoral Act of 1923.

PR-STV has been implicitly or explicitly endorsed by the Irish electorate on three occasions. The first occasion was the approval of the new constitution in 1937. Éamon de Valera opted to include not just the principle of proportional representation in his draft constitution, as the 1922 constitution had done, but to spell out that this should be proportional representation by means of the single transferable vote (see Box 4.1). The matter did not give rise to extensive debate. Fine Gael had at one stage expressed some reservations regarding PR-STV (O'Leary, 1979: 25–6). However, in the Dáil debate on the draft constitution, John A. Costello of Fine Gael merely questioned why the details of the electoral system should go into the constitution rather than being left to the greater flexibility of ordinary legislation, to which de Valera replied that the matter was too important to be left to the vagaries of party warfare.

More than two decades later, on the eve of his retirement as Taoiseach, de Valera proposed the abolition of PR-STV and its replacement by the plurality system. Although Fianna Fáil had been in power for 21 of the previous 27 years, it had won an overall majority of the seats in only four of the nine elections involved, and, unless PR-STV were abolished, might have been thought less likely to do so in the future without de Valera as leader. Needless to say, the government did not put the case for change in such partisan terms. Instead, it argued, firstly, that proportional representation has a disintegrating effect, creating a multiplicity of parties and

---

Box 4.1 The constitution and the electoral system

The 1937 Constitution is quite specific about the Dáil electoral system. The main provisions are as follows:

Article 16.2.

1. Dáil Éireann shall be composed of members who represent constituencies determined by law.

   ...

3. The ratio between the number of members to be elected at any time for each constituency and the population of each constituency, as ascertained at the last preceding census, shall, so far as it is practicable, be the same throughout the country.

   ...

5. The members shall be elected on the system of proportional representation by means of the single transferable vote.
6. No law shall be enacted whereby the number of members to be returned for any constituency shall be less than three.

increasing the probability of governmental instability. The second argument was that, whereas the plurality system enables the electorate to make a clear choice between two competing alternative governments, proportional representation makes the formation of government a matter for post-election bargaining among parties, depriving the electorate of a direct say in the matter (for a useful summary of the Dáil debate on the issue, see FitzGerald, 1959).

Faced with the government proposal, Fine Gael stifled whatever doubts it may have had about PR-STV and led the opposition to change. Labour was also whole-heartedly against change. The opposition's counter-arguments emphasised the issues of proportionality and fairness, particularly the question of the representation of minorities. Opposition politicians also attacked the proposal on the grounds that it would perpetuate Fianna Fáil rule indefinitely and undermine the parliamentary opposition. The proposal to abolish PR-STV was narrowly defeated, with 48 per cent in favour and 52 per cent against (see Appendix 2h).

Obviously, Fianna Fáil took some encouragement from the narrowness of its defeat in 1959 (33,667 votes). Otherwise, it would be difficult to explain the party's decision to have another go just nine years later. An all-party Oireachtas committee, established in 1966 to review the constitution, failed to reach agreement on the question of the electoral system and simply set out the arguments for and against change (Committee on the Constitution, 1967). In the event, the government opted for the same proposal as in 1959, that is, to replace PR-STV with the single-member plurality system. A second amendment proposed at the same time dealt with the issue of the ratio of members of the Dáil to population in each constituency, proposing that a deviation of up to one sixth from the national average be allowed. The purpose of the change was to enable rural areas with declining populations to maintain their level of parliamentary representation. It did not go unnoticed, however, that the areas that would benefit from such a change tended to be areas in which Fianna Fáil had strong and stable support.

Essentially, the same forces were ranged against the government in this second referendum on PR-STV, the only difference being that the defenders of the status quo campaigned with more confidence and conviction (for a summary of the debate see O'Leary, 1979: 66–70). The outcome was also more decisive: the result on the question of PR-STV was 39 per cent in favour of abolition and 61 per cent in favour of retention, and the voting on the other proposed amendment was virtually identical (see the table of referendum results in Appendix 2h). The position of PR-STV in Ireland was undoubtedly greatly strengthened by this decisive popular endorsement. Certainly, nothing more is likely to be heard about moving to the British-style plurality system. However, plurality voting is not the only alternative and there has been spasmodic renewal of the debate about the consequences of the system and about the desirability of altering it. Before turning to consider those consequences and that debate, it is necessary to take a detailed look at how the PR-STV system works.

How PR-STV works

There are three distinct senses in which one can have an understanding of how PR-STV works: one can understand it by reference to what is involved in the act of voting, the logic of the system and the mechanics of the count.

The act of voting

From the voter's point of view, understanding the system is quite simple. The voter is presented with a list of candidates and is required to indicate his or her order of preferences among these (see the specimen ballot paper in Figure 4.1).[1] Voters must indicate a first

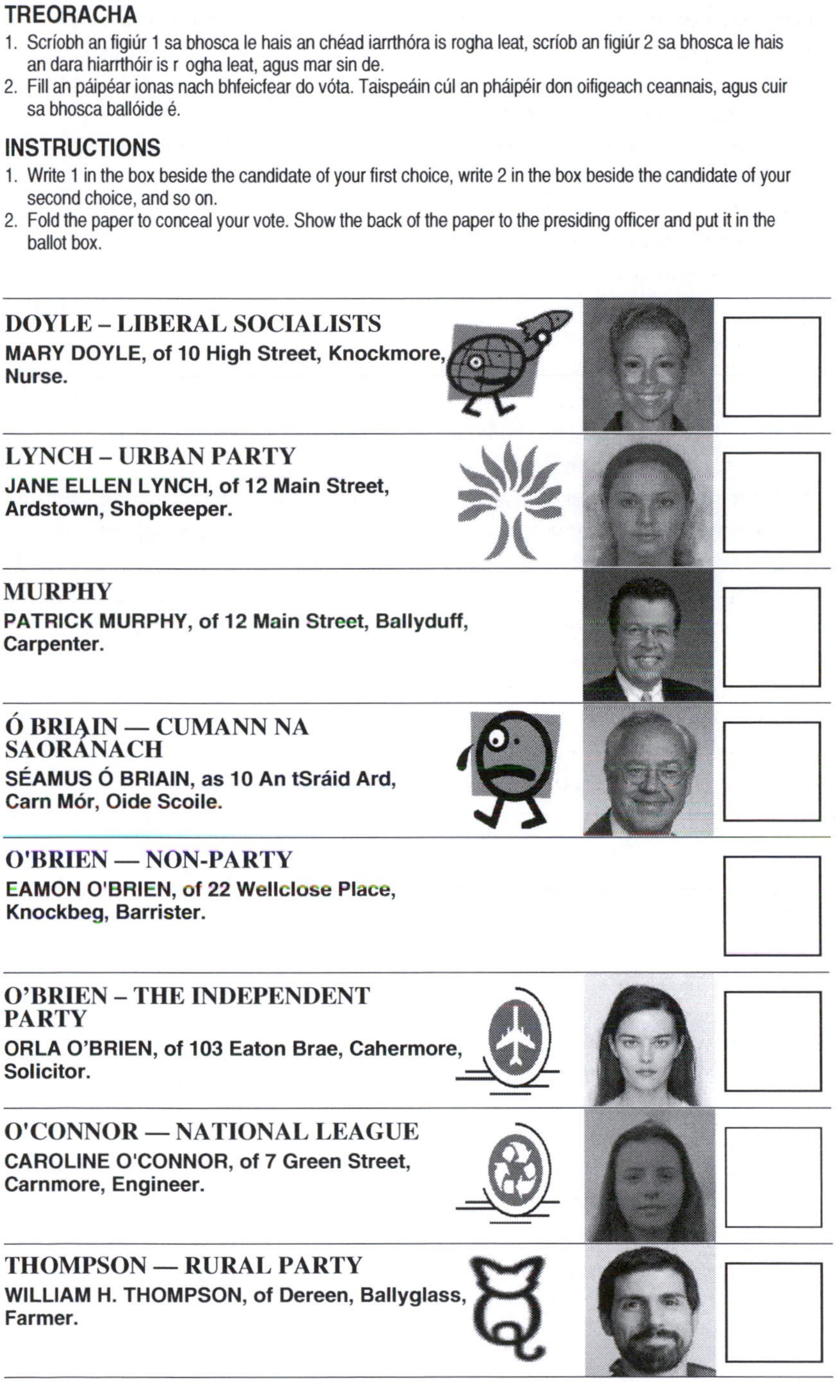

TREORACHA

1. Scríobh an figiúr 1 sa bhosca le hais an chéad iarrthóra is rogha leat, scríob an figiúr 2 sa bhosca le hais an dara hiarrthóir is r ogha leat, agus mar sin de.
2. Fill an páipéar ionas nach bhfeicfear do vóta. Taispeáin cúl an pháipéir don oifigeach ceannais, agus cuir sa bhosca ballóide é.

INSTRUCTIONS

1. Write 1 in the box beside the candidate of your first choice, write 2 in the box beside the candidate of your second choice, and so on.
2. Fold the paper to conceal your vote. Show the back of the paper to the presiding officer and put it in the ballot box.

DOYLE – LIBERAL SOCIALISTS
MARY DOYLE, of 10 High Street, Knockmore, Nurse.

LYNCH – URBAN PARTY
JANE ELLEN LYNCH, of 12 Main Street, Ardstown, Shopkeeper.

MURPHY
PATRICK MURPHY, of 12 Main Street, Ballyduff, Carpenter.

Ó BRIAIN — CUMANN NA SAORÁNACH
SÉAMUS Ó BRIAIN, as 10 An tSráid Ard, Carn Mór, Oide Scoile.

O'BRIEN — NON-PARTY
EAMON O'BRIEN, of 22 Wellclose Place, Knockbeg, Barrister.

O'BRIEN – THE INDEPENDENT PARTY
ORLA O'BRIEN, of 103 Eaton Brae, Cahermore, Solicitor.

O'CONNOR — NATIONAL LEAGUE
CAROLINE O'CONNOR, of 7 Green Street, Carnmore, Engineer.

THOMPSON — RURAL PARTY
WILLIAM H. THOMPSON, of Dereen, Ballyglass, Farmer.

Figure 4.1 Sample PR-STV ballot paper, 2016.

Source: www.housing.gov.ie/local-government/voting/d%C3%A1il-elections/sample-ballot-paper-general-election-2016.pdf preference for their vote to be valid and, after that, they may go on to indicate as many or as few further preferences as they wish. It must be emphasised that each voter has only one vote – hence the term *single* transferable vote. In essence the voter issues a set of instructions to the returning officer as to what to do with that one vote, i.e. to allocate it to each preferred candidate in the order that the voter has specified on the ballot paper.

The simplicity of PR-STV from the voter's perspective should be noted, because one superficially plausible objection to the system is the claim that voters will not be able to understand it. If one had in mind the second or third kind of understanding mentioned above, this might well be so. While the bulk of the voters may well appreciate the underlying logic of the system, it is unlikely that they fully understand its 'mechanics' in the sense that they would be able to conduct a PR-STV count if presented with a set of completed ballot papers. But all that is needed in order to use the system to the full is an understanding of the notion of ranking a set of candidates according to one's preferences. Of course, voters vary in their propensity to express preferences between candidates, and the average number of preferences expressed is relatively low. Thus, using data from the Irish National Election Study (INES), Marsh *et al.* estimate that the average voter expresses 3.9 preferences. They show that this depends on the number of candidates on the ballot paper, varying from an average of 3.5 preferences in constituencies with 6 candidates to 4.7 in constituencies with 17 candidates (Marsh *et al.*, 2008: 19). In a separate study based on real-world data made available as a result of a trial of computer voting in three constituencies in 2002, Laver (2004: 523) found that the mean number of preferences expressed was slightly higher, ranging from 4.4 to 5.0.

A particular quality of PR-STV concerns the factors that voters take into account when deciding how to rank the candidates. Voters can respond to cues from leaders about alliances with other parties (i.e. give their next preference to their favoured coalition partner), or vote on the basis of something other than party such as locality or perhaps candidates' views on issues that cut across party lines. The electoral system also incentivises candidates to seek personal support regardless of party, since even if the party vote were rock solid (which these days is less likely to be the case than it was in the past; see Gallagher, 2016b: 146), candidates still want to attract lower preferences from voters who are followers of other parties or none.

The logic of the system

The logic of PR-STV, or how it achieves what it achieves, is a somewhat more complex matter. In the case of the single-member plurality electoral system, the logic is clear: give the seat to the candidate with the most votes, regardless of what proportion of the total vote that is. The majority or two-ballot system, as used in, for example, French presidential elections, introduces a refinement on this rule: in order to win a seat a candidate must reach the threshold of 50 per cent plus one, i.e. an absolute majority. Again, the logic is clear. But what is the logic of PR-STV?

Understanding this is best approached by first considering how the system works when there is only a single seat to be filled, as in presidential elections and by-elections. Because multi-seat constituencies are an essential feature of PR – since a single seat cannot, obviously, be shared out proportionally – the system as used in presidential elections is not actually PR-STV.[2] However, starting with this simpler situation allows us to examine the logic of the system by illustrating the nature of the quota and of the process of transferring votes. We can then go on to see the effect of the introduction of multi-seat constituencies on both of these essential features.

Whatever the number of seats, PR-STV entails a quota – the number of votes that guarantees election. Once a candidate reaches this quota, he or she is declared elected. The quota is calculated as follows:

$$\text{Quota} = \frac{\text{Total number of valid votes}}{\text{Number of seats} + 1} + 1$$

Any fractional remainder arising from this calculation is disregarded. When there is only one seat available, this formula yields a threshold that is identical to that used in the French presidential election system, that is, 50 per cent of the votes plus one. STV in a single-seat contest is, in fact, simply a sophisticated version of the majority system. The sophistication lies in how the STV system deals with the problem that arises when no candidate reaches the required absolute majority, something that may well happen if there are more than two candidates. When this occurs in a French presidential election, all but the top two candidates are eliminated and the voters troop back two weeks later to choose between the remaining two candidates. This amounts in effect to asking those who voted for eliminated candidates to register a second preference. STV does not, as it were, waste the voters' time by asking them to come back later to register their second choice. Instead, it collects this information, along with information on third, fourth, fifth, et cetera, choices, all in one economical operation. Then, rather than disposing of all but the leading two candidates in one fell swoop, STV eliminates the lower-order candidates one by one, reassigning the votes of each eliminated candidate according to the next preferences they contain. This has the advantage of including information on the preferences of the voters across the full range of candidates rather than, as in the case of the French presidential system, merely as between the two candidates who are in the lead after the first round of voting.

PR-STV is not, however, just a refined version of the majority rule procedure, as it has the all-important additional feature of multi-seat constituencies. Multi-seat constituencies introduce two new elements into the logic of the system. The first is the systematic reduction of the quota as the size of the constituency (as measured by the number of seats) is increased. In the single-seat situation, the quota is half the votes plus one. A quick look at the formula shows that this principle can be easily extended, as follows: in a two-seat constituency, the quota is one third plus one, in a three-seater it is one quarter plus one, in a four-seater it is one fifth plus one, and so on. Thus, as the number of seats in a constituency is increased, the proportion of votes carrying an entitlement to a seat is progressively lowered – a nine-seat constituency would produce a quota of one-tenth plus one. The underlying inverse relationship between the number of seats in a constituency and the size of the quota is illustrated in Table 4.1.

Table 4.1 Quota by district magnitude in PR-STV

District magnitude (TDs per constituency)	*Quota, in per cent*
1	50.0 + 1 vote
2	33.3 + 1 vote
3	25.0 + 1 vote
4	20.0 + 1 vote
5	16.7 + 1 vote

The second feature introduced by moving to multi-seat constituencies is the transfer of the surplus votes of elected candidates – these being the votes of an elected candidate over and above the quota, that is, in excess of the number needed to guarantee a seat. If no such transfer were made, those who voted for such a candidate would not get the full share of representation to which, as a group, they are entitled. For example, suppose that, in a three-seat constituency, just over 50 per cent of the voters vote for candidate A, and that A's supporters represent a particular point of view. Since the quota in a three-seater is 25 per cent plus one, and since therefore A's votes are far more than needed to elect A, then, if A's surplus votes were not redistributed, the second 25 per cent of the voters supporting A's point of view would achieve no representation. The problem is solved by transferring A's surplus votes to the other candidates according to the second preferences of the supporters of A. This is the point at which the mechanics of the counting procedure become somewhat complex but, fortunately, the complexities, which will be examined presently, are not strictly relevant to grasping the logic of the system.

To summarise, the logic of PR-STV is that, by comparison with the plurality system, it increases the proportionality between share of the votes and share of the seats by:

- Lowering the cost of a seat by introducing multi-seat constituencies, each additional seat bringing about a reduction in the quota and in the percentage of votes that a candidate or party needs in order to win a seat;
- Eliciting extra information on the voter's wishes, that is, on his or her order of preference among the competing candidates;
- Using this additional information on preferences both to redistribute the votes of the lowest candidates and also to distribute any surplus votes, that is, votes that a candidate may have over and above the quota. Distribution of surplus votes is necessary in order to deal with what would otherwise be the under-representation of those who supported a candidate whose votes exceed the quota.

The mechanics of PR-STV

Understanding the mechanics of the system is best achieved by working through an example. Again, it is best to begin with the simple, albeit non-proportional, situation – a single-seat contest involving the transfer of the votes of an eliminated candidate. The presidential election of November 1990 provides a good illustration (see Table 4.2). The valid vote in that election amounted to 1,574,651, which, when divided by the number of seats plus one (i.e., by 2), yields 787,325.5. Disregarding the fraction and adding 1 to this number gives a quota of 787,326 votes. The Fianna Fáil candidate, Brian Lenihan, was in the lead on the basis of first preference votes, but his vote total fell short of the quota. Hence, the returning officer proceeded to eliminate the candidate with the lowest number of votes (Currie, the Fine Gael candidate) and to distribute his votes in accordance with the second preferences indicated by Currie's supporters. On the second count[3] about three-quarters (205,565) of Currie's votes were found to carry a second preference for Robinson (an independent candidate supported by the Labour Party). This gave Robinson a total of 817,830 votes, or 52 per cent of the total valid vote. This exceeded the quota and Robinson was declared elected. Lenihan received only 14 per cent of Currie's second preferences, while nearly 10 per cent of those who supported Currie did not award a second preference and their ballots appear in the 'non-transferable papers' row.

Table 4.2 The Irish presidential election, 1990

Candidate	First preferences	Transfer of Currie's votes	Second count result
Currie, Austin (FG)	267,902	−267,902	
Lenihan, Brian (FF)	694,484	+36,789	731,273
Robinson, Mary (Ind)	612,265	+205,565	817,830
Non-transferable papers		+25,548	25,548

Valid votes: 1,574,651. Quota: 787,326.

Because PR-STV involves multi-seat rather than single-seat constituencies, counting the votes in Irish general elections is a somewhat more complicated business. Again, the process is best explained by working through a particular count. The Limerick City constituency in the 2016 election (see Table 4.3) illustrates the key points. In this election, Limerick City was a four-seat constituency with a valid poll of 46,761 votes. When the number of valid votes was divided by the number of seats plus one (i.e., by 5) and, disregarding the fraction, 1 was added to the result, the quota came out at 9,353 votes. One candidate (Willie O'Dea, Fianna Fáil) exceeded the quota on the first count by a margin of 3,646 votes and was deemed elected.

The next step in the process was the distribution of O'Dea's surplus.[4] The destination of that surplus was determined by re-examining the entire set of 12,999 first preference votes for O'Dea. This was done by arranging O'Dea's votes in 'sub-parcels' beside the name of each of the continuing candidates according to the second preferences indicated on them. The total number of *transferable* votes (i.e. ignoring those that were non-transferable because they contained only a first preference for O'Dea and no second preference) was used as the base for calculating each continuing candidate's proportionate share of O'Dea's second preferences. These proportions were then applied to the 3,646 surplus votes that were to be transferred. Thus, if candidate X had obtained 50 per cent of the second preferences among O'Dea's transferable votes, he or she would have been entitled to 50 per cent of the 3,646 surplus votes. In the event, given that O'Dea did not have a Fianna Fáil running mate, the preferences were distributed quite evenly among four of the remaining candidates: Noonan, O'Sullivan, Prendiville and Quinlivan each received 17–18 per cent of O'Dea's second preferences and so were entitled to equivalent proportions of the surplus (e.g. in Noonan's case, 615 votes). The remaining portions of the surplus were distributed among the other candidates.

A significant and little understood aspect of the process of transferring surplus votes relates to which actual ballot papers are transferred and which remain with the elected candidate. The rule specifies that the particular papers to be transferred from each sub-parcel (i.e. from each set of O'Dea's second preferences lined up beside the name of each continuing candidate, as described above) shall be those 'last filed' in that sub-parcel. In other words, the surplus votes are physically transferred to each of the continuing candidates by taking the appropriate number of votes from the top of the relevant pile.

The defence of this procedure is that the counting process requires that the papers be thoroughly mixed at the outset and that, therefore, the set of papers transferred in the manner just described is a random sample of the entire sub-parcel. However, it can be argued that the sample may not be strictly random and that it would be worth the extra effort to transfer all the papers in each sub-parcel at the appropriate fraction of their value, thereby avoiding any risk of bias or distortion. This procedure is known as the 'Gregory method' and is the procedure used in the counting of votes at Seanad elections and at Northern Ireland Assembly elections

Table 4.3 Counting and transfer of votes in Limerick City, 2016 general election

	First count	Second count Transfer of O'Dea surplus		Third count Transfer of Bennis, Gaffney, Hayes and Riordan votes		Fourth count Transfer of Hennelly votes		Fifth count Transfer of Prendiville votes		Sixth count Transfer of Quinlivan surplus	
Bennis, Nora (CD)	673	(+150)	823	(−823)	–	–		–		–	
Gaffney, James (GP)	964	(+117)	1,081	(−1,081)	–	–		–		–	
Hayes, Des (Non-Party)	254	(+60)	314	(−314)	–	–		–		–	
Hennelly, Sarah Jane (SD)	2,747	(+292)	3,039	(+581)	3,620	(−3,620)	–	–		–	
Noonan, Michael (FG)	7,294	(+615)	7,909	(+312)	8,221	(+370)	8,591	(+427)	9,018	(+293)	9,311
O'Dea, Willie (FF)	12,999	(−3,646)	9,353		9,353		9,353		9,353		9,353
O'Donnell, Kieran (FG)	6,047	(+498)	6,545	(+285)	6,830	(+347)	7,177	(+335)	7,512	(+337)	7,849
O'Sullivan, Jan (Lab)	5,227	(+611)	5,838	(+328)	6,166	(+835)	7,001	(+721)	7,722	(+465)	8,187
Prendiville, Cian (AAA-PBP)	4,584	(+660)	5,244	(+252)	5,496	(+1,228)	6,724	(−6,724)	-	–	
Quinlivan, Maurice (SF)	5,894	(+633)	6,527	(+124)	6,651	(+374)	7,025	(+3,492)	10,517	(−1,164)	9,353
Riordan, Denis (Non-Party)	78	(+10)	88	(−88)	-	–		–		–	
Non-transferable	–	(+0)	0	(+424)	424	(+466)	890	(+1,749)	2,639	(+69)	2,708

Valid votes: 46,761; Number of seats: 4; Quota: 9,353

Elected: Willie O'Dea (FF), Maurice Quinlivan (SF), Michael Noonan (FG), and Jan O'Sullivan (Labour)

Note: votes of elected candidates in italics; distribution of transfers in brackets.

(for discussions of this point, see Coakley and O'Neill, 1984; Farrell and McAllister, 2003; Gallagher and Unwin, 1986). Implementation of this more precise approach would of course be greatly facilitated by the introduction of electronic voting. Had electronic voting been introduced in the early part of the millennium (after a trial in three constituencies in the 2002 election), it is likely that the Gregory method would have been introduced. However, in the light of concerns that were raised over the method of electronic voting being proposed the government shelved plans for its introduction (Murphy, 2008: 14–15).

As no-one reached the quota on the second count, the next step was to eliminate the lowest candidates. In this instance, there was a 'multiple elimination', which occurs whenever the votes for two or more candidates are such that they will be excluded in turn in any event, and where there is no possibility that they will reach the threshold for recouping their electoral expenses, which is one-quarter of the quota. The sum of Bennis's, Gaffney's, Hayes's and Riordan's votes was 2,306 (24.6 per cent of the quota and, therefore, below the threshold), and thus they were excluded together and their votes were transferred in accordance with the next available preferences. The transfer of votes from eliminated candidates is a simpler operation as there is no need to calculate proportions or to select which papers are to be transferred. In the event, 424 votes (18 per cent) were non-transferable; the largest block of transferable votes went to the Social Democratic candidate (Hennelly), with the rest divided among four other candidates.

The votes transferred to Hennelly still left her well below the other continuing candidates, so the returning officer proceeded to eliminate her and to redistribute her 3,620 votes. A third of these went to the AAA–PBP candidate, Prendiville (1,228 votes), bringing his total tally to 6,724. This still left him the weakest of the remaining candidates and since, yet again, no other candidate had managed to pass the quota, the next count involved the exclusion of Prendiville and the transfer of all of his votes to the remaining candidates. More than half of this AAA–PBP's candidate's votes (nearly 52 per cent) went to the Sinn Féin candidate, Maurice Quinlivan, resulting in his vote tally increasing to 10,517, 1,164 votes over the quota, making him the second candidate to be elected.

Quinlivan's election left two seats to fill, and the outcome would be decided by the distribution of Quinlivan's surplus. The approach to the distribution of a surplus that arises on a later count is slightly different from the distribution of a first-count surplus. The votes that are examined for next preferences are not the entire block of votes credited to the elected candidate at that stage but the votes in the 'sub-parcel last received' by him or her, that is, the 3,492 votes Quinlivan (SF) received from Prendiville (AAA–PBP). This procedure involves substantial savings in time and effort. Its rationale is that the votes that elected the candidate are precisely those votes in the 'sub-parcel last received' and, accordingly, it is these votes that should determine the destination of the surplus. It can also be argued, however, that the procedure involves a potential distortion in that the frequency distribution of next available preferences in the vote received by Quinlivan from Prendiville might well be different from the frequency distribution of preferences in the entire Quinlivan vote and, arguably, all those who voted for an elected candidate should have a proportionate say in the destination of the surplus in question (for more on this, see Farrell and McAllister, 2003). In the event, Quinlivan's 1,164 surplus votes split quite evenly between the two Fine Gael candidates (293 to Noonan and 337 to O'Donnell), with the largest portion going to O'Sullivan (465, or 40 per cent of the total). The two leading candidates, Noonan and O'Sullivan, were elected without reaching the quota; the third remaining candidate, O'Donnell, lost out (his elimination would have been pointless, since there were only two remaining candidates for the two remaining seats).

On this occasion, the vote-management efforts of Fine Gael to win two seats (which in large part have contributed to the party's vote–seat bonuses in recent elections; see Gallagher, 2011, 2016b) failed, though quite narrowly so. The strategy of seeking to spread the first preference votes as evenly as possible between the two candidates (Noonan's first preference tally was 7,294, whereas O'Donnell's was 6,047) had given O'Donnell a fighting chance, but in the end he was not able to pick up enough transfers to win a seat.

In summary, understanding how PR-STV works is quite simple in so far as the act of voting is concerned and the system has a rather elegant logic in the way it seeks to achieve a match between voters' preferences and the distribution of seats. On the other hand, the system can be quite complex when it comes to knowing how a surplus that has accrued on a count subsequent to the first count is transferred, though understanding this aspect of the matter is really only essential for returning officers and party strategists (and students of political science!). Be that as it may, as well as understanding how the system works, we also need to understand its political consequences.

The political consequences of PR-STV

This section explores the possible consequences of PR-STV in three areas: the proportionality between votes and seats, the stability of the party system and of governments, and the role of the elected representative. A concluding section assesses the arguments for and against PR-STV.

Consequences for proportionality

Disproportionality is measured by comparing parties' shares of the votes with their shares of the seats and noting the discrepancies. This is not quite as simple as it seems. First of all, the matter is complicated in the case of the STV version of PR, given the system's focus on individual candidates rather than parties, and given also the way in which transferred votes and not just first preference votes are a vital part of a party's overall level of support and can have a decisive effect on who wins a seat (Farrell and Katz, 2014). While acknowledging these difficulties, if we wish to examine the degree of proportionality achieved under PR-STV, we have, in fact, no option but to compare a party's share of the first preference vote with its share of the seats.

On average, in elections over the period 1948–2016, Fianna Fáil's vote–seat deviation (its share of seats minus its share of votes) has been overwhelmingly positive, at +3.1 percentage points (the singular exception being in 2011 when, in the light of its electoral meltdown, the party recorded a vote–seat deficit of –5.9). This 'bonus' has often been enough to put the party over the crucial threshold of 50 per cent of the seats, or at least to put it in a position to form a minority government. Fine Gael has generally also benefited from the system, though not to the same extent as Fianna Fáil, either in terms of the consistency of obtaining a bonus or of the average size of the bonus obtained (an average of 2.1 percentage points; though in 2011 the party achieved a record-breaking vote–seat bonus of +10.0). Labour, on the other hand, has obtained a share of the seats that is smaller than its share of first preference votes in 12 of the 20 elections in the period 1948–2016, its average deficit being –0.04 percentage points. The minor parties and independents as a group have tended to be even more consistent losers in the vote–seat proportionality stakes.

A more systematic way of assessing the proportionality of PR-STV is to use an index of proportionality, such as the least squares index, generally known as the Gallagher index (see

Lijphart, 1994: 58–62), which shows an average level of disproportionality in Irish elections from 1922 to 2016 of 4.2 – ranging from a low of 1.7 in February 1982 to a high of 8.7 in 2011 (computed from Gallagher, 2016a). In a comparative analysis using this measure, Irish election outcomes in the postwar period are more proportional than those held under first-past-the-post and other non-proportional systems, but in general, PR-STV scores quite poorly on proportionality compared to other PR systems, leading some to categorise this system as 'semi-proportional' (Farrell and Katz, 2014: 14; Farrell and McAllister, 2006: 83–90). Such a categorisation depends, however, on perspective; Gallagher (2014: 20), for example, argues that the record shows PR-STV as having been relatively proportional – more proportional, indeed, than several list systems.

Consequences for the party system and government stability

The classic case against proportional representation, argued mainly on the basis of case histories of Weimar Germany and of France and Italy in the 1950s, was that it leads to a proliferation of parties and thus to political instability or at least stalemate. These alleged effects of PR have been the subject of prolonged debate. In so far as the effect of PR on the number of parties is concerned, a consensus has emerged that can be summed up in Duverger's famous proposition that PR tends to result in multi-party systems (Duverger, 1964).

Distinguishing between two-party and multi-party systems, and even the matter of determining the number of parties in a system, are not as straightforward as they might seem. In addressing these problems, Laakso and Taagepera (1979) have proposed an index, called the 'effective number of parties', that takes account of both the number and the relative size of the parties in a system. This index is particularly useful for comparing the level of party fragmentation in different party systems, or in the same system at different points in time. The effective number of parties in Ireland (as measured by their seat share rather than their vote share) declined from a peak in June 1927 and remained low throughout the 1930s. It rose sharply twice in the 1940s, but then fell back and settled down at a low level from 1965 to 1982. In 1987, it began a rise that has continued ever since (with the slight exception of 2007 when it dropped back), reaching a record high level of 4.9 in 2016, meaning that Ireland's party system has recently become more fragmented (Farrell and Suiter, 2016; for more see Chapter 5). It is clear from this that the number of parties is not simply a function of the electoral system. Ireland has had the same electoral system since the foundation of the state but the number of parties has fluctuated considerably.

Looking at the matter in comparative terms, the average effective number of parties in parliament in 30 European democracies during the first decade of this millennium was 4.0; in Ireland the number in the same period was 3.1. This puts Ireland in twenty-third place on a scale of party fragmentation. The countries with the most fragmented systems were Belgium (7.8), Netherlands (5.7) and Lithuania (5.6). The least fragmented were Malta, which also uses PR-STV, with a score of 2.0, Hungary (2.2), and the United Kingdom (2.4) (figures from Gallagher *et al.*, 2011: 391). Given this ranking, and given the fluctuations in the effective number of parties in Ireland over time, the most we can conclude is that PR-STV in Ireland has, to use Sartori's terms (1976), facilitated moderate multi-partyism (or perhaps even extreme multi-partyism more recently) when other factors were leading in that direction.

It should also be noted that a preoccupation with the number of parties and with the alleged problems of multi-partyism seems to be based on an assumption that multi-party systems lead to unstable government. This has two dimensions. One is the suggestion that parliamentary party groups in a PR-STV system will necessarily be disunited and incohesive; the second is that in a fragmented parliament, government formation and maintenance become more challenging. On the first of these, as the Constitution Review Group pointed out, in the postwar European experience, any dangers that might arise from the presence of small parties have been countered by effective party discipline, an experience that is confirmed by the Irish case (Constitution Review Group, 1996: 58; Farrell *et al.*, 2015). In this regard, the Irish experience would seem to run counter to any suggestion that PR-STV leads to weaker party discipline and party organisation. For example, Taagepera and Shugart (1989: 28) argue that 'if strength of party organization is desired, STV is inappropriate, because either list PR (even with preference voting) or plurality (in the absence of US-style primaries) gives far more leeway to party elites in deciding who the party's representatives may be'.

This, however, is a relative observation. It does seem likely that, other things being equal, a list system of PR will lead to stronger party organisation. This does not mean that parties under PR-STV will be weak in some absolute sense. Katz (1980: 34) puts forward a more absolute version of the theory, hypothesising that 'Where intraparty choice is allowed, parliamentary parties will tend to be disunited' and noting that 'In the case of small districts this will be manifested in personalistic fractionalization' (1980: 34; see also Blais, 1991). He points to the prevalence of intra-party personalistic competition in the area of constituency service as evidence for this theory, but is unable to account for the evident high levels of party unity shown by Irish parliamentary parties (see Chapter 7), referring to this, though without additional explanation, as 'illusory' (Katz, 1980: 107). It would seem more sensible to note that intense intra-party competition in the area of constituency service can coexist with a very substantial degree of party cohesion and party discipline in the Dáil, and that the latter are products of constitutional structure and inherited modes of politics, and are not necessarily undermined by PR-STV (Farrell *et al.*, 2015).

Turning to the issue of fragmentation and its impact upon government stability, it should be noted that the Constitution Review Group's discussion focused exclusively on parties. By ignoring the way in which PR-STV facilitates the election of independent or non-party candidates, it may indeed have taken too sanguine a view of the Irish experience. The fact is that six Irish governments since the start of the 1980s have been explicitly dependent on the support of independent TDs, none more so than the government that took office in 2016. Two of these (those formed after the 1981 and February 1982 elections) collapsed within nine months. While this threat to the stability of government is occasional, since it depends on the parliamentary arithmetic after an election, no amount of party discipline can counter it. PR-STV contributes to the threat by increasing the probability of minority governments that may be tempted to rely on the support of a few independents, rather than including another party in a coalition arrangement (though arguably, following the 2016 election, it was the refusal of mainstream parties to enter government together that left the independents in so pivotal a position). It also facilitates the election of independents in the first place by focusing on individual candidates, by encouraging competition between deputies and candidates in the provision of local constituency service and, through the mechanism of the multi-seat constituency, by lowering the threshold of representation to a point at which it is within the reach of non-party candidates (Bowler and Farrell, 2017). In short, while it is true that PR-STV does not lead to unstable government by undermining party discipline, or, arguably, by facilitating the parliamentary presence of a multiplicity of parties, it does increase the probability of government reliance on independent deputies whose support may be delivered at a disproportionate price and even then may or may not be durable.

Consequences for the role of the TD

The issue of whether PR-STV imposes an excessive burden of constituency work on TDs hardly figured at all in the debates of 1959 and 1968. For example, a pamphlet by a civic-minded study group that aimed to provide an objective assessment of the arguments in 1959 devoted a page and a half to the issue of the quality of TDs, but only five lines of this dealt with the question of constituency service (Tuairim, 1959: 19–20). In contrast, the subsequent increase in the burden of constituency work led Farrell (1985: 14) to note in the mid-1980s that 'there is an evident consensus among deputies that the competition in constituency service has got out of hand'. The current Irish debate about PR-STV focuses mainly on the question of how far the electoral system is a cause of this preoccupation with constituency service and whether the system should be abandoned because of it. The fact that, over the years, the issue has been raised by current or former prominent politicians from a range of parties (see, for example, FitzGerald, 2003; Martin, 1991; Halligan, 2014; Hussey, 1993) suggests that there is a prima facie case to be examined.

Academic support for the proposition that the Irish electoral system leads to excessive emphasis on constituency work is not hard to find. Katz (1984: 143–4) argues that interpersonal competition tends to supersede interparty competition with the result that, ultimately, 'competition between parties tends to be on the basis of services rendered, rather than policy differences'. Carty emphasises the fact that PR-STV allows the voter to combine two criteria at once – party and personal service. He sees the electoral system as an independent contributory factor that adds to the already-existing cultural impetus towards brokerage: 'This dimension of electoral politics – local brokers competing for a party vote – has been institutionalised in Ireland by the electoral system ... With little to distinguish themselves from their opponents (particularly party colleagues), politicians are driven to emphasise their brokerage services to constituents, thus reinforcing cultural expectations' (Carty, 1981: 134).

The hypothesis underlying the above views is certainly plausible. The argument goes like this: the main competition for seats is between candidates of the same party. Since such candidates cannot differentiate themselves from one another on the basis of party policy, party record in government or party leadership, they compete on the basis of service to their constituents. This involves the kind of activity discussed more fully in Chapter 8: handling a large volume of casework, holding regular 'clinics' throughout the constituency, attending meetings of residents' associations and local pressure groups of all sorts, and being seen at local gatherings and functions from sporting events to funerals.

The report of the Constitution Review Group (see Chapter 3) cautiously concluded that 'the present PR-STV system has had popular support and should not be changed without careful advance assessment of the possible effects'. It went on to note that, if there were to be change, a list system of proportional representation or a dual system that combines proportional and non-proportional components would 'satisfy more of the relevant criteria than a move to a non-PR system' (Constitution Review Group, 1996: 60).

The report of the Constitution Review Group had not been intended to be definitive. That challenge was left to the subsequent All-Party Oireachtas Committee on the Constitution, which issued its report dealing with the role of parliament and, consequently, with the electoral system, in 2002. The main research report considered by the committee (Laver, 1998) dealt with the likely consequences of a switch to a mixed system (with some TDs elected from single-member constituencies and others from regional party lists, on the German model; for more on mixed systems see Farrell, 2011: ch. 5). It concluded that, whatever the other merits of such a system, and bearing in mind that that system would probably leave the broad party balance much as it would be under PR-STV, 'it seems likely that Fianna Fáil would win almost all the constituency seats, with the other parties winning all or most of their seats from the list-PR element of the system' (quoted in All-Party Oireachtas Committee, 2002: 17). Though the starkness of this prediction was queried in other evidence presented to the committee (All-Party Oireachtas Committee, 2002: 22), the assumption of a degree of skewness in the distribution of constituency and list seats between the parties almost certainly affected the committee's thinking.

In concluding, the committee summarised the pros and cons of PR-STV and mixed systems, emphasising in particular that there are two sides to the argument about the effects of PR-STV on the constituency service role of TDs and that a defining, unavoidable and undesirable aspect of the hybrid system is 'the resultant division of parliamentary representatives into two classes: constituency and list'. It argued against change on the grounds that PR-STV 'provides the greatest degree of voter choice of any available option' (All-Party Oireachtas Committee, 2002: 29).

A further process of review was established within only a few years of that report, this time under the auspices of a Joint Committee on the Constitution. In its report, published in 2010, the Joint Committee concluded that there was not 'a sufficiently compelling case' for changing the electoral system (Joint Committee on the Constitution, 2010: 160). It went on, further, to observe that, as 'the electoral system is an important part of the institutional framework in a democracy [it] should not be confined to the realm of party politics'. This led it to recommend the establishment of a citizens' assembly 'to examine the current operation of PR-STV in Ireland to determine if it continues to meet the needs of our democracy' (Joint Committee on the Constitution, 2010: 161). This followed the examples in the Canadian provinces of British Columbia and Ontario a few years earlier (see Fournier *et al.*, 2011).

The Joint Committee's recommendation was adopted by Fine Gael in its 2011 general election manifesto. The coalition of Fine Gael and Labour that was formed as a result of that election established a Convention on the Constitution in late 2012 comprising a mixture of 66 randomly selected citizens and 33 politicians from the Oireachtas and the Northern Ireland Assembly, led by an independent chair from the charity sector (Farrell *et al.*, 2017a). Reform of PR-STV was one of eight topics given to the Convention for it to consider. The Convention members voted overwhelmingly (by 79 per cent) against the adoption of a new electoral system (Convention on the Constitution, 2013), a recommendation that the government duly accepted. This would seem to have put to bed the question of replacing PR-STV with another electoral system for the foreseeable future (Farrell *et al.*, 2017b).

But that does not rule out the possibility of reforms to the operation of the existing electoral system, of which a number have been proposed. For instance, the Convention on the Constitution recommended that constituency sizes in Ireland (the smallest of any PR-STV jurisdiction – see Farrell and McAllister, 2006) should be increased. It also recommended that candidates should no longer be listed alphabetically on the ballot paper. This relates to a common concern among candidates that those with surnames located high (or low) on the alphabet are privileged electorally, with those whose surnames begin with letters around the middle of the alphabet being under-represented (see Farrell, 2011: 148–49). Both proposals were rejected by the government on this occasion. Other reform proposals that emerge from time to time concern the counting rules relating to vote transfers (see the discussion above about the Gregory method), whether to replace by-elections by another method for filling vacant parliamentary seats (none of the other PR-STV jurisdictions uses by-elections, though there is no entirely satisfactory alternative) or coming up with a more conventional method to determine constituency boundaries in Ireland (see Coakley, 2013: 171–202).

Perhaps more significant are the long-standing debates over the proposal to establish an electoral commission in Ireland. The electoral system – the focus of this chapter – is only one aspect (albeit a central one) of the broad topic of the regulation of electoral competition. The additional regulatory aspects include drawing constituency boundaries, accepting and validating nominations, and overseeing campaign finance and other aspects of campaigning in both elections and referendums. This regulatory process currently involves three separate commissions – the Constituency Commission, the Standards in Public Office Commission and the Referendum Commission – as well as a range of other administrative agencies and individuals. Successive governments since 2007 have promised to establish an electoral commission to integrate the work of these different agencies, but this has yet to occur (for discussion, see Buckley and Reidy, 2015; Farrell, 2015). This was also a recommendation of the Constitutional Convention, and on the eve of the 2016 election the Oireachtas Joint Committee on Environment, Culture and the Gaeltacht produced a detailed report on a proposed Electoral Commission, calling for its establishment 'without delay' (Joint Committee, 2016: 116). Given the expected remit of an Irish Electoral Commission, its establishment is likely to see renewed debates over reforms to specific features of PR-STV – notably the process of constituency boundary revisions and the structure of ballot papers, and possibly also issues relating to constituency size and details of the vote counting rules.

The balance sheet

PR-STV is a highly distinctive electoral system. It differs fundamentally from the other two major types of electoral systems – from the plurality system by virtue of its proportionality, and from PR list systems by virtue of putting the emphasis on individual candidates rather than on political parties. Both of these distinctive features are seen as weaknesses by critics of PR-STV. The first line of criticism – that it produces results that are too proportional and that are conducive to unstable government – is easily dealt with. PR-STV (combined with the small size of constituencies in Ireland) produces moderate rather than extreme proportionality (Farrell and Katz, 2014). For the most part, Irish governments have been relatively stable, and certainly there is no evidence to suggest that the electoral system has had an impact on the stability of Irish governments over time.

The second main line of criticism – that it devalues parties – raises more fundamental issues. Katz (1984: 145) argues that 'the choice offered by [list system] PR ... is a choice within party, while the choice offered under STV is a choice without regard to party'. It may be that the party versus non-party dilemma is overstated by Katz in the phrase 'choice without regard to party'. It is true that the choice in PR-STV is not tied to party; rather, it is open and flexible, because it elicits more information from the voter and places less constraint on the kind of information that can be transmitted. But this means that voters can vote on a party basis if they wish, and historically the evidence from the analysis of transfer patterns suggests that many do, albeit in gradually reducing amounts in recent elections (Gallagher, 2016b; Sinnott, 1995: 208–16).

The other side of the coin of the alleged devaluation of parties is the argument that PR-STV is responsible for the 'excessive' constituency orientation of TDs. That TDs do a great deal of constituency work is undeniable. That this is due in some definitive way to the electoral system is debatable. For one thing, it is clear that there are other causes of the constituency service role, among them being aspects of the political culture, the small size of Irish society, inadequate parliamentary resources and procedures, problems in the administrative system and the weakness of local government (see the discussion in Chapter 8). In short, it is clear that the constituency service role is due to a number of different factors, and it is likely that the electoral system is a contributory factor but not the main determinant. It should also be noted that the constituency service role can have positive as well as negative aspects, namely that of keeping public representatives in touch with the real problems of ordinary people, enhancing their input into future legislative proposals and contributing to the accountability of the system. This is a reminder that, in evaluating the system, one must look not just at its alleged negative consequences but also at its positive aspects.

We should also look at the alternatives that might be put in its place (Gallagher and Mitchell, 2008). For a variety of reasons, the plurality system, which has been twice rejected by the electorate, is a non-starter. At the other end of the spectrum, the list system is also unattractive for two main reasons – a closed list system would by definition do away completely with the candidate choice to which Irish voters are accustomed and attached; an open list system (allowing voters to support particular candidates within parties) would not do away with the intra-party competition at the electoral level that is alleged to be the main disadvantage of PR-STV. As noted in the constitutional reviews that have dealt with this issue, the prime remaining candidate is the mixed system. But it is not clear that such a system would eradicate inter-personal constituency-level competition. Experience in Germany, New Zealand, Scotland and Wales suggests that many list members aspire to become constituency members and, with this in mind, informally attach themselves to a constituency; it also suggests that members of parliament attach high importance to the constituency service role, whatever the electoral system (Gallagher and Suiter, 2017; see Chapter 8, pp. 200–1). Thus, one could well have a situation in which two or even three TDs would be assiduously cultivating a particular constituency; all the evidence indicates that in Ireland such competition would mainly take the form of provision of constituency service.

Finally, although the issue does not figure much in public or political debate about PR-STV, a balance sheet of the arguments for and against PR-STV should mention the problem of what might be described as alleged theoretical flaws in the system. The flaws are theoretical because they are identified for the most part by imagining the preferences of a small set of hypothetical voters and showing that the outcomes can vary with minor changes in the assumed preferences in ways that violate certain abstract principles of how an electoral system ought to function (see, for example, Dummett, 1997: 89–108, 138–57; Nurmi, 1997). The most important such violation is the phenomenon of 'non-monotonicity'. Monotonicity is the requirement that any increase in a candidate's vote should not diminish his or her chances of being elected. Because of the importance of the order of elimination in determining the outcome in PR-STV, the possible violation of this principle can be readily demonstrated with a hypothetical set of preferences. Furthermore, rare but real violations of the principle can be found in PR-STV election results (for example, Gallagher, 1999: 145–6). In assessing the significance of such issues from the voters' point of view, one must bear in mind that they depend either on assumptions or on retrospective knowledge about the order of elimination of the candidates and of the transfer behaviour of the voters. Such knowledge is not available to the voters and cannot enter into their calculations. This means that complex tactical voting under PR-STV can be imagined or retrospectively constructed; it cannot be realistically pursued by the voter. In summary, proponents of PR-STV should be wary of claiming that it is perfectly logical or that it disposes completely of the issue of tactical voting; at the same time, the problems identified in this regard remain in the realm of theory rather than practice and certainly do not justify Dummett's claim that the system is 'quasi-chaotic' (Dummett, 1997: 143; see Farrell and McAllister, 2006).

Conclusion

In the early years of the twentieth century, PR-STV appeared to be the natural choice as the electoral system for the emerging Irish state. It offered the possibility of minority representation, it suited the anti-party mood of the time and, most importantly, it was familiar. Described simply as 'the system of proportional representation' without further specification in the 1922 constitution, it was spelled out as PR-STV in the new constitution in 1937. This constitutional embodiment meant that any change to the system would require a referendum. Change was rejected by the people on both of the occasions on which it was attempted – and by a very substantial majority on the second occasion. However, the merits of the system have been the subject of debate since the late 1990s, in part on the initiative of a number of individual politicians seeking solutions to the problem of the burden of constituency service on elected politicians, in part through the work of a series of constitutional reviews.[5]

The criticisms of PR-STV are quite various. It is frequently criticised by observers unfamiliar with it on the basis that it is difficult for voters to understand. This is not a persuasive point. In the first place, what the voter actually needs to grasp is quite simple and, secondly, both its underlying logic and its (admittedly somewhat complex) mechanics can be made readily intelligible. It has also been argued that the system produces results that are too proportional and that, consequently, it undermines the stability of government. This argument is not sustainable. Likewise, there seems to be little support for the related argument that the system is destructive of party cohesion, though it must be conceded that it is conducive to the election of independent deputies and that this can have consequences for government stability.

This brings us to the most frequent and, superficially, the most plausible criticism of the system – that it imposes an excessive burden of constituency service upon those who are elected to the Dáil. There are two problems with this criticism. The first is that, in some of its versions at least, it appears to assume that all constituency service is a bad thing, that TDs should be legislators and nothing else, and that constituency service has no positive effect on the TD's legislative role. The second and the main problem with the criticism is that, rather than being due simply and solely to PR-STV, the excessive burden of constituency service experienced by TDs is due to a range of factors, as discussed in Chapter 8. Rather than treating alteration of the electoral system as a panacea, the more appropriate response would be to deal with the other contributory factors first. If this were done and if TDs still could not find an appropriate balance between their legislative and constituency service roles, there would be a case for re-examining the range of alternative electoral systems to see if one of them could do better on this *and* on the other criteria of a good electoral system.

Notes

1   The ballot paper used in the 2016 election was slightly different from previous elections. The main change was that the space for including the political party emblem was moved from the left to the right-hand side of the ballot paper, next to the candidate's photograph. This change was made to reduce the risk of voter confusion: when the party logos were on the left-hand side, there were blank boxes against non-party candidates and, in the past, some voters put their preferences in those boxes (inadvertently or deliberately), thus spoiling their vote. This was the first change to Irish ballot papers since the introduction of candidate photographs in 1999 and party logos in 2001 (Buckley *et al.*, 2007).

2   Technically, the single transferable vote in a single-seat contest is known as the alternative vote. It is worth emphasising that this is not PR because, in debate about electoral reform in Ireland, the option of so-called 'PR in single-seat constituencies' is sometimes put forward. What is being

referred to is, in fact, the alternative vote, which, as will become clear, cannot be a proportional system. The constitution, which describes the system under which the President is elected as 'proportional representation by means of the single transferable vote' (Article 12.2.3), contributes to this confusion, by naming an electoral system that cannot apply to the filling of a single vacancy.

3   As Tables 4.2 and 4.3 show, the counting of the votes proceeds through a number of stages. Perhaps confusingly, each stage is commonly referred to as a 'count', and that term will be employed in this chapter, to conform with prevailing usage in Ireland.

4   Distribution of a surplus is postponed if the surplus is less than the difference between the votes of the two lowest candidates, and if this distribution could not help any candidate to reach the threshold for reimbursement of electoral expenses (one quarter of the quota).

5   This debate over electoral reform has been, in large part, elite driven. There is no evidence from opinion poll data that the public would favour electoral reform (Coakley, 2013: 15–16; Farrell *et al.*, 2017a).

References and further reading

All-Party Oireachtas Committee on the Constitution, 2002. *Seventh Progress Report: Parliament.* Dublin: All-Party Oireachtas Committee on the Constitution.

Blais, André, 1991. 'The debate over electoral systems', *International Political Science Review* 12:3, pp. 239–60.

Bowler, Shaun and Todd Donovan, 2013. *The Limits of Electoral Reform.* Oxford: Oxford University Press.

Bowler, Shaun and David M. Farrell, 2017. 'The lack of party system change in Ireland in 2011', in Michael Marsh, David M. Farrell and Gail McElroy (eds), *A Conservative Revolution? Electoral Change in Twenty-First-Century Ireland.* Oxford: Oxford University Press, pp. 83–101.

Buckley, Fiona and Theresa Reidy, 2015. 'Managing the electoral process: insights from, and for, Ireland', *Irish Political Studies* 30, pp. 445–53.

Buckley, Fiona, Neil Collins and Theresa Reidy, 2007. 'Ballot paper photographs and low-information elections in Ireland', *Politics* 27:3, pp. 174–81.

Butler, David, 1981. 'Electoral systems', in David Butler, Howard R. Penniman and Austin Ranney (eds), *Democracy at the Polls: A Comparative Study of Competitive National Elections.* Washington DC: American Enterprise Institute for Public Policy Research, pp. 7–25.

Carstairs, Andrew McLaren, 1980. *A Short History of Electoral Systems in Western Europe.* London: George Allen and Unwin.

Carty, R. K., 1981. *Party and Parish Pump: Electoral Politics in Ireland.* Waterloo, Ontario: Wilfrid Laurier University Press.

Coakley, John, 2013. *Reforming Political Institutions: Ireland in Comparative Perspective.* Dublin: Institute of Public Administration.

Coakley, John and Gerald O'Neill, 1984. 'Chance in preferential voting systems: an unacceptable element in Irish electoral law?', *Economic and Social Review* 16:1, pp. 1–18.

Committee on the Constitution, 1967. *Report* (Pr. 9817). Dublin: Stationery Office.

Constitution Review Group, 1996. *Report of the Constitution Review Group.* Dublin: The Stationery Office.

Convention on the Constitution, 2013. *Fourth Report of the Convention on the Constitution: Dáil Electoral System.* Dublin: Convention on the Constitution. www.constitution.ie/AttachmentDownload.ashx?mid=fdf70670-030f-e311-a203-005056a32ee4

Dummett, Michael, 1997. *Principles of Electoral Reform.* Oxford: Oxford University Press.

Duverger, Maurice, 1964. *Political Parties.* London: Methuen & Co.

Farrell, Brian, 1985. 'Ireland: from friends and neighbours to clients and partisans: some dimensions of parliamentary representation under PR-STV', in Vernon Bogdanor (ed.), *Representatives of the People? Parliaments and Constituents in Western Democracies.* Aldershot: Gower, pp. 237–64.

Farrell, David M., 2011. *Electoral Systems: A Comparative Introduction*, 2nd edn. Basingstoke: Palgrave Macmillan.

Farrell, David M., 2015. 'Conclusion and reflection: time for an electoral commission for Ireland', *Irish Political Studies* 30, pp. 641–6.

Farrell, David M. and Ian McAllister, 2003. 'The 1983 change in surplus vote transfer procedures for the Australian Senate and its consequences for STV', *Australian Journal of Political Science* 38, pp. 479–92.

Farrell, David M. and Ian McAllister, 2006. *The Australian Electoral System: Origins, Variations and Consequences.* Sydney: UNSW Press.

Farrell, David M. and Richard S. Katz, 2014. 'Assessing the proportionality of the single transferable vote', *Representation* 50, pp. 13–26.

Farrell, David M. and Jane Suiter, 2016. 'The election in context', in Michael Gallagher and Michael Marsh (eds), *How Ireland Voted 2016: The Election That Nobody Won.* Basingstoke: Palgrave Macmillan, pp. 277–92.

Farrell, David M., Peter Mair, Séin Ó Muineacháin and Matthew Wall, 2015. 'Courting but not always serving: perverted Burkeanism and the puzzle of Irish parliamentary cohesion', in Richard Johnston and Campbell Sharman (eds), *Parties and Party Systems: Structure and Context.* Vancouver: UBC Press, pp. 92–107.

Farrell, David M., Clodagh Harris and Jane Suiter, 2017a. 'Bringing people into the heart of constitutional design: the Irish Constitutional Convention of 2012–14', in Xenophon Contiades and Alkmene Fotiadou (eds), *Participatory Constitutional Change: The People as Amenders of the Constitution.* London: Routledge, pp. 120–35.

Farrell, David M., Jane Suiter and Clodagh Harris, 2017b. 'The challenge of reforming a "voter-friendly" electoral system: the debates over Ireland's single transferable vote', *Irish Political Studies* 32, pp. 293–310.

FitzGerald, Garret, 1959. 'PR – the great debate', *Studies* 48, pp. 1–20.

FitzGerald, Garret, 2003. *Reflections on the Irish State.* Dublin: Irish Academic Press.

Fournier, Patrick, Henk van der Kolk, R. Kenneth Carty, André Blais, and Jonathan Rose, 2011. *When Citizens Decide: Lessons from Citizen Assemblies on Electoral Reform.* Oxford: Oxford University Press.

Gallagher, Michael, 1999. 'The results analysed', in Michael Marsh and Paul Mitchell (eds), *How Ireland Voted 1997.* Boulder CO: Westview Press and PSAI Press, pp. 121–50.

Gallagher, Michael, 2008. 'Ireland: the discreet charm of PR-STV', in Michael Gallagher and Paul Mitchell (eds), *The Politics of Electoral Systems*, revised ed. Oxford: Oxford University Press, pp. 511–32.

Gallagher, Michael, 2011. 'Ireland's earthquake election: analysis of the results', in Michael Gallagher and Michael Marsh (eds), *How Ireland Voted 2011: The Full Story of Ireland's Earthquake Election.* Basingstoke: Palgrave Macmillan, pp. 139–71.

Gallagher, Michael, 2014. 'Electoral institutions and representation', in Lawrence LeDuc, Richard Niemi and Pippa Norris (eds), *Comparing Democracies 4.* London: Sage, pp. 11–31.

Gallagher, Michael, 2016a. Election Indices. www.tcd.ie/Political_Science/staff/michael_gallagher/ElSystems/Docts/ElectionIndices.pdf.

Gallagher, Michael, 2016b. 'The results analysed: the aftershocks continue', in Michael Gallagher and Michael Marsh (eds), *How Ireland Voted 2016: The Election That Nobody Won.* Basingstoke: Palgrave Macmillan, pp. 125–58.

Gallagher, Michael and A. R. Unwin, 1986. 'Electoral distortion under STV random sampling procedures', *British Journal of Political Science* 16:2, pp. 243–53.

Gallagher, Michael and Paul Mitchell, eds, 2008. *The Politics of Electoral Systems*, revised ed. Oxford: Oxford University Press.

Gallagher, Michael and Jane Suiter, 2017. 'Pathological parochialism or a valuable service? Attitudes to the constituency role of politicians', in Michael Marsh, David M. Farrell and Gail McElroy (eds), *A Conservative Revolution? Electoral Change in Twenty-First-Century Ireland.* Oxford: Oxford University Press, pp. 143–71.

Gallagher, Michael, Michael Laver and Peter Mair, 2011. *Representative Government in Modern Europe*, 5th ed. New York: McGraw-Hill.

Halligan, Brendan, 2014. *Our Worst Preference: Reforming the Electoral System*. Dublin: Scathan Press.

Hussey, Gemma, 1993. *Ireland Today: Anatomy of a Changing State*. Dublin: Townhouse / Viking.

Joint Committee on the Constitution, 2010. *Fourth Report: Article 16 of the Constitution. Review of the Electoral System for the Election of Members to Dáil Éireann*. Dublin: Houses of the Oireachtas.

Joint Committee on Environment, Culture and the Gaeltacht, 2016. *Report of the Joint Committee on the Consultation on the Proposed Electoral Commission*. Dublin: Houses of the Oireachtas.

Katz, Richard S., 1980. *A Theory of Parties and Electoral Systems*. Baltimore and London: The Johns Hopkins University Press.

Katz, Richard S., 1984. 'The single transferable vote and proportional representation', in Arend Lijphart and Bernard Grofman (eds), *Choosing an Electoral System: Issues and Alternatives*. New York: Praeger, pp. 135–45.

Laakso, Markku and Rein Taagepera, 1979. '"Effective" number of parties: a measure with application to West Europe', *Comparative Political Studies* 12:1, pp. 3–27.

Laver, Michael, 1998. *A New Electoral System for Ireland?* Dublin: The Policy Institute and The All-Party Oireachtas Committee on the Constitution.

Laver, Michael, 2004. 'Analysing structures of party preference in electronic voting data', *Party Politics* 10:5, pp. 521–41.

Lijphart, Arend, 1994. *Electoral Systems and Party Systems: A Study of Twenty-Seven Democracies, 1945–1990*. Oxford: Oxford University Press.

Marsh, Michael, Richard Sinnott, John Garry and Fiachra Kennedy, 2008. *The Irish Voter: The Nature of Electoral Competition in the Republic of Ireland*. Manchester: Manchester University Press.

Martin, Micheál, 1991. 'Fianna Fáil has a problem – it's time to deal with it', *Sunday Tribune* 4 August, p. 12.

Murphy, Gary, 2008. 'The background to the election', in Michael Gallagher and Michael Marsh (eds), *How Ireland Voted 2007: The Full Story of Ireland's General Election*. Basingstoke: Palgrave Macmillan, pp. 1–18.

Nurmi, Hannu, 1997. 'It's not just the lack of monotonicity', *Representation* 34:1, pp. 48–52.

O'Leary, Cornelius, 1979. *Irish Elections 1918–1977: Parties, Voters and Proportional Representation*. Dublin: Gill and Macmillan.

Renwick, Alan and Jean-Benoit Pilet, 2016. *Faces on the Ballot: The Personalization of Electoral Systems in Europe*. Oxford: Oxford University Press.

Sartori, Giovanni, 1976. *Parties and Party Systems: A Framework for Analysis*. Cambridge: Cambridge University Press.

Sinnott, Richard, 1995. *Irish Voters Decide: Voting Behaviour in Elections and Referendums since 1918*. Manchester: Manchester University Press.

Taagepera, Rein and Matthew Soberg Shugart, 1989. *Seats and Votes: The Effects and Determinants of Electoral Systems*. New Haven and London: Yale University Press.

Tuairim Research Group, 1959. *P.R. – For or Against?* Dublin: Tuairim.

Websites

www.environ.ie/en/LocalGovernment/Voting/
Information on elections, from the Department of the Environment.

www.tcd.ie/Political_Science/staff/michael_gallagher/ElSystems/index.php
Michael Gallagher's electoral systems page.

www.electoral-reform.org.uk/voting-systems
Detailed discussion of electoral systems.

5 Parties and the party system

Liam Weeks

Politics in a parliamentary democracy generally operates through the conduit of parties. The exceptions, such as several Pacific island states that follow a non-partisan model, are very few in number (Weeks, 2015b). Some of the Irish state's founding fathers envisaged a system that, instead of relying on parties as the building blocks of democracy, would be forged on the basis of a direct connection between representatives and voters (O'Leary, 1979: 14). Although this ambivalence to parties remains in some quarters in the Irish political system, particularly in the persistence of independent or non-party deputies, and although the constitution makes no reference to parties, they remain the dominant mode through which politics operates in Ireland. Parties structure the political world and by a study of their organisations, and the dynamics both within and between them, we can gain an enhanced understanding of the political process and its workings.

This chapter outlines the key actors in the party system and the evolution of competition between them. First, the origins of the party system are examined from a comparative perspective, with a discussion of some of the debates about its formation. This is followed by a consideration of each of the durable parties, before a classification of the system as a whole in terms of its evolution, concluding with an assessment of the changes that have taken place in the early twenty-first century.

As well as the competition between parties, we also need to understand the internal mechanics of party organisations, especially since these can dictate the nature of the party as a whole. A later section of this chapter therefore examines the structure and workings of parties. It details how party organisations in Ireland function and where power lies within parties. The chapter concludes with an evaluation of the role of parties within the political system.

Parties and party systems

Fitting Irish parties into the categories generally employed in comparative analysis has proved challenging, as they lack features common to the European experience. For example, the party system has been dominated by two parties with almost incomprehensible names, Fianna Fáil and Fine Gael, between whom the differences have often been almost indiscernible (for the meanings and connotations of party names see Coakley, 1980). The unusual nature of the party system derives partly from its distinctive origins. This motivated John Whyte (1974: 648) to note some time ago that 'it is then perhaps a comfort to comparative political analysis that Irish party politics should be *sui generis:* the context from which they spring is *sui generis* also' (see also Carty, 1981). From this perspective, an understanding of the genesis of the Irish parties is required to comprehend the dynamics and patterns of party competition, both past and present.

Origins of the Irish party system

Most approaches to explaining the origins of the Irish party system focus on the period 1916–23. As was explained in Chapter 1, an insurrection in 1916 sparked off a movement for independence that culminated in the birth of the Irish Free State in 1922. The key political actor during most of this period was Sinn Féin, which replaced the Irish Parliamentary Party as the dominant political movement in Ireland. At the December 1918 UK general election, Sinn Féin won 70 of the 75 seats in the 26 counties that now constitute the Republic of Ireland, following which it set up a breakaway parliament (the first Dáil) in January 1919. A war of independence ensued, and a subsequent settlement (the Anglo–Irish Treaty of 1921) that granted Ireland a form of dominion rule split Sinn Féin, resulting in a civil war. Those in the party defending the treaty formed the first provisional government in the state, and established the pro-treaty party Cumann na nGaedheal in 1923. Those opposed to the treaty did not recognise the new government and initially abstained from parliamentary politics. These anti-treaty Republicans further fragmented in 1926, when party leader Éamon de Valera left to form Fianna Fáil, which entered the Dáil in 1927. Cumann na nGaedheal merged with two other parties in 1933 to form Fine Gael. Since then, Fianna Fáil and Fine Gael have been the dominant actors in Irish politics. In the period 1922–2016, Fianna Fáil and its precursors won on average 41 per cent of the vote and Cumann na nGaedheal/Fine Gael 31 per cent, with every government being led by one of these two parties. To summarise the party system's origins, then, the traditional argument is 'in the beginning was the treaty'. The importance of these origins is evident in that the main electoral competitors in the 1920s (Sinn Féin and its various splinters, plus Labour, plus independents) remain the main contenders in the 2010s. This is particularly unusual in a European context, and indicates a presence of stability alongside some tumult.

It is not just its nationalist origins that makes the Irish party system exceptional in a European context. Another line of argument stresses that party competition in Ireland had diverged from the more common European pattern even before the twentieth century. Before the mobilisation of the electorate in the mid-nineteenth century, the evolution of the Irish party system had developed along fairly conventional conservative–liberal lines. However, the political mobilisation of the Catholic population – which eventually took the form of a mass party (Coakley, 2004: 142) – interrupted this pattern, resulting in the emergence of a divide along nationalist/Catholic versus unionist/Protestant lines in the latter half of the nineteenth century. Garvin (1981: 137) therefore suggests that the 1916–23 period was not in fact a great watershed in changing the shape of Irish politics; rather, the party system resulting from the struggle for independence was a 'second-generation' system. Both O'Connell and Parnell had led broad pan-nationalist movements during the nineteenth century, and the Sinn Féin party inherited this mantle after 1916, confirming its dominance at the mobilising election of 1918 (see Chapter 1). The unionist/Protestant side of the nineteenth-century party system disappeared in the new state, as it was quite a small minority, dwindling further as many Protestants emigrated both across the border, where their side of the cleavage was in a majority, and across the Irish Sea.

It is possible that there is an element of truth in both of these conflicting theories: that a completely new party system began with Sinn Féin's electoral triumph in 1918 (Carty, 1981), and that there was a significant degree of continuity between this party system and the nineteenth-century model (Garvin, 1981). The logic is that these theories constitute two sides of the same coin; while Fianna Fáil and Fine Gael as specific parties certainly bear scarcely any resemblance to the political formations of the nineteenth century, their roots stem from the two issues that had shaped the party systems of the previous century, namely land agitation and national sovereignty. Fianna Fáil historically represented small farmers and strong nationalists, with Fine Gael representing large farmers and moderate nationalists. The twentieth-century party system is therefore both new and old.

Undoubtedly, a major factor explaining alignments in the post-independence state was the unresolved nature of the nationalist issue. The treaty became the polarising issue that split Sinn Féin, with the two sides' mobilisation in large part stemming from attitudes to Ireland's relationship with Britain (Garvin, 1981: 135). While there were few, if any, socio-economic differences between the TDs on either side of the split, the question of whether the division was purely political, or also had a class component, is still debated. Those opposing the treaty were more prominent in the economic and geographical peripheries of the country (predominantly the western seaboard). Thus, on one line of argument, there was a social dimension to the split, which was also reflected in the policies of anti-treaty Sinn Féin (and later Fianna Fáil), which reiterated some of the social doctrines of the democratic programme adopted by the first Dáil in 1919, and was particularly appealing to small farmers and the working class (see Moss, 1933: 18–19). At the same time, these policies and a predilection for revolutionary nationalism amongst a group of 'accidental politicians' initially alienated the more privileged sectors of Irish society from anti-treaty Sinn Féin. These sectors, especially those with financial links to the British Empire, preferred the more conservative pro-treaty wing of Sinn Féin (later to become Cumann na nGaedheal); they came from a tradition of constitutional nationalism in the Irish Parliamentary Party (Meehan, 2010). Sinnott (1995: 114–34), however, questions this; while support for Fianna Fáil was higher amongst some social groups, he finds little evidence of a class divide in the first half of the 1920s, a conclusion reinforced by the weak social basis to the Cumann na nGaedheal vote. Whatever the fundamental explanation for the different support bases of these parties, the difficulty of defining the differences between Fianna Fáil and Fine Gael is a remarkably persistent feature of the Irish party system, and is discussed at length below (on the parties and the party system generally, see Gallagher, 1985; Mair, 1987; McGraw, 2015; Sinnott, 1984, 1995).

The parties

Three parties in various guises have dominated the political stage in the post-independence state (see Figure 5.1). They constituted what was sometimes described as a 'two-and-a-half party system', with Fianna Fáil and Fine Gael the two main players, along with a smaller half, the Labour Party. It is necessary to understand these actors and their evolution before analysing their interaction in the form of the party system.

Fianna Fáil and Fine Gael

The Tweedledee and Tweedledum who agreed to have a battle, Fianna Fáil and Fine Gael are the inheritors of opposite sides of the treaty split in Sinn Féin, the party that monopolised representation in the first two Dála. Given their shared origins, it is useful to examine their evolution collectively.

Up until its nadir election of 2011, Fianna Fáil had been the dominant party of Irish politics (O'Malley and McGraw, 2017). After first coming to office in 1932, it was in government for

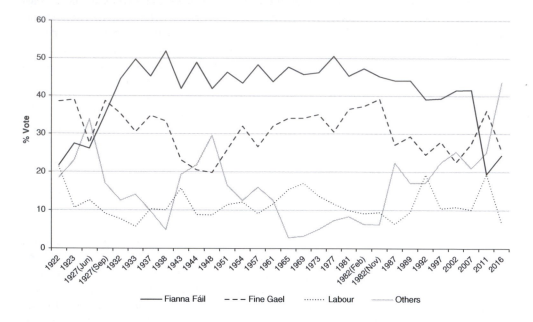

Figure 5.1 Electoral support for Irish parties, 1922–2016

Source: Calculated from Appendix 2b.

60 of the next 79 years. Fianna Fáil achieved this dominance thanks to an almost chameleon-like quality that enabled it to easily adapt to the nature of the prevailing political environment. The other vestige of the civil war, Fine Gael, has traditionally been perceived as a party of law and order, owing to its legacy as defender of the 1921 treaty and founder of the first Free State government. Its parent party, Cumann na nGaedheal, governed for the first ten years of the state; it never won a majority of the total number of seats, although *de facto* it was a majority government between 1923 and 1927 due to the anti-Treatyites' refusal to take their seats in parliament.

With their origins lying in a civil conflict, it is not surprising that Fianna Fáil and Fine Gael shared an animosity akin to that of the Tramecksan and Slamecksan parties in Swift's Lilliput, who neither ate, drank nor spoke with each other. However, while those two parties could be distinguished by the length of the heel of their shoes, at times it has not been as easy to differentiate Fianna Fáil from Fine Gael. The extent of their differences was most keenly felt in the early decades of the state, when memories of the civil conflict were still fresh, accentuated by the presence in parliament of a generation of civil war veterans up to the 1960s. Fianna Fáil claimed to represent the 'men of no property' (Lee, 1989: 160), and Fine Gael was more readily associated with the merchant and middle classes. Whether a coincidence or a consequence of such representation, Fine Gael was also seen as the more fiscally conservative party, preferring prudent economic management, whereas Fianna Fáil tended to be less cautious, often adopting more populist fiscal measures.

These differences are reflected in the parties' respective positions on the traditional left–right spectrum since 1948, on which they can be seen to have swapped positions a number of times (O'Malley and Kerby, 2004: 44–5). According to analysis of manifesto pledges, Fine

Gael was to the right of Fianna Fáil up until the 1960s, when the two parties switched positions as Fine Gael embraced social democracy and Fianna Fáil a corporatist ideology (Mair, 1987: 140). The latter developed a closeness to the property sector, in particular to builders and developers, earning the party the new moniker of the 'men in the mohair suits'. More switches have taken place in the years since, but the general pattern since the late 1980s is of a policy convergence between Fianna Fáil and Fine Gael. This reflects the evolution of an all-party consensus, particularly in relation to Northern Ireland and to management of the economy. Even among party members, whom we might expect to be more radical than either voters or TDs, a plurality of Fine Gael members surveyed in 1999 saw no real difference between the parties (Gallagher and Marsh, 2002: 180–9). While the differences between the parties have subsided, the enmity, although not on a par with that of their Lilliputian counterparts, remains. This was one of the factors in Fianna Fáil's rejection of overtures from Fine Gael to form a coalition government after the 2016 election, even though the reasons for such mutual coolness are no longer apparent. The division between the two parties now seems little more than what Carty described as a 'symbolic, ritualised conflict' (1981: 108).

Considering the two parties in a comparative perspective, it is particularly difficult to fit both Fianna Fáil and Fine Gael into established typologies. A common means of classifying parties is into party 'families' on the basis of origin and policy orientation. The two party families on the centre-right in Europe are conservatives and Christian democrats; the significant presence of one usually accounts for the weakness or absence of the other (Gallagher *et al.*, 2011: 260). While Christian democratic parties are usually prevalent in countries with a significant Catholic population (such as Ireland), neither Fianna Fáil nor Fine Gael can be considered orthodox Christian democratic parties because neither formed to defend the Catholic church's interests; rather, each has origins within a radical independence movement. Catholicism and nationalism had already been successfully fused in the nineteenth century, so neither creed was a threat to the other in post-independence Ireland. Indeed, the hegemony enjoyed by the church for many decades after independence was such that it did not need any party to defend its interests. This also explains why no anti-clerical liberal party emerged in Ireland until the 1980s, when the first cracks in the church's authority appeared.

Although comparative analyses treat Fine Gael as a Christian democratic party, and although it sometimes refers to itself as such (reflected in its membership of a number of transnational Christian democrat federations, including the European People's Party (EPP) and the European Union of Christian democracy), the party is not viewed as a defender of religious interests. While there was a strong element of Catholic conservatism within Fine Gael up until the 1970s, this was a reflection of the prevailing religious ethos of the country rather than a specific raison d'être of the party.

Despite a high level of religious conservatism within Fianna Fáil up to the 1980s (as traditionally espoused by its leader de Valera and later expressed in the morality debates on divorce, contraception and abortion), few if any classification schemes have placed the party in the Christian democrat category. However, Fianna Fáil is no further from the archetypal Christian democrat party than Fine Gael; the main reason why Fianna Fáil did not join any transnational Christian democrat movement may well be simply that Fine Gael got in first, joining the EPP when Ireland joined the EU in 1973. Fianna Fáil has been a member of a number of groups in the European Parliament, including the 'Union for Europe of the Nations', which the party leadership deemed to be too far to the right, resulting in its joining the 'Alliance of Liberals and Democrats' in 2009. Fianna Fáil's sole MEP elected in 2014 decided to sit with the European Conservatives and Reformists, however, resulting in his losing the party whip.

Since neither Fianna Fáil nor Fine Gael is a fully fledged Christian democrat prototype, some have reached the conclusion that they must both be secular conservatives (von Beyme, 1985, places Fianna Fáil in this category). Certainly, both Fianna Fáil and Fine Gael exhibit a streak of nationalism common to other conservative parties such as the Polish Law and Justice party or the British Conservatives. However, neither expresses the Euroscepticism of this strand of conservative parties, nor the mild opposition to state interventionism of the Scandinavian conservatives. The primary difficulty with classifying Fianna Fáil and Fine Gael is that they are not always clearly on the right of the political spectrum. As was shown, both have tended to converge on the centre of the ideological spectrum, sometimes switching sides between left and right. This has resulted in their promoting policies with flavours of conservatism, Christian democracy and social democracy, but not to the extent that either fits clearly into any of these categories. The best classification at which we can arrive, then, is that both Fianna Fáil and Fine Gael are what Kirchheimer (1966) called 'catch-all' parties, appealing above class and ideological divisions before the term 'catch-all' was even devised (Gallagher, 1985).

Labour

Ireland has traditionally not been fertile ground for parties of the left. The mean aggregate vote for such parties fluctuated between 10 and 20 per cent from the 1920s up to the 2000s, less than half that attracted by their counterparts in western Europe. The main protagonists of the left in most European countries have been members of the social democratic family, often the largest parties in their respective jurisdictions. In contrast, the Irish member of this family, the Labour Party, has traditionally been the 'half-party' of the Irish party system, winning a mean of just 11 per cent of votes at Dáil elections over the period 1922–2016, earning it a reputation as the Cinderella of social democracy in Europe.

Although reputedly the oldest party in Ireland, having been formed as the political wing of a trade union movement in 1912, Labour has been continuously in the shadow of the civil war parties, for which a number of explanations have been cited (see Gallagher, 1982; Mair, 1992). The first is that the pre-eminence of nationalist issues in the formative years of the Irish state relegated all other concerns to the sidelines. This meant that parties representing sectional interests, such as Labour, were at a major disadvantage.

A second factor was that, given the pre-industrialised nature of the economy, the working class was relatively small. It had no clear sense of class action and was willing to welcome socialist ideas generally only when these went hand-in-hand with the nationalist ideal (Rumpf and Hepburn, 1977: 67). For various reasons, many working-class voters were more likely to vote for Fianna Fáil, whose social programme was attractive to potential Labour voters. Indeed, unlike most left-wing parties in developed countries, Labour's support base was largely rural, being drawn mainly from the agricultural labourers in the farming heartlands, and the personal fiefdoms of Labour politicians; its appeal did not extend to urban areas until the mid to late 1960s, when it adopted a clear socialist programme (Garvin, 1981: 170).[1]

A third reason sometimes suggested is Labour's decision to stand aside from the 1918 election. Given the large number of first-time voters and the radical shift in support (or 'realignment') from the Irish Parliamentary Party to Sinn Féin, Farrell (1970) has argued that this can be considered what is sometimes termed a 'critical' election as it defined the pattern of party competition for the new state (see Coakley, 1994). According to this argument, Labour missed out on the possibility of putting socialist issues onto the agenda in 1918 (as it also did in the election to the second Dáil in 1921), and allowed the nationalist question to subsume all others.

An understated factor for Labour's Cinderella status has been its failure to develop an adequate organisation and electoral strategy. In the early decades of its existence, Labour had no election machine, instead comprising 'lazy deputies, an ineffectual organiser, [and] an insipid programme', where personality clashes and fractionalism were continually to the fore (Puirséil, 2007: 33, 10). Divisions over the radical orientation of the party contributed to the weak organisation, with more time spent debating ideology than building up a grass-roots network – notwithstanding the evidence that most of the party's successful candidates were elected despite, not because of, their socialism. Therefore, while party leader Brendan Corish was declaring nationally that 'The Seventies will be Socialist' during the 1969 election campaign, rural Labour deputy Dan Spring adopted the less ideological and more clientelistic slogan of 'He helps you. Now you help him' (Gallagher, 1982: 91).

Aside from Labour's specific mistakes, other factors accounting for the weak left include the rural, agricultural nature of the Irish labour force, the moral authority of the Catholic church and high levels of emigration. The land-holding peasantry is traditionally the most conservative of social groups, and any party with a tinge of socialism in its policies had little chance of attracting its support. The agricultural labourers who supported Labour were too few in number to replicate the experience in Scandinavia, where parties of the left experienced some electoral success in rural regions. If voters were left in any doubt about the evils of socialism, they were frequently reminded of these from the pulpit. Those remaining who still felt affection for the left tended to be from more disadvantaged sections of society, who historically emigrated in large numbers.

A decline in emigration and an increasingly urban, liberal and more secular population might have been expected to contribute to a revival in the fortunes of the left, but this did not materialise until an economic recession that began in the late 2000s. Even then, the Labour Party did not profit to the extent that its more optimistic supporters hoped. Although outpolling Fianna Fáil in the 2011 election, Labour's vote was little more than it had achieved in 1992, and less than the 1922 treaty election, when constitutional issues had been to the fore. In addition, the gains made were wiped out in 2016 when just seven Labour TDs were elected, its lowest-ever proportion of Dáil seats. Despite Labour's cyclical performances, support for the left as a whole has increased in recent elections. This includes some of the smaller parties and independents detailed in the next section, who between them attracted the support of approximately one-third of the electorate in 2011 and 2016.

Other parties

There has been a considerable range of minor parties, most of which have come and gone (see Coakley, 2012; Weeks and Clark, 2012). The current wave of such parties with parliamentary representation include a republican party (Sinn Féin), some left-wing parties (the Social Democrats and Solidarity–People Before Profit) and an environmental party (the Greens). A conventional European liberal party, the Progressive Democrats, although the most successful of the smaller parties, having served in four governments, formally wound up in 2008. The Green Party, founded in 1982, did not achieve parliamentary representation until 1989 and first entered government in 2007, but lost all its seats in 2011, though it regained a Dáil presence in 2016.

While these parties could all be termed 'minor', Sinn Féin threatens a serious breakthrough and an end to the civil war duopoly. Although in a power-sharing executive in Northern

Ireland on and off since 1999, Sinn Féin has yet to enter government south of the border. This is due to both a refusal of Fianna Fáil and Fine Gael to countenance sharing power with it and to Sinn Féin's awareness of the fate of other minor parties in government, which tend to be 'smothered' (O'Malley, 2012). Rather than a rapid rise (and an equally speedy fall, such as that experienced by other minor parties), Sinn Féin has instead been focused on incremental growth. As recently as 1990, it was suggested that Sinn Féin's future in the south was bleak, as it was then barely more popular amongst voters south of the border than amongst northern Protestants (Gallagher, 1990: 77). The party won its first Dáil seat in 1997, and advanced to five in 2002 and 14 in 2011. By 2016, Sinn Féin had firmly established itself as the third largest party in the state, approximately half the size of the two civil war parties in terms of seats, but much closer when it came to votes. In 2017, the party gave the first informal indications that it might be prepared to enter government as a junior partner, having previously ruled out such arrangements. If such an eventuality materialises, it will have a significant impact on the dynamics of competition within the party system.

At the 2016 Dáil election, there were three new party competitors with roots in parliament (Murphy, 2016). First, Renua was formed by a number of former Fine Gael TDs who had left that party in 2013 over a bill that introduced a restricted form of abortion. Its three incumbent TDs all lost their seats in 2016. Second, the Social Democrats were established in 2015 by three independent TDs, two of whom had a history of association with left-wing parties. All three comfortably held their seats in 2016, but they failed to have any other of their candidates elected, and one of the party's three co-leaders left the party later that year, before joining Fianna Fáil in 2017. Third, Anti-Austerity Alliance–People Before Profit came within one seat of Labour in 2016. As its name suggests, this was an alliance between two different groups, created for electoral purposes in 2015, and it mobilised on a programme of democratic socialism. The two individual components of the party emerged from the Socialist Party (which campaigned as the Anti-Austerity Alliance, before adopting the label 'Solidarity' in 2017) and the Socialist Workers' Party respectively. It is noticeable that none of the three new parties at the 2016 election was entirely new in the sense of having no associations with previously existing parties. In addition, all three emerged from within parliament, indicating how difficult it is for new parties to form without the advantages and resources brought by incumbency.

One notable absence from the contemporary Irish party stage is a party of the radical right (McDonnell, 2008). Although some have argued that Sinn Féin is, in certain respects, an Irish variant of such movements (O'Malley, 2008), it lacks an anti-immigrant appeal, which is a core message for many populist parties, and its programme is distinctly left-leaning. One possible manifestation of populism in Ireland comes in the form of independent politicians, who lie outside the party system. Ireland is exceptional in still having independents in its national parliament, long after they have disappeared from most other jurisdictions. Indeed, the numbers of independents elected to the Dáil in recent years have been greater than the combined number elected to other western parliaments. At the first four Dáil elections of the twenty-first century, a mean of 14 independents was elected, comprising almost 10 per cent of parliamentary representation.

One reason why few independents run for political office at the national level in other countries, and even fewer win seats, is that under the list electoral systems used by most European countries, independent candidacies are made very difficult, if not impossible. In addition, in many countries political competition and culture is centred on parties, with the consequence that many voters have little awareness of the local candidates. In contrast, as discussed in Chapter 4, Ireland uses a highly candidate-centred electoral system, proportional

Box 5.1 The role of independents

Between 1992 and 2016 the numbers of independents elected to the Dáil increased at every election bar one, to the point that following the 2016 election, only Fine Gael and Fianna Fáil had a stronger collective presence in the Dáil. The presence of independents has provoked some normative debate about their contribution, particularly in a parliamentary democracy, given the widespread assumption that disciplined parties are essential to its functioning and effectiveness (Weeks, 2016: 218–23).

Those critical of independents argue that:

- They are populist free-riders, who oppose everything and avoid the responsibility of governing.
- They cause instability because of their failure to follow a whip. This is especially to the fore when a minority government is dependent on independents' support for survival. Such independents can prioritise local over national concerns, undermining the effectiveness of the government and the interests of society as a whole.
- They demand patronage, or 'pork-barrel' constituency projects, in return for their support. This skews the allocation of national resources, without regard to priorities and needs. This can also affect the coherence of national programmes if independents make demands that run contrary to the tenet of such policies.
- This patronage tends to come in the form of secret deals between the party leaders and the independents. The details of such deals are often not even made known to cabinet, let alone to parliament. Governments use public money to buy an independent's vote, the cost of which is unknown, making such arrangements neither accountable nor transparent.

Those supportive of independents say that:

- In most cases where independents' votes are needed by minority administrations, they provide consistent support in the Dáil. The mean length of such governments is almost three years, slightly less than majority administrations, but not short by comparative standards.
- Free of the shackles of a whip, independents are free to speak their own mind, and are not simply voting fodder. This also makes parties and governments more responsive to parliament.
- Independents' seeking of largesse for their constituencies means they are responsive to the demands of their constituents, and are replicating the behaviour of most TDs. The amount of largesse independents receive is also most likely exaggerated, and can often pale into insignificance compared with the amounts that government ministers attract for their local constituency.
- Independents are not the only individuals in politics to negotiate secret deals, as it is never known what rebellious TDs demand from their leaders in return for their support. The secretive nature of these arrangements ensures that governments can limit what they grant independents. In contrast, when such deals are published, as was the case for the 'Gregory Deal', negotiated by independent Tony Gregory in 1982, they may disclose a large amount of information. At the time, this was estimated to cost more than £200 million, most of which was not delivered, as the government lasted just nine months.

representation by the single transferable vote (PR-STV). Combined with a political culture, described in Chapter 6, where voters' top priority at elections in Ireland has been to choose a candidate to look after the needs of the local constituency, this creates conditions conducive to the emergence and election of independents.

Another factor in the success of independents is their ability to achieve relevance via their involvement in the formation and maintenance of minority governments. Approximately 40 per cent of governments since the foundation of the state have relied on the support of independents in the Dáil, with the price of their support tending to be patronage-type arrangements for their respective constituencies (see Box 5.1). Independents achieved a different kind of relevance in 2016, as they were directly involved in the formation of a government (O'Malley, 2016), with three independents being appointed to cabinet in a Fine Gael-led minority administration, and a further three being given junior ministerial posts (for more on independents see Weeks, 2009, 2011, 2014, 2015a, 2016, 2017).

Classification and evolution of the party system

Political scientists often classify party systems, both in order to explain party behaviour and to provide a simplified method of explaining a complex model (Ware, 1995: 148); such classification is also useful in understanding the place of the party system in the wider comparative context. One common basis of classification is the sociological approach, pioneered by Lipset and Rokkan in the 1960s, according to which the number of parties and the nature of competition in Europe was determined by two revolutions. The first concerned the formation of the modern nation-state, and centred on battles between different groups for control of the state apparatus, while the second was the industrial revolution. Most party systems in Europe are structured around cleavages emanating from these revolutions, with the four main conflicts being between owner and worker, church and state, urban and rural areas, and centre and periphery interests (Lipset and Rokkan, 1967).

This approach does not explain the Irish party system, however, as none of these social conflicts has been particularly manifest in Ireland, primarily due to the absence of the aforementioned revolutions. Instead, the two main parties, as has been outlined, stem from a civil war fought within a nationalist power bloc. The only comparable case in Europe is in Finland, where a party system also evolved from a civil war that followed a conflict with a powerful imperial neighbour. The Finnish experience, however, had a strong class dimension, which was absent in the Irish case (Coakley, 1987). Critics of the sociological approach have argued that it misdirects the nature of the relationship between parties and identities (Boix, 2009: 503). They have argued that it is, rather, political elites who shape the interests of voters, evidence of which can be found in the Irish experience. There were few, if any, socio-economic divisions in the first and second Dála, but the split that ensued was created by elites, and persists to the present day. This explains why commentators often speak, usually disparagingly, of 'civil war politics' to explain the nature of political competition in Ireland, even though memories of the conflict have long since faded.

While these unique origins might explain why the Irish party system is seen as exceptional, its distinctiveness lies only in the nature of the conflict. The idea that early patterns of party competition are frozen into place around the key cleavages at the time of the introduction of the mass suffrage, and may well remain in place long after the conflict has abated, is not an experience exclusive to Ireland. The social cleavages identified by Lipset and Rokkan had the same freezing effect on party systems in western Europe. The relevance of this model to the Irish party system has been the source of some dispute, with Coakley (2004) arguing that the patterns of evolution of the Irish party system have more in common with central and eastern Europe than with western Europe.

Another approach is to focus on the number of parties. This is important to the extent that it indicates the level of fragmentation of power, and also affects the interaction between the parties. This approach entails more than simply counting the number of parties contesting elections, or even those with elected representatives; we also need to take account of their size, 'relevance' (Sartori, 1976: 121–3), and the nature of competition between the parties (for some classifications see O'Leary, 1979; Mair, 1979). One means of doing so involves counting the 'effective number' of parties, which considers parties' relative size and strength. This is not a proxy for the number of parties, but rather indicates the level of fragmentation. As is evident in Figure 5.2, the effective number of parties has varied considerably, being higher in the early years of the state, before declining, apart from an interrupted period of further fragmentation in the 1940s, up until the 1980s. Since this time, the figure has steadily increased; by 2016 it was more than double its level in 1982.

A more systemic approach takes into account this level of fragmentation, but also the nature and direction of competition between the parties. Party systems can range from two-partism where there is low party fragmentation and narrow ideological distance between parties, to polarised multipartism where fragmentation is high between parties, and these are ideologically far apart. While a two-party system is a feature of Anglophone democracies, the introduction of proportional representation proved an obstacle to its emergence in Ireland.

In the 1930s, the decline in the effective number of parties and the entry of Fianna Fáil into office, plus the subsequent consolidation of its power, marked the emergence of what Sartori (1976: 125, 198) labels a predominant party system. Fianna Fáil was in government for 35 of the 41 years between 1932 and 1973, with two spells of 16 uninterrupted years in

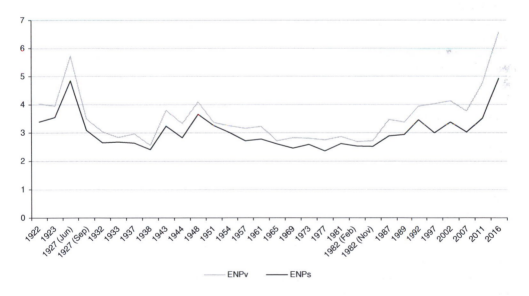

Figure 5.2 Effective number of parties in Ireland, 1922–2016

Source: Gallagher, Michael, 2017. Election indices dataset at www.tcd.ie/Political_Science/staff/michael_gallagher/ElSystems/index.php, accessed 6 December 2016.

Note: ENPv denotes the effective number of parties at the electoral level, ENPs at the parliamentary level.

office (1932–48 and 1957–73). The party was not dominant in the sense that it regularly won a majority of seats (it did so at only six Dáil elections). However, it apparently saw itself, and behaved, as a party in such a position, with Chubb (1992: 95) labelling it an example of, in Duverger's phrase, a *parti à vocation majoritaire*. The dominance of a party derives also from its location within the system, and often from its ability to play one side of the system off against another. Following its accession to power in 1932, for example, Fianna Fáil began to consolidate its pre-eminent position, in particular by moderating its radical vestiges to avoid alienating middle-class voters. Having built up a substantial plurality, if not a majority, of support within most social strata by the 1940s, Fianna Fáil was consequently able to present itself as the party of Ireland.

There were a number of challenges to Fianna Fáil's dominance, first in the 1940s and 1950s, when an increase in the effective number of parties signalled a potential fragmentation of the party system. New parties in the form of Clann na Poblachta and Clann na Talmhan appeared, and these pooled their resources to form an inter-party government in 1948. Unlike the 1920s, when the pluralism was of a polarised fashion, this was a more moderate format, as none of these parties wanted to overthrow the system. Within ten years, this potential fragmentation had dissipated, following which a two-and-a-half party system of Fianna Fáil, Fine Gael and Labour emerged. For almost three decades, the three parties together won nearly all of the seats at Dáil elections, with government alternating between Fianna Fáil and coalitions of Fine Gael and Labour. This pattern prevailed until the 1980s, when new parties in the form of the Greens, the Workers' Party and, most significantly, the Progressive Democrats emerged. They all constituted variants of party families that were already present in Europe, and signalled a shift in competition from two-and-a-half party to a multi-party system, both of which suggested a move towards a more European model. A further shift in this direction came with Fianna Fáil's reluctant embrace of the principle of coalition government in 1989. Having previously refused to contemplate taking part in any such arrangement, it entered a government with the Progressive Democrats, a party formed in 1985 by, amongst others, a number of former senior Fianna Fáil figures, including its first two leaders, Desmond O'Malley and Mary Harney. While this new strategy meant that Fianna Fáil was just another party, it also ensured that the party could maintain its dominance even with declining levels of support. It remained in office for the next 22 years, apart from a short-lived hiatus between 1994 and 1997, forming governments with Labour (in 1993), the Progressive Democrats (in 1989, 1997, 2002 and 2007), the Greens (in 2007), and with the assistance of some independent TDs (in 1989, 1997 and 2007).

The changing party system?

Writing over thirty years ago, Mair wrote of the Irish party system that 'the most compelling picture is one of increasingly precarious parties competing for an increasingly pragmatic and instrumental electorate, with their most striking characteristic being their sheer vulnerability' (1987: 228). Little seems to have changed since then to make parties seem any less precarious, and, if anything, their vulnerability has only increased. The Progressive Democrats, who threatened to break the mould at the time of Mair's writing, subsequently folded, while combined support for the two traditional main parties fell below 50 per cent for the first time in 2016. Mair also noted that the process of change he was describing in the 1980s was not a new experience for the Irish party system. It has always been in a state of transformation and evolution, adapting to a changing environment and electorate. What has distinguished the most recent mode of party system change, however, has been the level of convergence by the parties. What began in the 1980s accelerated during the 'celtic tiger' years, as parties battled for the median voter, a phenomenon particularly acute at the 2007 Dáil election, when even parties of the left, specifically Labour and Sinn Féin, advocated tax cuts to compete with, rather than to challenge, a centre-right neo-liberal consensus.

The greatest threat to the party system came with the economic recession of 2008–13 that threatened to shatter this consensus. The most dramatic consequence was the collapse in support for Fianna Fáil in 2011. While this earthquake threatened to tear down the party system, this instead remained standing as voters initially preferred to switch to the traditional opposition – Fine Gael and Labour – rather than to any new parties. The most significant feature of this era of party system change has been the increased level of volatility of the Irish voter, with 2011 the third most volatile parliamentary election in postwar western Europe, and 2016 the eighth most volatile (Farrell and Suiter, 2016: 279). The increasing fragmentation, as captured by the increase in the effective number of parties, suggests what has been called a 'Balkanisation' of the party system (Gallagher, 2016: 126). The primary beneficiaries of this tumult have been forces outside the party system, however, with increasing numbers of independents elected, as already noted. The fact that the root cause of this turmoil was an economic crisis, rather than any fundamental shift in alignments, suggests that it might be premature to speak of significant and durable change in the party system. The success of non-aligned candidates over that of new parties also suggests that the roots of change might not run as deep as might have been imagined. Party voters may have switched to independents as a protest, but they have not yet crossed the Rubicon by transferring their partisan allegiance to new parties. Granted, we are likely to continue to see significant electoral shocks of the sort that befell Fianna Fáil in 2011 and Labour in 2016, but to date this has remained within the confines of an established coterie.

Party organisation

Up to this point, we have looked at inter-party behaviour, but of equal significance are intra-party dynamics, which can have a strong bearing on how parties interact with each other. Historically, internal party machinations have been shrouded in mystery, with parties reluctant to disclose to the outside world anything more than is necessary. Parties were able to maintain this secret garden because they were private organisations. However, as they have moved closer to the state, in what has been termed a 'cartelisation' fashion (Katz and Mair 1995), parties have had to open up, which allows us to peer into their organisations and their activities.

Types of party organisation

The comparative literature distinguishes between different 'ideal types' of party organisation. One of the earliest to emerge was the cadre party, formed in nineteenth-century parliaments by political elites, whose 'members' were personal supporters of particular parliamentarians, rather than card-carrying adherents of the party itself. These were followed in the early twentieth century by mass parties, which began life as extra-parliamentary organisations, with an emphasis on a strong grass-roots network. As a party formed in parliament, Cumann na nGaedheal displayed some of the features common to a cadre party (Mair, 1987: 114). Centred on its local notables and formed from the top down (Meehan, 2010: 14–15), the party's TDs were loath to participate in grass-roots canvassing, were opposed to the notion of mass membership, and had a generally disdainful attitude to party politics (Regan, 2001: 129–44; Gallagher and Marsh, 2002: 41–55). Instead, Cumann na nGaedheal preferred to rely on the strength of its 'moral superiority' rather than its party structure (Dunphy, 1995: 83). This pattern of behaviour is in line with a theory propounded by Maurice Duverger (1956), an early scholar of the subject, that parties formed within parliament tend to be less centralised, coherent and disciplined than those formed outside parliament.

Although it can be argued that Fianna Fáil was also initially formed in a top-down manner by the actions of an elected elite, its greater emphasis on a strong extra-parliamentary organisation can still be seen as broadly in line with what Duverger predicted. For example, Sinn Féin's years in abstentionist isolation convinced its leader, Éamon de Valera, of the necessity of being responsive to public opinion and having a strong organisation (Garvin, 1981: 157). The first years of Fianna Fáil's existence were spent building up the party's grass roots, using the rural networks of the old IRA. This helped to establish an extensive network of resources, in respect of both personnel and funding, that the party could draw on at election time, and which provided it with a considerable advantage (for a general discussion on Fianna Fáil's foundations see Whelan, 2011: 17–30). While across Europe the earliest mass parties tended to originate on the left, Fianna Fáil was perhaps the closest equivalent to such a model in the Irish case, although in time all parties adopted elements of the mass party structure. Some have argued that Fianna Fáil has demonstrated features more associated with the cartel model of party organisation (Bolleyer, 2009), one that relies on close links to the state to maintain a position of dominance. Such features include a dependency on state resources to maintain the party's dominance, permeable organisational boundaries, and a flexible and strategic recruitment policy regarding candidate selection. Following the electoral shock of 2011, however, the party embraced characteristics more associated with traditional mass party structures, such as a more centralised party organisation, a fee-paying membership and greater extra-parliamentary structures (Bolleyer and Weeks, 2017). Since the models of party organisation are ideal types, it is not surprising that Irish parties do not correspond neatly with specific categories, although they have exhibited characteristics of most party models, including the electoral–professional party (in that they function to maximise electoral gain) and the franchise party, in which local entrepreneurs have a high degree of autonomy (McGraw, 2015: 172).

Party structure

The basic unit of an Irish party is the local branch, termed a *cumann* in Fianna Fáil and Sinn Féin. Usually, there are a number of these units per constituency, though in the Greens, the lowest level of organisation is a constituency-based body, sometimes subdivided into local groups. While branch size varies, each party requires a formal minimum membership (ten for Fianna Fáil, nine for Fine Gael, and five for Sinn Féin and the Greens while Labour stipulates ten for urban areas and five for a rural branch). These branches are responsible for sending delegates to constituency councils, national conferences, and for election to national executives. The supreme policy-making body within all the parties is the *ard-fheis* (so called in Fianna Fáil, Fine Gael and Sinn Féin) or national conference, which comprises delegates from each local branch, elected representatives and party officials. At the national conferences, party officers are elected, motions are discussed and party policy is formally agreed on. While this suggests an image of grass-roots democracy in action, much of what goes on at national conferences consists of the party hierarchy paying lip-service to taking on board the views of its members.

In practice, national conferences are little more than social rallies for the party faithful. They help to maintain the faith and commitment of the rank and file, and allow the party to demonstrate unity and enthusiasm to the outside world. Policy is typically made in a far more exclusive setting; where possible, the party executive prefers to keep controversial issues off the conference agenda. Because power tends to be decentralised to a greater extent within smaller parties, such as the Greens, and because of a greater commitment to internal party democracy, their conferences can sometimes have a greater policy impact.

Between one national conference and the next, management of the party rests in the hands of an executive committee (variously called, e.g. *ard chomhairle* in Fianna Fáil and Sinn Féin, and executive council in Fine Gael), comprising officials elected by delegates at a national conference, some *ex officio* posts and, to afford the parliamentary party a level of influence, Oireachtas members. This committee liaises with both the party front bench and its central headquarters to guide the running of the party. Historically, central office had a limited role vis-à-vis the branches of the party. TDs and councillors treated their localities as personal fiefdoms, controlling the branch network and limiting the flow of information to party head-quarters. Consequently, central office knew little about the grass roots of the party, limiting its ability to co-ordinate party matters.

This image of fragmented and inefficient party organisations was borne out by many internal party investigations. One such report within Fianna Fáil, written in 2005 by its dep-uty leader Brian Cowen, portrayed the party as a rural, elderly and inactive organisation. Almost half of its active members were over 55 years of age, one quarter of its branches were inactive, and half of them met once a year or less. Almost 60 per cent of branches had attracted no new members in three years, with total party membership being overestimated by as much as 200 per cent (Fianna Fáil, 2005). It is unlikely that this experience was unique to Fianna Fáil (see Gallagher and Marsh, 2002: 56–114, on a similar experience in Fine Gael). All parties, aided by the availability of public funding, have made greater efforts in recent years to centralise their organisations. This necessitated giving headquarters an increasingly important role in the management of parties, while working in tandem with the party leader. Central office is headed by a general secretary, who is the equivalent of the party's chief operating officer and works closely with the party leader in the running of the organisation. General secretaries tend to survive longer in their posts than party leaders and are powerful figures within the organisation, a position enhanced by their usually close relationship with leaders. They are responsible for executing the plans of the party and the leader, and are *de facto* the eyes and ears of the latter within the party machine.

Party membership

An aspect in which Irish parties historically lacked mass party characteristics was in the looseness of their membership boundaries. Branches alone were responsible for recruiting and registering members, a task they were not very enamoured with, except when selection conventions came around.

Since it was not until the professionalisation of parties in the 1970s that the first serious attempts were made to register members, data on party membership is available only for the period since then. Even then, the figures were probably exaggerated, both because of a loose-ness as to the definition of membership, and because greater numbers were thought to lend a sense of legitimacy. Consequently, the numbers presented in Table 5.1 need to be treated with a little scepticism. Nevertheless, they indicate a significant decline in party membership that, until recently, was consistent with the experience of other countries. So, while total party membership in Ireland in 1985 was estimated at 130,000 or 5 per cent of the electorate, in 2014 it was just under 70,000 or approximately 2 per cent of the electorate. Attempts have

Table 5.1 Party membership in Ireland, 1985–2014

Year	Fianna Fáil	Fine Gael	Labour	Progressive Democrats	Greens	Workers' Party	Sinn Féin	Democratic Left	Total
1985	80,000	40,000	6,200			3,000			129,200
1990	75,000	20,000	7,500	6,000	1,200	2,800	3,000		115,500
1995	70,000	20,000	7,000	8,000	1,000	800	3,000	1,400	111,200
2000	50,000	23,500	5,719	2,800					82,019
2004	55,000	34,219							89,219
2008	65,000	35,000	7,500	4,000	2,000		5,000		118,500
2014	20,000	35,000	5,606		800		8,054		69,460

Source: Data yearbooks of *Irish Political Studies* and previous editions of *Politics in the Republic of Ireland*.

Note: Figures are provided at five yearly intervals where possible.

been made to arrest this decline in recent years via a series of reforms in several parties to give grass-roots members some tangible powers in internal decision-making, although as yet it is difficult to determine the consequences of this greater level of inclusivity.

It is the norm within most parties across Europe that grass-roots members have little say in the development of a party's policy despite, or perhaps because of, their reputation for being more ideological than the political elites. While the Irish case does not deviate greatly from this pattern, the level of input afforded to party members varies according to party ideology, party size, and the perceived value of such a process. Not surprisingly, the Greens' emphasis on grass-roots democracy results in their adopting a more inclusive approach, and local branches are afforded opportunities to promote policies and have them debated at national conferences. Given the logistics that would be involved in such a process, neither Fianna Fáil nor Fine Gael extends similar opportunities to its members to set the policy agenda of the party. However, Fianna Fáil, in 2013, gave its members the authority to decide on whether the party should enter a coalition government, replicating a practice already in place within Labour and the Greens, and imitated by newly formed parties, including Solidarity–People Before Profit and the Social Democrats.

It is debatable to what extent this power results in members genuinely dictating coalition policy to their parliamentary party, or whether in reality the grass-roots can be 'guided' in a particular direction by the parliamentarians. Fianna Fáil TDs claimed that party members' opposition to government with Fine Gael (as expressed in a non-binding motion passed at the party's *ard-fheis* in 2015) was a key factor in their refusing overtures to form a grand coalition in 2016 (Bolleyer and Weeks, 2017: 14). However, had the party leadership really wanted to take part in such a government, it seems likely that it would have been able to convince the grass roots of the merits of such an arrangement (O'Malley, 2016: 258). Nevertheless, the very fact that members had a role to play at all was part of a wide range of significant reforms that have taken place within parties since the 1990s. Their aims were to arrest declining membership numbers by giving members a meaningful role, and also to revamp party structures that were seen as outdated and not conducive to the recruitment of high-quality candidates. The image of parties was one of cliques where members needed to be in the organisation for a long time to have influence, and where access to networks of influence was limited to a select few (Hughes *et al.*, 2007: 281). With the aid of public funding, some of the parties sought to improve this image by creating policy forums, providing different forms of membership, encouraging a higher rate of turnover within the officer posts and promoting younger candidates. One of the more substantial reforms concerned handing the membership some real powers, specifically in the processes of selecting candidates for public office and electing the party leader.

Candidates are selected at local conventions organised on a constituency basis. They need to be ratified by a national executive, which reserves the right to veto any local choice and/ or to add a name or names to the party ticket. Adding a name happens much more frequently than the vetoing of a locally selected individual. In the past, conventions were organised on a delegate basis, with each party branch represented by a number of members. This system was open to abuse, as incumbents in Fianna Fáil and Fine Gael in particular were sometimes guilty of securing the selection of weak running-mates to minimise the threat to their re-selection. In addition, 'ghost' or paper branches proliferated, guaranteeing a ready-made bloc of votes at conventions. This system negated genuine intra-party competition and also alien-ated ambitious party members. Consequently, reforms have taken place in all parties, in line with the comparative experience (Cross and Pilet, 2015), to open up the selection process and extend the franchise to all members at conventions.

At the same time, this level of democratisation paradoxically took place alongside an aforementioned greater level of centralisation within party organisations, as there has been an increasingly influential role for central party executives. Fianna Fáil took this process of centralisation furthest, with the establishment of a 'central constituencies committee' to manage candidate selection. This level of centralisation became particularly evident with the introduction of candidate gender quotas for the 2016 Dáil election, when parties had to field tickets of at least 30 per cent of both genders or face losing half of their state funding (see pp. 221–2 below). Fifteen of Fine Gael's 89 candidates and 16 of Fianna Fáil's 71 were added to the ticket by the party's national constituency committee (Reidy, 2016). In addition, constituencies were sometimes carved up into geographically defined sub-units for selection conventions, resulting in uncontested nominations that deprived members of an opportunity to exercise their franchise (Bolleyer and Weeks, 2017: 15).

Party leaders

Party leaders are generally quite powerful figures, especially within Fianna Fáil and Fine Gael, where such leaders are potential Taoisigh. In the past, most parties allowed only par-liamentarians to play a direct role in the election of a leader. The rationale was that a leader worked closely with, and needed to have the confidence of, his or her parliamentary party. In addition, only those working within the political system understood what qualities party leaders needed, and consequently TDs (and possibly senators and MEPs as well) were best placed to wield this power of selection.

However, just as with candidate selection, the leadership election process has become more inclusive. Fine Gael adopted an electoral college format in 2004 under which the par-liamentary party has 65 per cent of the votes, local representatives (councillors and Údarás na Gaeltachta members) 10 per cent, and the party membership 25 per cent. This was first used in June 2017, when Leo Varadkar's strong lead among parliamentarians (he won 51 of the 73 votes) and comfortable lead among the local representatives outweighed the two-to-one vic-tory of his only rival Simon Coveney among the members, giving Varadkar an overall major-ity of 60 per cent of the electoral college vote to Coveney's 40 per cent. Fianna Fáil adopted a similar model in 2015, although its voting weights are more favourable to party members, who comprise 45 per cent of the college, TDs make up 40 per cent, with senators, MEPs, local councillors and members of the *ard chomhairle* comprising the remaining 15 per cent.

Both Labour and the Greens have a wider franchise still, having adopted the OMOV (one member one vote) system. Although Labour first adopted these rules in 1989, it was not until 2002, with the election of Pat Rabbitte, that this mechanism was first activated. While the Greens avoided having a single leader for the first two decades of their existence, they bowed to the inevitable in 2001, when Trevor Sargent was elected to this position. The Social Democrats allow for a co-leadership, with OMOV in place for leadership contests, while the Solidarity–People Before Profit Alliance eschews the principle of party leadership. Alone amongst the parties, Sinn Féin has retained the delegate-based method to pick its leader, who is chosen (or ratified) at each annual *ard-fheis*. As with candidate selection, there are limits to the extent to which the process of leadership election has been democratised. Candidacies are usually restricted to TDs, who need the support of at least one other member of the parliamentary party. Nominations in Fianna Fáil require the support of five TDs, and in Fine Gael of 10 per cent of the parliamentary party. As for Labour, although Alan Kelly wanted to challenge Brendan Howlin for the leadership in 2016, he was unable to attract a nomination from another TD, meaning that Howlin was elected unopposed without the need for a ballot of the party membership.

The increased personalisation of politics has given party leaders in most countries more power, and Ireland is no exception to this rule. Party leaders constitute the face of the party, which is particularly evident during election campaigns when posters of party leaders bedeck telegraph poles and billboards nationwide. In the past, Fianna Fáil used slogans such as 'Let's back Jack [Lynch]' and had a campaign anthem for the 1981 election that asked voters to 'arise and follow Charlie [Haughey]'. Likewise, the Progressive Democrats tried to convince voters that 'Dessie can do it', while in 2011, and in less subtle fashion, Labour talked of 'Gilmore for Taoiseach'. The greater role of the media and its focus on leaders has only increased the importance of the latter, one example of which is the apparent significance of televised leaders' debates during Dáil election campaigns (see Chapter 12, pp. 311–13). Initially restricted to alternative Taoisigh, in the form of Fianna Fáil and Fine Gael leaders, all parties with parliamentary representation featured in separate debates during the 2016 campaign.

Parliamentary parties

In most parties the precise role of the parliamentary party group (PPG) is not defined by the party constitution. The parliamentary parties of Fine Gael, Fianna Fáil and Labour comprise their members of the Dáil, Seanad and the European Parliament. Sinn Féin's internal rules make no reference to a parliamentary party, but dictate that parliamentary members co-ordinate their work under the direction of the party's *ard chomhairle*. Likewise, the Green Party's PPG comprises those elected north and south of the border (TDs, Senators, MEPs, members of the Northern Ireland Assembly and, should it arise, members of the UK House of Commons). Although the rules of most parties give extra-parliamentary organisations, such as a national executive or party conference, some authority over the parliamentary party, this is rarely realised in practice. The PPG tends to have a degree of autonomy within the organisation provided it does not deviate too far from the general preferences of the party. Parliamentary parties have lost their former complete control over the election of the party leader, as mentioned above, though the parliamentarians retain a dominant role in Fianna Fáil and Fine Gael and in most parties the leader must be a TD and requires supporting nominations from a number of parliamentarians to be a candidate in a leadership election. In most cases, removing a party leader is also at the behest of the PPG.

PPGs tend to be fairly unitary organisations, as evidenced by their behaviour in parliament. Party bloc voting across all the parties is the norm; it is a rare event for TDs to vote against the party whip. There were 17 cases of such breaches of unity between 1993 and 2010, with eight of these coming in the crisis-hit Dáil of 2007–11 (Gallagher, 2010: 137). The consequence of such defections is usually automatic expulsion from the parliamentary party, and only one of the aforementioned eight expelled in the 2007–10 period was re-admitted. One reason why rebellions are so infrequent is the absence of factions within Irish parties. Although parliamentary parties have been split in the past, most notably Fianna Fáil under the leadership of Charles Haughey in the 1980s, there is no sense of an organisational basis to such divisions, which acts as a deterrent to their manifestation. Those contemplating a rebellion know they will be on their own. TDs are also aware that the benefits of voting the party line far outweigh any advantage to be had from not doing so. Almost uniquely in Europe, ministers in Ireland are recruited pretty much exclusively from the lower house of parliament (see Chapter 10). Most TDs have ministerial ambitions and know that party loyalty is necessary to curry favour with the party leadership. Consequently, the few who rebel tend to be those who feel they have little prospect of promotion to higher office.

Given the high levels of cohesion within PPGs, it is sometimes assumed that ordinary members of parliament have little power vis-à-vis the party leadership. Certainly, when it comes to making policy, it is generally the party's front bench that takes responsibility, with little input from backbenchers. This applies to parties both in government and in opposition. When a party is not in government, members of its front bench are usually allocated particular government ministries to 'shadow' and are the party's mouthpiece on these areas. In effect, they are the respective ministers' rivals, collectively constituting the alternative government. In part owing to the oligarchic nature of party organisations, and in part due to the lack of research facilities available to TDs, these spokespersons constitute the real policy-making body within the party. While weekly meetings of the parliamentary party can occasionally keep shadow cabinets in check, their activity tends to be of a reactive nature. When parties enter government, policy-making becomes even more centralised, at the level of individual ministers or the cabinet as a whole, marginalising the PPG further. This can lead to occasional stirrings, such as a so-called 'five-a-side-club' in Fine Gael of first-time TDs elected in 2011, who were unhappy with the party's direction in government.

Party finance

Political parties need money to operate. Where in previous decades they could rely on a core of faithful volunteers during election campaigns, such assistance is no longer enough. Fewer people are willing to participate in party activities, and campaigns are now almost semi-permanent in their nature and have taken on a higher degree of professionalisation, all of which demands more financial resources. The five general elections held in the 1980s were estimated to have cost Fianna Fáil almost IR£7.5 million, and Fine Gael close to IR£4 million, around €9.5 million and €5 respectively (Byrne, 2012: 193). Where parties got their money to pay these bills was always a mystery. Fundraising events, such as national church gate collections, raised impressive sums, but were still a long way short of what was required to run a modern party organisation. One source of finance was the state, with public funding in existence since the 1930s, in the form of parliamentary party 'leader's allowances' (in place since the Ministerial and Parliamentary Offices Act of 1938), travel and postal allowances, funding for registered parties with at least seven TDs, as well as financial support to hire research and administrative staff (Farrell, 1994: 235).

However, until the 1990s, state funding of political parties was relatively low by European standards. Members of the parliamentary party also contributed a portion of their salaries, but the reality was that parties and politicians had to look to private donors for assistance, and this raised questions about what was expected or promised in return for such donations. In the wake of revelations of corruption emanating from parliamentary tribunals of inquiry in the 1990s, a considerable package of reform legislation was introduced.[2] This was designed to provide greater transparency and accountability and to lessen parties' reliance on private donors. One element of this legislation involved increased levels of public subsidies for reg- istered parties winning over 2 per cent of first preference votes at the previous Dáil election.[3] The reform may also have been motivated by the strain placed on party resources by the increased professionalisation and centralisation of party organisations. Indeed, prior to the introduction of such legislation, political parties had accrued substantial debts, with Fianna Fáil reported to owe IR£3 million to the banks in 1993, Fine Gael IR£1 million, and Labour IR£120,000 (Laver and Marsh, 1993: 110).

The direct public funding of parties has two components. The first is a contribution to parties' annual running costs (excluding election expenses): each of the qualified parties receives a basic sum of approximately €130,000, plus a proportionate share (the basis for determining this being its first preference votes at the previous Dáil election) of a fund that in 2017 stood at almost €5 million; it increases annually in line with inflation. The second concerns the aforementioned allowances to party leaders, whose purpose is to cover expenses arising from parliamentary activities. The allowance for each leader is based on the size of their parliamentary party, and, to lessen the gap in resources between government and oppo- sition, these allowances are reduced by one-third for government parties, because of their access to civil service support. Since 2001, independent members of the Oireachtas have also been entitled to receive this payment, now known as a 'parliamentary activities allowance'. This amounts to €37,037 for independent TDs and €21,045 for independent senators.

The total sums payable to Irish parties from the public purse are considerable. They amounted in 2015 to almost €4.7 million to Fine Gael, €2.9 million to Labour, €2.7 million to Fianna Fáil, and €1.7 million to Sinn Féin; the smaller parties received €330,000 and the 27 independent members of the Oireachtas a combined total of €814,268 (Standards in Public Office Commission, 2016c). Parties with parliamentary representation also receive finan- cial support in the form of staff allocation, which amounted to almost €4 million in 2015. These figures do not include the partial reimbursement of general election expenses, up to a maximum of €8,700 for every candidate achieving a minimal degree of success.[4] After the 2016 Dáil election this amounted to €2.7 million. Combining all these figures, the sum total (not including all the additional allowances, such as free postage and free broadcasting time during elections) received by parties and candidates in 2015 was over €16 million of public money (see Table 5.2). This amounts to 84 per cent of parties' total income and indicates the extent to which they have become dependent on the state for survival. With regard to the income the parties generate themselves, approximately 40 per cent comes from fundraising and 40 per cent from membership subscriptions, with the remainder from donations and other sources.

Accompanying the increase in public subsidies has been the implementation of a greater regulation of campaign expenditure and political donations. Anonymous donations of more than €100 are prohibited, with candidates required to declare all donations in excess of €600, and parties to declare all donations in excess of €1,500. Moreover, candidates may not accept donations from any one individual in a single year exceeding €1,000, nor can candidates or parties accept donations from non-Irish citizens resident outside the island (not the state)

Table 5.2 Income of political parties in Ireland, 2015 (€)

Party	Exchequer funding	Leader's allowance	Parliamentary staff	Fundraising	Membership fees	Donations	Other income	Total
Fine Gael	2,281,055	2,394,394	1,332,000	736,635	429,190	31,277		7,204,551
Fianna Fáil	1,167,856	1,538,415	1,276,000	272,373	623,782	67,797	161,493	5,107,716
Labour	1,287,267	1,590,770	764,000		163,717	4,806	52,960	3,863,520
Sinn Féin	719,919	975,919	605,000	180,205	68,952	20,215	33,919	2,604,129
Renua Ireland				44,672	5,600	43,688		93,960
AAA–PBP		64,368	16,095		1,830		95	82,388
Green Party				25,982	11,235	33,420		70,637
Social Democrats						16,792		16,792
Total	5,456,097	6,563,866	3,993,095	1,259,867	1,304,306	217,995	248,467	19,043,693

Source: Standards in Public Office Commission (2017).

Note: Parliamentary staff refers to value of staff allocated to parties in parliament.

of Ireland. Donations from Irish citizens abroad, of whom there are many, especially in the USA, are permitted. This regulation has increased the element of transparency, albeit from a very low base. Irish parties do not attract a great deal of donations from corporate and business interests. Fine Gael, for a short while in the 2000s, refused to accept corporate donations, while Labour has traditionally been reluctant to look to such sources. Labour has instead benefited from its ties to trade unions (comprising two-thirds of donations). Fianna Fáil and the Progressive Democrats, in office for much of the 'celtic tiger' economic boom, were far more welcoming to donations from business and industry, with 85 and 70 per cent respectively of their donations coming from such sources (McGraw, 2015: 183).

The smaller left-wing parties have followed a different path to source finance, instead looking to their elected representatives. Solidarity–PBP and Sinn Féin require their TDs to take only the equivalent of the industrial wage from their parliamentary salary, donating the rest to the national party organisation. Sinn Féin has the added advantage of being able to rely on donations from overseas, which are estimated to constitute the overwhelming majority of the party's total donations (McGraw, 2015: 182–5). In general, though, the degree of private donations to parties is now pretty low, amounting to just €173,000 in 2015 (Standards in Public Office Commission, 2016b). It may be that public funding has achieved its goal, in that parties no longer need to seek donations, or that donors seeking undue influence are put off by the increased regulation.

The restrictions on expenditure are, in theory, equally prohibitive. At general elections, candidates are limited to specific maximum expenditure during the election period of €30,150 in a three-seat constituency, €37,650 in a four-seater and €45,200 in a five-seat constituency. However, one significant caveat is the legal definition of such a period: from the dissolution of the Dáil until polling day, a period of 24 days in 2016. In total, €8.4m was declared in 2016, down by 10 per cent on the comparable figure for the 2011 election. Fine Gael spent €2.8 million, Fianna Fáil €1.7 million, independents €1.2 million, Labour €1.1 million, Sinn Féin €650,000, AAA–PBP €267,000, the Social Democrats €191,000 and the Greens €147,000 (Standards in Public Office Commission, 2016a). Outside of the formal campaign period, there are no restrictions on what selected or intending candidates may spend. With regard to what the parties spend the money on, Fine Gael, Fianna Fáil and Sinn Féin in 2015 each employed around 50 full-time staff, which cost the former two parties over €2.5 million each, but Sinn Féin just €1.2 million. Labour employed 31 staff, paying €1.7 million in salaries. Fianna Fáil, Labour and Sinn Féin in 2015 each spent over €1 million on administrative costs, approximately half the €2.4 million spent by Fine Gael.

Conclusion

This chapter has described the pattern of party competition in Ireland from its origins to the present day. It is a picture of stability and volatility. The party system seems stable in that it has been dominated by the same actors since the 1920s. Challenges to their omnipotence have come and gone, with the 'civil war parties' and Labour remaining at the heart of the Irish party system. Even the independents, who pose a challenge to the raison d'être of party politics, are not a new phenomenon, having been an ever-present in parliamentary life. The volatility constitutes the swings in these parties' electoral fortunes and the occasional emergence of new parties. The climate of the party system following the 2011 and 2016 general elections certainly leans towards volatility, as the system is still recovering from the shock meted out to Fianna Fáil in 2011. Without the dominance of this pillar, which had held the party system together, its foundations seemed less secure than in previous generations.

However, at both of these elections no new force rushed in to occupy the gap left by a much depleted Fianna Fáil. Certainly, Sinn Féin grew in strength, but in a piecemeal fashion. New parties entered the Dáil, but failed to grow beyond the sum of their original constituent components. In the meantime, Fianna Fáil, which fell to as low as 10 per cent in opinion polls after the 2011 election, slowly began to recover. The party more than doubled its seat return in 2016 (albeit still delivering the second worst election performance in the party's history), with opinion polls later that year indicating that it had overtaken Fine Gael to become the most popular party. The future of the party system remains uncertain, but given the ability of the established parties to fend off challenges in the past, it would be a brave punter who bets against their doing so again.

The workings of party organisations have also been examined in this chapter, and it is obvious that most are top-down structures where the elites control much of the agenda. It was shown that different forces appear to be at work within the parties, with the tension between democratisation and centralisation sometimes spilling over into the public sphere. In light of the aforementioned challenges to parties, internal reforms to give members a more meaningful role have taken place in recent years. In this context, change has been occurring not just between the parties, but also within them. Whatever happens to the parties and the party system, it is clear that political parties are central to the understanding of the workings of Irish democracy. Not only are parties shaped by their institutional and societal environment; they are also pragmatic independent actors, with an ability to shape the outcome and maintain their predominant role.

Notes

1   For a revealing analysis of these particular Irish problems within the comparative context of class mobilisation, and in particular for a comparison of the Irish and Finnish cases, see Bartolini (2000: 441–54).
2   These included the Electoral Act 1997 and the Electoral (Amendment) Acts of 1998, 2001 and 2002.
3   To be included on the Register of Political Parties, a party has to demonstrate that it possesses a formal structure (including a party constitution, an executive committee, and an annual general meeting) and at least 300 signed-up members.
4   That is, who was either elected, or whose votes exceeded one-quarter of a quota at some stage during the count.

References and further reading

Bartolini, Stefano, 2000. *The Political Mobilization of the European Left, 1860–1980.* Cambridge: Cambridge University Press.

Boix, Carles, 2009. 'The emergence of parties and party systems', in Carles Boix and Susan C. Stokes (eds), *The Oxford Handbook of Comparative Politics.* Oxford: Oxford University Press, pp. 499–521.

Bolleyer, Nicole. 2009. 'Inside the cartel party: party organisation in government and opposition', *Political Studies* 57:3, pp. 579–99.

Bolleyer, Nicole and Liam Weeks, 2017. 'From cartel party to traditional membership organisation: the organisational evolution of Fianna Fáil', *Irish Political Studies* 32:1, pp. 96–117.

Byrne, Elaine, 2012. *Political Corruption in Ireland 1922–2010: A Crooked Harp?* Manchester: Manchester University Press.

Carty, R. K., 1981. *Party and Parish Pump: Electoral Politics in Ireland.* Waterloo, Ontario: Wilfrid Laurier University Press.

Chubb, Basil, 1992. *The Government and Politics of Ireland*, 3rd ed. London: Longman.

Coakley, John, 1980. 'The significance of names: the evolution of party labels', *Études Irlandaises* 5, pp. 171–81.

Coakley, John, 1987. 'Political succession during the transition to independence: evidence from Europe', in Peter Calvert (ed.), *The Process of Political Succession.* London: Macmillan, pp. 59–79.

Coakley, John, 1994. 'The election that made the First Dáil', in Brian Farrell (ed.), *The Creation of the Dáil.* Dublin: Blackwater Press, pp. 31–46.

Coakley, John, 2004. 'Critical elections and the prehistory of the Irish party system', in Tom Garvin, Maurice Manning and Richard Sinnott (eds), *Dissecting Irish Politics: Essays in Honour of Brian Farrell.* Dublin: UCD Press, pp. 134–59.

Coakley, John, 2012. 'The rise and fall of minor parties in Ireland, 1922–2011', in Liam Weeks and Alistair Clark (eds), *Radical or Redundant? Minor Parties in Irish Politics.* Dublin: History Press, pp. 46–78.

Cross, William and Jean-Benoit Pilet (eds), 2015. *The Politics of Party Leadership: A Cross-National Perspective.* Oxford: Oxford University Press

Dunphy, Richard, 1995. *The Making of Fianna Fáil Power in Ireland 1923–1948.* Oxford: Clarendon Press.

Duverger, Maurice, 1956. *Political Parties: Their Organisation and Activity in the Modern State*, 3rd ed. London: Methuen.

Farrell, Brian, 1970. 'Labour and the Irish political party system: a suggested approach to analysis', *Economic and Social Review* 1:4, pp. 477–502.

Farrell, David M., 1994. 'Ireland: centralization, professionalization and competitive pressures', in Richard S. Katz and Peter Mair (eds), *How Parties Organise.* London: Sage, pp. 216–41.

Farrell, David M. and Jane Suiter, 2016. 'The election in context', in Michael Gallagher and Michael Marsh (eds), *How Ireland Voted 2016: The Election That Nobody Won.* Basingstoke: Palgrave Macmillan, pp. 277–92.

Fianna Fáil, 2005. *Report to the Ard Chomhairle: Organisation.* Dublin: Fianna Fáil.

Gallagher, Michael, 1982. *The Irish Labour Party in Transition, 1957–82.* Manchester: Manchester University Press.

Gallagher, Michael, 1985. *Political Parties in the Republic of Ireland.* Manchester: Manchester University Press.

Gallagher, Michael, 1990. 'The outcome', in Michael Gallagher and Richard Sinnott (eds), *How Ireland Voted 1989.* Galway: Centre for the Study of Irish Elections and PSAI Press, pp. 68–94.

Gallagher, Michael, 2010. 'Parliamentary parties and the party whips', in Muiris MacCarthaigh and Maurice Manning (eds), *The Houses of the Oireachtas: Parliament in Ireland.* Dublin: Institute of Public Administration, pp. 129–52.

Gallagher, Michael, 2016. 'The results analysed: the aftershocks continue', in Michael Gallagher and Michael Marsh (eds), *How Ireland Voted 2016: The Election That Nobody Won.* Basingstoke: Palgrave Macmillan, pp. 125–57.

Gallagher, Michael and Michael Marsh, 2002. *Days of Blue Loyalty: The Politics of Membership of the Fine Gael Party.* Dublin: PSAI Press.

Gallagher, Michael, Michael Laver and Peter Mair, 2011. *Representative Government in Modern Europe*, 5th ed. Maidenhead: McGraw-Hill.

Garvin, Tom, 1981. *The Evolution of Irish Nationalist Politics.* Dublin: Gill and Macmillan.

Hughes, Ian, Paula Clancy, Clodagh Harris and David Beetham, 2007. *Power to the People: Assessing Democracy in Ireland.* Dublin: Tasc at New Island.

Katz, Richard S. and Peter Mair, 1995. 'Changing models of party organisation and party democracy: the emergence of the cartel party', *Party Politics* 1:1, pp. 5–28.

Kirchheimer, Otto, 1966. 'The transformation of western European party systems', in Joseph LaPalombara and Myron Weiner (eds), *Political Parties and Political Development.* Princeton: Princeton University Press, pp. 177–200.

Laver, Michael and Michael Marsh, 1993. 'Parties and voters', in John Coakley and Michael Gallagher (eds), *Politics in the Republic of Ireland*, 2nd ed. Limerick: PSAI Press, pp. 104–26.

Lee, J. J., 1989. *Ireland 1912–1985: Politics and Society.* Cambridge: Cambridge University Press.

Lipset, Seymour M. and Stein Rokkan, 1967. 'Cleavage structures, party systems, and voter alignments: an introduction', in S. M. Lipset and Stein Rokkan (eds), *Party Systems and Voter Alignments*. New York: The Free Press, pp. 1–64.

McDonnell, Duncan, 2008. 'The Republic of Ireland: the dog that hasn't barked in the night?', in Daniele Albertazzi and Duncan McDonnell (eds), *Twenty-first Century Populism: The Spectre of Western European Democracy*. Basingstoke: Palgrave Macmillan, pp. 198–216.

McGraw, Seán, 2015. *How Parties Win: Shaping the Irish Political Arena*. Ann Arbor: University of Michigan Press.

Mair, Peter, 1979. 'The autonomy of the political: the development of the Irish party system', *Comparative Politics* 11:4, pp. 445–65.

Mair, Peter, 1987. *The Changing Irish Party System: Organisation, Ideology and Electoral Competition*. London: Frances Pinter.

Mair, Peter, 1992. 'Explaining the absence of class politics in Ireland', in J. H. Goldthorpe and C. T. Whelan (eds), *The Development of Industrial Society in Ireland*. Oxford: Oxford University Press, pp. 383–410.

Meehan, Ciara, 2010. *The Cosgrave Party: A History of Cumann na nGaedheal, 1923–33*. Dublin: Royal Irish Academy.

Moss, Warner, 1933. *Political Parties in the Irish Free State*. New York: Columbia University Press.

Murphy, Gary. 2016. 'The background to the election', in Michael Gallagher and Michael Marsh (eds), *How Ireland Voted 2016: The Election that Nobody Won*. Basingstoke: Palgrave Macmillan, pp. 1–26.

O'Leary, Cornelius. 1979. *Irish Elections 1918–1977: Parties, Voters and Proportional Representation*. Dublin: Gill and Macmillan.

O'Malley, Eoin, 2008. 'Why is there no radical right party in Ireland?', *West European Politics* 31:5, pp. 960–77.

O'Malley, Eoin, 2012. 'Wipeout! Does governing kill small parties in Ireland?', in Liam Weeks and Alistair Clark (eds), *Radical or Redundant? Minor Parties in Irish Politics*. Dublin: History Press, pp. 94–109.

O'Malley, Eoin, 2016. '70 days: government formation in 2016', in Michael Gallagher and Michael Marsh (eds), *How Ireland Voted 2016: The Election That Nobody Won*. Basingstoke: Palgrave Macmillan, pp. 255–76.

O'Malley, Eoin and Matthew Kerby, 2004. 'Chronicle of a death foretold? Understanding the decline of Fine Gael', *Irish Political Studies* 19:1, pp. 39–58.

O'Malley, Eoin and Seán McGraw, 2017. 'Fianna Fáil: the glue of ambiguity', *Irish Political Studies* 32:1, pp. 72–95.

Puirséil, Niamh, 2007. *The Irish Labour Party 1922–1973*. Dublin: UCD Press.

Regan, John M., 2001. *The Irish Counter-Revolution 1921–1936: Treatyite Politics and Settlement in Independent Ireland*. Dublin: Gill and Macmillan.

Reidy, Theresa, 2016. 'Candidate selection and the illusion of grass-roots democracy', in Michael Gallagher and Michael Marsh (eds.), *How Ireland Voted 2016: The Election That Nobody Won*. Basingstoke: Palgrave Macmillan, pp. 47–73.

Rumpf, Erhard and A. C. Hepburn, 1977. *Nationalism and Socialism in Twentieth-Century Ireland*. Liverpool: Liverpool University Press.

Sartori, Giovanni, 1976. *Parties and Party Systems: A Framework for Analysis*. Cambridge: Cambridge University Press.

Sinnott, Richard, 1984. 'Interpretations of the Irish party system', *European Journal of Political Research* 12:3, pp. 289–307.

Sinnott, Richard, 1995. *Irish Voters Decide: Voting Behaviour in Elections and Referendums since 1918*. Manchester: Manchester University Press.

Standards in Public Office Commission, 2016a. *Dáil General Election 26 February 2016*. Dublin: Standards in Public Office Commission; also available at http://www.sipo.gov.ie/.

Standards in Public Office Commission, 2016b. *Donations to Political Parties in 2015*. Dublin: Standards in Public Office Commission; also available at http://www.sipo.gov.ie/.

Standards in Public Office Commission, 2016c. *Exchequer Funding of Political Parties in 2015 under the Electoral Legislation*. Dublin: Standards in Public Office Commission; also available at http://www.sipo.gov.ie/.

Standards in Public Office Commission, 2017. *Political Parties' Statements of Accounts*. Dublin: Standards in Public Office Commission; also available at http://www.sipo.gov.ie/

von Beyme, Klaus, 1985. *Political Parties in Western Democracies*. Aldershot: Gower.

Ware, Alan, 1995. *Political Parties and Party Systems*. Oxford: Oxford University Press.

Weeks, Liam, 2009. 'We don't like (to) party: a typology of independents in Irish political life, 1922–2007', *Irish Political Studies* 24:1, pp. 1–27.

Weeks, Liam, 2011. 'Rage against the machine: who is the independent voter?', *Irish Political Studies* 26:1, pp. 19–43.

Weeks, Liam, 2014. 'Crashing the party: does STV help independents?', *Party Politics* 20, pp. 604–16.

Weeks, Liam, 2015a. 'Why are there independents in Ireland?', *Government and Opposition* 51:4, pp. 580–604.

Weeks, Liam, 2015b. 'Parliaments without parties', *Australasian Parliamentary Review* 30:1, pp. 61–71.

Weeks, Liam, 2016. 'Independents and the election: the party crashers', in Michael Gallagher and Michael Marsh (eds), *How Ireland Voted 2016: The Election That Nobody Won*. Basingstoke: Palgrave Macmillan, pp. 207–26.

Weeks, Liam, 2017. *Independents in Irish Party Democracy*. Manchester: Manchester University Press.

Weeks, Liam and Alistair Clark (eds), 2012. *Radical or Redundant? Minor Parties in Irish Politics*. Dublin: History Press.

Whelan, Noel, 2011. *Fianna Fáil: A Biography of the Party*. Dublin: Gill and Macmillan.

Whyte, John H., 1974. 'Ireland: politics without social bases', in Richard Rose (ed.), *Electoral Behavior: A Comparative Handbook*. New York: The Free Press pp. 619–51.

Websites

www.electionsireland.org
Contains details of election results dating back to 1922.

www.sipo.gov.ie/en/
Site of the Standards in Public Office Commission, with details about the funding of political parties.

Party websites:
www.fiannafail.ie/
www.finegael.ie/
www.sinnfein.ie/
www.labour.ie/
www.greenparty.ie/
www.socialdemocrats.ie
www.antiausterityalliance.ie
www.peoplebeforeprofit.ie

6   Voting behaviour

Kevin Cunningham and Michael Marsh

The previous two chapters on the electoral system and the party system provide an understanding of the context within which elections take place. We now place our focus directly on elections and voting behaviour. This chapter deals with the voters and examines some theories and evidence to help us understand their behaviour in elections.

We start by looking briefly at different types of evidence for why people vote as they do at general elections, and then move on to consider three major approaches to explaining voting behaviour: the social psychological approach, the sociological approach and a third set of approaches centred on issues. This is followed by a discussion of several more specific aspects of voting behaviour: the role of leaders and candidates, the characteristics of voting behaviour at other types of polls (such as local and European elections), and finally, a consideration of why many people do not vote at all.

Analysing voting behaviour

There are two major sources of evidence about electoral behaviour. The first comes from election results themselves. These can be analysed in a number of ways, for a number of purposes. If we are interested in how voters rate parties, we can learn much from the ways in which packages of votes are transferred between candidates (Gallagher, 1978). If we are interested in what makes for a successful candidate, we can examine the degree of success of different types of candidates, such as those with or without a background in local government (Marsh, 1987). If we want to know what sorts of people support each party, we can examine the social make-up of districts where a party does well and those where it does badly (Laver, 1986a). This last type of analysis is somewhat limited as we are analysing the relationship between data sets at a high level of aggregation. Electoral data is typically only available at a constituency level, so the validity of the analysis is dependent on a considerable degree of homogeneity within constituencies and high levels of heterogeneity across constituencies. Since areas as large as Dáil constituencies are inevitably not homogeneous, the conclusions that we draw can also suffer from what is called 'the ecological fallacy'. What is observed at an aggregate constituency level may not be the case at an individual level. For example, we may observe greater levels of anti-immigrant sentiment in constituencies where foreign-born migrants are more numerous, even though as individuals they are the least likely to hold such views. Informal 'tally' data collected by party workers at a lower polling district level can ameliorate this to some degree (early examples are Sacks, 1976: 145–60; and Parker, 1982; a recent example is Kavanagh, 2015). However, this data is not always complete nor always available.

The second major source of information comes from large-scale surveys. Most of these have been commercial. These typically ask few questions and are designed to provide headlines rather than analysis, but they have proved useful, particularly in establishing the social basis of party support (Laver, 1986b). The Eurobarometer series of polls carried out for the EU since the early 1970s has also provided insights into voting behaviour, but these are not designed specifically to answer questions about Irish voting behaviour and do not usually coincide with elections. Not until 2002 was funding available for a full-scale academic survey, the first Irish National Election Study (INES). This was designed to test the adequacy in an Irish context of a wide range of academic theories about voting (Marsh *et al.*, 2001). This post-election survey was supplemented by four more waves of surveys of the same respondents, the last after the 2007 election. There have also been further post-election surveys for the 2011 and 2016 general elections. This chapter is based largely on this data, which provides us with many opportunities for developing our knowledge of why Irish people vote as they do.[1]

Before going on to assess the value in an Irish context of general theories about voting behaviour, we may use these data to analyse stability and change in the political system and consider how this might relate to voting behaviour. While the party system remained remarkably stable over its first 90 years, the elections of 2011 and 2016 saw striking volatility, as measured by fluctuations in electoral support for the parties (see Chapter 5). In 24 consecutive elections between 1932 and 2007, Fianna Fáil was the largest party, receiving between 39 per cent and 52 per cent of the vote. But in 2011, support for the party fell to 17 per cent in an election ranked as the third most volatile in long established European democracies since 1945 – all the more noteworthy since voters migrated between existing parties rather than turning to any significant new party (Mair, 2011: 287–8). In the 2016 election, volatility fell, but only marginally so. This was still the second most volatile of all Irish elections and ranked as the eighth most volatile of all elections in western Europe since 1945 (Farrell and Suiter, 2016: 279–83). While the volatility is clear and unmistakeable, the changes in vote shares at an aggregate level may still mask the true nature of the underlying volatility of voting behaviour, especially where parties may draw support from different types of people at different times.

This collapse in support for government parties was all the more remarkable given that the period was marked by substantial economic recovery. It has been argued that the 2016 election offered evidence of a de-alignment in Irish politics, with voters abandoning long-term political affiliations (Marsh and McElroy, 2016: 179). Approximately 70 per cent of those supporting a party between 1997 and 2002 and between 2002 and 2007 gave their first preferences to the same party on both occasions (Garry *et al.*, 2003: 122–4; see also Marsh *et al.*, 2008: 15–6). However, since then the ability of political parties to retain support from one election to the next has fallen considerably, down to 54 per cent in 2007–11. The tremors of the 2011 election were still apparent in 2016, when just 51 per cent reported voting for the same party that they had voted for in 2011 (Marsh and McElroy, 2016: 160).

While the volatility of the 2011 and 2016 elections was considerable, the difference between the party system at the start and end of the 2007–16 period was not as drastic. The period 2007–16 saw both the rapid collapse and subsequent revival of Fianna Fáil and the equally dramatic expansion and subsequent collapse of the Labour party. While the shape of the party system changed at each election, 2016 saw a number of voters returning to the party they had voted for prior to the crisis. As shown in Table 6.1, 47 per cent of those who voted for a party in 2007 stayed with, or returned to, the same party in 2016.

However, even the low degree of stability in individual voting behaviour indicated here may be an overestimate. Most of our estimates are based on a comparison between how people say that they voted in the most recent election and their recall of how they had voted five years previously. There is a known propensity for people to report past behaviour in line with their present behaviour (Markus, 1986; Van Elsas *et al.*, 2013; Dassonneville and Hooghe, 2017), meaning that inter-election retention of party support is typically over-estimated. In

Table 6.1 Stability of the vote 2011–16 and 2007–16

Vote in 2016	First preference vote in 2011				First preference vote in 2007			
	Fianna Fáil	Fine Gael	Sinn Féin	Labour	Fianna Fáil	Fine Gael	Sinn Féin	Labour
Fianna Fáil	61	13	7	11	45	7	4	10
Fine Gael	13	52	2	8	18	58	4	11
Sinn Féin	4	4	73	13	6	7	79	14
Labour	3	7	0	30	6	8	0	26
Other	5	10	7	24	9	5	7	22
Independent	14	14	11	15	15	15	7	17

Source: Authors' analysis of RTE/INES Exit Poll 2016.

Note: Those who could not remember and those too young to vote in 2007 were excluded. Since the 2016 poll was an exit poll, by definition it did not include non-voters.

2006, only three out of every four of those saying that they voted for Fianna Fáil or Fine Gael in 2002 had reported doing so when first asked in 2002. The proportions were even lower for other parties.[2] In the context of the underlying uncertainties of this stability and change in Irish voting behaviour, this chapter seeks to explain why voters choose one party over another, and why voters who consider no alternative to 'their' party feel that way.

Explanations of voting choice

In this section, we will discuss three major approaches to explaining party choice (see Box 6.1) and start with an account that seems best suited to explain the stability of vote choice.

The social psychological model

The most popular explanation for aggregate stability across successive generations of elec-tors is that voters tend to stay with the same party, and furthermore that the pattern of voting for a particular party is itself transmitted through generations within families: people vote as their mothers and fathers voted. This idea echoes a common view about voting in Ireland, at least until very recently, which is that a large part of the electorate is essentially 'Fianna Fáil' or 'Fine Gael' and that the roots of such attachment lie in the family. The academic version of this was developed most clearly in the USA over half a century ago by Angus Campbell and his colleagues in *The American Voter* (Campbell *et al.*, 1960). The main elements of this thesis were that:

- Most voters have an enduring link with a particular party ('party identification');
- Typically, this is 'inherited', in the sense of being passed on through the family;
- It is further bolstered by the behaviour of voting for the same party in successive elections;
- Moreover, party identification tends to screen out negative messages or information about one's own party, further helping to reinforce a stable, positive view of that party.

Carty (1981: 78) argued that party identification provided the only plausible account of the stability of Irish party support. He was relying on opinion poll data from the 1960s, which showed a high level of party attachment in the electorate, but his argument could still have

Box 6.1 Role of social background, party and issues in different explanations of vote choice

Social Psychological: Enduring party loyalties are central to vote choice. These are typically inherited and reinforced by voting history, and by the manner in which the external world is filtered through party loyalties, meaning that a voter's evaluations of leaders and issues will be influenced significantly by pre-existing positive evaluations of parties. Social background plays no direct role, although the parent-to-child transmission will tend to maintain differences between social groups to some degree. This theory is sometimes called the party identification model, or the Michigan model, after the location of the researchers who advanced the idea.

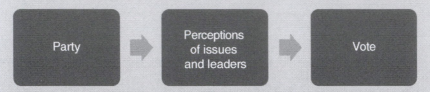

Sociological: This locates both issue preferences and predispositions towards parties in major social groups; people are mobilised to support parties by related organisations that target specific social groups. This approach is associated with Seymour Martin Lipset and Stein Rokkan, and is used to explain not just voting behaviour but also the set of parties between which voters choose.

Issue-based: This makes issues central to choice, arguing that voters assess parties on the basis of the significant issues of the election. The most common version is associated with Anthony Downs and sees voters as choosing the party whose position on issues is closest to their own – an approach known as the 'spatial model of voting'. A different theory, which also makes issues central, argues that voters choose the party they see as most competent to deal with those issues. In neither case does social position or party loyalty play any part in the explanation.

Table 6.2 Party identification, 2016

Party closeness	%
Close	30.6
Very close	*10.6*
Somewhat close	*17.8*
Not very close	*2.2*
Closer to one than any other	36.4
Not close at all	33.0
Total	100.0

Source: Authors' analysis of INES 2016 post-election survey questions: cross section weighted, N = 1,000.

been true 20 years later. Now that we see instability, we should see lower levels of attachment. The typical measure of this attachment in Ireland has been a question asking people if they feel close to a particular party and, if so, how close. A further question, asked only of those who say they do not feel close, inquires whether someone is closer to one party than the others. This gives us a five-point scale, ranging from very close to not close at all. Table 6.2 displays the distribution of voters on this scale in 2016.

Just under a third (31 per cent) of all those who voted in 2016 say they feel close to a party, whereas a second third (36 per cent) said they were closer to one party than the others, and a final third (33 per cent) seem to be completely unattached, lacking any identification with a party. While this could offer some explanation for the stability of voting in a subset of the voting population, the widespread lack of any firm attachment is exactly what we might expect in an electorate showing volatility. The figure of 31 per cent for those feeling close to a party, however, is not new: it is similar to levels found throughout the twenty-first century, as the high levels found in the 1970s declined after 1980 (Mair and Marsh, 2004: 240–2). It is also remarkably low by comparison with responses to the same question in other countries: across countries in western Europe, and in the USA, Canada, New Zealand and Australia, between 50 and 80 per cent express some attachment to a political party (Marsh *et al.*, 2008: 63). The extent of this decline, which far exceeds the general decline seen elsewhere (Dalton, 2014: 194–96), is also curious. While the low level of attachment is quite consistent with the striking levels of volatility seen in 2011 and 2016, the underlying decline in party attachment took place well before 2008, when just 26 per cent felt close. The marginal increase since then might suggest that the economic crisis led to a hardening of political affiliations among some voters. There is some evidence that the economic crisis created a new set of attachments among some people, most notably for Sinn Féin, but significant differences in survey methodology between 2011 and 2016 prevent any firm conclusions on this.

When we analyse levels of party identification across parties, we see some variation. Sinn Féin voters are most likely to say that they are close to their party (44 per cent) as against 38 per cent of Fianna Fáil voters, 37 per cent of Labour voters, 33 per cent of Fine Gael voters and 26 per cent of supporters of the Anti-Austerity Alliance–People Before Profit (AAA–PBP).

It is worth emphasising that party attachment is not the same thing as voting preference. While people tend to vote in a manner that is consistent with their stated party identification, they do not always do so. Whereas 79 per cent of those describing themselves as close to Fianna Fáil voted for that party in 2016, 16 per cent voted for other parties, with 5 per cent not voting. The corresponding figures for Fine Gael are 71, 22 and 7 per cent, for Sinn Féin 92, 6 and 2 per cent, and for Labour 63, 33 and 4 per cent (INES post-election survey).

Table 6.3 Vote by normal party preference of respondent's father, 2007

Vote in 2007	Father's normal party preference			
	Fianna Fáil	Fine Gael	Labour	Other/DK etc
Fianna Fáil	46	17	34	21
Fine Gael	12	50	15	16
Labour	6	7	19	7
Other	14	9	16	22
Did not vote	22	18	17	35
Total	100	100	100	100

Source: Authors' analysis of Irish national election study 2002–07; cross section weighted, N = 1,298.

It is possible that even if people do not reveal an attachment in their response to this question, they may still have a strong bias towards a particular party, and one that is in some sense inherited. The 2002–07 INES (described earlier) asked respondents how their parents voted. A minority did not remember or did not know, but 42 per cent said that their father usually voted for Fianna Fáil, 18 per cent for Fine Gael and 8 per cent for Labour, with small numbers mentioning each of several other parties, or saying their father did not vote, or voted for different parties. There is evidence of a significant association between parents and children in their voting preferences, at least among those who recalled a Fianna Fáil or Fine Gael bias in paternal behaviour.[3] Those recalling a Fianna Fáil father were more than twice as likely as those who do not to vote Fianna Fáil, and the relationship was even stronger in the case of Fine Gael; but in the case of Labour, father's voting preference seems to be of little importance (see Table 6.3). This relationship is somewhat weaker than a comparable one found in a survey carried out in the late 1960s and discussed by Carty (1981: 82).

The social psychological or party identification model is far from being universally accepted, either in the USA or in Europe. There have been a number of important criticisms. The first is that attachment these days is by no means as stable as implied in *The American Voter*. Some go so far as to argue that it changes with the vote, to the extent that vote choice determines attachment rather than the reverse (Thomassen, 1976: 72). Others have suggested that it is best seen as the outcome of a continuous process of evaluating parties and so may vary in direction and strength over time (Fiorina, 1981: 97). Using INES panel data Thomson (2017: 131–6) finds clear evidence of instability in attachment in Ireland between 2002 and 2007, concluding that change was due in part to evaluations of government performance. But Campbell and his colleagues did not rule out any change. On the contrary, they detected significant movements in party support and, most importantly, changes in the bases of party support in the form of electoral dealignments and realignments, periods of change in which individuals and groups moved away from one party and towards another. The decline of attachment in Ireland since the 1970s certainly seems to point to a process of dealignment, one that is consistent with the rise (and fall) of new parties.

The sociological model

The social psychological approach to voting choice focuses on how people develop and reinforce enduring patterns of behaviour. It pays relatively little attention to the content of politics: to the issues and ideals that might motivate parties and voters to come together. A popular alternative in Europe has been what we might call the sociological model. This sees different parties as representing different social groups, who are linked to 'their' parties by common interests and through networks of social institutions. In his chapter on Ireland in a comparative project on electoral behaviour inspired by this approach, John Whyte (1974) analysed one of the first Irish surveys to ask people about their vote and concluded that the Irish case provided the unusual picture of politics 'without social bases'. While elsewhere class, religion and urban–rural location might provide a good guide to how someone might vote, this proved to be of little help in predicting the behaviour of the Irish voter.

Several studies since then have sought to refine, qualify or confirm this interpretation. Mair (1979: 459–60) qualified the analysis by pointing out that Whyte had concentrated on what was then the major political division in terms of government formation: Fianna Fáil versus the rest. Given that Fianna Fáil was something of a catchall party, it was natural that the undifferentiated opposition would also be broadly based, but this perspective ignored real social differences between support for Fine Gael and for Labour, particularly in respect of class. Later analyses have served to develop that critique, one that has become potentially more significant as the party system moves away from the relative simplicity of the late 1960s. In 2016, the social basis of support was considerably more developed, as support for Sinn Féin had both increased considerably and become more closely aligned with working-class voters.

Figure 6.1 shows support for the three parties that were traditionally the largest, for Sinn Féin, and for independents, over the period 1969–2016, broken down by social grade (a set of conventional categories used by opinion poll companies). We just show the two extremes: AB is the better-off middle class, DE unskilled and dependents. We have not shown C1 (lower middle class) and C2 (skilled workers), but in almost all cases they fall between the lines shown. This exaggerates class differences, but also allows us to say that if nothing much shows up in this comparison there is, in fact, little to see.

Fine Gael and Sinn Féin have contrasting profiles, with their (higher) middle-class and (lower) working-class support bases respectively; the solid AB and long dashed DE lines have diverged. In the case of the Labour Party, the AB line has actually crossed the DE line, meaning that the party has more support among middle-class voters than it does among working-class voters. Fianna Fáil remains more consistent and broad-based, although arguably more working-class than its main rival, Fine Gael. A separate category, farmers, remains a little more distinctive in its behaviour, although it is a far smaller group than it was in 1969. Farmers tend overwhelmingly to vote Fine Gael or Fianna Fáil, with larger farmers – at least when these are identifiable – more drawn to Fine Gael.

Arguably, the greater instability that we now see provides an opportunity for clearer class divisions as people move away from traditional loyalties. Tilley and Garry (2017: 21–2) pointed out that the substantial defections from Fianna Fáil in 2011 saw the middle classes move to Fine Gael and working class voters to Labour, while Labour's losses in 2016 saw working-class defections to Sinn Féin. If the pattern is hardly new, the scale of the collapses makes the impact of class defections more substantial. In particular, 'class' politics becomes more likely when Fianna Fáil or Fine Gael loses support.

One major limitation of studies based around social grade is their questionable suitability for political analysis. Market research categories are chosen for their relevance to consumption patterns rather than political behaviour, and it has been argued that more sophisticated categories would show a stronger pattern (see Laver and Sinnott, 1987; see also Marsh *et al.*, 2008: 32–7; Tilley and Garry, 2017). Social grade is typically estimated from occupations whose relative importance has changed since the 1970s. In the absence of major industries, a homogenous industrial working class, the archetype of social grade C2DE, did not exist in

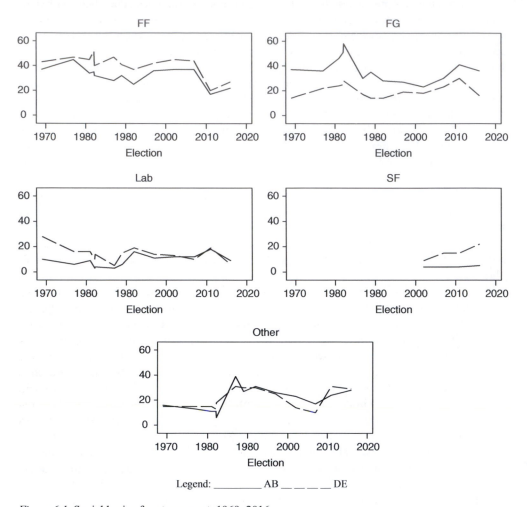

Figure 6.1 Social basis of party support, 1969–2016

Source: 1969–2002, as detailed in Marsh *et al.* (2008: 57 note 3); 2007 from Lansdowne/RTÉ Exit Poll; 2011 and 2016 from B&A Exit polls for RTÉ and RTÉ/INES.

Note: Social categories A and B include the more senior professional and business people, D and E are semi- and unskilled workers and dependents. All data are percentages.

Ireland to the same extent as it did in the UK. Furthermore, the size of the demographic groups have also changed over time; the proportion of skilled manual, semi-skilled and unskilled manual workers (C2DE) declined from 54 per cent in 1986 to just 36 per cent in 2011.[4]

Other measures, such as educational attainment, can be more consistently estimated. When we simplify educational attainment to distinguish those with a university-level education from those without, we can observe clear differences between the parties that are not too dissimilar from what would be expected based on the analysis of social grade. Whereas 37 and 34 per cent of Fine Gael and Labour Party supporters have a third-level education (level 6 or higher), this figure falls to 29 per cent for supporters of Fianna Fáil, 28 per cent for supporters of independent candidates, and to 17 per cent for supporters of Sinn Féin (RTÉ/INES Exit Poll 2016).

The divisions between churches, or between church and state, that have been so important in the European party system and voter alignments are not generally evident in the same way in Ireland. However, if we take religious practice as an indicator of support for the views of the Catholic church, we do see some significant differences in party choice between regularly practising Catholics and others: Fianna Fáil was supported by 34 per cent of practising Catholics and only 17 per cent of others, while the respective percentages for Sinn Féin were 11 and 18 (see Table 6.4). For Fine Gael, there was scarcely any difference between the two groups. This sort of contrast between Fianna Fáil and Fine Gael existed briefly in the 1980s, at a time of bitter referendum campaigns on divorce and abortion, but has generally been absent since then. This is a difference as pronounced as anything we see for occupational social class, and remains strong even if we allow for the fact that Fianna Fáil's support is stronger among older people, who are also more likely to be regular church attenders. Furthermore, as current trends point to continued decline in the proportion of practising Catholics, we may expect to see this polarisation play out to an even greater degree in defining party support.

In combination, some of these sociological differences do indicate greater contrasts between parties (see Marsh and McElroy, 2016: 166–8 on class differences in Dublin). Support for Fianna Fáil rises to 35 per cent among retirees living outside Dublin and falls to 7 per cent among single people living in Dublin. Support for Fine Gael rises to 36 per cent among farmers and those in the highest (AB) social grade and falls to 8 per cent among working-class C2DE people, who are either unemployed or working part-time. Support for Sinn Féin rises dramatically to 70 per cent among those living outside Dublin who are unemployed and are without a university degree, and falls to 3 per cent among middle-class people in the highest AB social grades in full-time employment in Dublin or Munster. If we were to identify combinations giving smaller, but better defined, clusters of voters, the results would be much more striking (see Laver, 2005: 199–201). But for these sorts of analysis to really carry much weight in explaining voting behaviour, we would need to see bigger differences between the larger groups, and this is simply not the case in Ireland.

By and large, however, all such analysis here seems to confirm the general conclusion that social grade is a better determinant of party support than it has been in the past. While Fianna

Table 6.4 Vote choice by church practice, 2016

Vote choice	Non-Catholic or irregular	Monthly or more frequent, Catholic
Fianna Fáil	17	34
Fine Gael	25	27
Sinn Féin	18	11
Labour Party	7	6
AAA–PBP	4	2
Green Party	4	1
Social Democrats	4	2
Renua	2	2
Independent	19	14
Others	1	2
Total	100	100
Sample size	758	671

Source: Authors' analysis of 2016 RTÉ/INES Exit Poll: weight adjustment to reflect result.

Fáil and Fine Gael resemble one another, the latter has moved towards becoming somewhat more middle class (again), while Sinn Féin is much more distinctive and increasingly represents a homogenous group of working-class and younger voters (O'Malley, 2008: 970). However, the overall explanatory power of the sociological approach remains rather limited.

Issue-based approaches

In contrast to the concerns of the party identification or sociological models, the media often talk about campaigns as if issues are the primary concern of voters. Elections allow the people to choose politicians, who then make decisions that have some impact on the rest of us. The rationale for a campaign period is that politicians can explain their own positions and voters can concentrate, for just a brief period, on what is being said. At the end of that time, voters can make their choice, and in doing so express their collective wish about future policy directions.

One query that arises about this sort of account concerns the ways in which voters might respond to the fact that they may be concerned about a number of issues, but they have only one first-preference vote. If a voter likes the position of Fianna Fáil on, say, health, but prefers Sinn Féin's position on social equality, how should she vote 'on the issues'? There are many answers to this, but a common assumption is that there are what we can call ideologies, a broad set of principles into which most other issues fit. The most widely used concept here is the notion of left and right. A left–right policy dimension can be seen as a kind of ideological marker, providing a reference point for people's standpoints on other issues. Typically, left and right are seen in economic terms with the left favouring more redistribution of wealth and a stronger role for the state in the economy, but in many countries, the left is also associated with a more secular or liberal view on moral issues such as abortion and divorce. We would expect those who see themselves as ideologically on the left to vote for left-wing parties, while those on the right will support parties on the right.

For voters, this simplification of political competition solves a major problem, that of having adequate information to make a choice. An ideology is a useful short-cut. This is not to say that political competition necessarily occurs on only one dimension, or is based around only one ideology. There may well be more than one, although in many countries a major dimension often coexists with other minor ones. However, if we assume for now a single dimension, Downs (1957) suggested that voters would choose the party closest to their own position, an approach that has been broadly described as the spatial model of voting. This way of thinking has generated huge interest among students of elections and parties. It lends itself to very sophisticated theories that promise to link two often separate questions that should be considered together: the strategies chosen by parties and the choices made by voters.

Research in this tradition in an Irish context is relatively limited, largely because of the absence of data until recently. An early analysis by Laver *et al*. (1987: 113–26) concluded that there was limited scope for such explanations in Ireland, as evaluations of party positions seemed independent of voters' own positions (but see Bowler and Farrell, 1990). However, if parties and voters are placed in a space defined by policy dimensions, much evidence suggests that the space is a very small one. Marsh *et al*. (2008: 49–52), using the 2002–07 election study, showed that voters see most parties as very similar in policy terms, a conclusion that holds for quite a wide range of broad policy areas, including taxes versus spending, the constitutional position of Northern Ireland, abortion (the last of these being an indicator of a broader set of moral issues), the EU and the environment. Only the Greens and Sinn

Féin appeared to convey a distinctive message, and then only on certain issues. Marsh *et al.* (2008: 52–3, 164–79) also demonstrate that the views of voters on these same areas, even when each is measured using a number of different questions, are generally associated very weakly with vote choice. Their analysis does not consider directly which party is closest to each voter, although it might be assumed, for instance, that if people who want 'a united Ireland' now tend to support Sinn Féin, it is because they see that party as representing their views on that issue.

However, a different analysis carried out by Benoit and Laver (2005), also using data from the 2002 election study, finds clearer evidence of policy- or issue-related voting. They used questions on public versus private ownership and on Northern Ireland from the election study to draw two-dimensional maps of the electorate on 'meta-issues' of economic left–right and the national question, and on economic left–right and moral issues (abortion, homosexuality), and then located parties on those maps, using separate surveys of experts, who were asked about party policies. The fact that the bigger parties are located close to most of the voters and the smaller parties are located where there are few voters provides some support for the argument that voters do choose parties according to such broad policy principles. Although this analysis makes some big assumptions about the possibilities of combining results from expert surveys and mass surveys, the area obviously justifies more research.

Many analyses elsewhere have ignored particular issues and simply asked voters to identify themselves as more or less 'left' or 'right', and have often asked voters to locate parties in a similar way. This technique, whether using self-placement (by a party's voters) or placements of parties by voters, tends to produce quite a clear pattern in Ireland, with Fine Gael and Fianna Fáil identified as right of centre and Labour, the Green Party, the Social Democrats, Sinn Féin and the AAA–PBP all identified as being on the left to varying degrees. Notably, the difference between Sinn Féin and Fine Gael is comparable to that between the Conservative and Labour parties in the UK.

When voters are asked to place themselves on the left–right scale, we observe that their self-placement tends to be close to the position of the parties they support. When the party system consisted of Fianna Fáil, Fine Gael and Labour, this extended over a narrow ideological dimension. This space has expanded considerably since support for Sinn Féin has increased significantly and the far left has organised itself into a more coherent group, in the form of Solidarity–PBP (formerly the AAA–PBP). Figure 6.2 graphically portrays the distribution of estimates of where each party is on the left–right scale. It is clear that there is little difference between Fianna Fáil and Fine Gael and that among left-leaning parties Labour is closest to the centre, followed by Sinn Féin, with the AAA–PBP furthest away. The graphic also highlights the variance, or spread, of the estimated party positions. Notably, these are sufficiently narrow to suggest that there is some certainty among voters as to what a left-wing party is and what a right-wing party is. For example, hardly any voters diverged from conventional perceptions by placing the AAA–PBP to the right of Fine Gael or Fianna Fáil.

As voters place themselves towards the centre-right of the left–right scale, there must also be a question mark over what it means to describe a voter as being on the left or the right. Does someone regard themselves as left-wing because they have left-wing positions on a set of issues, or because they vote Sinn Féin, and they know that it is generally regarded as a left-wing party? The evidence is against the first interpretation, as voters' self-placement on a left–right scale seems to be only weakly related to their views on questions of redistribution or public ownership. Moral issues are more closely linked, but even that relationship is not strong (Marsh *et al.*, 2008: 39–42; McElroy, 2017: 69–75).

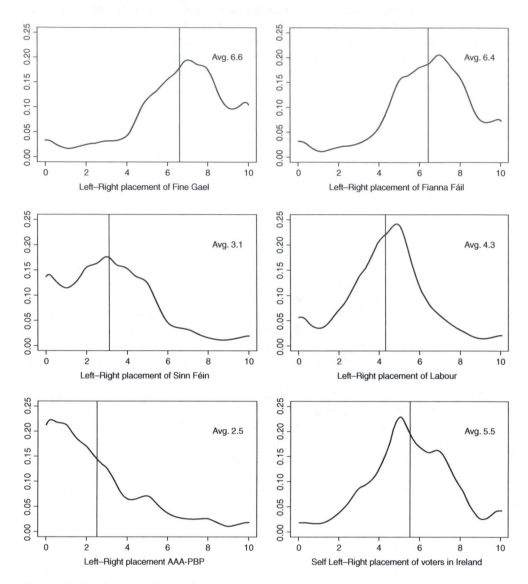

Figure 6.2 Distributions of respondents' interpretations of each party's left–right position and their left–right position, 2016

Source: INES/CSES 2016 post-election survey.

Note: The data are proportions.

A very different approach to the role of policy or issues in electoral behaviour arises from concerns about how far there are strong policy differences between parties and between voters. An early critique of Downs's work suggested that the sort of political competition he identified was no longer typical. For Downs, parties offer different solutions to issues, and the voter picks the party that best corresponds to her own preference. Stokes (1963: 372–4) queried how far parties do take different positions – that is, offer different solutions. Rather, he argued, most parties have similar views on what should be done. Where they differ is in the credibility of their promises to do it effectively. Many of the most important issues, Stokes argued, are 'valence issues' rather than 'position issues'. Almost everyone agrees that inflation, or unemployment, or pollution, or poverty are undesirable, but people differ on whom they trust to tackle these issues most competently. This approach focuses attention on party competence, and how parties might develop or lose a reputation for being able to get things done. Arguably, valence issues are particularly important in Ireland, in the absence of clear debate over the content of policy, and so party competition often comes down to disputes over how far governing parties should be given credit or blame for what has occurred during their term of office (Marsh *et al.*, 2008: 85–102; Marsh and Tilley, 2010).

This naturally raises again some of the problems that arise with any explanation of vote choice by reference to issues: which issues, how many issues, and how do voters balance what may be a difference of competence across issues? The same solution outlined above, a focus on ideological positions, is typically adopted in this approach as well. The economy is normally one of these issues, with everyone assumed to want economic growth. In most recent elections, voters have been asked what they regard as the most important issue in the election, or the most important issue for them personally, or the one that had most impact on their vote.

The major issues since 1997 are summarised in Table 6.5. In 1997, before rapid economic growth had the impact seen later, the major issues were unemployment and taxation, along with crime. In 2002 and 2007, the main issues were health, then crime, with many mentions related to the economy in general such as the cost of living and, to a lesser extent, unemployment and taxation. Although the survey in 2011 only allowed respondents to mention a single issue, it is clearly evident that, in the context of a major economic downturn, the economy became the most important issue. In 2016 normal service had almost been resumed: unemployment and the economy remained a focus, but health returned as a major issue.

Even so, the picture looks fragmented, with more than 20 different concerns reported as important for at least small groups of voters. Analyses linking these issues to party choice have

Table 6.5 Issues mentioned as influencing vote, 1997–2016

Issue	1997	2002	2007	2011	2016
Health	9	39	45	2	36
The economy	14	22	23	49	31
Water charges	0	0	0	0	17
Unemployment, jobs	39	6	3	6	16
Stable government	12	5	5	<1	16
Housing and homelessness	3	9	11	1	18
Taxation, cost of living	38	19	22	2	12
Crime, law and order, drugs	52	41	31	<1	10
Local issues	9	10	10	2	10
Education	9	8	8	1	7
Abortion	<1	<1	<1	<1	4
Childcare	<1	<1	<1	<1	4
Environment	6	8	13	<1	<1
Immigration	<1	<1	2	<1	<1

Source: Authors' analysis of exit polls 1997, 2002, 2007, 2011 and 2016.

Notes: The question asked was, 'What were the issues or problems that most influenced your decision as to which party to vote for? (PROBE) What other issues influenced you?' So, 45 per cent of respondents in 2007 mentioned health as one of their three issues and 55 per cent did not mention health at all. In 2011, respondents were asked to record one issue, and in 2016 respondents were asked to record two issues.

tended to see significant, if fairly weak, relationships between what people thought was important and how they voted (Marsh and Sinnott, 1999: 163–9; Garry *et al.*, 2003: 135–7; Marsh,
2008: 118–20). In 2016, these relationships were considerably stronger. For instance, 50 per cent
of Fine Gael voters mentioned managing the economy; this fell to 24 per cent for Fianna Fáil
voters and 21 per cent for Sinn Féin voters. Another 35 per cent of Fine Gael voters mentioned a
stable government as one of the two most important issues. This was mentioned by just 12 and 4
per cent among Fianna Fáil and Sinn Féin voters respectively. On the other hand, water charges
were mentioned by 38 per cent of Sinn Féin voters and 42 per cent of AAA–PBP voters as
compared with 5 per cent of Fine Gael and Labour voters. Housing and homelessness were mentioned by 22 and 27 per cent of Sinn Féin and AAA–PBP voters, as compared with 7 and 10 per
cent of Fine Gael and Labour voters. Issues such as health, education, crime and taxation were
less divisive. Fianna Fáil voters were also far more likely to mention issues within their constituency, with 17 per cent naming such a concern in their top two issues as compared with 7 per
cent for Sinn Féin or Fine Gael. A number of these associations are striking, and undoubtedly
the result of effective campaigning around single issues and positions identified by the parties.

One important strand of work in electoral behaviour within this tradition has focussed
on the economy, arguing that the health of the economy is central to other judgements.
Essentially, the argument is that strong economic growth – with consequent benefits from
employment levels and wages – will boost the government parties and weak performance
will hurt them. There is widespread evidence that a strengthening economy tends to boost
the incumbent's electoral fortunes (Powell and Whitten, 1993; Duch and Stevenson, 2008;
Lewis-Beck and Stegmaier, 2013), although the effects are arguably contingent on several
structural factors, like the openness of the economy and the fragmentation of the government
(Anderson, 2007; Kayser, 2014). Evidence for an 'economic vote' in Ireland has been mixed.
Mair (1987: 76–7) suggested that incumbent support was linked to changes in real disposable
income, but Harrison and Marsh (1998) found no similar pattern in opinion poll data. Fianna
Fáil did seem to benefit from growth in 2002 and 2007, and were punished heavily for the
crash in 2011 (Marsh *et al.*, 2008: 81–109; Marsh and Mikhaylov, 2012, 2014; Leyden and
Lewis-Beck, 2017). The failure of the 2011–16 government to reap any obvious benefits
from the 'recovery' is problematic here, but arguably, while real growth was certainly taking
place, too few people actually were better off than they had been in 2011, and many were
still worse off than they had been in 2008 (for a discussion see Marsh and McElroy, 2016:
168–71; Marsh, 2017: 199–205).

Leaders and candidates

The analysis so far has focussed on parties, but it may be that a vital element in the voter's
calculation is the individuals who carry the party flags. The most important of these is the
party leader. There are two main questions here: whether leaders are important factors in
the choices made by a voter and, if so, what attributes make a leader electorally effective. A
similar set of questions may be asked about a further category of individuals who carry party
labels: ordinary candidates for elective office.

Party leaders

There is ample potential for a leader to have a considerable impact on Irish elections. First of
all, the electorate is open to persuasion: the long-term influences of political values, social

cleavages, family traditions and even party attachments are relatively weak. Second, parties focus a lot of attention on leaders in their campaigns, particularly when they feel they have an electoral asset. For the two main parties, their leader is their candidate for Taoiseach. The media like to concentrate on leaders: major journalists are often sent to follow leaders, and leaders' photos dominate the pictorial landscape of the press. The parties themselves usually encourage this perspective. In some instances, this is a function of the nature of party organisations and in others it is a function of robust research. Typically, any new leader installs his or her loyal team to direct media communications and strategy while the slightly more permanent apparatchiks, free to make calculated decisions on the basis of research, are left in charge of the somewhat more complex task of election organisation. In the 2016 election, the dominance of Micheál Martin posters told a distinctive story about how Fianna Fáil understood its advantage, with the leader dwarfing the party: big Micheál, small Fianna Fáil (Leahy, 2016: 93). In the 2016 election survey, voters were asked to estimate how much they liked each leader on a 0 to 10 scale and 37 per cent awarded Martin a score of seven or more; only 23 per cent awarded Fine Gael leader and Taoiseach, Enda Kenny, such a score.

Arguably, for the electorate, the media and the parties, it is easier to simplify the contest in terms of comparisons between potential leaders, rather than comparisons between nuanced and detailed policy proposals. Indeed, the attributes of leaders may be more significant and more relevant in an era where public trust in policy proposals and manifestos remains low. Most campaigns, and 2016 was no exception, feature a debate between the rival leaders (see Chapter 12, pp. 311–13). Election debates, and particularly the first such debate in a series, are unique in that the viewership of such debates vastly exceeds any other current affairs programme. This debate is often the only occasion on which otherwise uninterested, undecided, less strongly affiliated voters engage with politics. The debate therefore has the potential to change a relatively large number of preferences. In 2016, there were three debates involving the leaders of each party, including one seven-way debate on RTÉ between the leaders of all major parties and groups represented in the Dáil. The impact of Micheál Martin was evident in this arena. The party's average poll rating across the three polls during the week before the debate was 18 per cent. In the three polls conducted in the week that followed the debate, support for the party increased significantly to an average rating of 21 per cent. While that would be within the margin of error for a single poll, the margin of error is much lower where we are analysing changes in the average of a number of polls.

Yet we might ask about how clearly voters distinguish leaders and parties, and the direction of any cause and effect with respect to popularity. The argument that leaders matter implies an effect that runs from leader to party: a voter likes a leader and therefore likes that leader's party. Yet the major Irish parties are long established, while leaders are relatively ephemeral. It is inconceivable that perception of a party leader would not be coloured significantly by party identification. In some countries, leaders build their own parties, institutions that are little more than vehicles designed to transport the leader into high office. This has not been the case in Ireland. Almost any leader of Fianna Fáil will normally have a reasonable level of popularity simply because of the prestige associated with the party leadership. In general, then, we would expect favourable attitudes towards parties to influence perceptions of leaders. Yet, it must also be accepted that some leaders may change the way many voters see their parties. Between 2002 and 2007, Bertie Ahern, it is often argued, made Fianna Fáil more widely acceptable, and even those who did not give Fianna Fáil a first preference were less hostile to the party than they once were, allowing it to win in 1997, 2002 and 2007 by getting more lower preference votes than it used to. Equally, Dick Spring may have done the same for Labour in 1992. By contrast, Fine Gael leader Enda Kenny arguably dragged down his party in 2016. These may be relatively marginal effects, but even marginal effects can be critical in some circumstances.

The scholarly literature on the electoral impact of leaders gives little support to those who see leaders as crucial to success and failure. A study across more than two dozen countries concluded that, in parliamentary systems, 'voters still make judgements about the collective merits of the parties as a whole rather than their leaders in particular' (Curtice and Hunjan, 2011), a finding confirmed by another more extensive study by Holmberg and Oscarsson (2011). Although all analyses show strong associations between leader and party popularity (Laver *et al.*, 1987: 127–37, Marsh and Sinnott, 1990: 103–7; Marsh and Sinnott, 1993: 102–5; Harrison and Marsh, 1994; Garry *et al.*, 2003: 128–40; Marsh, 2008: 119–28), the data generally available have not been sufficient to enable anyone to make much progress in establishing the direction of cause and effect. The most extensive Irish analysis was made using the 2002–07 election study. It assumed that the main direction of causality was from party popularity to leader popularity. The authors justified their assumption by pointing out that when party and leader ratings did not seem to point to the same choice of party, the party ratings proved much more decisive (Marsh *et al.*, 2008: 123–5; see also Thomsen and Suiter, 2016: 165–9). The results suggested that leadership probably made a difference of only a few percentage points to both Fianna Fáil and Fine Gael in 2002 (Marsh *et al.*, 2008: 164–72, 179–80).

Our second question was this: if leaders do matter, what attributes of a leader make him or her more effective? Is it simply the perception of competence, or are leaders valued for being caring, or trustworthy, for being close to the people, or being, in one sense or another, superior to them? Research across different political contexts finds that the most important characteristic is perceived competence (Nadeau and Nevitte, 2011; Ohr and Oscarsson, 2011). In Ireland, the 2002–07 election study included a battery of questions exploring assessments of each leader's honesty, capacity for being in touch with ordinary people and ability to run the country. The last of these has been considered the most important in previous research, as we have seen already, and it could be argued that this is what should matter most. Yet, being in touch with ordinary people could also be considered vital in a representative democracy. Not all leaders, even popular ones, might be considered strong in this respect. Honesty was included as a criterion because the activities of tribunals of inquiry into past misdoings of politicians (see Box 11.2, p. 287) have been potentially significant as an election issue. Analysis of the 2007 data suggested that competence was valued by voters as by far the most important quality in assessing leaders.

Candidates

Many observers of Irish elections think that local conditions and the candidates themselves, rather than the national parties and party leaders, are of critical importance. In most countries, it is assumed that voters at election time choose between the *parties*: while there may be some element of a 'personal vote' for some candidates, this is generally considered to be a small proportion of each party's overall support. However, conventional wisdom in Ireland sees the personal vote and the local context within which candidates compete as extremely important. The Irish electoral system does not provide for a party vote, only for a ranking of candidates, and when it comes to support for candidates from the larger parties, this means choosing between candidates of the same party. It is essential for understanding the nature of Irish electoral democracy to ask whether people are voting for parties (including leaders) or for candidates. It makes little sense to look for reasons why a particular voter supported Fianna Fáil, for instance, if that voter was simply supporting a particular Fianna Fáil candidate and would have done so regardless of that candidate's party label. As with leaders, there are two questions to ask here. The first is how far voters cast a personal rather than a party vote, and the second is what makes a candidate inherently more, or less, attractive.

Opinion polls have often asked voters to rank the importance for their vote choice of a number of things, including choosing a local candidate to look after the needs of the constituency. The other options include choosing a Taoiseach, selecting a group of ministers and picking between policies. While the wording varies, the results typically show only about 10 per cent voting to pick a Taoiseach, whereas close to half of all voters opt for choosing a candidate to look after local needs (see Sinnott, 1995: 168–71; Garry *et al.*, 2003: 125–6; Marsh and Cunningham, 2011: 185). In 2016, 42 per cent selected this option.[5] This suggests answers to both of our questions: a very substantial minority of voters are candidate-centred (rather than party-centred), and the main attribute for a candidate is a belief in his or her competence to look after local interests.

The evidence from several measures used in the INES surveys and exit polls points to the importance of the candidate, though with some variation from party to party. The responses to two questions asked of those who voted for a candidate from a political party are shown in Table 6.6. Thirty-one per cent of respondents said that the candidate was more important to them than the party and, moreover, that they would have voted for the same candidate even if that candidate stood with a different label. Twenty-nine per cent were on the other side, claiming the party as more important and saying they would not follow the candidate to a different party. But the remaining 40 per cent gave mixed responses, including those who said the candidate was more important but also that they would not follow the candidate to another party, or that it depended on which party the candidate moved to.

All of these analyses, like earlier ones using a question about voting for a candidate to protect the needs of the constituency, show that the importance of the candidate varies, according to the party voters choose. Historically, Fine Gael supporters are motivated much more by candidates than are Fianna Fáil voters, who are relatively strong on party. In 2007, for instance, 65 per cent of Fine Gael voters claimed that the candidate was more important to them than the party, compared with only 53 per cent of Fianna Fáil voters. This appears to have since reversed, with the 2016 figures being 47 and 57 per cent respectively.

Of course, an increasing number of voters in recent elections opted for an independent candidate. The success of independents is an unusual feature of Irish politics, one that is facilitated by the electoral system but is better explained by a growing rejection of parties and the previously discussed concern for local representation (see Chapter 5). Most independent

Table 6.6 Relative importance of candidate and party in voters' choice, 2016

Most important for vote	Would follow candidate to another party			
	Yes	*No*	*Depends*	*Total*
Party	10	29	6	45
Candidate	31	14	10	55
Total	41	43	16	100

Source: Authors' analysis of RTÉ/INES Exit Poll 2016.

Note: Cell entries are percentages of total, N = 1221, constituency weighting. Questions asked of those who voted for a party candidate.

voters in 2016 said it was the candidate that mattered, although for a quarter of such voters, the attraction was precisely that the candidate did not represent a party (although most of these would have voted for that candidate anyway).[6] Weeks (2011) has argued that independent voters are generally unremarkable in terms of social background and that the independent vote is more of an expression of indifference with respect to parties, rather than a specific antipathy.

More evidence about the relative importance of candidates and parties can be gleaned from an analysis of the way people mark their ballot papers, and the extent to which they vote for all the candidates of a party before moving to those of another party. If party is preeminent in their minds, we would expect voters to give preferences to running mates of the party of their first preference candidate above candidates from other parties. We would not expect the same to happen if candidate is preeminent. In the absence of access to the ballots themselves, we can learn something about voting patterns from vote transfers. If people vote on party lines, votes will tend to transfer to a candidate's running mates. Analyses of vote transfers show that this happens, and it happens in a majority of cases, but this trend is a declining one with no more than two-thirds of all transfers going to a running mate (when one is still available for transfers), compared to more than four-fifths forty years ago (Gallagher, 1978: 3–4, and 2016: 145–8; see also Sinnott and McBride, 2011: 210–11). Survey respondents have sometimes been asked to complete mock ballots and these can also be analysed directly to see how far party seems to determine the structure of preferences. Such analyses suggest even less party voting, with Marsh *et al.* (2008) showing that while a majority of voters do express a preference for all the running mates of their first choice candidate, less than 50 per cent do so in a perfect sequence: in many cases there is a deviation from what Americans would call a 'straight ticket' vote (Marsh *et al.*, 2008: 24; see also Bowler and Farrell, 1991: 312–14; Marsh and Plescia, 2016: 164–66, 173–5; Laver, 2004: 526–30).

Clearly, then, candidates are an important factor in voter choice. It would be unwise to suggest that this means that very many voters care little for parties, but the simple evidence discussed does indicate that a majority – 55 per cent in Table 6.6 – cares predominantly about the candidate. Arguably, however, we can only be sure a voter is motivated primarily by candidates rather than parties if the voter would be likely to select a different party in the absence of that candidate. Following this line of argument, only the 31 per cent who say they would vote for the same candidate regardless of that candidate's party are candidate-centred voters. One simulation of the 2002 election in which the weight of candidate factors was set to zero suggested that, in such a situation, only 20 per cent of voters would have chosen a different party, with Fine Gael being the main loser (Marsh, 2007: 123); indeed, when voters experience a clash between their favourite candidate and their favourite party, their vote choice is, in most cases, determined by their favourite candidate (Marsh and Schwirz, 2016; see also Thomsen and Suiter, 2016). This is a somewhat lower figure for candidate-centred voters than our previous discussion might suggest, but even if only 20 per cent choose their party because of the candidate, this still raises an important question: if candidates are so important, why has party support been relatively stable over such a long period?

One answer would be that it was not stable at all, even prior to 2011. The Fine Gael vote has fluctuated quite a lot over the period 1977–2016, as has that of the smaller parties. Only Fianna Fáil's vote has been very consistent, varying between 39 and 42 per cent over the four elections of the 1992–2007 period, before the economic crisis pushed its vote well below that in 2011, and 2016 saw only a relatively modest recovery. The second answer would be that the best candidates gravitate to the larger parties because they see those parties as the most promising vehicles for their political careers, and because the parties see the advantage to themselves in harnessing talent. A third, but related, answer is that membership of a bigger party helps to make a candidate more attractive to voters – to some degree, the best candidates are the best candidates because they are in the larger parties.

This raises a further question: what makes a candidate electorally attractive? Many studies have looked at the association between various candidate attributes and electoral success, as measured by votes won. All studies show that political experience is important (recent examples are Redmond and Regan, 2015: 250–52; Gallagher, 2016: 128–9). Higher levels of campaign spending also seem to help (Benoit and Marsh, 2008: 886–7). However, gender does not seem to be a factor (McElroy and Marsh, 2010, 2011; Buckley *et al.*, 2016). These analyses generally tend to use secondary information about candidates, but it is also possible to use survey evidence to find out what it is that voters like about candidates. Marsh *et al.* (2008: 156, 185–6) look at the association between general ratings of candidates by voters and ratings on three more specific scales: how good the candidate is at working for his or her area, his or her contribution to national political debate, and being close to the respondent's political views. The first of these factors, working for the area, was much more closely associated with general candidate evaluations than was either of the other two; the last was not important at all.

Other aspects of voting

In addition to general elections, Irish electors also vote in local elections as well as in elections to the European Parliament and presidential elections (Gallagher and Marsh, 1992; van der Brug *et al.*, 2000; O'Malley, 2012). Their behaviour here differs slightly from that in general elections. We also need to consider a matter to which these voting occasions draw particular attention: that of electoral turnout.

European and local elections

Since 1999, European and local elections have taken place simultaneously, largely to ensure higher turnout in both sets of elections. These take place using the same electoral system (PR-STV – see Chapter 4), with candidates nominated and presented by the same political parties, but we must ask whether the determinants of voting – partisanship, issues, the economy, leaders and candidates – are the same ones, and whether they have the same impact. It has become common to see these as 'second order national elections', a label that implies that these elections are treated by voters and parties as akin to general elections, but with much less at stake (Reif and Schmitt, 1980). If such a designation is correct, we would see the same parties winning much the same vote as they do in general elections, subject to three exceptions. First, small parties do better. Any tendency to support larger parties at the expense of small parties that are ideologically closer to the voter will be weakened when government formation is not at stake. Second, some voters will treat the relatively unimportant election as a referendum on the government, and an opportunity to punish it, especially in mid-term periods of government unpopularity. Third, turnout will be lower, as voters do not care as much, and parties make less effort. The particular issues that might be expected to be appropriate to the different type of election will be of little importance, unless they are important in general elections. While the concept of second order national elections and the assumptions underpinning it have been criticised (the strongest critique is Blondel *et al.*, 1998: 13–18), there is little evidence that vote choice in these elections is driven substantially by issues that might be peculiar to that arena (van der Brug *et al.*, 2008: 597–8; Marsh and Mikhaylov, 2010).

The Irish experience broadly supports the implications of the 'second order' thesis: smaller parties and independents have tended to do well at such elections, governing parties have tended to fare poorly, and turnout has been low. In 1994, when local elections were not held at the same time as the European Parliament election, turnout fell below 50 per cent. Local elections have been little studied, and then only with aggregate data as no dedicated surveys have been available. Gallagher (1989) concluded that Fianna Fáil usually did worse in local than in general elections, a result not inconsistent with the second-order concept, not least because that party was usually in government (see also Sinnott, 1995: 254–6). However, it is apparent from the results that when local and European elections are held at the same time, as they have been since 1999, people do behave very differently in each of them. For 2014, we have data from the RTÉ exit poll. Of those who reported voting in the 2014 local and European Parliament elections, held at the same time, only 58 per cent voted for the same party in each – and that is treating small parties (apart from Labour) as a single group. One explanation for the remarkably high level of instability is that this is a consequence of the different type of candidates standing in the two arenas. Independents usually perform much better in local elections than in others and candidates may also be a little more important than parties in those. When people were asked at different elections whether candidate or party mattered more, 58 per cent said the candidate in relation to the 2007 general election, 63 per cent said the candidate with respect to the European Parliament elections in 2004, while 71 per cent identified the candidate as primary in the case of the local elections of 2004.[7] Even so, this degree of instability underlines the fragile hold that Irish parties now have on the voters.

Turnout

Turnout in referendums and local and European Parliament elections is typically much lower than in general elections, where turnout seems to have been falling for some time, from around 76 per cent in 1981 to somewhere between 62 and 69 per cent since the late 1980s. It was 65 per cent in 2016, down from 69 per cent in 2011 (see Appendix 2b). While some of this recent decline is due to an increasingly inaccurate electoral register, it seems probable that turnout is lower than it once was (Coleman and Flynn, 2006; see also O'Malley, 2001, 2014).

There are many explanations of turnout, most of them echoing some of the explanations for voter choice already discussed. The first argument follows the rationalistic approach of Downs and explains voting and non-voting in *instrumental* terms: people vote to make a difference. There is of course a paradox here, since the chance of any one vote making a difference is infinitesimally small. However, taking a broader view of motivations, it is still sensible to suggest that changes or variations in voting will be, in part, a function of variations in the likely impact of the vote (Grofman, 1993: 94–5). On this account, where people see little difference between the parties, or where the outcome seems in no doubt, they will be less likely to vote. Turnout in this version has a lot to do with the parties themselves and what they offer. International evidence supports this argument: turnout is typically lower where elections seem to make little difference to the composition of government (Blais, 2006).

Of course, the parties themselves may work much harder to get out the last vote when elections are more competitive. This is central to a second explanation, which focuses on the various agencies of *mobilisation* and their links with voters (Rosenstone and Hansen, 1993). Turnout will be higher when parties are deeply rooted in social institutions, which themselves will work to get people to the polls. Again, this explanation highlights the importance of the social and political context, but we would also see those with weaker links to parties and politically-related institutions, such as trade unions, being less likely to vote.

A third account deals more specifically with individuals, arguing that turnout is a function of the resources available to an individual (Brady *et al.*, 1995). Those who find it easiest to access information about politics and the election will be most likely to vote. Hence, we would expect those with less information, as well as those with less education, to be more likely to abstain.

A fourth argument is about duty: that for most of those who do vote there is a feeling that they should do so (Blais, 2000: 92–114; and in an Irish context Blais *et al.*, 2017). All these explanations get some support from Irish evidence, although it is clear that none provides anything like a complete explanation.

This suggests that we might also look more closely at the meaning of non-voting. How far is it a deliberate act? It is possible that while some people decide that they will not vote, others may simply be distracted, or may be unable to get to the polls on the day. Blondel *et al.* have distinguished between 'circumstantial' and 'voluntary' abstention, and argued that while those in the latter group might resemble the non-voters in our previous accounts, the former group will look much more like voters (Blondel *et al.*, 1998: 40–54; see Marsh, 1991: 8–10).

One of the more striking patterns of turnout is the association with age. This seems almost universal: the tendency to turn out increases with age, only to fall back amongst the elderly. Marsh *et al.* (2008: 200) showed turnout in 2002 increasing steadily from 54 per cent among those 18–24, to 79 per cent in the 55–64 group, but then declining to 67 per cent among those over 74 years old. In 2011, the pattern seems to have been similar, with less than half of those under 25 voting, and then turnout rising with age.[8] We can see this as an outcome of a process in which people acquire more political knowledge and affiliations with age, as well as becoming more settled in their immediate communities, until in advanced age factors such as mobility become a problem. An alternative explanation is that voting becomes a habit, one engendered by repetition (Plutzer, 2004; Franklin, 2004: 204–5).

The tendency for abstention to be greater in the youngest generations is, by this first explanation, something that is normal; but the second account raises more serious concerns, given the falling numbers of young people voting today, suggesting that these will persist and that this will lead to a greater decline in turnout over the generations. This argument underpins a case that could be made for lowering the voting age, a proposal supported by the Constitutional Convention before the 2016 election. Turnout among the young is low, it is argued, because their first vote comes at a time when they are often separated from traditional supports. Were people to reach voting age when they were still at school, rather than often away from home, schools and families, they could and would be agents of mobilisation. This would see more people voting when they first get the opportunity, with long-term consequences for habitual turnout in later life (for some Austrian evidence see Wagner *et al.*, 2012).

A particular feature of Irish turnout is the geographical contrast between elections and referendums. The highest turnout in general elections tends to be in predominantly rural areas (Kavanagh *et al.*, 2004: 179–84). In referendums, however, turnout is highest in middle-class urban areas. It seems likely that in the absence of the extensive door-to-door canvassing by candidates and their representatives that we see in national elections, the individual characteristics of voters – whether duty or resources – have more of an impact.

Conclusion

There are few simple answers to the questions we have about party choice in Ireland. Although each of the three main approaches provides some valuable insights, it is evident that none of them provides a complete explanation of behaviour. Many people appear to have no party attachment, there is no strong social basis to patterns of choice, while accounts based on ideology or even specific issues do not get us very far. Some features of Irish electoral politics cut across all these accounts and make them less powerful than they may be elsewhere: for example, the fact that the largest two parties have a similar outlook on many issues, narrowing the dialogue about policy options and ideology, and significant localism, as reflected in the importance of the candidate. This is not to assert that Irish electoral politics is simply *sui generis* and requires an explanation unique to Ireland. Rather, we should be aware that the nature of party competition will itself have an impact on how people make their choices, and in Ireland that competition is less ideological and more local than it generally is elsewhere.

Notes

1   The data from all surveys from the 2002–7 Irish election study are available from the Irish Social Science Data Archive at UCD. A web-based interactive version, along with a list of publications and papers, is available at www.tcd.ie/ines.
2   Authors' analysis of INES 2002–7 data.
3   For a more extensive analysis of vote choice in 2002, looking at mothers as well as fathers, see Marsh *et al.* (2008: 72–7).
4   Calculations based on Central Statistics Office website, www.cso.ie/multiquicktables/quickTables. aspx?id=cna07.
5   Authors' analysis of RTÉ/INES Exit Poll.
6   Authors' analysis of RTÉ/INES Exit Poll.
7   Authors' analysis of the 2002–7 Irish election study, using only respondents who replied in all five waves.
8   Authors' analysis of 2012 European Social Survey.

References and further reading

Anderson, Christopher, 2007. 'The end of economic voting? Contingency dilemmas and the limits of democratic accountability', *Annual Review of Political Science* 10: 271–96.
Benoit, Kenneth and Michael Laver, 2005. 'Mapping the Irish policy space: voter and party spaces in preferential elections', *Economic and Social Review* 36: 83–108.
Benoit, Kenneth and Michael Marsh, 2008. 'The campaign value of incumbency: a new solution to the puzzle of less effective incumbent spending', *American Journal of Political Science* 52: 874–90.
Blais, André, 2000. *To Vote or Not to Vote: The Merits and Limits of Rational Choice Theory*. Pittsburgh: University of Pittsburgh Press.
Blais, André, 2006. 'What affects voter turnout?', *Annual Review of Political Science* 9: 111–25.
Blais, André, Carol Galais and Theresa Reidy, 2017. 'In the line of duty: the moral basis of turnout in the 2011 Irish election', in Michael Marsh, David M. Farrell and Gail McElroy (eds), *A Conservative Revolution? Electoral Change in Twenty-First-Century Ireland*. Oxford: Oxford University Press, pp. 172–91.

Blondel, Jean, Richard Sinnott and Palle Svensson, 1998. *People and Parliament in the European Union: Democracy, Participation and Legitimacy*. Oxford: Oxford University Press.

Bowler, Shaun and David Farrell, 1990. 'Irish voter rationality: the 1987 Irish general election revisited', *Economic and Social Review* 21, pp. 251–68.

Bowler, Shaun and David Farrell, 1991. 'Voter behaviour under STV-PR: solving the puzzle of the Irish party system', *Political Behavior* 13, pp. 303–20.

Brady, Henry, Sidney Verba and Helen Schlozman, 1995. 'Beyond SES: a resource model of political participation', *American Political Science Review* 89, pp. 271–94.

Buckley, Fiona, Yvonne Galligan and Claire McGing, 2016. 'Women and the election: assessing the impact of gender quotas', in Michael Gallagher and Michael Marsh (eds), *How Ireland Voted 2016: The Election That Nobody Won*. Basingstoke: Palgrave Macmillan, pp. 185–206.

Campbell, Angus, Philip E. Converse, Warren E. Miller and Donald E. Stokes, 1960. *The American Voter*. New York, NY: John Wiley & Sons.

Carty, R. K., 1981. *Party and Parish Pump: Electoral Politics in Ireland*. Waterloo, Ontario: Wilfrid Laurier University Press.

Coleman, Shane and Odran Flynn, 2006. 'Electoral register out by 860,000', *Sunday Tribune* 26 February.

Curtice, John and Sarinder Hunjan, 2011. 'Elections as beauty contests: do the rules matter?' in Kees Aarts, André Blais and Hermann Schmitt (eds), *Political Leaders and Democratic Elections*. Oxford: Oxford University Press, pp. 91–107.

Dalton, Russell, 2014. *Citizen Politics: Public Opinion and Political Parties in Advanced Industrial Democracies*, 6th ed. Washington, DC: CQ Press.

Dassonneville, Ruth and Marc Hooghe, 2017. 'The noise of the vote recall question: the validity of the vote recall question in panel studies in Belgium, Germany, and the Netherlands', *International Journal of Public Opinion Research* 29:2, pp. 316–38.

Downs, Anthony, 1957. *An Economic Theory of Democracy*. New York: Harper.

Duch, Raymond M. and Randolph T. Stevenson, 2008. *The Economic Vote: How Political and Economic Institutions Condition Election Results*. Cambridge: Cambridge University Press.

Farrell, David M. and Jane Suiter, 2016. 'The election in context', in Michael Gallagher and Michael Marsh (eds), *How Ireland Voted 2016: The Election That Nobody Won*. Basingstoke: Palgrave Macmillan, pp. 277–93.

Fiorina, Morris P., 1981. *Retrospective Voting in American National Elections*. London: Yale University Press.

Franklin, Mark N., 2004. *Voter Turnout and the Dynamics of Electoral Competition in Established Democracies since 1945*. Cambridge: Cambridge University Press.

Gallagher, Michael, 1978. 'Party solidarity, exclusivity and inter-party relationship in Ireland 1922–1977: the evidence of transfers', *Economic and Social Review* 10, pp. 1–22.

Gallagher, Michael, 1989. 'Subnational elections and electoral behaviour in the Republic of Ireland', *Irish Political Studies* 4, pp. 21–42.

Gallagher, Michael, 2016. 'The results analysed: the aftershocks continue', in Michael Gallagher and Michael Marsh (eds), *How Ireland Voted 2016: The Election That Nobody Won*. Basingstoke: Palgrave Macmillan, pp. 125–57.

Gallagher, Michael and Michael Marsh, 1992. 'The presidential election of 1990', in Ronald J. Hill and Michael Marsh (eds), *Modern Irish Democracy: Essays in Honour of Basil Chubb*. Dublin: Irish Academic Press, pp. 62–81.

Garry, John, Fiachra Kennedy, Michael Marsh and Richard Sinnott, 2003. 'What decided the election?', in Michael Gallagher, Michael Marsh and Paul Mitchell (eds), *How Ireland Voted 2002*. Basingstoke: Palgrave Macmillan, pp. 119–42.

Grofman, Bernard, 1993. 'Is turnout the paradox that ate rational choice theory?', in Bernard Grofman (ed.), *Information, Participation, and Choice: 'An Economic Theory of Democracy' in Perspective*. Ann Arbor, MI: University of Michigan Press, pp. 93–106.

Harrison, M.J. and Michael Marsh, 1994. 'What can he do for us? Leader effects on party fortunes in Ireland', *Electoral Studies* 13, pp. 289–317.

Harrison, M.J. and Michael Marsh, 1998. 'A re-examination of an Irish popularity function', *Public Choice* 94, pp. 367–83

Holmberg, Sören and Henrik Oscarsson, 2011. 'Party leader effects on the vote', in Kees Aarts, André Blais and Hermann Schmitt (eds), *Political Leaders and Democratic Elections*. Oxford: Oxford University Press, pp. 35–51.

Kavanagh, Adrian, 2015. 'An end to "Civil War politics"? The radically reshaped political landscape of post-crash Ireland', *Electoral Studies* 38, pp. 71–81.

Kavanagh, Adrian, Gerald Mills and Richard Sinnott, 2004. 'The geography of Irish voter turnout: a case study of the Irish 2002 general election', *Irish Geography* 37, pp. 177–86.

Kayser, Mark A., 2014. 'The elusive economic vote', in Lawrence LeDuc, Richard G. Niemi and Pippa Norris (eds), *Comparing Democracies 4: Elections and Voting in a Changing World*. Thousand Oaks, CA: Sage, pp. 112–32.

Laver, Michael, 1986a. 'Ireland: politics with some social bases: an interpretation based on aggregate data', *Economic and Social Review* 17, pp. 107–31.

Laver, Michael, 1986b. 'Ireland: politics with some social bases: an interpretation based on survey data', *Economic and Social Review*, 17, pp. 193–213.

Laver, Michael, 2004. 'Analysing structures of party preference in electronic voting data', *Party Politics* 10, pp. 521–41.

Laver, Michael, 2005. 'Voting behaviour', in John Coakley and Michael Gallagher (eds), *Politics in the Republic of Ireland*, 4th edn. London: Routledge and PSAI Press, pp. 183–210.

Laver, Michael, Michael Marsh and Richard Sinnott, 1987. 'Patterns of party support', in Michael Laver, Peter Mair and Richard Sinnott (eds), *How Ireland Voted: The Irish General Election 1987*. Swords: Poolbeg, pp. 99–140.

Leahy, Pat, 2016. 'Campaign strategies: how the campaign was won and lost', in Michael Gallagher and Michael Marsh (eds), *How Ireland Voted 2016: the Election that Nobody Won*. Basingstoke: Palgrave Macmillan, pp. 75–97.

Lewis-Beck, Michael and Mary Stegmaier, 2013. 'The VP-function revisited: a survey of the literature on vote and popularity functions after over 40 years', *Public Choice* 157, pp. 367–85.

Leyden, Kevin M. and Michael Lewis-Beck, 2017. 'The economy and the vote in Irish national elections', in Michael Marsh, David M. Farrell and Gail McElroy (eds), *A Conservative Revolution? Electoral Change in Twenty-First-Century Ireland*. Oxford: Oxford University Press, pp. 28–41.

McElroy, Gail, 2017. 'Party competition in Ireland: the emergence of a left–right dimension?' in Michael Marsh, David M. Farrell and Gail McElroy (eds), *A Conservative Revolution? Electoral Change in Twenty-First-Century Ireland*. Oxford: Oxford University Press, pp. 61–82.

McElroy, Gail and Michael Marsh, 2010. 'Candidate gender and voter choice: analysis from a multi-member preferential voting system', *Political Research Quarterly* 63, 822–33

McElroy, Gail and Michael Marsh, 2011. 'Electing women to the Dáil: gender cues and the Irish voter', *Irish Political Studies* 26, pp. 521–34

Mair, Peter, 1979. 'The autonomy of the political: the development of the Irish party system', *Comparative Politics* 11, pp. 445–65.

Mair, Peter, 1987. *The Changing Irish Party System: Organisation, Ideology and Electoral Competition*. London: Pinter.

Mair, Peter, 2011. 'The election in context', in Michael Gallagher and Michael Marsh (eds), *How Ireland Voted 2011: The Full Story of Ireland's Earthquake Election*. Basingstoke: Palgrave Macmillan, pp. 283–97.

Mair, Peter and Michael Marsh, 2004. 'Political parties in electoral markets in postwar Ireland', in Peter Mair, Wolfgang C. Müller and Fritz Plasser (eds), *Political Parties and Electoral Change: Party Responses to Electoral Markets*. London: Sage, pp. 234–63.

Markus, G.B, 1986. 'Stability and change in political attitudes: observed, recalled, and "explained"', *Political Behaviour* 8, pp. 21–44.

Marsh, Michael, 1987. 'Electoral evaluations of candidates in Irish general elections, 1948–1982', *Irish Political Studies* 2, pp. 65–76.

Marsh, Michael, 1991. 'Accident or design: non-voting in Ireland', *Irish Political Studies* 6, pp. 1–14.

Marsh, Michael, 2006. 'Stability and change in structure of electoral competition 1989–2002', in John Garry, Niamh Hardiman and Diane Payne (eds), *Irish Social and Political Attitudes*. Liverpool: Liverpool University Press, pp. 94–112.

Marsh, Michael, 2007. 'Candidates or parties? Objects of electoral choice in Ireland', *Party Politics* 13, pp. 501–28.

Marsh, Michael, 2008. 'Explanations for party choice', in Michael Gallagher and Michael Marsh (eds), *How Ireland Voted 2007: The Full Story of Ireland's General Election*. Basingstoke: Palgrave Macmillan, pp. 105–31.

Marsh, Michael, 2017. 'After 2011: continuing the revolution', in Michael Marsh, David M. Farrell and Gail McElroy (eds), *A Conservative Revolution? Electoral Change in Twenty-First-Century Ireland*. Oxford: Oxford University Press, pp. 192–207.

Marsh, Michael and Richard Sinnott, 1990. 'How the voters decided', in Michael Gallagher and Richard Sinnott (eds), *How Ireland Voted 1989*. Galway: PSAI Press, pp. 68–93.

Marsh, Michael and Richard Sinnott, 1993. 'The voters: stability and change', in Michael Gallagher and Michael Laver (eds), *How Ireland Voted 1992*. Dublin/Limerick: Folens/PSAI Press, pp. 93–114.

Marsh, Michael and Richard Sinnott, 1999. 'The behaviour of the Irish voter', in Michael Marsh and Paul Mitchell (eds), *How Ireland Voted 1997*. Boulder: Westview, pp. 151–80.

Marsh, Michael and Slava Mikhaylov, 2010. 'European Parliament elections and EU governance', *Living Reviews in European Governance* 5:4, doi:10.12942/lreg-2010-4.

Marsh, Michael and James Tilley, 2010. 'The attribution of credit and blame to governments and its impact on vote choice', *British Journal of Political Science* 40:1, pp. 115–34.

Marsh, Michael and Kevin Cunningham, 2011. 'A positive choice, or anyone but Fianna Fáil?', in Michael Gallagher and Michael Marsh (eds), *How Ireland Voted 2011: The Full Story of Ireland's Earthquake Election*. Basingstoke: Palgrave Macmillan, pp. 172–202.

Marsh, Michael and Slava Mikhaylov, 2012. 'Economic voting in a crisis: the Irish election of 2011', *Electoral Studies* 31, pp. 478–84.

Marsh, Michael and Slava Mikhaylov, 2014. 'A conservative revolution: the electoral response to economic crisis in Ireland', *Journal of Elections, Public Opinion and Parties* 24, pp. 160–79.

Marsh, Michael and Gail McElroy, 2016. 'Voting behaviour: continuing dealignment', in Michael Gallagher and Michael Marsh (eds), *How Ireland Voted 2016: The Election That Nobody Won*. Basingstoke: Palgrave Macmillan, pp. 159–84.

Marsh, Michael and Carolina Plescia, 2016. 'Split-ticket voting in an STV system: choice in a non-strategic context', *Irish Political Studies* 31, pp. 1–18.

Marsh, Michael and Laura Schwirz, 2016. 'Exploring the non-alignment of party and candidate assessments in Ireland: do voters really follow candidates?', in Johan A. Elkink and David M. Farrell (eds), *The Act of Voting: Identities, Institutions and Locale*. London, Routledge, pp. 178–91.

Marsh, Michael, Richard Sinnott, John Garry and Fiachra Kennedy, 2001. 'The Irish national election study: puzzles and priorities', *Irish Political Studies* 16, pp. 161–78.

Marsh, Michael, Richard Sinnott, John Garry and Fiachra Kennedy, 2008. *The Irish Voter: The Nature of Electoral Competition in the Republic of Ireland*. Manchester: Manchester University Press.

Nadeau, Richard and Neil Nevitte, 2011. 'Leader effects and the impact of leader characteristics in nine countries', in Kees Aarts, André Blais and Hermann Schmitt (eds), *Political Leaders and Democratic Elections*. Oxford: Oxford University Press, pp. 128–46.

Ohr, Dieter and Henrik Oscarsson, 2011. 'Leader traits, leader image, and vote choice', in Kees Aarts, André Blais and Hermann Schmitt (eds), *Political Leaders and Democratic Elections*. Oxford: Oxford University Press, pp.187–214.

O'Malley, Eoin, 2001. 'Apathy or error? Questioning the Irish register of electors to question turnout decline', *Irish Political Studies* 16, pp. 179–90.

O'Malley, Eoin, 2008. 'Why is there no radical right party in Ireland?', *West European Politics* 31, pp. 960–77.

O'Malley, Eoin, 2012. 'Explaining the 2011 Irish presidential election: culture, valence, loyalty or punishment?', *Irish Political Studies* 27, pp. 635–55.

O'Malley, Eoin, 2014. 'Voter turnout data make many of our comparisons invalid'. https://politicalreform. ie/2014/09/19/voter-turnout-data-make-many-of-our-comparisons-invalid/ [accessed 24.1.2017].

Parker, A. J., 1982. 'The "friends and neighbours" voting effect in the Galway West constituency', *Political Geography Quarterly* 1, pp. 243–62.

Plutzer, Eric, 2004. 'Becoming a habitual voter: inertia, resources, and growth in young adulthood', *American Political Science Review* 96, pp. 41–56.

Powell, Bingham and Guy Whitten, 1993. 'A cross-national analysis of economic voting: taking account of the political context', *American Journal of Political Science* 37, 391–414.

Redmond, Paul and John Regan, 2015. 'Incumbency advantage in a proportional electoral system: a regression discontinuity analysis of Irish elections', *European Journal of Political Economy* 38, pp. 244–56.

Reif, Karlheinz and Hermann Schmitt, 1980. 'Nine second-order national elections – a conceptual framework for the analysis of European election results', *European Journal of Political Research* 8, pp. 3–44.

Rosenstone, Steven J., and J.M. Hansen, 1993. *Mobilization, Participation, and Democracy in America.* New York: Macmillan.

Sacks, Paul M., 1976. *The Donegal Mafia: An Irish Political Machine.* New Haven, CT and London: Yale University Press.

Sinnott, Richard, 1995. *Irish Voters Decide: Voting Behaviour in Elections and Referendums since 1918.* Manchester: Manchester University Press.

Sinnott, Richard and James McBride, 2011. 'Preference voting under PR-STV 1948–2011', in Michael Gallagher and Michael Marsh (eds), *How Ireland Voted 2011: The Full Story of Ireland's Earthquake Election.* Basingstoke: Palgrave Macmillan, pp. 205–221.

Stokes, Donald E., 1963. 'Spatial models of party competition', *American Political Science Review* 57, pp. 368–77.

Thomassen, Jacques, 1976. 'Party identification as a cross-national concept: its meaning in the Netherlands', in Ian Budge, Ivor Crewe and Dennis Farlie (eds), *Party Identification and Beyond.* London: John Wiley and Sons, pp. 63–79.

Thomsen, Søren Risbjerg and Jane Suiter, 2016. 'Candidates, parties and constituency relations', in Johan A. Elkink and David M. Farrell (eds), *The Act of Voting: Identities, Institutions and Locale.* London: Routledge, pp. 161–87.

Thomson, Robert, 2017. 'The malleable nature of party identification', in Michael Marsh, David M. Farrell and Gail McElroy (eds), *A Conservative Revolution? Electoral Change in Twenty-First-Century Ireland.* Oxford: Oxford University Press, pp. 123–42.

Tilley, James and John Garry, 2017. 'Class politics in Ireland: how economic catastrophe realigned Irish politics along economic divisions', in Michael Marsh, David M. Farrell and Gail McElroy (eds), *A Conservative Revolution? Electoral Change in Twenty-First-Century Ireland.* Oxford: Oxford University Press, pp. 11–27.

Van der Brug, Wouter, Cees van der Eijk and Michael Marsh, 2000. 'Exploring uncharted territory: the Irish presidential election 1997', *British Journal of Political Science* 30, pp. 631–50.

Van der Brug, Wouter, Mark Franklin and Gabor Toka, 2008. 'One electorate or many? Differences in party preference formation between new and established European democracies', *Electoral Studies* 27, pp. 589–600.

Van Elsas, Erika J., Rozemarijn Lubbe, Tom W.G. van der Meer and Wouter van der Brug, 2013. 'Vote recall: a panel study on the mechanisms that explain vote recall inconsistency', *International Journal of Public Opinion Research* 26:1, pp. 18–40.

Wagner, Markus, David Johann and Sylvia Kritzinger, 2012. 'Voting at 16: turnout and the quality of vote choice', *Electoral Studies* 31:2, pp. 372–83.

Whyte, John H., 1974. 'Ireland: politics without social bases', in Richard Rose (ed.), *Electoral Behavior: A Comparative Handbook.* New York: The Free Press, pp. 619–51.

Weeks, Liam, 2011. 'Rage against the machine: who is the independent voter?', *Irish Political Studies* 26, pp. 19–43.

Websites

www.tcd.ie/ines
Site of the 2002–7 Irish election study, which provides a facility to examine many tabulations of the data, as well as to download articles written using that data

nesstar.ess.nsd.uib.no/webview/
Browsable website for the European Social Survey, which covers Ireland and contains many politically relevant questions

www.tcd.ie/Political_Science/elections/elections.html
Archive of survey data on Irish elections and referendums

www.ucd.ie/issda/
Main archive of Irish survey and other socio-economic data, including the Irish election studies

electionsireland.org/
Highly detailed election results website

7   The Oireachtas

President and parliament

Michael Gallagher

The constitution defines the Oireachtas as consisting of two houses, Dáil Éireann and Seanad Éireann, and the president (Article 15.1.2). Of these three political actors, the Dáil is the most significant, and we shall concentrate upon it in this chapter. It currently consists of 158 members (see Appendix 2c) elected from 40 constituencies, while the upper house, the indirectly elected Seanad, has 60 members.

In this chapter, we shall first consider the role of the president, emphasising the almost complete disconnection of the office from the governmental process. We go on to outline the role ascribed to parliament by classical liberal-democratic theory, and then show how this role is severely qualified by the reality of political parties' domination of political life. We then examine the extent of the Dáil's involvement in the appointment and dismissal of governments, the making of laws and policies and the scrutiny of government. We discuss the impact of the Seanad on the political process before, finally, reviewing the reasons why parliament in Ireland has difficulty in holding the government to account, and tackling the issue of whether the Oireachtas should really be regarded as a weak parliament.

The president

The president is constitutionally defined as part of the Oireachtas but operates almost completely separately from the two houses of parliament. The office of the president (Articles 12 to 14) marked a major innovation in the 1937 constitution and during the debates on the constitution it aroused anxieties that proved to be out of all proportion to its actual political impact. The president plays no part in the day-to-day affairs of government. The direct election of the president qualifies Ireland for membership of the club of 'semi-presidential' regimes according to an influential definition, which states that such a regime 'may be defined as the situation where a popularly elected fixed-term president exists alongside a prime minister and cabinet who are responsible to parliament' (Elgie, 1999: 13). In terms of the political impact of the president, though, Ireland is much more 'centi-presidential' than semi-presidential.

The office is filled by direct election for a seven-year term in a nationwide vote using the alternative vote procedure (for which see Chapter 4, especially Table 4.2). The combination of direct election and few powers made the Irish presidency unusual for many years, though this combination is now more common (Elgie, 2012). The openness of the election process is qualified by the nomination provisions, which, prior to 2011, all but restricted candidacy to those backed by a major party, leading to suggestions that the process should be made more open. The emergence at the 2011 election of a total of seven candidates, including more minor party and independent candidates than at all previous presidential elections combined, appears to have taken this concern off the agenda (see Box 7.1).

Box 7.1 The nomination of presidential candidates

An outgoing or former president can nominate himself or herself for a second term, but any other aspirant needs to follow one of two routes. They need to be nominated by either:

- 20 members of the Houses of the Oireachtas (TDs or senators); or
- the councils of four cities or counties.

In either case, anyone without the backing of one of the traditional three main parties faced an uphill struggle to get onto the ballot paper before the party system began to fragment in the early years of the twenty-first century. Indeed, on six occasions (in 1938, 1952, 1974, 1976, 1983 and 2004) there was no election, because the main parties in effect agreed on a single candidate, who was declared elected without a contest. These parties' control of national and local elected bodies was such that no other candidate was able to gather sufficient backing to stand. Prior to 2011 only four independents had secured such nominations: in 1945 and 1990 independents backed by Labour stood for the office, and in 1997 two independent candidates managed to get onto the ballot paper without party backing. As a result, one common suggestion for reform of the presidency was to lower the nomination threshold.

In 2011, even though Fianna Fáil did not make a nomination, seven candidates stood (O'Malley, 2012). Sinn Féin had become strong enough to muster the requisite number of signatures from parliamentarians, and four independents each secured nominations from four councils. Now, concern was expressed that it was 'too easy' to stand, and that media coverage of the election, especially studio debates between the candidates, was rendered confusing for the electorate because of the need to give equal time to each of seven candidates.

Turning to the powers of the president, she or he is given six discretionary powers for use in specific situations (Coakley, 2013: 44–89; Gallagher, 2012). Four of these are fairly minor. Three give the president an adjudicatory role in certain disputes between Dáil and Seanad, should these arise; to date, they have not. A fourth (Article 13.2.3) empowers the president to convene a meeting of either, or both, of the Houses of the Oireachtas, a power that to date has been used only on quasi-ceremonial occasions. Before exercising any of these powers, or the power to refer a bill to the Supreme Court (referred to later), the president must listen to (but is not bound by) the advice of the Council of State, which contains a number of past and present senior political figures together with up to seven people whom she or he has personally appointed.

The remaining two powers are important and have been of practical effect. The first relates to the dissolution of the Dáil. Under normal circumstances, when a Taoiseach 'advises' the president to dissolve the Dáil and thereby bring about a general election, the president is bound to accede to this. However, the president, in the words of Article 13.2.2, 'may in his absolute discretion refuse to dissolve Dáil Éireann on the advice of a Taoiseach who has ceased to retain the support of a majority in Dáil Éireann'. A Taoiseach whose administration has lost a vote on a confidence motion is clearly covered by this article, but there is room for debate as to whether there are any other circumstances in which a president could turn down a Taoiseach's request for a dissolution – for example, what about a Taoiseach whose Dáil base has patently disappeared, but who has not actually been beaten there in a formal vote? This question was answered when President Mary Robinson 'let it be known' that if the Taoiseach, Albert Reynolds, leading a rump Fianna Fáil minority government in November 1994 following the collapse of his coalition with Labour, had asked her to dissolve the Dáil, she would have invoked Article 13.2.2 and refused to do so (Hogan, 1997). Reynolds did not make the request and instead resigned as Taoiseach. It seems, in fact, that the president has considerable discretion in deciding when this power may be exercised (Gallagher, 2012: 529). While the president might, then, have a role when a government's lifespan ends, the president has no role in the process of government formation, unlike some other European heads of state (Gallagher *et al.*, 2011: 416–17).

The other main power of the office is that the president, when presented with a bill passed by the Houses of the Oireachtas, can, instead of taking the usual course of signing it into law, refer it to the Supreme Court for a judgment on its compatibility with the constitution (see Chapter 3, pp. 67–8). On 15 occasions since 1937, a president has referred a bill to the Supreme Court for a decision on its constitutionality; eight times the court has upheld the legislation, and on seven occasions it has struck the bill down, either partly or in its entirety. The exercise of this power, while perfectly legitimate, embroiled President Ó Dálaigh in controversy in 1976, and led to his resignation after a minister who had called him a 'thundering disgrace' retained his position in the government (Rafter, 2012: 585–9). As noted in Chapter 3 (pp. 67–8), the existence of this power has both advantages and disadvantages.

In addition to these formal 'hard' powers, presidents also wield a certain amount of 'soft power', which is exercised primarily through the speeches they make and the causes that they seem to endorse through invitations they accept or visitors they receive. The election of Mary Robinson in 1990 is generally seen to have heralded a more active and energetic interpretation of the role, and the new president occasionally took steps against the wishes of the government, albeit ones consistent with conventional understanding of presidential behaviour (Galligan, 2012). After his election in 2011, Michael D. Higgins frequently made speeches that expressed the political views that he had held while a parliamentarian, and sometimes his remarks seemed at odds with government policy, though he took care not to criticise the government directly. For example, at the start of the 2016 election campaign, he expressed scepticism about the wisdom of tax cuts – which happened to be a central part of the election programme of the main government party, Fine Gael. Other public comments by the president were said to have provoked private 'fury' within the government (Mac Cormaic, 2016). However, the constitutional protection for the office is such that it would be very difficult for a government to constrain, let alone remove, a president who goes beyond the accepted bounds of the role, even if he or she were to breach the letter of the constitution (Gallagher, 2012: 534–6).

Every seven years (but only then), when presidential elections come around, there is debate about the office and whether it should be strengthened or further depoliticised. The Constitution Review Group did not favour bestowing additional powers on the office, clearly being supportive of the image of the president as being, as it put it, 'above politics' (CRG, 1996: 25–34). There is no pressure from any quarter for significant change in any aspect of the office.

Parliament and government: theory and practice

In a presidential system of government – which, as we have just seen, Ireland emphatically does not have – parliament and president come into existence through separate elections, have different mandates, have separate and defined roles and typically vie with each other for power. In a parliamentary system of government, things are different. Classical liberal democratic theory ascribes a key role to parliament in such systems. The people elect a parliament, which elects a government, makes laws and decides policies; the government then carries out these decisions of parliament and remains constantly accountable to it. This, in fact, is what enables democratic states to claim that they are democratic. However, as we see in the second part of this section, the central role of political parties has a huge impact on the way politics actually operates. Ireland has a system of weak – in fact, very weak – bicameralism, and we discuss the Seanad later in the chapter; for the moment we concentrate on the role of Dáil Éireann.

The role of parliament

Set against the theory just outlined, practice right across Europe can seem rather disappointing, because it appears that once a government gets into office, it can usually go its own way largely unchecked by parliament. And, even given these generally low expectations of how much control any parliament can really exercise over a government, together with the notorious difficulty of measuring the power of a parliament, it has frequently been argued that the Dáil is exceptionally weak. In the 1970s, Ward described it as 'supine', in the 1980s, Dinan declared it 'a woefully inadequate institution', and in the 1990s, Chubb saw it as 'a puny parliament peopled by members who have a modest view of their functions and a poor capacity to carry them out' (Ward, 1974: 241; Dinan, 1986: 71; Chubb, 1992: 189). In the rest of this chapter, we consider whether these summary judgements are reasonable, looking at what parliament is supposed to do and ask how well it does it. We focus primarily on Dáil Éireann, with discussion of the Seanad later in the chapter.

Arend Lijphart (2012: 2) identifies two diametrically opposite models of democracy: the majoritarian (or Westminster) model and the consensus model. When it comes to relations between parliament and government, and indeed in other ways too, Ireland displays features of both models, as we shall see during the course of the chapter (see also Bulsara and Kissane, 2009; Farrell and Suiter, 2016: 286–9). The Westminster model is characterised by, among other things, single-party and bare majority cabinets, cabinet dominance over parliament, a two-party system and unicameralism or unbalanced bicameralism (Lijphart, 2012: 9–29). In contrast, among the characteristics of the ideal-type consensus model are government by a broad coalition, a genuine separation of powers between government and parliament, a multi-party system and strong bicameralism (Lijphart, 2012: 30–45). Lijphart acknowledges, though, that it is difficult to measure executive dominance, and in practice he employs cabinet durability as a proxy for this (Lijphart, 2012: 117–23). Given the major impact of the British style of government on the Irish system at independence, it is no surprise that Ireland usually displays some features of the archetypal Westminster system, such as bare majority cabinets, no effective separation of power between government and parliament and unbalanced bicameralism – but it also possesses some characteristics of the archetypal consensus system, such as proportional representation (see Chapter 4) and a judicially-interpreted written constitution (see Chapter 3).

Turning to a closer examination of what parliament does, the constitution assigns two main functions to the Dáil. These are the appointment of the Taoiseach and the government (Articles 13 and 28), and law making, or more broadly policy making (Articles 15 to 27). The constitution also declares (Article 28.4.1) that 'The Government shall be responsible to Dáil Éireann'. This gives us three dimensions on which to assess the performance of the Dáil: the appointment of governments, policy making, and scrutiny of government behaviour. Before that, we need to face the implications of the reality that parliament is dominated by political parties.

Parties and parliament

Any assessment of the relationship between government and parliament in Ireland should start with the point that viewing the two as distinct bodies that vie for supremacy would be entirely unreal. Government and parliament are 'fused'. The government sits in parliament – in practice virtually all members of government at any time are TDs (members of the Dáil), as discussed in Chapter 10 – as opposed to being a body external to it. The government could be seen, as suggested by the nineteenth-century writer Walter Bagehot, as a committee of parliament, elected by it and acting in its name and with its authority. From this perspective, it is more realistic to see parliament as wielding power *through* the government that it has elected than to see it as seeking to *check* a government that has come into being independently of it.

Parliament, like every other aspect of modern political life, is dominated by political parties (Bowler *et al.*, 1999). When Dáil deputies vote on issues, they do so, in most cases, as members of a party, not as 158 atomised individuals. All around Europe, deputies follow the party line and, if anything, parliamentary party cohesion is even higher in Ireland than the European average. The norm is that every TD votes in accordance with the party line on every issue (Farrell *et al.*, 2013; Gallagher, 2010). There are powerful incentives to stay in line. TDs voting against the party whip, or even abstaining, can expect to find themselves summarily expelled from the parliamentary party group (PPG), with the prospect of remaining as independents until and unless the PPG agrees to readmit them. In addition, TDs know that rebellion will probably harm their chances of promotion within the party.

However, TDs' obedience to the party line is not primarily a matter of fear of draconian punishments if they stray. The rules of each PPG, after all, are made by its members, who choose voluntarily to bind themselves by such tight discipline. TDs of each party believe that if they act on every issue as a cohesive bloc of deputies they will be more powerful than if they acted as individuals. Deputies maintain discipline because they are reluctant to appear to be siding with the opposition, and because the party line is, in any case, likely to be broadly acceptable to them since they all joined the same party in the first place and, moreover, they have their say on it at meetings of the PPG. Their instincts are always to remain part of the party bloc, out of a sense of loyalty and common purpose. Moreover, the tough penalties imposed on defectors – provided these are universally applied – make life easier in some ways. They make TDs less vulnerable to pressure from outside the party; TDs cannot be picked off, one by one, by pressure groups or local interests, because everyone knows that any threats such bodies can make against a TD for not doing their bidding pale into insignificance against the punishment the party would impose for displeasing it. The norm of PPG bloc solidarity, ensured by the party whip, thus protects TDs against external pressures.

Although the Irish constitution makes no mention of political parties, these are recognised as 'groups' in the standing orders of the Dáil. Prior to 2016, the situation was that each registered party with at least seven TDs was able to constitute a group. All the other TDs (independents and minor party representatives) were permitted to form a 'technical' group, provided they could muster seven TDs, but only one such group was allowed. The fragmentation witnessed at the 2016 election led to some significant changes in these rules. The minimum size of a group was reduced to five TDs, and there was no limit on the number of technical groups. In the 32nd Dáil, there were nine groups: Fine Gael, Fianna Fáil, Sinn Féin, Labour, Solidarity–PBP, the Independent Alliance, Independents 4 Change, a Rural Technical Group and the Social Democrats–Green Party group.

This proliferation of groups has had implications for the way the Dáil allocates its time. Prior to 2016, government control of the parliamentary agenda in Ireland was high by comparative standards (Döring, 2004: 147–9; MacCarthaigh, 2005: 112–13, 133). This changed in the 32nd Dáil, where parliamentary time was allocated by the Business Committee, chaired by the Ceann Comhairle (speaker of the Dáil), on which Fine Gael had two members and each of the other eight groups had one. Thus, the government, and indeed the government and Fianna Fáil together, were in a minority. The government had, in effect, lost control of the parliamentary agenda, and while this increased speaking rights and bill initiation opportunities for TDs from smaller parties, there was a cost in legislative output, leading critics to brand the 32nd Dáil 'a do-nothing Dáil'. It remains to be seen whether a similar body would retain such power in a future Dáil in which the government commanded an overall majority and in the summer of 2017 the two main parties agreed, to their joint benefit, on a redistribution of speaking time under which the allocation would more closely reflect all groups' respective strengths.

The Ceann Comhairle is elected by TDs at the first meeting of each Dáil following an election. Votes for the position have traditionally followed party lines, and whenever a government has had a secure majority, it has used this to install one of its own TDs in the position. Only occasionally, when the government of the day has had a very slim majority or has been in a minority, has it preferred to allow another TD to take the position, rather than sustain a reduction in its own voting strength by supplying the Ceann Comhairle from its own side of the house. Typically, the Ceann Comhairle elected in times of majority government is a government TD who has built up a degree of seniority but has been passed over by the Taoiseach when government posts were allocated. Successive oppositions have felt that the Ceann Comhairle of the day was, consciously or unconsciously, unduly protective of the government, rather than seeing it as his (every past occupant of the position has been male) mission to enable TDs to hold the government to account. Thus, one suggestion for Dáil reform has long been the introduction of a secret ballot election for Ceann Comhairle, in the hope that backbench government TDs in particular would feel freer to vote for a candidate who would represent the parliamentary rank and file rather than the 'bosses', and this reform was introduced at the start of the 32nd Dáil in March 2016. The candidate elected, Seán Ó Fearghaíl of Fianna Fáil, was generally seen as 'independent of government and carrying greater authority' (Lynch *et al.*, 2017: 50).

However, whether this reform would have much significance in times of majority government remains to be seen. For one thing, government TDs might well be inclined to support 'one of their own' rather than back an opposition TD, even in a secret ballot, partly out of sympathy for a colleague passed over for a ministerial position, and partly because of the electoral advantage in holding the position, given that the outgoing Ceann Comhairle is automatically returned to the next Dáil without a contest. This privilege, it has been said, is not accorded to the parliamentary speaker in any other jurisdiction (O'Connor, 2010: 170).[1] Government backbenchers might, it is true, potentially support an independent-minded colleague in a secret ballot rather than one favoured by the leadership, but given that in 2016 both Fianna Fáil and Sinn Féin put forward a designated party candidate for the position of Ceann Comhairle, even this is not a foregone conclusion.

The fusion of executive and legislature in parliamentary systems means that to consider parliament and government as two separate bodies competing with each other is to ignore the reality of party domination of parliament and government. Any effective increase in the role or power of 'parliament' vis-à-vis government means, in effect, an increase in the role or power of the opposition, not of parliament as a collective body. The role of government backbenchers, willingly accepted, is to sustain the government rather than to act as independent scrutinisers of it; government backbenchers do not seek additional means of holding their own ministers to account through parliamentary procedures, though they do this at private meetings of the parliamentary party group, as discussed later. The ongoing battle of government versus opposition is paramount and tangible; the notion of a contest for power between government and parliament bears little relation to political reality.

The importance of parties is illustrated by the simple fact that, notwithstanding the sometimes high number of independent TDs (see Chapter 5), an overwhelming majority of TDs have been elected on a party ticket. Beyond that fact, the profile of TDs is similar to that in most west European parliaments. In the 32nd Dáil, which was elected in 2016, the average TD was aged 51, with only six under 30 and just three over 70 (details of TDs' backgrounds are based on Gallagher, 2016: 151–4). Almost half of all TDs have a professional occupation, with school-teachers the most common category; the great majority of TDs are, in practice, full-time politicians. A little over half of Dáil members have a university degree. TDs have very strong local roots; nearly all live in their constituency, most were born and raised there, and 82 per cent were members of local government before being elected to the Dáil. Women are markedly under-represented, albeit not to the same extent as prior to 2016 (see Chapter 9). In short, the archetypal TD is male, middle-aged, middle-class and locally implanted.

Appointment and dismissal of governments

The formal position, as laid out in Article 13.1 of the constitution, is that the Dáil nominates the Taoiseach and approves the composition of the government, whereupon the president appoints them. The Dáil can also dismiss a Taoiseach and a government by passing a vote of no confidence (Article 28.10). In Westminster-model countries, governments are typically determined directly by elections, and the vote of parliament after the election merely puts the seal on what the voters have decided. In consensus model countries, in contrast, government formation can be a more complicated and time-consuming process; coalition government is the norm, and it may take weeks or months of negotiation to produce one (see Gallagher *et al.*, 2011: 412–57).

Until the 1980s, government formation in Ireland was usually seen as a variant of Westminster practice, with coalitions and minority governments relatively rare. Certainly, there have been elections that conformed very well to the model. For example, at the 1977 election Fianna Fáil won a majority of the votes and 84 of the 148 seats, and when the new Dáil met, the Fianna Fáil leader, Jack Lynch, was duly elected as Taoiseach on the block vote of the Fianna Fáil TDs. But single-party majority government was not as common as was sometimes assumed prior to the 1980s, while since 1981 it has disappeared. Over the whole period of the state, single-party majority governments have been in office for only 37 per cent of the time. Between 1948 and 2016, only four of the 20 governments were single-party majority ones, and these governments held office for only about 17 of those 68 years, during which period majority coalition government was twice as common (see Table 7.1). No election since 1977 has produced a single-party majority government. While majority government is the norm, minority governments have been in office more than a quarter of the time.

Table 7.1 Number and duration of governments in Ireland, 1923–2016

	1923–2016			1948–2016		
	Number of governments	Days in office	% of total days in office	Number of governments	Days in office	% of total days in office
1-party majority	9	12,542	37.1	4	6,026	24.2
1-party minority	8	5,888	17.4	4	3,488	14.0
Coalition majority	9	12,111	35.8	9	12,111	48.7
Coalition minority	3	3,263	9.7	3	3,263	13.1
Majority governments	18	24,653	72.9	13	18,137	72.9
Minority governments	11	9,151	27.1	7	6,751	27.1
Total	29	33,804	100.0	20	24,888	100.0

Source: Details of governments from Appendix 3c.

Note: Governments are defined as lasting until either a change of partisan composition or an election. The three governments holding exactly 50 per cent of Dáil seats are classified as majority if the Ceann Comhairle (Speaker) was drawn from opposition ranks (1965 and 1989), or minority when the Ceann Comhairle was a government TD (1937).

There are three ways in which government composition might be settled: by an election at which a single party or a pre-agreed coalition wins a majority of seats; by political parties which, after an unclear election outcome, put together a majority coalition; or by the Dáil itself, which elects a government whose own strength alone does not suffice for a majority. In the first two cases, the Dáil's role could be seen as nominal, in that it is merely ratifying either a verdict of the people or a deal made among parties in what used to be referred to as smoke-filled rooms. Elections are less frequently the sole battleground that determines government composition: in the post-1948 period, only five elections have directly produced a government. On another nine occasions, governments have not been chosen directly by the electorate but have resulted from post-election agreements among parties (see Table 7.2). This leaves seven occasions when the role of the Dáil has been decisive. In four of these cases, the Dáil elected minority Fianna Fáil governments. The other three occurred in 1981, when a minority Fine Gael–Labour coalition emerged; in 1997, when a minority Fianna Fáil–Progressive Democrats (PDs) coalition government was formed; and in 2016, when a Fine Gael-dominated government, with three independent ministers, was elected by 59 votes to 49, with the remaining 50 TDs not voting.

When we turn to the Dáil's role in dismissing governments, a similar picture emerges: compliance neither with the purest version of the Westminster model nor with the consensus model. The Dáil has dismissed a government on only two occasions. The first was in November 1982, when the minority Fianna Fáil government was defeated by 82 votes to 80 on a confidence motion. The second was in November 1992, when the PDs left the government and joined the opposition benches, whereupon a motion of no confidence in the Fianna Fáil minority government was passed by 88 votes to 77. At first sight, then, the record might look like that of an archetypal Westminster system, where the support of parliament can generally be taken for granted by the government.

However, there have been nine other occasions when the Dáil has, in effect, terminated the life of a government, which has chosen to resign rather than continue in a situation where defeat on a confidence motion seemed imminent. This happened in August 1927, 1938 and 1944, when the minority governments of the day were in a weak position and preferred to call a general election at a time of their own choosing, rather than wait for the Dáil to pull

Table 7.2 Origins of governments, 1948–2016

Government composition settled by	Number of cases	Cases
Election: single party or pre-declared coalition wins majority of seats	5	1957, 1965, 1969, 1973, 1977
Parties: parties controlling a majority of seats put together post-election majority coalition	9	1948, 1954, Nov 1982, 1989, 1992, 1994, 2002, 2007, 2011
Parliament: Dáil elects government that controls only a minority of seats	7	1951, 1961, 1981, Feb 1982, 1987, 1997, 2016

the plug. Similarly, prior to calling the 1951 election, the first Inter-Party government had been losing support from some of its own backbenchers in the wake of the traumatic 'Mother and Child' affair (see pp. 22 and 47 above). Six years later, the same fate befell the second Inter-Party government, and this factor was coupled with a weakening of its Dáil position due to by-election defeats together with the fact that the government had more or less lost confidence in itself (Gallagher, 2009: 129). In January 1982, the minority coalition government resigned immediately upon being defeated in a vote on its budget. In January 1987, Labour pulled out of its coalition with Fine Gael, leaving its erstwhile partners with only 68 seats and facing inevitable defeat had the Dáil met again. In 1994, Labour again pulled out of a coalition, this time with Fianna Fáil, and the rump Fianna Fáil government faced certain defeat in a confidence motion; on this occasion, in an unprecedented development, the government resigned but the Taoiseach did not seek a dissolution, given the expectation that the president would not grant one if he requested it (as mentioned earlier). In early 2011, the Green Party withdrew from its coalition with Fianna Fáil, bringing about the collapse of that government. In other words, one reason why governments have so rarely been dismissed by the Dáil is that when they have seen defeat staring them in the face, they have usually jumped off the cliff rather than waiting to be pushed.

The Westminster model, then, does not adequately capture the reality of the Dáil's role in appointing and dismissing governments. However, it remains true that Irish governments do not routinely fear dismissal by the Dáil; they are not regularly made or broken on the floor of the house. In this, the Dáil is in line with virtually every other parliament in Europe. The idea of parliaments constantly making and unmaking governments is neither realistic nor attractive. The classic example of a parliament wielding this power occurred in France's Fourth Republic, where there were 28 governments in only 13 years. Few would recommend 'strengthening' the Dáil so that this pattern could be replicated. If parliament has a role, it must lie in one of the areas to which we now turn.

Making policy

The production of legislation

Once the government has approved a proposal requiring legislation, the secretary general to the government sends the Attorney General (the government's legal officer) a letter requesting that legislation be drafted in accordance with the memorandum for government. As in most common-law countries, the drafting of legislation is carried out by specialist barristers whose full-time duty this is, rather than by civil servants. Specifically, legislation is drafted in the Office of the Parliamentary Counsel to the Government, operating under the auspices of the

Attorney General. The Attorney General has a role in scrutinising the draft legislation to ensure that it is compatible with the constitution – as we saw in Chapter 3, the Irish courts are active in hearing and, where appropriate, upholding challenges to the constitutionality of pieces of legislation. Once the bill has passed through this process, it goes to parliament for discussion.

Inevitably, the calm and methodical process that a formal description implies may not always occur in practice. Those responsible for drafting legislation complain that political actors do not always allow them sufficient time to do their job thoroughly. There are suggestions that a minister who comes under political pressure over some issue may demand a bill hastily, even if it is not yet ready. Indeed, in 2006, the Chief Justice commented on the 'patent' weakness in some 'hastily-drafted legislation' that the courts had recently had to try to interpret (Mac Cormaic, 2006). Ministers, in turn, sometimes feel that the drafters can be excessively fastidious in their approach, and that, if left unpressured, they would take an unacceptably long time to complete their tasks to their own satisfaction. It is apparent from this account that legislation is typically initiated by governments, not by parliament, and that parliament discusses, not always with sufficient care, ministerial proposals for legislation, rather than producing its own.

Over the half-century from 1966 to 2015, 1,897 bills were passed – an average of 38 per year. The number of bills passed per year has increased in the twenty-first century; over the years 2000–15, the average has been 44 bills per year. There is some sign that bill production is linked to the electoral cycle, as, over the 50-year period, the average number of bills passed in the last full calendar year before an election was 42. One clear trend is that even though the number of acts passed by parliament is not increasing, the length of those acts is. The average number of sections per act rose from 14 in 1956 to 23 in 1976, 27 in 1996 and 35 in 2015.

In addition, the volume of 'delegated legislation' in the form of statutory instruments has been increasing, especially since Ireland joined the European Union (EU) in 1973. This arises when parliament passes an act that expresses a broad goal and allows another authority – usually a specific minister – to make the detailed regulations (Morgan, 1990: 107–11). The rationale is that the central political issue at stake is discussed and decided by parliament, and the technical or administrative details are left to specialised authorities to work out. The power given to a minister under these terms may be quite extensive, including, for example, the right to amend existing laws without being subject to parliamentary scrutiny (see Chapter 10, p. 258). The rate of issue of statutory instruments in the period 2009–16, at 644 per year, was more than twice that in the 18th and 19th Dála (1965–73), at 295 per year.

The Dáil's role in law-making

The constitution, by assigning law-making powers exclusively to the Oireachtas (Article 15.2.1), reflects one of the central tenets of classical liberal democratic theory: the legislature (parliament) makes laws and the executive (government) carries them out. In this Montesquieuan vision, the government is merely the striking arm of parliament, carrying out parliament's will whether it likes it or not. This is obviously not the case in reality, and it is more common to find the view expressed that parliament, in Ireland even more than in many other countries, has come to be a mere 'glorified rubber stamp' (Dinan, 1986: 76) for whatever proposals government puts before it. It is a slight, but only a very slight, exaggeration to say that all legislation passed by the Dáil emanates from the government, and that all legislation proposed by the government is passed by the Dáil. In the 32nd Dáil, practice was rather different from the pre-2016 norm because the government rested on the support of little more than a third of TDs, as we note at various points in the discussion.

In the area of policy making, we can again distinguish between the Westminster and consensus models. In the former, parliament is not seen as a real maker of laws but instead provides a forum where the issues raised by a government proposal can be fully aired. The government is obliged to justify its measure and the opposition gets the chance to make the case against it (and, generally, to keep the government on its toes), but ultimately, the government sees its plans approved by parliament pretty much as a matter of course. There is no feeling that the opposition's views need to be taken into account or that its agreement is required for the passage of legislation – after all, the opposition is the opposition precisely because it 'lost' the last election and the government won it. To bring the opposition fully into the policy-making process would reduce the significance of the choice made by the voters at elections. In the ideal-type consensus model (which, of course, may not be realised anywhere in reality), in contrast, government is (or, at least, feels) obliged to take seriously the wishes of parliament, including the preferences of the opposition. While in the last resort it is the government that governs, governments prefer not to railroad their legislation through against strong resistance; they try to find a consensus within parliament for their proposals and are willing to take on board constructive suggestions from the opposition.

Ireland's law-making procedure, at least prior to the 2016 election, has been closely based, in the letter and in the spirit, on that of Westminster. Bills can be introduced in either house – in the past, almost all government bills were introduced in the Dáil, but since the 1980s more have been initiated in the Seanad. The formal progress of a bill is the same through each house, but since in the event of a disagreement between Dáil and Seanad it is the former that prevails (see p. 184), we shall concentrate here on the Dáil (for details, see Caffrey, 2010). A five-stage process is provided for bills, though most bills bypass the first (see Box 7.2). The second stage is the general debate on the principle of the bill. The third (committee stage) involves a detailed examination of each section of the bill. The fourth and fifth stages consist of considering the outcome of the committee stage and formally passing the bill. After this, bills go to the other house and then to the president, who signs them into law or, very rarely, refers them to the Supreme Court for a decision on their constitutionality (see pp. 67–8). In effect, only the second stage (through outright rejection) and the third stage (through amendment) offer the house any real opportunity to affect the content of a bill.

The second stage debates tend to have a ritualistic quality about them. The relevant minister opens the event by outlining the rationale for the measure to be introduced, after which a succession of opposition deputies pour cold water on the bill under discussion or, at best, welcome the legislation but criticise the delay in bringing it forward. A government bill faces the prospect of defeat at the second stage only in a situation of minority government. Governments in a weak position, such as the Fine Gael-led administration elected in 2016, usually avoid such defeats simply by refraining from introducing legislation that is likely to be defeated.

TDs are not supposed to read speeches from a prepared text, but they may use 'notes', which are sometimes very extensive. Indeed, critics see Dáil debates as little more than an exchange of scripts (usually supplied by party support staff) that are read tediously and sometimes haltingly into the record (Hannon, 2004: 102). Not surprisingly, then, second stage speeches, at least once the minister and the main opposition spokesperson have had their say, are made to a nearly empty chamber. Most TDs are not present until a few minutes before they are due to speak. While some profess indignation at the low level of attendance in the Dáil chamber, it is hard to criticise those TDs and ministers who decide that they have more

Box 7.2 The stages of a bill initiated in Dáil Éireann

Stage	Matters decided
First stage	Formal introduction of bill, securing agreement that the bill proceed to second stage. Virtually all bills (government bills, and private members' bills introduced by a 'group' of at least five deputies) can be presented to the house without needing this formal agreement, and enter the process at the second stage.
Second stage	Debate on the broad principle of the bill. The details of the bill are not discussed at this stage, and the substance of the bill cannot be amended. The vote taken after the second stage debate (assuming there is one – a significant number of bills are passed by agreement of the house, without the need for a vote) determines whether the bill is allowed to proceed or is rejected.
Third stage	Committee stage. The bill is examined in detail by a specialist 7-member committee. The bill is discussed section by section. Amendments may be proposed, provided they do not conflict with the principle of the bill, since this was approved by the house at the second stage.
Fourth stage	Report stage. Usually a formal acceptance of amendments made at third stage, or further amendment of the bill. Some amendments may be introduced by the sponsoring minister in response to arguments raised at the third stage. New amendments may be proposed, provided that they do not effectively repeat amendments rejected at the third stage.
Fifth stage	The final and formal passing of the bill. Speeches at this stage tend to be shorter and more ritualistic versions of those at the second stage. The bill now goes to the Seanad for discussion.
Final stages	When it returns from the Seanad, the Dáil discusses the changes, if any, proposed by the Seanad. If it accepts them, the bill is sent to the president, for signing into law or, at the president's discretion, for referral to the Supreme Court for a verdict on its constitutionality. If the Dáil does not accept the Seanad's suggested amendments, it sends the bill back to the Seanad for reconsideration. The Seanad may fall into line with the wishes of the Dáil or it may reaffirm its amendments, in which case it can delay, but not veto, the passage of the bill.

Note: Bills can also be initiated in the Seanad. In this case, they then go to the Dáil after being passed, but, in the event of the Dáil's deciding to make amendments, they are treated as if they had been initiated in the Dáil (Article 20.2.2 of the constitution).

useful ways of spending their time. As Bertie Ahern once put it during his time as Taoiseach, 'if you're in the Dáil all day you wouldn't do any work' (RTÉ1, 'Ryan Tubridy Show', 13 May 2006). Debate can be brought to an abrupt halt by the government deploying the 'guillotine': using its majority to terminate debate and dispose of all remaining stages of a bill in a single vote (MacCarthaigh and Manning, 2010: 443; O'Dowd, 2010: 325). This can result in flawed legislation being passed because the opposition did not get the chance to examine a bill thoroughly or to have all of its proposed amendments discussed, and the Fine Gael–Labour government of 2011–16 encountered much criticism for alleged over-use of the guillotine, especially on legislation relating to water charges.

Dáil debates can thus be dialogues of the deaf, set pieces with a strong element of theatre, in which TDs speak for the record or in order to get publicity at local level. Deputies wonder whether anyone is listening to them, as indeed do parliamentarians in many countries, and hence whether there is much point in putting a lot of work into their contributions. The media suspects there is little public interest in routine Dáil debates or committee sittings; newspaper coverage of parliamentary proceedings is far less than it was in the 1980s and before. It seems that there is a vicious circle whereby TDs make little effort to produce interesting speeches because they believe the media will ignore them whatever they say, while the media feel justified in not reporting most speeches because they are uninteresting. More charitably to both, Ceann Comhairle John O'Donoghue once observed that the parliamentary process, especially the work of committees, 'does not often fit the daily news cycle' (O'Donoghue, 2008). When it does, as at times when a political story is high on the news agenda, there is much more media attention to what is said in the Dáil, at least by leading party figures. Oireachtas proceedings have been televised since 1991, and the introduction in September 2014 of Oireachtas TV, a dedicated channel that covers debates and committee hearings, enables interested citizens to follow developments without being reliant on editorial judgements made by mainstream media.

Government and opposition

The assumption made so far is that all legislation emanates from the government because, with rare exceptions, only government bills can expect to pass into law. Indeed, the constitution states (Article 17.2) that no motion or resolution shall be passed, or law enacted, that involves spending public money, unless the Dáil receives a written message, signed by the Taoiseach, recommending the measure on behalf of the government. This is a stipulation in many countries, the rationale being that were it not in force, parliament might vote for the spending of money but against government efforts to raise it. Moreover, governments have ways of dealing with legislation that manages to get passed against their wishes. When the 1987–89 Fianna Fáil government sustained Dáil defeats on motions apparently 'directing' it to take certain steps, it ignored the motions, dismissing them as being merely declaratory. Similarly, the 32nd Dáil passed a number of bills on which the Fine Gael-led government was outvoted (and others that it did not bother to vote against because it knew it would be defeated), but these disappeared into the thicket of the committee stage with little or no prospect of becoming laws. Dáil standing orders contain provision for 'private members' bills', which are usually introduced by an opposition deputy.[2] From 1937 to 2002, only 15 such bills were passed (MacCarthaigh, 2005: 110), and there were additional instances of governments accepting bills originating with the opposition. Such bills do not represent any temporary dominance of parliament over government, though, because unless the government is in an exceptionally weak position, as in the 32nd Dáil, they will be passed only if the government directs its own backbenchers to support them.

The opposition, then, is unlikely under normal (that is, pre-2016) circumstances to secure the defeat of a government bill or the passage of a bill of its own. If the Dáil is to make any impression on legislation, this must usually come at the third, 'committee', stage of a bill's progress, where the opposition can hope to have some influence on the final shape of the bill. Since 1993, bills have gone to the relevant specialist committee for their third stage scrutiny: health bills to the health committee, agriculture bills to the agriculture committee, and so on. The government would usually have a majority on these committees, reflecting its majority in the house as a whole, though in the 32nd Dáil the government was in a minority on every committee just as it was in the Dáil itself. Although discussion on the broad principle of the bill is ruled out, this having been settled at the second stage, TDs can raise points about specific sections: they can point out anomalies, inconsistencies, loopholes, imprecise phraseology, and so on. If the points raised are consistent with the basic intention of the bill, the minister might well accept them and undertake to modify the bill accordingly.

The atmosphere in a small committee may be less confrontational than in the full chamber and ministers may be readier to take opposition proposals on board. If the minister does not want to accept opposition amendments, then, provided that the government has a majority of seats in the Dáil, they will fail. Examining the periods 1969–73 and 1982–89, O'Dowd (2010: 327–8) found that 99 per cent of government amendments to bills, but only 3 per cent of those emanating from non-ministerial TDs, were passed. This might suggest that non-ministerial TDs are wasting their time by tabling amendments, but it needs to be borne in mind that some of the ministerial amendments were introduced precisely to incorporate suggestions made at committee stage by opposition TDs or by government backbenchers (O'Dowd, 2010: 333–7). Parliamentary committees have greater scope for influence if they can discuss bills before the whole house does so. Traditionally, in the Oireachtas, the plenary discussions have preceded the involvement of the relevant committee, but in 2011 a system of 'pre-legislative scrutiny' was introduced, under which the outlines of a bill go first for examination to the relevant committee. This reform marks a significant departure from past practice and holds the potential for a greater policy-making role for committees and hence for the parliamentary opposition.

Notwithstanding this change, the Dáil is still not fundamentally an active participant in the process of making laws, let alone broader policy. Governments are usually more concerned to bring the major interest groups round to their way of thinking (see Chapter 11) than to placate the Dáil, whose backing they tend to take for granted. The Dáil is often seen as legitimising legislation rather than really making it, though the role of legitimation should not be disparaged. Norton (1990: 147) points out that parliaments play an important symbolic role, and that for many people the fact that all legislation has to be passed by a parliament consisting of the elected representatives of the people is more important in making them feel that they are ruled democratically than the question of how much real power that parliament wields. Parliament in Ireland appears to be trusted by the population slightly more than the average across the EU; a Eurobarometer survey of November 2016 found that 40 per cent of Irish respondents, compared with an average of 32 per cent across the EU, tended to trust parliament, the tenth highest figure among the 28 EU member states (Eurobarometer, 2016: T49).

It would be an exaggeration, in any case, to say that Ireland suffers from 'cabinet dictatorship' or an 'elected dictatorship' between elections. Quite apart from the extra-parliamentary checks on government, such as the constitution, the Dáil cannot be disregarded. The Dáil will do what the government wants, provided, and only provided, the government has the backing of a majority of TDs. In situations of minority government, the government will be able to get its legislation through only if it takes care not to introduce any proposals that would induce the opposition to combine against it. For example, the minority Fianna Fáil–PD government of 1997–2002 suffered no defeats on any of its legislative proposals, but that was because it took care not to introduce proposals that would have been defeated, not because the Dáil was certain always to do its bidding. This constraint was also brought home repeatedly to the Fine Gael-led minority government elected in 2016.

Governments and their backbenchers

As well as these external constraints, we need to bear in mind that the government has to pay a price to retain the backing of its TDs. Relations between governments and their own backbenchers are central to any understanding of the relationship between government and parliament (Andeweg and Nijzink, 1995; King, 1976). The real action may be taking place within the government parliamentary parties, rather than in the Dáil chamber (Gallagher, 2010). Ministers have to show their backbenchers some respect in order to keep them trooping loyally through the government lobbies. When the party is in power, weekly meetings of its PPG (attended by TDs, senators and MEPs) hear from ministers about their plans, and they expect this to be a genuine process of consultation. If a TD raises a doubt or a question, the minister would be unwise to brush this aside as dismissively as an opposition TD might be dealt with in the Dáil chamber – ministers, after all, want to be personally popular with their own TDs, for a variety of obvious reasons.

The initiative in making policy lies with the government, not with backbenchers. But no government has a completely free hand from its own party; if a proposed policy or item of legislation arouses broad antagonism from government TDs at a PPG meeting, it is unlikely to be pressed further. For example, this occurred in 2005, when government proposals to introduce 'café bars' ran into Fianna Fáil backbench resistance, allegedly following heavy pressure from the publicans' lobby group, and in 2016–17, when Fine Gael backbenchers objected to ministerial proposals that shops be permitted to sell alcohol only in marked-off areas of their premises. Similarly, in the extremely rare event that government TDs are persuaded of a government measure's flaws by a critical speech from an opposition TD in the Dáil, this will be reflected not in their voting against the measure in the chamber but in private pressure on the minister to amend or rescind the proposal. An awareness of what the PPG will and will not stand for is bound to be a factor in determining what policies the government tries to introduce.

With this qualification, then, it is the government and not the rest of parliament that has the initiative in the shaping of laws and policies. Once again, the Irish pattern is not exceptional. Of course, in presidential systems of government, such as the USA, parliament can be quite strong, because the survival of a government is not at stake: if a presidentially-backed bill is defeated in Congress, the administration does not fall. But things are very different in the parliamentary systems of government by which most European countries are governed. When a government is elected by, answerable to, and dismissible by parliament, measures proposed by the government are very unlikely to be rejected by parliament. All that we might hope for is that the Dáil keeps a vigilant eye on what government is up to, the topic that we now examine.

Scrutinising the behaviour of government

The initiative in making policy, then, lies with government, rather than with parliament. However, this does not freeze parliament out of the political process entirely. Even if it does pass virtually all the government's proposals, it may still keep the government under careful scrutiny, monitoring whether it has adhered to its commitments and on whether public money has been spent as it promised, keeping it on its toes and exposing its mistakes. Debates on motions other than bills, such as motions of confidence or ad hoc motions on 'matters of urgent public importance', may serve this function (Caffrey, 2010: 268–71; MacCarthaigh, 2005: 106–15, 128–32), but the two main methods of trying to compel the government to justify its behaviour lie in parliamentary questions and in the use of committees.

Parliamentary questions

The Dáil normally sits on Tuesdays, Wednesdays and Thursdays when in session: from 2 pm to 10 pm on Tuesdays, from 12 noon to 10 pm on Wednesdays and from 12 noon until around 8 pm on Thursdays. These are not 'normal' working hours in most occupations, but finding the optimal weekly schedule for parliament is a perennial and ultimately unsolvable dilemma. One cross-party difficulty in extending sitting hours per week is a conflict between deputies based in or close to Dublin and those who cannot commute on a daily basis to Leinster House. The former would prefer the Dáil to sit for four days a week and to maintain a nine-to-five routine, while the latter want their sojourn away from their homes to be kept to a minimum and hence would prefer fewer but longer sitting days.

On each of the three sitting days, party leaders have half an hour to ask questions. The Taoiseach answers questions for a further 90 minutes each week, and over six hours are dedicated to questions to ministers, who take it in turn to face these. Questions must be put down in advance, to give the minister and departmental civil servants time to discover the information sought. Most questions seek a written answer, which the TD receives within three working days, but others are put down for oral answer, which means that the TD must wait until the relevant minister's day for answering questions comes around. Questions may seek very detailed information about an individual constituent or the constituency of the TD asking the question (this is characteristic of questions for written answer), or they may ask about a topic of national significance or a matter of government policy (characteristic of questions for oral answer). TDs can respond to the minister's reply to a question answered orally by asking a 'supplementary' question. A TD dissatisfied with the minister's reply can raise and elaborate upon his or her grievance during the time set aside for 'topical issues' (formerly known as the 'adjournment debate') that occupies the last 48 minutes of each day's sitting, and the minister is obliged to reply more fully. The order in which questions for oral answer appear on the order paper (which determines which ones will be reached, since time constraints mean that on average fewer than 20 questions are answered orally each day) is settled by lottery.

The number of questions asked per year has risen greatly over the decades, from around 1,200 in the mid-1930s to 4,000 in the mid-1960s and an average of 41,166 (1,507 answered orally and 39,659 answered in writing) in the period 2013–15. The 2013–15 figure represents an average of around 250 questions a year from each TD, which is more than twice as many as from MPs in any of a set of European parliaments examined by Rozenberg and Martin (2011: 401). Exactly the same pattern of a major increase in parliamentary questions over the years is found in several other west European countries (Gallagher *et al.*, 2011: 58; Rozenberg and Martin, 2011: 396). The fact that most questions are tabled by opposition TDs affirms the political motive of putting down a question – government deputies ask relatively few questions, even of a local nature.

Question time is highly politicised. Opposition TDs put down questions for oral answer not in an ingenuous search for information but, in most cases, as part of the ongoing war of attrition against the government, which they hope to be able to embarrass (Hannon, 2004: 103). Ministers treat question time in the same spirit, aiming to give away as little as possible. The culture is one of concealment, not of openness. The etiquette of parliamentary questions (PQs) requires not that answers be helpful or informative, but only that they not be untruthful. Answers to a number of possible supplementary questions are prepared, but the information contained in them is not disclosed unless the relevant supplementary is asked.

The chairman of the long-running Beef Tribunal (discussed further in Chapter 11) stated that if questions had been answered in the Dáil as fully as they had to be answered in the tribunal, the tribunal would not have been necessary. Relevant information that is not specifically asked for is not disclosed: a minister involved in the beef affair, Ray Burke, explained that if the opposition did not ask the right questions, they would not get the right answers (O'Toole, 1995: 256). John Bruton, while opposition leader in the 1990s, deplored this approach, as oppositions usually do. However, entering government may diminish such reforming zeal, and in February 1995, as Taoiseach, Bruton used exactly the same words as Burke when explaining on the radio that he had not disclosed a piece of information because the TDs questioning him had 'not asked the right question', to which the opposition responded that they could not possibly have asked the right question unless they had already known the answer (Kerrigan and Brennan, 1999: 38).

Logistically, the odds at question time are stacked in the ministers' favour. After all, they have had some days to come up with a reply and they need not answer supplementary questions at all. Opposition TDs in every Dáil tend to be dissatisfied with the operation of question time. A long-standing demand of advocates of Dáil reform has been that the Ceann Comhairle be empowered to insist that ministers answer the questions that they are asked, and a change to the rules to this effect was finally made in 2016 (Standing Order 44A). Moreover, a minister who blatantly evades a question risks giving the impression of having something to hide. The stature of a minister who seems unable to give convincing answers to questions will drop among both government deputies and journalists. Question time is the liveliest part of the Dáil schedule, so it gets relatively good media coverage; if a minister performs ineptly or appears shifty at question time, this may receive wide publicity. Consequently, parliamentary questions can be quite effective in probing some alleged ministerial misdemeanour. However, they are not designed to enable the monitoring of government policies on a continuous basis – if this is to be done, the most appropriate mechanism is a system of committees.

Oireachtas committees

Committees are a feature of almost all modern parliaments, but their significance varies greatly. Where government is not directly accountable to parliament, parliament may work mainly through committees: examples include the US Congress and the European Parliament. In a fully-fledged committee system, there are committees to monitor the performance of each government department. Strong committees have the power to insist that ministers and civil servants appear before them to explain their decisions, and they also need the resources to hire outside experts and research staff in order to examine subjects systematically. To work effectively they need to operate to some extent on non- or cross-party lines, as otherwise they will merely replicate the division on the floor of parliament. Sometimes 'small group psychology' creates an identification with the committee that rivals, though rarely displaces, identification with party. Ministers and civil servants know that they might one day have to give detailed justifications of the decisions they make and so, it is hoped, they take more care to make the right ones.

Realistically, the only way in which the opposition – and government backbenchers – can be given a more meaningful role in parliament is through a well-designed committee system. The pre-1980s committee system was generally acknowledged to be ineffective, with the possible exception of the Public Accounts Committee (see next paragraph). After some experimentation in the next four parliaments, a durable model was established after the 1997 election, and much the same structure was re-established after each of the next four elections – although with a tendency towards expansion, leading to concern that the committee system was becoming overstretched. The structure of committees closely matches the structure of the government, so there is more or less one committee per department (in practice, some committees might handle two departments, or two committees might be responsible for different aspects of one department's activities). Each of the departmentally-related committees monitors the activities of its department, discusses its estimates, and deals with the third stage of legislation within the area of the department. The committees sit as joint committees (in other words, both TDs and senators take part) most of the time, but when they discuss the third stage of legislation that is passing through the Dáil, only TDs may participate. If the government has a majority in the Dáil then it will have a majority on each committee, but the weak position of the government in the 32nd Dáil meant that it was in a numerically weak position in every committee. In that Dáil, there were 32 committees, eight of them concerned with matters internal to the Houses of the Oireachtas and the other 24 outward-facing. Typically, the latter consisted of seven TDs and four senators, and of the TDs only two would be from Fine Gael, with another two from Fianna Fáil.

The Public Accounts Committee (PAC), which is a 'standing' committee (in other words, it is automatically re-established in every new Dáil), is generally regarded as the most powerful committee of all. It has the function of considering the accounts of government departments in the light of the annual reports of the Comptroller and Auditor General (C&AG), who checks that public money has been spent in the way that the Oireachtas decided it should be. Its role was enhanced following a modernisation and extension of the remit of the C&AG in 1993 (O'Halpin, 1998: 132; Mitchell, 2010; see also Chapter 10, p. 263). The PAC consists only of TDs and is always chaired by an opposition member.

TDs are able to express preferences as to which committees they wish to serve on, and those who want to be on a particular committee have a good chance of being selected for it. There is some tendency for TDs with sectoral knowledge to secure positions on the relevant committee (farmers on the agriculture committee, teachers on the education committee, and so on) but otherwise there are no discernible patterns (Hansen, 2011: 356–7). Unlike their counterparts in the US Congress, Oireachtas committee members do not have any power to direct 'pork' (public spending) towards their own constituencies. In the last analysis, the party leader, acting through the whip, assigns TDs to committees and, where applicable, chooses the chairs, and any TD exhibiting disloyalty knows what to expect. In January 2013, the Dáil voted (at Labour's behest) to remove Colm Keaveney from three committees, following his expulsion from the party's PPG after he voted against a budget item, and (at Sinn Féin's behest) to remove one of that party's TDs, Peadar Tóibín, from a committee after he voted contrary to the party line on abortion. Fianna Fáil criticised this as 'Stalinist' behaviour, though it had done just the same when one of its TDs, Joe Behan, resigned from the party in October 2008. The rationale is that TDs have the role of representing the PPG in committees and that a TD who has left his or her PPG can obviously no longer be trusted to do this. In the past, the government insisted on most committees being chaired by a government TD, but one of the reforms introduced in the 32nd Dáil provided, for the first time, for allocation of chair positions in proportion to the parliamentary strength of each PPG.

The post-1997 committee system is generally seen as having been more effective than its forerunners. The investigation by the Public Accounts Committee in 1999 of the non-payment of tax on certain non-resident accounts held in banks and building societies was regarded as a triumph for the entire committee system, bringing in well over €800 million for the exchequer, a sum far greater than the cost of the related inquiries (Byrne, 2012: 180–1; Mitchell, 2010: 136). Another step in the strengthening of the capacity of the committee system has been the expansion in library and research services for members and committees, following the creation of the Houses of the Oireachtas Commission in January 2004.

The precise powers of Oireachtas committees have sometimes been matters for decision by the courts. In November 2001, the High Court, in a judgment (generally known as the Abbeylara judgment) confirmed by the Supreme Court the following April, ruled that the Oireachtas does not have the power to set up enquiries that are likely to lead to findings of fact or expressions of opinion adverse to the good name of individuals not belonging to the

Dáil or Seanad (MacCarthaigh, 2005: 174–81). A proposal to change the constitution so as to permit each house of the Oireachtas to conduct inquiries that could result in findings regarding individuals was rejected in a referendum in October 2011 by a 53–47 margin; opinion polls had suggested that there would be a majority in favour, but doubts were raised, and with the referendum overshadowed by a presidential election on the same day, many voters were left with the feeling that the arguments had not been adequately aired and a majority opted for the status quo (O'Leary, 2014). Moreover, committees do not have the power to compel individuals to appear before them and give evidence. While committees may occasionally receive media coverage if they are investigating a matter on the current news agenda, most meetings are low-key events.

However, in January 2017 the High Court, in a case in which Angela Kerins alleged that she had been unfairly treated when she had appeared before the PAC in 2014 in her capacity as the head of a well-known charity, concluded that the hurtful and indeed damaging remarks made had merely been 'utterances', not conclusions, and that the constitution makes clear (Article 15.12) that TDs and senators are not 'amenable' to any court for these.[3] In the eyes of critics, this gave Oireachtas members licence to level abuse at anyone they chose, subject only to the ineffectual policing by the Oireachtas of its members' behaviour; indeed, some parliamentarians and parliamentary officials were said to have regarded the approach of certain members of the PAC as motivated by self-publicity, extremely aggressive and straying 'beyond acceptable behaviour' (Kelly, 2017). Whereas committees might be expected to operate through teamwork and collegiality, certain members of Oireachtas committees have been accused of using their positions to 'grandstand', with the main aim of achieving maximum publicity for themselves.

Despite the generally positive evaluation of the post-1997 committee system, it would be unrealistic to expect dramatic consequences to flow from any reorganisation of the committees (Lynch, 2017). Despite the extensive reforms introduced since the late 1990s, relations between government and parliament may be slightly adjusted by a well-designed committee system, but will never be fundamentally changed. The first reason is that most governments have not been keen to see a particularly probing committee system emerge. Government ministers, like everyone else, would prefer not to have to work under close scrutiny.

Second, those who would most benefit from such a system have ambivalent views on the matter. Opposition frontbenchers would like to see the government on the rack, but they look forward to being in government themselves in the future, and thus have some reluctance to see too many checks on ministers. Likewise, ambitious backbenchers dream of one day being a government minister, not of becoming a committee chair. In Ireland all ministers must be members of parliament, in contrast to certain European countries (notably France, the Netherlands, Norway and Sweden) where the offices of MP and government minister are incompatible. Whereas in Ireland only two of the approximately 200 ministers since 1922 were not former or current TDs upon their appointment (one in 1933 and one in 1981), the average European figure was calculated some years ago to be 25 per cent (De Winter, 1991: 48–50). In some countries, there are, to some extent, different parliamentary and governmental career structures, and a greater psychological separation between parliament and government. In Ireland, certainly as far as government backbenchers are concerned, there is little or no such separation. A sizeable proportion of TDs will be promoted; at the start of the Dáil elected in 2016, for example, 56 of its members (35 per cent of the total) were current or past cabinet or junior ministers. Hence, able TDs who are capable of dealing with national political issues know that they have a good chance of becoming ministers some day. TDs who are not in that category are unlikely to be interested in an effective committee system. A strong committee system would be of most appeal to TDs who, while interested in some aspect of the policy process, do not hope or expect to be ministers, and such TDs are rare.

Third, there are questions as to how far a strong committee system can be reconciled with a parliamentary system of government. A prudent government backbencher who wants promotion might well decide that going along with the party line is a safer option than becoming a trenchant inquisitor of his or her own party leaders in government.

Fourth, while the resources available to TDs have improved greatly since the 1970s, committees may have to share clerks and lack research support. In the absence of adequate resources, many TDs will continue to feel they cannot afford to spend too much time on committee work to the neglect of their constituency duties (for which, see Chapter 8). We will return to the question of the overall weakness of parliament later, but first we turn to the role of the Seanad.

Seanad Éireann

Our discussion so far has concentrated mainly on the Dáil but, as we mentioned at the start of the chapter, parliament also has an upper house, Seanad Éireann (Coakley, 2013: 90–136; Manning, 2010). The lifespan of each Seanad matches that of the Dáil; Seanad elections take place a couple of months after the corresponding Dáil election. The Seanad has 60 members, who are elected in a particularly convoluted manner (see Box 7.3). The election of 43 members from quasi-vocational panels might give the impression that the Seanad consists largely of representatives of interest groups. However, the reality is otherwise, because of the composition of the electorate (which is defined by law and not by the constitution). Not surprisingly, since the great bulk of the voters are practising party politicians, so too are the people they elect. By and large, the senators elected from the panels are similar in background to TDs – indeed, they are often former or aspiring TDs, or both. The presence of the university senators remains contentious, with the principle of special graduate representation being criticised as elitist, compounded by the fact that graduates from newer universities and from other third-level institutions are excluded from the franchise (Coakley, 2013: 121–2). The main argument in favour of the university seats is that these six senators, most of whom are not

---

Box 7.3 The composition of Seanad Éireann

Of the 60 senators, 43 are elected from five 'panels', six are elected by university graduates and the other 11 are appointed by the Taoiseach.

The five panels are Agriculture, Culture and Education, Industry and Commerce, Labour, and Public Administration, and those nominated for a panel are required to have 'knowledge and practical experience' of its subject (Article 18.7.1 of the constitution). The electors for the 43 panel seats are members of city and county councils, the newly-elected Dáil and the outgoing Seanad. At the 2016 Seanad election, the electorate for the panel seats comprised 1,160 people, of whom 874 were affiliated to one of the four main parties (Murphy, 2016: 240).

The six university senators are returned from two panels. Graduates of the National University of Ireland return three senators, with the other three elected by graduates of Trinity College Dublin. Graduates of all other third-level institutions are excluded from the election.

The remaining 11 senators are appointed by the Taoiseach.

members of a political party, are often an innovative and independent force in an Oireachtas that, usually, is otherwise firmly controlled by the parties. The 11 senators appointed by the Taoiseach are usually chosen so as to ensure that the government has a secure majority in the Seanad, and to give a boost to politicians who have a chance of winning an extra seat for the party at the next Dáil elections.

The Seanad is by far the weaker of the two houses. A few of the powers of the Houses of the Oireachtas, it is true, are shared equally between both chambers; thus, the declaration of an emergency (see pp. 62–3), the impeachment of a president or the removal of a judge (see p. 71) need acquiescence from both Dáil and Seanad. In the area of legislation, the Dáil is unequivocally the superior chamber. Bills come before the Seanad, but, at most, it can delay them for 90 days. If it rejects a non-money bill, reaches no decision or suggests amendments that are unacceptable to the Dáil, the Dáil can simply overrule it (Article 23.1 of the constitution). In the case of a money bill, the Seanad is given only three weeks in which to make its 'recommendations', which again the Dáil may overrule (Article 21). If it rejects a bill (other than a bill to amend the constitution) and the Dáil overrules it, it may invoke the 'Article 27 procedure', under which a majority of senators and a third of the members of the Dáil may petition the president not to sign the bill until it has been approved either by the people in a referendum or afresh by the Dáil following a general election. No such petition has ever been presented. Anecdotal evidence suggests that the minister sponsoring a bill is much more receptive to suggestions from senators if the bill is being introduced in the Seanad than in the case of a bill that goes to the Seanad after passing through the Dáil. The government nearly always has majority support within the Seanad, especially given the Taoiseach's right to nominate 11 of the senators, though in the Seanad elected in 2016 the government could rely on the support of only 21 of the 60 senators (Murphy, 2016: 246). The Seanad meets less frequently than the Dáil (for an average of 107 days a year in 2013–15, compared with the Dáil's 122 days) and it sits for fewer hours per day (during 2013–15 it sat for an average of 661 hours per year, compared with the Dáil's 991 hours).[4]

The Seanad is often dismissed as a mere 'talking shop', and some have called for its abolition, pointing out that comparable chambers were abolished, without noticeably adverse consequences, in Denmark (in 1953), New Zealand (1950) and Sweden (1970). Defenders of the Seanad argue that despite its lack of power, it plays a useful role in the legislative process, as debates on bills are usually conducted in a more reflective, constructive and non-party spirit than in the Dáil. In addition, the task of setting up an effective Oireachtas committee system would be even more difficult without the 60 senators. The matter came to a head in October 2013, when a referendum on Seanad abolition took place, at the initiative of the Taoiseach, Enda Kenny. The proposal was backed by the government parties (Fine Gael and Labour) and by Sinn Féin, but opposed by Fianna Fáil. The electorate was not greatly exercised, with a turnout of less than 40 per cent, and the proposal for abolition was defeated by a 52–48 margin (MacCarthaigh and Martin, 2015).

Opponents of abolition stressed that they did not want to retain the Seanad as it stood but favoured significant reform of the institution. This might entail widening its electorate by, for example, giving all Irish citizens, whether resident in Ireland or not, a vote for the 43 panel senators, and extending the franchise for the university seats to graduates of all third-level institutions. It might also entail increasing its powers, though the creation of a directly-elected second chamber with significant powers would represent a move towards strong bicameralism, an institutional model often seen as a recipe for gridlock (Gallagher, 2013). Many suggestions for reform have been made over the years (Coakley, 2013: 127–31; Murphy, 2016: 247–50), but none has yet been implemented; it remains to be seen whether the subject will rise to a position high on the political agenda.

A weak parliament?

From what we have said so far, it is evident that government is the dominant actor in its relations with the rest of parliament, but as its most powerful committee rather than as a body that competes with it – though in the increasingly frequent situation of minority government, the position is not quite so clear cut. There are many reasons for governmental dominance, some applicable to most parliaments – hence the frequent if vague assumption of a 'decline of parliaments' since the nineteenth century – and some specific to the Oireachtas.

For one thing, the role of the state, and hence of government, has grown considerably over the past hundred years. Government business has become much more complex, and it is more difficult for all but those directly and continuously involved to monitor its work. The level of specialisation and expertise required is such that everyone else, including the backbench member of parliament, is effectively an amateur in the policy-making process.

Second, the development of the mass media has provided an alternative and often more effective means of making governments accountable (see Chapter 12). Ministers cannot so easily wriggle out of awkward situations when being grilled by an interviewer on the television or radio as they can in parliament.

Third, new patterns of decision making virtually bypass parliament. In many European countries, including Ireland, the major interest groups, especially the employers' and farmers' organisations and the trade unions, play a central role in economic policy making (see Chapter 11). When the government agrees a package with these interests, parliament can do little except retrospectively discuss a *fait accompli*. Interest groups naturally concentrate their lobbying efforts on government ministers and senior civil servants, where the real power lies, leaving ordinary TDs with few interests to represent other than those of their constituents. In addition, a growing number of policies are made at EU level, again undermining the traditional notion of domestic parliaments as law-making bodies and increasing parliament's difficulty in maintaining effective oversight of executive action (Walsh, 2013; see also Chapter 14). Moreover, the courts, in their capacity as interpreters of the constitution, have at times imposed significant constraints on policy choices (see Chapter 3).

Fourth, as we have already observed, TDs have other demands on their time, especially constituency work (see Chapter 8). Even the most nationally-oriented deputies cannot spend all their political lives on parliamentary work, because they are expected to service the needs of their constituents and fear losing their seats if they neglect this work. Despite criticisms from some quarters that TDs spend too much time on constituency work and not enough on parliamentary business, voters would actually prefer them to spend less time than at present on national matters and more time on local ones (see Chapter 8, p. 202).

Finally, and most importantly, as we observed at the start of the chapter, deputies behave not as individuals but as members of a party. When it comes to the crunch, deputies in most parliaments follow the party line; when political life is dominated by political parties, as is the case throughout Europe, deputies' orientation to party is stronger than their orientation to an abstract notion of 'parliament'. Backbench government TDs want to back the government – indeed, ultimately to become members of it – and not to harass it. Giving government TDs more teeth will not alter the role of the Dáil if these TDs do not wish to bite the government. This is not necessarily a bad thing – to govern effectively, governments need to be able to rely on their own backbenchers to support them through thick and thin. In Ireland, government backbenchers have proved very reliable indeed.

It is tempting to imagine that the Dáil's difficulty in compelling answerability from the government might have contributed to the economic crash in 2008 and the policy mistakes that led up to this. Perhaps, if parliament had been able to constrain government, it could have prevented the adoption of policies that subsequently proved damaging in their consequences? In fact, there is no evidence to support such a view. The thrust of government policy leading up to 2008 – the narrowing of the tax base and the expansion of public spending – was not railroaded through by overbearing governments against the protests of the opposition, with their own backbenchers cowed by the party whip into giving their support. On the contrary, few dissenting voices were heard from any quarter (Donovan and Murphy, 2013: 144–67), and the opposition parties generally advocated even larger tax cuts and greater public expenditure. If the opposition had had greater input into the policy-making process, through some hypothetical rebalancing of the relationship between government and parliament, there is every reason to believe that the public finances would have drifted even more out of kilter and that the inevitable crash, when it happened, would have been even more drastic.

All of this makes clear that the factors that confine the Dáil to a scrutinising role, rather than a policy-making role, are common to legislatures in all parliamentary systems, in which parliament sustains a government. The cliché that the Dáil is 'the weakest parliament in Europe', or that it is a toothless watchdog, is frequently reiterated. But the criticisms made of it are levelled against many other parliaments. Writing about the UK House of Commons, Flinders and Kelso criticise the 'lazy thinking' that underlies similar statements about that institution. They argue that parliament was not designed or intended to play a pro-active scrutiny role, let alone a policy-making role; that the fusion of executive and legislature exists by design, rather than being a sign that something has gone wrong; and that governments are constrained by intra-party control mechanisms that take place out of public view within the PPGs (Flinders and Kelso, 2011). Assessing the power of the opposition in parliament across a number of countries, Garritzmann (2017: 17) estimates scores for 21 countries and places Ireland joint 13th on this criterion. This judgement was made before a number of developments since 2011 that could be expected to strengthen the Dáil's position. As well as the increased use of pre-legislative scrutiny, and the election by secret ballot of the Ceann Comhairle, which we have already discussed, the 2016 programme for government promised the establishment of an independent 'Budget Office' within the Oireachtas, which would enable members of the Dáil to cost proposals, draw on financial expertise independent of the Department of Finance, and have an input to the budget. This office, it was intended, would be fully up and running by 2018.

Moreover, while it is sometimes assumed that it would be unambiguously a good thing to increase the Dáil's capacity to make policy, or to constrain the government in its ability to do this, in fact such a step comes at a cost. The 32nd Dáil, elected in 2016, took over two months to elect a government, which, when it took office, had the support of just 59 of the 158 TDs; Fianna Fáil with 44 seats, had an arrangement with the government under which it would support it on its budget and on confidence motions, but would decide its stance on other matters on a case-by-case basis. Optimists saw this as the 'new politics' they had long hoped to witness: the government would no longer be able to ram its legislation through parliament but would have to seek the agreement of some of the opposition and build a degree of consensus behind its proposals. Critics of the 32nd Dáil in operation, though, saw it as illustrating the dangers of adjusting the balance between government and legislature too far, arguing that it was dominated by short-termism, with the government unable to do anything that might be unpopular in the short term, even if it would make sense in a longer-term perspective, because no opposition party would support such a measure. The guillotine was undoubtedly over-used in previous Dála, but without the possibility of debates being brought to an end by the guillotine in the 32nd Dáil, the pace of law-making was very slow.

Conclusion

The president, while by constitutional definition part of the Oireachtas, is in practice deliberately at a remove from parliament and government, and the debates around the role of the Oireachtas principally concern the relationship between government and parliament, specifically the Dáil. This relationship is often seen in adversarial terms, and the question is asked: which controls which? We have argued in this chapter that the question makes little sense in the context of a political system where government sits in parliament and is backed, as a matter of principle rather than on an ad hoc basis, by a majority of deputies.

If government and parliament were seen as competing for power then, clearly, we should have to conclude that government has the upper hand, at least under 'normal' pre-2016 circumstances. Virtually all government bills are passed, with opposition amendments taken on board only as the government sees fit, while hardly any legislation originating with the opposition is passed – certainly not against the wishes of the government. Extracting information from the government that it does not wish to disclose is an uphill struggle. Other than in times of minority government or coalition break-up, the government need not fear being ejected from office by the Dáil.

Nonetheless, Irish government does not amount to cabinet dictatorship. The Dáil's provisions for scrutiny of government allow the opposition to harass the government and to bring into the light matters that the government might prefer to keep concealed. The government also has to pay a price for the continued loyalty of its own backbenchers; it usually has to clear its plans with its TDs in advance, and takes care not to introduce measures that its TDs indicate they could not support. Even when the Dáil arithmetic means that government legislation is virtually certain to be passed, the opposition has plenty of opportunities to state its own criticisms.

If it were desired to make the Dáil a more significant actor, the most obvious step would be to build on the existing committee system and to use committees to discuss legislation before, rather than after, it goes to the full parliament. The reforms instituted since the 1997 election, and especially those introduced in 2016, implement some of these ideas, yet it is clear that changes to the rules alone will never transform the position of parliament. Parliament would become more powerful if TDs of the government parties ceased to see their main role as supporting the government and became, instead, quasi-neutral observers of the political process, ready to back or oppose the government depending on their view of the issue at hand. Such a development, which is improbable in the extreme, would undoubtedly transform the role not only of parliament but of the entire process of government – and not necessarily for the better.

Notes

1 For example, in 2011, the 31st Dáil elected Seán Barrett, a Fine Gael TD for Dun Laoghaire, as Ceann Comhairle. This resulted in Fine Gael's winning two more seats at the 2016 election than if a Fianna Fáil TD had been chosen as Ceann Comhairle in 2011.

2 Private members' bills should be distinguished from private bills, which differ from public bills in that they apply only to certain bodies or localities (an example is The Royal College of Surgeons in Ireland (Charters Amendment) Act, 2003). Private bills, of which there are only a handful per decade, must be introduced in the Seanad and have a distinctive method of enactment (for details see Morgan, 1990: 103–4; Dooney and O'Toole, 1998: 60–1).

3 The fact that the courts 'simply do not have a role in policing parliamentary utterances', in the words of the judge, was re-asserted in a High Court judgment two months later, in a case taken by businessman Denis O'Brien.

4 Details on sitting days and hours from *Annual Reports* of the Houses of the Oireachtas Commission.

188   *Michael Gallagher*

References and further reading

Andeweg, Rudy B. and Lia Nijzink, 1995. 'Beyond the two-body image: relations between ministers and MPs', in Herbert Döring (ed.), *Parliaments and Majority Rule in Western Europe*. Frankfurt and New York: Campus Verlag and St Martin's Press, pp. 152–78.

Bowler, Shaun, David M. Farrell and Richard S. Katz, 1999. 'Party cohesion, party discipline, and parliaments', in Shaun Bowler, David M. Farrell and Richard S. Katz (eds), *Party Discipline and Parliamentary Government*. Columbus: Ohio State University Press, pp. 3–22.

Bulsara, Hament and Bill Kissane, 2009. 'Arend Lijphart and the transformation of Irish democracy', *West European Politics* 32:1, pp. 172–95.

Byrne, Elaine, 2012. *Political Corruption in Ireland 1922–2010: A Crooked Harp?* Manchester: Manchester University Press.

Caffrey, Richard, 2010. 'Procedure in the Dáil', in Muiris MacCarthaigh and Maurice Manning (eds), *The Houses of the Oireachtas: Parliament in Ireland*. Dublin: Institute of Public Administration, pp. 257–84.

Chubb, Basil, 1992. *The Government and Politics of Ireland*, 3rd ed. Harlow: Longman.

Coakley, John, 2013. *Reforming Political Institutions: Ireland in Comparative Perspective*. Dublin: Institute of Public Administration.

Constitution Review Group, 1996. *Report*. Dublin: Stationery Office.

De Winter, Lieven, 1991. 'Parliamentary and party pathways to the government', in Jean Blondel and Jean-Louis Thiébault (eds), *The Profession of Government Minister in Western Europe*. Basingstoke: Macmillan, pp. 44–69.

Dinan, Des, 1986. 'Constitution and parliament', in Brian Girvin and Roland Sturm (eds), *Politics and Society in Contemporary Ireland*. Aldershot: Gower, pp. 71–86.

Donovan, Donal and Antoin E. Murphy, 2013. *The Fall of the Celtic Tiger: Ireland and the Euro Debt Crisis*. Oxford: Oxford University Press.

Dooney, Seán and John O'Toole, 1998. *Irish Government Today*, 2nd ed. Dublin: Gill and Macmillan.

Döring, Herbert, 2004. 'Controversy, time constraint, and restrictive rules', in Herbert Döring and Mark Hallerberg (eds), *Patterns of Parliamentary Behavior: Passage of Legislation across Western Europe*. Aldershot: Ashgate, pp. 141–68.

Elgie, Robert, 1999. 'The politics of semi-presidentialism', in Robert Elgie (ed.), *Semi-Presidentialism in Europe*. Oxford: Oxford University Press, pp. 1–21.

Elgie, Robert, 2012. 'The President of Ireland in comparative perspective', *Irish Political Studies* 27:4, pp. 502–21.

Eurobarometer, 2016. *Public Opinion in the European Union*, Standard Eurobarometer 86. Brussels: European Commission.

Farrell, David M. and Jane Suiter, 2016. 'The election in context', in Michael Gallagher and Michael Marsh (eds), *How Ireland Voted 2016: The Election That Nobody Won*. Basingstoke: Palgrave Macmillan, pp. 277–92.

Farrell, David M., Peter Mair, Séin Ó Muineacháin and Matthew Wall, 2013. 'Courting but not always serving: perverted Burkeanism and the puzzle of Irish parliamentary cohesion', in Richard Johnston and Campbell Sharman (eds), *Parties and Party Systems: Structure and Context*. Vancouver: UBC Press, pp. 92–107.

Flinders, Matthew and Alexandra Kelso, 2011. 'Mind the gap: political analysis, public expectations and the parliamentary decline thesis', *British Journal of Politics and International Relations* 13:2, pp. 249–68.

Gallagher, Michael, 2009. *Irish Elections 1948–77: Results and Analysis*. Abingdon: Routledge and PSAI Press.

Gallagher, Michael, 2010. 'Parliamentary parties and the party whips', in Muiris MacCarthaigh and Maurice Manning (eds), *The Houses of the Oireachtas: Parliament in Ireland*. Dublin: Institute of Public Administration, pp. 129–52.

Gallagher, Michael, 2012. 'The political role of the President of Ireland', *Irish Political Studies* 27:4, pp. 522–38.

Gallagher, Michael, 2013. 'Would a reformed Seanad be the worst outcome of all?'. https://politicalreform.ie/2013/09/03/would-a-reformed-seanad-be-the-worst-outcome-of-all/.

Gallagher, Michael, 2016. 'The results analysed: the aftershocks continue', in Michael Gallagher and Michael Marsh (eds), *How Ireland Voted 2016: The Election That Nobody Won*. Basingstoke: Palgrave Macmillan, pp. 125–57.

Gallagher, Michael, Michael Laver and Peter Mair, 2011. *Representative Government in Modern Europe*, 5th ed. New York and London: McGraw-Hill.

Galligan, Yvonne, 2012. 'Transforming the Irish presidency: activist presidents and gender politics, 1990–2011', *Irish Political Studies* 27:4, pp. 596–614.

Garritzmann, Julian L., 2017. 'How much power do oppositions have? Comparing the opportunity structures of parliamentary oppositions in 21 democracies', *Journal of Legislative Studies* 23:1, pp. 1–30.

Hannon, Katie, 2004. *The Naked Politician*. Dublin: Gill and Macmillan.

Hansen, Martin Ejnar, 2011. 'A random process? Committee assignments in Dáil Éireann', *Irish Political Studies* 26:3, pp. 345–60.

Hogan, Gerard, 1997. 'Ceremonial role most important for President', *Irish Times* 21 October.

Kelly, Fiach, 2017. 'TDs feel ruling vindicates tough questions: questioning at times strayed beyond acceptable behaviour', *Irish Times* 1 February.

Kerrigan, Gene and Pat Brennan, 1999. *This Great Little Nation: The A–Z of Irish Scandals and Controversies*. Dublin: Gill and Macmillan.

King, Anthony, 1976. 'Modes of executive–legislative relations: Great Britain, France, and West Germany', *Legislative Studies Quarterly* 1:1, pp. 11–34.

Lijphart, Arend, 2012. *Patterns of Democracy: Government Forms and Performance in Thirty-Six Countries*, 2nd ed. New Haven and London: Yale University Press.

Lynch, Catherine, 2017. 'The effect of parliamentary reforms (2011–16) on the Oireachtas committee system', *Administration* 65:2, pp. 59–87.

Lynch, Catherine, Eoin O'Malley, Theresa Reidy, David M. Farrell and Jane Suiter, 2017. 'Dáil reforms since 2011: pathway to power for the "puny" parliament?', *Administration* 65:2, pp. 37–57.

MacCarthaigh, Muiris, 2005. *Accountability in Irish Parliamentary Politics*. Dublin: Institute of Public Administration.

MacCarthaigh, Muiris and Maurice Manning, 2010. 'Parliamentary reform', in Muiris MacCarthaigh and Maurice Manning (eds), *The Houses of the Oireachtas: Parliament in Ireland*. Dublin: Institute of Public Administration, pp. 432–47.

MacCarthaigh, Muiris and Shane Martin, 2015. 'Bicameralism in the Republic of Ireland: the Seanad abolition referendum', *Irish Political Studies* 30:1, pp. 121–31.

Mac Cormaic, Ruadhán, 2006. 'Warning by Chief Justice of law drafted too hastily', *Irish Times* 26 April.

Mac Cormaic, Ruadhán, 2016. 'Higgins raises eyebrows with tax cuts criticism: the president is pushing out the boundaries with his latest comments', *Irish Times* 3 February.

Manning, Maurice, 2010. 'The Senate', in Muiris MacCarthaigh and Maurice Manning (eds), *The Houses of the Oireachtas: Parliament in Ireland*. Dublin: Institute of Public Administration, pp. 153–66.

Mitchell, Gay, 2010. *By Dáil Account: Auditing of Government, Past, Present and Future*. Dublin: Institute of Public Administration.

Morgan, David Gwynn, 1990. *Constitutional Law of Ireland*, 2nd ed. Blackrock: Round Hall Press.

Murphy, Mary C., 2016. 'The Seanad election: second chamber, second chance', in Michael Gallagher and Michael Marsh (eds), *How Ireland Voted 2016: The Election That Nobody Won*. Basingstoke: Palgrave Macmillan, pp. 227–53.

Norton, Philip, 1990. 'Conclusion: legislatures in perspective', in Philip Norton (ed.), *Parliaments in Western Europe*. London: Frank Cass, pp. 143–52.

O'Connor, Tom, 2010. 'An Ceann Comhairle', in Muiris MacCarthaigh and Maurice Manning (eds), *The Houses of the Oireachtas: Parliament in Ireland*. Dublin: Institute of Public Administration, pp. 169–83.

O'Donoghue, John, 2008. 'Does Dáil Éireann do a good job for the Irish people?', *Irish Times*, 3 March.

O'Dowd, John, 2010. 'Parliamentary scrutiny of bills', in Muiris MacCarthaigh and Maurice Manning (eds), *The Houses of the Oireachtas: Parliament in Ireland*. Dublin: Institute of Public Administration, pp. 358–76.

O'Halpin, Eunan, 1998. 'A changing relationship? Parliament and government in Ireland', in Philip Norton (ed.), *Parliaments and Governments in Western Europe*. London: Frank Cass, pp. 123–41.

O'Leary, Eimear Noelle, 2014. 'Oireachtas inquiries referendum', *Irish Political Studies* 29:2, pp. 318–29.

O'Malley, Eoin, 2012. 'Explaining the 2011 Irish presidential election: culture, valence, loyalty or punishment?', *Irish Political Studies* 27:4, pp. 635–55.

O'Toole, Fintan, 1995. *Meanwhile Back at the Ranch: The Politics of Irish Beef*. London: Vintage.

Rafter, Kevin, 2012. 'Redefining the Irish presidency: the politics of a "non-political" office, 1973–1990', *Irish Political Studies* 27:4, pp. 576–95.

Rozenberg, Olivier and Shane Martin, 2011. 'Questioning parliamentary questions', *Journal of Legislative Studies* 17:3, pp. 394–404.

Walsh, Alice, 2013. 'Oireachtas scrutiny of EU legislation: still a work in progress after 40 years', *Irish Jurist* 50, pp. 138–65.

Ward, Alan J., 1974. 'Parliamentary procedures and the machinery of government in Ireland', *Irish University Review* 4:2, pp. 222–43.

Websites

www.oireachtas.ie/parliament/
Houses of the Oireachtas site: one of the most informative sites possessed by any national parliament, containing all debates, legislation passed and other data.

www.irishstatutebook.ie
The complete text of all legislation passed since the founding of the state.

www.president.ie
Site of the President of Ireland.

presidential-power.com/
Site maintained by Robert Elgie of Dublin City University and others, covering all aspects of presidentialism and semi-presidentialism.

8   The constituency role of Dáil deputies

Michael Gallagher and Lee Komito

In Chapter 7 we examined the legislative and scrutinising roles of Dáil deputies. In this chapter we concentrate on a different aspect of the work of TDs, looking at the business on which they spend a lot of their time, namely constituency work. Some people wonder whether constituency work is really part of the duties of a TD at all; after all, the Irish constitution says nothing about it. Yet, judging by the large amount of time it occupies, it seems in practice to be more important in the working life of a TD than narrowly-defined parliamentary duties such as speaking in the Dáil chamber or examining legislation. In most countries, it is taken for granted that parliamentarians will work assiduously to protect and further the interests of their constituents, and that constituency work forms part of an MP's parliamentary duties rather than conflicting with them, but in Ireland there is a body of opinion that sees a constituency role as aberrant and outdated, labels it 'clientelism', or believes that it is taken to excess. We shall ask whether there is anything distinctive about Irish practice in this area, looking at the reasons why TDs do so much constituency work, and then consider the consequences it has for the political system.

The nature of constituency work

In all parliaments, members have both a formal, national, parliamentary role and a local, often more informal, constituency role. In the former, they are expected to play a part in legislative business and in monitoring government behaviour, as was discussed in the previous chapter. In their local role, they keep in touch with the people who elected them, looking after the interests both of their constituencies generally and of individual constituents. This role has several components (Searing, 1994: 121–60; Norton, 1994: 706–7). First, there is a 'welfare officer' role, in which the deputy sorts out, usually by interceding with the local or central civil service, a problem on behalf of an individual or group. Second, there is the 'local promoter' role, the deputy being expected to advance the interests of the constituency generally, by helping to attract industry to the area, avert factory closures, secure public investment, and so on. Third, the deputy has the role of 'local dignitary', and will be invited to, and expected to attend, a variety of functions in the constituency. The first two of these require some elaboration, though it is worth making the point that whereas in Britain Searing concluded from his work in the 1970s that most constituency-oriented MPs consciously choose either the welfare officer role or the local promoter role, in Ireland most TDs feel that they have little choice but to try to fulfil both. Having explored these two roles, we then consider the question of whether TDs' constituency work can be regarded as 'clientelistic', before placing deputies' constituency-related activities in comparative perspective.

The Dáil deputy as welfare officer

Those labelled 'welfare officers' by Searing are those 'whose primary focus falls on individual constituents and their difficulties' (Searing, 1994: 124). This may involve advising constituents about the benefits for which they are eligible; advising them how to get one of these benefits (such as a grant, allowance, pension or livestock headage payment); taking up with the civil service an apparently harsh decision or a case of delay; and helping, or seeming to help, someone to obtain a local authority house or even a job. Some of these activities allegedly involve pulling strings, for example in smoothing the path for dubious planning applications, so for some observers constituency work has negative associations because it is regarded as using undue influence to give particular people unfair advantages. Whatever it entails, it is very time-consuming. A former TD, Máire Geoghegan-Quinn, graphically describes the way in which the welfare officer role imposes on the life of a TD:

> Once you get elected you instantly become public property. You are on call 24 hours a day, 365 days a year ... As a TD you become responsible for whatever it is that any one of your 100,000 constituents wants you to be responsible for. They will raise these issues with you when you are out shopping, relaxing in the pub on Sunday night or at any other time they happen to run into you. Alternatively they might decide to, and indeed often do, call to your home to discuss their problems ... the Dáil only really operates from Tuesday to Thursday. But working in the Dáil alone doesn't tend to get you re-elected. So on Friday, Saturday and Monday you will find TDs criss-crossing their constituencies holding clinics, attending meetings and dealing with local problems. If they are based in any of the larger constituencies they will put up more than a thousand miles a week in their cars. Their evenings are spent at a mixed bag of political and public functions.
>
> (Geoghegan-Quinn, 1998)[1]

TDs do a lot of constituency work. Indeed, they probably spend most of their time doing it; as well as holding clinics, they exchange emails or phone calls with constituents and with officials to follow up cases. TDs surveyed in 2009 estimated that they spent 53 per cent of their time on constituency work, of which 40 per cent was devoted to casework and 24 per cent to local promoter activity, with the rest spent either on what seemed to be publicity for themselves or in asking parliamentary questions (Joint Committee on the Constitution, 2010: 36–7). These days, most TDs use public funding to maintain a constituency office staffed by an assistant, meaning that the TD does not have to be personally involved in every case. The main subject matter of the cases they receive are housing, social welfare and health (O'Leary, 2011: 336).

Who contacts TDs, how, and why? Successive Irish National Election Study (INES) surveys have found that, on average, approximately 16 per cent of respondents say that they have contacted a TD over the previous 12 months (see Table 8.1). There is some variation

Table 8.1 Extent of contact between citizens and TDs, 2002–16

	2002	*2006*	*2011*	*2016*
Contacted TD	21.4	15.6	12.0	15.8
N	2,642	1,061	1,818	1,000

Source: For 2002–11, Gallagher and Suiter, 2017: 154; for 2016, Red C INES survey, Q2a.

Note: In 2002, figures refer to the percentage of respondents contacting a TD in the previous five years, while in 2006, 2011 and 2016 they refer to a one-year period.

across the four surveys (conducted in 2002, 2006, 2011 and 2016), but we can identify a few general patterns. Making contact with a TD is a practice that crosses social and geographical boundaries; in most of the surveys social class, education, public/private sector employment and gender have little impact on the likelihood of contacting a TD. In the 2002 and 2016 surveys, rural dwellers were more likely to make contact than their urban counterparts, though there was no such pattern in 2006 or 2011. Generally, the youngest and oldest age groups are the least likely to contact a TD. Making such contact is positively correlated with other measures of political activity and engagement. In 2011, for example, of those who reported having followed the election campaign closely 21 per cent had contacted a TD in the previous year, compared with only 3 per cent who had followed it 'not at all closely' (Gallagher and Suiter, 2017: 153). Similarly, those who are most knowledgeable about politics, and those who vote, are more likely to make contact with a TD than those with the opposite characteristics.

Constituents may make contact with TDs by one of a number of routes. These days, it is not common for constituents to turn up on the doorstep of a TD's house, as used to happen in past decades, and writing a letter to a TD is also a dying practice. The 2016 INES survey found that email has become the most common method of making contact: 36 per cent of respondents had made contact this way, with 31 per cent doing so by phone and 24 per cent at a clinic (Farrell *et al.*, 2018). Email is used especially by middle-class respondents, by those with a university education and by younger respondents, while those living in local authority accommodation are particularly likely to make contact by attending a TD's clinic. Contact is made most frequently about a personal matter (58 per cent in 2011, 38 per cent in 2016), with community matters in second place and matters of national policy the least likely to be raised (Farrell *et al.*, 2018). Middle-class respondents are most likely to be making contact about a community issue, and working-class respondents, especially those living in local authority accommodation, about a personal matter.

Evidently, then, there is a lot of contact between TDs and constituents, and TDs devote a great deal of time to constituency work. Does all this activity serve any useful purpose – do people benefit from asking TDs for assistance? Jaundiced conventional wisdom might have it that TDs have considerable power; they can install an associate in a position of power locally and use him or her thereafter. In contrast, the American political scientist Paul Sacks, who conducted research in County Donegal, concluded that politicians could achieve very little. They nonetheless managed to create and retain bodies of support by dispensing what he called 'imaginary patronage' – that is, they convinced people that they had achieved something for them even though in reality they had not (Sacks, 1976: 7–8). Nearly all the constituency work TDs did was carried out, he implied, solely to create the impression that the TD was making an effort. Certainly, some of it might be of this nature: many requests concern cases where the constituent will get the benefit anyway without anyone's help (such as an old-age pension) or will not get it as he or she is simply not eligible. However, it might seem implausible that TDs can build up, and preserve for many years, a reputation as hard-working and effective constituency politicians simply by dispensing imaginary patronage, unless their constituents are exceptionally gullible.

Moreover, despite the cynical conventional wisdom that we mentioned earlier, there is not much evidence to back up claims of widespread 'string-pulling'. Of course, it is possible that there is more such activity than meets the public eye. When a former minister, Michael Lowry, fell from grace (at national level) in 1997, with a tribunal finding that he had been receiving substantial payments on which he had avoided tax (Murphy, 2016: 82–3), reporters found considerable local support for him from people who saw him as helpful in various though not precisely specified ways. In the words of one: 'He will help secure finances for certain things. He will help you if you are buying land or setting up your own business. Whatever it is, you can go to Michael, he will be there and if he can he will sort it out'. One supporter insisted that Lowry did not get people things to which they were not entitled; he was simply 'an absolute master at cutting through red tape' (quotes from Ingle, 1997). Whatever form his assistance took, it was very well received by his constituents; standing as an independent, Lowry headed the poll at each election in the period 1997–2016. Another Tipperary TD, Noel Davern, who had first been elected in 1969, said many years later that some of the improper favours that TDs are alleged to be able to secure may have been possible in the past but that TDs were now much more constrained by a number of factors and 'you wouldn't even think of doing that now' (quoted in Hannon, 2004: 56). These days, the likelihood of discovery is greater, and the public mood towards such behaviour is less tolerant. TDs themselves, when interviewed in 2009, downplayed their ability to get decisions overturned, though significant minorities believed that they could do this, and felt that for the most part their intervention simply got a case speeded up (O'Leary, 2011: 338–9).

Assistance from TDs may result from their control of, or access to, private rather than state resources. The two Healy-Rae brothers, Danny and Michael, were both elected as independent TDs in the Kerry constituency in 2016, and assistance from another member of the clan was cited by one voter as the reason for supporting them: 'I needed a track machine to clear a drain and Johnny had it down to me with a driver in two days, all free' (Nolan, 2016).

Overall, politicians' scope for pulling strings is not great, and is certainly less than it once was. The principle of appointment in the civil service on merit, rather than through string-pulling, was established early on, with the creation in the 1920s of the Civil Service Commission and the Local Appointments Commission. Over the years, the writs of these bodies have been progressively extended. Politicians cannot secure jobs for people, and voters do not expect them to do that.

In other words, it is very unlikely that much of the constituency work of TDs involves pulling strings on behalf of constituents, if only because ordinary TDs do not have many strings to pull. It is true that government ministers have the power to make decisions that will benefit or damage individuals, and there have been allegations and tribunal decisions that string-pulling and corruption have surfaced at this level (Byrne, 2012). Moreover, at local level, scope for enrichment exists because rezoning of land may result in a substantial financial gain for the landowner, and charges of corruption in this area have led to tribunals of inquiry and to criminal prosecutions (Byrne, 2012: 169–71). Even so, all the evidence is that the bulk of the constituency work conducted by ordinary backbench TDs is more mundane and less ethically questionable than this. A consensus has emerged that TDs can be helpful to constituents, but not by getting them things to which they are not entitled. Instead, the value of contacting a TD lies in the fact that this can enable people to find out about the existence of – and/or how to obtain – benefits, grants or rights of which they would otherwise have been unaware, or would have found difficult to secure without assistance.

This was the conclusion of research conducted in Dublin in the late 1970s and early 1980s. It found that the claim of politicians 'to power or influence rested on their ability to monopolise and then market their specialist knowledge of state resources and their access to bureaucrats who allocated such resources' (Komito, 1984: 174). Politicians could tell people what they were eligible for and how to secure it; this involved little work for the politician but saved constituents, many of whom are 'bureaucratically illiterate', a lot of work. In addition, a TD's intervention sometimes forced a case to be reviewed, a decision to be speeded up or a service to be provided (Komito, 1984: 182–3).

Kelly found much the same from her analysis of the caseload of Michael D. Higgins, then a Galway West TD (and subsequently President of Ireland). Despite the picture presented by O'Toole and Dooney (2009: 341–2), according to which representations from politicians rarely have any effect, Kelly (1987: 145) found that in many instances the TD was able to secure a benefit for people after they had initially been turned down by the civil service, and he also got cases speeded up. He achieved this not by pulling strings but because of his expertise: his knowledge of how best to present the case and of what sort of supporting documentation was needed. Some people had been corresponding with the wrong department, while others had omitted steps such as quoting their social welfare number or obtaining a doctor's certificate to back up their case. The same conclusion, that politicians can make a difference, either because they know the rules better than the constituent, or because they know more about the constituent's circumstances than a bureaucrat would glean from the standard application form, was reached by Hourigan (2015: 102–3). Through experience, TDs probably can be of genuine assistance: as one TD put it, 'there is hardly a Deputy in this House who is not at least as conversant with the supplementary welfare allowance scheme as are the community welfare officers' (Proinsias De Rossa, *Dáil Debates* 428: 834, 25 March 1993).

The point that some people really do benefit from contacting a TD was put colourfully in 1997 by a renowned exponent of constituency work, P. J. Sheehan, a Fine Gael TD for Cork South-West between 1981 and 2011. During his successful re-election campaign, he outlined his analysis and posed the rhetorical question:

> In rural Ireland, many don't have the confidence, or the knowledge about where to go or how to fight for their rights ... as long as we have the present system and bureaucracy exists, there will be a need for a helping hand and a friendly ear. If this service isn't needed, why are my clinics from the Head of Kinsale to the Dursey Sound overflowing with people every weekend?[2]
>
> (*Southern Star,* 31 May 1997: 3)

As in Canada, constituents may be relieved to 'reach someone real' after their experience of speaking with a different bureaucrat each time they call and having to give their file number every time (Peter Macleod, quoted in Franks, 2007: 34).

While the articulate and resourceful members of the commentariat may be well able to tackle their own problems, or call on a professional acquaintance for advice, or do not have such problems in the first place, and can thus afford to look down disdainfully at what they term 'clientelism', there are others for whom TDs perform an invaluable role. As a former minister puts it, 'For many people unfamiliar with the intricacies of a state bureaucracy, their deputy is their only accessible and sympathetic intermediary' (Quinn, 2005: 409). In a Seanad debate in 2007, responding to suggestions from a university senator that TDs should prioritise their legislative role, the former Fianna Fáil minister Mary O'Rourke said 'Let Senator Norris try to work through the bureaucracy of a county council without the assistance of someone who knows what approach to take' (*Seanad Debates* 185: 1664, 1 February 2007). Political commentator Noel Whelan observes that even though a lot of information is now available online and state bureaucracy is more user-friendly than it was in the past, 'many people still choose or need someone they know to tackle this bureaucracy with them' (Whelan, 2015). A Dublin deputy, Róisín Shortall, then of the Labour party, related:

> I represent an area with a very high level of unemployment, poverty, housing problems, and people who spend their lives in queues, trying to sort out social welfare issues. I get

up to 250 letters a week, and the follow-up on all these takes time. I wish it were not so. I wish people were sufficiently empowered to sort out their own problems. I wish they could go to their citizens' advice bureau and get the help they need. But this doesn't happen.

(*Irish Times*, 13 June 1995: 11)

So, researchers have not found evidence of TDs interfering on a major scale with the equitable operation of the political or administrative system but, equally, it is not true that TDs cannot achieve anything and that those who attend their clinics are suffering from a collective delusion. The picture to which most research points is that constituency work mainly involves rather routine activity, attending many clinics and local meetings, writing letters, helping people to sort out their social welfare problems and so on, rather than anything more corrupt or devious. The TD's welfare officer role, in fact, resembles that of a lawyer, who operates not by bribing the judge or jury but by ensuring that the case is presented better than the ordinary citizen would be able to present it.

The Dáil deputy as local promoter

The local promoter role is concerned primarily with making representations about 'the constituency's collective needs, which may be economic, environmental, or social' (Searing, 1994: 130). It may involve activity on behalf of a community, town, or residents' association, for example to persuade central or local government to improve water or sewerage services, street lighting, or roads ('fixing potholes' has become a standard summary of this activity for those who take a negative view of TDs' focus on constituency work). As when acting in the welfare officer role, this might involve the TD in contacting civil servants to try to get a decision reversed or speeded up, or in putting down a parliamentary question. Another aspect of the local promoter role is that a TD is expected to fight to increase the constituency's share of whatever cakes exist: that is, to attract new industries to the area, to prevent existing industries closing, to get state backing for local projects, and generally to ensure that the constituency does well out of the disbursement of government resources.

Voters in many constituencies seem to feel that their area is hard done by, so at elections TDs and other candidates invariably stress their determination to rectify matters. A recurrent theme in the campaigns of non-incumbents is that the sitting TDs have failed to 'deliver' for the constituency (or a part of it), which has been neglected for many years, and most candidates imply that the amount of resources flowing to a constituency is partly a function of the pressure exerted by its TDs. For example, after winning a by-election in Longford–Westmeath in 2014, Gabrielle McFadden stated:

The promise that I made to the people of Longford–Westmeath during the campaign was that I would fight very hard and shout very loud for Longford–Westmeath, and I will do that ... I think a lot of the recovery is happening in the Dublin area and I want some of that obviously for Longford–Westmeath, so I will be there every step of the way fighting to make sure that if there's money coming out of government for anything, that Longford–Westmeath will get it, that if there's a possibility of a company to come to this country, to invest in this country, I will be fighting for it to come to Longford or Westmeath, that's my way ... I mean it's he who shouts loudest and all of that, you know?

(RTÉ Radio 1, Marion Finucane Show, 25 May 2014)

Box 8.1 Irish politicians and the perceived delivery of largesse

Between 1997 and 2002, the minority Fianna Fáil–Progressive Democrat administration reached agreements with four independent TDs, under which the latter would support the government in exchange for spending on specified projects in their constituencies. Similarly, after the 2007 election, Bertie Ahern, prior to his re-election as Taoiseach, secured the support of a number of independent TDs in exchange for commitments that were not made public (O'Malley, 2008: 210–11; Weeks, 2017: 235–41). The minority government elected in 2016 was also dependent on independent TDs, and there were plenty of rumours and allegations that some of these had sought to extract particularistic benefits for their home patch, though it was difficult to establish the truth or otherwise of these.

Critics from other constituencies argued that it was wrong that money that should have been spent in the national interest was going disproportionately to certain constituencies simply because these TDs were in a pivotal position. At the same time, others suggested that there was no evidence that the TDs could claim legitimate credit for the projects, and that the government was securing the support of the independent TDs without actually doing anything it would not have done anyway. While it would be very difficult to establish the objective truth of politicians' ability to influence spending decisions, there is little doubt that there is a widespread public perception, encouraged by many politicians and commentators, that this is the case.

For example, in December 2003 the government announced a plan to decentralise government departments from Dublin to locations around the country. The junior minister Tom Parlon immediately issued leaflets in his constituency headed 'Parlon Delivers! 965 jobs!', listing the five towns concerned and the number of jobs each was set to receive – though it was later alleged that he had played no part in the decision but had merely got wind of it before it was announced. In the event, the decentralisation programme was widely criticised as ill thought out and was largely unfulfilled, and Parlon lost his seat at the next election. Likewise, in September 2012 a junior minister at the Department of Health, Róisín Shortall, resigned in protest after a list of areas where new primary care centres were to be set up was amended by the Minister for Health, James Reilly, who *inter alia* added two in his own constituency on the basis of far-from-transparent criteria – but Reilly lost his seat at the next election.

Ministers are expected to secure largesse for their home base or for the constituency as a whole. Names such as Pádraig Flynn in Castlebar, Michael Lowry in Thurles, Ray MacSharry in Sligo and Dick Spring in Tralee are often cited in this context. Waterford has had only two cabinet ministers since the 1980s, and one commentator at the 2016 election was in no doubt about the impact of one of these in particular: 'We have chopped and changed our TDs, but it was only with the advent of Martin Cullen and to a much lesser extent Austin Deasy that we saw what cabinet influence can do. There are still foolish people out there who deny the reality of the huge investment that came Waterford's way during Cullen's tenure and expect you to believe that this stuff appeared by magic without his persistent lobbying at the cabinet table' ('Phoenix', 2016).

At the 2016 election, the chair of a Portlaoise business group, in contrast, expressed dissatisfaction with the lack of largesse his county had received: 'He said he could not see what difference having a Minister has made to Laois but he has seen the impact and benefit Tullamore achieved by having Brian Cowen at a senior level in government over many years' (Kiernan, 2016). In a similar vein, Fine Gael was seen to be losing support in Mayo in 2015 because, even though it was the Taoiseach's constituency, a 'perceived lack of government delivery' was identified in an internal party assessment (Kelly, 2015).

Essentially the same sentiments are expressed by many other candidates around the country at every election.

Given his or her very limited power, though, there is not a great deal that the ordinary TD can achieve – unless they happen to be an independent TD holding the balance of power (Weeks, 2017: 205–51). One member of the 31st Dáil, explaining his decision to retire at the 2016 election, said that he had been able to achieve more as a councillor, such as 'parks, swimming pools and so on', than he had as a TD (Michael Conaghan, quoted in Minihan, 2015). Notwithstanding that, a significant minority of voters believe that TDs can have an impact on the geographical distribution of expenditure: 24 per cent in 2002 of respondents to the INES (and 29 per cent in 2007) said that in their view local TDs were most responsible for 'any improvements in the economic situation around here over the last five years', only slightly behind the percentage attributing this to government policies. On the whole, though, TDs can do little except to lobby hard those, primarily ministers, who make the important decisions. If a TD becomes a minister, constituents' expectations will rise accordingly, as there is a widespread belief that a minister who is sufficiently hard-working and adroit can 'deliver' in a big way for the constituency. In the 2007 INES survey, 75 per cent of respondents agreed that 'a constituency represented by a cabinet minister will have more money spent in it by the government', and research concludes that ministers can exercise some power, if only at the margins, as to where public money is spent (Manton, 2016; Suiter and O'Malley, 2014a, 2014b). Examples abound of ministers who are said to have secured largesse – 'pork', in American terminology – for their constituency, or at least for their own base within it (see Box 8.1).

In this way, voters have an incentive, when choosing their TDs, to elect candidates of perceived ministerial ability. As we saw in Chapter 4, intra-party competition for electoral support is inherent in the Irish electoral system, and supporters of the largest parties usually have a choice of candidates. Despite suggestions that voters' desire for good constituency representation might lead them to choose active locally-oriented representatives at the expense of people of national ability, and hence lower the calibre of parliamentarians (part of the argument of Carty, 1981: 137), in fact voters making their choices purely on the basis of local considerations have a strong incentive to support candidates of ministerial ability, because a minister can deliver the goods locally on a much grander scale than a permanent backbencher. Ironically, then, a desire for good local representation can lead to the election of nationally-oriented politicians.

Constituency work and clientelism

Some people use the term 'clientelist politics' to describe politics in Ireland; journalists and politicians alike are prone to speak, usually disapprovingly, of 'our clientelist system'. The picture painted is one where politicians deliver tangible benefits (or imaginary ones according to Sacks) and, in return, are rewarded by a vote at the next election. The suggestion is that politicians gradually build up a sizeable and fairly stable 'clientele' of people who are under some obligation to them; the politicians are able to 'call in the debts' at election time. Most voters, it is implied, are part of some politician's clientele.

However, the word 'clientele' would not be very apposite to describe those who give a first preference vote to a particular Dáil candidate. TDs simply do not possess 'clienteles'. Most people, as we saw earlier (Table 8.1), do not contact TDs at all. Moreover, even those who are helped by a TD cannot be taken for granted. For one thing, some of them 'do the rounds' of the clinics, hoping to improve their chances by getting several TDs to chase up their case; the

2006 INES found that around a third of those who had contacted a TD had contacted more than one TD (Gallagher and Suiter, 2017: 155). For another, even if a TD does something for a constituent, the secrecy of the ballot means that he or she has no way of knowing whether the favour is returned at the ballot box. Many of the key characteristics of clientelism, such as the solidarity binding 'clients' and 'patrons', are simply not present in Irish electoral politics (Farrell, 1985: 241; Collins and O'Shea, 2003: 88–90).

Clientelism is conventionally defined in the academic literature as entailing much more than mere routine constituency work. As it has been expressed, 'clientelistic accountability represents a transaction, the direct exchange of a citizen's vote in return for direct payments or continuing access to employment, goods and services' (Kitschelt and Wilkinson, 2007: 2). The kind of activities regarded as characterising clientelism, such as the distribution of public housing, special welfare benefits for supporters, public sector jobs, or the issuing of a birth certificate or a disability pension (Kitschelt, 2000: 849; Piattoni, 2001: 6), are simply not in the gift of TDs. In Ireland, constituents are typically seeking access to, or simply information about, universal benefits, rather than attempting to secure selective benefits that are not available to non-members of a politician's 'clientele'. An essential feature of a genuinely clientelistic system is that elected politicians in effect control the hiring, firing and advancement of career officials (Piattoni, 2001: 7). The Civil Service and Local Appointments Commissions, to which we referred on p. 194, mean that this is simply not the case in Ireland.

Thus, an earlier study concluded that 'politicians believed that they were inevitably dependent on the votes of anonymous constituents with whom they could have no direct links' (Komito, 1984: 181). Far from resting comfortably atop pyramids of loyal supporters, they come across as 'professional paranoids', permanently insecure, always busy at constituency work but never sure that any of it will pay electoral dividends. They promote a high community profile, advertise clinics, turn up at residents' association meetings and so on, not to build up a clientele – which is impossible – but simply to earn a reputation as hard-working people. They hope that even people who never actually need their services are impressed and will conclude that the TD will be there if they ever need him or her.

This being so, the word 'clientelism' is simply not appropriate to describe what TDs do in their role as constituency representatives. It is more realistic to see TDs as being engaged in 'brokerage', a distinct concept. A broker deals in access to those who control resources, rather than directly in the resources themselves; there might be situations in which a person wants something but is unable or unwilling to obtain it direct from the actor who has it, in which case the services of a broker may be useful. Once the service has been provided, the brokerage relationship ends. Clientelism, in contrast, implies a more intense, more permanent relationship. It involves 'clients', people who are in some way tied in to the person who does things for them, whereas 'brokerage' implies a relationship that is not institutionalised. 'To describe a political system as clientelistic is to imply persistent and diffuse relations of exchange in a closed system where all participants are either leaders or followers, and never simply uninvolved' (Komito, 1984: 176). To say that Irish politics is characterised by brokerage would imply that there are many people who do not have any dealings with TDs, and that even the people who do use TDs as brokers are not under any direct obligation to them as a result. Although the loosely-used term 'clientelism' has caught on in some circles as a way of describing constituency work, most reliable research suggests that brokerage rather than clientelism, as defined earlier, is the appropriate term to characterise TDs' constituency activities.

The term 'clientelism' may be used by some commentators partly because of its pejorative and nefarious connotations; it has overtones of manipulation and string-pulling, of a mode of behaviour that some feel Ireland should be moving away from, in contrast to the more neutral 'brokerage'. Eisenstadt and Roniger (1984: 18) observe that the tendency develops in many societies to perceive less formalised relations of this kind as 'slightly subversive to the institutionalised order, to fully institutionalised relationships or to membership of collectivities'. As we shall see later, constituency work in Ireland has been criticised on precisely these grounds.

Constituency work in comparative perspective

Before going on to examine the reasons why TDs engage in so much constituency work, we will look briefly at patterns in other countries. This should dispel any illusion that the constituency role of Irish parliamentarians is somehow unusual or that a heavy constituency focus is an example of Irish exceptionalism (Gallagher and Suiter, 2017: 145–8). 'Grievance chasing' is part of the role of the parliamentarian virtually everywhere. In the USA, an early study of the way public representatives spent their time noted: 'Providing constituent services and doing case work constitute for many representatives more significant aspects of their representational role than does legislative work like bill-drafting or attending committee hearings' (Eulau and Karps, 1977: 243–4). Michael Mezey notes that running errands for individual constituents and lobbying for funds for one's constituency are common to legislators around the world, and 'are in many ways the core of what we consider to be "representative democracy"' (Mezey, 2008: xi). More broadly, relationships (which may or may not be of the patron–client form) based on personal linkages tend to exist in all types of society – modern or traditional, western or eastern, developed or pre-modern (Eisenstadt and Roniger, 1984).

A comparison in the 1990s between TDs and members of the UK House of Commons found that the latter did less constituency work than the TDs, but not very much less; for example, they spent 47 per cent of their time on constituency work compared with 58 per cent for TDs (Wood and Young, 1997: 221). Most TDs believed that their re-election prospects would be damaged if they cut back on their constituency work, but most MPs did not believe this. Why, then, do MPs in Britain do so much constituency work? The main factor, another study concludes, is the psychological satisfaction that comes from doing it, 'combined with a general sense that casework is an important public duty of representatives' (Norris, 1997: 47). Research into the behaviour of MPs in the UK finds a continuing rise both in constituents' demand for local service from their MP and in constituency orientations among MPs (Campbell and Lovenduski, 2015: 696–7).

The same conclusion was reached by a study of Canadian MPs, which found that constituency work takes up more of their time than any other activity (Franks, 2007: 32). Parliament adjourns every fourth or fifth week to enable MPs to spend more time in their constituencies. As in Britain, MPs do this not primarily for electoral motives – in fact, those who regard it as unimportant to their re-election prospects actually do more of it than those who regard it as electorally important – but because it is seen as part of the job and as a 'satisfying' activity (Franks, 2007: 30). Surveys conducted in 2004 in the recently-established legislatures in Scotland and Wales found that virtually all members of these bodies considered helping to solve constituents' problems as very important, 'exceeding the perceived importance of all the other roles open to members' (Bradbury and Mitchell, 2007: 126). A cross-national survey of backbench MPs in five countries found that TDs in Ireland expressed a lower degree of constituency focus than their counterparts in Australia, Canada, New Zealand and the United Kingdom (Heitshuisen *et al.*, 2005: 39). Given the suggestion that the intra-party competition generated by PR-STV is the cause of TDs' constituency workload in Ireland (see pp. 204–5), it is worth making the point that none of the other countries mentioned in this section employs an electoral system under which candidates of a party are competing for votes against running mates.

Given this pattern, it would be very surprising if Irish members of parliament did *not* have heavy constituency workloads. Defending and promoting the interests of one's constituents to the best of one's abilities is 'part of the job' for a member of parliament, and it is hard to imagine a job specification for TDs that does not include this role. Collins and O'Shea (2003: 106) suggest that the contrary view may derive partly from a 'deeply-held' bureaucratic idea that politicians, certainly ministers, should confine themselves to broad issues of policy and that any involvement in administration is thus inappropriate interference. The constituency role is recognised by law, even if not in the constitution, in that some of the payments and facilities made available to TDs are expressly for the purpose of carrying out their constituency work (O'Halpin, 2002: 113). Perhaps, indeed, what requires explaining is not why TDs do a lot of constituency work but, rather, why anyone should think it strange that they do. However, this question, interesting as it is, falls outside the scope of the present chapter.

Causes of constituency work

Even though members of parliament almost everywhere have a heavy constituency load, the perception of Irish politics as 'clientelist' and somehow anomalous seems to be so widespread that it is worth trying to explain the high volume of casework descending on TDs. Four factors, in particular, are frequently mentioned: political cultural attitudes to the state, the small scale of society, the electoral system and the nature of the Irish administrative system. The potential impact of the ever-wider use of new technology is also discussed.

Political culture

Two aspects of Irish political culture are relevant to the constituency role of TDs. First, past attitudes to the state may still have a bearing on current attitudes. Second, the nature of elite political culture means that TDs regard serving their constituents as one of their most important roles.

First, historical factors may have led to some alienation from the state. In all peasant societies, the capital city and the machinery of central government tend to be looked on with some suspicion, and in Ireland this was reinforced by the perceived non-indigenous nature of the ruling elite. Chubb (1992: 210) suggests that brokerage is

> deeply rooted in Irish experience. For generations, Irish people saw that to get the benefits that public authorities bestow, the help of a man with connections and influence was necessary. All that democracy has meant is that such a person has been laid on officially, as it were, and is now no longer a master but a servant.

Prior to Irish independence, MPs of the Irish Parliamentary Party at Westminster were noted for their exceptionally strong focus on constituency matters (McConnel, 2013: 36). Coakley (2013: 152–3) gives the example of an MP in 1912, and a TD in 1969, asking very similar parliamentary questions about improvements to the harbour at Cahirciveen in County Kerry. The argument, then, is that the political culture of the nineteenth century and before, when central government was, for obvious reasons, perceived as alien, remote and best approached via an intermediary, has carried on into the post-independence state. Former Taoiseach Garret FitzGerald once commented that Dublin 'is still widely perceived in rural Ireland as if it were even today a centre of alien colonial rule' (FitzGerald, 1991: 364). Given that so many other aspects of pre-independence political culture have a bearing on contemporary politics (see Chapter 2), this is perfectly plausible, and indeed surveys have testified to people's belief that a TD is the best person to approach if one wants to be sure of getting one's entitlements (Farrell, 1985: 243; Komito, 1992).

This cultural explanation would become dubious, however, if linked too closely with the notion of a 'dying peasant culture' or with a suggestion that people's tendency to approach their TDs springs from an atavistic misconception of the way in which officialdom works. After all, the volume of brokerage seems to be increasing rather than decreasing as urbanisation and the decline of agriculture proceed. Political culture and the legacy of the past are part of the explanation, but we need to look also for causes in present-day Ireland: 'rather than an outmoded style of behaviour, brokerage is an effective solution to a particular set of problems' (Komito, 1984: 191). Thus, there is no reason to expect brokerage work to go away as 'modernisation' continues.

More broadly, successive INES datasets show how deeply rooted in Irish political culture is the expectation that TDs will give high priority to the constituency representation role. When given the proposition 'The assumption that TDs should provide a local service is a strength of the Irish political system', 52 per cent in 2011 and 62 per cent in 2016 agreed. Respondents in 2011 felt, in fact, that at present, TDs spend too little time on constituency work and too much time on national issues – though before conclusions are drawn about a supposedly exceptionally locally oriented Irish political culture, it is worth noting that Irish respondents wanted their parliamentary representatives to divide their time equally between local and national matters, whereas British voters would prefer theirs to devote 60 per cent of their time to constituency work and only 40 per cent to national matters (Gallagher and Suiter, 2017: 160–1). Attitudes to the role of the TD are not uniform across society. Generally, the better-off, those with more education, those who regard national and international events as more interesting than local ones, and readers of the *Irish Times* are the least enthused by TDs' local role, with those with opposite characteristics being the most enthusiastic (Gallagher and Suiter, 2017: 161–2; Farrell *et al.*, 2018). The cynical view of one commentator is that, even if TDs do sometimes apply pressure to have a constituent given preferential treatment, this is primarily a reflection of an ambivalence within the wider political culture: when it 'works' for someone, he or she regards the TD as a good constituency worker, but 'when it works for someone else, it's called cronyism' (Sheridan, 2014).

Second, elite political culture leads TDs to regard local and constituency representation as an integral part of their job rather than as something that 'takes them away from their proper role'. TDs interviewed at the start of the century reported that their constituency, rather than the nation as a whole or a specific sectional group, was their main representational focus (O'Sullivan, 2002: 206–7). When TDs were asked what they had hoped to achieve when they entered politics, a plurality replied 'promote the interests of the local area' (O'Sullivan, 2002: 209). Some TDs had drifted away from this aim and had come to prioritise national issues, while others, finding their initial national-level goals to be unachievable, acquired a stronger local focus over time (O'Sullivan, 2002: 211–12). TDs did not, though, see the local role as excluding a nationally-oriented one, for more of them identified 'legislating and influencing policy' as being among the most important duties and responsibilities of a TD than identified 'represent the constituency' (O'Sullivan, 2002: 237). When surveyed in 2009, TDs tended to rate the constituency aspects of their role as more important than activity related to legislation (Joint Committee on the Constitution, 2010: 38). First-time TDs, interviewed three years later, found constituency work to be 'satisfying and important' while being hugely time-consuming (Murphy, 2013: 10). In other words, TDs accept that active constituency representation comes with the job, though they do not see this as being incompatible with a nationally-focused role.

Small size of society

In all societies, informal networks of trust exist within and alongside formal structures. Such networks may be particularly significant in small societies where many people have some kind of direct or indirect access to decision makers that bypasses the formal structure. The Republic of Ireland is clearly, in relative terms, a small society, with only 4.8 million people, and this has an impact on people's perceptions of their deputies' role. At the 2016 election, for example, there was one deputy for every 20,918 electors and for every 13,499 valid votes. Very few other countries have as high a ratio of deputies to voters.

One might expect that the fewer people each member of parliament represents, the lower his or her constituency workload will be. Yet, at the same time, the fewer people each member represents, the more contact voters are likely to expect with him or her. In the USA, it has been found that the smaller the number of people represented by each senator, the more those people are likely to define the senator's role in pork-barrel terms, and the more contact they are likely to have with their senators (Hibbing and Alford, 1990). With such a small number of voters to represent, it is hardly surprising that deputies find themselves asked to play the role of 'mediator-advocate vis-à-vis the local and national administrative bureaucracies', as Farrell (1985: 242) put it. The 2002 INES found that 69 per cent of voters had spoken personally to the candidate to whom they gave their first preference vote (Marsh *et al.*, 2008: 256).

A reinforcing factor in Ireland is the high degree of centralisation of decision making, nearly all of which takes place in Dublin. Local government is weak – indeed, the lowest tier, town councils, was abolished in 2014 – with very few powers, and there are no meaningful intermediate (regional or provincial) tiers of government. The casework loads of Belgium's national MPs dropped dramatically once federalism was introduced in the mid-1990s (De Winter, 2002: 100). The upshot of the absence of significant sub-national government in Ireland is that national parliamentary representatives get requests for assistance with what in many other countries would be purely local matters. This is reinforced by the fact that the great majority of TDs (82 per cent of those elected in 2016, as noted on p. 170 above) come to the Dáil via local government, where they may be socialised into a casework-oriented role. Indeed, according to the 2002 election survey, TDs are contacted much more than councillors; only 11 per cent of voters had contacted a councillor in the previous five years (and a mere 2 per cent had contacted a senator), compared with 21 per cent for TDs. The outlawing in June 2004 of the 'dual mandate' (whereby individuals were able to be simultaneously TDs and members of a county or city council) was intended, in part, to reduce TDs' interest and involvement in local matters. However, in practice, the assiduity with which TDs keep an eye on the grass roots does not seem to have abated since then, and many have close relatives or associates sitting on local councils to ensure that they are kept fully informed about local developments by someone who, they hope, will not try to replace them.

The electoral system

Calling for a number of political reforms, Elaine Byrne asked: 'Should we introduce a new electoral system? One which produces national parliamentarians instead of provincial ombudsmen?' (Byrne, 2008). This neatly encapsulates a view expressed by a number of critics of PR-STV to the effect that, first, TDs spend too much time on activities they should not be spending their time on; second, TDs do not spend enough time on what they should be doing; and third, the electoral system is the cause of this state of affairs (for other examples see Hourigan, 2015: 100–1; O'Leary, 2014; O'Toole, 2011: 40–7, 73–80). Each of these assumptions is very much open to question (as was argued many years ago by one of the authors – see Gallagher, 1987).

The reason why the electoral system is sometimes suggested as a cause of brokerage is that, as we saw in Chapter 4, PR-STV puts candidates of the same party in competition with each other and thereby compels them to establish an edge over their so-called running mates. Running mates are a definite danger. Between 1922 and 1997, 34 per cent of all TDs who suffered defeat at an election, and 56 per cent of defeated Fianna Fáil TDs, lost their seat not to a rival party's candidate but to one of their running mates (Gallagher, 2000: 97). Among TDs surveyed in 2009, the more running mates a TD had at the last election, the higher the proportion of their time they spent on constituency work (Joint Committee on the Constitution, 2010: 42). Moreover, as we saw in Chapter 7, backbench deputies cannot easily make their mark as outstanding parliamentarians, so they cannot feasibly try to fight internal party battles on that terrain. Thus, once the demand for brokerage activity arises, TDs feel they have to respond to it. When surveyed by Wood and Young (1997: 221), 60 per cent of recently-elected TDs said they felt they could lose their seat if they reduced their constituency work.

TDs are probably right to believe that their electoral fortunes are affected by their reputation as constituency workers. Surveys have consistently shown that voters, when asked to rank a number of factors as determinants of their votes, attach more importance to choosing a TD who will look after the local needs of the constituency than to anything else (Farrell *et al.*, 2018). Even if some of those who say they want a TD who will look after the constituency are in fact expressing a choice *within* party, rather than a choice regardless of party, it is clear that voters attach importance to this role. Party members, too, certainly in Fine Gael, regard the local brokerage role as more important than the national parliamentary one (Gallagher and Marsh, 2002: 131–2). Newly-elected TDs, as part of their informal socialisation process in the Dáil, learn the conventional wisdom among politicians that ignoring constituency work in order to concentrate on delivering eloquent speeches in the chamber would be a recipe for electoral suicide (Murphy, 2013: 9).

The electoral system gives TDs a strong incentive to respond with alacrity to the demand that they do constituency work, but it does not really explain where this demand comes from in the first place. Even accepting that TDs eagerly advertise their availability and actively seek problems to solve, and may thereby generate more constituency work than would arise otherwise, this still leaves a lot that arises from other causes.

Emphasis on the electoral system as a significant cause of the constituency role of TDs implies that under a different electoral system, the volume of constituency work might diminish significantly. This is very doubtful; as we saw on pp. 200–1, members of parliament in countries with a range of completely different electoral systems undertake a lot of constituency work. Even if Ireland moved to a closed list PR system, where the voters simply had to accept the candidates selected by the party organisation without being able to choose between them, MPs might still do a lot of constituency work, as Belgian MPs did under what was in effect a closed list system in the 1990s. They did this in order to discharge what was felt to be a duty, together with the gratification that comes from achieving something tangible for a constituent, as well as establishing one's position as a VIP in the constituency, in contrast with the anonymity of life as a backbencher. In addition, the candidate selectors, that is, the local party members, when deciding how to order the candidates on the party list, favoured candidates who were active in dealing with casework, and just as in Israel, which also uses closed list PR, deputies must be very active at local level in order to build up support among the candidate selectors even though the voters cannot express a preference for them (De Winter, 1997). Müller, reviewing evidence from a number of countries, concludes that the impact of electoral systems should not be over-estimated: 'candidate-centred systems produce incentives for individual behavior, but it seems it depends on the circumstances how strong these effects are and what kind of behavior they cause' (Müller, 2007: 273). The evidence does not support a belief that a different electoral system would reduce, let alone remove, the burden of constituency work.

Administrative structures

The argument here is essentially that some citizens need brokers to obtain their entitlements. This is the conclusion of Roche and Komito and implicitly of others, such as Valerie Kelly, as well as TDs such as Róisín Shortall and P. J. Sheehan whom we quoted earlier. As Roche (1982: 103), who later became a TD himself, puts it: 'Irish complaint behaviour is a manifestation of a breakdown at the interface level between Ireland's public institutions and the Irish public'. In other words, some people turn to TDs to help them due to the frustration that results from their own direct dealings with the state apparatus.

This arises because of the nature of the machinery with which citizens come into contact. All bureaucracies tend to develop certain characteristics, such as inflexibility, rigid adherence to the rules and, perhaps, impatience with people who do not fully understand these rules. In Ireland, there is very little occupational mobility between the public service and the wider economy. There may be a bureaucratic tendency to send out standard replies that do not address a specific query, not to explain fully what someone is entitled to or why some application has been turned down – and, inevitably, there will be cases of delay. In an interview, one TD stated that 'a lot of the work you get is a matter of red tape and ... really we shouldn't be dealing with it – if officials at various levels were more consumer friendly ... we wouldn't have half the workload we have' (O'Sullivan, 2002: 291). In 1962, a senator characterised the constituency work of TDs as 'going about persecuting civil servants', a phrase that was later used as the title of a very influential article (Chubb, 1963) and still resonates. In 2007 the leader of the Seanad, Mary O'Rourke, said 'One paper suggested our job is to persecute civil servants. I agree. We need to persecute them, to make many approaches and to do much banging on doors' (*Seanad Debates* 185: 1665, 1 February 2007).

All of this leaves many people wanting assistance from someone willing to help them, and contacting a TD often seems the most attractive option. The main alternative is to seek assistance from a Citizens Information Centre (CIC). There are 112 such centres around the country; they operate under the auspices of the state-funded Citizens Information Board and are run largely by volunteers, of whom there were almost 1,100 in 2015 (Citizens Information Board, 2016: 48). CICs not only give information on social welfare entitlements (social welfare accounts for about half of the questions they receive), but, where appropriate, also take up cases with the relevant office or department; when queries were analysed in the late 1990s, it was found that the great majority of cases involved only imparting information (Browne, 1999: 34). In 2015, CICs dealt with almost a million direct queries, with another 153,000 queries arriving by phone, though scarcely any were sent by email (Citizens Information Board, 2016: 9, 54). This is clear evidence of public demand for assistance in dealing with the state bureaucracy. However, the restricted opening hours of CICs, and, perhaps, the limited ability of their volunteers to persuade public officials to reverse a decision, mean that these centres and services clearly do not meet the full demand.

A valuable channel for obtaining rectification of grievances is the office of the Ombudsman, which was established in January 1984 (see Chapter 10, and Morgan, 2012: 239–73, for the powers and operation of the office). However, many cases coming to TDs result from a lack of information as to how best to utilise the administrative system (or just disgruntlement with a decision) and do not involve possible maladministration; as John Whyte (1966: 16) put it half a century ago, they are problems on 'a humbler scale' than would warrant the attention of the Ombudsman. In the words of the National Social Service Board, 'the problem for most people in writing to the various Departments seems to be (i) not knowing exactly which section to address their letter to and (ii) the standard letter of reply may not deal satisfactorily with their enquiry' (NSSB, *Annual Report 1991*: 7). Consequently, over the period 2012–16 the office of the Ombudsman received, on average, 3,369 valid cases a year, plus a further 1,403 that fell outside its jurisdiction (all figures calculated from the *Annual Reports* of the Ombudsman), whereas TDs collectively are contacted by around half a million people per year (Gallagher and Suiter, 2017: 155). When the Ombudsman's 1996 annual report was debated in the Dáil, TDs commented tartly that the average TD deals with about the same number of cases per year as the Ombudsman does. One added that when the Ombudsman solves someone's problem, his or her work is praised as vindicating the rights of the ordinary citizen, yet when TDs do the same, their activities are frowned upon and dismissed as 'an antiquated practice of parish pump politics' (Michael Noonan, *Dáil Debates* 480: 1483–4, 2 October 1997). Details of some of the cases outlined in the annual reports of the office show how difficult it has sometimes been even for the Ombudsman, endowed as the office is with statutory powers to demand all the files relating to a case, to persuade the bureaucrats concerned that they should review a decision, highlighting the difficulties that ordinary citizens can encounter.

So, almost by default, people wanting assistance turn to public representatives, who cannot afford to be abrupt or offhand – TDs' jobs, unlike those of civil servants, may depend on how helpful and approachable they are. Nor is there much risk that TDs will loftily declare cases to be 'outside their jurisdiction'. TDs are very visible, available, highly responsive and possessed of relevant expertise.

To suggest that the nature of the Irish administrative system is part of the explanation for the high volume of brokerage demands made to TDs might seem to imply that civil servants are not doing their jobs perfectly. In one sense this is true, in that if the Irish public service dealt with all cases effectively, promptly and to the complete satisfaction of the citizen, there would be no need for brokers. But no large organisation does or ever will work this way, so such a standard is unrealistic. Individual civil servants may not have enough training to be as helpful to the public as they would like to be, and besides, as Collins and O'Shea (2003: 105) observe, traditionally 'the public servant is not rewarded for being helpful and approachable'.

Civil servants could stifle the brokerage system only by refusing to entertain any representations from politicians. They do not do this, partly because that system suits both politicians and civil servants, especially at the local level (Komito, 1984: 188–9). It protects the bureaucrats to some extent, since politicians form a barrier between them and the public. Without politicians acting as brokers, many more people would be tackling them directly; as it is, politicians form an unofficial complaints tribunal. In this capacity politicians also provide an unpaid monitoring service; they can differentiate those who have been dealt with harshly, or have lost out on the benefit of the doubt, from those whose complaint is groundless. If a TD or councillor then makes a firm complaint about a particular case, the official can be fairly sure that it has some basis, since politicians will not risk jeopardising their ongoing relationship with the official on behalf of an undeserving constituent. So, in effect, politicians do some preliminary screening of cases and then present the strongest among them in a manner tailored to the expectations of the civil service, which helps the officials.

In return, civil servants may well give special priority to representations from TDs and respond more sympathetically than to letters of complaint or injury from ordinary members of the public. For over two decades, there has been a special exclusive 'hotline' in the Department of Social Welfare to enable TDs to enquire about individual cases (statement by Minister for Social Welfare – *Dáil Debates* 421: 778–9, 23 June 1992). Similarly, when Irish Water was established in 2014, it set up a 'helpdesk' to deal exclusively with queries from public representatives (D'Arcy, 2015). It is not known whether, as in Canada, experienced and skilled bureaucrats deal with the cases referred by TDs, while less qualified staff give slower and less personal attention to the complaints coming direct from ordinary citizens (Franks, 2007: 33). In addition, officials consider politicians to be more 'trustworthy'. Politicians have a stake in maintaining good relations with officials, so officials can rectify errors without any adverse comment. Members of the public, having no stake in the status quo, cannot be similarly trusted; officials are less likely to admit, and hence to rectify, errors.

Impact of new technology

In principle, we could expect new technology to reduce the need for TDs' brokerage assistance. The problems people experienced in dealing with the state bureaucracy were exacerbated in the 1960s and 1970s by the rapid growth in both the number of services being provided and the number of people looking for these services. Long delays in processing a social welfare claim, for instance, were the result of increases in the number of people applying for assistance and of an increasingly complex application procedure to decide eligibility. More recently, though, new technology has alleviated some of the difficulties. Structural improvements (such as computerisation) have reduced processing delays; the result may not suit the applicant, but at least the answer is known more quickly. This has reduced the scope for brokerage interventions by politicians – their ability to get fast answers is now a less valuable commodity.

New technology and the advent of the 'information society' might reduce the need for politicians' assistance still further, by changing the relationship between government, TDs and voters. The amount of information made available has increased dramatically in recent years. The government has invested in web-based information systems that enable citizens to discover what their entitlements are and, in some cases, to apply for these electronically. This has reduced the monopoly that politicians previously enjoyed over information about entitlements and claiming procedures. Individuals can apply for services and benefits and monitor the progress of their application without recourse to politicians or even officials. Even those without access to the internet can use freephone or lo-call numbers to access officials directly, and these officials can provide immediate answers to individual queries. This is due partly to a changed attitude in the civil service, which is now more encouraging about citizen queries, but it also results from a change in the information system that enables civil servants to answer such queries for a relatively low 'transaction cost'. Part of the reason for going to politicians before was that the 'cost' of answering a query was relatively high. The person dealing with the query had to be located, the necessary file had to be dug out, details might have to be checked with other bureaucrats, and so on. Only a politician was important enough to warrant such an investment of time. With new office technologies, the cost of dealing with the query has been significantly reduced, so answering a citizen's query is now affordable.

There is also, perhaps partly as a result of corruption investigations and tribunals, more transparency in how scarce resources (such as public housing) are allocated to applicants, and so less scope for political intervention in the administrative process. This seems to have increased the level of general policy interventions that politicians are requested to make (as opposed to interventions for personal services). However, local queries on matters such as parking and the painting of railings in public buildings still arrive for TDs.

New technologies are also having an impact on communication between politicians and constituents. An increasing number of politicians have their own websites, containing contact details, in order to enhance their visibility. Many TDs, especially in urban areas, encourage constituents to contact them electronically and, as noted earlier, by 2016 email had become the most common method by which constituents contacted TDs (Farrell *et al.*, 2018). This reduces their workload, as electronic queries can be received and processed by administrative assistants and the outcome of the query can simply be communicated electronically to the constituent. In addition, it helps the TD build up a database of names to whom newsletters and personalised mail shots can be sent, providing a cost-effective means of maintaining visibility in the constituency. On the other hand, it enables individuals to mass-mail all 158 TDs with a click of a button and, together with the emergence of interactive social media, with which most TDs feel they have to engage, means that TDs are much more easily contactable than ever before (Murphy, 2013: 13; O'Leary, 2011: 333).

New technology does not render the constituency role of TDs redundant, though. The increase in efficiency has not been matched in most areas by any marked increase in transparency: the rules for determining eligibility remain complex, and thus the need for the assistance of someone who understands the system remains. Technological advances can result in 'more complex modes of delivery', increasing, rather than reducing, demand for the assistance of TDs when dealing with state bureaucracies, as has been noted in the UK (Campbell and Lovenduski, 2015: 691). Those citizens whose resources for dealing with the bureaucracy are fewest are also the least likely to be able to make meaningful use of the information society. Furthermore, there has been no great increase in the amount of trust extended to civil servants and their activities, and thus the need for someone who can be trusted to act on one's behalf remains. Politicians provide a 'one-stop shop' for voters and can be relied upon to do their best, if only for self-interested reasons, to secure a successful outcome; citizens may not feel equally confident that an unknown bureaucrat will make the same effort.

Consequences of TDs' constituency work

Some of the consequences of the constituency role of TDs are highly tangible, while others are less so. Brokerage work affects the operation of the political and administrative systems, and some suggest that it plays a part in shaping political culture. We shall look at its impact on the Dáil, the government and the civil service, and consider its effects on people's attitudes towards politics generally.

Impact on the Dáil and the government

This is the most obvious and tangible area in which brokerage has an impact. Dealing with casework reduces the time available for formal parliamentary duties, such as examining legislation and discussing policy, which weakens the Dáil's ability to provide effective scrutiny of government and to contribute to policy formation, and for these reasons some deplore TDs' immersion in constituency duties. However, as we saw in Chapter 7, there are obviously many other reasons why the Dáil is less powerful than the government, and it is open to question how much stronger it would be if TDs had less constituency work. Moreover, there is no reason why, with an adequate provision of support staff, politicians should not be able both to provide a service for constituents and to be active parliamentarians (Chubb, 1992: 210).

It is also sometimes suggested that even ministers are overburdened with constituency work and are unable to devote enough time to government business (FitzGerald, 2003: 93). However, ministers tend to use civil servants to do most of their constituency work for them. A series of parliamentary questions tabled by Fine Gael TDs in December 2008 and January 2009 asked about the size of each minister's private office and constituency office. It turned up the information that the 15 cabinet ministers and 20 ministers of state collectively had 403 civil servants in their private offices and looking after their constituency work, at a cost of around €18.7 million a year (the findings are summarised in O'Halloran, 2008, 2009). Of the 216 staff employed by cabinet ministers, 76 were specifically described as looking after the ministers' constituency work, but the line between this and the 'private office' may not be clear-cut; indeed, one minister acknowledged in 1993 that 'staff are not formally divided between constituency and other duties. The situation varies from day to day in each office and staff carry out appropriate duties as the need arises' (Joe Walsh, Minister for Agriculture, *Dáil Debates* 427: 1854, 11 March 1993). Given that each cabinet and junior minister has, therefore, an average of 12 civil servants, paid for by the taxpayers, to assist in his or her constituency and political work, it is hard to believe that brokerage can be a major burden on the shoulders of ministers. On a more modest scale, individual TDs now receive allowances towards the cost of running a constituency office, and it may well be that, as in Canada, 'more office staff leads to more constituency service work, not to more time and attention devoted to broad policy matters' (Franks, 2007: 40).

Impact on the work of the civil service

The constituency work of TDs serves many useful functions for citizens, but this does not mean that all of its consequences are beneficial, or that there is no such thing as excess. We noted earlier that TDs may do some preliminary screening of cases before deciding which ones to take up with officials. However, even if a TD realises that a particular case is hopeless, he or she may not want to say this bluntly to the constituent. The safer option is to forward the case to the civil service, perhaps even putting down a parliamentary question, though of course without burning up credit with contacts in the civil service by flagging it as a deserving case. When this happens on a large scale, there is an obvious cost to the civil service in time and money. Each question has to be followed up fully and all the details have to be investigated, even if the answer turns out to be something straightforward such as the person's simply not being eligible. Tales abound of civil servants or ministers, faced with even minor decisions, discovering that the matter is the subject of correspondence from several TDs and perhaps councillors too. Sometimes, undoubtedly, TDs do make representations even if they can see that a case is 'a dead duck' because 'it can be the only way to get people off your back'; only a response in writing will satisfy the constituent that nothing more could have been done (Éamon Ó Cuív TD in *Irish Times*, 13 April 2002). Examining these representations also costs civil servants time that could be spent dealing with other things so, ironically, some TDs, by clogging up the works with pointless representations, described by Fintan O'Toole as a Kafkaesque 'whirling blizzard of paper-pushing', may exacerbate the very delays about which they complain (O'Toole and Dooney, 2009: 341–2; O'Toole, 2011:

42). Whether it really follows that citizens would get a better service were it not for TDs taking up the cudgels on their behalf is, of course, another matter.

Individualisation of social conflict

Michael D. Higgins (1982: 133) has argued that clientelism 'disorganises the poor'; it encourages them to seek an individual solution to a problem, such as poverty, rather than to see the problem as fundamental to society and take part in collective action to try to redress it. It fosters vertical links, from the TD to the constituent, rather than horizontal ones between people in the same position, such as the poor or the unemployed. Clientelism engenders competition rather than cooperation between people in similar vulnerable positions, each one seeking privileged treatment rather than equality. Thus, he concluded (p. 135), it is 'exploitative in source and intent'. Its origins lie in the dependency of the poor, 'the structural fact of poverty', and in the uneven distribution of resources such as wealth, knowledge and access, and it perpetuates this dependency by heading off any demand for more fundamental changes. Hazelkorn has also argued that clientelism redirects incipient class conflict into channels that emphasise the role of individuals rather than of classes: 'the effect has been to retard the political development and consciousness of the economically dominated classes' (Hazelkorn, 1986: 339). She suggested that for left-wing TDs 'to operate in constituencies through clinics could be politically disastrous in the long-term', as this would reduce the chances of horizontal class links building up among the dominated classes (Hazelkorn, 1986: 340).

It is not clear, though, what exactly is meant by 'clientelism' in these accounts. Hazelkorn seemed to regard all the constituency work of a TD as clientelism: 'Irish clientelism involves individuals who seek out their TD ... in order to acquire some benefit or service which they feel they would not receive by their own, or their group's efforts' (Hazelkorn, 1986: 327; cf. Higgins, 1982: 118–19). If politicians who help constituents to sort out problems that the constituents could not resolve by themselves are behaving in a 'clientelistic' fashion, then clientelism exists in virtually every country in the world and cannot explain much about Ireland specifically. Higgins became a TD in 1981 and in that role was once asked on television whether he now engaged in the clientelistic practices that he had earlier deplored. His answer drew a distinction between, on the one hand, politicians attempting to give the impression that they were achieving results through manipulation and, on the other hand, politicians helping people to obtain their rights (RTÉ1, Prime Time, 25 February 1997). The feeling remains that the term 'clientelism' is being used very loosely in these arguments.

TDs' readiness to offer helpful advice to constituents would come well down the list as an explanation for the absence of socialism in Ireland. It may well be that politicians' brokerage work reduces the level of alienation among those who seek their assistance, and thereby acts as a force for the stability, rather than for the radical transformation, of a social structure marked by clear inequalities. However, it is far-fetched to imagine that if politicians refused to help constituents with their problems, the result would be an unstoppable build-up of demand for collective action that would rectify many of society's ills. It is hard to see how someone concerned about a delay in their pension payment, say, can tackle the immediate problem except in individual terms, and it is not necessarily irrational for individuals to seek to solve their own short-term problems rather than to try to transform society first. Although it is true that the 'welfare officer' role of members of parliament involves solving the problems of individuals – as it does in every country – the 'local promoter' role entails work for collectivities. The case against constituency work on the ground that it is a barrier to the left in Ireland remains unproven.

Impact on perceptions of the political system

There is some disagreement about how constituency work affects perceptions of the political system. Some feel that it performs a linkage role and has an integrative effect; it brings citizens and the central state machinery closer together. TDs, by providing a 'helping hand and a friendly ear', as P. J. Sheehan (quoted above) put it, can serve the functions of humanising the state in the eyes of people who would otherwise see it as remote and countering the cynicism that attaches to 'politicians' generically. As has been noted in Britain, the effect is to build support for the political system by making people feel that there is at least someone who will listen to their problem and is 'on their side' (Norton and Wood, 1993: 50–5). Moreover, through constituency work, information is transmitted in both directions; politicians are kept fully in touch with their constituents, and will be quickly alerted to any general problems, for example about the way in which a department is implementing a policy. A Labour TD commented 'I learn more about the impact our economic recession is having on our country and its people from constituency clinics and local meetings than I ever could from articles or books' (Joanna Tuffy, *Irish Times,* 12 March 2009).

Others take a negative view, believing that brokerage perpetuates a mistaken belief that government and the civil service do not work in a fair and rational manner. Dick Roche, a public administration specialist as well as a TD for a number of years, has argued that the practice of approaching a politician with complaints about the civil service has had 'a corrosive impact on political life. It undermined the confidence in the administrative system and its impartiality, and it also gave rise to the view that just about everything could be fixed' (*Dáil Debates* 482: 929, 6 November 1997; cf. O'Toole and Dooney, 2009: 342). Sacks (1976: 221–5) also believes that much constituency work propagates the notion that citizens improve their chances of getting something from the state by approaching it via a TD, and this perpetuates citizens' negative and suspicious views of the political system. In turn, this reinforces personalism and localism, the tendency to trust only those with whom one has some personal or local connection, which Sacks regarded as important and pre-modern elements in Irish political culture. However, as we pointed out earlier, the bureaucratic view according to which people's use of TDs is irrational has been challenged by detailed research, according to which TDs can be of genuine help to constituents, not by 'fixing' matters improperly but by securing the legitimate redress of grievances or, at least, obtaining a satisfactory explanation of a decision.

Conclusion

Irish citizens expect their members of parliament to be active constituency representatives, taking up their personal or communal problems or grievances with the relevant government department. Although some have sought distinctively Irish explanations for this, a heavy constituency workload is the norm for parliamentarians around the world, and the main reason tends to be the same everywhere: quite simply, representing one's constituents is a central part of the job of a member of parliament in every country. The volume of constituency work takes time that TDs could, at least in theory, devote to their formal parliamentary responsibilities, and also has an impact on the functioning of the civil service. Among some commentators on Irish politics, constituency work tends to be regarded as a negative phenomenon. It is often branded 'clientelism', a term with a multitude of unfavourable connotations (largely due to the private and individual, rather than public and collective, nature of politician–voter interactions), yet it is clear that Irish politics is not clientelistic in the conventional sense of the term. As in other countries, constituency work has both negative and positive consequences:

it may weaken the ability of parliament to provide effective scrutiny of government and to make an input to policy-making, yet it provides a vital link between citizen and state, reduces alienation, and provides feedback on the effects of government policies. The constituency role of TDs is a central aspect of the Irish political system, and its consequences continue to generate argument and discussion.

Notes

1   Máire Geoghegan-Quinn was a Fianna Fáil TD for Galway West from 1975 to 1997. In the 1990s, the constituency was represented by five TDs, with a population at the 1997 election of 100,251 people. Most TDs hold 'clinics' in their constituency, setting aside a certain amount of time at designated places where constituents can come and discuss their problem with the TD.
2   The two places mentioned are approximately 130 kilometres apart.

References and further reading

Bradbury, Jonathan and James Mitchell, 2007. 'The constituency work of members of the Scottish Parliament and National Assembly for Wales: approaches, relationships and rules', *Regional and Federal Studies* 17:1, pp. 117–45.

Browne, Michael, 1999. *Citizens' Information: Theory, Current Practice and Future Challenge*. Dublin: National Social Service Board.

Byrne, Elaine, 2008. 'When a nation's thinking gets trapped by institutions', *Irish Times*, 23 December.

Byrne, Elaine, 2012. *Political Corruption in Ireland 1922–2010: A Crooked Harp?* Manchester: Manchester University Press.

Campbell, Rosie and Joni Lovenduski, 2015. 'What should MPs do? Public and parliamentarians' views compared', *Parliamentary Affairs* 68:4, pp. 690–708.

Carty, R. K., 1981. *Party and Parish Pump: Electoral Politics in Ireland*. Waterloo, Ontario: Wilfrid Laurier University Press.

Chubb, Basil, 1963. '"Going about persecuting civil servants": the role of the Irish parliamentary representative', *Political Studies* 11:3, pp. 272–86.

Chubb, Basil, 1992. *The Government and Politics of Ireland*, 3rd ed. Harlow: Longman.

Citizens Information Board, 2016. *Annual Report 2015*. Dublin: Citizens Information Board.

Coakley, John, 2013. *Reforming Political Institutions: Ireland in Comparative Perspective*. Dublin: Institute of Public Administration.

Collins, Neil and Mary O'Shea, 2003. 'Clientelism: facilitating rights and favours', in Maura Adshead and Michelle Millar (eds), *Public Administration and Public Policy in Ireland: Theory and Methods*. London: Routledge, pp. 88–107.

D'Arcy, Ciaran, 2015. 'Irish Water helpdesk set up for politicians: eight-person helpdesk to deal with queries from senators, TDs and councillors', *Irish Times*, 27 August.

De Winter, Lieven, 1997. 'Intra- and extra-parliamentary role attitudes and behaviour of Belgian MPs', in Wolfgang C. Müller and Thomas Saalfeld (eds), *Members of Parliament in Western Europe: Roles and Behaviour*. London: Frank Cass, pp. 128–54.

De Winter, Lieven, 2002. 'Belgian MPs: between omnipotent parties and disenchanted citizen–clients', in Philip Norton (ed.), *Parliaments and Citizens in Western Europe*. London: Frank Cass, pp. 89–110.

Eisenstadt, S. N. and L. Roniger, 1984. *Patrons, Clients and Friends: Interpersonal Relations and the Structure of Trust in Society*. Cambridge: Cambridge University Press.

Eulau, Heinz and Paul D. Karps, 1977. 'The puzzle of representation: specifying components of responsiveness', *Legislative Studies Quarterly* 2:3, pp. 233–54.

Farrell, Brian, 1985. 'Ireland: from friends and neighbours to clients and partisans: some dimensions of parliamentary representation under PR-STV', in Vernon Bogdanor (ed.), *Representatives of the People? Parliaments and Constituents in Western Democracies*. Aldershot: Gower, pp. 237–64.

Farrell, David M., Michael Gallagher and David Barrett, 2018. 'What do Irish voters want from and think of their politicians?', in Michael Marsh, David M. Farrell and Theresa Reidy (eds), *The Post-Crisis Irish Voter: Voting Behaviour in the Irish 2016 General Election*. Manchester: Manchester University Press.

FitzGerald, Garret, 1991. *All in a Life: An Autobiography*. Dublin: Gill and Macmillan.

FitzGerald, Garret, 2003. *Reflections on the Irish State*. Dublin: Irish Academic Press.

Franks, C. E. S., 2007. 'Members and constituency roles in the Canadian federal system', *Regional and Federal Studies* 17:1, pp. 23–45.

Gallagher, Michael, 1987. 'Does Ireland need a new electoral system?', *Irish Political Studies* 2, pp. 27–48.

Gallagher, Michael, 2000. 'The (relatively) victorious incumbent under PR-STV: legislative turnover in Ireland and Malta', in Shaun Bowler and Bernard Grofman (eds), *Elections in Australia, Ireland, and Malta under the Single Transferable Vote: Reflections on an Embedded Institution*. Ann Arbor: University of Michigan Press, pp. 81–113.

Gallagher, Michael and Michael Marsh, 2002. *Days of Blue Loyalty: The Politics of Membership of the Fine Gael Party*. Dublin: PSAI Press.

Gallagher, Michael and Jane Suiter, 2017. 'Pathological parochialism or a valuable service? Attitudes to the constituency role of Irish parliamentarians', in Michael Marsh, David M. Farrell and Gail McElroy (eds), *A Conservative Revolution? Electoral Change in Twenty-First-Century Ireland*. Oxford: Oxford University Press, pp. 143–71.

Geoghegan-Quinn, Máire, 1998. 'Loss in salary and privacy price of becoming a TD', *Irish Times*, 28 March.

Hannon, Katie, 2004. *The Naked Politician*. Dublin: Gill and Macmillan.

Hazelkorn, Ellen, 1986. 'Class, clientelism and the political process in the Republic of Ireland', in Patrick Clancy, Sheelagh Drudy, Kathleen Lynch and Liam O'Dowd (eds), *Ireland: A Sociological Profile*. Dublin: Institute of Public Administration, pp. 326–43.

Heitshuisen, Valerie, Garry Young and David M. Wood, 2005. 'Electoral context and MP constituency focus in Australia, Canada, Ireland, New Zealand, and the United Kingdom', *American Journal of Political Science* 49:1, pp. 32–45.

Hibbing, John R. and John R. Alford, 1990. 'Constituency population and representation in the US Senate', *Legislative Studies Quarterly* 15:4, pp. 581–98.

Higgins, Michael D., 1982. 'The limits of clientelism: towards an assessment of Irish politics', in Christopher Clapham (ed.), *Private Patronage and Public Power*. London: Frances Pinter, pp. 114–41.

Hourigan, Niamh, 2015. *Rule-Breakers: Why 'Being There' Trumps 'Being Fair' in Ireland*. Dublin: Gill and Macmillan.

Ingle, Róisín, 1997. 'Tipperary voters stand by their man despite damning report from tribunal', *Irish Times*, 30 August.

Joint Committee on the Constitution, 2010. *Results of Survey of Members of Both Houses of the Oireachtas: The Electoral System, Representative Role of TDs and Proposals for Change*. Dublin: Houses of the Oireachtas.

Kelly, Fiach, 2015. 'Fine Gael faces voter backlash over "lack of delivery in Mayo", party report says', *Irish Times*, 27 March.

Kelly, Valerie, 1987. 'Focus on clients: a reappraisal of the effectiveness of TDs' interventions', *Administration* 35:2, pp. 130–51.

Kiernan, Lynda, 2016. 'Portlaoise "not served by its politicians"', *Leinster Express*, 2 February.

Kitschelt, Herbert, 2000. 'Linkages between citizens and politicians in democratic polities', *Comparative Political Studies* 33:6/7, pp. 845–79.

Kitschelt, Herbert and Steven I. Wilkinson, 2007. 'Citizen–politician linkages: an introduction', in Herbert Kitschelt and Steven I. Wilkinson (eds), *Patrons, Clients, and Policies: Patterns of Democratic Accountability and Political Competition*. Cambridge: Cambridge University Press, pp. 1–49.

Komito, Lee, 1984. 'Irish clientelism: a reappraisal', *Economic and Social Review* 15:3, pp. 173–94.

Komito, Lee, 1992. 'Brokerage or friendship? Politics and networks in Ireland', *Economic and Social Review* 23:2, pp. 129–45.

McConnel, James, 2013. *The Irish Parliamentary Party and the Third Home Rule Crisis*. Dublin: Four Courts Press.

Manton, Richard, 2016. 'Spokes or strokes? Clientelism and cycling funding in Ireland', *Irish Political Studies* 31:4, pp. 443–60.

Marsh, Michael, Richard Sinnott, John Garry and Fiachra Kennedy, 2008. *The Irish Voter: The Nature of Electoral Competition in the Republic of Ireland*. Manchester: Manchester University Press.

Mezey, Michael L., 2008. *Representative Democracy: Legislators and Their Constituents*. Lanham, MD: Rowman and Littlefield.

Minihan, Mary, 2015. 'Labour TD confirms he will not contest next general election', *Irish Times*, 30 June.

Morgan, David Gwynn, 2012. *Hogan and Morgan's Administrative Law*, 4th ed. Dublin: Thomson Reuters.

Müller, Wolfgang C., 2007. 'Political institutions and linkage strategies', in Herbert Kitschelt and Steven I. Wilkinson (eds), *Patrons, Clients, and Policies: Patterns of Democratic Accountability and Political Competition*. Cambridge: Cambridge University Press, pp. 251–75.

Murphy, Gary, 2016. *Electoral Competition in Ireland since 1987: The Politics of Triumph and Despair*. Manchester: Manchester University Press.

Murphy, Mary C., 2013. *At Home in the New House? A Study of Ireland's First-Time TDs*. London: Hansard Society.

Nolan, Dónal, 2016. 'Game of thrones as Healy-Raes rise', *Kerryman*, 2 March.

Norris, Pippa, 1997. 'The puzzle of constituency service', *Journal of Legislative Studies* 3:2, pp. 29–49.

Norton, Philip, 1994. 'The growth of the constituency role of the MP', *Parliamentary Affairs* 47:4, pp. 705–20.

Norton, Philip and David M. Wood, 1993. *Back from Westminster: British Members of Parliament and Their Constituents*. Lexington: University of Kentucky Press.

NSSB (National Social Service Board), *Annual Reports*. Dublin: National Social Service Board.

O'Halloran, Marie, 2008. 'Ministers' offices are "A and E ward" of state', *Irish Times*, 13 December.

O'Halloran, Marie, 2009. 'Kenny criticises €10.5m ministers' spend on staff', *Irish Times*, 31 January.

O'Halpin, Eunan, 2002. 'Still persecuting civil servants? Irish parliamentarians and citizens', in Philip Norton (ed.), *Parliaments and Citizens in Western Europe*. London: Frank Cass, pp. 111–27.

O'Leary, Eimear, 2011. 'The constituency orientation of modern TDs', *Irish Political Studies* 26:3, pp. 329–43.

O'Leary, Olivia, 2014. 'It's time our TDs were free to forget about Mrs Murphy's bed', *Irish Times*, 14 February.

O'Malley, Eoin, 2008. 'Government formation in 2007', in Michael Gallagher and Michael Marsh (eds), *How Ireland Voted 2007: The Full Story of Ireland's General Election*. Basingstoke: Palgrave Macmillan, pp. 205–17.

O'Sullivan, Mary-Clare, 2002. *Messengers of the People? An Analysis of Representation and Role Orientations in the Irish Parliament*. Trinity College Dublin: unpublished PhD thesis.

O'Toole, Fintan, 2011. *Enough is Enough: How to Build a New Republic*. London: Faber and Faber.

O'Toole, John and Seán Dooney, 2009. *Irish Government Today*, 3rd ed. Dublin: Gill and Macmillan.

'Phoenix', 2016. 'What have we learned?', *Waterford News and Star*, 9 February.

Piattoni, Simona, 2001. 'Clientelism in historical and comparative perspective', in Simona Piattoni (ed.), *Clientelism, Interests, and Democratic Representation: The European Experience in Historical and Comparative Perspective*. Cambridge: Cambridge University Press, pp. 1–30.

Quinn, Ruairí, 2005. *Straight Left: A Journey in Politics*. Castleknock: Hodder Headline Ireland.

Roche, Richard, 1982. 'The high cost of complaining Irish style: a preliminary examination of the Irish pattern of complaint behaviour and of its associated costs', *IBAR – Journal of Irish Business and Administrative Research* 4:2, pp. 98–108.

Sacks, Paul M., 1976. *The Donegal Mafia: An Irish Political Machine*. New Haven and London: Yale University Press.

Searing, Donald, 1994. *Westminster's World*. Cambridge, Mass: Harvard University Press.

Sheridan, Kathy, 2014. 'Cronyism is at the heart of Irish society', *Irish Times*, 7 October.

Suiter, Jane and Eoin O'Malley, 2014a. 'Yes, minister: the impact of decision-making rules on geographically targeted particularistic spending', *Parliamentary Affairs* 67:6, pp. 935–54.

Suiter, Jane and Eoin O'Malley, 2014b. 'Chieftains delivering: testing different measures of "pork" on an Irish data set of discretionary sports grants', *Journal of Elections, Public Opinion and Parties* 24:1, pp. 115–24.

Weeks, Liam, 2017. *Independents in Irish Party Democracy*. Manchester: Manchester University Press.

Whelan, Noel, 2015. 'In defence of the Irish county councillor', *Irish Times*, 11 December.

Whyte, John, 1966. *Dáil Deputies: Their Work, Its Difficulties, Possible Remedies*. Dublin: Tuairim pamphlet 15.

Wood, David M. and Garry Young, 1997. 'Comparing constituent activity by junior legislators in Great Britain and Ireland', *Legislative Studies Quarterly* 22:2, pp. 217–32.

Websites

www.oireachtas.ie
Site of the Oireachtas, from which there are links to the sites of those TDs who have personal websites.

www.citizensinformation.ie
Site of organisation overseeing Citizens Information Centres and source of a great deal of online information about dealing with the state.

ombudsman.gov.ie/
Site of the Ombudsman.

9 Women in politics

Yvonne Galligan and Fiona Buckley

The centenary commemorations of the women's suffrage campaign and associated Acts, notably the Representation of the People Act, 1918, and the Parliament (Qualification of Women) Act, 1918, shine a spotlight on women's political representation over the past 100 years. Suffragists thought that their victory heralded the end of inequality in political life for women. Yet, women's political under-representation persisted, and by the mid-1990s gender equality in public office became a test of democratic legitimacy and accountability for feminists and advocates of political reform. This framing of the democratic deficit was reinforced by the United Nations (UN) World Conference on Women in 1995, at which women's empowerment was a central theme. Thereafter, the Irish government was one of over a hundred governments held accountable to the UN for its commitment to realising gender equality in power and decision-making.

Thus, at the close of the twentieth century, the paucity of women in politics gradually became a litmus test for the health of democracy. The structural exclusion of one half of the citizenry from an equal share of power created a strong normative claim for redress, based on justice and equality as the fundamental principles of democracy. Important though this normative argument is for a focus on women, Irish parties have paid variable attention to the representativeness of parliament, and the presence of women in the Oireachtas remains low by European standards. Perhaps this lack of urgency reflects public indifference to the representative nature of the Dáil, as the 2011 and 2016 Irish National Election Surveys (INES) would seem to indicate. When asked what characteristics were important in a TD (such as being of the same social class, having the same level of education, being of the same age), being of the same gender as the respondent was the least important, though it was still somewhat more relevant for women than for men (Farrell *et al.*, 2018).

This raises the question, then, as to why we should be concerned about gender as a representative characteristic in political life. Yet, perhaps this snapshot in time provided by the INES survey does not reflect public indifference to the gender of elected representatives. Instead, it may be that the public thinks this issue is now addressed and that it is time to incorporate other diversity characteristics into the electoral sphere. This is quite a typical view among voters in Britain (Cowley, 2013), and could have echoes among the Irish public. Or, it may also be that the public – male and female – think that their interests are adequately represented, and so the sex of politicians is not an issue. Whatever the explanation, there is evidence to show that the public was attentive to the gender of politicians in previous times. In 2007, on the eve of the economic crash that was to send shock waves through the Irish economy and society, 60 per cent of those surveyed in a similar INES poll indicated that 'things would improve if there were more women in politics'. While just about half of men agreed, 71 per cent of women did so, indicating a pent-up demand among the female public for better descriptive representation. Moreover, in 2011, even though respondents attached little importance to the idea of having a TD of the same gender as themselves, 62 per cent believed that there should be more women TDs, with 29 per cent wanting no change and only 3 per cent saying they wanted fewer female TDs (Farrell *et al.*, 2018). That pressure for greater female presence in politics was articulated further in the 2014 Constitutional Convention report on women in public life, where an overwhelming majority (97 per cent) of the 100 citizens and political participants wanted to see government take more action to encourage women's public and political engagement.[1]

The public view, an important aspect in understanding the politics of presence and its underlying drivers, can differ also on policy. In a study of voters' and politicians' attitudes on policy issues in a European Parliament election, female voters in Ireland were found to be more progressive than males on the four policy issues interrogated – same-sex marriage, abortion, women and paid work, and the welfare state (McEvoy, 2016: 766). This finding points to women and men collectively holding different views on policy issues, and by extension it can be argued that these policy differences should be represented in parliament. The same research shows that women MEPs hold more liberal views on abortion, as well as on women and paid work, than their male counterparts. Interestingly, it also finds that as more women enter the European Parliament, men become more liberal in their policy positions, and both women and men then more fully represent women's interests and positions (McEvoy, 2016: 772–6).

The discussion above highlights the complex dynamics of gender politics in practice, making it relevant for our understanding of how group-based interests are expressed in representative politics. Gender – male, female and non-binary – infuses all representative characteristics. In studying women/gender politics in Ireland, we draw attention to one aspect of representative politics, and in so doing highlight the working of Irish democratic processes and practices from a viewpoint that adds nuance to the rich knowledge base provided by other perspectives. We begin this chapter by taking a detailed look at the pattern of women's representation in social and political decision-making. This is followed by an exploration of the causes and the consequences of women's absence from public life. We chart the gradual inclusion of women's interests – some old, others new – in the political agenda, before concluding with a general assessment of current patterns and future challenges.

Women in society

The dearth of women in positions of political power in Ireland is only part of the wider pattern of women's absence from, or under-representation in, decision-making centres generally. Socio-cultural research confirms a positive link between women's access to legislatures, female employment levels and societal attitudes towards gender equality (Alexander and Welzel, 2007; Inglehart and Norris, 2003; Inglehart *et al.,* 2002). These are factors in the persistent under-representation of women in Irish politics also.

The early years of the state saw the passage of discriminatory constitutional provisions and laws that restricted women's access to employment, accentuated their role in the private sphere, banned birth control and facilitated the second class status of women (Beaumont, 1997). These included Article 41.2.1 of the current (1937) constitution: 'In particular, the State recognises that by her life within the home, woman gives to the State a support without which the common good cannot be achieved.' Even in 1937, this provision was hotly contested by a coalition of feminists and trade union activists (Luddy, 2005). By the 1970s, however, women's subservient role and status was challenged (Galligan, 1998; Connolly 2002). Restrictions on women's employment were lifted and legislation outlawing unequal pay was introduced. In subsequent decades, the proportion of women in the labour force increased. In 2015 the female employment rate stood at 63 per cent with the corresponding figure for men at 75 per cent (Eurostat, 2016a). Thus, one of the background reasons for women's under-representation – their low labour force participation – was less relevant.

Caring responsibilities have regularly been identified as depressing women's political and civic participation. The same goes for women's employment patterns. In 2016, employment rates of women and men aged 20–44 were much the same when they had no children (approximately 86 per cent). However, the figure falls to 60 per cent for women when their youngest child is aged three years or under. The comparable figure for men is 82 per cent, representing a gender gap of 22 percentage points (IBEC, 2016: 8). Given the high costs of childcare in Ireland, estimated to be €16,500 per annum in a two-child household (Barry, 2014: 11), it is little surprise that some parents opt out of the labour force. This care work largely falls on women to perform, indicating the persistence of traditional gender roles in Ireland. Many women balance family life and work by engaging in part-time employment. In 2013, women constituted 73 per cent of those working 19 hours per week or fewer, often in low paid jobs (CSO, 2014). The varied level of women's engagement with the workforce, as compared with men's high and continuous employment patterns, goes some way to explaining the persistence of a gender pay gap, measuring 14 per cent in 2014 (Eurostat, 2016b). However, policy measures to ease the cost of childcare since 2010 have resulted in a significant growth in publicly-funded childcare places, amounting to over 100,000 places for three- and four-year-olds in 2017 (Ní Aodha, 2017).

Since the 1970s, women have made significant inroads in the professions. This is especially evident in the areas of law and justice. In March 2017, the Minister for Justice, Attorney General, Chief State Solicitor, Garda (police) Commissioner, Director of Public Prosecutions, Chief Justice and chairperson of the Policing Authority were all women. In 2015, female solicitors (4,623) outnumbered male solicitors (4,609), reputed to be 'the first time a female majority has existed in any legal profession anywhere in the world' (Kelly, 2015). The proportion of female gardaí increased to 26 per cent in 2016, up from 19 per cent in 2006, while the number of female sergeants, inspectors, superintendents and chief superintendents doubled in the same time period (*Dáil Debates* 345:16, 28 September 2016). Over a third of all judges were women in 2017, up from 23 per cent in 2009 (see Table 9.1). However, the judicial arena is not immune from sexism. A 2016 Bar of Ireland survey found that just 16 per cent of all senior counsel were women, while two-thirds of women barristers recounted experiencing discrimination during their careers (Keena, 2016).

Table 9.1 Women in the judiciary, 2009–17

Court	2009		2017	
	Total number of judges	Women N (%)	Total number of judges	Women N (%)
Supreme Court	8	2 (25.0)	7	2 (28.6)
Court of Appeal	n/a	n/a	10	3 (30.0)
High Court	38	5 (13.2)	40	14 (35.0)
Circuit Court	38	12 (31.6)	40	17 (42.5)
District Court	62	15 (24.2)	64	23 (35.9)
Total	146	34 (23.3)	161	59 (36.7)

Source: www.courts.ie (last accessed 1 September 2017).

Note: at the time of writing, there were three vacancies in the Supreme Court.

The public service is a key employer of women in Ireland, offering job security and flexibility. However, within the highest rank of the civil service, a gender imbalance persists, despite improvements over the years. In 2007, four women occupied the top position of secretary general (25 per cent), while a further twelve (13 per cent) held the position of deputy secretary general or assistant secretary (CSO, 2007: 22). Since the economic crisis, the civil service workforce has reduced in size, but women retained and increased their presence in senior positions: in January 2017, 29 per cent of secretary general positions, and 28 per cent of deputy secretary general or assistant secretary positions, were held by women (see Table 9.2). Furthermore, over a third of posts at principal officer level were held by women, indicating a strong supply of women well positioned to contest future promotional opportunities. Yet, there is no room for complacency. As Table 9.2 demonstrates, there is a 'largely pyramidal [structure] with relatively few women compared to men rising to senior positions' (National Women's Strategy, 2013: 10, 51). In January 2017 the Minister for Public Expenditure and Reform announced measures to address the under-representation of women at the senior levels of the civil service, including a 50–50 gender target for appointments at senior levels.

Statistics on state board membership in 2013 indicated that 36 per cent of positions were held by women; close to, but still short of, the target of 40 per cent originally set by government as far back as 1993. To accelerate gender balance on state boards, in 2014, the government introduced new measures, which included the development of a talent bank of women willing to serve as board members, as well as a renewed commitment to the 40 per cent target, accompanied by an aim to achieve this by the end of 2016.[2] However, in January 2017 a survey revealed that just over half (54 per cent) of boards had yet to reach the 40 per cent target (Doyle, 2017).

Women's representation on company boards also remains low. In 2016, just 13 per cent of board members of Ireland's largest publicly listed companies were women, below the EU average of 21 per cent (European Commission, 2016). To address the under-representation of women on company boards, the EU set targets to ensure that at least 40 per cent of board members of publicly listed companies are women by 2020. In Ireland, a potential pool of suitably qualified women is available to fill these positions, as evidenced in the proportion

Table 9.2 Civil service grades by biological sex, 2013–17

Grade	Women		Men	
	N	%	N	%
Secretary general (2017)	5	29.4	12	70.6
Deputy and second secretary (2015)	5	23.8	16	76.2
Assistant secretary (2015)	60	28.0	155	72.0
Principal officer (2015)	452	36.2	798	63.8
Assistant principal (2015)	1,518	44.2	1,915	55.8
Administrative officer (2013)	123	56.2	96	43.8
Higher executive officer (2013)	1,686	53.2	1,484	46.8
Executive officer (2013)	3,338	66.6	1,674	33.4
Staff officer (2013)	1,239	78.6	338	21.4
Clerical officer (2013)	8,383	77.3	2,457	22.7

Sources: 2017 figure authors' own; 2015 figures calculated from information available from *Dáil Debates* 885: 2, 2 July 2015; 2013 figures from Central Statistics Office (www.cso.ie/en/releasesandpublications/ep/p-wamii/womenandmeninireland2013/socialcohesionlifestyleslist/socialcohesionlifestyles/#d.en.65499), accessed 27 February 2017.

of female graduates. Women accounted for 52 per cent of all graduates in 2014 (Higher Education Authority, 2016a). Yet, just 14 per cent of Irish companies are headed by a female chief executive, and while 34 per cent of junior level management positions are held by women, their representation falls off at each subsequent senior grade (Taylor, 2016). In addition to childcare, organisational culture, in the form of gender biases, acts as a barrier to women's career advancement. This is very evident in the field of academia, where high profile cases have exposed gender discrimination in the area of promotion.[3] While gender balance exists at lecturer level, just 19 per cent of professors are women. To address the lack of women in senior levels of academia, the Higher Education Authority (HEA) supports the introduction of mandatory gender quotas for promotion in higher education institutions (Higher Education Authority, 2016b).

Women in political institutions

In the late nineteenth century, Irish women campaigning for the vote saw it as the key to increasing women's influence in national life. The Irish suffrage movement, strongly influenced by the women's franchise campaign in Britain, sought to bring a feminist voice to Irish politics. However, the strengthening independence movement led to this aim being joined, and arguably overshadowed, by the demand for national sovereignty promoted by prominent Sinn Féin women (Cullen, 1997: 272). The supremacy of the nationalist discourse over that of feminism is important in understanding the low representation of women subsequent to independence. While winning the vote in 1918[4] was presented as a victory for feminists in Britain, the extension of the franchise to women in Ireland was interpreted as a step on the way to self-government. From this point on, women's place in political life was linked to their association with the 'national question', and among the few women who made it to political office in the post-1918 decades, many had close family and personal connections with the revolutionary era (Galligan, 2017: 159–63). In the following sections, we trace the participation of women in Irish political life to the present, focusing on their representation in national and local politics, and their involvement in political parties.

National level

When people are asked to reflect on the role of women in Irish politics, the names of Constance Markievicz, Mary Robinson and Mary McAleese readily come to mind. Their accomplishments serve as milestones in the history of women's political representation in Ireland. Constance Markievicz was the first woman parliamentarian in Ireland, and her appointment as Minister for Labour in 1919, though largely a symbolic appointment, placed her among the first women worldwide to achieve such political office. Mary Robinson's election as the country's first female president in 1990 made Ireland only the second country in Europe (after Iceland) to have a woman head of state elected by popular vote. In 1997, Mary McAleese became the first woman in the world to follow another woman into the office of elected head of state (see Appendix 3 for biographical details of leading political figures). These achievements placed women firmly on the political map in Ireland and brought international recognition to the country for the advancement of women in politics. However, these highlights are more symbolic than substantial. The role of president is primarily ceremonial (see Chapter 7), and Markievicz's appointment as Minister for Labour in 1919 was emblematic of the contemporary fusion of the nationalist and suffrage causes. It would be 60 years before another woman served in cabinet.

The reality is that women have been grossly under-represented in Irish politics. Of the approximately 1,300 people elected to Dáil Éireann between 1918 and 2016, just 114 (9 per cent) were women. Between the 1992 and 2011 general elections, the number of women TDs increased by a mere five, to 25 (see Table 9.3). With only 15 per cent of women TDs, Ireland was in 107th position in a global league table for women's parliamentary representation at the end of 2011, a significant drop from its 1996 position (39th).[5] The drop of nearly 70 places is primarily due to the surge in countries adopting affirmative measures, such as gender quotas, following the United Nations (UN) Fourth World Conference on Women in Beijing in September 1995.

The stagnation in growth in Irish women's political representation, up to and including the 2011 general election, drew attention from international observers. In the comments on Ireland's progress under the UN's Convention on the Elimination of Discrimination against Women (CEDAW), concern was expressed about the 'significant under-representation of women in elected political structures, particularly in the Oireachtas' (United Nations, 2005: 8). It encouraged the State 'to take sustained measures to increase the representation of women in elected bodies' (United Nations, 2005: 8). In Ireland though, despite much rhetoric about the need for more women in politics, politicians and political parties largely shied away from advocating equality measures such as gender quotas, preferring instead the softer strategy of gender targets (Galligan and Wilford, 1999; Buckley, 2013).

The economic downturn of 2008 was a catalyst for change. In the febrile political atmosphere that followed the banking and financial crisis, there were ubiquitous demands for political reform.[6] Oireachtas committees[7] were established to review the political system. To address the under-representation of women in politics, proposals to introduce gender-balancing mechanisms in candidate selection processes were made, recommending that state funding of political parties be tied to the proportion of women candidates.[8] These recommendations were to be pivotal in the legislation that followed (Buckley, 2013). In May 2011, the Fine Gael–Labour coalition government announced its intention to link the public funding of political parties to the proportion of women candidates selected at general elections. The

Table 9.3 Women candidates and TDs at elections, 1977–2016

Election	Candidates			Deputies		
	Total	Women	%	Total	Women	%
1977	376	25	6.6	148	6	4.1
1981	404	41	10.1	166	11	6.6
1982 (Feb)	366	35	9.6	166	8	4.8
1982 (Nov)	365	31	8.5	166	14	8.4
1987	466	65	13.9	166	14	8.4
1989	371	52	14.0	166	13	7.8
1992	482	89	18.5	166	20	12.0
1997	484	96	19.8	166	20	12.0
2002	463	84	18.1	166	22	13.2
2007	470	82	17.4	166	22	13.2
2011	566	86	15.2	166	25	15.1
2016	551	163	29.6	158	35	22.2

Sources: Authors' calculations For 2007 figures, Gallagher (2008: 80).

Note: the actual number of women contesting the 1987 general election is distorted due to the fact that one independent candidate, Barbara Hyland, ran in thirteen constituencies. For 2007 figures, Gallagher (2008: 80).

Electoral (Amendment) (Political Funding) Act, 2012, incentivises political parties to select women candidates by specifying that payments to political parties 'shall be reduced by 50 per cent, unless at least 30 per cent of the candidates whose candidatures were authenticated by the qualified party at the preceding general election were women and at least 30 per cent were men'. The 30 per cent gender threshold came into effect at the 2016 general election and is due to rise to 40 per cent from 2023 onwards.

Candidate selection quotas are primarily used in European and South American states and can be adopted through legislation or voluntarily by a political party. Aside from Ireland, nine other EU member states use legislative candidate gender quotas for elections to their lower houses of parliament: Belgium, Croatia, France, Greece, Luxembourg, Poland, Portugal, Slovenia and Spain. Like Ireland, Croatia, France, Luxembourg and Portugal use financial provisions to incentivise parties to comply with gender quota laws. In Belgium, Greece, Luxembourg, Poland, Slovenia and Spain political parties that do not select the requisite proportion of women candidates face rejection of their list as invalid. Voluntary gender quotas are more frequently used in Scandinavian countries, where they have been in use since the late 1970s. A third form of gender quota – the reserved seat quota – is primarily used in African and Asian contexts. This quota specifies that a certain number or proportion of seats in parliament are reserved for women. Quotas are usually adopted via a country's constitution. Following the passage of UN Security Council Resolution 1325 in 2000, which specified the inclusion of women in peace negotiations, it is not uncommon to see reserved seats adopted in post-conflict societies, such as Afghanistan. To ensure the effectiveness of gender quotas, a growing number of political parties and nation-states worldwide have introduced extra features to their quota regimes, including placement mandates that specify where on the ballot paper women candidates are to be listed, and recommendations that women candidates are selected in winnable seats.

The introduction of gender quotas in Ireland proved a success in 2016 (Buckley *et al.*, 2016). The number of women candidates increased by 90 per cent compared with 2011, and the number of women elected by 40 per cent. Following the election, women's political representation in Dáil Éireann was 22 per cent, demonstrating the capacity of gender quotas to engender fast-track change in women's descriptive political representation (Buckley *et al.*, 2016: 201). However, there is no room for complacency. When we place Ireland in a comparative context, it is clear that a male super-majority still exists in Irish politics. Comparing the proportion of women in Dáil Éireann with that of the lower houses of parliament in other EU member states in 2017, the Dáil emerges as one of the least gender-balanced legislatures (see Table 9.4).

Male domination of Irish politics is also clear to see when reviewing government office-holding. Of the 199 people appointed cabinet ministers between 1919 and June 2017, 91 per cent were men. Only 18 women had ever served in cabinet up to that time. With the exception of the largely symbolic appointment of Constance Markievicz as Minister for Labour in 1919, no woman held a cabinet post until December 1979, when Máire Geoghegan-Quinn (Fianna Fáil) became Minister for the Gaeltacht. Although the proportion of woman attaining ministerial office has grown (see Table 9.5), government in Ireland continues to be a male-dominated space. Despite Taoiseach Enda Kenny's pledge in December 2014 to have gender parity in ministerial appointments following the 2016 general election,[9] some 75 per cent of his ministerial appointees (cabinet and ministers of state) were men.

When women are appointed to cabinet government in Ireland, a gendered pattern is evident in the ministerial portfolios assigned to women, with female cabinet ministers more likely to receive portfolios relating to social affairs (48 per cent of cases) than economic

Table 9.4 Women's representation in lower houses of parliament in EU28, 2017

Country	% female representation
Sweden	43.6
Finland	42.0
Spain	39.1
France	38.8
Belgium	38.0
Denmark	37.4
Germany	37.0
Slovenia	36.7
Netherlands	36.0
Portugal	34.8
United Kingdom	32.0
Italy	31.0
Austria	30.6
Luxembourg	28.3
Poland	28.0
Estonia	26.7
Bulgaria	23.8
Republic of Ireland	*22.2*
Lithuania	21.3
Romania	20.7
Czech Republic	20.0
Slovakia	20.0
Croatia	18.5
Greece	18.3
Cyprus	17.9
Latvia	16.0
Malta	11.9
Hungary	10.1

Table 9.5 Ministerial office-holding by gender, 1977–2017

Government	Year	Men (N)	Women (N)	Women (%)
Fianna Fáil	1977	21	1	4.5
Fianna Fáil	1979	29	1	3.3
Fine Gael–Labour	1981	26	2	7.1
Fianna Fáil	1982	24	1	4.0
Fine Gael–Labour	1982	28	3	9.7
Fianna Fáil	1987	28	2	6.7
Fianna Fáil–PDs	1989	27	3	10.0
Fianna Fáil–PDs	1992	28	3	10.0
Fianna Fáil–Labour	1993	25	5	16.7
Fine Gael–Labour–Democratic Left	1994	24	6	20.0
Fianna Fáil–PDs	1997	26	5	16.1
Fianna Fáil–PDs	2002	28	4	12.5
Fianna Fáil–Greens–PDs	2007	29	6	17.1
Fianna Fáil–Greens–Independents	2008	30	5	14.3
Fine Gael–Labour	2011	24	6	20.0
Fine Gael–Independents	2016	25	8	24.2
Fine Gael–Independents	2017	27	7	20.6
All		449	68	13.2

Source: Authors' own calculations.

Note: Ministerial office-holding includes cabinet ministers and ministers of state.

Box 9.1 Firsts for women in politics

1918	Women over 30 entitled to vote for the first time in parliamentary elections; first woman elected (Constance Markievicz, Sinn Féin)
1919	First woman government minister (Constance Markievicz), though the position was largely symbolic as Ireland was not self-governing
1923	Votes for all women
1937	First woman party leader (Margaret Buckley, Sinn Féin)
1969	First woman on a parliamentary committee (Evelyn Owens, Labour)
1977	First woman junior minister (Máire Geoghegan-Quinn, Fianna Fáil)
1979	First woman government minister (Máire Geoghegan-Quinn, Fianna Fáil)
1982	First woman Cathaoirleach (speaker) of the Seanad (Tras Honan, Fianna Fáil)
1982	First woman chairperson of a parliamentary committee (Nora Owen, Fine Gael)
1990	First woman president (Mary Robinson)
1993	First woman leader of a party with Dáil representation (Mary Harney, PDs)
1997	First woman Tánaiste (Mary Harney, PDs)
2011	First woman Attorney General (Máire Whelan)

ones (24 per cent). Male ministers have been less likely to hold social affairs portfolios (17 per cent) while, in contrast, they dominate economic and foreign policy briefs (52 per cent). According to Connolly (2013: 376), the continuing tendency to engage in gender clustering of ministerial portfolios in Ireland is high by international standards. Given that ministerial appointments are made within the context of party interests and dynamics, Connolly (2013) argues that the type of portfolio assigned to women is a function of their position within their parties, as well as the gendered ethos of those parties, party leaders and government, rather than a conscious act of discrimination.

Local government

The pattern of women's representation in local government has been similar to that at national level. Women's local council representation has been consistently low, reaching a modest 21 per cent in 2014. This wide gap in gender representation on local councils is relevant as local government service is one of the main routes to national politics. Following the 2016 general election, close to 90 per cent of women elected were local councillors at some stage in their political careers. The corresponding figure for male TDs was 85 per cent, indicating the significance of local government service to both women's and men's electoral prospects. However, as seen in Table 9.6, men dominate local councils, meaning that few women have an opportunity to acquire the political experience and networks essential for candidate selection and election at the national level (Buckley *et al.*, 2014; 2015). The legislative gender quota does not apply at local elections. However, there are signs of a quota diffusion effect (Buckley and Hofman, 2015). At the 2014 local elections, female candidacies increased as political parties set informal gender targets as they prepared for the implementation of gender quotas at the 2016 general election. Gender targets ranged from 25 per cent (Fine Gael) to 33 per cent (Fianna Fáil). Smaller, newer and leftist parties tended to meet their targets more easily than the long-established and centre-right parties of Fianna Fáil and Fine Gael, emphasising the role of political parties in encouraging or encumbering women's candidacy.

Table 9.6 Women councillors elected at local elections, 1974–2014

Election year	Women's seat-holding (%)
1974	6
1979	6
1985	8
1991	12
1999	15
2004	19
2009	17
2014	21

Source: Buckley and Hofman (2015: 89); Manning (1987: 158–60).

Political parties

By 2010, Irish political parties had come to recognise that interventions were required to secure women's place on candidate lists. However, few were willing to commit to a definite gender quota, preferring instead the more fluid concept of 'gender targets'. The reluctance to adopt gender quotas often stemmed from 'rank and file' opposition, often at odds with the party leadership on the best way forward to facilitate women's candidacy. Evidence of divergent views on gender quotas was apparent. In 2010, the Fine Gael leadership proposed the introduction of gender quotas in its political reform statement 'New Politics'. However, the proposal was widely resisted within the party, with objectors claiming 'that the introduction of gender quotas would contravene the principles of equal opportunity, fairness and democracy' (Buckley, 2013: 347). Consequently, Fine Gael rolled back on a commitment to gender quotas in its 2011 general election manifesto. Similarly, in Fianna Fáil, a motion to support electoral gender quotas, supported by the party's elected representatives, 'was defeated at the party's Ard Fheis in March 2012 with delegates preferring the notion of "merit" as grounds for selection' (Buckley, 2013: 351). Even within Labour, a party that has supported the use of interventionist measures since the 1980s, and which negotiated the inclusion of legislative gender quotas in the 2011 Fine Gael–Labour Programme for Government, some resistance was evident; Joanna Tuffy, one of the party's TDs, was among the most vocal opponents of gender quotas.

All parties formally supported the Electoral (Amendment) (Political Funding) Act 2012, but the grassroots resistance outlined here was to re-emerge in the course of selection conventions for the 2016 general election (discussed later). However, of 155 selection conventions held across the four main political parties, just 12 directives from party headquarters specifying the gender of the candidates to be selected were issued. In effect, party managers and electoral strategists were able to ensure that the convention process would deliver an outcome in line with party gender plans. Thus, the inaugural roll-out of legislative gender quotas in Ireland was a relatively smooth process (Buckley *et al.,* 2016).

Besides the electoral arena, there has been a growing consciousness among political parties of the need to bring more women into internal decision-making fora too. Research indicates that party service at national executive level enhances women's electoral ambitions, mainly through socialising prospective candidates into the norms and rules of political decision-making, providing future candidates with a profile within the party and enabling party leaders to evaluate the electoral potential of senior female party members (Kittilson,

2006). The level of women's participation in party politics has remained broadly static in terms of membership since the 1990s, with women comprising between 25 and 40 per cent of party members, a common pattern across the world (Buckley and McGing, 2011; Gauja and van Haute, 2015: 194).

In recent years, all parties have become more aware of the institutional obstacles to women's political ambitions and have undertaken various publicly funded projects to address these issues. The heightened consciousness of the gender makeup of parties has benefited women in the senior ranks. Fianna Fáil's powerful Committee of 20, elected at its annual conference, returns equal numbers of women and men through elections based on separate male and female slates for 10 seats each. Labour has a 30 per cent gender quota for membership of its executive board and central council positions, while of the six executive board members elected by party members, three must be women. At least 30 per cent of Sinn Féin's *ard chomhairle* must be women (through co-option, if necessary). Of the 12 *ard chomhairle* members chosen by the party membership, equal numbers of women and men must be elected. Fine Gael's national executive also shows some signs of gender balancing, with parliamentary and regional representatives including at least one woman in each case. Gradually, the numbers of women holding positions on the national executives of political parties have come to reflect their party membership rates; as of March 2017, 50 per cent of members of the national executive of the Green Party were female, with the figures for other parties being 43 per cent for Sinn Féin, 37 per cent for Labour, 33 per cent for Fine Gael and 28 per cent for Fianna Fáil (data supplied by the respective parties).

Awareness of the need to support women seeking political office has also grown. All political parties engage in capacity-building programmes, encouraging women's candidacy through training and mentoring programmes, as well as working with Women for Election, a non-partisan organisation offering support programmes to women seeking political office. However, party expenditure on the promotion of women remains low. In 2015, just three per cent of all expenditure went on women's participation in politics.[10]

Women's hold on constituency officer positions shows little change from the traditional pattern, according to which women have held supportive rather than leadership positions. In 2017, women held just 15 per cent of constituency chair positions within Fine Gael, yet occupied half (51 per cent) of constituency secretary posts. In Labour, one fifth (21 per cent) of constituency chair positions are held by women while women account for 35 per cent of constituency secretaries. In Sinn Féin, only 17 per cent of constituency chair positions are held by women whereas women predominate among constituency secretary positions (72 per cent). While a breakdown of constituency office-holding in Fianna Fáil is unavailable, of the total of 935 positions within Fianna Fáil's constituency and cumann organisations, 213 (23 per cent) are held by women.

The under-representation of women in constituency leadership positions may be indicative of traditional expectations regarding women's political involvement at the grassroots level. These attitudes contribute to a local reluctance to encourage the ambitions of aspiring women candidates, stymieing women's access to local council politics. *The National Strategy for Women and Girls 2017–2020*, published in April 2017 (Department of Justice and Equality, 2017), acknowledged the need for action to 'be taken to increase the participation of women in local government' (57). However, it did not commit to concrete initiatives, such as gender quotas, to redress the continuing under-representation of women in local politics, preferring instead a loose commitment to 'investigate potential supports to promote the participation of women' (59) in future local elections.

Box 9.2 Leading women politicians

Irish politics has been largely male-dominated since the foundation of the state. Only since the late 1970s have women politicians gained access to any of the levers of power. Some of the prominent women in Irish politics include:

Mary Robinson (born 1944) was the first woman elected President in 1990, with the backing of Labour, the Workers' Party and the Green Party. She had previously served as Senator between 1969 and 1989, elected via the University of Dublin constituency. During her time in the Seanad, as well as during her career as a barrister, she was an advocate for law reform on a number of gender equality issues, including equal pay and access to contraception. Between 1997 and 2002, she served as UN High Commissioner for Human Rights.

Mary McAleese (born 1951) was elected President in 1997, standing as the Fianna Fáil candidate with the support also of the Progressive Democrats. She was returned unopposed for a second term in 2004.

Máire Geoghegan-Quinn (born 1950) was appointed to cabinet in 1979. She was the first woman to hold such office since the largely symbolic appointment of Constance Markievicz to cabinet in 1919. She was TD for Galway West from 1975 until her retirement from electoral politics in 1997. During her time in politics, she held various ministries including Gaeltacht, Transport and Communications, and Justice. After national politics, she went on to have a prominent career in Europe, serving on the European Court of Auditors between 2000 and 2010 and as EU Commissioner for Research, Innovation and Science between 2010 and 2014.

Mary Harney (born 1953) was the first woman appointed Tánaiste in 1997. Originally a member of Fianna Fáil, she left the party in 1985 and became a founding member of the Progressive Democrats. She served as its party leader between 1993 and 2006. Following the disbandment of the party in 2009 she became an independent TD and, in the process, became the second independent TD to hold a cabinet position in the history of the state. She served as TD for the constituencies of Dublin Mid-West and Dublin South-West over a 30-year period from 1981 to 2011. She held a number of cabinet ministries, including Enterprise, Trade and Employment and Health and Children.

Mary O'Rourke (born 1937) was a Fianna Fáil TD for the constituencies of Longford–Westmeath and Westmeath between 1982 and 2002, and again from 2007 to 2011. During her time in national politics, she served in a number of cabinet ministries including Education, Health, and Public Enterprise. She was the first woman to serve as deputy party leader of Fianna Fáil.

Mary Coughlan (born 1965) was a Fianna Fáil TD for Donegal South-West between 1987 and 2011. She is one of just four women to serve as Tánaiste, and the second woman to be appointed to this position, serving in the role between 2008 and 2011. Of the 18 women who have served in cabinet in Ireland, she has held the highest number of cabinet ministries, including Social and Family Affairs; Agriculture, Fisheries and Food; Enterprise, Trade and Employment; and Education and Skills.

Joan Burton (born 1949) was first elected as a Labour TD for Dublin West in 1992, and though she lost her seat in 1997, she regained it in 2002 and held it at each of the next three elections. In 2014 she became the first woman to be elected leader of the Labour Party and the third woman to be appointed Tánaiste. She served as Minister for Social Protection from 2011 to 2016.

Frances Fitzgerald (born 1950) was re-elected as a Fine Gael TD for Dublin Mid-West in 2016, having first taken a seat there in 2011. She previously served as TD for the constituency of Dublin South-East between 1992 and 2002. In May 2016, she was appointed Tánaiste. During her political career she has served as Minister for Children and Youth Affairs, Minister for Justice and Equality, and Minister for Business, Enterprise and Innovation.

Katherine Zappone (born 1953) was elected an independent TD for Dublin South-West in 2016. In May 2016, she was appointed Minister for Children and Youth Affairs, becoming the first openly gay woman to serve in cabinet in Ireland. She also became only the second independent woman TD to hold a cabinet ministry and the sixth person to hold a ministry as a first-time TD in the history of the state.

Causes of the under-representation of women

So far, we have examined the extent of the under-representation of women in politics and other centres of decision-making. We now look at possible reasons for this under-representation. In doing so, we will discuss some of the factors that have acted as barriers to women's participation in public life, beginning with socio-cultural attitudes. We follow this with a review of party selection practices to assess the extent of gender inequality in party institutional structures. We then outline the barriers that women face in creating a local presence, which is an essential first step to a career in politics.

Socio-cultural attitudes

To understand women's under-representation in politics in Ireland, one needs to understand Irish political culture (see Chapter 2 for a general overview of this). The turbulent decades at the beginning of the twentieth century afforded women the opportunity to integrate a feminist consciousness within nationalism. But as noted in the earlier pages of this chapter, the policies and laws of the new state unravelled women's status as equal citizens, and bestowed on men a patriarchal dividend (Connell, 1996) that reinforced their dominant position in the gender order in Irish society (Buckley *et al.,* 2013).

The influence of Roman Catholic teachings conveyed a traditional view of women's social role and prioritised home and family-based duties (Randall and Smyth, 1987). The role of wife and mother was valorised, essentially marginalising women from the public sphere. These socially conservative views shaped attitudes towards women in politics, as is evident in some male politicians' comments on women politicians. Laffan (2014: 166) notes that when republican women campaigned against William T. Cosgrave's re-election as president of the executive council in 1923, he is reported to have said they 'should have rosaries in their hands or be at home with knitting needles'. Similarly, Ferriter (2008: 189) recounts the views of Fianna Fáil TD Timothy O'Connor who, when asked for his thoughts on women's participation in politics in a Women's Political Association survey in 1977, advised 'in my own county the women are doing a great job of work in keeping their homes going and bringing up their families. This I think is just what Almighty God intended them to do'.

Faced with such socio-cultural attitudes, it is not surprising that so few women put themselves forward for election in the period between 1922 and 1977. During this time, just 24 women were elected to Dáil Éireann, 80 per cent of whom were related to a former male TD. Women were heavily reliant on male networks to enter politics, an access route that Galligan *et al.* (2000) describe as the 'widow's and daughter's inheritance'. From 1977 to 1992, there was a perceptible increase in the number of women contesting and winning Dáil elections, with the proportion of women candidates and TDs increasing threefold, though from a low base (see Table 9.3). However, as noted previously, progress stagnated after this period of growth. Perplexingly, this stagnation coincided with an era of greater equality for women and the growing feminisation of the workforce, factors usually associated with increased women's participation in politics (Buckley *et al.*, 2015).

For mothers with political ambitions, the practicality of pursuing this time-consuming career in tandem with child-rearing is an issue of greater significance than it is for their male colleagues. Data from a comprehensive survey of women legislators pointed to family responsibilities as the most significant source of difficulty in pursuing a political career – demands that are exacerbated when a politician is from a constituency outside Dublin (Galligan *et al.*, 2000). It indicates the continuing influence of traditional cultural attitudes in Ireland, even among women who have managed to get elected to the highest legislative office, confirming that culture is an important ingredient in shaping women's political opportunities.

However, culture is just one of the causes of the under-representation of women in Irish politics and, indeed, cannot solely explain why gains in women's political representation between 1977 and 1992 were not continued in the following years (Buckley *et al.*, 2015). Thus, we must widen our analytical gaze to examine institutional factors, such as party candidate selection procedures, and how they interact with informal institutional dynamics, such as localism, to stymie women's access into politics.

Candidate selection

Explanations for women's political under-representation have focused on internal party selection processes as the single most important obstacle to women's political participation (Elgood *et al.*, 2002). As the gate-keepers to political office, political parties exercise considerable influence on the extent of women's candidacy. In comparison to single-member district election systems, studies suggest that PR-STV has the potential to increase female candidature due to the availability of more opportunities in constituencies with higher seat magnitudes (Buckley *et al.*, 2014: 473; McGing, 2013; Matland and Taylor, 1997; Kaminsky and White, 2007; Kittilson and Schwindt-Bayer, 2012). However, constituency size is relatively small, ranging from three to five seats (see Chapter 4), encouraging political parties to favour established and incumbent candidates, usually male, rather than risk fragmenting the party vote excessively by running additional candidates. While women's membership of the four main political parties averaged 34 per cent in 2011, their average rate of female candidacy was just 19 per cent in that year's general election. Of course, not all party women (or men) will put themselves forward for selection at conventions, but the gap between women's membership and candidacy rates indicates that women are overlooked in favour of their male party colleagues.

Viewing candidate selection through a feminist analytical lens uncovers the gendered underpinnings of the informal practices that guide this institutional process. Emphasis is placed on localness and incumbency, characteristics that tend to favour 'local sons' (Kenny, 2013). Developing a local base and network requires time and money. As highlighted in earlier sections of this chapter, women continue to be the primary care providers in Irish families and many opt out of paid employment to undertake these responsibilities. Thus, in comparison to men, women have unequal access to the key political resources of time and money to develop local bases, which places them at a disadvantage in selection contests. Likewise, incumbency disadvantages women. Incumbency confers instant name recognition and track record on the bearers, garnering them levels of support that challengers find difficult to muster (Benoit and Marsh, 2008). Given that the majority of incumbents are men, female candidates operate at a disadvantage in both selection and election contests.

To address this gender inequality in candidate selection processes, political parties were legally bound to implement the quota law passed in 2012. The selection of women candidates in this context led to claims that women were unmerited candidates, selected solely on the basis of their biological sex rather than ability and political experience. However, as Buckley *et al.* (2016: 192) show, some 51 per cent of women candidates were political office-holders at the time of the general election in comparison to 60 per cent of male candidates, demonstrating that the women who ran were already politically experienced. The issuing of gender directives by party headquarters at the 2016 general election led to tensions with the party grassroots, but this is nothing new in Irish politics. At election after election, constituency level parties strive to protect their selection autonomy against what they perceive as centralised democracy within political parties (Reidy, 2016).

Local base and networks

In an Irish context, one of the most important determinants of political success is the strength of a candidate's local base (Kavanagh, 2007: 186). One of the most effective methods of establishing this is through local government service. In 2017, 86 per cent of TDs in the 32nd Dáil were councillors at some stage of their political careers (Gallagher, 2016: 153). However, as we have seen, there are relatively few women in local government. One way of overcoming this disadvantage is through the development of local networks based on occupation. Professions such as teaching, medicine, law and business are generally seen as conferring status within a local community. They involve extensive interaction with the local electorate, and can be used as a foundation for personal bailiwick-building. In addition, these occupations bring economic independence and relative flexibility of time, two additional advantages for a person ambitious to hold political office. It is no accident then that teaching is the most prevalent occupation among the women TDs in the 32nd Dáil. Just under 30 per cent of women TDs are teachers, an occupation that provides aspirants with significant local networking opportunities, and the time in which to consolidate these networks (Buckley *et al.*, 2016: 200). However, women TDs' working lives are diverse, including other occupations with the potential to generate a high profile, such as trade union organisers, lawyers, and business women. These forms of employment combine three important factors facilitating political career-building: income security and financial independence, opportunities for local contact, and time in which to pursue support-building activities.

Consequences of the under-representation of women

The term 'representation', when used in the context of women's presence in parliamentary assemblies, is taken to have two different, yet related, meanings. One is the representation of interests, or substantive representation: do women represent women's concerns, are they expected to do so by the voting public, and do they feel they have a specific responsibility to speak for women's interests? The second addresses the representativeness of the legislature, descriptive representation – is a parliament truly democratic if it excludes women or only minimally incorporates them among its members? In this section, we focus on these questions to assess their application in an Irish context before going on to examine the extent to which women's interests have been institutionalised and mainstreamed into the policy agenda in Ireland.

Substantive representation – representing women's interests

Studies of women parliamentarians appear to indicate that women legislators seek in some way to speak and act for women in the community, and they also show that there is some expectation among women voters that women politicians will share their concerns (Celis, 2014: 59–61). Indeed, many of the discriminatory policies enacted against women in Ireland, from 1922 onwards, are often seen as the product of a male-dominated political order. It is clear that during the 1970s, when women's parliamentary representation was almost negligible, government and parliament were, at best, only partially responsive to the growing voice of gender reform. The articulation and representation of women's rights fell to the emerging feminist movement, a reform-minded judiciary (see Chapter 3), and the European Commission (see Chapter 14). These agencies were more important catalysts in the initiation of change in the status of women than either politicians or parliament, suggesting that the political system was forced to respond to external pressures rather than initiating change. While European directives on employment and judicial decisions on individual rights acted as an important spur to specific legislative changes, the re-emergence of the women's movement in the early 1970s prompted a public discussion of discrimination against women in law and public policy.

It can be argued that women's lobby groups have had a more immediate influence on specific aspects of public policy than the efforts of women TDs. In 1972, the Commission on the Status of Women recommended that action be taken to remove discrimination against women in the areas of the home, employment, social welfare, taxation, family law, jury service, public life and education. Over four decades later, the issues have evolved, with consideration given to issues such as advancing socio-economic equality for women and girls, women in leadership, embedding gender equality in decision-making, and enhancing women's and girls' mental and physical health and active citizenship (Department of Justice and Equality, 2016).

One issue that has remained contentious is that of abortion. Since the constitution was amended in 1983 in a way that was intended to prohibit any legalisation of abortion, the issue has been the subject of repeated court cases, the findings of which have called for political responses (Bacik, 2013). One sad case above all mobilised public support for change. Savita Halappanavar presented to a hospital in Galway in October 2012 suffering from a miscarriage and died from complications shortly thereafter. The crux of the issue was that medical doctors treating her refused to perform an abortion due to uncertainty around the legal protection for those performing terminations. Media attention to the tragic story mobilised widespread support for the deceased woman, and the government responded by introducing legislation to clarify the protection available to doctors. However, it was not a sufficient response to satisfy a new generation of citizens. Halappanavar's death re-mobilised a coalition of civil society groups that had lain dormant for two decades along with a new generation of citizens in a coalition to repeal the eighth amendment to the constitution. This amendment, passed in 1983 after a bitter campaign, provided for the equal right to life of mother and unborn child, and it was interpreted by the Supreme Court in the 1992 X case in a manner not foreseen by proponents of the amendment (see Box 3.2, p. 64).

The emergence of a repeal coalition also spurred pro-life groups to mount a vigorous defence of the constitutional status quo. In 2015, a private members' bill tabled by independent socialist TD Clare Daly sought to provide for abortion in cases of fatal foetal abnormality. The bill was defeated, with Fianna Fáil, Fine Gael and Labour voting against it, guided by the advice of the Attorney General that the bill was unconstitutional, and Sinn Féin abstaining. Yet, the issue remained a live one. It was raised during the 2016 election campaign, with a pledge to repeal the eighth amendment in the Labour, Sinn Féin and Green Party manifestos. The Fine Gael manifesto committed to referring the issue to a citizens' assembly, with a view to determining the extent of a consensus for constitutional change (Fine Gael, 2016: 71–2). At the same time, some independent candidates spoke against reform of the constitution. Nonetheless, it remained a party commitment, and became part of the negotiations on government formation (O'Malley, 2016: 270). In the following months, the United Nations Human Rights Council recommended a repeal of the restrictive abortion provision (Fitzgerald, 2016) and some members of the government openly favoured a repeal of the eighth amendment. Following a defeat of a private members' bill on 27 October 2016, seeking to repeal this amendment, proposed by Ruth Coppinger of the Anti-Austerity Alliance (subsequently renamed Solidarity), the citizens' assembly at its inaugural meeting on 26–27 November 2016 agreed to dedicate four of its meetings to the topic. In April 2017, the citizens' assembly recommended a liberalisation of the state's abortion laws.

Of importance too is the internationalisation of the domestic gender equality agenda, influenced by government commitments to progress on United Nations and European Union equality policies. The importance of international obligations is that they require the Irish government to respond in a proactive manner to progressively effect gender equality. The UN Committee on the Elimination of Discrimination Against Women repeatedly exhorted Ireland to adopt 'temporary special measures' to increase women's legislative representation. This external pressure, aligned with national debates and lobbying, resulted in the adoption of gender quotas in Irish political life. In September 2016, Ireland accepted, in full or in part, 84 per cent of the 262 policy recommendations from the UN evaluation of the government's sixth and seventh combined periodic reports to the Committee on the Elimination of Discrimination Against Women. Of the 41 recommendations not accepted, almost one half (19) dealt with issues of reproductive rights and abortion.[11] These external fora also provide women's civil society representatives and equality institutions independent of government (such as the Irish Human Rights Commission) with a platform to present alternative analyses of women's situation to that of the state. These shadow reports are considered carefully by the relevant international body, and their contents are used to frame critical questions to Irish government representatives.

Descriptive representation – women in parliament

For long, then, the representation of women's interests has largely been conducted by voices outside the legislative system, through lobbying, pressure, and international frameworks, forcing a generally reluctant government to respond. Nonetheless, there have been feminist voices within the Dáil seeking to address women-specific issues in health, family matters, gender-based violence, employment opportunities and, less frequently, women in decision-making. As more women enter national politics, and as the number of women and men from centre-left parties increases, gender equality issues have come more distinctly to the fore, of which the issue of repeal of the eighth amendment is but one example. Other issues to come onto the floor of the 32nd Dáil, following the 2016 election, included gender reassignment, pension equality, gender balance in decision-making and equality proofing of budgets, all demonstrating the diversity of issues being raised by representatives. Thus, there is a range of evidence emerging to indicate that having more women in parliament can have an effect on the style and substance of political debate. In January 2017, a women's caucus was established in Leinster House, led by Green Party TD Catherine Martin. This initiative followed hot on the heels of a similar move in the Northern Ireland Assembly, and reflects a growing trend in specialised parliamentary bodies dealing with gender equality matters (Sawer and Grace, 2016).

However, as more women enter parliaments across the world, there is no consistent evidence of a continual move towards more gender equality policy outputs. Indeed, Dahlerup (2014: 155) notes in relation to Scandinavia that there was a greater commitment to feminism and feminist values among women representatives in the 1980s than in the 2000s, even though there are more women in parliament now. She argues that progress in terms of women's numerical representation cannot be automatically linked with a more woman-friendly parliament and with parliamentary outcomes sensitive to the redress of gender inequalities. This also underlines the complex relationship between gender, ideology and 'competing' identity interests that, as the case of Northern Ireland illustrates, fragments women's political claims (Galligan, 2013).

The institutionalisation of women's interests

Gradually, as issues of women's rights and status in society came onto the political agenda in Ireland, political structures evolved and institutionalised the expression of these demands. Since 1993, there has been a cabinet minister for equality, with this brief constituting part of a larger portfolio, usually Justice. Recent commitments to gender mainstreaming have brought about renewed efforts to combat domestic, sexual and gender-based violence. In January 2017, the Minister for Justice and Equality announced plans to introduce legislation to define sexual consent (Bardon, 2017), gender proofing of national budgets and the gender proofing of fiscal plans. The Gender Recognition Act and Marriage Act (legalising same-sex marriage) were passed in 2015, and there is a promise in the 2017–2020 National Women's Strategy to provide the institutional arrangements within government to support the delivery of gender-sensitive policymaking (Department of Justice and Equality, 2016: 8).

However, structures for supporting gender mainstreaming in policy did not emerge from the austerity years unscathed. Public sector bodies were targeted for savings in an effort to place the public finances on a viable footing after the fiscal crisis. Over 2009–10, the budget of the Equality Authority was cut by 43 per cent, and that of the Human Rights Commission by one quarter. The Equality Authority was merged with the Irish Human Rights and Equality Commission (IHRC) in 2013, with a consequent reduction in expertise and personnel. Also closed in 2009 were the Women's Health Council and the Crisis Pregnancy Agency (merged with the Health Service Executive). The closure of the gender equality unit of the Department of Justice, Equality and Law Reform predated the crisis. Its activities were 'mainstreamed' into the general working of the Department of Justice, Equality and Law Reform in 2006. The National Employment Action Plan (NEAP), too, had a gender mainstreaming requirement, as a result of European policy on equal opportunities for women and men in employment. However, this initiative also came to an end in 2006. Public funding for the peak women's civil society organisation, the National Women's Council of Ireland, was repeatedly cut. Since 1997, a restructuring of parliamentary committees led to the stand-alone women's affairs committee being subsumed into the committee on justice and equality and, within that, the creation of a sub-committee on women's rights in 1998. In 2016, the Committee on Justice and Equality had no sub-committee on women's rights. Thus, the separate standing of women's rights has never been restored, and in recent times has disappeared, making it more challenging for gender issues to be explored in a parliamentary context, as happens in Finland (Hoppania and Holli, 2015). Though there has been some restoration of funding for equality agencies and women's organisations, the depth of the row-back on equality institutions during the economic crisis reflects the contingent hold of the field in Irish governance.

Conclusion

The relationship between women and politics in Ireland has become more complex over time. Women considering a career in public life continue to do so in a cultural environment that expects them also to fulfil traditional home-based duties. In partial response to these pressures, women are postponing having their first child until later in life and the fertility rate, at 1.96 in 2014, was below replacement level.[12] While Ireland still ranked low on the European scale in terms of women's representation in political life, the candidate quota began to take effect at the 2016 election. Thus, unlike earlier assessments that were pessimistic about an increased presence of women in elected office, the affirmative action measure is expected to continue improving women's political presence.

Significant progress has been made in policy terms also. A range of issues raised by women since the 1970s, particularly those relating to women's rights within the family and in employment, have largely been addressed. A number of institutional reforms have taken place that have impacted on gender equality issues. Alongside the courts, the internationalisation of Ireland's gender equality agenda has led to important shifts in policy focus, bringing renewed opportunities for coalition-building between external equality organisations and internal civil society activists, to effect change. Furthermore, women continue to forge ahead in all aspects of Irish economic and social life. A new generation of women is taking its place in Irish decision-making fora. Considerable numbers of highly educated, experienced, talented women are not prepared to settle for a second-place role in Irish society. The effect of these patterns combined is to influence politics and political parties to be more responsive to, and inclusive of, women and women's issues. The challenge for the future is to maintain, and improve on, gender equality in all its aspects, while taking account of the intersectional complexities of gender-related issues. On this point, parties and politics have a long road to travel.

Notes

1 www.constitution.ie/AttachmentDownload.ashx?mid=268d9308-c9b7-e211-a5a0-005056a32ee4 (accessed 18 March 2017).
2 www.genderequality.ie/en/GE/Pages/State_Boards (accessed 20 January 2017).
3 In 2014, the Equality Tribunal found that the National University of Ireland Galway (NUIG) had discriminated against Dr Micheline Sheehy Skeffington because of her gender, overlooking her for promotion.
4 The Representation of the People Act, 1918, granted the vote to women aged 30 and over who met certain property qualifications, while all men aged 21 and over were entitled to vote. Women and men in Ireland gained equal suffrage rights under Article 14 of the Constitution of the Irish Free State, 1922. This came into effect at the 1923 general election.

5 Figures adapted from the Inter-Parliamentary Union – www.ipu.org/wmn-e/world.htm (accessed 27 February 2017).

6 An alliance of groups called for the introduction of gender quotas, including the 5050 Group, the National Women's Council of Ireland and the women's section of the Labour Party.

7 A sub-committee of the Joint Committee on Justice, Equality, Defence and Women's Rights, namely 'Women's Participation in Politics', was convened in April 2009. In September 2009, the Joint Committee on the Constitution conducted a review of the electoral system to assess its performance against a range of criteria, including the representation of women.

8 Gender quotas for TDs, whereby a certain proportion of seats in Dáil Éireann would be reserved for men and a certain proportion of seats would be reserved for women, were not considered as this would contravene the constitution.

9 www.irishtimes.com/news/politics/enda-kenny-pledges-to-appoint-women-to-half-of-cabinet-posts-1.2043269 (accessed 24 March 2017).

10 Under the Electoral Act, 1997, political parties must detail their expenditure under a number of headings, including 'the promotion of participation by women'.

11 www.upr.ie/ (accessed 25 January 2017).

12 ec.europa.eu/eurostat/statistics-explained/index.php/File:Total_fertility_rate,_1960%E2%80%932014_(live_births_per_woman)_YB16.png (accessed 25 January 2017).

References and further reading

Alexander, Amy C. and Christian Welzel, 2007. 'Empowering women: four theories tested on four different aspects of gender equality'. Paper presented at the Midwest Political Science Association, Chicago.

Bacik, Ivana, 2013. 'The Irish Constitution and gender politics: developments in the law on abortion', *Irish Political Studies* 28:3, pp. 380–98.

Bardon, Sarah, 2017. 'Sexual consent legislation to be submitted for cabinet approval', *Irish Times*, 24 January.

Barry, Ursula, 2014. *Economic Crisis and Gender Equality: Ireland and the EU.* Brussels: Foundation for European Progressive Studies.

Beaumont, Caitriona, 1997. 'Women, citizenship and Catholicism in the Irish Free State, 1922–1948', *Women's History Review* 6:4, pp. 563–85.

Benoit, Kenneth and Michael Marsh, 2008. 'The campaign value of incumbency: a new solution to the puzzle of less effective incumbent spending', *American Journal of Political Science* 52:4, pp. 874–90.

Buckley, Fiona, 2013. 'Women and politics in Ireland: the road to sex quotas', *Irish Political Studies* 28:3, pp. 341–59.

Buckley, Fiona and McGing, Claire, 2011. 'Women and the election', in Michael Gallagher and Michael Marsh (eds), *How Ireland Voted 2011: The Full Story of Ireland's Earthquake Election.* Basingstoke: Palgrave Macmillan, pp. 222–39.

Buckley, Fiona and Hofman, Caroline, 2015. 'Women in local government: slowly moving in from the margins', *Administration* 63:2, pp. 79–99.

Buckley, Fiona, Yvonne Galligan and Claire McGing, 2013. '"Someday, girls, someday": legislating for candidate gender quotas in Ireland', paper presented at the *41st ECPR Joint Sessions of Workshops*, Johannes Gutenberg Universität, Mainz, Germany, 11–16 March.

Buckley, Fiona, Mack Mariani and Timothy J. White, 2014. 'Will legislative gender quotas increase female representation in Ireland?: a feminist institutionalism analysis', *Representation* 50:4, pp. 471–84.

Buckley, Fiona, Mack Mariani, Claire McGing and Timothy White, 2015. 'Is local office a springboard for women to Dáil Éireann?', *Journal of Women, Politics and Policy* 36:3, pp. 311–35.

Buckley, Fiona, Yvonne Galligan and Claire McGing, 2016. 'Women and the election: assessing the impact of gender quotas', in Michael Gallagher and Michael Marsh (eds), *How Ireland Voted 2016: The Election That Nobody Won.* Basingstoke: Palgrave Macmillan, pp. 185–205.

Celis, Karen, 2014. 'Representation', in Rosie Campbell and Sarah Childs (eds), *Deeds and Words: Gendering Politics after Joni Lovenduski*. Colchester: ECPR Press, pp. 51–72.

Connell, Raewyn, 1996. 'Politics of changing men', *Australian Humanities Review*, http://www.australianhumanitiesreview.org/archive/Issue-Dec-1996/connell.html (accessed 10 January 2017).

Connolly, Eileen, 2013. 'The Oireachtas as a gendered institution', *Irish Political Studies* 28:3, pp. 360–79.

Connolly, Linda, 2002. *The Irish Women's Movement: From Revolution to Devolution*. Basingstoke: Palgrave Macmillan.

Cowley, Philip, 2013. 'Why not ask the audience? Understanding the public's representational priorities', *British Politics* 8, pp. 138–63.

CSO (Central Statistics Office), 2007. *Women and Men in Ireland 2007*. Dublin: Stationery Office. PM A7/2266.

CSO, 2014. *2013 Women and Men in Ireland Report.* Cork: Central Statistics Office.

Cullen, Mary, 1997. 'Towards a new Ireland: women, feminism and the peace process', in Maryann Gialanella Valiulis and Mary O'Dowd (eds), *Women and Irish History*. Dublin: Wolfhound Press, pp. 260–77.

Dahlerup, Drude, 2014. 'The critical mass theory in public and scholarly debates', in Rosie Campbell and Sarah Childs (eds), *Deeds and Words: Gendering Politics after Joni Lovenduski*. Colchester: ECPR Press, pp. 137–64.

Department of Justice and Equality, 2016. *Towards a New National Women's Strategy 2017–2020*, http://www.genderequality.ie/en/GE/Public%20Consultation%20Paper%20-%20NWS.pdf/Files/Public%20Consultation%20Paper%20-%20NWS.pdf (accessed 22 January 2017).

Department of Justice and Equality, 2017. *National Strategy for Women and Girls 2017–2020*: *Creating a better society for all*, http://www.justice.ie/en/JELR/National_Strategy_for_Women_and_Girls_2017_-_2020.pdf/Files/National_Strategy_for_Women_and_Girls_2017_-_2020.pdf (accessed 15 June 2017).

Doyle, Kevin, 2017. 'More than half of Government's State boards fail to meet gender quota', *Irish Independent*, 3 January.

Elgood, Jessica, Louise Vinter and Rachel Williams, 2002. *Man Enough for the Job?: A Study of Parliamentary Candidates*. Manchester: Equal Opportunities Commission.

European Commission, 2016. *The EU and Irish Women*. Dublin: European Representation in Ireland: http://ec.europa.eu/ireland/node/684_en

Eurostat, 2016a. Employment Statistics, http://ec.europa.eu/eurostat/statistics-explained/index.php/Employment_statistics (accessed 22 January 2017).

Eurostat, 2016b. *Gender Pay Gap Statistics*. Luxembourg: European Union. http://ec.europa.eu/eurostat/statistics-explained/index.php/Gender_pay_gap_statistics#Further_Eurostat_information (accessed 30 December 2016).

Farrell, David M., Michael Gallagher and David Barrett, 2018. 'What do Irish voters want from and think of their politicians?', in Michael Marsh, David M. Farrell and Theresa Reidy (eds), *The Post-Crisis Irish Voter: Voting Behaviour in the Irish 2016 General Election*. Manchester: Manchester University Press.

Ferriter, Diarmaid, 2008. 'Women and political change in Ireland since 1960', *Éire–Ireland* 43:1, pp. 179–204.

Fine Gael, 2010. *New Politics: Fine Gael Political Reform Statement*. Dublin: Fine Gael.

Fine Gael, 2016. *Fine Gael General Election Manifesto 2016: Let's Keep the Recovery Going*. Dublin: Fine Gael.

Fitzgerald, Cormac, 2016. 'Ireland has been told by the UN Human Rights Council to change its abortion laws', http://www.thejournal.ie/ireland-hum-rights-2768942-May2016/ (accessed 9 January 2017).

Gallagher, Michael, 2008. 'The earthquake that never happened: analysis of the results', in Michael Gallagher and Michael Marsh (eds), *How Ireland Voted 2007: The Full Story of Ireland's General Election*. Basingstoke: Palgrave Macmillan, pp. 78–104.

Gallagher, Michael, 2016. 'The results analysed: the aftershocks continue', in Michael Gallagher and Michael Marsh (eds), *How Ireland Voted 2016: The Election That Nobody Won.* Basingstoke: Palgrave Macmillan, pp. 125–57.

Galligan, Yvonne, 1998. *Women and Politics in Contemporary Ireland: From the Margins to the Mainstream.* London: Pinter.

Galligan, Yvonne, 2013. 'Gender and politics in Northern Ireland: the representation gap revisited', *Irish Political Studies* 28:3, pp. 413–33.

Galligan, Yvonne, 2017. 'Persistent gender inequality in political representation, north and south', in Niall Ó Dochartaigh, Katy Hayward and Elizabeth Meehan (eds), *Dynamics of Political Change in Ireland: Making and Breaking a Divided Ireland.* London: Routledge, pp. 159–77.

Galligan, Yvonne and Rick Wilford, 1999. 'Gender and party politics in the Republic of Ireland', in Yvonne Galligan, Eilís Ward and Rick Wilford (eds), *Contesting Politics: Women in Ireland, North and South.* Oxford: Westview Press, pp. 149–68.

Galligan, Yvonne, Kathleen Knight and Una Nic Giolla Choille, 2000. 'Pathways to power: women in the Oireachtas 1919–2000', in Maedhbh McNamara and Paschal Mooney (eds), *Women in Parliament, Ireland: 1918–2000.* Dublin: Wolfhound Press, pp. 27–69.

Gauja, Anika and Emilie van Haute, 2015. 'Conclusion: members and activists of political parties in comparative perspective', in Emilie van Haute and Anika Gauja (eds), *Party Members and Activists.* London: Routledge, pp. 186–201.

Higher Education Authority, 2016a. *2014–15 Statistics.* Dublin: Higher Education Authority.

Higher Education Authority, 2016b. *Report of the Expert Group Review of Gender Equality in Irish Higher Education Institutions.* Dublin: Higher Education Authority.

Hoppania, Hanna-Kaisa and Anne Maria Holli, 2015. 'States of gender democracy: variation on a theme in Finland', in Yvonne Galligan (ed.), *States of Democracy: Gender and Politics in the European Union.* Abingdon and New York: Routledge, pp. 50–66.

IBEC, 2016. *Labour Market Participation of Women.* Dublin: Irish Business and Employers' Confederation.

Inglehart, Ronald, Pippa Norris and Christian Welzel, 2002. 'Gender equality and democracy', *Comparative Sociology* 1, pp. 321–45.

Inglehart, Ronald and Pippa Norris. 2003. *Rising Tide: Gender Equality and Cultural Change Around the World.* Cambridge: Cambridge University Press.

Kaminsky, Jackie and Timothy J. White, 2007. 'Electoral systems and women's representation in Australia', *Commonwealth and Comparative Politics* 45:2, pp. 185–201.

Kavanagh, Adrian, 2007. 'Elections and voting', in Brendan Bartley and Rob Kitchen (eds), *Understanding Contemporary Ireland: A Geographic Analysis.* London: Pluto Press, pp. 185–96.

Keena, Colm, 2016. 'Two in three women barristers face discrimination, study finds', *Irish Times*, 21 April.

Kelly, Teri, 2015. 'Profession's perfect parity', *Law Society Gazette*, Jan/Feb, pp. 20–1.

Kenny, Meryl, 2013. *Gender and Political Recruitment: Theorizing Institutional Change.* Basingstoke: Palgrave Macmillan.

Kittilson, Miki Caul, 2006. *Challenging Parties, Changing Parliaments: Women and Elected Office in Contemporary Western Europe.* Columbus, OH: The Ohio State University Press.

Kittilson, Miki Caul and Leslie A. Schwindt-Bayer, 2012. *The Gendered Effects of Electoral Institutions: Political Engagement and Participation.* Oxford: Oxford University Press.

Laffan, Michael, 2014. *Judging W. T. Cosgrave: The Foundation of the Irish State.* Dublin: Royal Irish Academy.

Luddy, Maria, 2005. 'A "sinister and retrogressive" proposal: Irish women's opposition to the 1937 draft constitution', *Transactions of the Royal Historical Society* 15, pp. 175–95.

McEvoy, Caroline. 2016. 'Does the descriptive representation of women matter? A comparison of gendered differences in political attitudes between voters and representatives in the European Parliament', *Politics & Gender* 12, pp. 754–80.

McGing, Claire. 2013. 'The single transferable vote and women's representation in Ireland', *Irish Political Studies* 28:3, pp. 322–40.

Manning, Maurice, 1987. 'Women and the elections', in Howard R. Penniman and Brian Farrell (eds), *Ireland at the Polls, 1981, 1982, and 1987: A Study of Four General Elections.* Durham: Duke University Press, pp. 156–66.

Matland, Richard E. and Michele M. Taylor, 1997. 'Electoral system effects on women's representation', *Comparative Political Studies* 30:2, pp. 186–210.

National Women's Strategy, 2013. *Towards Gender Parity in Decision-Making in Ireland: An Initiative of the National Women's Strategy 2007–2016.* Dublin: Gender Equality Unit, Department of Justice and Equality.

Ní Aodha, Gráinne, 2017. 'Demand for crèches: for the first time, there are over 100,000 children in free childcare', http://www.thejournal.ie/free-childcare-ireland-3199393-Jan2017/ (accessed 22 January 2017).

O'Malley, Eoin, 2016. '70 days: government formation in 2016', in Michael Gallagher and Michael Marsh (eds), *How Ireland Voted 2016: The Election That Nobody Won.* Basingstoke: Palgrave Macmillan, pp. 277–92.

Randall, Vicky and Ailbhe Smyth, 1987. 'Bishops and bailiwicks: obstacles to women's political participation in Ireland', *Economic and Social Review* 18:3, pp. 189–214.

Reidy, Theresa, 2016. 'Candidate selection and the illusion of grass-roots democracy', in Michael Gallagher and Michael Marsh (eds), *How Ireland Voted 2016: The Election That Nobody Won.* Basingstoke: Palgrave Macmillan, pp. 47–73.

Sawer, Marian and Joan Grace (eds), 2016. 'Specialised parliamentary bodies and gender representation (special section)', *Parliamentary Affairs* 69:4.

Taylor, Charlie, 2016. 'Just 14% of Irish companies have women leaders', *Irish Times*, 11 February.

United Nations, 2005. *Concluding Comments: Ireland.* New York: UN Committee on the Elimination of Discrimination against Women.

Websites

www.cso.ie/en/statistics/womenandmeninireland/
Central Statistics Office website links to the various editions of *Women and Men in Ireland* reports.

www.qub.ac.uk/cawp
Centre for Advancement of Women in Politics in Queen's University Belfast, which provides data on women in politics in the Republic of Ireland, Northern Ireland and Britain, including women candidates at elections. The site also makes available a range of documents on women and politics and has links to other women and politics sites.

http://ec.europa.eu/justice/gender-equality/gender-decision-making/database/index_en.htm
Maintained by the European Commission's Directorate General on Justice and Consumers. It collates data on women and men in decision-making across the European Union.

www.quotaproject.org/
The quota project is a joint project of the International IDEA (International Institute for Democracy and Electoral Assistance), the Inter-Parliamentary Union and Stockholm University, collating data on gender quotas worldwide.

www.genderequality.ie/en/GE/Pages/WomenPublicSector
Provides data on women in Ireland and maintained by the Gender Equality Division of the Department of Justice and Equality.

www.unwomen.org/en
UN Women is an entity of the United Nations, responsible for gender equality and the empowerment of women.

www.womenforelection.ie/
Hosted by Women for Election, a non-partisan organisation that encourages women to run for politics and provides capacity training to achieve this aim.

Part III
Policy and administration

10   The government and the Taoiseach

Eoin O'Malley and Shane Martin

On independence, Ireland became a parliamentary democracy, inheriting from Britain a system of government that has operated there in the same basic form for nearly two centuries. In this system, the cabinet or government is 'a committee of the legislative body selected to be the executive body' (Bagehot, 1963 [1867]: 66). Constitutional theory would suggest that the parliament was charged with making law and the government would oversee its implementation. This is not how it tends to operate in Ireland or in any other parliamentary democracy. Unlike in presidential systems, there is limited separation of powers; parliament and the government are fused and often stand and fall together. The government is selected by a Taoiseach who is chosen by the Dáil, and his (the office has so far been held only by men) selection of ministers is then approved by the Dáil. The government then depends on the confidence of the Dáil. Though cabinet is in practice a committee of Dáil Éireann, for a variety of reasons, many of which are dealt with in Chapter 7, the relationship between the government and the Dáil is one in which the cabinet dominates the Dáil. Laws tend not to originate in, nor are they shaped by, the Dáil. Rather, they are usually brought to the Dáil as bills by government.

This changed during the 32nd Dáil, which came into being following the 2016 election. The government formed in May 2016 fell far short of a Dáil majority, and so depended on the main opposition party, Fianna Fáil, for support. That government no longer had a reasonable expectation of passing its bills. Furthermore, the government was now in a position where it had to accept bills from the opposition that it would not have introduced of its own volition. It is likely that in a future time of majority government the usual pattern of government dominance would resume, though some rule changes are likely to mean that the opposition would retain some of its increased power.

There is much more to government than the 15 men and women who collectively comprise the cabinet and individually head departments of state. There are ministers of state (often known as junior ministers), tasked with easing the burden on cabinet ministers; senior civil servants, permanent officials, political neutrals who advise ministers and are often charged with implementing policies; special advisers to ministers who offer government ministers alternative, more political, advice; and the heads of the numerous state agencies. Together, these might be referred to as the 'core executive' (Rhodes, 1995), and any consideration of government is incomplete without them. Government, or the 'core executive', is not a unified actor. It might be better conceived as a collection of power centres. This chapter will consider these actors, their roles and relationship, how they co-ordinate, and the division of power between them.

Of the many models used to describe the distribution of power *within* governments, two of the most prominent are *prime ministerial government* and *cabinet government*. The former implies that governments are led by a dominant prime minister, while according to the latter a collegial cabinet is the apex of power (Crossman, 1972). At least three other models can be added: *ministerial government*, where ministers are autonomous policy-makers in their own departments (Laver and Shepsle, 1994); the *bureaucratic government* model, according to which the civil service as the 'permanent government' controls policy (Niskanen, 1971); and the *segmented model* of government, which posits that different actors will be prominent in different policy areas, so we might see prime ministerial government on Northern Ireland policy, for example, but ministerial autonomy with little cabinet or prime ministerial interference in tourism policy (see Elgie, 1997 for a full overview).

It is questionable whether any model gives a complete picture of what actually happens in government, given that all models ignore the important inputs of interest groups (see Chapter 11), advisers and agencies. They also ignore another vital actor: political parties. Coalition governments – an increasingly common feature of Irish politics – are composed of different parties, each of which places different demands on the government's resources and will have differing preferences on contentious policies. Party government is the idea that the executive is subject to the control of well-organised political parties (Blondel and Cotta, 2000). We can see the centrality of party politics in the distribution of power in the core executive, and this starts with the formation of governments.

We begin the chapter by examining that process, including the selection of ministers, and then we discuss the nature of government decision-making in cabinet and the role of the Taoiseach. The chapter examines the position of ministers within their departments, and ministers' relationship with the civil service. Finally we consider the ways in which government is held accountable for its actions.

Government formation

The basic framework for the formation of a government is laid out in the constitution, according to which the Dáil selects a Taoiseach, who is appointed by the President (Article 13.1.1). The Taoiseach then selects ministers, who are approved by the Dáil and appointed by the President (see Martin, 2014 for a detailed overview). The constitution makes no mention of a fundamental part of the Irish political system, namely the party system. For much of the last century, government formation meant that the leader of the largest party, nearly always Fianna Fáil, would be appointed Taoiseach and submit to the Dáil the names of his cabinet, who would be supported by that party's TDs. These single-party Fianna Fáil governments were interposed with coalition governments of other parties who could put aside policy differences for the opportunity to break the Fianna Fáil hegemony.

Election results now rarely produce clear government outcomes. Since 1981, no Fianna Fáil leader has had the automatic support of a majority in the Dáil, so either he or the leader of Fine Gael must look for support among other parties or get the agreement of independents to allow their government to take office. But which party will coalesce with which is the result of post-election negotiations about which the electorate has no say and little foreknowledge. Up to 1989 Fianna Fáil refused to contemplate taking part in any coalition government, and on a number of occasions it formed a minority government. In 1989, Charles Haughey broke with that strategy, forming a government with the Progressive Democrats (see Chapter 5, p. 122; see Appendix 5 for biographical details of leading political figures). Fianna Fáil's decision to enter coalition politics may have made it more difficult for voters hoping to influence the formation of particular governments. Green Party voters in 2007 might have been surprised to find that their vote had the effect of re-electing Bertie Ahern as Taoiseach, despite the Green leader having described the Fianna Fáil leader as a political 'dead man walking' a few weeks earlier (O'Malley, 2008: 209). Similarly, in 2016, Shane Ross, the *de facto* leader of the Independent Alliance, described Enda Kenny as a 'political corpse' a few weeks before supporting Kenny's nomination as Taoiseach (Ross, 2016).

So, putting a government together in Ireland is no longer a mere formality of confirming the outcome of the election (see also Table 7.2, p. 172). A number of factors dictate which (if any) government will be formed. The simple arithmetic is important. Those forming coalition governments often prefer to have a majority of seats tied in to a coalition agreement, as this gives a degree of certainty and stability to the government. It is normal, and expected, that majority coalition governments will be 'minimum winning coalitions' – that is, they do not contain more parties than are necessary to form a majority. The rationale for this expectation is that government involves the divisions of spoils, both of policy and office, and having more parties than necessary would mean making more concessions than a minimum winning coalition would have to.

Some combinations of parties produce stable majorities and others do not. For example, Labour and Fine Gael might have planned to form a government after the 2016 election, but the two parties' parliamentary strength simply did not make that possible. The arithmetic of the parties' support usually gives one party a clear advantage in negotiations. This is not always the largest party; the range of options available to each party is more important. In 1993 the Labour Party was able to choose between alternative coalitions led by Fianna Fáil or by Fine Gael. In 2007 Fianna Fáil was able to choose with whom it wished to negotiate. The outgoing Taoiseach, Bertie Ahern, chose to form an oversized coalition – one in which there are more parties than strictly necessary to form a majority government. The advantage of this for the larger party is that any threats made by surplus parties to leave the government have no immediate consequences for the stability of the government. Even if one party leaves, the government will still retain a majority in the Dáil. It can also happen that governments are appointed without a stable Dáil majority. This is difficult, given the need for a majority in the investiture vote (in other words, following an election a new government needs to be explicitly endorsed by the Dáil as opposed to being able to survive until it is voted out, as is the case in Scandinavian countries), but in 2016 a minority government was formed. This was possible not just because the majority needed is only of those voting, not an absolute majority of all TDs, but also because other parties could not agree an alternative government. Fianna Fáil came to a 'confidence and supply' agreement with Fine Gael, under whose terms it formally agreed to abstain in crucial votes (including the investiture vote), to allow a Fine Gael-led minority government to take office (see O'Malley, 2016 for more details). Unusually, this government included independent (non-party) TDs. On previous occasions when such TDs had been willing to provide external support to the government, this had usually been in return for constituency rewards. Each additional party or group provides an extra fault-line for the government, threatening the durability of the more complex governmental arrangements. Minority government may also come about because parties are unwilling to spread the rewards of office more thinly. Policy and office rewards are important issues in forming the government. The negotiations centre on agreeing a programme for government and on the division of posts within that government.

Agreeing the programme for government

Programmes for government have increased in size and detail over time. Whereas in the 1973–77 coalition the agreement between Fine Gael and Labour was a pre-election 'fourteen-point programme' of about 1,000 words (*Irish Times*, 8 February 1973), the programme agreed after the 2016 election by Fine Gael and independents ran to 42,000 words. Programmes usually emerge as a compromise between the various parties' manifestos, the raw material for programmes for government. These are themselves written with the post-election negotiations in mind; if they are not it may cause problems. In the opinion of one senior Labour strategist, part of the party's problem in 2016 was that it did not consider what promises it would have to concede to enter government when it drafted its 2011 manifesto (interview with Ed Brophy, 18 January 2017).

Programmes for government are determined by the negotiating skills of the usually moderate larger party in tempering the more radical demands of its potential partners. Smaller parties and alliances of independent TDs push for the inclusion of as many projects as they can, and for the removal of items in the larger party's manifesto that they regard as unacceptable. The degree of success of each side depends on its negotiating strength, itself partially dependent on the implications of each side's alternative or 'outside' options (see Muthoo, 2000).

The time taken on the programme is testimony to its great importance, and once agreed it informs the work of government. Senior civil servants treat it as the agenda of work for their departments. The programme informs cabinet work; Albert Reynolds is reported to have said in a cabinet debate on an issue that was causing division, 'if it's in the programme, then it's a deal; if not, it's up for discussion' (private interview).[1] A system of 'programme managers', put in place in 1993 to oversee its implementation, subsequently reduced in scale, is widely credited with making the process of government more efficient and less politically contentious. Being in the programme is one of the factors that make it much more likely that an election pledge is fulfilled (Costello *et al.*, 2016: 38).

Selecting ministers

The process of constructing a cabinet goes hand-in-hand with the negotiations on the formation of coalition government. Constitutionally, the Taoiseach alone chooses the cabinet, albeit from a very restricted pool, but his choice must be approved by the Dáil. Therefore, Taoisigh must consider the durability of the government when constructing cabinets. Under the constitution (Article 28.1) the government may have at most 15 members. Unusually, compared with other European countries, all must come from one or other house of parliament, with at most two being senators. With just two exceptions (one in 1957, one in 1981), since 1937 all ministers have been TDs. The reasons for the almost complete absence of non-TDs as ministers are not entirely clear. Both cases of senatorial appointments were problematic, causing resentment within the parliamentary party, and some logistical problems in government as senators do not take office until many weeks after the Dáil meets and therefore cannot take up ministerial office immediately. However, given the long time it took to form a government in 2016, this was not an obstacle; yet even though the pool of government TDs to choose from was the smallest ever, the Seanad option was not used.

The question of whether ministers should or can be responsible both to the Dáil for their executive acts and to their constituents for their acts as TDs has been the subject of some debate. The Convention on the Constitution, which met in 2013, recommended to government that the constitution should require that deputies who are appointed ministers must resign their Dáil seats. The logic is that ministers would then concentrate solely on the ministerial function. Coakley (2013: 234–5) points out that this would immediately create vacancies that would be have to be filled through by-elections, which might well jeopardise the majority of the new government. Furthermore, if the ministers wanted to be re-elected, they would most probably continue to pay close attention to their constituencies.

In practice, given the need to form and maintain governments that have the support of the Dáil, and given that power in parties tends to be concentrated in the parliamentary party (see Chapter 5), whose members see career progression almost solely in terms of governmental appointment, government leaders need to satisfy parliamentary party demands for ministerial posts. TDs, on whom the leader relies for support, tend to have local power bases independent of the party leadership, and the party leader has some resources to help garner that support. One is his or her control of the careers of TDs through ministerial appointment, so Taoisigh may be unwilling to relinquish this resource by appointing outsiders. Within one's own party, it means that senior figures from other factions must be accommodated. For example, Enda Kenny might not have wanted to appoint Leo Varadkar to his cabinet when he became Taoiseach in 2011, as the two men's relationship was poor, but there was a sense that it would be too politically dangerous to leave Varadkar on the backbenches. In coalition government, the Taoiseach has a veto over appointments but the leaders of the coalition parties effectively select the ministers coming from their own parties. The number of posts tends to be distributed more or less proportionally to the comparative sizes of the parliamentary parties (this is known in the academic literature as Gamson's Law), but in Ireland smaller parties have been over-represented (O'Malley, 2006: 328–9), reflecting their relatively strong bargaining position. That Taoisigh depend on their position as party leader to make appointments was forcefully shown in 1948, when the only person to hold the post of Taoiseach who was not leader of his party, John A. Costello, was chosen to head a coalition government only *after* the party leaders had agreed the distribution of cabinet posts (McCullagh, 1998: 32–3).

The selection of ministers is important not just as an office reward for parties, but also because it allows parties some control of policy in those portfolios. The model of ministerial government (Laver and Shepsle, 1994) assumes that parties occupying a portfolio can control policy output. The evidence from a large number of interviews with Irish ministers is that ministerial autonomy is restricted by the need for cabinet approval for many decisions, but there is no doubt that parties have more influence where they hold the portfolio than where they do not (Costello *et al.*, 2016: 37). Former Labour leader and Tánaiste Éamon Gilmore (2016: 135) claims he placed Pat Rabbitte in the Department of Communications, Energy and Natural Resources as a precaution against likely calls to part-privatise the ESB and Bord Gáis. It is also clear that some portfolios are seen as especially important to certain parties. Thus, it was common for left-wing parties to provide the Minister for Social Protection, as Labour did in 2011. This has some advantages for the government as a whole. It will have in place ministers who are active and interested, and will inevitably force those ministers and their parties to compromise themselves; they will be compelled, by considerations of feasibility, to take decisions that they might otherwise have criticised their colleagues in government for taking. Departments can be reorganised with some ease to suit the policy priorities of incoming governments, so the Department of the Environment, Community and Local Government became Housing, Planning, Community and Local Government in 2016, to reflect the new government's priorities (see Appendix 4).

When ministers are selected, this also reflects their seniority within the party and/or how favourably the party leader views them. Sometimes there may be an attempt to demote someone who is out of favour by putting them in a relatively insignificant department. There is a clear if unofficial ranking of departments. The Minister for Finance is both legally and politically the most important position after the Taoiseach (see Considine and Reidy, 2012). Like the Tánaiste and Taoiseach, the Minister for Finance must, under the constitution, be a TD (Article 28.7.1). In 2011 Finance's spending function shifted largely to a new department, Public Expenditure and Reform, which reduced its pre-eminence, though in June 2017 the two departments were functionally re-integrated. Foreign Affairs has also traditionally been seen as important, though this may be an overestimate of its real power, as much of the Northern Ireland and European Union work is co-ordinated by the Taoiseach's department. For instance, when Brexit came closer to reality following the 2016 UK referendum, there was some pressure to have a separate Brexit minister, but the Taoiseach indicated that he would take on the co-ordinating responsibilities. Some portfolios are regarded as good sources of political patronage; for example, the Department of the Environment was associated with infrastructural projects, such as roads, which in the past ministers were able to use to direct resources to their own constituencies (though this is now somewhat restricted by the transfer of some powers to executive agencies). Both cabinet and junior ministers responsible for sport, it has been shown, are able to locate investment in their own constituencies (Suiter and O'Malley, 2014). Other departments, such as Defence, are regarded as less important. In the government formed in 2016, the Taoiseach assigned Defence to himself, with day-to-day management carried out by a junior minister.

A number of criteria may be important in choosing a cabinet. Leo Varadkar suggested 'ability and the capability of people to do the job' as the most important, but added: 'After that I'll take into account ... the need for a degree of regional balance, a degree of gender balance and of course the core issue of trust' (McQuinn, 2017). Though there is little evidence for any need for geographic balance (O'Malley, 2006), it is conventional wisdom that ministerial office can be a boon to the electoral prospects of the minister's party – though the experience of incumbent ministers in 2011 might raise considerable doubts about this – and so there may be an unwillingness to leave some regions unrepresented in cabinet. One factor that is *not* important is expertise in the specific policy area of the department. Irish ministers tend to be generalists rather than specialists in their fields. So although at times a TD with a background as a lawyer heads the Department of Justice, or a former teacher may be in Education, there is no expectation that ministers generally would have any portfolio-specific expertise. Perhaps for this reason, the 2013 Convention on the Constitution recommended that ministers without a seat in parliament be allowed. This was ignored by the government, perhaps for the reasons discussed earlier: ministerial office (and the expectation of future office) is an important component in maintaining the support of the parliamentary party.

Taoisigh must also consider the need to have competent ministers. Smith and Martin (2017) find that TDs whose relatives served in cabinet are more likely to be promoted to cabinet, evidence for what they see as a dynastic advantage in ministerial selection. Incompetent loyalists, though pliable, make mistakes. And, for political reasons, ministers – even incompetent ones – cannot easily be dismissed, despite the clear constitutional right of a Taoiseach to dismiss any minister. O'Malley (2006) found that the atmosphere in the Dáil resembles that of a small village, so new TDs may be regarded with suspicion and their immediate promotion can lead to jealousy. It is a place where Taoisigh will have to live with any dismissed minister, making reshuffles personally awkward and politically costly. Governments cannot afford to lose TDs, given their usually tight Dáil majorities, if they have a majority at all. Former ministers can be irregular attendees in the Dáil and have less to lose from party or government censure. Following Alan Shatter's resignation as Minister for Justice in 2014, under heavy pressure from the Taoiseach, he was frequently critical of the Taoiseach and the government.

In situations of low ministerial turnover and increased professionalisation of politics, with most TDs regarding politics as a career, Taoisigh could find that impatience on the backbenches generates calls for leadership turnover to effect promotions. In part to overcome these demands, there was ongoing expansion of the number of ministers of state, or 'junior ministers', to 20 by 2007 (it was reduced to 15 during the economic crisis, but increased again to 18 in 2016). The increase was defended on the basis of the expanded work of the government. This argument, which has been repeated by successive Taoisigh, is little more than a paper-thin defence of increasing patronage to satisfy backbench demands for jobs. However, junior ministers increasingly perform important roles with distinct policy responsibilities important to the work of government, often easing the demands on cabinet ministers' time.

Taoiseach and cabinet

The idea of the cabinet emerged from eighteenth-century English politics, where the ministers met individually with the King in his closet or cabinet, a small private room. Ministers met collectively in advance of these meetings to agree on an identical story that they would each convey to the King. The cabinet meeting developed into one where the ministers met collectively with the King, and eventually the King ceased to attend cabinet meetings. From these beginnings a number of norms emerged, with the doctrine of ministerial responsibility at its core as the central plank of cabinet government (Marshall, 1989).

In Ireland, as elsewhere, there are few codified rules for the operation of government. There is a *Cabinet Handbook* that outlines cabinet procedures, but these can be ignored if the serving Taoiseach so wishes or finds himself unable to prevent them from being broken. The constitutional rules for cabinet are sparse, running to five pages and covered in just one article (28). This compares to the 12 articles and almost 30 pages detailing the rules of the Houses of the Oireachtas in the constitution. Even this article is limited in its impact: Farrell has argued that 'the Constitution, as a rulebook, has only tangential connection with the Irish political and governmental game' (Farrell, 1987: 162). The rules on government deal mainly with appointment and dismissal. The only significant constitutional rules on the running of government relate to ministerial responsibility and, though codified, are left vague and seemingly unenforceable in practice.

Doctrine of ministerial responsibility

The doctrine of ministerial responsibility guides how ministers act both individually and collectively as a government. Three political principles make up the doctrine of ministerial responsibility: confidence, unanimity and confidentiality. The *confidence principle* is the requirement that the government must retain the confidence – that is, support – of the Dáil. If it loses a confidence vote – that is, a vote on whether the Dáil retains confidence in the government – the Taoiseach must resign (which under the terms of Article 28.11.1 means that all other members of the government are also deemed to have resigned), or ask the President to dissolve the Dáil. One interpretation of this principle implies that any vote can be a confidence vote, and in practice a Taoiseach can declare that any vote is a vote of confidence, as the threat of an election tends to concentrate minds of recalcitrant TDs. But some votes are less important, and nowadays a government defeat, though unwelcome and once rare, is no longer regarded as a test of confidence in the government. Only twice (in 1982 and 1992) has a government been defeated on a formal confidence motion. More often, governments pre-empt inevitable defeats by seeking a dissolution. For example, in late 2010 the Green Party indicated it would be withdrawing support from the government once the budget had been passed. The Taoiseach, Brian Cowen, called an election before a Labour motion of no confidence could be voted on.

The confidence principle also refers to the need of government to be accountable to the Dáil: to answer questions, submit proposals for debate and be subject to Dáil votes. As part of this, ministers are regarded as individually responsible for their departmental actions, and so they are politically responsible to the Dáil for the actions of their departments. This political responsibility in part emanates from a minister's formal legal responsibility, where the minister is the legal embodiment of the department's activities and decisions (see below). A strict reading of this suggests that ministers must resign for sufficiently grave errors in their departments, even when they might not have had any part in these or even been aware of them. Practically, this means that ministers can be put under pressure for their departmental actions by opposition parties tabling motions of no confidence, but they will resign only if it is politically advantageous for the Taoiseach to insist on this. So, when opposition parties put down a motion of no confidence in the PD Minister for Health, Mary Harney, in late 2007, her position was not under threat because the government did not want to lose a minister who could act as a lightning conductor for unpopular government policies, or to deprive itself of the two Dáil votes her party brought. The individual responsibility of ministers is limited by a seemingly contradictory principle of collective responsibility or unanimity.

The *unanimity principle* is the idea that regardless of what positions ministers take in cabinet discussions, once a government decision is made, all ministers are required to publicly support it and accept collective responsibility for it – or else resign from government. This is important because it ensures that governments divided on an issue will not reveal that division, and will not be weakened publicly. This is not merely a convention, but has constitutional force through Article 28.4, which stipulates that the government meets and acts as a collective authority. Though this is normally maintained, there have been occasions when it has been strained to the point of breaking. In 1974, the Taoiseach, Liam Cosgrave, with another minister, Dick Burke, and a handful of other Fine Gael TDs, voted against a bill presented by his own government that would have allowed the limited sale of contraceptives. This led to the government being defeated on the vote. The Taoiseach had allowed a free vote on the issue, but for some of his colleagues it was a breach of the unanimity principle (Collins, 1996: 169). The unanimity principle means that the cabinet as a whole is politically responsible for the activities of the government. This has an important impact on how government operates, forcing ministers to bring politically contentious issues to cabinet even where there is no legal requirement to do so. This limits the autonomy that ministers have to dictate policy in their own portfolio.

A corollary of the unanimity principle is that ministers do not declare their position on an item due to go to government in advance of that decision. At times, ministers set out a proposed policy in advance of cabinet discussions to bring public pressure to bear on the cabinet discussion. Media frequently report what the cabinet is expected to discuss, and how parties in government stand on each issue in a way that could bias or pre-empt the decision. For instance, it was easy to know in advance of the decision in October 2016 of Enda Kenny's second government on an AAA–PBP bill to repeal the eighth amendment to the constitution (outlawing abortion) that some of the Independent Alliance ministers wished to support the bill, because they announced this. The issue, which the Programme for Government had agreed would be sent to a Citizens' Assembly to make recommendations to government, went to cabinet, where a government decision was taken to oppose the bill. The Alliance ministers duly opposed the bill, but the Irish public was left in no doubt how they felt.

In order to make unanimity possible, a third principle is necessary. The *confidentiality principle* ensures that discussions in cabinet are confidential. As well as enabling unanimity, for if discussions were publicised unanimity could not realistically be maintained, it also enables frank discussions. In the context of the economic collapse, where it was prudent to consider 'nightmare' scenarios, such as a collapse of the euro and a reversion to the Irish pound, a high level of secrecy was necessary, lest sensible contingency planning became a self-fulfilling prophesy. While the principle is taken seriously, it cannot be as strictly applied as the Supreme Court in 1992 wished it, prohibiting disclosure of cabinet discussions and finding that confidentiality is 'not capable of being waived by any individual member of a government' (Attorney General v. Hamilton [1993] *Irish Reports* 250: 272). This interpretation, described by a former senior judge and cabinet minister as 'very odd' (Lindsay, 1992: 164), disallowed any disclosure of cabinet discussions. A 1997 constitutional amendment (Article 28.4.3) eased the restrictions very slightly, by allowing cabinet discussion to be revealed, if the High Court so directs, if a tribunal of inquiry requests this or where the administration of justice by a court requires it. The Court's decision, proceeding on 'largely artificial premises with regard to the separation of powers' (Hogan, 1993: 134), showed little concern for the necessities of governance and the subsequent constitutional amendment failed to bring the law into line with political practice. We know that ministers frequently inform their senior civil servants and special advisers of cabinet discussion (see Finlay, 1997 and Walshe, 2015 for examples); the constitution is ignored in the interests of efficient government. More oddly, the decision and subsequent amendment might preclude a minister who is resigning from outlining his or her reasons for resigning if these relate to cabinet discussions. In practice, some ministers get away with leaks or announcements if they are politically powerful or if this behaviour has been sanctioned by the Taoiseach. The significance of leaks of this sort varies with political circumstances and according to relations within government. Greater levels of disagreement between, and more particularly *within,* government parties can lead to increased leaking as an attempt to frame the media debate.

In general, we can see that the rules on ministerial responsibility, though observed, are enforced only insofar as they are politically practicable. In July 2016, three Independent Alliance ministers supported an opposition bill to allow abortion in cases of fatal foetal abnormalities, against the government's legal advice. In other circumstances this might have been seen as a reason to dismiss those ministers, but political necessities meant that their actions were tolerated. Some have argued that collective responsibility increases the power of the government over the parliament (Crossman, 1963: 22; Farrell, 1987: 168–9) by making it more difficult to divide the government and providing constitutional protection for a culture of secrecy. Within cabinet, it might strengthen those already strong in cabinet by ensuring that the winning position is defended by all.

The operation of cabinet government

The procedure outlined in the *Cabinet Handbook* indicates that cabinet is, in theory at least, the apex of power in Ireland. Box 10.1 sets out the procedure in detail. What is discussed at cabinet is a matter for the Taoiseach, but it usually includes all government-sponsored legislation, any major policy change and anything with financial implications. The Department of the Taoiseach sets the agenda from items submitted by ministers. While it would be difficult for a Taoiseach to prevent an item from being discussed that ministers wished to be on the agenda, one former Taoiseach said 'if there was something you were totally against, you could control it. You could control it by not having it at the cabinet table; you could control it by having it at a cabinet sub-committee where it's thrashed out' (private interview, 8 September 2009).

Box 10.1 Cabinet procedure

Due to the constraints of collective responsibility, the *Cabinet Handbook* requires 'that Ministers should inform their colleagues in advance of proposals they intend to announce … in particular … proposals for legislation that can be initiated only after formal approval by Government … Government approval is required for significant new or revised policies or strategies'. Furthermore, it demands that ministers make no public mention of issues to be raised at government as this may prejudice the decision of government.

Ministers wishing to raise a matter for decision by the government will circulate a draft memorandum to the various interested departments, always including the Departments of the Taoiseach and Finance, which will give observations. In coalition governments, the offices of party leaders must also be informed. A minister may or may not accept these observations, but they must be addressed in the formal memorandum that goes to the government secretariat, which will check it and seek to resolve any inter-departmental disputes before the item goes to cabinet. The Minister for Finance, notably, is exempt from the normal requirements of prior consultation that the cabinet procedures impose on ministers. A minister can also introduce a memorandum for information, in order to report to cabinet on a politically topical issue of an ongoing nature that does not require a decision of government.

Government or cabinet meetings are normally held from 10 each Tuesday morning when the Dáil is in session and each Wednesday when it is in recess. The main agenda is available to ministers from Friday morning. There is also a supplementary agenda for urgent business finalised at 4 on the afternoon preceding the meeting. Urgent business is accepted at the Taoiseach's discretion.

Meetings are attended by cabinet ministers, along with the chief whip, the Attorney General (AG) and the Secretary General (SG) to the Government, who takes notes. Since 1994, another of the junior ministers, unofficially known as a 'super-junior', has also been permitted to be present; the number of super-juniors was increased to two in 2016 and three in 2017. The AG, SG, chief whip and super-juniors may not speak unless specifically called upon, though the SG may advise the Taoiseach privately during the course of a meeting. Everyone is expected to be present, so permission is sought for absences. There are no formal rules about the operation of cabinet, and how it proceeds depends on the Taoiseach's style, but it tends to be formal, with contributions being addressed through the Taoiseach and ministers being referred to by their title. On average, each meeting may have between 20 and 30 items on the agenda, many of which are formal items that can be dealt with quickly. On more substantial issues, the relevant minister will be invited to introduce an item, and then other ministers will question him or her. Quite how the decision is arrived at is uncertain. A Taoiseach takes the sense of the meeting, and announces a decision. Some decisions are deferred for 'further consideration', which is often a polite way of indicating that the proposal was rejected. Votes never happen on contentious issues, as they would be expected to divide on party lines, thus exacerbating any existing tensions in government. Decisions, but not discussions, are formally recorded but are sent only to the office of the relevant ministers. The minister can then question the recorded decision if he or she feels that it did not reflect the decision taken. The full minutes of decisions taken are then read at the following week's cabinet, but the written minutes are not supplied. The SG allegedly takes notes of the cabinet discussions but these do not seem to have ever been released. The absence of such material means that academics must rely on interviews and memoirs in order to study cabinet government in Ireland.

What happens once an item gets to cabinet? Cabinet is a black box – we know what goes in as agenda items and comes out as decisions, but we have little understanding of what happens inside other than by what is reported by ministers (Quinn, 2005, ch. 1, gives an insider's overview of the cabinet procedure in operation). Cabinet operation varies considerably by Taoiseach. Garret FitzGerald, Fine Gael Taoiseach during the 1980s, had a style regarded by more than one minister as 'dysfunctional', with items that were thought urgent given priority over items that, while generally thought important, never required immediate attention, and discussion took place without a view to making a decision and thus could last 12 hours or more. Other Taoisigh were more business-like in their approach, and under Bertie Ahern few meetings lasted more than three hours. Brian Cowen's and Enda Kenny's cabinet meetings were sometimes longer, in part because of the crisis these governments faced. But this did not make the cabinet a more effective place for decisions or even for imparting information. John Gormley, the leader of the Green Party in government, complained that it was 'very difficult to get a clear picture at Cabinet' (Boyle, 2012: 217).

While most items are formal and can be dealt with in a few minutes, there will commonly be perhaps two or three items that require substantial discussion. In private interviews, former ministers indicate that about a third to a half of ministers might speak on each of these items. Many of those speaking will relay their departmental rather than personal opinions, though some ministers make significant personal contributions, which may, in fact, differ from the department's observations. It seems to be the case that the Department of Finance will have strong opinions about any item that has funding implications and former Finance ministers agree with the suggestion that they, in effect, have veto power within cabinet, though one they use sparingly.

Farrell (1994) found that ministers regarded cabinet as more than a mere rubber stamp – that cabinet is a real constraint. His evidence from interviews was based on experiences in the 1980s where severe financial restrictions meant that ministers essentially competed with each other for funds. More recent interviews indicate that while many ministers still regard cabinet as important, and a forum where a proposal will get 'a decent grilling', it is also clear that much of the discussion now takes place in advance of cabinet and that many of the objections are now either accommodated or dismissed through meetings of ministerial advisers by the time an item reaches cabinet. The decision is then on the principle of the proposal and its political implications. Cabinet has been described by a former Taoiseach as a forum to 'politically-proof' proposals, and it is regarded as having failed if it does not foresee public backlash to a proposal. For instance, the reaction to the Cowen government's proposal to withdraw medical cards to the over-70s in October 2008 showed that while it might have been good policy, it was bad politics, and backbenchers let their unhappiness with the cabinet be known. The government quickly had to reverse the decision.

There are a number of reasons for the move away from detailed policy formation and debate at cabinet. One is that less contentious items are cleared for agreement in advance by the team of special advisers, especially those of the Taoiseach and Tánaiste. Another is the expansion of the cabinet committee system. Once barely in operation in Ireland, the use of cabinet committees expanded slowly under Taoisigh Albert Reynolds and John Bruton. Bertie Ahern introduced a much-expanded set of cabinet committees in which ministers and senior officials in both departments and agencies would meet. The logic of this is that where an issue crosses departmental boundaries, it can focus collective minds when all relevant actors are present – for instance, the cabinet sub-committee on health includes the head of the Health Service Executive – and ministers would be removed from their 'departmental bunker'. Emerging issues would be addressed by new committees with the capacity to give focus to the government's response. In 2016, for example, a Brexit committee was established, alongside the nine others already in place, in such areas as housing and health. Some of the committees cover areas that seem so broad that it is not clear that they allow for much specialisation, examples being social policy and public sector reform. Others appeared unnecessary as they hardly cross-cut departments, for instance, Arts, Irish and the Gaeltacht. These may be a way to signal that a government cares about an issue. Some civil servants felt that there were too many committees, and that the large number did not allow for the centre of government to genuinely target priority policy areas (private interviews). When Leo Varadkar became Taoiseach in June 2017, he appears to have agreed there were problems with the committee system, as he halved the number he inherited from Enda Kenny.

A decade earlier the committee system had been restricted to ministers and one senior official after Brian Cowen became Taoiseach in 2008 (*Irish Times*, 9 June 2008). Enda Kenny's first government in 2011 introduced an Economic Management Council (EMC), which one participant dubbed the 'War Cabinet' (Gilmore, 2016: 1). It consisted of the Taoiseach, the Tánaiste, the Minister for Finance and the Minister for Public Expenditure and Reform, their main advisers and certain senior officials – about 13 people in all. It could also call upon other officials and ministers for briefings. The EMC was initially meant to meet weekly *after* cabinet meetings, to avoid the perception that it was pre-empting the cabinet, but during the height of the crisis it met more frequently. Many, including cabinet ministers, complained that it was the presumptive cabinet, and some suggested even that it might be unconstitutional (*Irish Times*, 7 November 2014). Those on the inside reject this claim, and felt it was essential for the efficient running of the state in a time of crisis, but it would obviously be hard for other ministers to successfully counteract a proposal where all relevant ministers and party leaders, as members of the EMC, were backing it.

The criticisms of the EMC were probably unjustified as it merely formalised what had always been the case: that the Taoiseach and Minister for Finance, and in coalition governments party leaders, had met to co-ordinate and agree policy in advance of formal government meetings. Up to the 1990s these occurred informally in most coalitions. In 1993 Dick Spring, the Labour leader and Tánaiste, insisted on more formal arrangements. Nowadays party leaders tend to meet in advance of cabinet to discuss and agree solutions to, or defer decisions on, intractable policy disputes between parties. One former party leader, recently in government, said that on only one occasion was an item brought to cabinet against his wishes. There was some agreement among interviewees that the role of senior advisers had become more important and that these were now central to the co-ordination and smooth running of government.

The role of the Taoiseach

A British prime minister, on taking office, noted that after an initial flurry of activity, 'I sat back and realised I had nothing to do' (Callaghan, 1987: 403). No Taoiseach would complain that there was nothing to do, but the role of the Taoiseach, who has no line department to run, is nowhere precisely specified. As we have seen, the first duty of a Taoiseach is to choose his cabinet and junior ministers and he may wish to direct them in some way as to the priorities of the government, taking account of a party manifesto or programme for government agreed between coalition parties. After that, the Taoiseach will oversee the process of government. Seán Lemass (1968: 3) described the role as one that would facilitate the taking of decisions by the government. Former Taoiseach Garret FitzGerald (2004: 66) wrote of the role that cabinet business has to be organised, and the Taoiseach has to chair and lead the government, initiating policy development and also encouraging this process amongst his cabinet members. He has to decide on priorities for legislation; settle parliamentary business through his chief whip; and establish from time to time *ad hoc* cabinet committees with appropriate membership to deal with issues involving more than one department.

To carry out these functions, he is supported by a Department of the Taoiseach. Before the 1980s, this was regarded as procedurally important, enabling the co-ordination of government by moving paper around, but not central to policy-*making*. The top civil servants there were meticulous about rules, and tended to draw a clear distinction between the role of politicians and of civil servants. Charles Haughey and Garret FitzGerald, both activist Taoisigh with broad interests, expanded the Department: from about 30 people in 1977 (including cleaners and messengers) to 130 in 1984, and as of 2017, it stood at just over 200 people (Department of An Taoiseach, 2016). This suggests, according to Hardiman *et al.* (2012), that there has been no 'hollowing out' of state capacity to co-ordinate policy responses. As issues move up the political agenda, the department assumes a role. Although Taoisigh have always monitored Northern Ireland policy closely, the Northern Ireland unit was moved from the Department of Foreign Affairs into the Taoiseach's department on a formal basis in 1997, as the peace process consumed more and more of the Taoiseach's time. An issue that needs to be addressed in a sustained and co-ordinated manner may also be given special focus by the Taoiseach's department. So in 2016–17 it was agreed that the Taoiseach would effectively become the 'Minister for Brexit' and any responses would be co-ordinated by his department. As of early 2017, the Taoiseach's department had seven sections, five devoted to policy areas: Britain and Northern Ireland, EU business, the economy, social policy, and international affairs. The Taoiseach also co-ordinates communication of government policy: his department houses the Government Information Service, which communicates with political correspondents of the media and informs them of government decisions (see Chapter 12).

Chairman or chief? Sources of the Taoiseach's authority

Taoisigh are usually expected to offer political leadership, and are not mere facilitators. The central role 'equips the Taoiseach to exercise better-informed powers of surveillance over his Government's activity' (Morgan, 1990: 55). It has been argued that within his own system, the Taoiseach 'is potentially more powerful than any other European prime minister, with the exception of his British counterpart' (O'Leary, 1991: 159). One former civil servant with experience in five departments, including that of the Taoiseach, says of the office and the department that 'it is amazingly powerful, all significant decisions flow through there' (private interview). In the only book-length study of Taoisigh, Farrell (1971: 83–4) argued that 'no single actor … can compare in influence with the Taoiseach: what he says … will be listened to and what he wants achieved', though he concluded that the styles of the men who held the office show 'a remarkably close attachment to the chairman's role'. Farrell used the images of 'chairman' and 'chief' to distinguish between Taoisigh who are 'prepared to allow others share resources, responsibility and publicity, reluctant to move beyond established procedures' and those with a tendency 'to accumulate political resources, concentrate decision making or control of decision making in their own hands, and – above all – make use of their strategic position to mobilise the machinery of government for action' (Farrell, 1996: 179–80). In this assessment of early office holders, only Seán Lemass emerged clearly as a 'chief'.

Of the recent holders of the office, Bruton and Ahern can probably be thought of as chairmen who were primarily concerned with the stability and durability of their governments. Bruton had been affected by his inability to form a government after the November 1992 election, and though usually thought of as being right-wing, he repositioned his party to align it to his coalition partners. Ahern was a conservative but consensus-seeking politician, who rarely pushed a policy that differed from the status quo, and was primarily concerned with keeping his party, coalition partners and the social partners happy. He worked very hard at managing the government, and ministers report that there were rarely rows at cabinet, because he had done the groundwork in advance. Interviews with cabinet colleagues of Haughey, FitzGerald and Reynolds suggest that those Taoisigh resemble chiefs in that they took leadership positions on many significant issues, and involved themselves directly in the work of ministers. However, in most cases and times, they were also in political positions that necessitated compromise.

Brian Cowen might be the least successful Taoiseach ever. Temperamentally he appeared to be a chief and colleagues complain that he surrounded himself with a 'team of friends', relying on a clique of senior ministers and advisers. His behaviour changed on becoming Taoiseach, and a once collegiate Minister for Finance became a more assertive Taoiseach. His blunt style led to more showdowns in government, and one participant felt that even if the economic crisis had not hit Ireland, the Cowen government would have fallen. He spent less time than others on the mechanical side of reaching agreed decisions. That temperament was ill-suited to the type of coalition he led, which relied on his own party (Fianna Fáil), the Green Party and a number of independents. There were reports in the press that some ministers felt the cabinet was 'railroaded' by him into important decisions, such as the nationalisation of Anglo Irish Bank (*Sunday Independent*, 18 January 2009). However, in his attitude to social partnership, it appeared that he was a conciliator and facilitator; he was eventually defeated by his cabinet on a decision as to whether to agree to further social partnership talks. He hoped to bring unions along with the crisis-induced public sector pay cuts, but most of his cabinet, especially Brian Lenihan, felt that this was unlikely to yield benefits, and would have just slowed down the necessary responses to the crisis (see Lee and McConnell, 2016: 161–6).

When Enda Kenny entered office as Taoiseach in 2011, expectations were low. Though he never soared in public popularity, his colleagues were more impressed. Many regarded him as 'much under-rated', in that he performed as a fair and efficient chair of cabinet meetings and government business. He is said to have approached issues with a reasonably open mind, to have been good at delegating, and to have lacked an ego that would make taking defeat or changing his mind difficult. His premiership can be viewed positively, given the position of the country when he took over and its position when he left, yet even towards the end of his tenure he failed to inspire confidence and his confused accounts in early 2017 of a Garda whistleblowers scandal, which first emerged in 2014, probably accelerated his departure. Even so, his retention of the office for so long in spite of poor election results demonstrates Kenny's significant political skill. Leo Varadkar, who became Taoiseach in 2017, having won the leadership of Fine Gael, was perceived as relatively activist. At the time of his accession he set out a vision of sorts, indicating that he was part of the 'new European centre', and that Ireland would become a 'Republic of Opportunity'. While his ministerial appointments were somewhat conservative – with just one minister demoted from the cabinet – in the Dáil speech on 14 June 2017 in which he nominated his cabinet members he outlined an agenda for each minister, including what he saw as their policy priorities.

Another criterion on which to assess Taoisigh is their capacity to determine policy. The literature would suggest that Taoisigh are remarkably powerful. O'Malley and Murphy (2017) found examples where Fianna Fáil Taoisigh undoubtedly moved policy in ways that alternative Taoisigh would not have. We can see that the Taoiseach can control others around him; by potentially choosing what government is formed, selecting and dismissing ministers, setting the agenda for cabinet, calling decisions at cabinet and through the ability to observe the entirety of government. But Taoisigh can be constrained by factions within their party (as Haughey was in the early 1980s) and by the demands of coalition government, which cannot be ignored (as Reynolds twice found out to his cost, when his governments broke up in 1992 and 1994).

Even a usually dependable parliamentary party can find a voice if an issue is seen as electorally important. It is probably the position as party leader more than anything else that determines the strength and power of the Taoiseach. The variation in relationships between ministers and the Taoiseach is explained when we compare those ministers for whom the Taoiseach is party leader and those for whom he is a coalition colleague. In the operation of government, ministers usually report first to their party leader. Party leaders are strong because they can command a certain number of votes in the Dáil without which the government would fall (save perhaps in the case of oversized coalitions). The Taoiseach, as party leader, in turn commands those votes when he is seen as a political or electoral asset for the party. When Enda Kenny ceased to be considered an electoral asset, following the 2016 election, he was put under considerable pressure to resign. We might conclude that a person becomes Taoiseach in part because he is powerful, and controls sizeable support in the Dáil, though the office of Taoiseach undoubtedly offers means to enhance that power. But even the office of Taoiseach is not enough to dominate politics. The experience of the minority Kenny government elected in 2016 would seem to bear this out. That government was forced to accept many policy defeats and though Fine Gael dominated *within* the government, it could not be said to have dominated policy formation.

We might also expect that as coalition government became the norm, the position of Taoiseach might have diminished in importance. Government appears to be populated by a series of veto players, and the Taoiseach can veto policies from ministers. He can put ministers in departments where the two share opinions. So Bertie Ahern effectively vetoed plans for the deregulation of bus services in Dublin in 2004 when he removed the minister who was pushing this. Coalition means that fewer portfolios will be controlled by the Taoiseach's party and his party's preferred policies are much more vulnerable to veto by a coalition partner. It makes a difference to the power of a Taoiseach in that in a coalition government he must deal with a well-organised group of TDs that can effectively veto any new proposals by threatening to leave government. Though it is rare that such threats are made explicit, coalition partners are always aware of this ultimatum. For example, because of the insistence of some of its coalition partners, Fine Gael was forced in 2017 to proceed with a bill on judicial appointments that it was known not to favour. By contrast, party groupings may be less disciplined and more vulnerable to a Taoiseach's ability to offer deals to individuals within that group. That said, one thing is clear from one insider's account of a coalition; Boyle (2012) shows how the Greens discovered that small concessions were easy to make and to justify to oneself and to one's supporters, but that the decision to withdraw support was immensely hard. While it is difficult to make an overall assessment of the power or importance of Taoisigh or prime ministers more generally, longevity might be a measure of their effectiveness. On that basis, we would say that Ahern and Kenny were powerful. Still, we can point to areas where they lost policy battles. Perhaps, then, the characterisation of the Taoiseach as utterly dominant is wrong.

Ministers and departments

Though the office of the Taoiseach may be thought of as the apex of political power in the Irish system, most policy making effectively takes place within departments. Ministers are the political heads of government departments and it is up to each minister to set the department's broad policy parameters and priorities. Policies emerging from a government department are almost certain to have the approval and backing of the minister. In fact, policy might get decided at the departmental rather than cabinet level. This can happen for a number of reasons. First, ministers are gate-keepers, in that policies relevant to their jurisdiction usually need their sponsorship. It would be unheard of for policy proposals regarded as falling within the remit of one department to emerge from another. Second, ministers as heads of departments charged with implementing policy can control how a policy is administered. Third, given that ministers are judged primarily on their own departmental record, they may cede policy autonomy to each other. Ministerial 'logrolling' – trading of authority and support – occurs when ministers agree to support each other's policies. As one former Taoiseach noted, 'most cabinet ministers spend 90 per cent of their time immersed in their own departments, with only 10 per cent concerned with the rest of government' (John Bruton, *Irish Times*, 1 November 2014). Bruton's assessment of ministerial focus is corroborated by accounts in the autobiographies and memoirs of former ministers (O'Malley and Rafter, 2018).

Ministers are also empowered by the use of statutory instruments. These are one of the means by which legislative functions are delegated by the Oireachtas to the executive. It is often the case that policy is made in the Oireachtas but that it delegates the power to implement and amend its operation, if not its principle, to a minister. By leaving the relevant minister to decide many of the specific details, the Oireachtas is providing the minister with something of a free hand to shape public policy. Furthermore, the EU imposes a great deal of law on governments through its directives. These directives need to be transposed into Irish law, but, given their extent and nature, it may be not be practical for the Oireachtas to deal with all this in primary legislation, so the European Communities Act, 1972, allows ministers to make regulations. There has been a marked increase in the use of statutory instruments. The average annual number used in Ireland in the 1960s was 284; this rose steadily to the 1990s where there were on average 445 a year. In the period 2010–16, the average annual number rose to 650. When compared to the number of Acts of the Oireachtas per year (on average 45 between 2010 and 2016), the number of such ministerial orders may suggest a great importance, but in practice many of these orders are short and relatively inconsequential. However, one does find statutory instruments that run to over 50 pages, which might then be construed as shifting some policy-making power from the Oireachtas to the government. Indeed, this was what the Supreme Court found in Laurentiu v Minister for Justice (Ní Mhuirthile *et al.*, 2015: 105).

Despite the legal freedom of ministers to act, even energetic and able ministers can be restricted from introducing significant policy innovations by a coalition's programme for government and by the need to get political approval from cabinet. We might also expect that those providing them with advice can act as a constraint. The civil service plays a critical role both by advising politicians on policy formulation and in implementing legislative and ministerial decisions. At the core of the bureaucratic model of governance is the idea that civil servants can shape the development and implementation of policy in a way that undermines the power and influence of politicians. The Irish civil service is relatively small by European standards, with around 35,000 full-time equivalent civil servants, representing just under 2 per cent of the total labour force (Department of Public Expenditure and Reform, 2014a). As in other countries, the relationship between senior civil servants and their political masters is the outcome of an implicit bargain based on formal and informal rules and norms. Hood (2000: 8) defines the public service bargain as 'any explicit or implicit understanding between (senior) public servants and other actors in a political system over their duties and entitlements relating to responsibility, autonomy, and political identity, and expressed in convention or formal law or a mixture of both' (see also Hood and Lodge, 2006). In Ireland (like the UK), this means that civil servants are guaranteed secure employment, with promotion based on merit and not patronage. Furthermore, they are shielded from the public eye, though civil servants are now required to face Oireachtas committees.

In return, civil servants are expected to promote the interests of the ministers regardless of their own preferences. Historically, and as provided for in the 1924 Ministers and Secretaries Act, the minister was head of department and its 'corporation sole', so civil servants acted only in the name of the minister. Ministers were responsible for all actions of their departments and, in effect, civil servants never did anything independently of the minister. The 'corporation sole' principle has been used by some civil servants in the past as an excuse for refusing to face parliamentary committees (Zimmerman, 1997). This tradition, inherited from the British civil service model, laid great emphasis on civil servants as neutral players, offering advice to ministers and acting to promote a minister's preferences regardless of their own. Such a model was seen to serve democracy well, given that ministers were accountable to the Oireachtas and indirectly to the electorate, while civil servants as permanent employees of the state effectively enjoyed immunity from accountability.

The level of influence of Irish civil servants over government ministers remains something of an unanswered question. The traditional view of the civil service is imperfect on a number of grounds. One can question the degree to which it is practical for a government minister to be able to control and oversee everything that is happening in his or her department. This inability to monitor and control every aspect of civil servants' work becomes even greater if we accept that individual civil servants are likely to have independent ideas and preferences that may be less than completely aligned with the preference of the minister. What one is left with is a classical problem of delegation. A minister must rely on civil servants to both advise on and implement policy. What civil servants bring to the attention of the minister has significant agenda-setting consequences. In terms of implementation, even greater levels of delegation are called for: ministers cannot implement policy in any real sense, but must rely both on their senior civil servants and on front-line staff in the public sector more generally.

The potential to influence is stacked heavily in favour of the civil service. As agents of the minister, civil servants have a number of distinct advantages compared to their principal. Senior civil servants are likely to possess more information about the subject matter of policy than the minister. While ministers come and go, civil servants enjoy longer tenures of service and this alone gives them an enormous informational advantage. Senior civil servants also have direct access to other levels of the service with which the minister may find it difficult to communicate easily. Ministers face competing demands on their time. Collective responsibility requires them to maintain interest in policies outside their own department, at least in principle. While civil servants are free to focus on departmental matters, government ministers must balance ministerial work with parliamentary party and constituency obligations. Ministers cannot afford to neglect their own parliamentary seats (Martin, 2014). These competing demands and ministers' heavy workloads may well significantly reduce the ability of ministers to influence policy change within their portfolios. In reality, civil servants are unlikely to be as removed from policy formation as the traditional British model might expect us to believe.

It is acknowledged that senior civil servants have significant influence since, among other factors, they are the point of contact in the governmental system for interest groups and they have the capacity to filter what gets to the minister. Farrell (1994: 83) notes that most ministers regarded a high level of collaboration as usual and civil service obstruction as unusual. Former ministers do, however, seem to reserve most negativity for the role and performance of the Department of Finance. As in other systems, this department enjoys a co-ordinating role, giving it the right to vet proposals with a spending element from other government departments. As Considine and Reidy (2012: 98) note, Finance is 'overly concerned with management of the expenditure process' to the detriment of good economic management. In his autobiography, Garret FitzGerald points to a number of instances of civil servants opposing proposed policy changes in areas such as taxation, healthcare and new multi-denominational education provisions (FitzGerald, 1991: 386).

Yet, in general, FitzGerald and subsequent Taoisigh tend to have a positive attitude towards the civil service. In identifying the need for significant public sector reform, Kingston (2007: 72) identifies ministerial control over senior civil service appointments as a motivation for civil servants to be sensitive to the wishes and preferences of their political masters. Quinn (2007: 218) found that a lack of self-confidence and a fear of failure in the civil service led to an over-reliance on outside consultants and an unwillingness to innovate. Ultimately, the relative influence of a minister and senior civil servant is likely to depend on the personality of both and the strength of preferences each may have over certain policies or procedures.

Rules governing the relationship between ministers and civil servants provide at least a baseline to understand the intertwined existence of minsters and bureaucrats. In the Irish case, the legal basis of this relationship has shifted somewhat in recent times in an attempt to recognise the inadequacies of the pure ministerial model. This resulted in significant legislation that undermined the British model as represented by the original Ministers and Secretaries Act of 1924. The Public Service Management Act, 1997, refined our understanding of ministerial government by explicitly dividing responsibilities between the minister and the senior civil servant in each department. Beyond renaming the post of departmental secretary 'secretary general', the Act devolved a significant managerial role to the secretary general, who now became responsible for human resource issues for the lower and middle ranks of the department. Whereas previously the minister formally hired, promoted, and managed junior civil servants, now the secretary general formally performs this role. Moreover, the act required individual departments to undertake and publish strategic plans with the aim of improving performance, efficiency and effectiveness. These reforms were born out of the new public management philosophy that placed greater emphasis on managerialism. The initiative for such reforms came largely from within the civil service itself (Hardiman and MacCarthaigh, 2008). The economic and fiscal crisis led to further demands for, and facilitated, reforms of the civil service as well as a shrinking of the state (MacCarthaigh, 2017; see Box 10.2). The establishment of the Department of Public Expenditure and Reform in 2011 removed the responsibility for expenditure from the Department of Finance. The new department sought to streamline and renew the civil service at a time when public sector budgets were shrinking (Department of Public Expenditure and Reform, 2014b). Reform of the civil service occurs within the context of broader public sector reform. Post-crisis public sector reform focused on issues such as reducing costs, improved service delivery, digital government and greater openness, transparency and accountability in public administration (Department of Public Expenditure and Reform, 2014c). The Rafter Report (Department of Public Expenditure and Reform, 2014c) recommended changes to increase further the accountability of civil servants, including the creation of an Accountability Board.

Box 10.2 Public sector reform

It could be suggested that the system of public administration in Ireland contributed to the banking and economic crisis that began in 2008. The Joint Committee of Inquiry into the Banking Crisis found that 'The oversight, challenge and effective scrutiny by the Oireachtas of the Government and its policy decisions in relation to fiscal policy, financial stability and the system of financial regulation was inadequate in the pre-crisis years' (Committee of Inquiry into the Banking Crisis, 2016: 15). Indeed, very few bodies – including government departments, the mainstream media or political parties – contemplated the consequences of the government's economic and fiscal policies in the run-up to the 2008 crisis. Government policy on public administration had been focused on agencification – the process of delegating certain functions from a government department to a specialist agency. The expectation was that agencies would improve effectiveness and efficiency, having greater policy and managerial autonomy than if they were embedded within a government department. The Irish experience had been criticised even before the economic crisis by the OECD, which noted that 'in Ireland, the objectives of agencification are unclear, mixed and not prioritised, resulting in sub-optimal governance structures' (OECD, 2008: 298).

One response to the banking crisis and recession was to reform the public sector. Most immediately, the fiscal situation and the conditions attached to Ireland's International Monetary Fund Programme demanded a retrenchment in the number of people working in the public sector. De-agencification, involving rationalisation of the number of state agencies, became a priority for the coalition government elected in 2011 (Dommett *et al.*, 2016). Wider public sector reform involved changing work practices and a renewed emphasis on more effective and efficient public management, driven by the newly-created Department of Public Expenditure and Reform. As a result, the civil service became somewhat leaner in terms of size, with the work of some departments subject to better monitoring. For example, the quasi-autonomous Irish Fiscal Advisory Council, created in 2011, assesses and comments on forecasts prepared by the Department of Finance and reports publicly on the degree to which the government is meeting its own income and expenditure targets.

The right given under the 1997 legislation to Oireachtas committees to hear testimony from and to question senior civil servants shifted the public administration practice in Ireland away from the ministerial government model towards the bureaucratic model. These developments give greater recognition to the role of civil servants – in particular at senior level – not only in internal management but also in advising ministers and implementing government policy.

Yet, despite the change in legislation that brought the internal structures and processes of the civil service more closely into line with the reality of civil service influence, one could overstate the case for bureaucratic government in Ireland. The minister still remains the head of department. Moreover, politicians have increasingly come to rely on non-civil servants to provide advice. In particular, the role of special adviser has become more important in Irish government. Unlike civil servants, special advisers are appointed only for the period of tenure of particular ministers. While some special advisers have come from within the civil service, it is more common for ministers to recruit advisers from outside the service. Noting that the appointment of the first special adviser could be traced to the inter-party government of 1954–57, Connaughton (2010: 354) found that special advisers in more recent times 'were drawn from a variety of backgrounds including political activists, company directors, union officials, consultants, accountants, elected local councillors and public servants.' Advisers act as an extension of the minister, often providing a buffer between minister and civil servant. Moreover, ministerial advisers may meet on a cross-departmental basis in a way that senior civil servants rarely do. In many ways, the growth of special advisers has reduced the influence of senior civil servants and shifted the balance of power back in the direction of the minister. The role of special advisers was institutionalised in the Public Service Management Act, which provided a legal basis for each minister and minister of state to have a special adviser. Ministers may also bring in other help from outside the civil service, possibly to head their private office but also to act in roles such as departmental press secretary. As we will see later in this chapter, special advisers serve an important additional role in coalition government.

Monitoring Irish government

The electorate holds governments accountable for their actions at election time by rewarding or punishing incumbent government parties. A number of other avenues also exist by which the government is held accountable. Most monitoring mechanisms are external to the government itself. However, the increased frequency of coalition government has seen the need for parties within government to monitor each other. External monitoring comes from six main sources: the Oireachtas and its committees, the Ombudsman, the Comptroller and Auditor General, tribunals of inquiry, the media, and freedom of information legislation.

As noted earlier, the ability of the Oireachtas to hold the government accountable is severely restricted by the fusion of the executive and legislature under Ireland's parliamentary system of government. Question time and the use of written parliamentary questions remain limited as tools of executive oversight (see Chapter 7). Reform of political institutions in the aftermath of the banking crisis and recession presented opportunities to enhance parliament's role in monitoring the government. Today, Oireachtas committees are much stronger than has historically been the case. Committee appointments are no longer the sole preserve of party leaders. The parliamentary agenda is shaped by a business committee, rather than by the government chief whip. Pre-legislative scrutiny – the process by which planned legislation is considered and evaluated by Oireachtas committees prior to the formal legislative process – is now an option for committees and departments. As was noted before, the emergence of a minority government following the 2016 general election meant that the executive, no longer able to depend on majority support, instead had to build legislative coalitions to get its policies enacted. Thus, political reform combined with the lack of a solid parliamentary majority has meant that the Oireachtas has become more relevant to monitoring the government. At the same time, it would be easy to overstate the impact of political reform; in Ireland, the government very much continues to dominate parliament.

The Office of Ombudsman, established under the Ombudsman Act, 1980, has the power and duty to investigate complaints of maladministration in government departments, local authorities, the health service and publicly-funded third level education institutions. The Ombudsman can investigate an action where a complaint has been made, and can initiate investigations. During 2015, the office received 3,641 complaints considered to lie within its jurisdiction. Over 60 per cent of all complaints against the civil service in 2015 were accounted for by the Department of Social Protection, and in particular, its decisions regarding social welfare entitlements (Office of the Ombudsman, 2016). Typically, public bodies accept the decision of the Ombudsman although they are not legally required to do so.

Under Article 33 of the Constitution, the Comptroller and Auditor General (C&AG) reports to the Oireachtas on the administration of money by public bodies, including government departments and state agencies. The office of C&AG suffered for many decades from a lack of resources and from a general culture of non-cooperation from the civil service (O'Halpin, 1985). In more recent years, however, the desire of some politicians for public sector reform has seen a more robust exercise of powers by the C&AG. Public servants, politicians and the media now closely observe the contents of C&AG reports to the Dáil Public Accounts Committee (PAC). This in turn has increased both the credibility of the role of C&AG and the readiness of the public service to cooperate with audits and investigations. As with the Ombudsman, the C&AG is capable of producing reports highlighting shortcomings, inefficiencies and ineffectiveness in the public sector. Annual reports are now replete with audit concerns and negative conclusions about the value for money of certain public programmes. While the C&AG and the PAC can probe into misspending or accounting malpractice, they are more limited in investigating whether monies spent on public programmes actually achieve stated policy goals.

The Oireachtas can also establish tribunals of inquiry, under United Kingdom legislation dating from the period before formal independence. The Tribunals of Inquiry (Evidence) Act 1921 provides for the Oireachtas to initiate public inquiries. These inquiries are headed by a judge and operate in a quasi-judicial manner with the right to order the production of documentation and to compel and examine witnesses. In the early 1990s, tension within the Fianna Fáil–Progressive Democrats coalition led to the creation of the Beef Tribunal under the chairmanship of Justice Liam Hamilton. That tribunal investigated allegations of political favouritism and its report was a contributory factor in the break-up of the Fianna Fáil–Labour government in 1994. Although criticised for excessive costs and inconclusive evidence of political wrongdoing, tribunals of investigation have become a significant source of monitoring in Irish politics. For example, the McCracken tribunal was to uncover covert payments to politicians, while the Flood/Mahon tribunal exposed corruption in the planning process. In 2008, Bertie Ahern resigned as Taoiseach following revelations at the Mahon tribunal concerning payments allegedly made to him by a number of businessmen. Tribunals are reactive by nature, typically created on an ad hoc basis to further investigate events and processes that have been uncovered by a different 'police patrol' (ongoing routine monitoring) or 'fire alarm' (reactive oversight of executive failures).

In most democracies, the media are considered to play a key role in monitoring the activities of government (see Chapter 12). Commonly referred to as the 'fourth estate' of democracy, the media often fill the vacuum of oversight in circumstances where other political institutions are unable or unwilling to investigate and/or to expose administrative and political errors. Of course, the government also tries to 'handle' the media and each government department and agency typically has at least one press officer and, sometimes, a small staff to work on media relations. The ability of the media, traditional and new (and of public and interest groups more generally), to access information on the actions of government has greatly increased in recent decades. State papers, such as cabinet minutes and papers, are released to the public after 30 years (although some exceptions apply on the basis of national security and foreign relations). Given this, the importance of the National Archives is primarily historical and does not enable monitoring of incumbent governments. That said, some politicians may be keenly interested in how historians judge them.

A much more significant development for the external oversight of government was the inception of a freedom of information (FOI) culture in Ireland. The Freedom of Information Act, 1997, establishes a legal right for members of the public to access records held by most public bodies. Almost 28,000 requests were made to public bodies under the Act in 2015, with journalists accounting for 20 per cent of requests (Office of the Information Commissioner, 2016). In addition to making access to information and documents easier, the FOI Act may contribute to changing the traditional culture of secrecy within government. This made possible, for example, our discovering the extent of the lobbying by lawyers' interest groups against proposed reforms in the period 2011–15 (see Chapter 11, p. 282). On the other hand, FOI laws sometimes have the effect of increasing secrecy by making actors reluctant to put too much in writing. A number of organisations and types of documents are exempt from the Act, such as recent cabinet papers, the papers of individual politicians and those of certain public bodies, such as the Garda Síochána.

The economic crisis brought into sharp focus the degree to which institutions are capable of monitoring the government. A lack of monitoring and oversight, it could be argued, permitted the production of poor public policy, which at the very least exacerbated the banking and economic crises. In response to such arguments, the government established new forms of extra-legislative monitoring, particularly in the realm of economic policy-making. Amongst the most significant is the Irish Fiscal Advisory Council (Box 10.2).

The above are examples of external monitoring. Internal monitoring can also be important, particularly in the case of coalition government. The nature of monitoring has tended to be very different in cabinets composed of ministers from different parties. Where parties around the cabinet table disagree on policy, an individual minister may have an incentive to deviate from the programme for government. In single party government, such problems are assumed not to exist, as all government ministers are from the same political party, and hence share similar policy preferences. In coalitions, typically, some form of intra-cabinet monitoring is necessary to enable each party in government to monitor and control the actions of other parties in government.

We observe a number of potential intra-coalition monitoring mechanisms in politics. Thies (2001) shows that junior ministers from one party may monitor the behaviour and actions of cabinet ministers from other parties. Evidence indicates that political parties in multiparty governments allocate junior ministerial positions in such a way as to shadow each other's senior ministers. In Ireland, there is a well-established system of junior ministerial positions, but while it is difficult to conclude that Irish junior ministers are strategically placed to shadow senior ministers from different parties, at least one party leader has claimed that the positions have been used in this way (private interview). André *et al.* (2016) suggest that Oireachtas committees play a role in helping parties in coalition government to keep tabs on each other. According to this perspective, the strengthening of parliamentary committees is directly related to the shift from single-party to coalition government and, in particular, to the desire of the smaller coalition party to be able to monitor the larger party's ministers.

In some countries, deputy prime ministers play a significant role in the monitoring of coalition cabinets. In Ireland, the traditional role of the Tánaiste is to deputise for the Taoiseach when the latter is out of the country, for example. In more recent years, however, the role of Tánaiste has changed due, in part, to the increased frequency of coalition government. In recent coalition governments, with the exception of those of 1989–92 and 2007–11, the leader of the second party in government has been Tánaiste. We can differentiate between two different models of Tánaiste; one where the office-holder is a senior member of the Taoiseach's own party and deputises for the Taoiseach, and a second where the Tánaiste is a party leader and shares a leadership, co-ordination and monitoring role with the Taoiseach.

As noted above, more formal mechanisms such as programme managers and special advisers have been in place since 1993 to monitor the implementation of the programme for government, which is particularly useful for the smaller government party or parties without 'eyes and ears' in many departments, and as such they are an important source of intra-government monitoring. Ultimately, a strong system of programme managers may lead to stronger ministerial government, though after 1997 the system was cut back to one where just the party leaders have programme managers. The post of special adviser continues to perform many of the same functions, the advisers collectively operating in effect as a lower-level cabinet. The overall picture that emerges is of greater levels of post-recession monitoring, from both outside and within government.

Conclusion

As a result of the economic crisis, it became clear that much of the pre-crisis supposed expansion in the Irish economy had been illusory and that there had been massive failures of planning and oversight in a number of areas of the economy, not least the banking sector. The Irish government's accounting practices were shown to be poor and economic forecasting was over-optimistic, if not unsophisticated. In that context, there was a debate on whether the Irish governmental system is fit for purpose.

Some of the various official investigations into the crash found failings not just in policy, but also in the way policy was formulated. Wright (2010) noted that social partnership (see Chapter 11) 'overwhelmed' the policy process, especially given the financial demands that it placed on government. He observed that the Department of Finance (and we can assume that this is the case for all departments) lacked specialist, technical capacity, and did not act in a strategic manner. While the Department of Finance was found to have issued reasonable advice to ministers, it did not do so forcefully enough and did not vary the tone of the advice. Nyberg (2011) concluded that all actors in the Irish financial system, including the regulator, central bank and politicians exhibited 'irrational' behaviour, in particular 'herding' and 'groupthink'. He found a culture and organisation in the Irish public institutions with a 'strongly empowered leader gradually eliminating independent critical analysis among staff' (Nyberg, 2011: 9).

Important issues arose for consideration in the aftermath of the recession, including whether a system in which ministers can only really be selected on the basis of local electoral popularity is wise, or whether a civil service system that encourages blame-avoidance can encourage innovation and excellence. None of the reforms and changes subsequently made was radical. Lobbying legislation was introduced (see Chapter 11), a Fiscal Advisory Council was created, and expertise within the civil service was increased, but in many ways the changes were a response to the last crisis rather than an attempt to prevent what might be a future, different crisis. We also noted that monitoring institutions are limited to investigating malpractice, but not the effectiveness of public spending. These issues are ripe for debate.

This chapter has examined the Irish government system with a view to uncovering how it operates and identifying where policy-making power lies. Although Ward (1994: 296) finds that power is concentrated in the government, it is not clear *where* power lies within the government. Cabinet, ministers and the Taoiseach are all potentially powerful actors, though all are constrained significantly, not least by each other, but also by the bureaucracy and through increasingly important systems of external monitoring. Both the bureaucracy and systems of government monitoring have undergone significant changes in recent years. For the civil service, and the public sector more generally, the challenge remains to deliver quality and value for money. Enhanced monitoring made possible by political reform within and outside the Oireachtas mean a much higher level of scrutiny than governments have been traditionally accustomed to. When greater levels of intra-cabinet monitoring and the emergence of a minority government following the 2016 general election are added to this, one is left with the impression of more open government. Despite this, much is still to be learned about the operation of government in Ireland.

Note

1   This chapter is based, in part, on a series of interviews conducted by Eoin O'Malley with former and existing Taoisigh, ministers, civil servants and advisers. The interviews are usually conducted on the basis of confidentiality. Eoin O'Malley has also been given access to recorded interviews of ministers by the late Brian Farrell. These are held in UCD Library.

References and further reading

André, Audrey, Sam Depauw and Shane Martin, 2016. 'Trust is good, control is better: multiparty government and legislative organization', *Political Research Quarterly* 69:1, pp. 108–20.

Bagehot, Walter, 1963 [1867]. *The English Constitution*, edited by Richard Crossman. London: Fontana.

Blondel, Jean and Maurizio Cotta (eds), 2000. *The Nature of Party Government: A Comparative European Perspective*. London: Palgrave.

Boyle, Dan, 2012. *Without Power or Glory: The Greens in Government.* Dublin: New Island.

Callaghan, James, 1987. *Time and Chance.* London: Collins.

Coakley, John, 2013. *Reforming Political Institutions: Ireland in Comparative Perspective.* Dublin: Institute of Public Administration.

Collins, Stephen, 1996. *The Cosgrave Legacy.* Dublin: Blackwater Press.

Committee of Inquiry into the Banking Crisis, 2016. *Report of the Joint Committee of Inquiry into the Banking Crisis, Volume 1.* Dublin: Houses of the Oireachtas.

Connaughton, Bernadette, 2010. '"Glorified gofers, policy experts or good generalists": a classification of the roles of the Irish ministerial adviser', *Irish Political Studies* 25:3, pp. 347–69

Considine, John and Theresa Reidy, 2012. 'Department of Finance', in Eoin O'Malley and Muiris MacCarthaigh (eds), *Governing Ireland: From Cabinet Government to Delegated Governance.* Dublin: Institute of Public Administration, pp. 88–105.

Costello, Rory, Paul O'Neill and Robert Thomson, 2016. 'The fulfilment of election pledges', in Michael Gallagher and Michael Marsh (eds), *How Ireland Voted 2016: The Election That Nobody Won.* Basingstoke: Palgrave Macmillan, pp. 19–32.

Crossman, Richard H.S., 1963. 'Introduction', in R.H.S. Crossman (ed.), *The English Constitution by Walter Bagehot.* London: Fontana, pp. 1–56.

Crossman, Richard H.S, 1972. *Inside View: Three Lectures on Prime Ministerial Government.* London: Jonathan Cape.

Department of An Taoiseach, 2016. *Department of An Taoiseach Annual Report 2015.* Available at http://www.taoiseach.gov.ie/eng/Publications/Publications_2016/Department_of_the_Taoiseach_Annual_Report_2015.pdf

Department of Public Expenditure and Reform, 2014a. *Civil Service Renewal Plan.* Dublin: Department of Public Expenditure and Reform.

Department of Public Expenditure and Reform, 2014b. *Public Service Reform Plan 2014–2016.* Dublin: Department of Public Expenditure and Reform.

Department of Public Expenditure and Reform, 2014c. *Strengthening Civil Service Accountability and Performance.* Dublin: Government Reform Unit, Department of Public Expenditure and Reform.

Dommett, Katharine, Muiris MacCarthaigh and Niamh Hardiman, 2016. 'Reforming the Westminster model of agency governance: Britain and Ireland after the crisis', *Governance* 29:4, pp. 535–52.

Elgie, Robert, 1997. 'Models of executive politics: a framework for the study of executive power relations in parliamentary and semi-presidential regimes', *Political Studies* 45:2, pp. 217–31.

Farrell, Brian, 1971. *Chairman or Chief? The Role of Taoiseach in Irish Government*. Dublin: Gill and Macmillan.

Farrell, Brian, 1987. 'The constitution and the institutions of government: constitutional theory and political practice', *Administration* 35:4, pp. 162–72.

Farrell, Brian, 1994. 'The political role of cabinet ministers in Ireland', in Michael Laver and Kenneth A. Shepsle (eds), *Cabinet Ministers and Parliamentary Government*. New York: Cambridge University Press, pp. 73–87.

Farrell, Brian, 1996. 'The government', in John Coakley and Michael Gallagher (eds), *Politics in the Republic of Ireland*, 2nd ed. Limerick: PSAI Press, pp. 167–89.

Finlay, Fergus, 1997. *Snakes and Ladders*. Dublin: New Island Books.

FitzGerald, Garret, 1991. *All in a Life*. Dublin: Gill and Macmillan.

FitzGerald, Garret, 2004. 'The role of the Taoiseach: chairman or chief?', in Tom Garvin, Maurice Manning and Richard Sinnott (eds), *Dissecting Irish Politics: Essays in Honour of Brian Farrell*. Dublin: UCD Press, pp. 66–81.

Gilmore, Éamon, 2016. *Inside the Room: The Untold Story of Ireland's Crisis Government*. Sallins: Merrion Press.

Hardiman, Niamh and Muiris MacCarthaigh, 2008. *The Segmented State: Adaptation and Maladaptation in Ireland* [Geary Institute Discussion Paper Series]. Dublin: Geary Institute, University College Dublin.

Hardiman, Niamh, Aidan Regan and Mary Shayne, 2012. 'The core executive: the Department of the Taoiseach and the challenge of policy coordination', in Eoin O'Malley and Muiris MacCarthaigh (eds), *Governing Ireland: From Cabinet Government to Delegated Governance*. Dublin: Institute of Public Administration, pp. 106–27.

Hogan, Gerard, 1993. 'The cabinet confidentiality case of 1992', *Irish Political Studies* 8, pp. 131–7.

Hood, C., 2000. 'Paradoxes of public-sector managerialism, old public management and public service bargains', *International Public Management Journal* 3:1, pp. 1–22.

Hood, Christopher, and Martin Lodge, 2006. *The Politics of Public Service Bargains: Reward, Competency, Loyalty and Blame*. Oxford: Oxford University Press.

Kingston, William, 2007. *Interrogating Irish Policies*. Dublin: Dublin University Press.

Laver, Michael and Kenneth A. Shepsle (eds), 1994. *Cabinet Ministers and Parliamentary Government*. New York: Cambridge University Press.

Lee, John and Daniel McConnell, 2016. *Hell at the Gates: The Inside Story of Ireland's Financial Downfall*. Cork: Mercier Press.

Lemass, Seán, 1968. 'Lemass on government', *Léargas* 12, pp. 2–19.

Lindsay, Patrick, 1992. *Memories*. Dublin: Blackwater Press.

MacCarthaigh, Muiris, 2017. *Public Sector Reform in Ireland: Countering Crisis*. London: Palgrave.

McCullagh, David, 1998. *A Makeshift Majority: The First Inter-Party Government, 1948–51*. Dublin: Institute of Public Administration.

McQuinn, Cormac, 2017. '"Trust" will be at the core of Varadkar's considerations for new cabinet', *Irish Independent*, 9 June.

Marshall, Geoffrey, 1989. 'Introduction', in Geoffrey Marshall (ed.), *Ministerial Responsibility*. Oxford: Oxford University Press, pp. 1–13.

Martin, Shane, 2014. 'Government formation in Ireland: learning to live without a majority party', in Bjørn Erik Rasch, Shane Martin and José Antonio Cheibub (eds), *Parliaments and Government Formation: Unpacking Investiture Rules*. Oxford: Oxford University Press, pp. 121–35.

Martin, Shane, 2016. 'Policy, office, and votes: the electoral value of ministerial office', *British Journal of Political Science* 46:2, pp. 281–96.

Morgan, David Gwynn, 1990. *Constitutional Law in Ireland*, 2nd ed. Dublin: Round Hall Press.

Muthoo, Abhinay, 2000. 'A non-technical introduction to bargaining theory', *World Economics* 1:2, pp. 145–66.

Ní Mhuirthile, Tanya, Catherine O'Sullivan and Liam Thornton, 2015. *Fundamentals of the Irish Legal System: Law, Policy and Politics*. Dublin: Round Hall

Niskanen, William, 1971. *Bureaucracy and Representative Government*. Chicago: Aldine Atherton.

Nyberg, Peter, 2011. 'Misjudging risk: Causes of the systemic banking crisis in Ireland'. Available at http://www.bankinginquiry.gov.ie/Documents/Misjuding%20Risk%20-%20Causes%20of%20 the%20Systemic%20Banking%20Crisis%20in%20Ireland.pdf [accessed 3 March 2017].

OECD, 2008. *Ireland: Towards an Integrated Public Service*. Paris: OECD.

Office of the Information Commissioner, 2016. *Annual Report 2015*. Dublin: Stationery Office.

Office of the Ombudsman, 2016. *Annual Report 2015*. Dublin: Stationery Office.

O'Halpin, Eunan, 1985. 'The Dáil committee of public accounts, 1961–1980', *Administration* 32:4, pp. 483–511.

O'Leary, Brendan, 1991. 'An Taoiseach: the Irish prime minister', in G. W. Jones (ed.), *West European Prime Ministers*. London: Frank Cass, pp. 133–62.

O'Malley, Eoin, 2006. 'Ministerial selection in Ireland: limited choice in a political village', *Irish Political Studies* 21:3 pp. 319–36.

O'Malley, Eoin, 2008. 'Government formation in 2007', in Michael Gallagher and Michael Marsh (eds), *How Ireland Voted 2007: The Full Story of Ireland's General Election*. Basingstoke: Palgrave Macmillan, pp. 205–17.

O'Malley, Eoin, 2016. '70 Days: government formation in 2016', in Michael Gallagher and Michael Marsh (eds), *How Ireland Voted 2016: The Election That Nobody Won*. Basingstoke: Palgrave Macmillan, pp. 255–76.

O'Malley, Eoin and Gary Murphy, 2017. 'The leadership difference? Context and choice in Fianna Fáil's party leadership', *Irish Political Studies* 32:1, pp. 118–40.

O'Malley, Eoin and Kevin Rafter, 2018. 'The memoirs of male politicians in independent Ireland', in Liam Harte (ed.), *A History of Irish Autobiography*. New York: Cambridge University Press.

Quinn, Ruairí, 2005. *Straight Left – A Journey in Politics*. Dublin: Hodder Headline.

Quinn, Ruairí, 2007. 'Is our public service ready for the future? A response from the political arena', in Mark Callanan (ed.), *Ireland 2022: Towards 100 Years of Self-Government*. Dublin: Institute of Public Administration, pp. 214–21.

Rhodes, R.A.W., 1995. 'From prime ministerial power to core executive', in R. A. W. Rhodes and Patrick Dunleavy (eds), *Prime Minister, Cabinet and Core Executive*. Basingstoke: Macmillan, pp. 11–37.

Ross, Shane, 2016. 'An awful truth dawned: we're talking to a political corpse', *Sunday Independent*, 6 March.

Smith, Daniel M. and Shane Martin, 2017. 'Political dynasties and the selection of cabinet ministers', *Legislative Studies Quarterly* 42:1, pp. 131–65.

Suiter, Jane and Eoin O'Malley, 2014. 'Yes, minister: the impact of decision-making rules on geographically targeted particularistic spending', *Parliamentary Affairs* 67:4, pp. 935–54.

Thies, Michael F., 2001. 'Keeping tabs on partners: the logic of delegation in coalition governments', *American Journal of Political Science* 45:3, pp. 580–98.

Walshe, John, 2015. *An Education: How an Outsider Became an Insider – and Learned What Really Goes on in Irish Government*. Dublin: Penguin.

Ward, Alan J., 1994. *The Irish Constitutional Tradition: 1782–1992*. Dublin: Irish Academic Press.

Wright, Robert, 2010. *Assessing the Capacity of the Department of Finance*. Available at http://www. finance.gov.ie/sites/default/files/deptreviewwight.pdf [accessed 3 March 2017].

Zimmerman, Joseph F., 1997. 'The changing roles of the Irish department secretary', *Public Administration Review* 57:6, pp. 534–42.

Websites

www.taoiseach.gov.ie

The Department of the Taoiseach's website contains information on the personnel of cabinet, the organisation of government and the Cabinet Handbook.

www.oireachtas.ie/parliament/oireachtasbusiness/parliamentarydebates/
Access to all parliamentary debates.

www.irishstatutebook.ie
Complete list of laws and statutory instruments.

irlgov.ie
Government of Ireland website.

ombudsman.gov.ie/
Website of the Office of the Ombudsman.

www.oic.gov.ie
Website of the Office of the Information Commissioner.

audgen.gov.ie
Website of the Comptroller and Auditor General.

www.isad.ie/
The Irish State Administration Database, which captures the establishment, growth and evolution of Ireland's state administration from the foundation of the Irish Free State in 1922 to the present.

11 The policy-making process

Gary Murphy

Who makes public policy in Ireland and how do they do it? We will answer these apparently simple but devilishly tricky questions in this chapter, which examines the policy-making process, assesses how decisions are made, and considers who influences them. It analyses the structures through which public policy is made, implemented and monitored and discusses the crucial role that interest groups play when it comes to national policy making within the Irish state. It also reviews the steps governments have taken to ensure that policy making is open and transparent to the public, something that was not at all apparent during the greater part of the Irish state's existence. While such secrecy is not unique to Ireland, there can be little doubt that until recently the policy process in Ireland was opaque and secretive. This had the effect of preventing adequate oversight of government policy (O'Malley, 2011: 101).

Since independence in 1922, the Irish state's experience of national policy making has been somewhat random and haphazard. Policy making is an extremely complex business. While governments make policies, the process by which the decision to actually go ahead and introduce any particular policy is made can be tortuous and will normally involve many different stakeholders. These can include politicians, both in government and in opposition, the media, interest groups of various kinds, and individual citizens. Policy making can be made more complex by bureaucracy at the local, national and European level, and by the ability of various groups and citizens to exercise their right of recourse to the courts. The constitution imposes certain constraints and can be used as an excuse for inaction, and policy making also takes place in the context of Ireland's status as a member of the European Union, with the obligations that that entails (see Chapter 14). The result has been that governments have sometimes faced difficulties both in actually making decisions in the first place, and then in implementing them successfully. The desired results are not always achieved, and governments may not even be sure what results they want from their policies in the first place. Sometimes governments introduce policies and then either fail to follow them through with any great commitment or even renege on them. This is not necessarily a matter of bad faith but more a realisation of the difficulties governments face in implementing policies once the decision has been taken to introduce them.

Public policy and bureaucracy

The policy process consists of a set of arrangements under which the government sets out a framework of legislation that it wants to introduce and then implements a strategy to do so. Hill (2013: 7) compares this to going on a journey where one determines where one wants to go, works out the best way to get there, goes on the journey, and then reflects on that process for future reference. The government identifies its intended destination through its programme for government, particularly since coalition government became the norm in Ireland in the 1980s. Then the civil service, often in conjunction with advice from consultants, develops numerous and frequently extremely detailed plans of how any particular policy will work and what its impact on society will actually be. Various organised interested groups and individual citizens lobby, often vociferously, on the particular scheme in an effort to have it changed, enhanced or perhaps withdrawn altogether. The introduction and subsequent abolition of water charges in Ireland between 2013 (when the utility Irish Water was established) and 2016 (when charges were suspended) is a good example of the impact of such lobbying, whose targets are usually members of the Oireachtas and civil servants. Finally, the legislation goes for debate to the Dáil and the Seanad, where it is subject to amendment; the parliamentary debate is invariably influenced by the lobbying to which all Oireachtas members are subject.

Once the particular policy is passed into law, it goes onto the statute book. That, of course, is not the end of the matter as even then the law can very soon encounter public protest, which might lead to modification or complete retraction. Examples include the reversal of the automatic entitlement to a medical card for those over 70, which was announced in 2008, and the introduction of water charges in 2015, as outlined earlier. In both cases, significant changes were made to public policy after decisions had been reached in cabinet (in the first example) or by the Oireachtas (in the second). By the time the policy journey has been completed, the original shape of the intention could well be quite different from what ultimately transpired. This is because the journey has been affected by various interactions along the route with stakeholders, such as civil servants and lobby groups, who may have persuaded the government to change the envisaged route, to veer off course or perhaps to abandon it altogether.

The effectiveness of public policy in Ireland has been hampered by a number of weaknesses inherent in the political system. The Irish state and the various governments that have served it have long been hostages to the short-termism and localism that have plagued policy making since independence. Long-term planning has rarely been to the forefront of governmental or even civil service thinking when it comes to policy making, while localism and constituency nursing have almost always taken priority for governments. The lack of experts at almost all levels of government has also constrained effective policy making. In January 2010 the Minister for Finance, Brian Lenihan, revealed that only two economists in his department held PhDs.[1]

This lack of expertise was highlighted during the economic crash in 2008 and subsequently, when it emerged that the government and the civil service were ill-equipped to deal with the crisis. Once the Fianna Fáil-led government became aware, or at least more aware than previously, of the scale of the banking crisis in the autumn of 2008, it was compelled to rely almost entirely on consultants, receiving advice from the financial firm Merrill Lynch, for instance, up to and including the day of the bank guarantee scheme, on how to deal with the ramifications of the solvency issues of the banks and their implications for the Irish state. Relying on such advice, on the night of 29–30 September 2008 the government took perhaps the most dramatic public policy decision in the history of the state when it guaranteed the deposits, loans, obligations and liabilities of the six Irish banks, a total sum of over €440 billion, more than twice the country's gross national product at the time (Donovan and Murphy, 2013: 200). This decision was taken without the government or the civil service having complete information on the solvency difficulties the banks faced or on the consequences that this particular public policy decision would have for the state and its citizens.

Due to the sheer scale of the banking crisis and the difficulties it caused for Irish citizens, the government agreed in January 2010 to a framework of inquiry into the crisis and commissioned three reports for consideration by the Dáil. All were severely critical of public policy making in the Irish state. The first, by former IMF officials Klaus Regling and Max Watson, concluded that the banking meltdown was a result of domestic decisions, rather than the global economic crisis: 'Ireland's banking crisis bears the clear imprint of global influences, yet it was in crucial ways "home-made"' (Regling and Watson, 2010: 5). The then Governor of the Central Bank, Patrick Honohan, concluded that in its budgetary and macroeconomic policy, the government had relied to an unsustainable extent on the construction sector and other transient sources for revenue (Honohan, 2010: 6). In the third report, the former IMF economist Peter Nyberg found that the main reason for the crisis was 'the unhindered expansion of Ireland's property bubble', the attendant risks of which 'went undetected or were at least seriously misjudged by the authorities whose actions and warnings were modest and insufficient' (Nyberg, 2011: 91). These reports are damning indictments, portraying the policy-making process as complacent, haphazard and at times downright wrong.

There is a large comparative literature on the public policy process (Dodds, 2013; Hill, 2013; Howlett and Ramesh, 2003). One useful way of examining public policy is through the *bureaucratic* model. This model suggests that public policy is determined by a combination of civil servants and politicians, with the civil servant leading the minister though the maze of the policy process to the decision that the official thinks most appropriate for the state. In this model, the permanent civil service knows best, guiding, with a relatively invisible hand, transient ministers and governments through their tenures in office, ensuring that the state is not traumatised by profligate politicians wishing to make their mark through extravagant spending from the public purse. While some ministers are more powerful and demanding of civil servants than others, in this view the permanent civil service ensures continuity and stability in public policy over time. The public can then rest safe in the knowledge that political expediency can never become the raison d'être of policy making: the civil service builds up enduring and secure relationships with the major economic interest groups, trade unions and business organisations in particular, and these outlast individual governments, thus ensuring a certain continuity in public policy. As long as relatively centrist parties are returned to power at general elections, the relationships between government, the bureaucracy and the relevant sectional interest groups should be mostly harmonious and public policy, especially in respect of the economy, should be fairly predictable.

The reality, of course, is somewhat different. When Charlie McCreevy was Minister for Finance between 1997 and 2004 he adopted an 'if I have it I spend it' approach to the public finances, with ultimately disastrous results (Lee and McConnell, 2016: 109; Murphy, 2016a: 104–5). While the civil service might wish to adopt a long-term approach to policy making and the public good, governments in Ireland have almost always been short-term in their thinking. Ministers sometimes simply ignore the advice of civil servants. In one famous instance, the Beef Tribunal in the mid-1990s found that Albert Reynolds, as Minister for Industry and Commerce, was legally entitled to make all the decisions he had done in relation to export credit insurance, which benefited the businessman Larry Goodman, and had done so in good faith. The tribunal found that Goodman, Ireland's largest beef exporter, had fairly ready access to members of the government for the purpose of discussing his plans for the development of his companies and his exports (Collins and O'Raghallaigh, 1995: 706). The result was a policy whereby Reynolds continually increased export credit insurance, using his discretionary ministerial powers, systematically overruling the advice of his senior civil servants (O'Toole, 1995: 79–85). The final cost to the Irish taxpayer was a loss of €83 million (Byrne, 2012: 125).

Over a decade later, during the economic boom, the very few contrarian voices in the civil service, external bodies and the media to suggest that the state was inevitably heading for an extremely hard landing once the property bubble burst were routinely ignored. One former Minister for Finance, Ray MacSharry, subsequently maintained that the culture of the time seemed to be to spend the revenue without giving a second thought as to whether the same level of revenue would be available the following year. As MacSharry recounted it, McCreevy in one conversation said to him '"I have two billion of a surplus. Do you think I should leave that there?" I replied "yes I do" but he just laughed at me' (MacSharry, 2014: 105–6).

With the collapse in the Irish economy in late 2008, the Taoiseach, Brian Cowen, admitted that, with the benefit of hindsight, certain policy errors had been made during the boom years and these had deepened the crisis. He insisted, however, that all policy decisions had been based on the best advice available at the time. On one level, this seems to preclude or deny a role for politics in political decision making and reduces Irish politics to a contest over who can best manage the economy (Barry, 2010: 28). On another level it seems to absolve the political class and the governments of which Cowen was first a senior figure and later leader to the role of passive participant in the policy process, taking advice and following it slavishly without any consideration of its political consequences. Within the civil service, there were very few voices of caution, and those that did raise concerns, such as Marie Mackle, a relatively junior official in the Department of Finance, were told to disregard their fears of a property crash in 2006 and to instead toe the consensus line that a crash could never happen. Mackle's superiors told her instead to issue positive statements on the state of the economy and the housing market.[2] In this we see a classic example of the bureaucratic model of policy making, where both senior civil servants and the political class agreed on a certain course of action and could not be dissuaded by any contrarian voices, whether more junior civil servants or former members of the political class.

Public policy and interest groups

Defining an interest group

The second approach to policy making revolves around interest groups, which can be divided into two broad categories. The first consists of those groups that have a sectional base and represent large sections of society, such as trade unions, farmers, business organisations and self-regulating professional bodies, such as those for doctors and lawyers. The second comprises cause-centred groups, which lobby in support of various causes, such as questions of morality or the environment, for instance. These groups can be permanent or transient. Both sectional and cause-centred groups make inputs into the policy-making process across the political and bureaucratic spectrums and are clearly central to the whole process.

The study of interest group politics involves assessing the 'organisation, aggregation, articulation and intermediation of societal interests that seek to shape public policies' (Beyers *et al.*, 2008: 1103). Interest group activity in Ireland was associated in the public mind for many years with the process of social partnership, under which the major sectional groups played a central role in the economy between 1987 and 2009 (see below). While these groups were sidelined when social partnership came to an end in the midst of the financial crisis, they remain important players in public policy making. The various cause-centred groups have attempted to influence outcomes in specific areas, and in specific and sometimes diverging directions, across the full gamut of policy areas, including issues of morality, the environment, climate change, the health services, immigration, sport and Ireland's position on the international stage.

Understanding how interest groups work is crucial to knowing how modern democracies function. Defining an interest group remains problematic, yet necessary. One influential study (Beyers *et al.*, 2008: 1106) noted that the diverse terminology used to refer to such groups makes this a challenge: 'interest groups, political interest groups, interest associations, interest organisations, organised interests, pressure groups, specific interests, special interest groups, citizen groups, public interest groups, non-governmental organisations, social movement organisations, and civil society organisations' have all been used. As a formal definition, the decades-old view of Kimber and Richardson (1974: 1) remains useful: that an interest group 'may be regarded as any group which articulates demands that the political system or subsystem should make an authoritative allocation'. Adding the rider that such groups do not themselves seek to occupy positions of political authority enables us to distinguish interest groups from political parties (Murphy, 2010a: 564). While political parties of course try to influence public policy, their main focus is electoral politics and attempting to gain public office. A satisfactory definition of an interest group will stipulate two criteria: that the organisation has some autonomy from government, and that it tries to influence policy outcomes (Wilson, 1991: 8).

In Ireland, some groups have attempted to straddle the divide by putting forward their own members as candidates for election at both national and local level, with varying degrees of success, because of their perception that they have little chance of influencing the political process from the outside. Election to Dáil Éireann therefore becomes a sign of their importance as a mature and influential group with an important cause. Being inside the Oireachtas tent is often seen as a better way of influencing policy than being on the outside competing with other disaffected groups (Murphy, 2010a: 579). Once the position of the traditionally dominant parties was eroded in the elections of 2011 and 2016, the attraction of Dáil Éireann as a focal point for such groups increased exponentially. This is reflected in particular in the rise of independents as a major factor in Irish electoral politics (see Chapter 5), and it has ensured that candidates representing such organisations, such as hospital action groups and those disaffected with austerity, have an arena in which to air their grievances, beyond simply protesting to governments.

A further feature of policy making in Ireland in recent years has been the increasingly vigorous lobbying on behalf of business or private interests, in an attempt to influence specific government policy, as distinct from the sectional demands of the wider business community. This was a feature of evidence heard at the Flood/Mahon and Moriarty Tribunals of inquiry into land rezoning in County Dublin and payments to politicians that ran from 1997 until 2011 and 2012 respectively (Byrne, 2012: 143–91). Thus any discussion of interest groups now has to take into account private business interests as well as the cause-centred and sectional groups with which interest group study has traditionally been concerned.

The approach taken by interest groups is also shaped by the crucial questions of the opportunities for access through which influence may be exerted, and the expectations that interest groups have from their dealings with government. While politicians and civil servants have a responsibility to hear the concerns of interest groups and to allow them access to the machinery of government, it is also their responsibility to temper the expectations of such groups (Murphy, 2010b: 503). The main channels of access available to interest groups are the civil service, parliament, the courts, political parties, the mass media and various supranational bodies (Heywood, 2013: 304). Ultimately, the existence of interest groups places constraints on governments in that the 'process of governing societies always involves some accommodation of the wishes of pressure and interest groups' (Richardson, 1993: 11). But the centrality of interest groups to the political process is clear, as much of the process of governance can be seen as the management of the interface between governments and groups.

Models of interest group activity

When thinking about the role of interest groups in public policy, it can be useful to compare their behaviour with certain 'models'. While such models in their pure form may not exist in reality, they outline different possible situations with which any one country's actual position can be compared. These models are analytic, not prescriptive: proponents of a particular model of policy making argue that it is the model that best captures the reality of policy making, not that it represents the way in which policy making *should* take place. Using models of interest group behaviour helps us in determining how such groups operate within the political system. Within the decision-making subsystem, two models of interest group behaviour are particularly useful: corporatism and pluralism.

The *corporatist* model suggests that interest groups are closely associated with the formal political process and play a critical role in both the formulation and the implementation of major political decisions. Thus, large and powerful interest groups monopolise the representation of the interests of a particular functional section of the population, such as organised labour, farmers and employers. Moreover, these interest groups are organised in a hierarchical manner, typically with a powerful major or peak organisation at the top. In the Irish case, examples would include the Irish Congress of Trade Unions (ICTU), the Irish Business and Employers Confederation (IBEC) and the Irish Farmers' Association (IFA), co-ordinating strategy at the top of a pyramid of organisations. These organisations proceed to negotiate with each other and with government to produce an agreed outcome that both minimises social and economic disruption and provides stability for both government and the groups involved.

One of the main problems associated with corporatism as a concept, however, is that different scholars have used it in different ways, so there are multiple definitions. One scholar reckoned that 24 different working definitions of corporatism alone were used by various authors between 1981 and 1997 (Siaroff, 1999). For Siaroff, working from his review of these definitions, corporatism involved, 'within an advanced industrial society and democratic polity, the co-ordinated, co-operative and systematic management of the national economy by the state, centralised unions, and employers (these latter two co-operating directly in industry), presumably to the relative benefit of all three actors' (Siaroff, 1999: 177). Such a definition unjustifiably excludes the peak farming organisations. What sets corporatism fundamentally apart as a model of interest group activity is the stress it places on policy implementation. We should therefore include peak farming organisations if they are comprehensive in their representation of the particular sector of society they represent, and are able both to protect their members' interests and to control these members.

The *pluralist* model maintains that individual interest groups apply pressure on political elites in a competitive manner, and attributes power in policy making to individual groups operating in particular areas at particular times. The study of pluralism was heavily influenced by Dahl (1961), who argued that although the politically privileged and economically powerful exerted greater power than ordinary citizens, no ruling or political elite was able to dominate the political process. A key feature of politics was that the competition between parties at election time, and the ability of interest groups to articulate their views freely, established a reliable link between the government and the governed and created an effective channel of communication between the two. Thus, the level of accountability and popular responsiveness in place was sufficient for the political system to be regarded as democratic.

Competition, as it relates to interest groups, is usually disorganised, and its main essence is for various groups to succeed in influencing government while at the same time excluding other groups from the policy process. Schmitter's classic definition of pluralism states that it is

> a system of interest representation in which the constituent units are organized into an unspecified number of multiple, voluntary, competitive, non-hierarchically ordered and self-determined (as to type or scope of interest) categories which are not specifically licensed, recognized, subsidized, created or otherwise controlled in leadership selection or interest articulation by the state, and which do not exercise a monopoly of representational activity within their respective categories.
>
> (Schmitter, 1974: 96)

Unlike corporatism, pluralism offers no formal institutional role to interest groups in decision making or implementation of policy. Interest groups are assumed to be self-generating and voluntary. This allows government a critical role in mediating between groups that are competing with each other to represent the interests of the same classes of people in similar areas of economic and social activity. Indeed, group activity may be fragmented and group membership may only be a small proportion of the potential total. Moreover, groups in the same field of interest may be poorly co-ordinated by peak organisations, or not co-ordinated at all, resulting in the emergence of a pluralist rather than a corporatist model of behaviour.

In the pluralist model, better organised interest groups with more resources and more strategic social, economic and political positions than others can be relatively powerful influences on government. In theory, although not all groups have equal levels of power or resources, the fact that it is relatively easy to form a group should ensure at least some access to the levers of political power (Smith, 1990: 309). In a pluralist system, new groups can emerge and be accommodated within the system by adapting, by other groups adapting, and by the inherent openness of pluralist democracy. The key question to be answered, however, is what influence such groups can have. Most pluralists accept that the market in political influence is imperfect and contains actors with differing capacities to alter public policies. They also accept that under different governments, some groups can have more success than others. So, for instance, trade unions are more likely to be influential under governments of a social democratic persuasion than under governments of a Christian democratic or conservative hue. The situation is likely to be the opposite for business interests.

There is a third model that needs to be mentioned, which is that of policy networks. This approach examines interest groups not as free-standing entities but as members of wider networks (Cole and John, 1995: 90). With the proliferation of interest groups in recent years, policy making has taken on an increased complexity and the policy network approach is based upon the idea that decision making in liberal democracies is rarely limited to key actors in a single organisation but, rather, involves a whole range of actors across many bodies trying to seek agreement. In the Irish case, agricultural policy can be viewed as a network. The IFA has had an official input into government policy on agriculture since 1964, and the close relationship that it has with the Department of Agriculture allows privileged access to one sector of the community and, more importantly, can limit or restrict the access of outsiders. Moreover, while personnel within the network may change positions, they rarely move outside its rarefied confines. The result has been that Irish agricultural policy maintains a stable network capable of limiting the access granted to outsiders (Evans and Coen, 2003: 14). When it comes to farming, the Department of Agriculture and the IFA need each other to operate successfully and thus are mutually dependent. It is clear that the Department of Agriculture has long seen itself as a supporter of the farm sector as distinct from being a representative of all citizens, as a 2016 report into pesticides in crop management made clear.[3] While the agricultural policy network is significant, the centrality of governments in policy change remains clear, as such a change cannot happen without some governmental initiative (Greer, 2002: 471).

Interest groups in Ireland: a profile

Now that we have established what interest groups are and how they work in theory, we turn our attention to their form and function in Ireland. A casual look at the numbers of interest groups would suggest that they play an important role in Irish society and provide a vital outlet for the concerns of their members. Considering sectional groups, in 2016 there were 17 agricultural organisations, 24 educational organisations, 22 professional health organisations, six civil service associations, two different Garda (police) representative bodies, three defence force representative bodies, seven local government organisations, 45 trade unions affiliated to ICTU, four unions not affiliated to ICTU, and some 300 other trade and professional bodies that were organised to represent the interests of their members. Within these, there were a number of distinct business organisations, with IBEC, for instance, having over 21 separate sectoral associations affiliated to it (Institute of Public Administration, 2017: 168–70, 294–321).

As regards cause-centred groups, in 2016 there were 64 different arts and cultural organisations, 75 health support organisations, 18 Irish language organisations, 12 women's interest groups, 35 youth organisations and numerous other organisations espousing various social, political and cultural causes (Institute of Public Administration, 2017: 170–6, 332–49). We can categorise some of these organisations as occasional interest groups, in that, while their main function is not political, they often end up lobbying governments. Chief amongst these groups would be the Catholic Church, which lobbies on a range of issues, such as abortion, stem cell research and same-sex marriage; and various sporting organisations, which have had significant financial success in lobbying governments for funding in relation to both their day-to-day business and the redevelopment of various stadia throughout the country.

Sectional groups

In this section, we first assess the influence of sectional groups in relation to social partnership and economic policy making in general. We then examine the impact of a number of specific groups on the policy-making process.

Social partnership

Ireland has had a tradition of tripartite consultation in the public policy sphere since the early 1960s. It was during this era that the economic interests (farmers, trade unions and business associations) were invited to participate in the work of a number of national bodies that were concerned with formulating a new approach to economic management (Horgan, 1997: 228–49; Murphy, 2003a: 105–18). This approach – co-ordinated by the Taoiseach Seán Lemass and tripartite in nature – had the ultimate aim of entry to the European Economic Community in mind.

In the 1970s, the focus of state policy shifted; corporatist policies in the economic sphere were dropped and the process was no longer directly aided by government financial support (Hardiman, 1988). Notwithstanding this, the continuing high level of state intervention in the economy ensured an ongoing and important role for the Confederation of Irish Industry (McCann, 1993: 51). To a lesser degree, this was also the case with the trade unions and the farmers' organisations. While the sectional groups were not central to economic decision making, they were far from isolated voices in the wilderness. The trade union movement in particular in this period was seen by all governments as a type of expedient friend who could be brought into the charmed circle of power and then brusquely dismissed when circumstances changed (Murphy and Hogan, 2008: 596).

Circumstances certainly had changed by the time a minority Fianna Fáil government came to power in 1987. The deep depression in the mid-1980s saw the so-called 'social partners' (trade unions, business interests and the farming organisations), acting in the tripartite National Economic and Social Council (NESC), agree a strategy to overcome Ireland's dire economic situation. The *Strategy for Development* (NESC, 1986) formed the basis upon which, in 1987, the new Fianna Fáil government and the social partners negotiated the Programme for National Recovery. This was followed by six other agreements (see Box 11.1). What made these agreements different from those of the 1960s and 1970s was that they were not simply centralised wage mechanisms but agreements on a wide range of economic and social policies, such as tax reform and the evolution of welfare payments, with the Department of the Taoiseach responsible for the overall negotiation and implementation of these agreements.

The consensual approach associated with social partnership mirrored that of northern European social democracies such as Sweden, Norway and Denmark. In the decade from 1997 to 2007, the Irish state, whose whole economic policy-making structure was based around social partnership, experienced the kind of economic success that was previously associated with these Nordic countries. But this success did not last and social partnership was not able to prevent the collapse of the Irish economy in the wake of the global financial crisis of 2008; in fact, it became one of the victims of the crisis. Nevertheless, the Taoiseach, Brian Cowen, tried to renegotiate another social partnership agreement in early 2009 but, faced with a revolt from his Minister for Finance, Brian Lenihan, and indeed a majority of his Fianna Fáil parliamentary party, he changed course (Lee and McConnell, 2016: 159–60). The Cowen government pushed ahead with its national recovery plan even after the trade unions refused to accept a public sector pension levy and withdrew from talks designed to frame a co-ordinated response from all the social partners. This in effect ended social partnership, although Cowen rather curiously continued to declare that social partnership was alive and well.

The social partnership agreements had evolved considerably from 1987, when the first agreement was developed strictly as a means of responding to a grave fiscal crisis. They developed into a strategy for facilitating steady growth, and the inward investment that fuelled such growth, over a much longer time period than was originally expected, and this strategy was central to the successes of the Irish economy from the mid-1990s onwards. The fourth agreement, Partnership 2000, in an attempt to tackle social exclusion, even brought in a number of groups from the charity and development sector, although it is not clear how much weight the government and the sectional social partners attached to the contribution of these groups. Social partnership spawned a large and diverse academic literature, with one left-wing view being that it was simply a myth to sustain inequality in Ireland and to benefit the leadership of peak organisations to the detriment of the ordinary membership, particularly in trade unions (Allen, 2000). Another approach (Roche and Cradden, 2003: 80–7) suggested that it was best understood as a theory of competitive corporatism that prioritised the

---

Box 11.1 Social partnership and pay agreements in Ireland since 1987

A number of broadly tripartite agreements have been made between governments and the main economic interest groups since the mid-1980s, under the auspices of NESC (the National Economic and Social Council, an advisory body through which employers, trade unions, farmers and senior civil servants analyse policy issues). The first of these agreements represented a strategy to escape from the circle of economic stagnation, rising taxes, increasing debt and massive unemployment that surrounded the Irish economy in the mid-1980s. Its success paved the way for further agreements in the 1990s, and these agreements were widely seen as a major explanation for the rapid economic growth that Ireland enjoyed from 1994 to 2007 (the so-called 'Celtic Tiger' economy). The main agreements have been:

- Programme for National Recovery (PNR) 1987–90
- Programme for Economic and Social Progress (PESP) 1990–93
- Programme for Competitiveness and Work (PCW) 1994–96
- Partnership 2000 for Inclusion, Employment and Competitiveness 1997–2000
- Programme for Prosperity and Fairness (PPF) 2000–03
- Sustaining Progress 2003–05
- Towards 2016 (agreed in June 2006; in September 2008 a review and transitional agreement covering pay was agreed).

The last of these agreements effectively collapsed at the end of 2009, when the government imposed pay cuts of between 5 per cent and 8 per cent upon about 315,000 public servants in its budget.

The negotiation of each of these social partnership agreements was preceded by a NESC strategy report, which set out the shared perspective of the social partners on the achievements and limits of the previous programme and the parameters within which a new programme would be negotiated.

Once social partnership ended, the government enacted three specific pay deals with public sector trade unions in which they agreed that, in return for efficiencies in the public sector, and agreed reductions in pay in the 2013 agreement, there would be no compulsory redundancies.

- Croke Park Agreement (The Public Service Agreement 2010–14)
- Haddington Road Agreement (The Public Service Stability Agreement 2013–16*)
- Lansdowne Road Agreement (The Public Service Stability Agreement 2015–18*)

*These two agreements were reached before the previous agreement had run its full term.

---

enhancement of national competitiveness, having sustainable levels of public expenditure, reforming taxation and welfare systems, and upskilling the labour force. In that context the social partnership pacts of the 1990s can be seen as examples of competitive corporatism, which has also been termed 'supply side' or 'lean' corporatism. Ireland's social partnership experiment since 1987 was one of a number of similar agreements across the EU. Nine of the 15 members of the European Union at that time – Belgium, Finland, Germany, Greece,

Ireland, Italy, the Netherlands, Portugal and Spain – put in place social partnership pacts of this competitive neo-corporatist kind in the 1980s and 1990s.

When social partnership was brought to an end, temporarily at least, its advocates could claim that it had served Ireland well in the two decades between 1987 and 2007, but its death was little mourned, as it had failed to provide the state with an economic system that was sufficiently robust to successfully weather the global recession. If anything, two decades of social partnership had left the Irish state with a shortage of expertise when it came to dealing with the consequences of that recession. The unions called for extra spending, while the government's only solution seemed to be to cut public services and increase taxation, without any real idea of what the consequences would be for the state and its people.

The major sectional groups in action

While social partnership is over for the time being, the impact of interest groups on policy making remains. Crucial to their degree of success is the question of access. All interest groups, which pursue their aims and exercise their influence on policy through public or private channels, need access, direct or indirect, to the ultimate decision makers. Thus, the major sectional economic interests have representatives on the boards of state companies, on various advisory and review bodies, and at European level. They have adequate resources to carry out their own research and to analyse relevant decisions that might be taken at various levels. They have excellent access to the bureaucracy at both the national and international level and they lobby continuously. As an illustration, we will look at the main sectional interest groups: the IFA, ICTU and IBEC.

The IFA represents about 75,000 members and is organised into 945 branches country-wide and, in turn, 29 county executives. In a leadership election in March 2016, exactly 75,501 paid-up members of the association were eligible to vote.[4] It has over 3,000 elected voluntary officers who work with individual branches to ensure that local views are received by the leadership and that 'well thought out and democratically decided policy is pursued' (Greer, 2005: 55). For its members, the greatest benefit of the IFA is its strong representative voice on issues of concern to Irish farmers, both in Ireland and in Europe. The IFA spends nearly half of its income from farmers every year on its European lobbying efforts and claims that its influence in Europe is far greater than its numerical strength would indicate. This influence is achieved by maintaining a permanent office in Brussels manned by the IFA's director of European affairs who plays a vital role in promoting and defending Irish farmers' interests in Europe and acts as an effective communications link with EU decision makers. The IFA is also a member of COPA (the Committee of Agricultural Organisations), which is an organisation of farmers and their co-operatives within the European Union.

The structures put in place by organisations such as the IFA are of little benefit unless they can be used effectively to influence decision makers in the government, the EU and agri-business. Like similar farming organisations worldwide, the IFA seems to have retained its influence in the policy process despite the shrinking size of the agricultural sector. It does this through a variety of means. The IFA has both formal and informal links with Fianna Fáil and Fine Gael, at professional and voluntary levels. At local level, the IFA uses its voluntary officers and links with individual political parties, whether backbenchers or county councillors, to lobby on various issues, using these political representatives to try to secure its objectives.

The other main economic interest groups, the trade unions and the business organisations, have similar access to the decision-making process and employ lobbying techniques akin to those of the farming organisations. While the Irish trade union movement was substantially weakened during the early 1980s, as it was in Britain and the United States (Murphy and Hogan, 2008: 589–95), its re-emergence as a central player in the social partnership context after 1987 made it an intrinsic part of the fabric of public policy in Ireland. ICTU's main function is to co-ordinate the work of trade unions operating in Ireland both north and south, and to represent the interests of workers to government in respect of economic, employment, taxation and social protection issues. It is represented on government advisory bodies; it proposes and names representatives of labour for nomination to a number of such bodies. ICTU styles itself as the largest civil society organisation on the island of Ireland, and it is the central authority for the trade union movement in the Republic, with 98 per cent of trade union membership in the country affiliated to it.[5]

In early 2017, there were 44 unions affiliated to ICTU, a decline of eleven in a decade. Nearly three quarters of a million workers were enrolled in unions affiliated to ICTU: 527,048 in the Republic and 196,928 in Northern Ireland.[6] This is a decline of some 50,000 since 2008. It is also noteworthy that there has been a major decline in trade union density (the number of workers who are members of trade unions) since the mid-1990s. In 1994, union density was 46 per cent. By 2003, this had fallen to less than 38 per cent, and in 2014, it stood at just under 28 per cent, though that was still slightly ahead of the EU average of 23 per cent.[7] Decline in density has been common internationally during the last decade, with Ireland just one of a number of countries to see a marked drop. The average annual drop in density for OECD countries was 0.3 per cent per year between 1999 and 2012, while Ireland's was in the region of 0.7 per cent per year (Walsh, 2015: 86). While ICTU remains an enormously powerful body, its shrinking membership and density are clearly worrisome for it. It does, however, have a strong international voice, being the sole Irish affiliate of the European Trade Union Confederation, the representative body for trade unions at European level, and it is also affiliated to the International Trade Union Confederation.

The business community is represented through IBEC, which believes that industry's bargaining position is strengthened through representation of the widest range of members across the fullest range of issues in a single organisation. IBEC represents and provides economic, commercial, employee relations and social affairs services to its constituent companies and organisations from all sectors of economic and commercial activity, and is, in general, the umbrella body for Ireland's leading sectoral groups and associations. It reported a membership in 2017 of 7,500 firms consisting of both home-grown and multinational companies, big and small, spanning every sector of the economy, and employing over 70 per cent of the private sector workforce in Ireland.[8] This number has been relatively steady since 2008.

IBEC sees itself as the national voice of Irish business and employers. It attempts to shape policies and influence decision making in a way that develops and protects its members' interests, which it does by representing these interests to government, state agencies, trade unions, other national interest groups and the general public. IBEC is also active on the European level, working through its Brussels office, the Irish Business Bureau, on behalf of business and employers to try to ensure that European policy is compatible with IBEC's own objectives for the development of the Irish economy. These objectives are to create and sustain a competitive business environment that encourages enterprise and growth.

Despite the demise of social partnership, ICTU and IBEC remain important lobby groups in the Irish policy-making arena. Their access to the structure of decision making gives them powerful leverage in their attempts to protect their members' interests. While neither of them is currently involved with the government in terms of policy implementation, they remain major players in the interest group game.

Self-regulating professional bodies, such as the Irish Medical Organisation and the Law Society, which defend the interests of their predominantly middle-class members but are not strictly trade unions, constitute another important sectional grouping – one that has the ear of government. They can be just as important in thwarting proposed reforms as in lobbying in favour of specific pieces of legislation. For instance, the Bar Council of Ireland (representing barristers) and the Law Society of Ireland (representing solicitors) were both very worried in 2011 about plans by the newly-elected Fine Gael–Labour government to reform the legal profession through the Legal Services Regulation Bill. A key objective of this bill, a condition of Ireland's bailout programme by the Troika in 2010, was to lower legal costs. From the moment the Minister for Justice, Alan Shatter, published the bill in the autumn of 2011, both organisations began a vigorous lobbying campaign to oppose the legislation, as records obtained under Freedom of Information legislation later revealed.[9]

While the Bar Council had already expressed its concerns to Shatter, it was able to take its case directly to the Taoiseach, Enda Kenny, demonstrating its power of access. In a series of meetings with Kenny and other ministers between 2011 and 2015, these groups managed to persuade the government to water down the bill significantly. They both campaigned and lobbied against key parts of the legislation, and managed to secure major concessions when late amendments were made in advance of the final legislation going through the Oireachtas. Ken Murphy, director general of the Law Society, wrote to Mr Kenny in December 2011, to express 'very deep concerns' about the Bill:

> You also gave me very strong reassurance when I expressed the Society's fear that, despite the total absence of consultation in relation to the contents of the Bill in advance of its publication, that the fundamental policy of the Bill could not be changed. You said emphatically that any of the contents of the Bill could be changed.
>
> (*Irish Times*, 31 December 2015)

The ultimate result was that both the Bar Council and the Law Society secured major concessions. They retained important powers despite the creation of a new independent regulator and there was in effect no real reduction in legal fees.

Economic commentator Dan O'Brien bemoaned such influence, stating that the Fine Gael–Labour government of 2011–16, despite the enormous political capital that it had in the form of the biggest Dáil majority in the history of the state, had been far too timid in its dealing with powerful interest groups that had sought to prevent it from making changes that would benefit all citizens: 'From the legal profession to the health service, reforms that could have improved the functioning of the economy and saved taxpayers money have too often been shied away from' (*Irish Independent*, 28 January 2016). It is notable that the examples he cites, those of lawyers and doctors, are the two most powerful self-regulating bodies in the state, with easy access to the levers of power and policy making.

Cause-centred groups

Cause-centred groups have been significant players in the policy process since the late 1970s. They can be divided into two categories: ad hoc groups formed to press for a single measure, as has become common in the area of moral politics, for instance, and organisations with a permanent mission such as Greenpeace or the Simon Community. The activities and influence of such groups have become much more visible in recent years. Their tactics range from the simple lobbying of local and national politicians to actually putting up group members for election. We will now look at some examples of cause-centred groups in action.

The politics of morality: abortion

Groups formed with the aim of getting a single piece of legislation enacted have become quite vocal since the 1980s, particularly in the area of moral politics, with active involvement in the abortion and divorce referendums of the 1980s and 1990s. The trend extended into the twenty-first century, as the Protection of Life during Pregnancy Act of 2013 and the same-sex marriage referendum of 2015 show. In the referendums of the 1980s, the forces of moral conservatism had shown themselves to be the kingpins in modern interest group techniques and they were far more effective than those who sought to liberalise Irish society. By the time the second divorce referendum was held in 1995, however, those groups in favour of the amendment, such as the Divorce Action Group and the Right to Remarry Group, had also proved themselves to be efficient operators in the game of interest politics. By the middle of the second decade of the twenty-first century, interest groups that advocated repeal of the eighth amendment to the constitution, inserted in 1983 in the hope of preventing abortion from being legalised, had begun to mobilise in large numbers, as had proponents of the legalisation of same-sex marriage.

In the early 1980s, groups wishing to impose a distinctly Catholic view of morality on the state, principally the Society for the Protection of the Unborn Child, were able to persuade the Fine Gael–Labour government of the day to call a referendum in 1983 with the purpose of introducing an amendment that would guarantee the rights of the unborn child and constitutionally outlaw abortion (Girvin, 1986). They were supported in this by the main opposition party, Fianna Fáil. Two further abortion referendums took place in 1992 and 2002. This was because the 1983 referendum had the opposite effect to that anticipated by those who had advocated the amendment (and probably all those who voted for it) when, in delivering its judgment in the X case in 1992, the Supreme Court found that the risk of suicide provided grounds for having an abortion in Ireland within the meaning of the amendment (see Box 3.2). The 1992 referendums saw the right to information and the right to travel enshrined in the constitution, but the government's proposed solution to the X case was defeated. The Taoiseach, Bertie Ahern, was the main driver behind the referendum in March 2002, whose purpose was to attempt to remove the possibility of suicide by the mother as a justifiable basis for abortion (Murphy, 2003b: 16). That referendum was narrowly defeated, and the abortion controversy that had stalked Ireland for close to two decades seemed to have been settled, although rather uneasily. The eighth amendment and the X case judgment remained in place, an abortion was in effect practically impossible to obtain in Ireland, and moral politics, while always on the radar, no longer convulsed Irish society.

All this changed completely with the tragic death from a septic miscarriage of a woman named Savita Halappanavar in Galway in October 2012. Having asked for and been refused an abortion, she delivered a stillborn child and died herself some four days later.[10] Her death gave rise to a range of public protests. Pro-choice groups, and her husband, claimed that her death was a result of the eighth amendment and the lack of clarity concerning the limited circumstances in which abortion was legal and available in Ireland (Holland, 2013: 70). Pro-life groups, in contrast, claimed that the eighth amendment and the ban on abortion had nothing to do with the specifics of Ms Halappanavar's medical case. Her death led to a number of investigations, and both parliament and, eventually, government responded. In January 2013 the Oireachtas health committee, under the chairmanship of Jerry Buttimer (a Fine Gael TD), held a series of public sittings at which it heard from legal and medical practitioners, religious representatives and groups advocating both anti-abortion and pro-choice views. The aim of these hearings was to provide a mechanism to help frame the legislation for the restricted introduction of abortion, based on the Supreme Court's decision in the X case. The result was the introduction of the government's Protection of Life During Pregnancy Act of 2013, which came into effect on 1 January 2014 and defined the circumstances and processes by which abortion can be legally performed in Ireland, including through a risk of suicide of the mother. Inevitably, the bill was criticised by both sides of the Irish abortion debate: the pro-choice view was that it was too restrictive, and the pro-life view was that it was not restrictive enough. This did not by any means settle the issue of abortion, and after the Citizens' Assembly in April 2017 recommended a fresh referendum to remove the eighth amendment (see Chapter 9), groups on both sides began once again to mobilise more actively.

The politics of morality: same-sex marriage

While abortion had been an ongoing issue for some three decades, the question of same-sex marriage was very much a phenomenon of the second decade of the twenty-first century. In June 2012, the Labour leader and Tánaiste, Éamon Gilmore, had described the right of gay couples to marry as the 'civil rights issue of this generation' (Gilmore, 2016: 216). After the Constitutional Convention (see Chapter 3) voted in April 2013 that the constitution should be changed to allow for civil marriage for same-sex couples, the Fine Gael–Labour government quickly agreed a timetable for the referendum, which took place in May 2015. With cross-party support and a large civil society input, the Yes campaign to allow for same-sex marriage built a wide-ranging coalition that enthused large swathes of Irish society. On a turnout of close to 61 per cent, 62 per cent voted Yes (see Appendix 2h).

The same-sex marriage referendum campaign tells us much about interest groups and policy making. Interest groups such as the Gay and Lesbian Equality Network (GLEN), the Irish Council for Civil Liberties (ICCL) and Marriage Equality had been campaigning for some time on the issue. They put their case to the Constitutional Convention in April 2013, while the Irish Catholic Bishops' Conference, the Knights of Columbanus and the Evangelical Association of Ireland presented the opposite view. Once the Convention recommended that there be a referendum allowing for civil marriage, the groups in favour of this position joined together under an umbrella group called Yes Equality, whose aim was to get the government to call such a referendum (Healy *et al.*, 2016: 23–4).

While GLEN, the ICCL and Marriage Equality were the three main players in Yes Equality, in total it included some 35 groups, including the youth wings of a number of political parties and student unions in different universities and colleges (Healy *et al.*, 2016: 187). Strong support within the cabinet from Gilmore and from Justice Minister Alan Shatter (before he resigned in 2014) ensured a relatively smooth passage through government, and the referendum was ultimately held on 22 May 2015. A full three decades after Catholic lobby groups had persuaded a different Fine Gael–Labour government to hold a referendum inserting a ban on abortion into the constitution, a number of lobby groups espousing a different set of social values persuaded first the Constitutional Convention and then the government to hold a referendum to insert a clause allowing for same-sex civil marriage.

Despite the overwhelming political support for a Yes vote, a number of lobby groups opposed it with no little fervour. Principal amongst these was the Catholic Church, which had been an effective advocate for its stated position on various social issues in Irish society since independence. It now argued that same-sex marriage should remain unconstitutional and that marriage basically entailed a relationship between a man and a woman. The Yes campaign later admitted that it underestimated the extent to which, and the intensity with which, the Catholic Church leadership would involve itself in the No campaign (Healy *et al.*, 2016:

121). Despite falling mass attendance (see Chapter 2), the voice of the Catholic Church still held powerful sway in many parts of Ireland. Other groups campaigning against the proposal included the Iona Institute, which had long campaigned on a series of conservative causes, and a new group called Mothers and Fathers Matter. The latter was established to oppose the government's Children and Family Relationships bill of 2014, and then stayed in existence to become a mainstay of the No campaign.

Both sides spent large amounts of money on the campaign. The legislative regulations governing referendum campaign expenditure prescribe that all donations have to be from Irish citizens and no individual may donate more than €2,500. Yes Equality estimated that it spent about €800,000 on its campaign, all of it funded by individual donations, including on-line crowd funding efforts, with the average individual donation to the Yes Equality campaign being about €75.[11] The Iona Institute spent nearly €195,000 on its campaign.[12]

In the No campaign, we saw two types of cause-centred group in action. On the one hand there was the Catholic Church, which has a permanent lobbying function and involves itself in areas as diverse as education and abortion, and on the other there was Mothers and Fathers Matter, a group that was set up to oppose a specific piece of government legislation and a referendum campaign, and that left the political scene once the referendum campaign concluded.

Beyond morality

It is important to stress that cause-centred interest group activity in the policy process stretches well beyond the politics of morality. Environmental issues have long been associated with interest group politics and environmental interest groups range from those with a continuing mission, such as Greenpeace, to those that campaign on single issues. Ad hoc groups have sprung up at various times to oppose particular industrial initiatives on environmental grounds. These groups can be extremely potent; chronologically, they range from those who opposed the building of a nuclear power plant at Carnsore Point in Wexford in the late 1970s, to those who some four decades later oppose the building of incinerators across the country to generate energy from waste material. Environmental groups have been vocal on issues such as the rezoning of land, and motorway construction on or near historic national sites such as Carrickmines Castle and the Hill of Tara. Opposition to the building of the Corrib gas pipeline by the Shell oil company in County Mayo saw heated protests for over a decade in the 2000s. Although protest groups have put significant pressure on governments, for the most part they have been unsuccessful in their quest to change policy. Indeed, critics have claimed that far from being motivated by environmental issues their overriding raison d'être is the principle of 'not in my backyard', or 'nimbyism'. Some protests have been effective, though; for example, since Carnsore Point, the nuclear power debate has been completely off the political agenda.

The 2017 debate about a decision by the national planning authority, An Bord Pleanála, to give approval to EirGrid, the state-owned electric power transmission operator, to build a new North–South electricity interconnector shows that such issues remain pretty much perennial in Irish politics. EirGrid's proposal to construct almost 300 pylons in Meath, Cavan and Monaghan was objected to by around 200 landowners on health and environmental grounds, and their campaign received widespread local support. Those groups with a mission of indefinite duration have almost no institutionalised access to power due to the fact that for the most part they have been happy to distance themselves from the political establishment and indeed have established a type of counter-cultural appeal (Gallagher *et al.*, 2011: 468–9).

Environmental groups that campaign on single issues can best be seen as corresponding to the pluralist model in that they are competing against other groups – typically, business interests.

While we have examined moral-issue referendums in some detail, we should also note that referendums on European issues (see Chapter 14) have attracted a variety of interest groups, many of which get involved in such campaigns to highlight, and to lobby on, issues other than the ostensible topic of the referendum. For instance, the Lisbon Treaty campaign of 2008 became a melting pot of sorts for a range of lobby groups, particularly for those on the No side (Quinlan, 2009: 111–2). These included Cóir (an offshoot of Youth Defence, another anti-abortion group), the Peace and Neutrality Alliance and a new economic interest group Libertas, which used the occasion to advocate a specific neo-liberal vision of the European Union. It also attracted a number of hospital action groups who, while admitting that the treaty had nothing whatsoever to do with their primary concern, nevertheless used it to highlight what they saw as the downgrading of hospitals in their local communities. Interest groups, it appears, will use every type of available mechanism to advance their cause, even if a mechanism is completely irrelevant to their issue of primary concern.

Lobbying and the democratic process

Investigating political lobbying

The question of access to decision making is crucial to interest group politics. For many years, the issue was intertwined with financial donations to individual politicians as well as to political parties. Both Fianna Fáil and Fine Gael received substantial donations from business interests over a long period. In its second interim report of September 2002, the Flood Tribunal into planning in Dublin ruled that former minister Ray Burke (who at different times had held the Foreign Affairs, Justice, and Communications portfolios) had received corrupt payments from a succession of builders (see Box 11.2). It also concluded that Burke, during his time as Minister for Communications in the late 1980s, had made decisions that were not in the public interest after receiving payments from a private radio station's main backer, Oliver Barry (Tribunal of Inquiry, 2002: 65). Burke was eventually jailed for six months in January 2005, becoming the first former minister to be imprisoned on foot of investigations undertaken by a statutory tribunal of inquiry. He pleaded guilty to two counts of lodging false tax returns and later made a settlement of €600,000 with the Criminal Assets Bureau (Byrne, 2012: 172). The link between business contributions to political parties – and by extension to the political process – and favourable treatment for such business interests was palpably proven to Justice Flood's satisfaction.

However, in 2015, three years after it had issued its final report, the tribunal, now known as the Mahon Tribunal, apologised to Ray Burke and a number of businessmen for finding that they had hindered and obstructed its work and said that all such findings of hindrance and obstruction made against individuals in its second and third interim reports would be removed. Burke and others were then entitled to claim full legal costs for their appearances at the tribunal (*Irish Times*, 15 January 2015). The tribunal's decision to reverse its finding arose from a Supreme Court decision in July of 2014 concerning the way the allegations made by the tribunal's key witness, James Gogarty, against Burke and a number of other people had been handled (Murphy, 2016a: 86–7).

There was, for long, a view that Fianna Fáil, in particular, had an especially close relationship with property developers and the construction industry. This was most important in relation to local planning, where county councillors charged with deciding on land rezoning were

Box 11.2 Tribunals of inquiry

The Oireachtas has the power to establish tribunals of inquiry to investigate certain matters of public importance. The original legislation dates from 1921 and has been amended on a number of occasions, most recently 2004. The legislation is known collectively as the Tribunals of Inquiry (Evidence) Acts, 1921 to 2004.

Since 1991, the following tribunals have been established:

- *Hamilton Tribunal* into beef processing industry (hence also known as the 'Beef Tribunal') – established 1991, reported 1994.
- *Finlay Tribunal* into the Blood Transfusion Service Board – established 1996, reported 1996.
- *McCracken Tribunal* into payments to politicians (Dunnes Stores) – established 1997, reported 1997.
- *Moriarty Tribunal* into payments to politicians and related matters – established 1997, final report 2011, in two parts. Part one deals mostly with Charles Haughey. Part two is divided into two volumes. Volume One deals with various payments to Michael Lowry and related issues. Volume Two deals with the decision to award the state's second mobile phone licence to Esat Digifone.
- *Mahon Tribunal* (formerly known as the *Flood Tribunal*) into planning matters, including rezoning by Dublin authorities – established 1997, final report 2013, in five volumes.
- *Lindsay Tribunal* into HIV and hepatitis C infection of persons with haemophilia – established 1999, reported 2002.
- *Barr Tribunal* into the shooting of John Carthy in Abbeylara, County Longford on 20 April 2000 – established 2002, reported 2006.
- *Morris Tribunal* into activity of certain gardaí in the Donegal division – established 2002, final report 2008, in eight volumes.
- *Smithwick Tribunal* into suggestions that members of An Garda Síochána or other employees of the state colluded in the fatal shooting of RUC members on 20 March 1989 – established 2005, reported 2013.
- *Disclosures Tribunal* into the Garda whistleblower scandal, opened in February 2017.

continuously and vigorously lobbied by developers, especially from the late 1960s onwards. The influence that the construction industry had with Fianna Fáil was aptly symbolised by the Fianna Fáil tent at the Galway races annual festival every July. This venue, which dated from the early 1990s, was a Fianna Fáil fundraising initiative and served as a sort of annual gathering of some of Ireland's richest property developers and construction company owners, who got the opportunity to mingle with Fianna Fáil politicians. At the height of the boom the tent was reckoned to have raised €160,000 a year for the party, but it was terminated after a 15-year run by Brian Cowen just over two weeks after he became Taoiseach in 2008 (*Irish Times*, 23 May 2008).

The question of financial donations and influence gained particular salience from the difficulties that beset Bertie Ahern after the *Irish Times* revealed in September 2006 that, as Minister for Finance in 1993 and 1994, he had accepted payments of somewhere between

€50,000 and €100,000 from a variety of business people and that the matter was being investigated by the Mahon Tribunal. Ahern went on to win the 2007 general election but, under pressure from a number of quarters in the wake of some unconvincing performances in the tribunal, he resigned as Taoiseach in May 2008, stating that the effects of the tribunal had taken its toll on him, his party and those closest to him, and insisting that he had done nothing wrong. He was severely criticised in the final Mahon report of March 2012, which found that much of the explanation provided by him as to the source of the substantial funds that he had received was 'untrue' (Mahon, 2012: 1473). Importantly for Ahern and his defenders, the tribunal did not make a finding of corruption against him and he quickly and publicly stated that he had never received a corrupt payment in his life and had always told the truth to the tribunal. In any event, Fianna Fáil started preparing to expel him from the party, but he resigned his membership before that ignominy could be visited upon him. Former minister Pádraig Flynn faced similar difficulties: the tribunal found that he had wrongfully and corruptly sought a payment of £50,000 from a developer and then proceeded to utilise the money for his personal benefit (Mahon, 2012: 2458). Flynn also resigned from Fianna Fáil after moves to expel him were initiated.

The Moriarty Tribunal, which reported in 2011, 13 years and six months after it was established, produced a main finding that Michael Lowry, a Fine Gael minister between 1994 and 1996, had been the recipient of direct financial contributions from businessman Denis O'Brien (as indeed had Fine Gael itself). In turn, it said, O'Brien had benefited from a decision made by Lowry's Department of Transport, Energy and Communications, namely the awarding of the state's second mobile phone licence to O'Brien's company, Esat Digifone. The tribunal found that a 'cocktail of irregularities' within the evaluation process was complemented by the 'insidious and pervasive influence' of Lowry, who 'not only influenced, but delivered, the result' (Byrne, 2012: 165–6; Moriarty, 2011: 1050). The tribunal was excoriated by both O'Brien and Lowry, who rejected its findings as biased, selective and not substantiated by evidence or fact, and who furthermore implied that Justice Moriarty had 'gone rogue and become obsessed with destroying Ireland's international reputation' (Byrne, 2012: 167).

Ireland is clearly not a corrupt country by comparative standards, being ranked as the nineteenth cleanest country out of 176, and the tenth cleanest in the EU, in Transparency International's 2016 Corruption Perceptions Index, with a score of 73.[13] Ireland's lowest rank since the foundation of this index in 1995 was twenty-fifth in 2012, with a score of 69, which would seem clearly to have been a consequence of the Moriarty and Flood Tribunal reports. From the Hamilton report into the beef industry in 1994, through McCracken in 1997 and Moriarty in 2011 into payments to politicians, to Flood/Mahon into planning corruption in Dublin in 2012, these tribunals of inquiry have uncovered vast, secret and complex payments to politicians. Having heard copious amounts of evidence, the judges in each case rejected at least some of the evidence given by certain politicians but, crucially, did not find politicians to have acted corruptly. They did find that an insidious nexus of builders, developers and politicians was at work, and that this had led to an unhealthy interlinking of business, private and public interests in Ireland, but they did not find that this was necessarily corrupt (Murphy, 2016a: 101).

Such a situation even pertained to the former Taoiseach Charles J. Haughey, who was the subject of two tribunals: the McCracken Tribunal, concerning payments from the businessman Ben Dunne to Haughey and Michael Lowry, and the Moriarty Tribunal into payments to politicians. Between them, these tribunals managed to track down payments of some IR£9 million (around €11.4 million) to Haughey during his public career. The McCracken Tribunal concluded that 'there appear[ed] in fact to have been no political impropriety' on the part of Haughey (McCracken, 1997: 73). This was despite the fact that the tribunal castigated Haughey, stating that it was 'quite unbelievable' that he would not have known of the illegal off-shore Ansbacher accounts through which these payments were funnelled and that much of his evidence was 'unacceptable and untrue'. Moreover, it stated that no Taoiseach 'should be supported in his personal lifestyle by gifts made in secret to him' (McCracken, 1997: 52, 72–3). For its part, the Moriarty Tribunal was of the view that 'inescapable conclusions must be drawn that he [Haughey] received a wide range of substantial payments falling squarely within the tribunal's terms of reference, and that certain of the acts or decisions on his part while Taoiseach were referable to some of those payments' (Moriarty, 2006: 543).

There is no evidence that the tribunals of inquiry have had an impact on people's voting preferences. Michael Lowry has had spectacular success as an independent politician at every election since 1997, since he and Fine Gael parted company in that year following revelations about money he had secretly received from Ben Dunne (Girvin, 1999: 24–5), while Fianna Fáil's meltdown in the 2011 general election resulted primarily from its mismanagement of the economy and had little to do with any perceptions of political corruption.

Since the 1990s, and mainly as a result of revelations at tribunals of inquiry, the Irish state has put in place measures aimed at ensuring that its politics is clean. The Ethics in Public Office Act of 1995, and the Standards in Public Office Act of 2001 that established the Standards in Public Office Commission, along with later legislation pertaining to freedom of information (2014), the protection of whistleblowers (2014), and the regulation of lobbyists (2015) have all gone some way to providing a robust framework for cleaner politics.

The Ethics in Public Office Act, 1995, established the independent Public Offices Commission and committees on members' interests in both Dáil and Seanad. It provided for the disclosure of interests by parliamentarians and public servants and for investigation of possible non-compliance with the requirements of the legislation. The Standards in Public Office Act, 2001, established the Standards in Public Office Commission to replace, and assume all of the functions of, the Public Offices Commission. It introduced a requirement that elected members of both houses of the Oireachtas and appointees to senior office in the public service furnish evidence of tax compliance, and made provision for the publication of codes of conduct for ministers, ordinary members of both houses, and public servants.[14] The Freedom of Information Act, 2014, building on legislation passed in 1997 and 2003, gave citizens a legal right to access official records held by government departments or other public bodies, as defined by the act. It also entitled each person to have official information relating to themselves amended where it is incomplete, incorrect or misleading and to be given reasons for decisions taken by public bodies that affect them.[15] The Protected Disclosures Act, 2014, provided a robust statutory framework within which workers can raise concerns regarding potential wrongdoing that has come to their attention in the workplace, offering protection if they are penalised by their employer or suffer other loss for doing this. The 2014 Act addressed the recommendation contained in the final report of the Mahon Tribunal for the introduction of pan-sectoral rather than piecemeal whistleblower protection legislation. The legislation pays particular attention to seeking as much as possible to protect the identity of a whistleblower, noting that the disclosure rather than the whistleblower should be the focus of attention.[16]

Regulating political lobbying

Regulating lobbying had been on the political agenda since 1999, and at various times Labour, the Progressive Democrats, the Green Party, Fianna Fáil and Fine Gael all expressed support for the idea. It was specifically mentioned in the Fianna Fáil–Green revised programme for government in 2009, and the Fine Gael–Labour coalition government promised to legislate for it in its 2011 programme for government, and ultimately did so some four years later (McGrath, 2011; Murphy *et al.*, 2011). The Regulation of Lobbying Act was signed into law in March 2015. It provides for a web-based Register of Lobbying to make information available to the public on 'the identity of those communicating with designated public officials on specific policy, legislative matters or prospective decisions.'[17] In broad terms, it is designed to provide information to the public about 'who is lobbying whom about what'.[18]

This legislation was a response to the growth of the lobbying industry in Ireland. Given the complexities of policy making and governance in Ireland, many groups, both sectional and cause-centred, professional bodies, businesses, and indeed private individuals have begun to hire lobbyists to lobby government on their behalf. Most lobbyists now working in Ireland have long experience of how the political and administrative system works; they include former government press secretaries, former officials of all the major parties, some ex-TDs and a host of former journalists. In general, lobbyists claim that they are simply providing advice and access to the decision-making process for business people or groups who are ignorant of the public policy process and need specialists to introduce them to the complex workings of government. Given the increasing prevalence of such lobbyists, the view of many transparency advocates internationally is that governments need to regulate lobbying to ensure that decision making is free from corrupt influence. The best way to do that is to provide a statutory register.

The Irish legislation covers practically the full spectrum of the lobbying industry. It has clear definitions of what lobbying (including grass-roots lobbying) involves, and of which policy makers and what policy issues are involved (Murphy, 2017: 203). The register is freely available on the internet, and it is easy for lobbyists to use as they may file their returns electronically. The act makes clear what information lobbyists must disclose, with delayed publication of information in specified circumstances only. Crucially, the establishment of an Office of Lobbying Regulation within the Standards of Public Office Commission, which is independent of both government and industry, would suggest that the Act will be thoroughly enforced.

The fact that the head of lobbying regulation has expressly delineated functions and responsibilities is designed to ensure that there is clear separation between regulators and lobbyists. This will be helped by the fact that there will be regular reviews of the system, reporting by both the head of lobbying regulation and the Minister for Public Expenditure and Reform, and significant penalties for not registering with the regulator and providing the necessary information. In its first year of operation there were over 1,100 registrants and close to 1,500 returns by lobbyists. The register is searchable and provides information on who the lobbyist was, what areas were covered in their lobbying activities, whom they lobbied and, perhaps most crucially of all, what the intended outcome of their lobbying initiative was. All this is radically new in the Irish context. The lobbying register clearly provides citizens with far more information on the lobbying process than ever before – an important step in the promotion of open and transparent policy making.

Across the globe, lobbying regulations usually include a 'cooling off period', whereby those who serve as politicians, advisors or civil servants cannot become lobbyists immediately after they have left public office (Chari *et al.*, 2010: 106–8). This is a necessary part of retaining citizens' trust in public life and ensuring that parliaments are not seen as cosy cartels for political insiders. These periods can range from one year to five years. The Irish act has gone for the most limited type of cooling-off period: former public officials may not lobby their former colleagues (either in the public body where the new lobbyist once worked, or in whatever public body their former colleagues have since moved on to) for one year. This poses the question as to whether restrictions should apply across all lobbying activities rather than simply in the specific area of the person's former public employment. It also raises questions about the privileges some people receive by virtue of their former public employment, whether as TD or adviser, such as an access pass to the Oireachtas, which brings with it the opportunity to meet with politicians on a daily basis. In any event, Ireland joins an increasing number of countries that have introduced lobbying regulation in the past two decades as part of their armoury to ensure openness, transparency and accountability in public life.[19]

Conclusion

We asked at the beginning of this chapter who makes policy and how they make it. We have seen that while interest groups are a central part of the policy-making process, governments ultimately make the final decisions. This is even the case in corporatist states, as governments make the decision as to who actually gets inside the corporatist tent to implement policy. Interest groups pursue their goals through a number of different channels, including public and private pressure on government, individual politicians, and other interest groups, along with use of the mass media. It is clear that the Oireachtas and its members remain the centre of attention for those attempting to influence public policy in Ireland; parliament is the centre for information, access and publicity for such groups. TDs have access to insider information, can generate publicity, may be able to influence the state bureaucracy, and are in a position to put pressure on governments and individual ministers by tabling parliamentary questions.

Having access to the governmental tent and being able to use it effectively is an important part of influencing policy in Ireland. Given that lobbying is now subject to public scrutiny through the register of lobbying website, where citizens can freely search for information on who is lobbying whom about what, the nature of policy making in Ireland has become more transparent and open. Governments are ultimately accountable to electorates and have to take responsibility for the decisions they make. They might make these decisions in conjunction with, or having consulted, both the civil service and a variety of interest groups. They might even blame the bureaucracy or lobby groups when things go wrong. But at the end of the day, policy making cannot happen without governments making decisions. The end process is often long and tortuous and involves enormous numbers of stakeholders. In that context, while policy making in Ireland is quite complex, the simple reality is that government remains at the centre of the process.

Notes

1   www.irisheconomy.ie/index.php/2010/01/29/economics-expertise-in-the-irish-government/
2   *Irish Times*, 4 July 2014, at www.irishtimes.com/business/economy/new-finance-chief-told-official-to-disregard-property-crash-fears-1.1854609 (last accessed 28 April 2017).
3   *Irish Examiner*, 27 February 2017, at www.irishexaminer.com/viewpoints/ourview/is-weedkiller-a-cancer-threat-443877.html (last accessed 28 April 2017)
4   www.agriland.ie/farming-news/ifa-membership/
5   www.ictu.ie/about/.
6   www.ictu.ie/about/affiliates.html
7   www.worker-participation.eu/National-Industrial-Relations/Across-Europe/Trade-Unions2
8   www.ibec.ie
9   *Irish Times*, 31 December 2015, at www.irishtimes.com/business/economy/lawyer-bodies-lobbied-taoiseach-on-bill-reforms-1.2480630

10 www.rte.ie/news/special-reports/2013/0418/382308-timeline-savita-halappanavar/
11 Correspondence from Noel Whelan of Yes Equality to the author, 15 March 2017.
12 fora.ie/iona-institute-marriage-ireland-2853811-Jun2016/
13 www.transparency.org/news/feature/corruption_perceptions_index_2016#table
14 www.sipo.gov.ie/en/about-us/legislation/
15 foi.gov.ie/faqs/what-is-foi/
16 www.per.gov.ie/en/protected-disclosures-i-e-whistleblowing/
17 www.sipo.gov.ie/Website/en/About-Us/Registration-of-Lobbying/
18 www.lobbying.ie/
19 The United States in 1946 became the first country to introduce lobbying regulation covering its federal government. It was followed by Germany (1951), Canada (1989), the European Parliament (1996), Poland (2005), Hungary (2006), Israel (2008), France (2009), Mexico (2010), Slovenia (2010), Austria (2012), Italy (2012), Netherlands (2012), Chile (2014) and Great Britain (2014). Australia introduced rules in 1983, abandoned them in 1996, and reintroduced them again in 2008.

References and further reading

Allen, Kieran, 2000. *The Celtic Tiger: The Myth of Social Partnership in Ireland*. Manchester: Manchester University Press.

Barry, Frank, 2010. 'Politics and economic policy making in Ireland', in John Hogan, Paul F. Donnelly and Brendan O'Rourke (eds), *Irish Business and Society: Governing, Participating and Transforming in the Twenty-First Century*. Dublin: Gill and Macmillan, pp. 28–43

Beyers, Jan, Rainer Eising and William Maloney, 2008. 'Researching interest group politics in Europe and elsewhere: much we study, little we know?', *West European Politics* 31:6, pp. 1103–28.

Byrne, Elaine, 2012. *Political Corruption in Ireland 1922–2010: A Crooked Harp?* Manchester: Manchester University Press.

Chari, Raj, Gary Murphy and John Hogan, 2010. *Regulating Lobbyists: A Global Comparison*. Manchester: Manchester University Press.

Cole, Alistair and Peter John, 1995. 'Local policy networks in France and Britain: policy co-ordination in fragmented political sub-systems', *West European Politics* 18:4, pp. 89–109.

Collins, Neil and Colm O'Raghallaigh, 1995. 'Political sleaze in the Republic of Ireland', *Parliamentary Affairs* 48:4, pp. 697–710.

Dahl, R.A., 1961. *Who Governs? Democracy and Power in an American City*. New Haven, CT: Yale University Press.

Dodds, Anneliese, 2013. *Comparative Public Policy*. Basingstoke: Palgrave.

Donovan, Donal and Antoin E. Murphy, 2013. *The Fall of the Celtic Tiger: Ireland and the Euro Debt Crisis*. Oxford: Oxford University Press.

Evans, Mark and Liam Coen, 2003. 'Elitism and agri-environmental policy in Ireland', in Maura Adshead and Michelle Millar (eds), *Public Administration and Public Policy in Ireland: Theory and Methods*. London: Routledge, pp. 1–19.

Gallagher, Michael, Michael Laver and Peter Mair, 2011. *Representative Government in Modern Europe: Institutions, Parties and Governments*, 5th ed. Maidenhead: McGraw-Hill.

Gilmore, Éamon, 2016. *Inside the Room: The Untold Story of Ireland's Crisis Government*. Dublin: Merrion Press.

Girvin, Brian, 1986. 'Social change and moral politics: the Irish constitutional referendum 1983', *Political Studies* 34:1, pp. 61–81.

Girvin, Brian, 1999. 'Political competition, 1992–1997', in Michael Marsh and Paul Mitchell (eds), *How Ireland Voted 1997*. Boulder, CO: Westview Press and PSAI Press, pp. 3–28.

Greer, Alan, 2002. 'Policy networks and policy change in organic agriculture: a comparative analysis of the UK and Ireland', *Public Administration* 80:3, pp. 453–73.

Greer, Alan, 2005. 'Farm interest groups in Ireland: adaptation, partnership and resilience', in Darren Halpin (ed.), *Surviving Global Change? Agricultural Interest Groups in Comparative Perspective*. Aldershot: Ashgate, pp. 51–70.

Hardiman, Niamh, 1988. *Pay, Politics and Economic Performance in Ireland 1970–1987*. Oxford: Clarendon Press.

Healy, Gráinne, Brian Sheehan and Noel Whelan, 2016. *Ireland Says Yes: The Inside Story of How the Vote for Marriage Equality Was Won*. Dublin: Merrion Press.

Heywood, Andrew, 2013. *Politics*, 4th ed. Basingstoke: Palgrave.

Hill, Michael, 2013. *The Public Policy Process*, 6th ed. Harlow: Pearson.

Holland, Kitty, 2013. *Savita: The Tragedy That Shook a Nation*. Dublin: Transworld Ireland.

Honohan, Patrick, 2010. *The Irish Banking Crisis: Regulatory and Financial Stability Policy 2003–2008*, available at http://www.bankinginquiry.gov.ie/

Horgan, John, 1997. *Seán Lemass: The Enigmatic Patriot*. Dublin: Gill and Macmillan.

Howlett, Michael and M. Ramesh, 2003. *Studying Public Policy: Policy Cycles and Policy Subsystems*. Oxford: Oxford University Press.

Institute of Public Administration, 2017. *Ireland – A Directory 2017*. Dublin: Institute of Public Administration.

Kimber, Richard and Jeremy J. Richardson (eds), 1974. *Pressure Groups in Britain*. London: Dent and Co.

Lee, John and Daniel McConnell, 2016. *Hell at the Gates: The Inside Story of Ireland's Financial Downfall*. Cork: Mercier Press.

McCann, Dermot, 1993. 'Business power and collective action: the state and the Confederation of Irish Industry 1970–1990', *Irish Political Studies* 8, pp. 37–53.

McCracken, Mr Justice Brian, 1997. *Report of the Tribunal of Inquiry (Dunnes payments)*. Dublin: Stationery Office.

McGrath, Conor, 2011. 'Lobbying in Ireland: a reform agenda', *Journal of Public Affairs* 11:2, pp. 127–34.

MacSharry, Ray, 2014. 'The poisoned chalice', in Brian Murphy, Mary O'Rourke and Noel Whelan (eds), *Brian Lenihan: In Calm and Crisis*. Dublin: Merrion, pp. 102–14.

Mahon, Mr. Justice Alan, 2012. *The Final Report of the Tribunal of Inquiry into Certain Planning Matters and Payments*. Dublin: Stationery Office.

Moriarty, Mr Justice Michael, 2006, 2011. *The Moriarty Tribunal Report. Report of the Tribunal of Inquiry into Payments to Politicians and Related Matters, Parts 1 and 2*. Dublin: Stationery Office.

Murphy, Gary, 2003a. 'Towards a corporate state? Seán Lemass and the realignment of interest groups in the policy process 1948–1964', *Administration* 51:1–2, pp. 105–18.

Murphy, Gary, 2003b. 'The background to the election', in Michael Gallagher, Michael Marsh and Paul Mitchell (eds), *How Ireland Voted 2002*. Basingstoke: Palgrave Macmillan, pp. 1–20.

Murphy, Gary, 2010a. 'Influencing political decision-making: interest groups and elections in independent Ireland', *Irish Political Studies* 25:4, pp. 563–80.

Murphy, Gary, 2010b. 'Access and expectation: interest groups in Ireland' in John Hogan, Paul F. Donnelly and Brendan O'Rourke (eds), *Irish Business and Society: Governing, Participating and Transforming in the Twenty-First Century*. Dublin: Gill and Macmillan, pp. 489–504.

Murphy, Gary, 2016a. *Electoral Competition in Ireland since 1987: The Politics of Triumph and Despair*. Manchester: Manchester University Press.

Murphy, Gary, 2016b. 'The background to the election', in Michael Gallagher and Michael Marsh (eds), *How Ireland Voted 2016: The Election That Nobody Won*. Basingstoke: Palgrave Macmillan, pp. 1–26.

Murphy, Gary, 2017. 'Ireland', in Alberto Bitonti and Phil Harris (eds), *Lobbying in Europe: Public Affairs and the Lobbying Industry in 28 EU Countries*. Basingstoke: Palgrave, pp. 195–206.

Murphy, Gary and John Hogan, 2008. 'Fianna Fáil, the trade union movement and the politics of macroeconomic crises, 1970–82', *Irish Political Studies* 23:4, pp. 577–98.

Murphy, Gary, John Hogan and Raj Chari, 2011. 'Lobbying regulation in Ireland: some thoughts from the international evidence', *Journal of Public Affairs* 11:2, pp. 111–19.

NESC, 1986. *A Strategy for Development, 1986–1990*. Dublin: National Economic and Social Council, Report No. 83.

Nyberg, Peter, 2011. *Misjudging Risk: Causes of the Systemic Banking Crisis in Ireland*, available at http://www.bankinginquiry.gov.ie/

O'Malley, Eoin, 2011. *Contemporary Ireland*. Basingstoke: Palgrave.

O'Toole, Fintan, 1995. *Meanwhile Back at the Ranch: The Politics of Irish Beef*. London: Vintage.

Quinlan, Stephen, 2009. 'The Lisbon Treaty referendum 2008', *Irish Political Studies* 24:1, pp. 107–21.

Regling, Klaus and Max Watson, 2010. *A Preliminary Report on Ireland's Banking Crisis*, available at http://www.bankinginquiry.gov.ie/

Richardson, Jeremy J. (ed.), 1993. *Pressure Groups*. Oxford: Oxford University Press.

Roche, William K. and Terry Cradden, 2003. 'Neo-corporatism and social partnership', in Maura Adshead and Michelle Millar (eds), *Public Administration and Public Policy in Ireland: Theory and Methods*. London: Routledge, pp. 69–87.

Schmitter, Philippe C., 1974. 'Still the century of corporatism?', *Review of Politics* 36, pp. 85–131.

Siaroff, Alan, 1999. 'Corporatism in 24 industrial democracies: meaning and measurement', *European Journal of Political Research* 36:6, pp. 175–205.

Smith, Martin J., 1990. 'Pluralism, reformed pluralism and neopluralism: the role of pressure groups in policy making', *Political Studies* 38:2, pp. 302–22.

Tribunal of Inquiry, 2002. *The Second Interim Report of the Tribunal of Inquiry into Certain Planning Matters and Payments* [Flood Tribunal]. Dublin: Stationery Office.

Walsh, Frank, 2015. 'Union membership in Ireland since 2003', *Journal of the Statistical and Social Inquiry Society of Ireland* 44, pp. 86–100.

Wilson, Graham K., 1991. *Interest Groups*. Oxford: Basil Blackwell.

Websites

www.lobbying.ie
The register of lobbying.

www.bankinginquiry.gov.ie
The 2010–11 Commission of Investigation into the Banking Sector in Ireland.

https://inquiries.oireachtas.ie/banking
The 2016 Houses of the Oireachtas Committee of Inquiry into the Banking Crisis.

www.ictu.ie
Irish Congress of Trade Unions.

www.ibec.ie
Irish Business and Employers Confederation.

www.ifa.ie
Irish Farmers' Association.

12 The media and politics

Kevin Rafter

The media plays a central role in modern democracies and, in particular, the work of journalism can help democracy to thrive (Schudson, 2008: 26). This 'public service' contribution of journalism has been distilled in numerous sets of principles, which include the role of journalists in providing information to the public, undertaking a watchdog role in identifying wrongdoing and adhering to professional concepts such as objectivity, fairness and impartiality (McQuail, 2003; Kovach and Rosenstiel, 2007). Moreover, successful political communication strategies assist politicians to win public support for their arguments, and ultimately assist in securing power where policies can be implemented.

Few political strategies can, however, be delivered without some degree of engagement with the media. It is not possible for political leaders to meet individually, or even in smaller groupings, with all members of the public. It is thus necessary for information to be mediated to the wider public, notwithstanding the emergence of social media platforms, including Facebook, Twitter and Instagram, as new tools for communicating politics.

From politicians using social media to win arguments to the sizable audiences watching televised leaders' debates, the media today, therefore, has a pivotal place in a modern political system. But how successful the media is in fulfilling its role in assisting the democratic process is strongly contested. Indeed, what is understood by the term 'media' is also a source of considerable ongoing debate given the emergence of a host of new online outlets with distinctive ideological leanings and little attachment to traditional news coverage values.

The relationship between the media and the political system in Ireland has also not been without controversy. The practice of journalism has had political impact, stretching from the *Sunday Independent*'s 1948 exclusive on Ireland's declaration as a Republic to corruption allegations involving leading political figures, including former taoisigh Charles Haughey and Bertie Ahern, which involved several tribunals of inquiry sitting from 1997 to 2012.

In considering the relationship of the media and politics in an Irish context, this chapter starts by briefly examining some of the arguments about the media and democracy. This section is followed by an overview of the media sector in Ireland, including the regulatory arrangements that are in place. We then turn to the role of media in parliament, with a focus on political journalism and the government communication system. The next section examines the media and elections not just as regards coverage of campaigns but also concerning the issue of bias and balance in reporting and televised leaders' debates. The following section considers the impact of advances in communication technologies and new communication platforms on how the media and political systems interact, with a specific focus on the use of social media and the bypassing of traditional rules on political advertising.

Media and democracy

The media operates as a channel of communication between politicians and the public. In an idealised world the core task of the media in a democratic society could be briefly summarised as helping to create a better informed public in the hope that 'a more informed citizenry will produce a better and fuller democracy' (Schudson, 2008: 204). But the media – and the news media specifically – seek to do more than just provide information. Other scholars have expanded the functions of the media in an 'ideal-type' democratic society to include not just informing and educating citizens but also acting as a platform for public discourse, being a watchdog and operating as a channel for the advocacy of different political viewpoints (Deuze, 2005).

How well the media does in achieving these aspirations is a matter of some debate, given that media organisations also have wider objectives, including commercial pressures to deliver profits. Strömbäck (2005) attempted to set out in some detail the standard required of the news media. He argued that journalism is expected to carry out several functions, including engaging the public in the political process, framing politics as being inclusive and providing basic information on political processes and other relevant issues. Significantly, in terms of an activist role for the news media, he also argued that the media must actively foster political discussions that are characterised by impartiality, rationality, intellectual honesty and equality among the participants (Strömbäck, 2005: 340). The frequency with which this ideal outcome is achieved is debatable.

It has long been recognised that the media is not just a passive participant but that it can shape the public agenda by deciding what stories are covered (McCombs and Shaw, 1972). Writing in 1922, Walter Lippmann focused on the power of the media in shaping public opinion, which, he argued, was often based on 'the pictures in our heads' that were commonly incomplete and distorted (Lippmann, 1922: 3). More specifically, the media can influence audiences by means of what is known as 'framing', that is, ensuring that certain aspects of news events are selected and made more salient. Where other aspects of policy debates are neglected, or even ignored by the media, inappropriate and biased decisions may be made, and the quality of democracy is thereby damaged.

The idealised world of media activity, in which democracy is enhanced by means of open discourse that creates informed citizens, however, clashes with many shortcomings inherent in the media, and news journalism in particular. The pursuit of professional ideals can clash with the need to generate profit, which often means that commercial news media has to 'try to supply what the news audience will accept and what advertisers will pay for' (Gans, 2003: 21). Pressure to generate profits – and, where these are insufficient, to accept reductions in newsroom budgets – can thwart attempts to achieve the democratic ideals of journalism. It may be simply easier to attract audiences, and thereby secure advertising and protect financial bottom lines, with sensational headline-grabbing reports and 'soft' entertainment-orientated news.

Driven by commercial considerations to secure greater audiences, the media may pay less attention to important but ultimately dull debates on policy, which rarely generate dramatic headlines. Instead, coverage may focus on the 'game of politics' evident in reports on personality differences between election candidates and winners and losers from the latest opinion poll. Many empirical studies have focused on the process of elections – the game frame – which concentrates on personalities, opinion polls and electoral tactics, rather than coverage of policy matters. The influence of commercial pressures on media coverage is a prominent theme in this literature.

The commercialisation of news, and pressure to generate profit, are seen as factors in pushing media outlets to prefer 'game' – or what is also labelled 'horse-race' – coverage. This reduces funding for serious but costly journalism, and replaces investigative work with 'talking heads' and punditry, a form of reporting whose merits have been widely debated (Salgado and Strömbäck, 2011). This development is most pronounced in the United States, where one study estimated that stories incorporating journalistic opinions were as high as 82 per cent on Fox News (Cushion, 2012: 101).

Such considerations have led many critical voices to argue that media interest in politics is 'insufficient as things stand and may well be in decline' (Higgins, 2006: 26). Even more seriously, some argue that media negativity contributes to voter disengagement with the political process (Cappella and Jamieson Hall, 1997; Patterson, 1994). This tendency can lead to a 'spiral of cynicism', where people exposed to ongoing negative news and coverage dominated by the game frame become even more cynical about the political process. Moreover, politicians who see game stories getting more coverage are incentivised to emphasise activities involving games stories for the media (Cappella and Jamieson, 1997). There has been periodic debate in Ireland about media negativity, although without consensus about where responsibility actually rests. For example, when Pat Rabbitte was Minister for Communications in 2013 he criticised media coverage of politics for its 'all-pervasive negativity' and for refusal to 'give a damn' about the consequences of political coverage (McGee, 2013). The comments, however, led one newspaper columnist to label Rabbitte the 'Minister with Responsibility for Vicious Slagging' while arguing that the real threat to democracy came not from the media but from opportunistic politicians (Kerrigan, 2013).

The Irish media sector

Irish people consume a high volume of news – 84 per cent of people say they access some news every day, while 53 per cent say they access news several times a day (Broadcasting Authority of Ireland, 2016). The Irish media sector comprises broadcast, print and online entities, including national services from RTÉ, TG4 and TV3, but also global news sources from a variety of digital providers. Globalisation is a reality as international companies such as the BBC, Sky and Liberty Global are active participants in information provision to Irish audiences. Their presence is on a much greater scale than in the past, but it is worth noting that the Irish media sector has for long been marked by the activity of external media organisations.

The print media

All newspaper groups in the Irish market are privately owned commercial operators. While the *Irish Times* and the *Irish Independent* are the two biggest selling daily titles (see Table 12.1), leading British newspaper groups have a significant presence in the Irish market largely due to historical ties and close geographical proximity. Throughout the 1920s, leading British newspapers sold strongly in the Irish market. The combined Irish circulation of the *Daily Mail* and the *Daily Express* was 49,119 copies in 1926; five years later, in 1931, the comparable figure was 60,707 (Morash, 2010: 139). By way of contrast, the leading domestic national daily newspaper – the *Irish Independent* – had sales in the region of 90,000 at this time.

By the early 1990s, British newspapers still had high circulations in Ireland. In the Sunday market at the end of 1991, the combined sales of the *News of the World*, the *Sunday Mirror* and the *Sunday People* were in the region of 300,000 copies or 32 per cent of the entire Sunday newspaper market. Figures supplied in a parliamentary debate on the newspaper

Table 12.1 Select newspaper circulation, 1990–2016

Title	Jan–Dec 1990	Jan–Dec 1999	Jan–Jun 2009	Jan–Jun 2014	Jan–Jun 2015	Jan–Jun 2016
Irish Independent	152,000	166,000	152,204	112,383	109,524	102,537
Irish Times	94,000	113,000	114,488	80,332	76,194	72,011
Irish Examiner	57,000	61,000	50,346	35,026	33,198	30,964
Irish Daily Mail*	4,000	6,000	52,144	50,032	50,037	46,578
Irish Daily Mirror	60,000	62,000	64,194	50,263	43,250	38,294

* An Irish edition of the *Daily Mail* was introduced in 2006.

Source: Data for 2009–16 from News Brands Ireland (newsbrandsireland.ie); data for 1990 and 1999 from Barrett, 2000.

industry in May 1995 indicated that since 1975, sales of all British titles in Ireland had grown by 40 per cent (*Dáil Debates*, 143: 727, 16 May 1995).

Regardless of whether they are classified as 'Irish-owned' or as 'Irish editions of British newspapers', all the leading national daily and Sunday titles are dependent on commercial revenue (from copy sales and advertising), and none receives public funding. Like their counterparts in other countries, newspapers in Ireland have had to cope with rapid change as a consequence of loss of readers, advertising and business value. Circulation and advertising have been undermined by the industry-wide impact of the internet. The collapse in the Irish economy after 2008, and the wider international financial crisis, compounded an already difficult situation. Nevertheless, through programmes of aggressive cost cutting, some publishers have succeeded in maintaining profitability, albeit at lower levels than previously.

The broadcast media

For over half a century after the foundation of the Irish state in 1922, the broadcasting sector in Ireland was rooted in state ownership and operated in a monopoly environment. Since the first regular radio broadcasts took place in 1926, the new service met strong official resistance and was starved of resources. As Savage (1996: 5–6) put it, 'the Department of Finance … saw the radio station as a waste of scarce resources. Finance seemed to have nothing but contempt for Radio Éireann and adopted a hostile attitude toward the station that endured for many years'.

Until the mid-1950s, Radio Éireann was considered the mouthpiece of the government of the day, offering time for ministerial broadcasts but avoiding even mildly contentious political coverage. The first unscripted political discussion programme was broadcast in 1951; in the same year, a weekly commentary on parliamentary proceedings was introduced. The emergence of politicians onto the airwaves in Ireland was a slow process: only one member of the Oireachtas participated in radio programmes in 1954, five in 1956, three in 1957, five in 1958 and six in 1959 (Horgan, 2004: 17).

Debate about establishing an Irish television service commenced in the early 1950s. Public interest in the new medium increased, spurred on by demonstrations in local electrical shops and by a sales push from manufacturers. Across the border, BBC television arrived in Northern Ireland early in 1953 and reached some 80 per cent of homes there by the end of 1955. Due to transmission signal spillover, it was possible for some households in the Republic along the east coast and in border areas to receive British channels. A commission was established in 1957 to report on the merits of establishing an Irish television service, although there was ongoing resistance from the Department of Finance due to the perceived costs involved. Seán Lemass originally favoured allowing the private sector to own and operate the new service (Savage, 1996: 209). Following government debates about the appropriate ownership model, however, Telefís Éireann (now RTÉ) first broadcast on 31 December 1961 as a station in public ownership.

The arrival of domestic television challenged a long established deferential attitude to politicians in the Irish media generally. Significantly, the legislation that established the new television service moved broadcasting away from direct government control, allowing it some autonomy as a semi-state entity. Nevertheless, there was a distinct political establishment presence when the service went on air at the end of 1961. The opening night viewing included a broadcast from President Éamon de Valera and speeches from Taoiseach Seán Lemass, the Minister for Posts and Telegraphs, Michael Hilliard, and the Archbishop of Dublin, John Charles McQuaid. De Valera captured the concerns of many people – and not just those in Ireland – about the impact of the new medium: 'Like atomic energy it can be used for incalculable good but it can also do irreparable harm. Never before was there in the hands of men an instrument so powerful to influence the thoughts and actions of the multitude' (quoted in Savage, 1996: xi).

Uneasy moments between the incumbent Fianna Fáil government and the new television service followed, as politicians were held to account by the broadcast media in a way not experienced previously, given that the relationship had been largely defined by passive radio news coverage. For example, Charles Haughey, the Minister for Agriculture, sought in October 1966 to interfere with the content of a news report, and amid subsequent controversy he told the Dáil that 'when I give that advice with all the authority of my office as Minister … that advice should be respected by the national television network' (*Dáil Debates* 224: 1085, 12 October 1966). A decision to send staff to cover the Vietnam War, including reporting from communist North Vietnam, was cancelled in 1967 following government intervention (Savage, 2010: 108). The most contentious interaction between the broadcast service and the political system concerned the use of Section 31 of the Broadcasting Authority Act, 1960. From 1971 to 1994, this section effectively prevented RTÉ – which was in a monopoly position as the only domestic news service for most of this period – from directly presenting the political views of paramilitary organisations or their political associates, thus banning Sinn Féin from the airwaves (Horgan, 2002: 337).

The new domestic television channel gave politics an increased level of importance and, with their frequent television appearances, politicians and the small group of political journalists in Leinster House started to emerge for the first time as well-known personalities. During the 1960s, politicians were held to account by the media in a way not experienced previously. Reporting was less deferential and the perspective of journalists was increasingly called upon as analysis and comment were given greater prominence alongside news reporting of political developments. From the first general election covered by RTÉ in 1965 onwards, the relative importance of print and broadcast changed.

Television is now the most popular platform for accessing news in Ireland at 73 per cent, followed by online media (70 per cent). RTÉ has the greatest reach at 64 per cent, followed by Independent News and Media (publisher of the *Irish Independent* among other titles) at 44 per cent, the *Irish Times* 37 per cent, and breakingnews.ie 24 per cent. Just over half (52 per cent) of Irish people say they use social media platforms as a source of news each week. Nevertheless, traditional print media remains an extremely important source of political information for the Irish public. For example, Table 12.2 shows the newspapers that Irish people used for political information in 2011.

Table 12.2 Newspapers regularly used for political information, 2011

Title	Total %
Irish Independent	34
Irish Times	19
Sunday Independent	14
Irish Star	12
Local/Freesheets	11
Examiner	10
Sunday World	10
Sunday Times	8
Herald	7
Irish Sun	7
News of the World	4
Sunday Business Post	3
Other	13
None	17

Source: Based on Marsh *et al.*, 2017: 225.

RTÉ's monopoly on domestic broadcasting services remained in place for almost three decades after the advent of television in the early 1960s. A second RTÉ television channel (RTÉ Two) first broadcast in November 1978, while cable providers – forerunner of today's digital companies – offered viewers in many urban areas paid access to the main British channels. The audience for the latter stations was higher still when consideration is given to the households accessing non-RTÉ services due to 'signal overspill' and illegal transmission deflectors. Policy change across Europe in the 1980s ultimately ended public broadcasting monopolies, with the promotion of commercial privately owned broadcast media. The emergence of a dual broadcasting system in Ireland, which followed the enactment of legislation in 1989 to deregulate the television and radio markets, was, therefore, not unique.

The Irish broadcasting landscape now contains a mixture of public and private, commercial and community licenced services operating at national, regional and local levels. In its role as a public broadcaster, RTÉ faces domestic competition in the television market from a number of free-to-air operators, most notably TV3, which went on air in September 1998 as a single-channel service but now operates three separate channels and is owned by Liberty Global, the international media group. The Irish language station TG4, a publicly owned television service, commenced broadcasting in October 1996. These free-to-air Irish stations operate in a highly competitive television market where the majority of households subscribe to a digital or satellite service from providers such as Sky and Virgin Media, giving them access to a wide variety of non-Irish television stations. Despite these major market changes, RTÉ has retained a significant place in Ireland's television landscape. But, as shown in Table 12.3, viewership is undergoing considerable change, with audience fragmentation across a range of the niche channels and the increasing availability of a myriad of popular online and streaming options, including YouTube and Netflix.

Yet, despite audience fragmentation and increased viewer choice, news and current affairs programmes continue to attract high audiences. For example, RTÉ's nine o'clock news on 27 February 2016 – the evening of the Dáil election count – had 721,400 viewers and was the most watched news bulletin in 2016. Among the channels now available to Irish viewers is Oireachtas TV, which provides coverage of the Dáil, Seanad and Oireachtas committees to 1.1 million households on a variety of digital platforms, as well as live web streaming. This

Table 12.3 Television audience, share of total viewers, 2005–15

Channel	2005	2010	2015
RTÉ One	27.8	24.8	19.9
TV3	13.4	12.8	8.4
RTÉ Two	11.1	9.8	6.3
UTV	5.9	4.0	7.0*
BBC One	7.1	4.7	3.8
3e	–	1.1	2.8
TG4	3.2	2.2	1.8
Channel Four	4.4	2.9	1.5
BBC Two	4.0	2.7	1.5
Sky Sports News	–	0.6	1.0
All others	23.1	34.4	46.0

* Combined figure for UTV and UTV Ireland.

Source: Nielsen Market Research.

Note: All figures are percentages, and total 100 vertically.

Table 12.4 Radio listenership, share of adults, 2010–16

Channel	2010	2012	2014	2016
RTÉ Radio 1	22.7	22.8	21.5	23.6
RTÉ 2FM	8.2	7.2	6.5	6.0
RTÉ Lyric FM	1.7	1.6	1.9	2.0
Today FM	9.3	9.4	8.7	7.6
Newstalk	4.0	4.4	6.4	5.9
Any regional/local	53.6	54.1	54.3	54.6

Source: BAI (Ipsos MBRI).

Note: Adults are defined as those aged 15 or more. The time of the day covered was 7am to 7pm. All figures are percentages.

dedicated channel commenced operation in September 2014, some 26 years after television cameras were first allowed into the houses of the Oireachtas.

The Irish radio market is as competitive as its television counterpart, due to the large number of licenced stations at local, regional and national levels. RTÉ Radio One and the privately owned Newstalk are the main national talk-based radio stations, although Today FM – a music-based station which has the same owner as Newstalk (Communicorp) – has a talk-based current affairs programme in the evening drive-time slot. Some 83 percent of those over 15 years of age – almost three million people – listened every weekday to radio in 2016. Table 12.4 confirms the strength of local radio in Ireland; it now has a larger combined audience than its national counterparts (the RTÉ stations, Today FM and Newstalk).

Regulation of the media

Since the enactment of the Broadcasting Act, 2009, the regulatory remit of the Broadcasting Authority of Ireland (BAI) has extended to all broadcasters within the jurisdiction of the Republic, but not to broadcasters licenced in the United Kingdom and elsewhere, even if their programme content is available to Irish viewers. As regulator, the BAI has statutory oversight over the two public broadcasters, RTÉ and TG4, and monitors their adherence to agreed strategy commitments in respect of programming and other key targets. Moreover, as the licensing authority for private broadcasters, the BAI monitors compliance with the various programme content commitments in licence contracts. Public complaints related to radio and television programming are considered by BAI's Compliance Committee against a range of statutory broadcasting codes. The 2009 legislation specifically deals with news and current affairs coverage, including coverage of elections. All broadcasters, irrespective of their ownership status, are legally obliged to report and present news in an objective and impartial manner and without any expression of the broadcaster's own views.

While commercial television and radio stations survive on advertising revenues, RTÉ is funded by a combination of licence fee and commercial revenue. The national licence fee is currently 'top-sliced', with 93 per cent of the annual payment (€160 for each household with a television set) ring-fenced for RTÉ and TG4. The remaining 7 per cent is allocated by tender for individual public service type programming on all licenced stations, irrespective of their ownership profile. It is not possible, however, to finance news and current affairs programming from this 'top-sliced' fund.

A separate regulatory regime exists for the newspaper sector, covering its print and online content. The Press Council of Ireland was established in 2007 and oversees an independent system of press regulation. In the absence of the type of legal obligations governing broadcast companies, newspapers are free to determine their own editorial direction. There are different ownership arrangements in Ireland's newspaper market, ranging from privately owned to publicly quoted (stock market) companies, to trust structures; all, of course, are profit orientated.

There have been longstanding concerns about the dominant market position of some media groups, specifically Independent News and Media (INM) and, more recently, Communicorp. These concerns have primarily concentrated on the position of a dominant proprietor – first Tony O'Reilly (at INM) and more recently Denis O'Brien (at both groups). When O'Reilly expanded the range of titles in the Independent stable during the 1990s, Séamus Dooley of the National Union of Journalists suggested that the business now had excessive influence over public and, ultimately, political opinion (Hughes *et al.*, 2007: 424). A contrasting view, however, emerged from a study prepared by the independent think tank Tasc, which concluded that, 'despite this concentration, there is enough variety of outlets and voices in the Irish media to facilitate democratic debate' (Hughes *et al.*, 2007: 409). Moreover, the same study noted that editorial interference by owners 'with the publication of stories of public concern very rarely occurs' (Hughes *et al.*, 2007: 409).

The centre of power at the INM group shifted from O'Reilly to O'Brien, who invested some €500 million between 2006 and 2012 to become the largest individual shareholder. The war of words between the two sides saw O'Brien complain that he had been unfairly treated by the Independent titles: 'the hostile reaction to my shareholding in INM has been seamlessly executed through the editorial pages of all their publications' (O'Brien, 2011). Unlike O'Reilly, whose media interests in Ireland were primarily in the national and local newspaper sectors, O'Brien has built a formidable presence in the Irish broadcast market also. His company, Communicorp, owns Newstalk and Today FM, as well as music stations Spin and 98FM.

The emergence of cross-media ownership has reopened consideration of the role of the proprietor in privately owned media, and the relationship between control, commerce and public interest. Most attention has focused on O'Brien due to his 29.9 per cent stake in INM and as principal shareholder in Communicorp. A 2016 study commissioned by Sinn Féin MEP Lynn Boylan identified concentration of media ownership in Ireland as 'high risk', although O'Brien rejected this claim (Doughty Street Chambers and KRW Law, 2016; Doyle, 2016).

There has been occasional government and parliamentary interest in the workings of the media, particularly in respect of ownership, standards and the funding of public broadcasting. A tribunal of inquiry was established in 1969 to examine an RTÉ current affairs report on moneylending, although this level of political interest in editorial content is the exception rather than the norm (Horgan, 2001). The Broadcasting Act 2009 does allow for a formal investigation of programme content that causes public concern (for example, in the case of an RTÉ report in 2011 that contained false allegations about clerical child abuse).

Following the collapse in 1995 of the Press group of newspapers (set up in the early 1930s to give a voice to Fianna Fáil), a Commission on the Newspaper Industry was established. The Commission reported on ownership and issues related to privacy, press freedom and reader redress. Its main contribution was to feed into the debate that ultimately led to the establishment of the Press Council of Ireland (mentioned earlier). More recently, a parliamentary inquiry into the Irish banking collapse addressed the question as to whether media reporting impacted on, or contributed to, the economic crisis, a topic taken up previously in other reports and studies (Nyberg, 2011; Donovan and Murphy, 2013: 144–70). The inquiry heard from eight senior media executives who held either commercial or editorial positions in four media organisations during the economic boom and subsequent collapse. Overall, however, its final report only provided a cursory reference to the relationship between the property sector and the media, and said nothing about interactions between politicians and journalists (Rafter, 2017).

Media, parliament and government

Until near the end of the eighteenth century, journalists and printers faced the threat of imprisonment for reporting on parliamentary debates at Westminster. There were, however, regular breaches of the publication prohibition and, following a reform campaign, the secrecy rule on the reporting of debates was relaxed. Throughout the nineteenth century, 'papers of record', including *The Times* and the *Daily Telegraph*, reproduced lengthy verbatim accounts of parliamentary debates as well as political developments in Ireland, including Daniel O'Connell's failed attempt to repeal the Act of Union and more successful campaigns for land reform and home rule.

Newspapers were the medium by which politics was brought to the masses and the political class acknowledged the power of the press. Irish Nationalist Party leader Charles Stewart Parnell – not unlike his successors today – cultivated journalists. One political reporter recalled in his memoir that Parnell, 'was always civil and courteous to journalists. He frequently travelled in the same compartment with the reporters when going to or returning from a meeting in the country' (Dunlop, 1911: 30). Moreover, during the revolutionary period there was a close overlap between the Irish media and politicians. For example, Arthur Griffith is best known as the founder of Sinn Féin in 1905 and also as a signatory of the Anglo–Irish treaty. But Griffith primarily earned his living as a newspaper publisher and was described as 'an extraordinarily clever journalist' by Augustine Birrell, Chief Secretary for Ireland in 1916 (Laffan, 1999:16).

Notwithstanding the emergence of a host of new communication platforms, political reporters in Leinster House, like their counterparts at Westminster or in Washington, still work in close proximity to power and those who wield it. These specialist reporters have traditionally been viewed as belonging to a journalistic 'elite' (Nimmo and Combs, 1990: 226), but whether this status still prevails is a moot point. Ultimately, the overlapping relationship between the two professions is defined by interdependence (Davis, 2009; Ross, 2010). In the words of a longtime spokesperson for former British prime minister Margaret Thatcher: 'they need each other. Journalists need stories and politicians need to be written about' (Ingham, 1994: 549).

The work of journalists has had an impact on the political system in Ireland. One of the biggest journalistic 'scoops' in the history of the Irish media was published on 5 September 1948 when an exclusive story in the *Sunday Independent* revealed that Ireland was to leave the Commonwealth (Rafter, 2012). Under the front-page headline 'External Relations Act to Go', Hector Legge, the author of the story, wrote with some authority that with repeal of the legislation in question, Ireland would be formally declared a republic. This revelation not only embarrassed Taoiseach John A. Costello – then on his first trip abroad since the formation of his inter-party government seven months previously – but also caused the formal announcement to be mired in political controversy.

The relationship between journalists and politicians reached a particular nadir during Charles Haughey's tenure as Fianna Fáil leader (1979–1992), with continuous leaks from cabinet and revelations that illegal taps had been placed on the phones of some political correspondents perceived to be hostile to Haughey. The source of Haughey's lavish lifestyle had long been a source of media interest, but he had retired from public life by the time media reports linked him to payments from businessman Ben Dunne. This and subsequent revelations led to the establishment of two tribunals of inquiry (first McCracken, then Moriarty) and, in many respects, fuelled further media activity that produced other official investigations into political corruption in Ireland.

Irish journalists have marginally more trust in parliament than in politicians or government (Rafter and Dunne, 2016). A 2016 survey found that 52 per cent of journalists had some trust in politicians, but 40 per cent said they have little or none. The equivalent figures for government were 51 per cent and 38 per cent, and for parliament, 57 per cent and 27 per cent. By way of contrast, a majority of Irish people (61 per cent) agree that their national media provides trustworthy information, a level higher than in the EU (53 per cent; Eurobarometer 2016). For Irish people, the broadcast media is perceived to be a more reliable source of news (television 71 per cent; radio 77 per cent) than newspapers (print and online) at 60 per cent, and online platforms at 35 per cent.

The working relationship of journalist and politician is marked by both conflict and cooperation. As described by Schudson (2008: 14), 'the job of the media ... is to make powerful people tremble'. Politicians, however, do not always welcome this type of reportage, as their specific objective is to secure positive coverage. This journalist–politician nexus is thus marked by 'two sets of mutually dependent and mutually adaptive actors, pursuing divergent (though overlapping) purposes' (Blumler and Gurevitch, 1981: 479). The evidence bears out this conclusion. In a British study, Davis found that relations between politicians and journalists at Westminster could be defined as 'cautious co-operation that benefited both sides' (2009: 210). A similar study in New Zealand identified a complicated, and often contradictory, relationship marked by an acknowledgement of the need to maintain 'at least cordial relations' (Ross, 2010: 287).

The institutionalised nature of the 'political beat', with close working and social interactions between journalists and sources, is evident wherever national parliaments are located. Critics have labelled these relations a version of 'pack journalism' (see Crouse, 1972) or a form of 'embedded journalism' (Davis, 2009). The term 'pack journalism' was coined during the 1972 American presidential election campaign when Timothy Crouse witnessed reporters moving in packs, dining and eating together as well as sharing and comparing notes with other colleagues over extended time periods. The problem with 'pack' journalism is that reporters jointly covering an institution or a campaign feed off one another and reinforce their joint focus. Many of these traits are evident in the parliamentary press gallery in Dublin, where reporters spend their working day in Leinster House removed from their newsdesks and working with colleagues from rival media organisations. As well as the risk of self-censorship, an excessively close relationship between journalist and politician may result in the former being 'metamorphosed from an active and critical observer of political affairs into a passive purveyor of government messages' (Franklin, 2004: 87).

This situation becomes even more problematic in the context of the sophisticated, professional and well-resourced public relations machinery that has become a stable feature of contemporary politics. Such is the powerful role that the media plays in the triangular relationship between journalists, politicians and the public that it has been argued that politicians have adjusted their strategies to the needs and requirements of the media (Strömbäck and Kaid, 2008). Evidence for this 'media logic' is seen in the behaviour, strategies and tactics of politicians, and in the near-permanent involvement of media advisers and 'spin doctors' in all areas of the political process (Louw, 2010). It has been argued that the growth of political public relations is matched by a sense of manipulation of journalists by their sources 'to a degree that is unhealthy for and damaging to the democratic process' (McNair, 2011: 148).

The extent to which media coverage actually has a direct impact on voter decision making is a debatable matter. In relation to the Irish elections of 2007 and 2011, Bernhagen and Brandenburg (2017) concluded that once standard predictors of vote choice including economic evaluations are considered, the Irish media did not have any effect on the decision to vote for an incumbent party.

The parliamentary press gallery

The parliamentary press gallery represents the interests of all journalists working in Leinster House. Membership is restricted to journalists formally accredited as representatives of their respective media organisations. Within the gallery, the political correspondents group represents the interests of specialist reporters who have the exclusive right to attend private daily briefings from representatives of the government. This system was originally modelled on arrangements in London at the time of independence, with the political correspondents group corresponding to the 'Lobby' at Westminster, although operating on a less formal basis.

In this earlier era, political journalists reported almost verbatim on Oireachtas contributions and public speeches delivered by politicial leaders. National newspapers paid particular attention to the sensitivities of politicians, evident in one anecdote relating to the now defunct *Irish Press*, which was in the control of the de Valera family. As a young reporter in the late 1950s, Michael Mills was sent to Leinster House, where, during a Dáil debate on Northern Ireland, Éamon de Valera uttered an obvious contradiction in a double-negative. Mills acted to make the speech comprehensible, but upon being made aware of the change his editorial superiors firmly told the young reporter that 'Mr de Valera does not contradict himself' (Burke, 2009: 2). As punishment, Mills was not given another Leinster House assignment for several years, although he went on to have a distinguished media career and later became Ireland's first Ombudsman.

The number of media outlets covering politics increased during the 1980s and 1990s, driven by deregulation of the broadcast market, which led to the licensing of privately owned local and national radio stations and a new national television station, TV3. Several British newspaper groups, seeking to increase profit in a growing Irish economy, also introduced dedicated Irish editions, including the *Sunday Times*, the *Irish Sun* and the *Irish Daily Mail*. They all employed political journalists based in Leinster House. There was a further increase in the number of journalists accredited to the parliamentary press gallery when established media outlets – RTÉ and the national newspapers – added to their reporting teams in Leinster House. From fewer than a dozen reporters in the late 1960s, gallery membership reached 20 by the end of the 1980s, and was just short of 100 journalists in 2000. The number reached 130 by 2009 and remains at this level. The gallery has autonomy over its own affairs within Leinster House, where reporters have office space and car parking free of charge, estimated to be worth approximately €300,000 (Special Group, 2009: 150).

The government press secretary

As a government minister during the Second World War (or the 'Emergency', as it was known in Ireland), Seán Lemass held regular meetings with senior journalists to brief them on rationing and on the supply of goods. In terms of government relations with the press, however, Lemass's actions were an exception. The 1973–77 Fine Gael–Labour coalition introduced regular non-attributable briefings for political correspondents. By contrast, from the 1930s correspondents at Westminster were receiving regular collective briefings, and the system was formalised into daily briefings after 1945; the role of the prime minister's spokesperson was long recognised.

The postion of government press secretary was created in the 1970s to manage relations with political journalists, and is an essentially political office. The government press secretary is the head of the Government Information Service, which oversees all aspects of government communications, and is the Taoiseach's principal media spokesperson. Most holders of this position have been recruited from the world of journalism or from the wider public relations industry. Their task is not just to represent the Taoiseach to the media but also to drive the government's news agenda, principally on behalf of the Taoiseach's party.

The political correspondents in Leinster House attend private briefings given by the Government Press Secretary. With coalition administrations now the norm, these briefings are generally given jointly by the Government Press Secretary and other media advisers representing the different political parties in office. So, for example, under the 2011–16 Fine Gael–Labour coalition, a spokesperson for each party attended the briefings while, following the formation of the Fine Gael minority coalition in 2016, the briefings were delivered by the Government Press Secretary – representing the Fine Gael side of government – while a Deputy Government Press Secretary spoke on behalf of the Independent Alliance and also the two non-aligned independent ministers.

Until recently, these briefings were held daily, but since 2011, the only formal briefing is held on the day the cabinet meets each week, with other briefings organised in a more *ad hoc* way. The formal post-cabinet briefings are held in private at varying times, generally between five and seven o'clock. The content is usually off-the-record, with attribution to 'government sources', although occasionally the material may be credited more specifically to 'a spokesperson for the government'; such spokespersons are rarely identified by name.

The press briefings – which remain one of the main political communication events in the relationship between government and the media – tend largely to be information flows where the Government Press Secretary and his or her colleagues make a series of announcements to a captive audience, such as news that the cabinet has approved certain appointments or authorised specific policy actions. The briefings also provide an opportunity for media questions on any issue of the day but, in general, the government spokesperson rarely departs from a prepared template of answers agreed in advance. A reporter with a scoop will never take his or her story into the briefing to tip off rivals. Developments in communication technology mean it is now possible for journalists to obtain information with far less direct face-to-face contact with their political sources. Moreover, with an increased number of political, policy and media advisers working for ministers, politicians and their staff brief journalists individually outside the formal government system.

The Irish system remains far less formalised than its counterpart at Westminster, and has not been reshaped by the type of reform experienced in London since the 1990s. The appointment of Alastair Campbell as Tony Blair's spokesman when Labour came to power in 1997 essentially ended the 70-year-old Westminster system of secret unattributable briefings for lobby reporters. Under the new regime, some briefings were held on-the-record. Transcripts with summaries of the daily briefings have been available online since 2000. Non-Westminster journalists and foreign correspondents are also invited to attend.

There have been some attempts at modernisation of this system in Leinster House. In his first period as Taoiseach (February–November 1992), Albert Reynolds introduced a new, weekly, on-the-record briefing to political correspondents. This innovation was, however, dropped when Reynolds was re-elected as Taoiseach following the November 1992 general election. The Fianna Fáil leader had previously enjoyed a relatively benign relationship with the media but, on becoming Taoiseach, was confronted by a more hostile engagement with journalists. One political reporter maintained that his colleagues failed to take advantage of the new briefing system, displaying their limitations 'by focusing almost entirely on getting a headline for the following morning's newspapers or a line for the next news bulletin, and showed little inclination to explore the issues of the day in a rounded fashion' (Collins, 2004: 206). In the aftermath of the 2016 general election, marked by criticism of a lack of accessibility to the media, then Taoiseach Enda Kenny hosted regular on-the-record briefings with political correspondents with cameras present, a policy continued by his successor, Leo Varadkar.

Media and elections

Irish voters rely heavily on the media for information about politics and election campaigns. Television remains the most popular platform for accessing news in Ireland (Reuters Institute for the Study of Journalism, 2016). Some 73 per cent of Irish people get their news from television. Older age categories (55 or more) are the highest news consumers across television, radio, print and websites, and one in five (21 per cent) of this age group use social media to get their news. By way of comparison, 59 per cent of males and 62 per cent of females in the 25–34 age category get their news via social media platforms. As elsewhere, the issue of media influence on elections remains an open question in Ireland, although the role of editorial coverage may best be captured in the assertion that the press 'may not be successful at telling people what to think, but it is stunningly successful in telling its readers what to think about' (Cohen, 1963: 13). The media can be influential, especially when deciding what stories to cover. In this regard, the concept of 'framing', as discussed earlier, usefully describes the media role in determining how an event is portrayed, and the resulting perception of the same event by the public. In framing news, journalists play a powerful agenda-setting role. Consequently, political reporters are important participants in the political process in their own right. Their work influences political debate and, ultimately, may shape voter decisions on who they want to represent them in parliament.

Media coverage

A considerable body of academic research has sought to distinguish between media coverage that frames an election as a contest or game, and coverage that focuses on a debate about policy (Strömbäck and van Aelst, 2010). Several studies have directly linked media focus on game reporting to increased voter cynicism and disengagement from politics (Patterson, 1994; Cappella and Jamieson, 1997; Brants *et al.*, 2010). Politicians complain that healthy scepticism has been replaced by biting cynicism. At the time of his resignation as British prime minister, Tony Blair spoke about the media acting like 'a feral beast, just tearing people and reputations to bits' (Blair, 2007). Yet, where politicians see negative reporting underpinned by increased trivialisation, reporters allege 'spin' and expanded political public relations manipulation of what is actually happening.

Empirical evidence to document this so-called 'spiral of cynicism' thesis, however, has produced mixed results. A Dutch survey found mutual cynicism among journalists and politicians, although politicians were more cynical about journalists, especially when they believed that the media had a political agenda (Brants *et al.*, 2010). The authors concluded that causality most likely existed in both directions (Brants *et al.*, 2010: 26).

A number of studies have focused on game and policy framing in reporting of Irish elections (presenting alternative perspectives on the election, whether as an electoral competition or as a policy contest). One analysis of *Irish Times* coverage over four elections (1973, 1987, 1989 and 1992), showed a sharp increase in the game frame over the policy frame between the 1973 election (12 per cent game; 85 per cent policy) and the 1987 election (32 per cent game; 66 per cent policy) with only slight variation in the two following contests (Farrell, 1993: 34). A comprehensive study of the coverage by 12 national newspapers of the 2011 election campaign found significant variation in whether the titles focused on game or policy frames, or whether they covered the campaign at all (McMenamin *et al.*, 2013). There was a wide difference between the title that had most policy focus in its coverage (*Sunday Business Post*) and the newspaper with the least coverage (*News of the World*). The former devoted over one third of all news and opinion articles to the election, whereas only 3 per cent of articles in the latter title focused on the campaign. A related content analysis of broadcast material from the 2011 election also found significant differences in news coverage in different Irish media organisations. In summary, the findings showed that there was more policy coverage on public television (RTÉ) than on private television (TV3) and that there was more policy on morning public radio (RTÉ) than morning private radio (Newstalk).

The hypothesis, so widely featuring in the academic literature, that public stations without a strong profit orientation provide more policy-orientated content clearly finds support in the Irish case. However, the results for election coverage on national radio in Ireland challenge the idea that public service news always contains more substantive policy coverage than private broadcasters. Overall, the content analysis from the 2011 general election on newspaper and broadcast coverage showed that differing editorial approaches were adopted across media outlets in the Irish market. Parties, candidates and voters were presented with a wide range of perspectives on radio and television as well as in print titles, although the analysis from 2011 made no comment on the tone of this content.

In a study of coverage of the 2016 general election, an attempt was made to address a more specific issue: to identify the presence of 'stability' and 'austerity' frames in newspaper and broadcast reporting (Courtney *et al.*, 2018). The study sought to determine whether the then Fine Gael–Labour coalition or the opposition of Fianna Fáil, Sinn Féin and other groups was more effective at delivering its campaign message through the media. Set against the backdrop of a nascent economic recovery in the aftermath of the 2008 economic crisis, Enda Kenny's government attempted to frame the election as a choice between continuing economic stability by their re-election, or instability arising from the entry into office of a disparate group of opposition parties. In turn, the opposition attempted to frame the election as a referendum on the coalition government's implementation of austerity measures since 2011. The findings from this study show that 43 per cent of media content in the 2016 campaign was coded as about stability against just over one third of coverage about austerity.

The same study of the 2016 general election campaign examined sentiment in media coverage. The content analysis focused on the relative proportion of positive to negative sentiment in election coverage in both newspapers and broadcast outlets. The *Irish Times*, *Irish Independent* and *Irish Examiner* were found to have a majority of negative coverage, although they were less negative than other outlets including the *Irish Daily Mirror*, which barely covered politics at all in the campaign, but was found to be the most likely to emphasise negativity. The study found that the broadcast sources clustered together on the higher end of the negativity scale with the exception of TV3, which was found to be relatively positive in its election coverage in 2016. The study concluded that while broadcasters were constrained by balance rules, their on-air interviewees injected sentiment – and primarily negative sentiment – into the coverage.

Balance and bias

Despite the significant changes in Irish politics and in wider Irish society in the first two decades of the twenty-first century, the available evidence from surveys compiled in 1997 and 2015–16 shows no significant shift in the political orientation of journalists in Ireland. Irish journalists collectively lean more to the left than to the right in their political outlook. Overall, 74 per cent of the voters in 2016 – when presented with a 0 to 10 left–right scale – described themselves as centre/left (they placed themselves somewhere in the range 0–6), as against 86 per cent of journalists who similarly positioned themselves (see Rafter and Dunne, 2016).

Achieving political balance in media content in the Irish media comes down to a combination of media routine and legislative intervention. The print – and, more recently, online – sectors generally follow the criterion of newsworthiness. The broadcast sector is overseen by additional regulation. As noted previously, the BAI has regulatory authority over private and public broadcasters within the jurisdiction of the Republic of Ireland, but not over broadcasters licenced in the United Kingdom and elsewhere whose programme content may be available to Irish viewers. All broadcasters within the state are legally obliged to report and present news in an objective and impartial manner and without any expression of their own views. The BAI also issues a code of election coverage, which essentially reaffirms the requirement that all programming during an election period is impartial and fair. RTÉ traditionally imposed a 24-hour news blackout prior to polling day in elections and referendums. The BAI, however, relaxed the eve of polling moratorium in 2011, so that a broadcast blackout of election coverage starts only at 2 pm on the day before voting. This policy remained in place at the 2016 general election.

Irish newspapers were usually politically partisan in the past. The *Irish Times* was 'formerly the unofficial organ of the Protestant and Unionist minority' (Chubb, 1992: 59), the *Irish Press* supported Fianna Fáil, while the *Irish Independent* traditionally leaned towards Fine Gael. The type of strident party political partisanship evident, for example, in newspapers in the United Kingdom has, however, never been particularly pronounced in the Republic of Ireland. There are notable exceptions, including the *Irish Independent*'s editorial on the eve of the 1997 general election, which backed, in particular, the taxation policies of Fianna Fáil and the Progressive Democrats. These two parties, then led respectively by Bertie Ahern and Mary Harney, had argued strongly for cuts in income tax rates, while the outgoing Fine Gael-led coalition favoured what it claimed were more equitable adjustments to tax allowances. The 1997 editorial was an unusual departure from past practice in that the *Irish Independent* published a front-page editorial on the eve of polling day under the headline, 'It's payback time', favouring the Ahern–Harney approach.

Those involved in writing this editorial denied that there had been any external intervention, despite suspicions that Tony O'Reilly, the then controlling shareholder, was penalising an incumbent government for decisions taken, or not taken, that had a negative impact on his commercial interests in the television reception business (Downey, 2009: 251). O'Reilly's response was to note that 'government always feel they are being maligned by it [media coverage], whatever government, and opposition feel that they are being ignored' (Cooper, 2015: 347). Brandenburg and Zalinski (2008: 169) concluded, however, that the front-page endorsement of a Fianna Fáil–PD government was 'a unique document in the modern Irish context insofar as it advocates party political endorsements on principle'.

In the same period, the Irish edition of the *News of the World* aligned itself with Fianna Fáil under the leadership of Bertie Ahern (Rafter, 2016). The newspaper – owned by Rupert Murdoch – did not explicitly advise its Irish readers whom to back in the 1997 election, but the message was clear on its pre-polling day edition, with the juxtaposition of an editorial calling for strong government to fight crime and cut taxes alongside an opinion article by Ahern headlined with his promise 'We'll go to war over jobs, crimes and taxes'.

Research in this area is generally focused on election news coverage to determine balance versus bias in visibility and success at securing attention for issues promoted by political parties and candidates. The extent of media bias in recent Irish elections has been investigated in several studies. For example, a pictorial analysis of Bertie Ahern's campaign as Fianna Fáil leader in 2002 showed an over-representation of not just Ahern's party but also his coalition partner, the Progressive Democrats, in overall pictorial coverage and in front-page coverage (Brandenburg and Hayden, 2003).

It is worth noting, however, that more coverage of a party leader or an election candidate does not automatically equate to more favourable coverage, as Bertie Ahern found out in the 2007 election. Ahern entered the campaign dogged by controversy about his personal finances and having to deal with an ongoing tribunal of inquiry. Ahern was mentioned in 70 per cent of front-page newspaper headlines in coverage of the 2007 campaign, compared to his coalition partner Michael McDowell, the PD leader, with 15 per cent of mentions, and Fine Gael leader, Enda Kenny, with 9 per cent of headline mentions. Yet, as Brandenburg and Zalinski (2008: 183) note, this intense concentration on Ahern 'might be seen by both Ahern and Fianna Fáil as unwelcome and indicating a bias against them'.

In order to ensure that they meet their statutory obligations in relation to balance in election coverage, broadcasters generally use a stopwatch approach, with necessary adjustments during the campaign to try to ensure that actual coverage adheres to the predetermined on-air allocations. RTÉ's long-established practice in allocating airtime between competing parties and candidates was to use the first preference vote secured by parties in the previous general election in determining the time allocation in the subsequent contest. There had always, however, been some flexibility to take account of local factors, changes in public opinion and the entry of new parties.

RTÉ's practice – even allowing for some flexibility – was, however, unable to take account of dramatic shifts in public opinion prior to the 2011 general election (Rafter, 2015). As a result, the station introduced a weighting system underpinned by four elements of equal importance (25 per cent each): first preference votes in the 2007 general election; percentage of seats held by the party at the calling of the election in 2011; an estimate of the number of candidates nominated by each party in 2011; an average of (a) mean opinion poll results from 2007 to 2011, (b) percentage of first preference vote in the 2009 European election, and (c) percentage of first preference vote in the 2009 local elections.

Throughout the 2011 campaign, RTÉ's internal data showed the Labour Party over-represented and independents and others under-represented in programme coverage. At the mid-point in the campaign, RTÉ's own monitoring data showed that coverage of the parties was close to that suggested by this formula, with Fianna Fáil in the 30–31 per cent range (the formula suggested a guideline of 31 per cent); Fine Gael at 25–27 (guideline, 27 per cent); Labour in the 20–25 range (guideline, 13 per cent); Sinn Féin in the range 9–12 (guideline, 7 per cent); Greens in the 5–8 range (guideline, 5 per cent) and others, 3–8 per cent (guideline, 18 per cent). This allowed significant adjustments to be made subsequently to ensure that coverage was more closely in line with the guidelines. Whereas at the 2007 general election, Fianna Fáil and Fine Gael were under-represented in RTÉ coverage and smaller parties were over-represented, the final outcome in 2011 meant that Sinn Féin and Labour were over-represented, with Fianna Fáil and Independents under-represented, illustrating the difficulty of rigidly applying the formula.

The RTÉ experience in 2011 illustrates the challenges faced by broadcasters in achieving 'balanced' coverage in an election campaign, a difficulty also experienced in recent referendum campaigns not just in Ireland but also in the United Kingdom. A study of media coverage of the Brexit referendum campaign in 2016 reported that most UK newspaper articles backed the Leave side. Broadcasters, including the BBC – operating under regulatory obligations similar to their Irish counterparts – offered equal airtime to both sides in the campaign. However, analysis of broadcast coverage found that 'while broadcasters may have been even-handed in terms of giving both sides equal time, they could have more independently scrutinised, challenged or contextualised many of the facts and figures that were used repeatedly by both sides' (Cushion and Lewis, 2016).

This British experience with Brexit shows how the presence of professional media codes and legislative obligations does not prevent accusations of bias in coverage, an outcome that illustrates the difficulty in achieving a state of balance that meets the requirements of all sides in an election or referendum campaign. A number of legal challenges have been taken to broadcast coverage in referenda in Ireland, including the Coughlan Supreme Court judgment (2000), which arose from the divorce referendum in 1995. The implication of the Coughlan judgment is that both sides in a referendum campaign are now given equal access to the airwaves (Barrett, 2011).

Televised leaders' debates

Irish voters have been able to judge the leaders of the main political parties in televised debates since February 1982 (see Table 12.5). The only exception was in 1989 when no agreement on a debate was reached. These debates have become central communication events in recent election campaigns. For the parties, they are the most effective way of reaching a sizeable audience. For example, the first RTÉ debate during the 2016 campaign was watched by 568,000 viewers, almost half of all those watching television at the time.

The question of whether third or other parties should be included in television debates dominated discussion prior to 2011. Long-time Labour Party adviser Fergus Finlay

Table 12.5 Irish leaders' debates, 1982–2016

Debate	Station	Parties	Participants
1982 (Feb)	RTÉ	FF, FG	Haughey, FitzGerald (Taoiseach)
1982 (Nov)	RTÉ	FF, FG	Haughey (Taoiseach), FitzGerald
1987	RTÉ	FF, FG	Haughey, FitzGerald (Taoiseach)
1989	No debate		
1992	RTÉ	FF, FG	Reynolds (Taoiseach), Bruton
1997	RTÉ	FF, FG	Ahern, Bruton (Taoiseach)
2002	RTÉ	FF, FG	Ahern (Taoiseach), Noonan
2007	RTÉ	FF, FG	Ahern (Taoiseach), Kenny
2011	TV3	FF, Lab	Martin, Gilmore
2011	RTÉ	FF, FG, Lab, Greens, SF	Martin, Kenny, Gilmore, Gormley, Adams
2011	TG4	FF, FG, Lab	Martin, Kenny, Gilmore
2011	RTÉ	FF, FG, Lab	Martin, Kenny, Gilmore
2016	TV3	FF, FG, Lab, SF	Martin, Kenny (Taoiseach), Burton, Adams
2016	RTÉ	FF, FG, Lab, SF, Social Democrats, Renua, AAA-PBP	Martin, Kenny (Taoiseach), Burton, Adams, Donnelly, Creighton, Boyd Barrett
2016	RTÉ	FF, FG, Lab, SF	Martin, Kenny (Taoiseach), Burton, Adams

(1998: 124) expounded on the disadvantage of exclusion: 'Being the third party in Irish politics has one major drawback. All the television concentration in an election campaign is on the Taoiseach and the alternative Taoiseach. Everyone else, no matter how good their campaign, gets squeezed'. As in other countries where televised debates have become a feature of election campaigns, voters tune in to learn where the candidates stand on key policies and to work out the differences between them. They also get a sense of what the candidates are like as people.

The seven debates between February 1982 and May 2007 share a number of common distinguishing features. First, participation was confined to the leaders of Fianna Fáil and Fine Gael. Second, there was a single televised debate in each campaign. Third, all the debates were hosted by RTÉ. Finally, the programme format was studio-based, featuring a table debate set with the leaders and a single moderator seated in close proximity behind a desk.

Following this period of continuity in format, the leader debates changed for the first time in the 2011 election. First, the number of debates increased to four, from a single debate in previous contests. Second, the number of host broadcasters increased to three from a single broadcaster previously. Third, one of the four debates in 2011 took place in the Irish language (all earlier debates had taken place in English); this was also the first debate to be pre-recorded, to allow time to apply English language subtitles. Fourth, there was some innovation with the debate format, with the use of stand-up lecterns in one debate, which was hosted before a live studio audience. Finally, and most significantly, the number of party leaders invited to participate increased.

Some of these developments were replicated in the 2016 general election debate – in particular, the idea that televised debates should involve leaders beyond Fine Gael and Fianna Fáil. It remains to be seen if any future reassertion of electoral dominance by the two main parties leads to a return of a direct 'head-to-head' encounter involving the two leaders most likely to be Taoiseach. Even if this did happen, given the changes in 2011 and 2016, it is likely that other debates would still continue to be televised, involving all party leaders, including those of smaller parties.

Alongside debates involving the main party leaders, broadcasters have also hosted debates involving deputy party leaders and finance spokespeople. The most famous televised debate in Irish electoral history took place not in the context of a general election but, rather, at the end of the 2011 presidential contest. During this debate on RTÉ One television (between seven candidates seeking to succeed Mary McAleese in Áras an Uachtaráin), incorrect information was broadcast during the live programme, based on an unverified tweet. A subsequent complaint by independent candidate Seán Gallagher – whose reputation had been challenged in the controversial tweet – was upheld by the BAI, which accepted that RTÉ's broadcast of the tweet was unfair. This finding, however, arrived long after the election result had been declared; Gallagher, who had been seen as potentially winning the election, ended as runner-up.

The media in a changing world

The history of online political communication is relatively short. Facebook first appeared in February 2004, YouTube arrived twelve months later, while Twitter went live in July 2006. Despite their short lifetimes since then, new media technologies have opened up the possibility of politicians connecting individually with every single voter with potentially 'profound implications for democracy' (Street, 2001: 212). In a similar vein, writing at the outset of the arrival of the so-called digital revolution, Coleman and Blumler (2009: 9–10) speculated optimistically about how the internet had the potential to 'revitalise our flagging political communications arrangements' through the creation of new online political spaces in which voters and politicians could meet to discuss policy. More soberly, Lilleker (2010: 186) noted that while 'the revolutionary predictions have largely not been met, however, the internet *has* had an impact on social and political relations'. This changing world has had an impact in a variety of ways, from allowing candidates and public representatives to connect in a new way with the public, to undermining longstanding legislative rules on political advertising.

Social media

The Obama US presidential campaigns in 2008 and in 2012 are credited with mobilising the Democratic candidate's supporters 'to become information brokers by creating and sharing their own content, reporting on the latest events of the campaign trail, organizing local and national events as well as collecting donations to support their candidate' (Baumann, 2010: 1). The use of Twitter by Donald Trump was one of the most distinctive elements in the 2016 campaign. The tone and content of Trump's online activity, first as a candidate and subsequently as president, marks a significant departure in online activity by a leading political figure.

Social media has also emerged as a communication tool for Irish politicians, although not on the scale of Obama's utilisation of new platforms, or with anything like the controversy of Trump's use of Twitter. New digital communications tools and platforms evident in US politics have been slower to have an impact on Irish politics, but their emergence is nonetheless real. By the time of the 2007 general election, it was concluded that the internet had played 'an important role both for the media and for the parties and the candidates' (Brandenburg and Zalinski, 2008: 171). Five years later, there was mention of 'remarkable changes' in digital political communications since the previous election in 2007 (Wall and Sudulich,

2011: 89). Whereas in 2007 only one in three candidates had a personal website, by 2011 three quarters of candidates had a Facebook profile, while just over half had a Twitter account (Wall and Sudulich, 2011: 100).

This development of social media usage in Irish political communications has not taken place without some political drama. The online intervention of Green Party senator Dan Boyle in early February 2010, via Facebook and Twitter, while Fianna Fáil minister Willie O'Dea was embroiled in controversy over his remarks about a constituency rival in Limerick, led to the latter's resignation as Minister for Defence. Some months later, in September 2010, Fine Gael TD Simon Coveney's tweet about the performance of Brian Cowen during a RTÉ interview forced the sitting Taoiseach to deny being hung-over during a peak-time radio interview.

The extent to which digital media had become regarded as normal by the time of the 2016 general election was captured by one commentator who described the campaign as 'the first truly social media election in Ireland', given the extent to which platforms such as Twitter and Facebook were 'used by candidates and parties to sell their messages, and by voters to converse about the issues' (Goodbody, 2016). To emphasise the arrival of digital communication in political terms in Ireland, one newspaper report recorded how Sinn Féin had 'gone from near zero in 2011 to almost 80,000 likes on Facebook'; Gerry Adams had a 'phenomenal' 100,000 followers on Twitter; while Mary Lou McDonald, with over 60,000 likes, was the party's most popular TD on Facebook (McGee, 2016). Moreover, Fine Gael had – according to the same report – 'more than quadrupled its reach' on Facebook since 2011, to 12,200, with Enda Kenny (41,400 followers) and Leo Varadkar (30,000) its major Twitter stars, while Fianna Fáil (20,000) and Labour (28,000) had 'experienced similar exponential growth on Twitter'.

Undoubtedly, more candidates than ever saw the need to have an online presence in 2016. For example, more than 70 per cent of candidates had a Twitter account in 2016, up from 57 per cent in 2011. Aside from the growth in online presence, little is as yet known about the type and impact of this virtual engagement. One early assessment, while showing the skewed nature of Twitter election activity (over 50 per cent of users were 15–24 years old and from urban areas), concluded that 'social media is certainly gaining in significance, but it's not a kingmaker – not yet' (Greene, 2016).

Political advertising

Scope for broadcast political advertising in Ireland has traditionally been limited, due to a longstanding legislative prohibition on paid broadcast advertising of a political nature on television and radio. Controversy about the blanket legislative prohibition has arisen periodically in connection with requests by charities and other non-governmental agencies to place radio advertisements deemed to be of a political nature (Rafter, 2009). Difficulties with political parties have been rare, given widespread acceptance of the existing regime. But the new online platforms have provided new ways of communicating political messages to the public. Early developments based on technological change included the first Obama campaign in 2008 (purchasing advertising space on home video games) and the Conservative Party in the UK in 2009 (running a campaign on Spotify to target younger voters).

The migration of television adverts to the internet has been evident in electoral contests in many countries. In Ireland, many political parties, candidates and interest groups are now using the internet to distribute advertising that cannot be placed on BAI-regulated television and radio stations. During the 2011 and 2016 general election campaigns, several parties, including Labour and the Greens, produced internet-only videos that could not be broadcast on television given the legislative rules on paid political advertising.

While the parties are likely to bypass these legislative rules increasingly, the traditional ban on paid political advertising on radio and television still remains alongside a system of free party political broadcasts (PPBs) during election and referendum campaigns for qualifying political parties. The Broadcasting Act, 2009, notes that PPBs are available only to political parties. The BAI has subsequently determined that PPBs can be offered only to political parties listed on the Register of Political Parties. Participating broadcasters are required to ensure that no party receives an unfair advantage when allocating time to PPBs. The BAI's election code also requires broadcasters to ensure that PPBs are transmitted 'at times that are aimed at achieving a similar audience for all such broadcasts' (2011: 7). In a post-election analysis in 2011, RTÉ left open the possibility of reducing the maximum PPB duration that was allowed, and noted that the scheduling of PPBs needed to be examined (Rafter, 2015). By the time of the 2016 general election, however, no changes had been introduced.

Sizeable audiences in Ireland watch PPBs, though we do not know what impact these have. The 16 television broadcasts during the 2007 general election campaign had an average viewership of 500,000 people. In a 2009 study, respondents were asked if they could recall any party political broadcasts from the previous general election campaign (Rafter, 2011). Almost six in 10 of all adults (58 per cent) could recall party political broadcasts from 2007 (39 per cent had no recollection). The same survey pointed to strong public support for the principle behind the current system. Asked for their view on the statement 'regardless of whether I watch or hear them myself, I think it is important that party political broadcasts are shown', almost six in 10 respondents (57 per cent) agreed. Despite these positive sentiments, there is no legal obligation on Irish broadcasters to air free election broadcasts. While RTÉ does make airtime available, most BAI-licenced stations opt not to do so.

Overall, there are rarely major surprises in the political advertising strategies of Irish parties and candidates; personality remains prominent, with posters largely free of policy and ideology. The one major standout broadcast was at the 2007 general election, with the appearance of Tony Blair, Bill Clinton and former US senator George Mitchell in a PPB endorsing incumbent Taoiseach Bertie Ahern. The trio of international political figures endorsed Ahern, with a focus on his role in the Northern Ireland peace process although they also referred to his leadership in creating the 'Celtic Tiger' economy, evidently unaware of the crash that was to follow just 16 months later. The so-called 'peace broadcast' was a significant departure from the traditional approach to broadcast political advertising in Ireland, not just with the external political endorsement but also the overwhelming presidential-style focus in a parliamentary system.

Conclusion

The media has a central place in a modern political system alongside the public and politicians. Whereas in earlier eras the media's role was primarily as a conduit of information directly from rulers to the masses, in contemporary democracies the nature of the media's role is far more complex, especially as information now moves in a multitude of different directions across a range of online and offline platforms, and does so instantaneously.

As seen in this chapter, the media has a role in the democratic process in both informing and educating the public about decisions made in the political arena and also in assisting voters to know more about candidates seeking their support to secure elected office. Achieving this type of ideal outcome, however, is not always easy, especially where media outlets grapple with combining a commercial drive to generate profits alongside public inter-est objectives. In the case of Ireland, studies of election coverage illustrate how both public and private media produce a mix of what we call game and policy coverage – yet we also know from research findings that striking the correct balance in this coverage, to ensure that elections are adequately covered and voters fully informed, is an ongoing challenge.

Debates about 'fake news' and data dumps, arising from the hacking of email and other online accounts, continue to attract international interest and concern. The emerging impact of new online communication platforms is still being played out. But we do not need to look beyond Ireland to find evidence of the ramifications of our changing media world, includ-ing the impact of unverified tweets that were broadcast on prime-time television during the 2011 presidential election, and new communication technologies allowing candidates and parties to bypass longstanding rules about broadcast political advertising. Given the role of the media in all of these different guises in contemporary life, ongoing analysis of reportage and its impact, as well as the interactions of media with the political system, must be of seri-ous interest to scholars of political science.

References and further reading

Barrett, Gavin, 2011. *A Road Less Travelled: Reflections on the Supreme Court Rulings in Crotty, Coughlan and McKenna (No. 2)*. Dublin: IIEA.

Barrett, Sean, D., 2000. 'Competitiveness and contestability in the Irish media sector' [Trinity Economic Paper Series paper no. 2000/3]. Dublin: Trinity College Dublin.

Baumann, Sabine, 2010. 'Election 2.0: how to use cyber platforms to win the US presidential elections – An investigation into the changing communication strategies of election candidates'. Available at: www.inter-disciplinary.net/wp-content/uploads/2010/02/baumannpaper.pdf.

Bernhagen, Patrick and Heinz Brandenburg, 2017. 'Economic voting through boom and bust: information and choice at Irish general elections, 2002–2011', in Michael Marsh, David M. Farrell and Gail McElroy (eds), *A Conservative Revolution? Electoral Change in Twenty-First-Century Ireland*. Oxford: Oxford University Press, pp. 42–60.

Blair, Tony, 2007. 'Reuters speech on public life', 12 June 2007. Available at: http://news.bbc.co.uk/2/hi/uk_news/politics/6744581.stm (Accessed: 23 January 2017).

Blumler, Jay G., and Michael Gurevitch, 1981. 'Politicians and the press', in Dan Nimmo and Karen Sanders (eds), *Handbook of Political Communication*. Beverly Hills: Sage Publications, pp. 467–93.

Brandenburg, Heinz and Jacqueline Hayden, 2003. 'The media and the campaign', in Michael Gallagher, Michael Marsh and Paul Mitchell (eds), *How Ireland Voted 2002*. Basingstoke: Palgrave Macmillan, pp. 177–96.

Brandenburg, Heinz and Zbyszek Zalinski, 2008. 'The media and the campaign', in Michael Gallagher and Michael Marsh (eds), *How Ireland Voted 2007: The Full Story of Ireland's General Election*. Basingstoke: Palgrave Macmillan, pp. 166–86.

Brants, Kees, Claes de Vreese, Judith Moller and Philip van Praag, 2010. 'The real spiral of cynicism? Symbiosis and mistrust between politicians and journalists', *International Journal of Press Politics* 15:1, pp. 25–40.

Broadcasting Authority of Ireland (BAI), 2016. 'Over half of Irish consumers (52%) now get their news via social media sites'. Available at: www.bai.ie/en/over-half-of-irish-consumers-52-now-get-their-news-via-social-media-sites/ (Accessed: 31 March 2017).

Burke, Ray, 2009. 'The *Irish Press* of the troubles: *Scéala Eireann* 1968–1995', paper delivered at the annual conference of the Newspaper and Periodical History Forum of Ireland, Dublin Institute of Technology, 20–21 November.

Cappella, Joseph and Kathleen Jamieson Hall, 1997. *Spiral of Cynicism: The Press and the Public Good*. Oxford: Oxford University Press.

Chubb, Basil, 1992. *The Government and Politics of Ireland*, 3rd ed. New York: Longman.

Cohen, Bernard, 1963. *The Press and Foreign Policy*. Princeton: Princeton University Press.

Coleman, Stephen and Jay G. Blumler, 2009. *The Internet and Democratic Citizenship: Theory, Practice and Policy*. Cambridge: Cambridge University Press.

Collins, Stephen, 2004. 'The parliamentary lobby system', in Tom Garvin, Maurice Manning and Richard Sinnott (eds), *Dissecting Irish Politics: Essays in Honour of Brian Farrell*. Dublin: UCD Press, pp. 198–211.

Cooper, Matt, 2015. *The Maximalist: The Rise and Fall of Tony O'Reilly*. Dublin: Gill and Macmillan.

Courtney, Michael, Michael Breen, Iain McMenamin, Eoin O'Malley and Kevin Rafter, 2018. *Media and Elections in Ireland since 1969*. Manchester: Manchester University Press.

Crouse, Timothy, 1972. *The Boys on the Bus*. New York: Random House.

Cushion, Stephen, 2012. *The Democratic Value of News: Why Public Service Media Matter*. Basingstoke: Palgrave Macmillan.

Cushion, Stephen and Justin Lewis, 2016. 'Scrutinising statistical claims and constructing balance: television news coverage of the 2016 EU referendum', in Daniel Jackson, Einar Thorsen and Dominic Wring (eds), *EU Referendum Analysis 2016: Media, Voters and the Campaign – Early Reflections from Leading UK Academics*. Poole: Centre for the Study of Journalism, Culture and Community, Bournemouth University, pp. 40–1.

Davis, Aeron, 2009. 'Journalist–source relations, mediated reflexivity and the politics of politics', *Journalism Studies* 10:2, pp. 204–19.

Deuze, Mark, 2005. 'What is journalism? Professional identity and ideology of journalists reconsidered', *Journalism* 6:4, pp. 442–64.

Donovan, Denis and Antoin E. Murphy, 2013. *The Fall of the Celtic Tiger: Ireland and the Euro Debt Crisis*. Oxford: Oxford University Press.

Doughty Street Chambers and KRW Law, 2016. *Report on the Concentration of Media Ownership in Ireland*. Brussels: European United Left/Nordic Green Left (GUE/NGL) Group of the European Parliament.

Downey, James, 2009. *In My Own Time*. Dublin: Gill and Macmillan.

Doyle, Kevin, 2016. 'Sinn Féin MEP calls for inquiry into ownership of the media in Ireland', *Irish Independent*, 25 October.

Dunlop, Andrew, 1911. *Fifty Years of Irish Journalism*. Dublin: Hanna & Neale.

Eurobarometer, 2016. *Media Pluralism and Democracy*. Fact Sheets Ireland. Special Eurobarometer 452, November.

Farrell, David, 1993. 'Campaign strategies', in Michael Gallagher and Michael Laver (eds), *How Ireland Voted 1992*. Limerick and Dublin: PSAI Press and Folens, pp. 21–38.

Finlay, Fergus, 1998. *Snakes and Ladders*. Dublin: New Island.

Franklin, Bob, 2004. *Packaging Politics: Political Communications in Britain's Media Democracy*. London: Arnold.

Gans, Herbert J., 2003. *Democracy and the News*. Oxford: Oxford University Press.

Goodbody, Will, 2016. #GE16 – The first real social media election here, rte.ie., 29 February. Available at: www.rte.ie/business/2016/02/29/ge16-the-first-social-media-election/ (Accessed: 10 March 2017).

Greene, Derek, 2016. 'Most candidates used Twitter but its influence unknown', 29 February. Unpublished report. Available at www.insight-centre.org/content/social-media-and-ge16-read-dr-derek-greene-irish-times (Accessed: 10 March 2017).

Higgins, Michael, 2006. 'Substantiating a political public sphere in the Scottish press', *Journalism* 7:1, pp. 125–44.

Horgan, John, 2001. *Irish Media: A Critical History Since 1922*. London: Routledge.

Horgan, John, 2002. 'Journalists and censorship: a case history of the NUJ in Ireland and the broadcasting ban 1971–94', *Journalism Studies* 3:3, pp. 377–92.

Horgan, John, 2004. *Broadcasting and Public Life: RTE News and Current Affairs 1926–1997*. Dublin: Four Courts Press.

Hughes, Ian, Paula Clancy, Clodagh Harris and David Beetham, 2007. *Power to the People? Assessing Democracy in Ireland*. Dublin: Tasc at New Island.

Ingham, Bernard, 1994. 'The lobby system: lubricant or spanner?', *Parliamentary Affairs* 47:4, pp. 549–65.

Kerrigan, Gene, 2013. 'Negative? Give us some good news, Pat', *Sunday Independent*, 6 January.

Kovach, Bill and Tom Rosenstiel, 2007. *The Elements of Journalism: What Newspeople Should Know and the Public Should Expect*, rev. ed. New York: Three Rivers Press.

Laffan, Michael, 1999. *The Resurrection of Ireland: The Sinn Fein Party, 1916–1923*. Cambridge: Cambridge University Press.

Lilleker, Darren, 2010. Book review: 'Stephen Coleman and Jay G. Blumler, *The Internet and Democratic Citizenship: Theory, Practice and Policy*', *European Journal of Communication* 25:2 pp. 186–7.

Lippmann, Walter, 1922. *Public Opinion*. New York: Harcourt, Brace & Co.

Louw, Eric, 2010. *The Media and the Political Process*. London: Sage.

McCombs, Maxwell E. and Donald L. Shaw, 1972. 'The agenda-setting function of mass media', *Public Opinion Quarterly* 36:2, pp. 176–87.

McGee, Harry, 2013. 'Rabbitte accuses media of damaging democracy by "denigrating" politics', *Irish Times*, 4 January.

McGee, Harry, 2016. 'Sinn Féin leads social media election race', *Irish Times*, 2 February.

McMenamin, Iain, Roddy Flynn, Eoin O'Malley and Kevin Rafter, 2013. 'Commercialism and election framing: a content analysis of twelve newspapers in the 2011 Irish general election', *International Journal Press/Politics* 18:2, pp. 167–87.

McNair, Brian, 2011. *An Introduction to Political Communication*, 5th ed. London: Routledge.

McQuail, Denis, 2003. *Media Accountability and Freedom of Publication*. Oxford: Oxford University Press.

Marsh, Michael, David M. Farrell and Gail McElroy (eds), 2017. *A Conservative Revolution? Electoral Change in Twenty-First-Century Ireland*. Oxford: Oxford University Press.

Morash, Chris, 2010. *A History of the Media in Ireland*. Cambridge: Cambridge University Press.

Nimmo, Dan and James Combs, 1990. *Mediated Political Realities*, 2nd edn. New York: Longman.

Nyberg, Peter, 2011. 'Misjudging risk: Causes of the systemic banking crisis in Ireland'. Available at http://www.bankinginquiry.gov.ie

O'Brien, Denis, 2011. 'Depiction of me as enemy of journalism undeserved', *Irish Times*, 15 November.

Patterson, Thomas, 1994. *Out of Order*. New York: Vintage.

Rafter, Kevin, 2009. 'Run out of the gallery: the changing nature of Irish political journalism', *Irish Communications Review* 11, pp. 93–103.

Rafter, Kevin, 2011. 'Hear no evil – see no evil: political advertising in Ireland', *Journal of Public Affairs* 11:2, pp. 93–9.

Rafter, Kevin, 2012. 'A tale of "womanly intuition": Hector Legge at the *Sunday Independent*, 1940–70', in Mark O'Brien and Kevin Rafter (eds), *Independent Newspapers: A History*. Dublin: Four Courts, pp. 119–32.

Rafter, Kevin, 2015. 'Regulating the airwaves: how political balance is achieved in practice in election news coverage', *Irish Political Studies* 30:4, pp. 575–94.

Rafter, Kevin, 2016. 'The Irish edition – from "filthy scandal sheet" to "old friend" of the Taoiseach', in Laurel Brake, Chandrika Kaul and Mark W. Turner (eds), *'Journalism for the Rich, Journalism for the Poor': The News of the World and the British Press, 1843–2011*. London: Palgrave, pp. 179–94.

Rafter, Kevin, 2017. '"Insufficient critique" – the Oireachtas banking inquiry and the media', *Administration* 65:2, pp. 89–107.

Rafter, Kevin and Stephen Dunne, 2016. *The Irish Journalist Today*. Dublin: Dublin City University. Available at: theirishjournalisttoday.com/Journalism2016.pdf.

Reuters Institute for the Study of Journalism, 2016. *Digital News Report*. Available at: www.digitalnewsreport.org.

Ross, Karen, 2010. 'Dance macabre: politicians, journalists, and the complicated rumba of relationships', *International Journal of Press/Politics* 15:3, pp. 272–94.

Salgado, Susana and Jesper Strömbäck, 2011. 'Interpretive journalism: a review of concepts, operationalizations and key findings', *Journalism* 13:2, pp. 144–61.

Savage, Robert, 1996. *Irish Television: The Political and Social Origins*. Cork: Cork University Press.

Savage, Robert, 2010. *A Loss of Innocence? Television and Irish Society 1960–72*. Manchester: Manchester University Press.

Schudson, Michael, 2008. *Why Democracies Need an Unlovable Press*. Cambridge: Polity.

Special Group on Public Service Numbers and Expenditure Programmes, 2009. *Volume 2: Report*. Dublin: Department of Finance.

Street, John, 2001. *Mass Media, Politics and Democracy*. Basingstoke: Palgrave Macmillan.

Strömbäck, Jesper, 2005. 'In search of a standard: four models of democracy and their normative implications for journalism', *Journalism Studies* 6:3, pp. 331–45.

Strömbäck, Jesper and Lynda Lee Kaid, 2008. *The Handbook of Election News Coverage around the World*. New York: Routledge.

Strömbäck, Jesper and Peter van Aelst, 2010. 'Exploring some antecedents of the media's framing of election news: a comparison of Swedish and Belgian election news', *International Journal of Press/Politics* 14:1, pp. 41–59.

Wall, Matthew and Maria Laura Sudulich, 2011. 'Internet explorers: the online campaign', in Michael Gallagher and Michael Marsh (eds), *How Ireland Voted 2011: The Full Story of Ireland's Earthquake Election*. Basingstoke: Palgrave Macmillan, pp. 89–106.

Websites

www.bai.ie
Broadcasting authority of Ireland, the national regulatory authority for broadcasting in Ireland.

www.presscouncil.ie
Press Council of Ireland: the national independent body, which adjudicates on complaints against newspapers in Ireland.

www.rte.ie
RTÉ: Ireland's public service broadcaster.

www.tv3.ie
TV3: Ireland's privately owned national television service.

Newstalk: www.newstalk.com
Ireland's privately owned talk-based radio service.

Other national media outlets include:
Irish Times (www.irishtimes.com), *Irish Independent* (www.independent.ie), *Irish Examiner* (www.irishexaminer.com), The Journal (online only at www.thejournal.ie), *Sunday Business Post* (www.businesspost.ie)

Part IV

Ireland in a wider world

13 Northern Ireland and the British dimension

John Coakley

When British voters opted to leave the European Union in June 2016, shockwaves went through the Irish political establishment. Political leaders had been planning for such a possibility, though not quite expecting this outcome to the referendum. The subsequent sustained campaign of the government to ensure that Irish interests were protected as much as possible in the context of British withdrawal from the EU draws attention to the unique relationship that Ireland has had with its large neighbour. Ireland's historical dependence on Great Britain and the decades-long dispute over Northern Ireland provided a distinctive dynamic to the Irish political process, as we have seen in Chapter 1, and they are explored further in this chapter.

As recently as 1985, when the Anglo–Irish Agreement was drawn up, each of the two parties to the agreement produced their own variants on the first words of the text, and both versions were signed by the two sides. The official British text described that agreement as being between the governments of 'the United Kingdom of Great Britain and Northern Ireland' and 'the Republic of Ireland'; the official Irish text described the two parties as the governments of 'the United Kingdom' and 'Ireland'. The shorter Irish version was no mere exercise in verbal economy. As a matter of principle, the Irish government was not prepared to acknowledge the *de jure* incorporation of Northern Ireland in the United Kingdom, something that is explicit in the full title of that state; and the British government did not wish to acknowledge the implicit claim to Northern Ireland in the official name of the Irish state. In the past, British official usage had referred exclusively to 'Éire' or to the 'Irish Republic', but from the 1970s onwards 'Republic of Ireland' gained currency among British officials as a way of referring to the 26 counties (Coakley, 2009).

Behind this apparently trivial battle over names lie centuries of conflict between communities and islands. Chapter 1 has already described the historical relationship between Ireland and Great Britain, and has examined the extent to which that has coloured the Irish political process. The present chapter narrows the focus to one of the most contentious features bequeathed by this relationship, the question of Northern Ireland. The first section of the chapter looks at the evolution of Northern Ireland as a distinct entity, with its own borders and political institutions. This evolution can best be understood in the broader context within which it operated: the changing relationship between Dublin and London after 1922, the topic we then address. Both this relationship and the domestic political system of Northern Ireland itself were fundamentally redefined in the late 1990s; the third section of this chapter therefore focuses on the nature of the Good Friday Agreement of 1998. The final section describes later institutional reforms within Northern Ireland and the political environment within which they took place.

Northern Ireland and the South

Novel though the concept of 'Northern Ireland' was in the early twentieth century, this new political entity quickly became familiar and eventually acquired an image of permanence. This process of bedding down took place in two respects: the normalisation of the very notion of partition, and the steady development of the devolved institutions that were put in place there in 1921, issues that we consider in turn.

The consolidation of partition

The roots of the partition of Ireland are deeply embedded in Irish history (for general historical background, see Laffan, 1983; Jackson, 1999; Bardon, 2005; Boyce and O'Day, 2006; English, 2007; Kennedy and Ollerenshaw, 2012). At one level, they lie in the seventeenth century 'plantations' that changed the face of Ulster, up to that point the most Gaelic of the provinces, giving it a largely Anglo–Scottish, Protestant character. By the nineteenth century, the northeastern area was further distinguished from the rest of the island by socio-economic differences. In addition to the long-standing privileged position of Protestants (and especially of Episcopalians, or members of the Church of Ireland), Ireland's industrial revolution had been substantially concentrated in the Lagan Valley, with the rapidly expanding city of Belfast as its focal point, and the economic growth of that region left the rest of the island well behind.

To these cultural and socio-economic differences were added political ones. As electoral mobilisation took off in the late nineteenth century, unionist Ulster became increasingly sharply differentiated from nationalist Ireland, as we have seen in Chapter 1. But there were further political differences between North and South. Organised unionism was itself divided: its main organisation, the Irish Unionist Alliance, extended after 1885 only over the three southern provinces, where unionist support was thinly spread. Northern unionism was organised separately, its electoral machine taking permanent shape with the formation of the Ulster Unionist Council (still today the controlling body of the Ulster Unionist Party) in 1905. There were differences within nationalism, too, but these became obvious only in 1918, when nationalist candidates in several northern constituencies managed to withstand the Sinn Féin tide that engulfed the South – though this was aided by an electoral pact brokered by the Catholic primate, Cardinal Logue.

When partition was finally legislated for in 1920, then, the British could present it as a recognition of political realities (see Hennessey, 1998; Duffy, 2009). Since religious affiliation at this time almost entirely determined political allegiance, we can use this as an indicator of political preference, relying on the 1911 census, which indeed formed the basis of later political calculations. By this measure, the new southern state comprised counties that were overwhelmingly nationalist; the county with the largest Protestant minority was Dublin (29 per cent). The new state of Northern Ireland contained two counties with large Protestant majorities, Antrim (79 per cent) and Down (68 per cent), and two with smaller but still significant majorities, Armagh (55 per cent) and Londonderry (54 per cent). But in the two remaining counties, Protestants were a minority: Tyrone (45 per cent) and Fermanagh (44 per cent). Overall, according to the 1911 census, Protestants accounted for 66 per cent of the population of the six counties that would form Northern Ireland, and Catholics for 34 per cent. In the nine-county province of Ulster overall, Protestants amounted to only 56 per cent of the population and Catholics to 44 per cent.

Partition clouded North–South relations over the following decades for three main reasons. First, nationalists claimed that it was wrong in principle: a clear majority of the people of Ireland had voted in 1918 for independence for the whole island, and the unionist minority had no right to block this democratic decision. Second, it had, in any case, been unfairly implemented: rather than seeking to draw a border that would follow the admittedly imprecise boundary between Protestant and Catholic Ireland, an effort had been made to maximise the territory of Northern Ireland, even though this meant incorporating some overwhelmingly Catholic areas adjacent to the South (but not so many as to place a Protestant majority at risk). Third, nationalists pointed out that partition was maintained from the 1920s onwards by policies of discrimination, gerrymander and oppression directed against the Catholic minority (McKittrick, 2012).

From the northern Protestant perspective, the picture appeared different. First, there was no particular reason why, if nationalist Ireland wished to opt out of the United Kingdom, Protestant Ulster could not opt out of nationalist Ireland; there was nothing sacred about using the island as the only decision making unit (Gallagher, 1990). Second, although the new state extended over some predominantly Catholic areas, these had been included to maximise the number of Protestants who would be able to retain the valued link with Britain. Third, some unionists simply denied that any discriminatory or other unfair practices were directed against Catholics, while others, if they admitted these, justified them on the ground that Northern Ireland was entitled to protect itself against subversion by a disloyal minority; and both groups alleged that, in any case, the South discriminated against its own small Protestant minority.

Against this background, the prospects for a productive political relationship between North and South were poor. But they were not non-existent, at least initially. Although it has been labelled the 'partition act', the Government of Ireland Act of 1920 sought to make provision for all-Irish institutions. Irish unity would continue to be symbolised by the continuance of certain long-established offices, and provision was made for a 40-member inter-parliamentary Council of Ireland, with 20 members each from the northern and southern parliaments. The responsibility of the Council was confined to a small range of matters initially, but provision was made for it to become an embryonic Irish parliament.

The Council of Ireland never met; it perished in two stages. First, it was overtaken by the Anglo–Irish treaty of 1921, which greatly extended the political autonomy of the South (instead of being a self-governing part of the United Kingdom, and thus a mirror image of Northern Ireland, it was given separate status as a British dominion, outside the United Kingdom, as we have seen in Chapter 1). This had the effect of bringing to an end the few offices that would have symbolised the unity of the island, such as those of Lord Lieutenant and Lord Chancellor, and it led to the disappearance of the Irish Privy Council, of which northern and southern government ministers would have been members. Second, an agreement in 1925 between the Irish, British and Northern Irish governments to 'freeze' the North–South border as it then stood was accompanied by a further agreement to shelve the idea of a Council of Ireland.

This ended whatever formal opportunities had existed for political contact between North and South. Northern unionists, who were to dominate the Northern Ireland parliament and monopolise its government for 50 years, had not been particularly keen on the Council of Ireland, but the Northern Ireland parliament had selected its representation on it. The government of the Irish Free State, however, had found the Council a distasteful reminder of partition, had shown no enthusiasm to get it up and running, and gladly scrapped it in 1925 when the occasion arose (Coakley, 2017: 198–200). In the decades that followed, political contact between the two parts of the island was close to non-existent. The gap was accentuated by the Second World War, in which the South expressed its independence by remaining neutral while Northern Ireland participated alongside the rest of the United Kingdom. The relationship reached a low point in the late 1940s, when the South not only left the Commonwealth but also began a vigorous and fruitless campaign to persuade the British to end partition (Kennedy, 1988). Cooperation between the two jurisdictions was minimal, covering only areas where it would have been difficult to avoid it (Kennedy, 2000). The first steps towards political 'normalisation' between North and South had to await the arrival of a new political generation. This was marked by a visit by Taoiseach Seán Lemass to meet his counterpart, Prime Minister Terence O'Neill, in Belfast in January 1965. But this development, and the thaw in relationships associated with it, was overtaken by events in Northern Ireland (McCann, 2015).

Devolution in Northern Ireland

Northern Ireland came into existence in 1921 with a set of political institutions defined in the Government of Ireland Act, 1920. The Northern Ireland Parliament consisted of a House of Commons elected initially by proportional representation, but by the plurality system from 1929, and a Senate elected mainly by the House of Commons; and the Government of Northern Ireland depended on the composition of the House of Commons, on the British model (on the old system of government in Northern Ireland, see Birrell and Murie, 1980). But the House of Commons was always controlled by the Unionist Party (which won 70 per cent of all seats over the 10 elections, 1921–69, to the Nationalist Party's 16 per cent); the Senate was even more overwhelmingly dominated by the Unionist Party; and the government was almost exclusively Unionist (on the two parties, see Walker, 2004; Norton, 2014).[1]

Unionist rule in Northern Ireland was marked by well-documented complaints of discrimination against Catholics, especially in such areas as local government (where there were notorious instances of electoral gerrymandering), the allocation of public sector housing, public and private sector employment, and the policing and security system. After years of fruitless complaining, the frustration of Catholics spilled over in 1968, a year of revolution throughout much of the world, behind a civil rights movement that aimed to win full equality before the law for all (see Purdie, 1990; Ó Dochartaigh, 2005; Prince, 2007; McKittrick, 2012). The subversive potential of the civil rights movement lay in the fact that it did not represent a full-frontal attack on the state, as pro-unity nationalist movements had traditionally done; instead of articulating long-standing nationalist arguments, it advocated equality for all, implying the extension of conventional British standards to Northern Ireland. This was a difficult demand for a unionist government to resist, and in 1968–69, under pressure from London, it agreed to a comprehensive reform package to address Catholic grievances in the areas of discrimination, gerrymandering and policing.

If the Northern Ireland problem had been simply about civil rights, it could have been resolved at a relatively early stage (for general background and analysis, see Whyte, 1990; McGarry and O'Leary, 1996, 2004; Ruane and Todd, 1996; Aughey and Morrow, 1996; Mitchell and Wilford, 1999; Tonge, 2002, 2005; Aughey, 2005; Dixon, 2008; McGrattan, 2010; Dixon and O'Kane, 2011; Cochrane, 2013). But much more than this was at stake: having exposed the vulnerability of the state, nationalists pressed home with more far-reaching demands. Since the 1970s, these have taken two very distinctive forms. First, a new mainstream nationalist party, the Social Democratic and Labour Party (SDLP), appeared in 1970, and since then has pushed a dual agenda: for power sharing between the two main communities within Northern Ireland, and for institutional recognition of the Irish identity of northern nationalists by the creation of an 'Irish dimension', such as some kind of all-Irish body (McLoughlin, 2010; Campbell, 2015). Second, a new force appeared at the same time: in December 1969 the Provisional Irish Republican Army (IRA) was created. The armed campaign that it waged until 1994 was accompanied by a political movement, Sinn Féin, in pursuit of a radical objective: the withdrawal of the British from Northern Ireland and the establishment of an all-Ireland republic (English, 2012).

This mobilisation on the nationalist side was matched by similar developments within unionism. As early as 1965, on the occasion of the Taoiseach's visit to Northern Ireland, a little-known clergyman, Reverend Ian Paisley, moderator of an even less well-known denomination, the Free Presbyterian Church of Ulster, made a vocal protest at Stormont, with placards reading 'No Mass, no Lemass' and 'IRA murderer welcomed at Stormont' (Moloney and Pollak, 1986: 119). A religious and political outsider, Paisley articulated the fears of many unionists in the face of political change and apparent 'surrender' to civil rights demands, and his Protestant Unionist Party took on a new lease of life when it was reorganised as the Democratic Unionist Party (DUP) in 1971. This challenged mainstream unionism, which itself was deeply divided, and grew steadily in electoral appeal through the 1970s. In March 1972, the Ulster Unionist Party received its biggest jolt, one from which it was never to recover, when the British government suspended Northern Ireland's devolved institutions, which had existed for over half a century. Direct rule from London followed, overseen by a new office holder, the Secretary of State for Northern Ireland, a member of the British cabinet (see Birrell, 2009).

Since the beginning of the 1970s, then, electoral politics in Northern Ireland has been dominated by two very distinctive forms of competition. First, nationalists have competed with unionists (though a small centrist party, the Alliance Party, has drawn some support from both communities since its foundation in 1970). After decades during which the combined representation of nationalists never exceeded a quarter of the seats in the Northern Ireland House of Commons, nationalist strength has been growing steadily, as discussed later, reflecting not just increased vote mobilising capacity on the part of the two nationalist parties but also a steady growth in the Catholic share of the population, from 35 per cent in 1961 to approximately 45 per cent in 2011 (by which date the Protestant share had dropped to 48 per cent). Second, there have been intense electoral struggles within the two communities. On the nationalist side, the SDLP inherited the mantle of the old Nationalist Party, seeing itself as the voice of its community and initially managing to beat off the Sinn Féin challenge that appeared in the early 1980s. On the unionist side, the Ulster Unionist Party, whose long-standing hegemony had been frittered away in the 1970s, nevertheless managed to remain ahead of the DUP for three decades. All of this was to change in November 2003, however, when the more militant parties on the two sides, Sinn Féin and the DUP, established a decisive lead within their respective blocs (see further discussion later).

The political parties in the Republic were by no means neutral bystanders in this process. The SDLP had a big impact in its early years on thinking within the major parties there. There was some early sympathy in the Republic, at both political level and among the general public, for Sinn Féin and the IRA, but this evaporated as the death toll from the IRA's armed campaign rose. From the early 1970s until the 1990s, Sinn Féin was not just regarded with hostility by Irish governments but was actively prevented from having open access to the southern state communications media (Sinn Féin members were not allowed to speak on radio or television from 1972 to 1994; see Chapter 12). To complete the picture, the Republic's relationship with all strands of unionism remained frosty until well into the 1990s, characterised more by mutual recrimination than by constructive dialogue.

The Irish–British relationship

As we have seen in Chapter 1, the relationship with Great Britain was a central, formative influence in Irish politics, leaving its imprint, in very different ways, on constitutional norms, party development and political behaviour. Over the life of the state, this relationship has gone through two broad phases that we consider in turn: up to the 1960s at least, an effort to establish complete independence of Great Britain, and, from the 1970s onwards, an attempt to renegotiate this relationship, in particular in response to developments in Northern Ireland.

The path to independence

In the early years of the state, the British–Irish relationship was a major issue of political dispute, as Irish governments – especially after 1932 – sought to extend the state's independence. The most important restrictions on Irish sovereignty were the continuing role of the King as head of state and Ireland's membership of the Commonwealth, both provided for in the Anglo–Irish treaty of 1921. Although these became less visible over time, each remained a formal reality until 1949, when the Republic of Ireland Act came into effect, breaking such links as remained with the monarchy and the Commonwealth.

The unique character of Ireland's position within the Commonwealth was clear from the outset. The unity of the early Commonwealth was symbolised by the crown, which was represented in each Commonwealth state by a governor-general, by tradition a British nobleman. But the Irish Free State broke with this tradition from the beginning: the first governor-general, Tim Healy (1922–28), appointed on the nomination of the Irish government, was neither British nor a nobleman; he was of West Cork middle-class background. Furthermore, he was discouraged by the Irish government from engaging in an active role. His successor was forced to resign in humiliating circumstances in 1932 by the new Fianna Fáil government, which then went on to secure the appointment of a new governor-general who was not only personally objectionable to the British but also fulfilled only the minimum constitutional functions of his office. Thus, the termination of this office in 1936, though of some symbolic significance, had few practical implications for the British–Irish relationship, which had already lost the kind of link that bound other Commonwealth governments to London (Coakley, 2012).

The restricted role of the governor-general was of considerable practical significance. In other Commonwealth states, the office of the governor-general at this time had many of the functions of a modern embassy; and the Commonwealth states, in turn, were represented in London by high commissioners, diplomats with quasi-ambassadorial status. Ironically, then, for almost two decades after 1922, Dublin had eyes, ears and a voice in London through its High Commission there, but London had no comparable formal channel of communication in Dublin. This position was rectified in September 1939, when the first British 'representative' in Dublin – his title deliberately vague – was appointed, just as the Second World War was breaking out. It was not until after 1949 that the holder of this post was designated an 'ambassador'.

Although the constitutional issue disappeared as a source of dispute after Ireland had finally severed its ties with crown and Commonwealth in 1949, the territorial issue remained contentious, not helped by British annoyance at Ireland's wartime policy of neutrality (a policy widely supported in Ireland, where participation in the war was commonly seen as not in Ireland's interest). The British responded to the Republic of Ireland Act with its own Ireland Act of 1949, which, while continuing to protect the position of Irish immigrants, declared that 'in no event will Northern Ireland or any part thereof ... cease to be part of the United Kingdom without the consent of the Parliament of Northern Ireland'. The question of partition continued periodically to inflame relations between the two governments, especially after a new all-party anti-partition campaign was launched in Dublin in 1949. But the relationship also had its positive moments. Earlier, for example, the Anglo–Irish agreements of 1938 had ended the financial dispute between the two states over repayments for loans under the pre-independence land acts, and resolved other outstanding differences, providing for British withdrawal from certain ports that had been retained under the terms of the 1921 Treaty (see Chapter 1). In 1965, the two governments signed the Anglo–Irish Free Trade Agreement, the most explicit acknowledgement of the need for practical cooperation up to that point, and a standing Irish–British Parliamentary Group was formally constituted in 1966 to bring British and Irish parliamentarians together (Coakley, 2017: 200).

The outbreak of the Northern Ireland troubles after 1968 once again cast a shadow on the Irish–British relationship – this time, at least initially, a substantial one (see Arthur, 2000; Craig, 2010; Williamson, 2017). Alongside the political rhetoric and, indeed, constitutional provisions that implied a territorial claim on Northern Ireland, public opinion was inflamed by the harsh treatment meted out to Catholics in such instances as the Derry civil rights march of October 1968, the Belfast riots of August 1969, the internment without trial of a large number of suspected IRA activists in 1971 and the killing of 13 unarmed civilians by British troops in Derry on 'Bloody Sunday' in January 1972. The resulting resentment was reflected in such episodes as the 'arms crisis' of 1970 (when prominent ministers were accused of colluding in an unsuccessful attempt to smuggle arms for use by northern nationalists) and the burning of the British embassy in 1972 (following sustained public protests in Dublin). But efforts by the Irish government to influence the course of events in Northern Ireland were brushed aside by the British government on the grounds that this was an internal United Kingdom affair, and thus no business of the Irish government (on the civil unrest, see Arthur and Jeffery, 1996; Bew *et al.*, 1996; for reference material, Elliott and Flackes, 1999; Bew and Gillespie, 1999; on the British perspective, Boyce, 1996; Cunningham, 2001).

The 'Irish dimension'

The suspension of the devolved institutions of government in Stormont and the introduction of direct rule from London in March 1972 transformed the context of the conflict. It became clear that the British government was moving closer to the SDLP position, implying acceptance not just of power sharing within Northern Ireland but also of involvement of the Republic in an institutionalised 'Irish dimension'. The outcome was the creation in 1973 of a new Northern Ireland Assembly that was required to produce an executive or government that would be 'broadly acceptable' throughout the community – code for power sharing between nationalists and unionists. Agreement on a three-party coalition comprising Ulster Unionists (themselves deeply divided on the issue), the SDLP and the Alliance Party was duly forthcoming, and in December 1973 an agreement at Sunningdale, England, between the Northern Ireland executive-designate and the British and Irish governments made provision for a Council of Ireland with significant executive powers. This would comprise a 60-member interparliamentary Consultative Assembly, an intergovernmental Council of Ministers and a permanent secretariat (Kerr, 2011; Hennessey, 2015; McCann and McGrattan, 2017).

The Council of Ireland agreed in 1973 was never to come into being. The Northern Ireland Executive did take up office in January 1974, but immediately ran into difficulties. Opponents of the Sunningdale Agreement took control of the Ulster Unionist Party in late January; an election to the British House of Commons in February 1974 registered a decisive majority in Northern Ireland for anti-Sunningdale unionists; and in May a political strike organised by the loyalist (or militant unionist) Ulster Workers' Council finally brought about the resignation of the executive (it was at this time, too, that the worst single set of incidents in all the troubles took place, when bombs in Dublin and Monaghan planted by loyalists killed 33 people). Subsequent efforts to revive devolution (such as a Constitutional Convention in 1975–76) failed, and the focus of British attention switched to security policy, expressed in a vigorous but unsuccessful attempt to defeat the IRA. As the 1970s advanced, the southern perspective, too, seemed to change, as politicians and the public lost their appetite for involvement in a conflict that was bloody, bitter and apparently intractable.

By the early 1980s, the time for a new initiative seemed right. The working relationship between the two governments had improved, partly because both were increasingly involved in joint decision making as a consequence of their accession to the European Community in 1973. There was a concrete political reason for seeking an alternative to a cycle of political violence that seemed unending. The two governments were worried by the rise of Sinn Féin. This had for long been a marginal force in electoral terms, but the deaths of 10 republican prisoners on hunger strike in 1981 resulted in a mobilisation of popular sympathy that gave the party a new lease of life. The British undertook their own initiative in 1982, with the creation of an assembly on which executive powers might be conferred if there was substantial consensus to this effect, in a so-called 'rolling devolution' scheme. This proved unsuccessful, since only two parties (the DUP and the Alliance Party) participated consistently in the assembly's affairs. Dublin, consigned to the sidelines, could do little other than reflect; but this it did with some energy. The government set up an inter-party New Ireland Forum that met in 1983–84, bringing together the three main southern parties and the SDLP (predictably, the unionist parties did not accept an invitation to attend). This sought to arrive at a nationalist consensus on the way forward, and its report, under pressure from Fianna Fáil leader Charles Haughey, identified a unitary Irish state as its preferred option. It also considered two other models: a federal or confederal state, and joint rule over Northern Ireland by the two sovereign governments (for a summary of the forum's conclusions, see Coakley, 2002: 170–4).

Although the constitutional models considered by the New Ireland Forum were each dismissed by British prime minister Margaret Thatcher, who listed the three options and declared that each was 'out', she nevertheless engaged in intense negotiations with the Irish side, and these led to a far-reaching agreement at Hillsborough, Co Down, in November 1985. This Anglo–Irish Agreement of 1985 was designed to bypass the capacity of either side in Northern Ireland to block it by simply excluding them from the new arrangements, which gave the Irish government a formal voice in Northern Ireland affairs. The agreement was vehemently rejected by unionists, who saw it as allowing the Irish government a foot in the door in Northern Ireland, but the IRA also continued with its military campaign (see Aughey and Gormley-Heenan, 2011; for the impact on unionism, Cochrane, 1997; Farrington, 2006).

The agreement did not come close to satisfying the stated preference of nationalist Ireland, stopping well short of even the notion of joint rule, but its provisions were nevertheless remarkable (for the text, see Elliott, 2002: 194–9). There was to be an Anglo–Irish Intergovernmental Conference that would meet regularly and frequently to discuss matters of common interest; it would have particular responsibility for a wide range of matters impinging on relations between the two communities within Northern Ireland. Although sovereignty would continue to reside with the British, the Irish government would be entitled to express its views and make proposals on all matters falling within the ambit of the conference, and in the event of disagreement between the two sides, 'determined efforts' would be made to resolve them. The work of the conference would be serviced by a standing secretariat drawn from the Irish and UK civil services. Significantly, international (and especially American) support for the deal was signalled by the creation of the International Fund for Ireland, which has offered substantial financial support for socio-economic development projects in Northern Ireland and the border counties, jointly administered by civil servants from Dublin and Belfast.

The mere existence of these structures was significant, but the definition of the areas to which they applied was even more striking. In general, these covered political, security and legal matters, including the administration of justice, and cross-border cooperation was also to be promoted. The language of the agreement made it clear that the two governments were moving increasingly towards recognition of Northern Ireland as having a binational character. The agreement was defined as comprising a framework 'for the accommodation of the rights and identities of the two traditions which exist in Northern Ireland', and for promoting 'reconciliation, respect for human rights, co-operation against terrorism and the development of economic, social and cultural co-operation'. It was agreed that the Intergovernmental Conference would consider 'measures to foster the cultural heritage of both traditions, changes in electoral arrangements, the use of flags and emblems, the avoidance of economic and social discrimination and the advantages and disadvantages of a Bill of Rights in some form in Northern Ireland'. The extent to which these measures were designed to improve the circumstances of nationalists, in particular, was underlined by the granting of an explicit right to the Irish government to make representations on behalf of the nationalist community. The agreement also went further than ever before in defining the circumstances under which Irish unity could come about, while also accepting current constitutional realities. It developed more explicitly one of the provisions of the Sunningdale Agreement, stating that

> The two Governments
> a affirm that any change in the status of Northern Ireland would only come about with the consent of a majority of the people of Northern Ireland;
> b recognise that the present wish of a majority of the people of Northern Ireland is for no change in the status of Northern Ireland;
> c declare that, if in the future a majority of the people of Northern Ireland clearly wish for and formally consent to the establishment of a united Ireland, they will introduce and support in the respective Parliaments legislation to give effect to that wish.

The agreement also endorsed the creation of a parliamentary body that would link the two jurisdictions, though this came into existence only in 1990.

The Good Friday Agreement

The Anglo–Irish Agreement of 1985 did not provide a solution to the problems of Northern Ireland, and was probably not intended to do so in any kind of permanent way. By attempting to enhance the status of the nationalist community, it strove to undermine support for the IRA, but that body continued its armed campaign. The agreement was perceived by unionists as damaging, unfair and one-sided, and they did their utmost to overturn it. But it had been designed to withstand the kinds of action that had brought down the power-sharing executive in 1974. The two governments in Dublin and London were far distant from Northern Ireland, and the new Anglo–Irish secretariat, though based just outside Belfast, was physically out of bounds to protesters. The result was that the agreement was able to survive street protests, strenuous objections in parliament and even the force of unionist opinion (all 15 unionist

MPs in the British House of Commons resigned their seats to force a set of by-elections on the issue in January 1986, though the net outcome was that one unionist seat was lost).

The agreement did, however, have a considerable impact on the positions of the various parties. For Sinn Féin, it was something of a setback: to the extent that it represented a victory for constitutional nationalism, it gave the SDLP an advantage. SDLP leader John Hume sought to build on this, engaging in talks with Sinn Féin leader Gerry Adams from 1988 onwards. These resulted ultimately in a document defining a shared nationalist position, and much of this was incorporated in the 'Downing Street declaration' of 1993, a joint statement by the British Prime Minister and the Taoiseach to the effect that talks would be held on an open-ended agenda regarding the future of Northern Ireland, and that all parties not engaged in violence could participate in them. This led ultimately to the IRA ceasefire of August 1994, which was quickly followed by a loyalist ceasefire (for background, see Gilligan and Tonge, 1997; Mallie and McKittrick, 1997; Hennessey, 2000; Moloney, 2002; Cox *et al.*, 2006). But the 1985 agreement also held out a carrot to unionists: it provided that the Anglo–Irish Intergovernmental Conference would not have jurisdiction over any matters that were the responsibility of devolved institutions within Northern Ireland. If, therefore, agreement could be reached on the establishment of such institutions (which the governments insisted would have to be based on the principle of power sharing), the Anglo–Irish Agreement would be undermined. Many unionists hoped that it would be possible to arrive at a new agreement that would supersede that of 1985; they thus had a vested interest in coming to the negotiating table (see Aughey, 1989; Cochrane, 1997).

Accompanying these shifting positions and perspectives was an intense process of discussion between the various parties (de Bréadún, 2008). The Irish government convened a Forum for Peace and Reconciliation in Dublin in 1994–96 that involved the previously marginalised Sinn Féin in a series of discussions with the SDLP, the Alliance Party and the southern parties. The British government organised elections to a Northern Ireland Forum (1996–98), whose main function was to provide teams for inter-party talks (most of these took place outside the Forum, which the nationalist parties in any case did not attend). With the assistance of a great deal of informal diplomacy and external mediation (notably by a team headed by former US senator George Mitchell), talks between the Northern Ireland parties and the two governments in 1997–98 finally resulted in agreement on Good Friday, 10 April 1998. This was approved by referendum on 22 May 1998, with the support of 94 per cent of those voting in the Republic and 71 per cent in Northern Ireland (where surveys showed support from more than 90 per cent of Catholics and more than 50 percent of Protestants).[2] It also formed part of a broader package of constitutional reform within the United Kingdom, with the introduction of devolved government in Scotland and Wales (Coakley *et al.*, 2005).

The Good Friday Agreement (also known as the Belfast Agreement) was remarkable for the range of parties that went along with its provisions and for the wide span of areas that it covered. The DUP had withdrawn from the talks process in 1997 when Sinn Féin was admitted, but all of the other significant parties, including Sinn Féin and two small parties close to the main loyalist paramilitary organisations, had joined the British and Irish governments in approving the final draft. The agreement covered not only the issues of power sharing within Northern Ireland and the 'Irish dimension' (now renamed 'strand one' and 'strand two' respectively), it also introduced a 'strand three' – the broader British–Irish relationship. But the agreement went even further than this, addressing long-term constitutional matters, short-term issues arising from decades of conflict and a number of areas of particular concern to one community or the other (see Box 13.1; for the text of the agreement, Elliott, 2002: 223–34; for analyses, Ruane and Todd, 1999; Wilford, 2001; McGarry and O'Leary, 2004; Cox *et al.*, 2006).

Box 13.1 The Good Friday Agreement, 1998

1. Strand one: devolved government for Northern Ireland

- A 108-member legislative assembly with consociational provisions
- A First Minister and a Deputy First Minister elected on a cross community basis
- An executive comprising up to 10 ministers chosen by the D'Hondt formula
- A committee system with chairs and deputy chairs chosen by the D'Hondt formula

2. Strand two: links between Northern Ireland and the Republic of Ireland

- A North/South Ministerial Council bringing together ministers from the two administrations
- A North–South secretariat comprising northern and southern civil servants (established in Armagh)
- Six North–South implementation bodies
- Six areas of cooperation between the two administrations

3. Strand three: links between Ireland and Great Britain

- A British–Irish Council linking eight administrations
- A British–Irish Intergovernmental Conference linking the two sovereign governments
- A British–Irish joint secretariat comprising British and Irish civil servants (established in Belfast)

4. Other provisions

Constitutional issues: The agreement acknowledged that a majority of the population of Northern Ireland wished to remain in the United Kingdom; the Irish government agreed to hold a referendum to drop its constitutional claim on Northern Ireland; and the British government agreed to facilitate Irish unity should a majority support this.

Equality: The governments acknowledged the divided nature of Northern Irish society and committed themselves to respecting the equality of the two cultures, including a right to opt for either British or Irish citizenship, or both, whatever the overall territorial arrangements.

Policing and human rights: An independent commission on policing would recommend on a police force acceptable to the two communities; the criminal justice system would be reviewed; and a commission on human rights would be established.

Addressing the legacy of conflict: There would be an accelerated programme of early release of prisoners; structures to assist victims of the violence would be established; the parties to the agreement pledged themselves to work in good faith to remove all paramilitary weapons; and the British government agreed to a reduction in the security force presence.

Strand one: domestic politics in Northern Ireland

The core of the new arrangements was a set of devolved institutions in Belfast that were given responsibility for most matters of domestic policy making. The key, in turn, to the functioning of these is the balance of political forces represented in a newly created Northern Ireland Assembly. This was to have 108 members, elected by the single transferable vote system of proportional representation (see Chapter 4), from 18 six-member constituencies (which correspond to those used as single-member constituencies in elections to the UK House of Commons).

In line with provisions commonly to be found in 'consociational' democracies, such as Belgium, where elaborate power- and resource-sharing measures are designed to overcome deep societal divisions, all members of the assembly (MLAs) are required either to designate themselves 'unionist' or 'nationalist', or to opt out and self-designate as 'other'. In a number of the most politically sensitive areas, the assembly is obliged to make its decisions 'on a cross-community basis', defined as enjoying support either by a majority of the assembly plus majorities within the unionist and nationalist blocs, or by a 60 per cent majority of the assembly plus support from at least 40 per cent of the members of each of these two blocs. In addition, a petition of concern invoking cross-community voting can be triggered by a 'significant minority' of MLAs (specified as 30 out of 108).

The main example of the first of these qualified majority systems in operation was the election of the First Minister and the Deputy First Minister. The agreement required them to be elected by means of a single vote, with a requirement of majority support within each of the two blocs (thus ensuring, in effect, that one post would go to each of the two communities). Other ministerial posts were to be allocated on the basis of the D'Hondt electoral system (a proportional representation formula commonly used for parliamentary elections in continental European list systems). The largest party is given the first seat, and subsequent seats are allocated following the conventional D'Hondt formula, each party selecting its preferred ministry as its turn arrives. Provision was also made for a strong committee system, the committees corresponding to government departments and reflecting party strength in the assembly. Their chairs and deputy chairs, too, were to be selected in accordance with the D'Hondt formula.

The first election to the new assembly took place in 1998, and led to the installation of a four-party executive, comprising the two main unionist and the two main nationalist parties. Because of prolonged haggling over other issues (with the failure of the IRA to 'decommission' weapons as a major stumbling block), the executive did not take office until December 1999. Even after that, though, it functioned in a stop–start way because of internal political pressures, until finally collapsing in 2002. It took almost five years for a new executive to get up and running, as discussed below.

Strand two: the North–South dimension

Although unionists were prepared to swallow a form of power sharing within Northern Ireland that went much further than that implemented in 1973–74, they had particular difficulties with any attempt to revive the Council of Ireland concept agreed at that time. The result was the creation of a set of bodies with a less ambitious political superstructure and a more practical focus, some of them building on existing systems of cross-border cooperation, much of it EU funded (on the EU dimension, see Tannam, 1999; Murphy, 2014). The most important of the new institutions is the North/South Ministerial Council, which has a small standing secretariat in Armagh. In February 2017, the secretariat was made up of 18 people, nine seconded from the civil service in Dublin and the rest from Northern Ireland.

The North/South Ministerial Council meets in three formats: plenary, sectoral and institutional. In its plenary form, it includes the Taoiseach and the Northern Ireland First Minister and Deputy First Minister as its core, but the practice in the 23 meetings that had taken place by the end of January 2017 has been for most members of the Irish government and the Northern Ireland Executive to attend. The agenda tends to focus on long-term planning for North–South collaboration, but with the United Kingdom's plans to leave the European Union acquiring particular prominence in 2016. The council has also met 10 times in 'institutional' format to consider business that did not fall under any other heading, including technical matters, such as appointments to boards.

The most common type of meeting of the council is the sectoral one. Sectoral meetings consist of the relevant southern minister, his or her northern counterpart, and a northern minister from the 'other' side (for example, if the responsible northern minister was a member of the DUP, a nationalist minister would also attend). Their agenda is highly focused, dealing with the work of a specific implementation body or area of cooperation. In the first phase during which the agreement was up and running (December 1999 to October 2002), a total of 60 sectoral meetings took place. During the long period of suspension of the devolved institutions in Belfast (October 2002 to May 2007), no meetings at all were organised, but the two governments monitored the work of the implementation bodies on a 'care and maintenance' basis, taking any necessary decisions regarding existing functions but not incorporating new ones. Normal business resumed in October 2007, and by 1 January 2017 a further 207 sectoral meetings had been held, though a number of these took place on the same day in the interests of efficiency.[3] Before 2010, meetings alternated between various towns in Northern Ireland (52 per cent of all meetings), with a further 33 per cent in Dublin and 15 per cent elsewhere in the Republic, mainly in the border counties; but since 2010, following the construction of a new, purpose-built headquarters to house the secretariat in Armagh, 80 per cent of meetings have taken place there.

The North/South Ministerial Council supervises two main types of activity: the work of implementation bodies, and areas in which the two administrations function separately but cooperate formally. Under the provisions of the agreement, six North–South 'implementation bodies' were set up. These are listed in Table 13.1, which also gives an indication of the staffing and the budget of each. Some of the bodies (such as Waterways Ireland, responsible

Table 13.1 North–South implementation bodies, 2016

Implementation body	Headquarters	Staff, 2016	Budget, 2016 (€m)
Waterways Ireland	Enniskillen	320	22.8
Food Safety Promotion Board	Cork	30	7.5
InterTrade Ireland	Newry	38	12.0
Special EU Programmes Body	Belfast	59	2.6
Language Body	Dublin and Belfast	72	13.2
Foyle, Carlingford and Irish Lights Commission	Derry	53	5.5

Source: Information supplied by the secretariat of the North/South Ministerial Council.

Note: There is also a de facto seventh implementation body, Tourism Ireland, with 148 staff and a budget of €52.7m.

for maintenance and development of all of the island's inland waterways, mainly for leisure purposes) have a relatively large staff and a highly visible impact. Others (such as the Special EU Programmes Body) have a small staff and budget, but have been responsible for administering much larger tranches of funds from the European Union. Some (such as the Food Safety Promotion Board – operating under the label Safefood – and InterTrade Ireland) are entirely new bodies; others (such as the Foyle, Carlingford and Irish Lights Commission) are based largely on existing ones. Indeed, in the latter case, one of the existing bodies, the Commissioners of Irish Lights, established in another form in 1786, has not been brought under the aegis of the Council (the fact that it forms part of a coastal protection system shared with Great Britain posed certain legal difficulties). In the case of the language body, there are two agencies. One, Foras na Gaeilge, was made up of existing Dublin-based bodies that now have a 32-county function and the second, the Ulster-Scots Agency, is an entirely new body whose mandate is to promote the Ulster Scots language and culture.

In addition to the areas where implementation bodies were established, it was agreed that in six other designated areas cooperation would take place through the medium of existing departments. The areas are agriculture, education, environment, health, tourism and transport. Actual levels of cooperation in these areas have been very uneven. In the area of tourism, for example, cooperation proceeded rapidly, though much of it had begun even before the Good Friday Agreement. The result was the creation in 2000 of a new all-Ireland tourist promotion company, Tourism Ireland Ltd – in effect, a seventh implementation body. In health, too, a good deal of progress has been made. In the transport sector, by contrast, where the case for coordinated planning is virtually unanswerable, cooperation has been relatively slow, though it was promoted by the British and Irish governments during the period of direct rule (2002–07; see Coakley and O'Dowd, 2007).

Although the impact of the North–South architecture created by the Good Friday Agreement is potentially great, since the mandate of the bodies is an all-Ireland one, its visibility has been low, largely because of the very specific areas to which its writ has been confined. The planned North–South parliamentary body finally appeared only in 2012, and then in the looser form of a North–South Inter-Parliamentary Association. It met twice-yearly in Dublin and Belfast in 2013–15, but in the election year of 2016, it met only once, in December. The North–South Consultative Forum planned in the agreement has not appeared at all, though it continues to feature on the agenda of meetings of the North/South Ministerial Council.

The origins of much of the momentum driving North–South cooperation in the early twenty-first century lie outside the structures created by the Good Friday Agreement. Thus, the Irish government reacted to the challenge posed by the United Kingdom's decision to leave the EU by launching a series of meetings, beginning on 2 November 2016, under the framework of an All-Island Civic Dialogue on Brexit. Designed to bring together affected interests from Northern Ireland and the Republic, its objective was to make recommendations to the government on dealing with the consequences of Brexit. At governmental level, the island-level response to the same challenge was organised formally through the North/South Ministerial Council, supplemented by *ad hoc* meetings between Northern Ireland officials and their southern counterparts.

Indeed, many of the most striking instances of North–South cooperation have taken place outside the framework of the agreement. Thus, for example, two important agencies promoting collaboration in health and social care services (Cooperation and Working Together and the Institute of Public Health in Ireland) date from 1992 and 1998 respectively (Pollak, 2017); the introduction of an all-Ireland free travel pass for those of pension age was introduced in 2007, by agreement between the Irish and British governments; much planning in relation to the road network has been organised on a similar basis; and so too has work on cooperation in the energy sector, culminating in the creation of an all-island single electricity market in 2007.

Strand three: the British–Irish dimension

In many respects, the strand three provisions of the Good Friday Agreement were seen as a trade-off for the strand two provisions: nationalists were particularly keen on links with the Republic, and unionists were to the fore in demanding a strengthening of links with Great Britain. Here, the most visible institution is a new British–Irish Council. This is intergovern- mental in structure, and links the administrations of eight territories of very uneven status for purposes of information sharing and policy co-ordination on matters of common inter- est: two sovereign states (the Republic of Ireland and the United Kingdom), three devolved administrations within the United Kingdom (Scotland, Wales and Northern Ireland), and three autonomous crown territories close to the UK (the Isle of Man and the Channel Islands of Jersey and Guernsey). By February 2017, 28 plenary meetings of the council had taken place, and modest progress had been made in a number of sectors (such as data collection and infor- mation sharing on the environment, drugs, transport, housing, energy and spatial planning) where a common approach appeared sensible (Coakley, 2014: 85–8). The British vote to leave the European Union aroused particular interest among members of the Council, which met in an extraordinary session in June 2016, immediately after the referendum; but, given political divisions and diverging priorities on the Council, as well as an absence of clarity on the full implications of Brexit, it was able to do little more than function as a forum for discussion.

The British–Irish Interparliamentary Body continued alongside these institutions. It was made up originally of 50 members drawn equally from the British and Irish parliaments, but its membership was enlarged to 68 in 2001, with the inclusion of representatives of the United Kingdom's three devolved regions and of the Channel Islands and the Isle of Man. The body has been useful as a bridge-building exercise and in constructing informal net- works among its members; by the end of 2016, 53 plenary meetings had taken place. Its work proceeded mainly through a committee system extending over four areas: security matters, European affairs, economic matters and the broad environmental and social area (Coakley, 2014: 82–5). Not surprisingly, the second of these – European affairs – acquired particular salience in the Brexit context.

The Good Friday Agreement also created a less visible agency that fits uncomfortably in strand three, the British–Irish Intergovernmental Conference, designed to bring together the two sovereign governments in respect of areas not devolved to the new institutions in Belfast. At first sight, it resembled its predecessor, the Anglo–Irish Intergovernmental Conference, established in 1985, but in principle it also contained representatives of the northern parties, and thus of unionism, since provision was made for participation in its affairs by 'relevant' members of the Northern Ireland Executive. Its role was limited by the fact that matters devolved to the Northern Ireland Assembly were excluded from its mandate, which was fur- ther reduced following the devolution of justice powers in 2010. In practice, the Conference met infrequently, and it has not met at all since 2007, when a sustained period of devolved government began. In 2012 the British side of the secretariat moved physically back to the Northern Ireland Office in Stormont, leaving the Irish side to continue to represent the Irish government in Belfast. Though no longer functioning as a joint secretariat except in name, the officials involved on the two sides meet periodically and act jointly when necessary. The Irish officials in the secretariat also fulfil a significant representational and symbolic function, playing a discreet role in liaising on behalf of the Irish government with a wide range of groups across the political spectrum (Coakley, 2014: 77–81). In many respects, the functions originally filled by the Conference are now managed by more extensive and intensive patterns of bilateral contact between the two governments. The challenges of Brexit may, however, give formal institutions of this kind a new lease of life, should the need for more structured cooperation arise.

Resolving issues of contention

Reaching an accommodation on the shape of major political institutions was an outstanding achievement in a society as divided as Northern Ireland, but the Good Friday Agreement went further, also addressing a range of other issues that were exceptionally contentious. These included long-term constitutional matters; the question of equality between the two communities in the economic, social, cultural and political domains; outstanding challenges in the area of security, policing and human rights; and the dilemma of making a transition from conditions of armed conflict, with its legacy of fundamental problems, to a more peaceful dispensation.

In the constitutional domain, nationalist Ireland made major concessions. Article 2 of the Irish constitution, which originally stated that 'the national territory consists of the whole island of Ireland, its islands and the territorial seas', was replaced following the 1998 constitutional referendum by a new wording that stated merely that 'it is the entitlement and birthright of every person born in the island of Ireland, which includes its islands and seas, to be part of the Irish Nation'. Article 3 was also amended to make it clear that Irish unity could come about 'only by peaceful means with the consent of a majority of the people, democratically expressed, in both jurisdictions in the island'. The agreement also sought to reassure nationalists by acknowledging that Irish unity would be implemented if majorities within Northern Ireland and the Republic supported this.

The agreement also acknowledged the divided nature of Northern Irish society, and the two governments committed themselves to respecting cultural equality and dual nationality, including the right of the people of Northern Ireland to opt for either British or Irish citizenship, or both. Specific reforms were planned in the areas of criminal justice, human rights and policing (of which the most visible outcome was the reorganisation of the Royal Ulster Constabulary in 2001 to form a new Police Service of Northern Ireland, with a more substantial Catholic membership and a more neutral ethos). A programme of accelerated release of prisoners and a set of measures designed to assist victims of the violence were also put in place. The issue of demilitarisation posed the biggest challenge of all. The decommissioning of the weapons of paramilitary groups, and especially of the IRA, became a central political issue that destabilised the Northern Ireland Executive, but the impasse was largely resolved when in September 2005 the IRA completed the process, begun in October 2001, of putting its arms beyond use. The British military presence was reduced in 2005–07 to 'garrison strength', as troops withdrew from their former security role.

Towards a stable political system?

While the Good Friday Agreement marked a significant normalisation in the North–South and British–Irish relationships, its provisions for the domestic government of Northern Ireland continued to come under challenge (for overviews, see Barton and Roche, 2009; Clancy, 2010; Mitchell, 2015). On the one hand, the original alliance between the more 'centrist' of the two unionist and the two nationalist parties that had dominated the power-sharing government, the Ulster Unionist Party and the SDLP, crumbled in the face of growing support for the two more radical parties within the respective communities, the DUP and Sinn Féin. On the other hand, the passage of time inevitably exposed gaps in the original Good Friday blueprint, requiring some patching up through supplementary agreements.

Political change

The pattern of party politics in Northern Ireland, as this had been consolidated in the 1980s and 1990s, survived in the early years after the Good Friday Agreement, with the SDLP supported by most Catholics and the Ulster Unionist Party as the dominant one among Protestants. Together, these parties headed the Northern Ireland Executive, which, as well as David Trimble of the Ulster Unionist Party as First Minister and Seamus Mallon of the SDLP as Deputy First Minister, included three other Ulster Unionist, three SDLP, two DUP and two Sinn Féin ministers. The life of this first executive was a stressful one. DUP ministers refused to attend its meetings, though working in their ministerial posts. A prolonged stand-off between the Ulster Unionists and Sinn Féin over the decommissioning of IRA weapons and related security issues precipitated several suspensions of the institutions, and ultimately the re-introduction of direct rule from London (this entailed the Secretary of State for Northern Ireland and junior ministers again taking responsibility for running the government of Northern Ireland). The first major period of direct rule extended over more than three months, from 11 February to 29 May 2000; but the institutions were again suspended indefinitely on 14 October 2002. A fresh assembly election in November 2003 did little to bring the institutions back to life; it simply confirmed that the DUP had overtaken the Ulster Unionist Party as the main party on the unionist side, and that Sinn Féin had overtaken the SDLP as the largest nationalist party (see Figure 13.1).

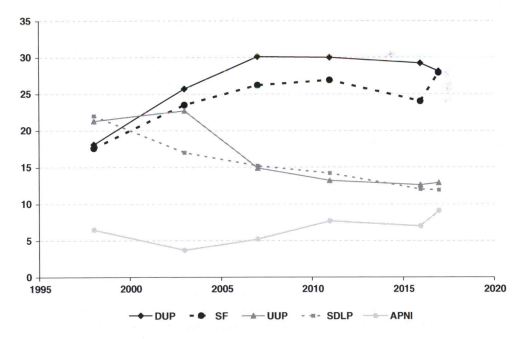

Figure 13.1 Northern Ireland Assembly election results, 1998–2017

Note: Only the largest five parties are included. The data points (election dates) are 1998, 2003, 2007, 2011, 2016 and 2017, and indicate percentages of the valid poll.

The rise of the DUP and Sinn Féin appeared to bode ill for implementation of the agreement, given their diametrically opposed perspectives on major policy matters. Nevertheless, following minor structural changes to the Good Friday Agreement negotiated in St Andrews, Scotland, in October 2006 – changes sufficient to allow the DUP to argue that it had now been replaced by a new agreement – the DUP agreed to share office with Sinn Féin, which in turn agreed to fully accept the police service. Fresh assembly elections in March 2007 further consolidated the lead of the DUP and Sinn Féin within their respective blocs, and a new executive, headed by Reverend Ian Paisley as First Minister and Martin McGuinness of Sinn Féin as Deputy First Minister, took office in May 2007 (it consisted of four other DUP ministers, three Sinn Féin, two Ulster Unionist and one SDLP minister). The North–South and British–Irish institutions, which had entered semi-dormant mode following the collapse of the power-sharing executive, were easily revived.

Notwithstanding considerable challenges and disagreements over policy issues, the executive put in place in 2007 survived for almost a decade with little change, reflecting a relatively stable balance of political forces in the assembly. Ian Paisley was replaced as First Minister by his DUP colleague, Peter Robinson, in June 2008, and Robinson was in turn replaced by Arlene Foster in January 2016. Martin McGuinness of Sinn Féin continued to be Deputy First Minister over this period. There were, however, some changes in the composition of the executive. To start with, the arithmetic in the assembly changed following a further election in 2011 – not much, but enough for the Ulster Unionist Party to lose one of its two seats to the Alliance Party. The Alliance Party also profited from agreement on the creation of a Justice Ministry in 2010. Given the sensitivity of this area, provision was made that the Justice Minister should be appointed by a cross-community vote rather than as part of the D'Hondt process, and the parties agreed that the Alliance Party leader would be offered this post. In yet another change, the Ulster Unionist Party withdrew from the executive in October 2015, and its seat passed to the DUP.

Although the balance of political forces in the assembly remained almost unchanged following the 2016 election, there was a much sharper shift in the composition of the

Table 13.2 Distribution of seats in the Northern Ireland Assembly, 1998–2017

Party	1998	2003	2007	2011	2016	2017
Democratic Unionist Party	20	30	36	38	38	28
Ulster Unionist Party	28	27	18	16	16	10
Other unionist	10	2	1	2	2	2
(Total Unionist designation)	*58*	*59*	*55*	*56*	*56*	*40*
Sinn Féin	18	24	28	29	28	27
Social Democratic and Labour Party	24	18	16	14	12	12
(Total Nationalist designation)	*42*	*42*	*44*	*43*	*40*	*39*
Alliance Party	6	6	7	8	8	8
Other	2	1	2	1	4	3
(Total Other designation)	*8*	*7*	*9*	*9*	*12*	*11*
Total	108	108	108	108	108	90

Note: The table takes account of party affiliations and designations immediately after each election, ignoring later changes. 'Other unionist' includes five UK Unionist Party in 1998 and one in 2003; two Progressive Unionist Party in 1998 and one each in 2003 and 2007; one Traditional Unionist Voice in 2011, 2016 and 2017; and three independent unionists in 1998 and one in 2011, 2016 and 2017. 'Other' includes two Women's Coalition in 1998; one independent in 2003 and 2007; one Green in 2007 and 2011, and two in 2016 and 2017; and two People Before Profit Alliance in 2016 and one in 2017.

executive. Following the introduction of arrangements to facilitate the formation of an official opposition on the Westminster model, the three smaller executive parties (the Ulster Unionists, the SDLP and the Alliance Party) did not participate in the D'Hondt ministerial allocation process, instead going into opposition. The outcome was an executive, now reduced in size, in which (apart from the First Minister and Deputy First Minister) there were four DUP and three Sinn Féin ministers; an independent unionist was elected Justice Minister. The life of this two-party coalition was, however, short and bitter. In addition to several unresolved issues inherited from the years of the conflict and unfulfilled commitments from earlier agreements, Sinn Féin accused the DUP of unwillingness to compromise in areas of dispute, notably over the handling of a scandal over a botched scheme to encourage use of more environmentally friendly heating fuel. Sinn Féin withdrew from the executive in January 2017, precipitating a fresh assembly election.

Following a rancorous campaign, and a big increase in turnout, especially in nationalist areas, the DUP lost out heavily in the March 2017 election, with Sinn Féin making big gains; its assembly party had only one member fewer than that of the DUP, a symbolically important consideration because of the entitlement of the largest party to the post of First Minister. For the first time ever, those designating themselves as 'unionist' failed to win a majority in the assembly, and both the DUP and Sinn Féin adopted positions that would make the formation of a new executive difficult. This electoral trend was a consequence not just of a significant mobilisation of nationalists, but also of demographic evolution, as the proportion of Catholics has risen steadily. Though survey evidence consistently shows that, in present circumstances, only a minority of Catholics support Irish unity, pro-union Catholics typically do not regard themselves as 'unionists', and only a tiny proportion of them vote for unionist parties (see Hayes and McAllister, 2013; Coakley, 2015).

Underlying the dynamics of these electoral changes has been a significant reconfiguration of the competing parties and political forces. On the nationalist side, the transformation of Sinn Féin from an uncompromising party of Irish unity to one prepared to accept (however grudgingly) the constitutional status quo has been remarkable (see Murray and Tonge, 2005; Bean, 2007; Frampton, 2009; Sanders, 2011; Spencer, 2014). But this ideological transition has come at a cost: as Sinn Féin has moved towards the middle ground, it has left space for 'dissident' republican groups to occupy the traditional republican position, however limited their capacity to disrupt the political settlement by violent action or otherwise (Frampton, 2011; Taylor and Currie, 2011; Horgan, 2013; Whiting, 2015). On the unionist side, the formal success of the Good Friday Agreement in securing the Union appears to have had limited impact on the parties. The Ulster Unionist Party, responsible for delivering this deal, has been punished electorally, reduced to a secondary position by the DUP (Patterson and Kaufmann, 2007; McAuley, 2010; Tonge *et al.*, 2014). At the same time, organisations such as the Orange Order and loyalist paramilitary groups continue to keep vigil against a perceived threat to the British identity of their community (Kaufmann, 2007; McAuley and Spencer, 2011; Reed, 2015; McAuley, 2016).

Institutional reform

The pattern of party politics in Northern Ireland evolved alongside a path of significant institutional developments. The Good Friday Agreement, for all the range of public life over which it extended, did not resolve all matters in dispute. In some areas, such as arrangements for devolved government in Northern Ireland, it provided a relatively detailed blueprint. In others, such as the North–South bodies, it outlined the broad pattern that was envisaged, leaving the details to be negotiated. In yet others, such as policing, it committed itself to general principles only, handing responsibility for specific arrangements over to a commission that would report later (on the new system of government, see Knox, 2010; Birrell and Gormley-Heenan, 2015).

Since the various components of the agreement were interlocking, it is not surprising that it took almost two years for the new institutions to be formally launched (on 2 December 1999). Even then, the institutions were overshadowed by the issue of IRA decommissioning, one finally resolved only in September 2005.[4] Other reforms (such as policing) took some time; some (such as the compilation of a bill of rights for Northern Ireland) were never completed. As well as these elements of unfinished business, the experience of operating the new institutions suggested modifications in certain areas. This resulted in a number of supplementary agreements, of which three were of particular importance.

First, for several years after the collapse of devolved government in 2002, the prospects of restoration appeared poor, given the diametrically opposed perspectives of the DUP and Sinn Féin. But a set of negotiations between the parties and the British and Irish governments at St Andrews, Scotland, concluding on 13 October 2006, led to a new deal that made minor changes to the Good Friday Agreement. These included measures designed to make the running of the executive more efficient, but in particular a new mechanism for appointing the First Minister and the Deputy First Minister. They would no longer be elected by joint vote of the assembly (thus sparing the DUP from having to vote for a Sinn Féin Deputy First Minister), but would emerge automatically: the leader of the largest party in the assembly would simply designate the First Minister, while the leader of the largest group in the other designation (unionist or nationalist) would nominate the Deputy First Minister.[5] With DUP agreement to share power on this basis, and Sinn Féin willingness to fully accept the police service, it was possible for a new executive to take office following fresh assembly elections in 2007.

Second, while the St Andrews Agreement made provision for the transfer to Northern Ireland of powers in the area of justice, the details were not worked out. This was a particularly sensitive area given the long history of antagonism between Sinn Féin and the police, and deep unionist suspicions of Sinn Féin. Following further discussions between the parties, agreement was reached at Hillsborough Castle on 5 February 2010 on the establishment of a new Justice Department whose minister would be elected in a cross-community vote (rather than being based on the D'Hondt process, as in the case of the other ministers). The agreement also tried to resolve other matters of dispute, notably that of contentious parades.

Third, following further tensions within the executive over both legacy issues arising from the conflict and new ones associated with UK-wide reduction in social welfare provisions, a further agreement designed to stabilise the executive was arrived at in Stormont House on 23 December 2014.[6] This made provision for mechanisms for dealing with clashes over cultural matters (such as flags and parades) and for unresolved matters arising from the civil conflict, as well as for additional funding and cost-saving measures. It was agreed that the size of the assembly would be reduced from 108 to 90 (as indeed it was for the 2017 election), that the size of the executive would be reduced by three, and, significantly, that provision would be made for an official opposition to accommodate parties entitled to places in the executive but unwilling to take these up. A 'Fresh Start' agreement almost a year later, on 17 November 2015, sought to secure implementation of the Stormont House Agreement and extended it in certain respects, but a range of deeply divisive issues remained unresolved.

Conclusion

The evolution of politics within Northern Ireland owes much to the stewardship of the British and Irish governments, which had been moving towards an agreed position on this matter since the early 1970s. But it also flowed from a steady moderation in the positions of the parties there, and especially of the more militant ones. Sinn Féin has moved to a position of unreserved support for peaceful methods to achieve political change, and the DUP has, in the past, shown itself capable of imaginative compromise. There has also been remarkable rapprochement on two other axes, the North–South and Irish–British ones. The Republic has not just dropped its territorial claim to Northern Ireland, but guaranteed in its constitution that Irish unity can only come about by democratic agreement. Nationalist opinion, North and South, appears content with a settlement in which the unity of the island is symbolised by a few all-island bodies of limited reach, perhaps reflecting declining commitment to Irish unity (see Chapter 2; Hayward, 2009; McGrattan and Meehan, 2012; Ó Dochartaigh *et al.*, 2017; Coakley, 2002, 2015, 2017).

The shared British–Irish intergovernmental position was, however, greatly facilitated by joint membership of the European Union, and came under severe pressure as measures to take the United Kingdom out of the European Union proceeded. This has big implications for the British–Irish relationship, and may lead to an enhanced role for existing bodies, such as the British–Irish Council and the British–Irish Parliamentary Assembly. But it has exceptional significance for the North–South relationship. The Good Friday Agreement took for granted a 'soft' North–South border that would facilitate cross-jurisdictional transactions and the work of the North–South bodies. The prospective emergence of a 'hard' border between North and South thus had the effect of further raising the stakes as regards the relationship between the Republic and its nearest neighbour, a matter that is addressed at greater length in the next chapter.

Acknowledgement

Thanks are due to officials from the Department of Foreign Affairs and Trade for their assistance with the research on which this chapter is based.

Notes

1 The only non-members of the Ulster Unionist Party ever appointed as ministers were Harry Midgley (1943–47; formerly of the Northern Ireland Labour Party, later an Ulster Unionist minister), David Bleakley (1971; Northern Ireland Labour Party), and one junior minister, G.B. Newe (1971–72; politically unaligned, and the only Catholic ever to become a minister).

2 A Northern Ireland Life and Times survey in 1999 showed 94 percent of Catholics and 55 per cent of Protestants stating that they had voted in favour of the agreement; www.ark.ac.uk/nilt/1999/Political_Attitudes/HOWVOTE.html.

3 On about 60 occasions, two meetings have taken place on the same day and in the same place, usually because ministers sensibly take advantage of an opportunity to do extra business as efficiently as possible. For example, SafeFood is normally discussed as part of the health sector, those dealing with Waterways Ireland usually coincide with meetings of the language bodies, and, since 2012, meetings on Tourism Ireland have normally coincided with those on InterTrade Ireland. Much of this may be put down to the fact that any one minister may wear different hats (so that, for example, the Irish Minister for Arts, Heritage, Regional, Rural and Gaeltacht Affairs was responsible both for the waterways and for language matters between May 2016 and June 2017).

4   This is the date at which the Independent International Commission on Decommissioning, established by the British and Irish governments, announced that it was satisfied that all IRA weapons had been placed beyond use. In the commission's final report in July 2011, it expressed the belief that the weapons of the remaining significant loyalist and republican groups, with the exception of 'dissident' republicans, had been placed beyond use.

5   In fact, the St Andrews agreement provided that the post of First Minister would not necessarily go to the largest party, but to 'the largest party in the largest designation'; since unionists outnumbered nationalists, this meant in effect that the DUP, as the largest unionist party, would get the post for the foreseeable future. However, following a later amendment agreed by the DUP and Sinn Féin, the legislation implementing this, the Northern Ireland (St Andrews Agreement) Act, 2006, made a significant change: the First Minister post would now go simply to 'the largest party', regardless of designation, thus opening up the possibility of Sinn Féin getting this post.

6   Stormont House, home of the Northern Ireland Office, is an early twentieth-century building on the Stormont estate on the outskirts of Belfast. It should be distinguished from the older Stormont Castle, home of the Northern Ireland Executive, and Parliament Buildings, the iconic structure which houses the Assembly and was built as Northern Ireland's parliament house in 1932.

References and further reading

Arthur, Paul, 2000. *Special Relationships: Britain, Ireland and the Northern Ireland Problem*. Belfast: Blackstaff Press.

Arthur, Paul and Keith Jeffery, 1996. *Northern Ireland since 1968*. Oxford: Blackwell.

Aughey, Arthur, 1989. *Under Siege: Ulster Unionism and the Anglo–Irish Agreement*. London: Hurst.

Aughey, Arthur, 2005. *The Politics of Northern Ireland: Beyond the Belfast Agreement*. London: Routledge.

Aughey, Arthur and Cathy Gormley-Heenan (eds), 2011. *The Anglo–Irish Agreement: Re-Thinking Its Legacy*. Basingstoke: Palgrave Macmillan.

Aughey, Arthur and Duncan Morrow (eds), 1996. *Northern Ireland Politics*. London: Longman.

Bardon, Jonathan, 2005. *A History of Ulster*, new ed. Belfast: Blackstaff.

Barton, Brian and Patrick J. Roche (eds), 2009. *The Northern Ireland Question: The Peace Process and the Belfast Agreement*. Basingstoke: Palgrave Macmillan.

Bean, Kevin, 2007. *The New Politics of Sinn Féin*. Liverpool: Liverpool University Press.

Bew, Paul and Gordon Gillespie, 1999. *Northern Ireland: A Chronology of the Troubles 1968–1999*, new ed. Dublin: Gill and Macmillan.

Bew, Paul, Peter Gibbon and Henry Patterson, 1996. *Northern Ireland, 1921–1996: Political Forces and Social Classes*, rev. ed. London: Serif.

Birrell, Derek, 2009. *Direct Rule and the Governance of Northern Ireland*. Manchester: Manchester University Press.

Birrell, Derek and Alan Murie, 1980. *Policy and Government in Northern Ireland: Lessons of Devolution*. Dublin: Gill and Macmillan.

Birrell, Derek and Cathy Gormley-Heenan, 2015. *Multi-Level Governance and Northern Ireland*. Basingstoke: Palgrave Macmillan.

Boyce, D. George, 1996. *The Irish Question and British Politics 1868–1986*, 2nd ed. Basingstoke: Palgrave Macmillan.

Boyce, D. George and Alan O'Day (eds), 2006. *The Ulster Crisis 1885–1921*. Basingstoke: Palgrave Macmillan.

Campbell, Sarah, 2015. *Gerry Fitt and the SDLP: 'In a Minority of One'*. Manchester: Manchester University Press.

Clancy, Mary-Alice C., 2010. *Peace Without Consensus: Power Sharing Politics in Northern Ireland*. Farnham: Ashgate.

Coakley, John (ed.), 2002. *Changing Shades of Orange and Green: Redefining the Union and the Nation in Contemporary Ireland*. Dublin: UCD Press.

Coakley, John, 2009. '"Irish Republic", "Eire" or "Ireland"? The contested name of John Bull's other island', *Political Quarterly* 80:1, pp. 49–58.

Coakley, John, 2012. 'The prehistory of the Irish presidency', *Irish Political Studies* 27:4, pp. 539–58.

Coakley, John, 2014. 'British Irish institutional structures: towards a new relationship', *Irish Political Studies* 29:1, pp. 76–97.

Coakley, John, 2015. 'Does Ulster still say "no"? Public opinion and the future of Northern Ireland', in Johan A. Elkink and David M. Farrell (eds), *The Act of Voting: Identities, Institutions and Locale*. London: Routledge, pp. 35–55.

Coakley, John, 2017. 'Adjusting to partition: from irredentism to "consent" in twentieth-century Ireland', *Irish Studies Review* 25:2, pp. 193–214.

Coakley, John and Liam O'Dowd (eds), 2007. *Crossing the Border: New Relationships between Northern Ireland and the Republic of Ireland*. Dublin: Irish Academic Press.

Coakley, John, Brigid Laffan and Jennifer Todd (eds), 2005. *Renovation or Revolution? New Territorial Politics in Ireland and the United Kingdom*. Dublin: UCD Press.

Cochrane, Feargal, 1997. *Unionist Politics and the Politics of Unionism since the Anglo–Irish Agreement*. Cork: Cork University Press.

Cochrane, Feargal, 2013. *Northern Ireland: The Reluctant Peace*. New Haven, CT: Yale University Press.

Cox, Michael, Adrian Guelke and Fiona Stephen (eds), 2006. *A Farewell to Arms? From Long War to Long Peace in Northern Ireland*, new ed. Manchester: Manchester University Press.

Craig, Anthony, 2010. *Crisis of Confidence: Anglo–Irish Relations in the Early Troubles, 1966–1974*. Dublin: Irish Academic Press.

Cunningham, Michael, 2001. *British Government Policy in Northern Ireland 1969–2000*. Manchester: Manchester University Press.

De Bréadún, Deaglán, 2008. *The Far Side of Revenge: Making Peace in Northern Ireland*, 2nd ed. Cork: Collins Press.

Dixon, Paul, 2008. *Northern Ireland: The Politics of War and Peace*, 2nd ed. Basingstoke: Palgrave.

Dixon, Paul and Eamonn O'Kane, 2011. *Northern Ireland since 1969*. London: Longman.

Duffy, Stephen M., 2009. *The Integrity of Ireland: Home Rule, Nationalism, and Partition, 1912–1922*. Madison: Fairleigh Dickinson University Press.

Elliott, Marianne (ed.), 2002. *The Long Road to Peace in Northern Ireland*. Liverpool: Liverpool University Press.

Elliott, Sydney and W.D. Flackes, 1999. *Northern Ireland: A Political Directory, 1968–1999*, 5th ed. Belfast: Blackstaff.

English, Richard, 2007. *Irish Freedom: A History of Irish Nationalism*. London: Macmillan.

English, Richard, 2012. *Armed Struggle. The History of the IRA*, new ed. London: Pan.

Farrington, Christopher, 2006. *Ulster Unionism and the Peace Process in Northern Ireland*. Basingstoke: Palgrave Macmillan.

Frampton, Martyn, 2009. *The Long March: The Political Strategy of Sinn Féin, 1981–2007*. Basingstoke: Palgrave Macmillan.

Frampton, Martyn, 2011. *Legion of the Rearguard: Dissident Irish Republicanism*. Dublin: Irish Academic Press.

Gallagher, Michael, 1990. 'Do Ulster unionists have a right to self-determination?', *Irish Political Studies* 5, pp. 11–30.

Gilligan, Chris and Jon Tonge (eds), 1997. *Peace or War? Understanding the Peace Process in Northern Ireland*. Aldershot: Ashgate.

Hayes, Bernadette C. and Ian McAllister, 2013. *Conflict to Peace: Politics and Society in Northern Ireland over Half a Century*. Manchester: Manchester University Press.

Hayward, Katy, 2009. *Irish Nationalism and European Integration: The Official Redefinition of the Island of Ireland*. Manchester: Manchester University Press.

Hennessey, Thomas, 1998. *Dividing Ireland: World War I and Partition*. London: Routledge.

Hennessey, Thomas, 2000. *The Northern Ireland Peace Process: Ending the Troubles?* Dublin: Gill and Macmillan.

Hennessey, Thomas, 2015. *The First Northern Ireland Peace Process: Power-Sharing, Sunningdale and the IRA Ceasefires 1972–76*. Basingstoke: Palgrave Macmillan.

Horgan, John, 2013. *Divided We Stand: The Strategy and Psychology of Ireland's Dissident Terrorists*. Oxford: Oxford University Press.

Jackson, Alvin, 1999. *Ireland 1798–1998: Politics and War*. Oxford: Blackwell.

Kaufmann, Eric P., 2007. *The Orange Order: A Contemporary Northern Irish History*. Oxford: Oxford University Press.

Kennedy, Dennis, 1988. *The Widening Gulf: Northern Attitudes to the Independent Irish State, 1919–1949*. Belfast: Blackstaff.

Kennedy, Liam and Philip Ollerenshaw, 2012. *Ulster since 1600: Politics, Economy and Society*. Oxford: Oxford University Press.

Kennedy, Michael J., 2000. *Division and Consensus: The Politics of Cross-Border Relations in Ireland, 1925–1969*. Dublin: Institute of Public Adminstration.

Kerr, Michael, 2011. *The Destructors: The Story of Northern Ireland's Lost Peace Process*. Dublin: Irish Academic Press.

Knox, Colin, 2010. *Devolution and the Governance of Northern Ireland*. Manchester: Manchester University Press.

Laffan, Michael, 1983. *The Partition of Ireland, 1911–25*. Dundalk: Dundalgan Press, for the Dublin Historical Association.

McAuley, James W., 2010. *Ulster's Last Stand? Reconstructing Unionism after the Peace Process*. Dublin: Irish Academic Press.

McAuley, James W., 2016. *Very British Rebels? The Culture and Politics of Ulster Loyalism*. London: Bloomsbury.

McAuley, James W. and Graham Spencer (eds), 2011. *Ulster Loyalism after the Good Friday Agreement: History, Identity and Change*. Basingstoke: Palgrave Macmillan.

McCann, David, 2015. *From Protest to Pragmatism: The Unionist Government and North–South Relations from 1959–72*. Basingstoke: Palgrave Macmillan.

McCann, David and Cillian McGrattan (eds), 2017. *Sunningdale, the Ulster Workers' Council Strike and the Struggle for Democracy in Northern Ireland*. Manchester: Manchester University Press.

McGarry, John and Brendan O'Leary, 1996. *Explaining Northern Ireland: Broken Images*. Oxford: Blackwell.

McGarry, John and Brendan O'Leary, 2004. *The Northern Ireland Conflict: Consociational Engagements*. Oxford: Oxford University Press.

McGrattan, Cillian, 2010. *Northern Ireland 1968–2008: The Politics of Entrenchment*. Basingstoke: Palgrave Macmillan.

McGrattan, Cillian and Elizabeth Meehan (eds), 2012. *Everyday Life after the Irish Conflict: The Impact of Devolution and North–South Cooperation*. Manchester: Manchester University Press.

McKittrick, David, 2012. *Making Sense of the Troubles: A History of the Northern Ireland Conflict*, rev. ed. London: Viking.

McLoughlin, P. J., 2010. *John Hume and the Revision of Irish Nationalism*. Manchester: Manchester University Press.

Mallie, Eamonn and David McKittrick, 1997. *The Fight for Peace: The Secret Story behind the Irish Peace Process*, rev. ed. London: Mandarin.

Mitchell, David, 2015. *Politics and Peace in Northern Ireland: Political Parties and the Implementation of the 1998 Agreement*. Manchester: Manchester University Press.

Mitchell, Paul and Rick Wilford (eds), 1999. *Politics in Northern Ireland*. Boulder, CO: Westview.

Moloney, Ed, 2002. *A Secret History of the IRA*. London: Allen Lane.

Moloney, Ed and Andy Pollak, 1986. *Paisley*. Dublin: Poolbeg.

Murphy, Mary C., 2014. *Northern Ireland and the European Union: The Dynamics of a Changing Relationship*. Manchester: Manchester University Press.

Murray, Gerard and Jonathan Tonge, 2005. *Sinn Féin and the SDLP: From Alienation to Participation*. Dublin: O'Brien Press.

Norton, Christopher, 2014. *The Politics of Constitutional Nationalism in Northern Ireland, 1932–70: Between Grievance and Reconciliation*. Manchester: Manchester University Press.

Ó Dochartaigh, Niall, 2005. *From Civil Rights to Armalites: Derry and the Birth of the Irish Troubles*, 2nd ed. Basingstoke: Palgrave Macmillan.

Ó Dochartaigh, Niall, Katy Hayward and Elizabeth Meehan (eds), 2017. *Dynamics of Political Change in Ireland: Making and Breaking a Divided Island*. London: Routledge.

Patterson, Henry and Eric Kaufmann, 2007. *Unionism and Orangeism in Northern Ireland since 1945: The Decline of the Loyal Family*. Manchester: Manchester University Press.

Pollak, Andy, 2017. 'Northern intransigence and southern indifference: North–South cooperation since the Belfast agreement', in Niall Ó Dochartaigh, Katy Hayward and Elizabeth Meehan (eds), *Dynamics of Political Change in Ireland: Making and Breaking a Divided Island*. London: Routledge, pp. 178–92.

Prince, Simon, 2007. *Northern Ireland's '68: Civil Rights, Global Revolt and the Origins of the Troubles*. Dublin: Irish Academic Press.

Purdie, Bob, 1990. *Politics in the Streets: The Origins of the Civil Rights Movement in Northern Ireland*. Belfast: Blackstaff.

Reed, Richard, 2015. *Paramilitary Loyalism: Identity and Change*. Manchester: Manchester University Press.

Ruane, Joseph and Jennifer Todd, 1996. *The Dynamics of Conflict and Transition in Northern Ireland: Power, Conflict and Emancipation*. Cambridge: Cambridge University Press.

Ruane, Joseph and Jennifer Todd (eds), 1999. *After the Good Friday Agreement: Analysing Political Change in Northern Ireland*. Dublin: UCD Press.

Sanders, Andrew, 2011. *Inside the IRA: Dissident Republicans and the War for Legitimacy*. Edinburgh: Edinburgh University Press.

Spencer, Graham, 2014. *From Armed Struggle to Political Struggle: Republican Tradition and Transformation in Northern Ireland*. London: Bloomsbury.

Tannam, Etain, 1999. *Cross-Border Cooperation in the Republic of Ireland and Northern Ireland*. Basingstoke: Macmillan.

Taylor, Max and P.M. Currie (eds), 2011. *Dissident Irish Republicanism*. London: Bloomsbury.

Tonge, Jonathan, 2002. *Northern Ireland: Conflict and Change*. London: Prentice Hall.

Tonge, Jonathan, 2005. *The New Northern Irish Politics?* Basingstoke: Palgrave Macmillan.

Tonge, Jonathan, Maire Braniff, Thomas Hennessey, James W. McAuley and Sophie Whiting, 2014. *The Democratic Unionist Party: From Protest to Power*. Oxford: Oxford University Press.

Walker, Graham, 2004. *A History of the Ulster Unionist Party: Protest, Pragmatism and Pessimism*. Manchester: Manchester University Press.

Whiting, Sophie A., 2015. *Spoiling the Peace? The Threat of Dissident Republicans to Peace in Northern Ireland*. Manchester: Manchester University Press.

Whyte, John, 1990. *Interpreting Northern Ireland*. Oxford: Clarendon.

Wilford, Rick (ed.), 2001. *Aspects of the Belfast Agreement*. Oxford: Oxford University Press.

Williamson, Daniel C., 2017. *Anglo–Irish Relations in the Early Troubles: 1969–1972*. London: Bloomsbury.

Websites

cain.ulst.ac.uk/index.html
Conflict archive on the internet (main source for background on the Northern Ireland conflict)

www.ark.ac.uk/elections/
ARK: Northern Ireland elections (comprehensive results)

www.northernireland.gov.uk/
Northern Ireland Executive (with links to departments)

www.niassembly.gov.uk/
Northern Ireland Assembly (with links to debates)

www.nio.gov.uk/
Northern Ireland Office (British government agency, with links to many useful documents)

www.dfa.ie
Department of Foreign Affairs and Trade, Dublin

www.northsouthministerialcouncil.org/
North/South Ministerial Council

www.britishirishcouncil.org/
British–Irish Council

www.britishirish.org/
British–Irish Parliamentary Assembly

14 Europe and the international dimension

Brigid Laffan and Ben Tonra[1]

Ireland, according to Article 5 of its constitution, is a 'sovereign, independent, democratic state'. This assertion of the state's legal right to conduct its own affairs is an inadequate description of the state's relationship with the rest of the world. Forces of Europeanisation and globalisation have greatly increased Ireland's interaction with the international system and have embedded the state, its economy and its society within that system. The 2016 KOF Index of Globalisation ranks Ireland second in the world in respect of economic, political and social globalisation.[2] It makes considerable sense, therefore, to adapt the terminology often used by economists, and to think of Ireland in global terms as a 'small open polity'.

Such an approach also reminds us that the national political system is not self-contained but is subject to complex interactions with its external environment. On the one hand, Irish policy makers seek to project their values, preferences and interests onto the European and global stages. On the other, European and global forces have a significant impact upon events and policy in Ireland. This is true of all small states, although, given the level of interdependence in the contemporary world, no state is contained within a hard shell.

Ireland's external environment is in the throes of profound change as this 'small open polity' faces considerable risk, uncertainty and turbulence in the years ahead. The strategy of successive governments has been to focus on Ireland's relations with three key sources of influence, the European Union (EU), the United Kingdom (UK) and the United States of America (USA). The relationship with the USA has broadened since the 2000s, and a new focus on Asia has emerged. None of Ireland's key relationships is predictable at this time of instability, as core features of the post-Cold War order, which are very important to small states, are threatened. The EU, which is central to an understanding of Ireland's place in the world, has experienced acute pressure since the onset of the global financial crisis in 2008. This trauma was followed by a divisive refugee crisis that did not impact greatly on Ireland, but did further strain relations among the member states.

From an Irish perspective, however, it was the June 2016 decision by the UK electorate to support leaving the EU, commonly referred to as 'Brexit', that brought the greatest dangers for Ireland. Joint UK and Irish membership of the EU played a major role in normalising relations between the two islands, by taking the hard edge off the Irish border and by supporting the peace process in Northern Ireland. All of this was placed at risk by the UK's withdrawal from the EU. The election of Donald Trump as President of the USA in 2016 brought added uncertainty. His promise to put 'America First' implied a fundamental change in the US commitment to international multilateral organisations and a change in attitude to US overseas investment and trade, which has been of critical importance to Ireland. He is also the first US president since the EU was established not to regard that institution as an essential part of the world order. In fact, the Trump presidency is characterised by a pivot towards protectionism.

Thus, the Irish government, parliament and people will have to navigate the uncertainties of twenty-first-century global and European politics in a volatile world.

For its part, the European Union is a complex political system whose influence on its members is pervasive and sometimes controversial. The effects of the EU can be felt in politics, public policy and more widely in the state's constitutional and legal system. EU membership is not a 'foreign policy' issue *per se*; in many respects it is an extension of national (or 'domestic') politics. Engagement with the Union creates a new type of politics that is neither international nor domestic, but shares elements of both. For this reason, following an overview of Ireland's traditional external relations in the next section, we consider the nature of Ireland's relationship with the EU and we review the interplay of forces and interests between Dublin, Brussels and Frankfurt (as home of the European Central Bank), before turning, in the last section, to consider the new challenges facing Ireland and the European Union.

The external environment

To begin, we can ask ourselves whether Ireland really has a 'foreign policy' in the sense implied in the constitutional claim to independence quoted earlier (Tonra *et al.*, 2012). To what extent, and employing what means, do Irish governments pursue their values and interests internationally? We shall see that much of this activity now takes place in conjunction with other EU states and through the complex web of multilateral networks that has been developed since the end of the Second World War. This raises questions about the nature of specific policy areas and even about the nature of the 'sovereign, independent state'.

Any state's external environment consists of all other international actors, together with the nature of the system formed by their relationships. Over time, the international profile and even role of any state evolves and changes, and Ireland is no exception. Whether the Irish state contributes to or contests such change, however, it has no option – by virtue of its power, capacity and/or sense of self-identity – but to adapt to these new realities. What is perhaps most interesting in looking at the historical evolution of the Irish state's international position is its success to date in negotiating the shoals and reefs of international politics.

Ireland in a world of great powers, 1922–48

From the establishment of the Irish Free State as a member of the British Empire (later 'Commonwealth') in 1922 until the late 1940s, the international system was dominated overwhelmingly by the actions of the great powers, almost unmediated by multilateral institutions or international law. Although the League of Nations provided the new state with the opportunity to establish and develop its international credentials (Keown, 2015), the attempt to organise an international rule of law through the League failed. International stability was eventually only re-established through war. At first sight, it seems paradoxical that Ireland's political independence was steadily consolidated during this period, but given that the overriding goal was one of independence, this result is perhaps not so surprising. British decline was a constant theme throughout the period, as the age of empire began slowly to give way to the age of superpowers. Irish government representatives worked assiduously at both bilateral and multilateral levels first to establish, and then gradually to strengthen, the attributes of independent sovereign statehood. Over time, Ireland's ambiguous constitutional position (as a British dominion) was successfully exploited to secure the maximum leverage over Ireland's external affairs and ultimately to lay the groundwork for the decision in 1948 to declare the state to be a republic.

These efforts began with multilateral negotiations within the British Commonwealth and the League of Nations, establishing the legal *bona fides* of the Irish state in international law and ultimately providing the basis for de Valera's unilateral revision of the 1921 Anglo–Irish Treaty in the 1937 constitution. Following a difficult period of bilateral conflict, including an economic 'war' with Britain (see Chapter 1), a resolution was achieved. This included – rather surprisingly, given the wider European context – the handing over to Irish control in 1938 of naval ports originally retained by the British government in the 1921 treaty to provide for the defence of the British Isles. The return of the ports was an absolute prerequisite for the successful pursuit of Irish neutrality in the Second World War (Fisk, 1983; Wills, 2007).

The comparative success of Irish neutrality over the course of the Second World War, and the way in which the concept of neutrality came to be defined as the very *leitmotif* of Irish independence and sovereignty, should not obscure the basic limitations of Ireland's international position coming into the postwar era. Notwithstanding formal political independence, the economy remained almost wholly dependent on the fortunes (or more often the misfortunes) of one of Europe's least successful economies, that of Britain. Moreover, partition was, if anything, even more firmly consolidated in spite of sporadic attempts to make it an international issue. Although neutrality had been pursued skilfully, its viability owed more to geopolitical realities than to government policy, and it left Irish negotiators somewhat in the cold when geopolitics changed dramatically with the outbreak of the 'Cold War' (Salmon, 1989; Fisk, 1983; O'Halpin, 2008; Kennedy, 2008).

Ireland in the age of superpowers, 1948–89

A different kind of international system came into being after the Second World War. This 'bipolar' system, although marked by international tension between the United States and the Soviet Union, came to acquire a much greater degree of stability than its predecessor. Against a background of unprecedented economic growth, 'international regimes' (a term that covers both formal organisations and looser arrangements) increasingly became the norm. Traditional distinctions between 'foreign policy' and 'domestic policy' lost some of their meaning, especially among the countries forming the core of west European integration.

Ireland was slow to adapt to this process. In the late 1940s traditional concerns with Anglo–Irish relations and partition seemed at least as important as the Cold War. Geopolitical irrelevance facilitated an even less clearly defined policy of neutrality when Ireland eventually joined the United Nations (UN) in 1955. Economic dependence on the United Kingdom inhibited a closer involvement in the emerging European integration process, as British governments remained aloof from 'Europe'. However, a fundamental reappraisal of economic policy in the late 1950s brought about a more active interest in European integration. A British application to join the European Economic Community (EEC) in 1961 caused Ireland also to apply, but this process was brought to an end in 1963 by a French veto against British membership.

'Europe' remained the focal point of government policy from the early 1960s onwards, for overwhelmingly economic reasons. When enlargement again became feasible in 1969, membership was negotiated and was approved in a referendum in 1972, by a majority of 83 per cent in a turnout of over 70 per cent (see Appendix 2h). Thus, from 1973, the effects of membership of the EEC (later the European Community [EC]) began to reach deep into Irish public life (Keatinge, 1991), including its foreign policy. Economic growth rates accelerated significantly while direct transfers from the European budget, initially through the Common

Agricultural Policy and later, and more broadly, through the structural funds (regional, social and 'cohesion'), further contributed to Irish economic development.

Ireland in the contemporary age

The collapse of communism in 1989 heralded a short-lived unipolar moment as *Pax Americana* appeared unassailable. This changed with the terrorist attacks against the United States on 11 September 2001 and subsequent terrorist attacks in Africa, Europe, Oceania and the Middle East. US unipolar power was also undermined by the rise of China and the re-emergence of Putin's Russia as a geopolitical rival.

The end of the Soviet Union opened the path towards reform and the continental enlargement of the EC. This had been transformed into the European Union (EU) by the Maastricht Treaty of 1992, which also created the pathway to the introduction of the euro as the single European currency through the Economic and Monetary Union. That project, and the many public policy choices driven by it, served to underpin a further period of rapid Irish economic growth in the 1990s. The dramatic increases in Irish growth rates in the second half of the 1990s (the so-called 'Celtic Tiger' phenomenon) caught most observers by surprise as the Irish economy appeared to outperform all others in the EU for more than a decade. This brought Irish per capita GDP from 66 per cent of the EC average in 1972 to 150 per cent of the average of the expanded EU in 2008.[3] Indeed, Ireland was regarded by many of the smaller states in Central and Eastern Europe as a model success story, and one to which they aspired in respect of their own membership of the EU, although admiration at the achievements of the Celtic Tiger economy waned from 2009 as the Irish economy went into a steep downward spiral.

The extent and speed of change in Ireland's external environment has been unparalleled and was for many years moderated by a set of well-entrenched multilateral organisations – the UN and its agencies, the Bretton Woods system (International Monetary Fund, World Bank and World Trade Organisation), collective security institutions (Organisation for Security and Cooperation in Europe, NATO), and regional political or economic groupings (such as the Organisation for Economic Cooperation and Development, the OECD). Contemporary global challenges have, however, placed these institutions under new pressures: how to accommodate rising powers such as China, how to address the challenges posed by a frustrated geopolitical actor such as the Russian Federation, how to manage the risks of the Trump presidency to global order, how meaningfully to address regional instability in the Middle East (and its associated consequences such as migration), and how to deal with immediate threats such as those of terrorism, cyber security and climate change. The existing institutional matrix of global and regional governance has abjectly failed in some cases and only partially succeeded in others.

For Ireland, the European Union has been a central institutional element in all of this, and thus it has been much more directly involved in the making of the global and regional system than had been the case earlier. In 2017, the 28-member European Union still produced more than one fifth of the goods and services consumed internationally and generated about one quarter of global wealth. It did so not only from its own resources but through its trading and economic relationships with the rest of the world. The Union has thus emerged as a powerful economic and trading actor, with the capacity to define the shape and policy of international institutions. It is not, however, itself immune to wider forces of global instability. The banking crisis of 2008 led directly to nearly a decade of continent-wide economic austerity and forced a partial redesign of banking and economic governance in the European Union. Irish policy makers also learned that policy errors (national and European) and decision-making delays could have catastrophic national implications. The Union also has to deal with its own sources of instability – most especially, those forces at both ends of the political spectrum that are profoundly critical of European political and economic integration to date. The 2016 decision of the UK electorate to leave the European Union is not only emblematic of the potential force of that dissatisfaction (which is evident in many member states), but is also itself a source of instability for the Union, and most especially for Ireland.

The evolving international system is not benign for small states such as Ireland. The orthodox prescription for Irish foreign policy is to cling even tighter to the moorings of international law and its institutional networks. For Ireland, the European Union continues to be the centre of that matrix and it has traditionally offered Irish policy makers their greatest capacity to participate in the shaping of world events, rather than simply being swept before them. With British departure from the EU, however, Irish policy makers now face the extraordinarily difficult task of negotiating alongside European partners to design a new EU–UK relationship that does not do irreparable damage to core Irish political, economic and strategic interests.

European Union institutions

Over the years, the EU has developed a constitutional framework and a set of institutions to govern co-operation among its member states. The Union's constitutional and legal framework consists of a series of treaties and an extensive corpus of laws that have been agreed within the framework of the Union's institutions. This section analyses the key characteristics of the European Union and the interaction between European institutions and Ireland (Laffan and O'Mahony, 2008). It begins with an assessment of the unique nature of EU membership as compared with other international affiliations, and goes on to review how Irish values and interests are represented within Union structures.

EU membership: a unique context

Since the establishment of the state, Ireland has signed numerous international treaties and accepted extensive international obligations. A commitment to intensive multilateralism is characteristic of small states, particularly of small European states that have a shared interest in a rule-bound and institutionalised international order. The Irish contribution to European integration from 1973 onwards has marked a commitment by Ireland to enter into a union of states and peoples that would have a substantial and significant impact on sovereignty, state identity and public policy. A number of distinctive features of the EU render membership qualitatively different from membership of traditional international organisations.

First, European treaties have added a further layer to the Irish constitution because of the wide applicability of European law, the jurisprudence of the European Court of Justice and a series of treaty reforms. Ireland's constitution is encased within the wider constitutional framework of the EU.

Second, the European Union is governed by a set of distinctive institutions, including the European Council, Commission, Council of Ministers, Parliament and Court of Justice, as well as the European Central Bank, the Court of Auditors and a host of agencies. Irish ministers, civil servants and representatives of interest organisations are drawn into a multi-level system of policy making that stretches from local government within Ireland to EU-level decision-making processes. Policy making may begin at home, but it may also begin in EU institutions and in other EU capitals.

Box 14.1 EU treaties

The main treaties (excluding accession and secession treaties) and their date of signature/date of effect:

- The Paris Treaty (establishing the European Coal and Steel Community), 1951/1952 (ceased 2002)
- The Rome Treaties (establishing the European Economic Community and Euratom), 1957/1958
- The Merger Treaty, 1965/1967 (ceased 1999)
- The Single European Act, 1986/1987
- The Treaty on European Union (Maastricht Treaty), 1992/1993
- The Treaty of Amsterdam, 1997/1999
- The Treaty of Nice, 2001/2003
- Treaty establishing a Constitution for Europe, 2004 (ratification failed)
- The Treaty of Lisbon, 2007/2009
- The Fiscal Stability Treaty, 2012/2013

Third, the policy remit of the European Union is very broad; it includes market regulation, budgetary affairs, social and employment affairs, the international role of the Union and many other areas. This takes the Union into the nooks and crannies of domestic politics. Ireland's decision to join the Eurozone from its inception under the 1992 Maastricht Treaty was a major shift of monetary regime, and in the context of economic policy sharing a currency with 19 other states greatly deepens Ireland's interdependent relationships with other EU states. Moreover, EU state aid and competition policy prohibit certain kinds of economic interventions by the member states.

Fourth, the EU has not reached a stable equilibrium in respect of either membership or its treaty framework (see Box 14.1). In fact, a series of events since 2009, notably the euro crisis, the refugee crisis and the prospect of Brexit, have greatly exacerbated tensions about 'how much EU?' and 'what kind of EU?'. The EU is thus a major presence in Irish politics: it is an issue in itself, it is a source of law and policy, and it is an arena of policy making. Beyond this, the EU is a source of rights for individual Irish citizens, a source of rights within Ireland for the citizens of other member states, and for some Irish citizens, it offers an additional social identity.

Representing Ireland in the EU

Like the other member states, Ireland has a voice and representation in all European institutions. Under existing treaty rules, the Irish government nominates one of the 28 members of the *European Commission*, the body that proposes European laws, manages European programmes (including the budget) and oversees the manner in which each member state meets its obligations under European law. Between 1973 and 2017, 10 Irish commissioners have served in the College of Commissioners (see Box 14.2). Each commissioner has responsibility for an area of European policy, not unlike ministers in a national government. Irish nationals have the opportunity of working in the Commission either as full time officials or as national experts for a number of years. Two Irish nationals, David O'Sullivan (2000–05)

Box 14.2 Ireland's EU commissioners, 1973–2017

Commissioners are nominated by the respective national governments, and to date all the commissioners appointed by Irish governments have been politically established figures. Apart from Peter Sutherland and David Byrne, each of whom was Attorney General prior to his appointment, all other Irish commissioners have been former ministers and senior politicians within their political parties. A commissioner is assigned a 'portfolio' in the Commission, much like a cabinet minister at national level, and there is considerable competition for the most significant positions.

Commissioner	Appointing government	Period	Portfolio
Patrick Hillery	FF	1973–76	Social Affairs
Richard Burke	FG–Labour	1977–81	Transport, Consumer Affairs, Taxation
Michael O'Kennedy	FF	1981–82	Personnel, Administration, Statistics
Richard Burke	FF	1982–84	Personnel, Administration, Statistics
Peter Sutherland	FG–Labour	1985–88	Competition
Ray MacSharry	FF	1989–92	Agriculture and Rural Development
Pádraig Flynn	FF	1993–99	Social Affairs and Employment
David Byrne	FF–PD	1999–2004	Health and Consumer Protection
Charlie McCreevy	FF–PD	2005–09	Internal Market and Services
Máire Geoghegan-Quinn	FF–Green	2010–14	Research, Innovation and Science
Phil Hogan	FG–Labour	2015–	Agriculture and Rural Development

and Catherine Day (2005–15), the first woman, have held the post of Secretary General of the Commission – a remarkable record given that there have only been five secretaries general since the establishment of the EEC in 1958. The Commission, with over 23,000 full time officials, is a relatively small organisation given the size of the EU. To augment its own resources and to ensure that it has an overview of conditions in each member state, the Commission services are surrounded by expert and advisory groups that assist it in developing legal and policy proposals that then go to the Council and Parliament for negotiation and approval (Kenealy *et al.*, 2015). Irish experts join their counterparts from other member states on Commission working groups.

The Council of Ministers and the European Council make up the decision-making forum of the member state governments. The *European Council*, which meets at least three times each year, brings together the heads of state or government – in Ireland's case, the Taoiseach – from the 28 member states to agree on priorities for the Union, both in Europe and internationally. The frequency and intimacy of summit meetings, particularly during crises, brings Europe's highest office holders into regular, intensive contact with one another, both in person and over the telephone. Following the ratification of the Lisbon Treaty (2009), the European Council has a permanent president based in Brussels.

The *Council of Ministers*, although legally a single institution, meets in different forms, depending on the policy area in question. Ireland is represented by the appropriate minister; for example, the Minister of Agriculture attends the Agricultural Council and the Minister for Justice attends the Justice and Home Affairs Council. Sitting around a table with the other 27 member state ministers, Irish ministers work to promote and protect Irish priorities in negotiations, and to reach agreement with other member states. Under existing EU rules, each member state holds the presidency of the Council for a period of six months on a rotating basis. Ireland last held the presidency in 2013 and is due to hold it again in the second half of 2026. The main responsibility of the presidency is to chair all Council bodies other than the European Council (which is chaired by its president) and meetings of foreign affairs ministers (chaired by the Union's High Representative for Foreign Policy, who is also vice-president of the Commission).

The EU is characterised by permanent negotiations among the member states as they seek to manage the challenging issues that cross national borders today, such as climate change or food safety. Preparations for meetings of the Council are conducted by committees of civil servants from the member states, meeting in working parties. The issues are channelled through the Council hierarchy until they reach the political level. Technical issues are often agreed by officials, whereas the more contentious political issues are dealt with by ministers in the Council. The Council works on the basis of well-established procedures and voting rules that serve to move its business along. Consecutive treaty changes have extended the number of issue areas where Council decisions can be taken under what is called 'qualified majority voting'. Under the Lisbon Treaty, this took the form of a new 'double majority' system of voting. This specifies that a qualified majority is reached if two conditions are met: (a) that 55 per cent of member states vote in favour, which in practice means 16 out of 28 states, and (b) that those states represent at least 65 per cent of the total EU population. The purpose behind the 'double majority' rule is to ensure that there is both a majority of states in favour of a measure and that those states represent a sizeable majority of Europe's overall population. Although the Council usually decides by consensus, formal votes are periodically called. In the period 2009–15, Ireland voted against fewer than 20 (2 per cent) of EU legislative proposals; 16 other member states found themselves more frequently in a losing minority (Hix, 2016). This suggests that Irish negotiators usually find a way of securing the accommodation of their preferences within the evolving consensus.

The *European Parliament* is the fourth major European institution and is directly elected by the citizens of the member states. Ireland has 11 members out of a total membership of 751. This is a very small number, but given the size of the population the country's representation is in fact generous; one Irish MEP represents just fewer than 350,000 people, whereas each German MEP represents 840,000. MEPs do not sit in national groupings but as members of transnational political groups representing the main political families in Europe. As of 2017, Irish MEPs were members of five of the Parliament's groups (see Table 14.1).

When Ireland became a member of the Community in 1973, its political parties had to decide which European Parliament group to join. This was relatively straightforward for Labour, which joined the Socialist group. For Fianna Fáil and Fine Gael the decision was more difficult – for one thing, they felt that they could not join the same group because of electoral competition at national level. Fine Gael joined the largest of the conservative groups, the European People's Party (the Christian Democrats).

Fianna Fáil, by contrast, was left without a political grouping for its first six months in the parliament. The advantages of belonging to a group – such as secretarial and research backup, speaking time and membership of committees – forced it ultimately to link up with the French Gaullists. There were no close party-to-party links of the sort found in the Christian Democratic group or the Socialists. The departure of the Gaullists to the European People's Party in 1999 left Fianna Fáil in a group called the Union for Europe of the Nations (UEN). In March 2009, Taoiseach Brian Cowen announced Fianna Fáil's intention to join the Liberals

Table 14.1 Irish party membership of European Parliament groups, 2017

European Parliament group	Total	Irish members	Irish party
European People's Party	216	4	Fine Gael
Alliance of Socialists and Democrats	190	1	Independent
Alliance of Liberals and Democrats for Europe	70	1	Independent
Greens/European Free Alliance	50	0	
Alliance of European Conservatives and Reformists	73	1	Fianna Fáil
European United Left/Nordic Green Left	52	4	Sinn Féin (3) Independent (1)
Europe of Freedom and Direct Democracy	46	0	
Europe of Nations and Freedom Group	39	0	
Non-attached	15	0	
Total	751	11	

Note: Fianna Fáil MEP Brian Crowley left the ALDE group in 2014, contrary to his party's wishes, and joined the ECR group. Fianna Fáil remains a member of the ALDE parliamentary group.

after the June 2009 European Parliament elections, a step that brought the party into a significant European Parliament grouping for the first time. Following the party's poor performance in the 2014 European elections, Brian Crowley, the only remaining Fianna Fáil MEP, refused to sit with the Liberals and instead opted for the UK Conservative-led European Conservative and Reformist grouping (which is expected to disappear after Brexit). Following the election of its first MEPs in 2004, Sinn Féin joined the confederal group of the European United Left, while Irish MEPs elected as independents have usually joined the group whose political stance is closest to their own.

Irish MEPs inhabit a rather different world from that of their counterparts in the Dáil or Seanad. They travel a lot, and spend two or three weeks of every month outside Ireland at plenary sessions of the parliament, attending committee meetings and dealing with the work of their political groupings – vital activities if they are to build up a profile for themselves in order to maximise their influence within the parliament. This makes it difficult for them to maintain contact with their very large constituencies and to maintain visibility in their political parties. Nevertheless, Irish MEPs have won prestigious positions. In January 2002, most notably, Pat Cox, a Munster MEP and member of the Liberal Group, was elected President of the Parliament for a period of two and a half years – the highest elected office that an Irish person has won in the European Union.

Since its establishment in 1998, but particularly since the final stage of creating the euro currency, the *European Central Bank* (ECB) has come to play a central role in Irish monetary and wider economic policy. The independence of the ECB and its role as a central bank make it a very powerful institution in the architecture of European institutions. The Governor of the Central Bank of Ireland is *ex officio* a member of the ECB's Governing Council. Apart from the core policy-making bodies, the EU also has a judicial arm, the *European Court of Justice* (ECJ); an auditing body, the *European Court of Auditors*; an *Economic and Social Committee*; and a *Committee of the Regions*. Ireland is represented on all of these.

The first body, the ECJ, is of particular significance, since its judgments have a direct impact on the Irish state, Irish companies and Irish citizens. Irish courts may seek rulings from the ECJ on the correct interpretation of EU law, and the Irish government and private citizens may find themselves before the court in Luxembourg. Ireland has been taken to court in such diverse areas as agriculture, fisheries, the internal market, taxation and the environment. Its record on infringement is better than the EU average, notwithstanding some outlier years (Nicolaides and Suren, 2007), but this varies from one policy area to another (Thomas, 2017). In 2015, for instance, the Commission issued 17 letters of formal notice and six reasoned opinions against Ireland (in each case, 2 per cent of the total). Both of these steps are part of the pre-litigation phase of infringement proceedings, whereby the Commission puts a member state on notice that it is in breach of its treaty obligations. By the end of December 2015, Ireland faced 35 outstanding cases at the Court, or 2.5 per cent of all outstanding cases (EU, 2016). EU law endows Irish citizens and groups with rights that they can pursue in the Irish courts, as well as at the ECJ. The Irish courts are obliged to ask the ECJ for a preliminary ruling on matters of EU law if these are raised by cases in the Irish system. Rulings from the ECJ have meant, for example, that the state has had to pay compensation to women for discrimination in social security legislation (Cousins, 2002:181), and has been penalised for late implementation of EU directives.[4]

Public opinion and attitudes towards Europe

Alongside the evolution of the European institutions, we need to consider also the manner in which the Irish public reacted to the various changes that have taken place as the scope of the EU was widened geographically and deepened in respect of its public policy implications. This section considers two aspects of this: the reaction of the electorate in successive EU-related elections and referendums, and public opinion more generally.

Popular involvement in the EU

Since 1979, Ireland's electoral cycle has included European Parliament elections (for the results of past elections, see Appendix 2e). Originally, Ireland was represented by 15 MEPs elected from four constituencies, but by 2014 the number had been reduced to 11, who were elected from three constituencies: Dublin with three seats, and four seats each in the South and the Midlands/Northwest constituencies. Election is by PR-STV, as in the case of Dáil elections (see Chapter 4). European elections have come to be categorised by political scientists as 'second order' ones – perceived by the electorate as less important than national parliamentary elections, which lead to government formation (see Chapter 6, p. 155). Nonetheless, Irish political parties take the elections very seriously, as they usually reflect their mid-term standing with the electorate.

Referendums are a pronounced feature of Ireland's engagement with the EU. Membership of the EU was endorsed by an emphatic 'Yes' vote in the initial 1972 referendum on membership, where accession was supported by the two largest parties, along with the employers' and farmers' organisations. The Labour Party, two small rival Sinn Féin parties and most of the trade union movement opposed membership in a campaign largely dominated by economic issues. Unlike the UK and Denmark, membership did not lead to divisive splits within political parties. Since the initial referendum, Ireland has voted a further eight times on European treaties. The referendum on the Single European Act (SEA) is noteworthy because of the so-called Crotty judgment, called after the activist economist who secured an injunction to prevent the government from lodging the instrument of ratification for the SEA. He successfully argued in the Supreme Court that it would be unconstitutional for the government to ratify the treaty through the Oireachtas because the constraints placed upon Irish foreign policy by the proposed treaty represented a material change to the terms of Ireland's original accession. The Supreme Court ruled that ratification of the SEA would require a constitutional amendment and, as we saw in Chapter 3, this, in turn, requires a referendum. This Supreme Court decision explains why every significant EU treaty since then has involved a referendum, even when parliaments in other member states can make the decision themselves.

The SEA referendum was followed, in turn, by referendums on the Treaty on European Union (known as the Maastricht Treaty), the Amsterdam Treaty and the Nice Treaty. The outcome of the Maastricht treaty referendum, with 69 per cent in favour (see Appendix 2h) endorsed Ireland's participation in the single currency. In May 1998, the Irish electorate voted on the Amsterdam treaty, but the outcome suggested an emerging hesitation among the electorate about the continuing process of treaty change: the proportion supporting the treaty fell to 62 per cent. This decline in the Yes vote was followed by the rejection of the Nice Treaty in June 2001 by a majority of 54 per cent, albeit on a low turnout of 34 per cent. This was a profound shock to the government, to its partners in the Union and to the candidate states in central Europe that were affected by this outcome. Rejection presented the government with a very difficult domestic and external agenda, to which it responded with a strategy of creating domestic conditions for a second referendum. It established a cross-party National Forum on Europe (autumn 2001), and brought forward new legislation to improve parliamentary scrutiny of Ireland's European policy (July 2002). It also sought to provide additional assurance to the electorate by securing EU agreement on the so-called 'Seville Declarations' (June 2002); one was a European Council statement that European treaties do not impose mutual defence commitments, the other a statement by the Irish government that participation in the EU's common foreign and security policy 'does not prejudice its traditional policy of military neutrality'.[5] Following its re-election in May 2002, the government re-ran the referendum in October 2002, securing a Yes vote of 63 per cent (see Appendix 2h).

A further treaty change in the EU was proposed in 2008. The Lisbon Treaty was ratified by national parliaments in all EU member states – except in Ireland, where the government was advised by its Attorney General that a referendum would again be necessary. On 12 June 2008, 53 per cent voted to reject the treaty, on a turnout of over 53 per cent. Opponents of the treaty were drawn from the right of the political spectrum, notably new campaign organisations Libertas and Cóir, as well as from the more traditional anti-EU left, including Sinn Féin and a number of small parties of the left. Working separately, these groups successfully defined the terms of the debate on the referendum and overcame the combined efforts of the major political parties, key interest organisations and most of the social partners (Quinlan, 2009; O'Mahony, 2009). Research following the referendum demonstrated that socio-demographic factors and party allegiance played an important role in voting behaviour. The highest No vote (65 per cent) was recorded among the unskilled working class, whereas among the more affluent middle-class group the Yes vote reached 64 per cent (Quinlan, 2009). Gender differences were also apparent, with women (56 per cent) more likely to vote No than men (51 per cent). Post-referendum research indicated that a majority of Fianna Fáil (63 per cent) and Fine Gael (52 per cent) supporters followed the party line, whereas 61 per cent of Labour supporters did not, instead voting against. A majority of Green Party supporters also voted No, as did the overwhelming majority of Sinn Féin supporters (Quinlan, 2009).

The referendum result brought the connection between politics within Ireland and the politics of the EU arena sharply into focus. The other member states, particularly those that had already ratified the treaty, were not prepared to say that the Lisbon Treaty was dead. It became clear that other member-state governments wished to proceed with ratification. The Irish government found itself in an isolated position, with an electorate that was uneasy about just what kind of EU it wanted and would sign up for. However, a renewed effort by the major parties, together with a set of political and legal assurances from the EU, helped to create the conditions for a second referendum. Now in the middle of an economic crisis, the electorate endorsed the treaty by a significant majority of 67 per cent in October 2009 (Quinlan, 2012). In a further referendum in 2012, a 60 per cent majority endorsed the Fiscal Stability Treaty, which was designed to tighten budgetary rules within the Eurozone (Costello, 2014).

Public opinion and the EU

Popular endorsement of treaty change does not mean that the Irish elite or electorate is over-whelmingly Euro-enthusiastic or Euro-federalist. Attitudes in Ireland, like those elsewhere in the EU, are complex and multi-dimensional. Irish nationalism has, to a large extent, been successfully nested within a popular, if sometimes inchoate, European identity (Coakley, 2005). Moreover, this identity is underpinned by a broadly favourable attitude towards EU membership and its benefits, in stark contrast to the attitudinal base in the UK. That said, there have been fractures at elite and popular levels. The two referendum defeats in 2001 and 2008 suggest that opposition to treaty change can be successfully mobilised, and enthusiasm for the EU dipped during the acute economic crisis. The Irish elite has always been more comfortable with an EU that does not impinge too deeply on politics and does not take on too many state-like qualities.

Benoit's analysis of Irish political parties and European integration pointed to 'subtle dif-ferences in party positioning on various aspects of support for the scope and pace of con-tinuing European integration' (Benoit, 2009: 447). He distinguished three clusters of parties. Fine Gael and Labour were the most pro-integration, and these were followed by Fianna Fáil and the Progressive Democrats; all four of these broadly supported integration. On the Eurosceptic side were Sinn Féin and the Green party. When the Green party entered govern-ment in 2007, its position on the EU shifted to a more pro-integration stance (Benoit, 2009). Sinn Féin has also moderated its position, and would now claim to be Euro-critical, not Eurosceptic; in Northern Ireland, it even campaigned against Brexit during the 2016 referen-dum. Opposition to the EU is most visible within smaller socialist and left-wing parties and groups, and among some independents.

Overall, public attitudes to the EU in Ireland are largely positive – indeed, rather more pos-itive than in most other member states, based on the evidence of successive Eurobarometer opinion polls over many decades. The level of support was, however, marked by a notice-able decline in supportive attitudes during the acute economic crisis of 2008–13 (see Figure 14.1). As the Irish economy began to recover, the image of the EU in Ireland appeared also to improve. By November 2016, 55 per cent had a favourable image of the EU and the percent-age with a negative image had declined to 13 per cent, one of the lowest negative ratings in the EU.

Public opinion in Ireland also differs significantly from that of the UK in particular. This may be seen from opinion polling in November 2016 in a number of areas, such as free move-ment of people (favoured by 90 per cent of Irish respondents, but only 68 per cent in the UK; the EU average was 81 per cent), the single currency (supported by 85 per cent, with the UK at just 24 per cent; the EU average was 38 per cent), and positive attitudes towards immigra-tion from the EU (81 per cent). Ireland was also one of only four EU countries with majority support (57 per cent) for immigration from outside the EU, though a significant proportion (38 per cent) held negative views of this. It is too early to predict what the long-term impact of Brexit on Irish attitudes will be, but Irish people are in no doubt as to the centrality of this issue. In the immediate aftermath of the UK referendum, 62 per cent said that Europe was more important to Ireland than the UK, with 25 per cent opting for the UK as the more

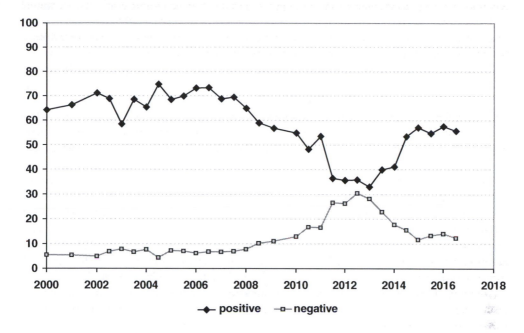

Figure 14.1 Images of the EU in Ireland, 2000–17

Source: Computed from Eurobarometer Interactive, ec.europa.eu/commfrontoffice/publicopinion/index.cfm/Chart/index.

Note: The question was 'In general, does the European Union conjure up for you a very positive, fairly positive, neutral, fairly negative or very negative image?'; lines include those with 'very' and 'fairly' positive, and those with 'very' and 'fairly' negative attitudes, respectively. All data are percentages.

important of the two, and 13 per cent were undecided.[6] As the costs of Brexit are felt in Ireland, North and South, it is not clear that a majority of the Irish population would prioritise relations with the UK over EU membership.

Public policy and European governance

The development of the EU is not just an issue of 'high politics' in a referendum campaign or of coping with Brexit; it has a continuing impact on a host of domestic public policy issues. This impact is felt through the Union's spending policies, especially in its agricultural and regional funds, through the demands of the single currency, and through European regulation. This impact was brought sharply home in November 2010 when Ireland entered into a bail-out under the EU, the ECB and the International Monetary Fund, and was subject to three years of supervision by these three bodies (the so-called 'Troika').

Key areas of public policy

Irish agricultural policy is almost entirely made in Brussels. Irish farmers, attracted by the prospect of improved farm incomes, strongly endorsed Ireland's membership of the EU in the 1970s. Since then, the Irish Farmers' Association and the Irish Creamery Milk Suppliers Association have acted as powerful lobbies in support of the common agricultural policy (CAP), a policy dating from the 1960s that was designed to secure and to maintain farm incomes. The high budgetary cost of the policy (consuming 50–60 per cent of the EU's annual budget since 1991) has led to sustained pressure for reform, but this has been resisted in particular by the Irish, French and the eastern member-state governments. A combination of budgetary pressures, successive enlargements and pressure within the General Agreement on Tariffs and Trade (GATT) and its successor, the World Trade Organisation (WTO), have nevertheless forced change in the financing and instruments of agricultural support in Europe. The eastern enlargement in May 2004 led to a decoupling of EU payments to farmers from agricultural production, but has not led to a reduction in the size of the agricultural budget in the Union. Financial flows from the CAP have meant that the subvention of farm incomes in Ireland has been paid for by the European budget and indirectly by European consumers, who pay higher prices for their food than they might otherwise do.

Other financial transfers from the EU budget have become part and parcel of distributive politics, especially since the 1980s. The structural funds represented a very significant transfer from the EU budget to Ireland, notably through Community Support Frameworks (CSFs), which spanned the periods 1988–93, 1994–99, 2000–06 and 2007–13. Central government invested heavily in the implementation of the various EU programmes, and Ireland is generally regarded as a state that has used structural funds effectively. Whereas the first CSF was developed and controlled by the Department of Finance, different regions, localities and community groups fought for influence subsequently. The flow of funding in the 2000–06 period represented a transition phase in Ireland's receipts of structural funds. For this period, the country was divided into two regions, the Borders, Midlands and West (known as the BMW region) and the Eastern region. The BMW region retained its status as one designated for a high level of EU subvention, whereas the Eastern region received considerably less support. Although Ireland's GDP per capita converged with, and then surpassed, the EU average, as we mentioned earlier, Ireland continued to be a net beneficiary of the EU budget. After 2006, Ireland's receipts from the structural funds dramatically changed, as EU transfers were increasingly directed to the new member states. Remarkably, Ireland in the 'Celtic Tiger' period of rapid economic growth (around the turn of the century) continued to be a net beneficiary from the EU budget because of the common agricultural policy. Notwithstanding an increased contribution from Ireland, the country remained a net beneficiary in 2015.[7]

The implementation of EU environmental law illustrates the manner in which Europe becomes part of the dynamic of politics at local level. The EU enacted two apparently innocuous environmental conservation directives – the Birds Directive in 1979 and the Habitats Directive in 1992 – that have proved very contentious and difficult to implement. These two directives altered the policy frame at national level by requiring the imposition of restrictions on private land use, thus impinging particularly on farmers. They are strongly supported by environmental organisations, notably BirdWatch Ireland and the Irish Peatland Conservation Council. Farmers, however, reacted angrily to the constraints imposed by the directives, with the result that their implementation was delayed. The Commission, in an attempt to ensure compliance and speed up implementation of the directives in this field, brought Ireland to court on five occasions between 1999 and 2008 (the ECJ found against Ireland in all five cases), and threatened Ireland's receipts from the structural funds.

During this period, successive governments found themselves mediating between angry farmers who were turning up in their hundreds to Irish Farmers' Association meetings, the Commission seeking implementation of agreed European law, and the environmentalists using Brussels to strengthen their hand in domestic politics. Within the administration, there was also a battle between scientific interests committed to areas of special conservation, the generalist civil servants dealing with Brussels, and the politicians, who were unwilling to impose an unpopular European directive on their constituents (even though they had originally consented to this).

The question of turf cutting was particularly emotive. Ireland had a ten-year derogation for domestic turf cutters; this ran out in 2009, re-introducing a highly contentious issue onto the agenda. In January 2011, the Commission began infringement proceedings against Ireland on this matter. In an effort to get local agreement and comply with the directive, the government established a Peatlands Forum, developed a compensation scheme and agreed a long-term peatlands management strategy that ensured that Ireland was not brought to court again. It did not, however, resolve the underlying argument; there were conflicting reports on the level of compliance among local turf cutters and ongoing arrests and court cases. The nature conservation directives are frequently cited in public as prime examples of unacceptable Brussels interference. Limitations on cutting turf are deeply resented in parts of Ireland and continue to impact on general election politics, as do restrictions in other areas, such as harvesting shellfish.

The single currency has had a fundamental impact on Irish public policy, and more recently on politics. Following the ratification of the Maastricht Treaty, successive Irish governments signalled their desire to join the single currency in the first wave. This had a direct bearing on the framing of the annual budget from 1992 onwards, as the goal of policy was to meet the criteria for participation in European monetary union. This implied tight control over the public finances and a fiscal policy designed to promote low inflation. The positions of the Central Bank and the Department of Finance were enhanced *vis-à-vis* the spending ministries, as the Department of Finance could hide behind these criteria in preparing the annual budgetary estimates. With the introduction of the euro as a common currency in 2002, EU economic governance became even more important as there is now considerable pressure to co-ordinate macro-economic policies, including taxation, at EU level. This has further served to strengthen the role of the Department of Finance in the Irish system. In addition to the euro, European state aid rules have had a major impact on government intervention in the economy. For example, the Irish government's guarantee of deposits in the banks in October 2008, at the outset of the global banking crisis, had to be framed in such a way that it did not discriminate between Irish banks and foreign-owned banks operating in the country, in order to secure Commission approval.

The financial market turmoil in 2008 brought Ireland's economic interdependence with the rest of Europe and the world sharply into focus. As a very open economy, Ireland benefited from high economic growth in the 1990s and in the first decade of the twenty-first century. However, the country was also more exposed to the global economic downturn that began with the crisis in financial markets in September 2008. The consequences of a global crisis were exacerbated in Ireland because of poor domestic policy choices and 'cheap' money from European financial markets. Combined, this heightened the exposure of the Irish banks to bad loans generated through excessive and high-risk lending to property developers, creating a construction boom. Fearing the possible failure of the domestic banking and financial system, the government offered a guarantee of all deposits in banks in Ireland in September 2008.

By November 2010, the rising costs of the bank guarantee, driven by the insolvency of Anglo Irish Bank, had effectively undermined the ability of the government to borrow on the financial markets to run the state. In addition, the Irish financial system was, by that stage, entirely reliant on short-term financing through the ECB to maintain liquidity. Support from EU-related sources amounted to 140 billon euro, or 80 per cent of the Irish gross domestic product. Interdependence in the EU was now being replaced by dependence.

In mid-November 2010, under enormous pressure from the ECB and other Eurozone states, Ireland sought a rescue package from the EU and the IMF; this amounted to 67.5 billion euro, and placed Ireland under Troika governance for three years, as described above. This was followed quickly by the collapse of the Fianna Fáil–Green coalition and the defeat of the participating parties in the 2011 general election.

Although Ireland was the first Eurozone country to exit such a 'Troika' programme, the three-year bailout was a period of sustained and harsh budget cutbacks and rising taxes, which in turn exacerbated an already troubled domestic economy. The bailout episode was undoubtedly the most traumatic period of Ireland's membership of the EU, as the design faults of the single currency project became manifest and the Union struggled to design effective policy responses. The experience undermined trust in the EU; for the first time, those thinking EU membership was a 'good thing' dipped below 70 per cent in Eurobarometer surveys, though this later recovered as the economy picked up again. However, the political turmoil of the crisis has left important legacies. The role of the ECB in insisting that the costs of the Irish banking bailout be borne entirely by Irish taxpayers – with no losses to unsecured bank bondholders – for long remained highly contested in Ireland, which had been forced to defer to the wishes of the ECB, given its dependence on that body for liquidity for the banks (Laffan, 2016: 184–9).

Government and parliament

EU membership has also had implications for Ireland's governmental and parliamentary system, which has had to respond to this extra layer of governance and politics. Like its counterparts in other member states, it did so within the broad contours of its political and administrative culture and institutional system. A cabinet sub-committee on European Affairs was added to the government's array of cabinet committees, a range of interdepartmental committees for the coordination of European issues was established, and the office of Minister of State for European Affairs was created. Within cabinet, the Taoiseach and the Minister for Foreign Affairs are traditionally the two most important political office holders in relation to European issues (Laffan, 2001). The Ministers of Agriculture and Justice are also key players, because of the importance of Europe to their respective portfolios. The Finance Minister has always had a critical role, for obvious reasons. During the period of Troika governance, the Taoiseach, Tánaiste, Finance Minister and Minister for Public Expenditure and Reform were the four key cabinet posts in relation to domestic and EU policy, and collectively constituted the government's Economic Management Council (2011–16), a new cabinet sub-committee, discontinued after the 2016 election, that was the equivalent of a war council during and after the economic crisis (see Chapter 10).

In the early years of EU membership, the Department of Foreign Affairs played a central role in managing European business and had oversight of Ireland's relations with the EU. The growing significance of the European Council in the EU system has greatly strengthened the role of the Taoiseach's department in European affairs, and in 2016 a dedicated division was established there, with responsibility for handling the implications of the UK's exit from the EU. The Minister of State for European Affairs is usually a joint appointment to both departments, but the office-holders tend to spend most of their time in the Taoiseach's department. The weakness of parliamentary scrutiny of European affairs emerged as an issue during the first Nice referendum in 2001. The government proposed a more substantive parliamentary process in response, and this was incorporated in the European Union (Scrutiny) Act, 2002. The procedures envisaged far more ministerial and official engagement with the Committee on European Affairs, both before and after meetings of the Council of Ministers. In addition, the lead department in any field was obliged to prepare 'notes' on all draft legislative proposals for Oireachtas committees. A 'note' identifies the importance of a particular European proposal (classifying it as having major significance, having some significance or being purely technical), an assessment of the implications for Ireland, an overview of the consequences for national legislation and the EU budget, and the likely timetable for negotiations and implementation. 'Notes' must also specify the legal basis of the proposal, the voting rules that apply to it and the role of the European Parliament. From 2007, this task was undertaken by a new Joint Oireachtas Committee on European Scrutiny, which uses these 'notes' to decide how it will scrutinise the proposals.

The post-Nice procedures have undoubtedly enhanced parliamentary scrutiny of European affairs. The 2009 Lisbon Treaty further enhanced the role of national parliaments by ensuring that they would receive EU documents at the same time as national governments, and by providing them with the possibility of working with other national parliaments to block certain EU proposals. Notwithstanding improvements in Oireachtas scrutiny, it remains challenging for all parliaments in Europe to hold their governments to account for their actions in Brussels. Moreover, the Irish electorate does not reward deputies for spending time on European topics, and these issues rarely provide any political payback for hard-pressed parliamentarians.

Emerging challenges

As the twenty-first century proceeds, Ireland faces major challenges in its external environment. The first arises from the rapidly changing character of the EU, as its central institutions acquire greater political weight and expand their reach in such areas as foreign affairs and defence. The second is an inevitable reconfiguration of Ireland's relationship with its nearest neighbour, given the outcome of the British referendum on EU membership. We consider these topics in turn.

Foreign and defence policy

If membership of the EU impinges to such an extent on what is conventionally thought of as domestic public policy, it might be asked whether we can expect a member state, especially a small one such as Ireland, to conduct its own foreign policy (Tonra, 2007; Tonra *et al.*, 2012). Not surprisingly, this activity does indeed largely take place in a collective setting, through the Common Foreign and Security Policy (CFSP) and the associated Common Security and Defence Policy (CSDP). Although it involves intensive consultations with all other member states, this policy area is a far less closely integrated form of policy-making than exists elsewhere in the EU.

Decisions on Irish foreign policy still ultimately rest with the government in Dublin, and the whole apparatus of national diplomacy – the Department of Foreign Affairs and Trade and its embassies abroad – has grown both in size and political importance. Indeed, a significant expansion in Ireland's diplomatic network occurred following the end of the 2008–14 economic crisis, with the opening or re-opening of five new embassies (in the Holy See in 2014, Bangkok in 2014, and in Jakarta, Zagreb and Nairobi in 2015). Three new consulates were also established in 2014–15.

At this level of generalisation, it may seem that an acceptable balance has been found between the way in which Irish governments see their national foreign policies and the obligations of EU membership. But as the Union has further developed its own foreign policy infrastructure and has sought to develop a military capacity to underpin it, Irish policy makers face a challenge: to support the creation of a more integrated and coherent EU policy in this area, or to insist on retaining maximum latitude in the pursuit of a distinctive Irish foreign policy.

An important institutional framework dedicated to the creation of an effective EU foreign policy has emerged: the ambassadorial-level Political and Security Committee; a dedicated EU military committee and military staff; the High Representative for EU foreign and security policy; and the diplomatic infrastructure provided by the EU's External Action Service. The Union's 2016 global strategy – effectively, a key EU policy document agreed by all member states that defines the goals of EU foreign policy – sees the strengthening of EU security and defence as a critical and popular initiative in an era of increased threats and insecurities. While Ireland has fully participated to date in this process, as in committing troops to the Union's multilateral battlegroups, national sensitivities related to military 'neutrality' or non-alignment persist. These require, for example, that Irish contributions to EU military operations be externally validated through the so-called 'triple lock', which requires Irish troops serving overseas to operate within an explicit UN mandate.

The challenge faced by Ireland in contributing to the development of a more effective EU foreign policy is shared by other member states to a greater or lesser degree, but is made all the more difficult by the Union's own weaknesses as an international actor. The deliberative, iterative and consensual style of policy making suitable to environmental, agricultural or transportation policy is singularly unsuited to addressing real-time security crises. The Union's lack of a sovereign, hierarchical and executive-style foreign policy capacity is never so obvious – and so debilitating – as in times of crisis. The Union's confused and slow response to the so-called Arab Spring in 2011 and the associated outbreak of the Syrian civil war, its failure to deal with Russia's 2014 invasion, occupation and annexation of parts of Ukraine, and its failure to address the 2015–16 migration crisis, all combine to limit confidence in the Union's capacity as an international actor. The expectation that the Union should itself be capable of acting in the world like a state may be part of the problem; it is, after all, an entity comprised of 28 sovereign states. It is not at all clear that Ireland would consent to the kinds of profound constitutional and political changes necessary to make the Union a truly effective international actor.

Brexit

The outcome of the UK referendum of June 2016 on the question of EU membership, when 52 per cent voted in favour of Brexit, had a profound impact on Ireland, its external environment and the context of EU membership. Joint membership of the EU since 1973 had framed British–Irish relations and played an important role in addressing the conflict in Northern Ireland and in normalising relations between the two islands. The Good Friday Agreement (which provided a framework for governance within Northern Ireland, and for relations between north and south and between the two islands) is predicated on joint membership of the EU (see Chapter 13). The agreement between the two governments specifically acknowledges their role as 'partners in the European Union' (Good Friday Agreement, 1998: preamble, fourth paragraph).

Participation by key actors from Ireland and the UK in all EU institutions provided additional arenas for informal bilateral dialogue, and helped in framing relations between them.

Brexit shifted one of the key anchors of Irish public policy and statecraft. Ireland was most affected because of its relationship with Northern Ireland, the intensity of the economic relationship with the UK, and the common travel area, agreed in 1922, to link Ireland and Great Britain. A majority of voters in Northern Ireland (56 per cent) voted to remain in the EU in the Brexit referendum; a majority there did not want to lose the benefits of EU membership. Northern Ireland had received a significant injection of EU funding under a special programme designed to support the peace process. More significant, however, was the question of the border between the two parts of the island. The nature and location of the post-Brexit border regime for goods, services and the movement of people is obviously dependent on the outcome of negotiations between the UK and the EU, designed to determine their long-term relationship. Brexit represented a major shock for Ireland and the wider Union, one that underlined the volatility evident in domestic politics in many member states. It added uncertainty at a time when the Union was already stretched by the legacy of the Eurozone crisis and the continuing refugee crisis.

Conclusion

Ireland's external environment has been an important influence on the state's political development. In the turbulent international system up to the end of the Second World War, the British connection provided the main focus; the new state's political independence was demonstrated by the policy of neutrality during the war. After the war, Ireland was gradually drawn into a broader, more stable and increasingly interdependent international system. Membership of the European Union since 1973 has provided this small open polity with a framework within which it could mediate the forces of growing interdependence and, later, globalisation. The EU was not just about managing the outside world, however, as membership had a major impact on political life in Ireland. Politics and public policy were moulded by engagement with the EU. As representatives of a small state, Irish policy makers will have to think on their feet as they navigate the new instabilities and insecurities that the Union and its member states are now facing. After more than 40 years of membership, those policy makers have built up considerable expertise, and this will be severely tested as the Union addresses its own internal and external challenges, and Irish diplomats have once more to focus on recasting Ireland's critical bilateral relationship with the UK from within a diminished European Union.

The collapse of communism in 1989, the terrorist attacks on the twin towers in September 2001 and the 2004 enlargement of the EU have all, in their own ways, altered the basic dynamics of world politics. The 2016 Brexit vote, and the rise of nationalist populism in key countries, may yet add to this. Certainly, they make the world a more complex and challenging place, especially for small open polities such as Ireland. The boundary between internal and external security has become blurred and security threats are deriving from unstable or failed states, from the proliferation of weapons of mass destruction and from the actions of highly motivated terrorists. In this new world order, Europe is itself challenged to respond in a way that resonates more positively with its own citizens, that finds agreement among its own member state governments and that, at the same time, garners respect from its international partners. There also remain difficult questions about Europe's wider role in the world and its relations with the United States and emerging global powers such as China. These questions and challenges will continue to have an impact on the substance and conduct of Irish foreign policy.

Notes

1   The authors would like to acknowledge the contribution made by Patrick Keatinge to this chapter. He was co-author with Laffan of the corresponding chapter in the earliest editions of the volume.
2   The KOF Globalisation Index is published annually by ETH Zurich and measures the three main dimensions of globalisation – economic, social and political – offering a comparative ranking: http://globalization.kof.ethz.ch/ (accessed 23 January 2017).
3   Gross Domestic Product (GDP) is traditionally used to measure comparative historic economic growth. However, this includes the value of goods and services produced by foreign multinational corporations and as a result, in the Irish case, this can distort year-on-year growth measurement in the domestic economy. Gross National Product (GNP) or Gross National Income (GNI) are today viewed as better indicators of contemporary Irish economic growth.
4   As an example, in C-374/11, European Commission v. Ireland, 19 December 2012, Ireland was fined €2 million plus €12,000 per day for each further day the state failed properly to transpose EU legislation on septic tank inspections.
5   European Council Conclusions, 21–22 June 2002, www.consilium.europa.eu/en/european-council/conclusions/1993-2003/.
6   www.newstalk.com/Brexit-Ireland-opinion-poll-Britain-economy-Northern-Ireland-referendum-EU (accessed 6 February 2017).
7   This is according to European Court of Auditor statistics; Ireland received over 2 billion euros and contributed just over 1.8 billion. According to the Department of Finance, Ireland became a small net contributor in 2014, but this is because the Department of Finance does not include research income gained by the universities, as this does not go through the exchequer. EU-level data, on the other hand, include all such financial flows. The data here was contained in a presentation made by Ireland's representative on the European Court of Auditors to the Joint Committee on EU Affairs on 29 November 2016; http://oireachtasdebates.oireachtas.ie/debates%20authoring/debatesweb-pack.nsf/committeetakes/EUJ2016112900002.

References and further reading

Benoit, Kenneth, 2009. 'Irish political parties and policy stances on European integration', *Irish Political Studies* 24:4, pp. 447–66.

Coakley, John, 2005. 'Irish public opinion and the new Europe', in Michael Holmes (ed.), *Ireland and the European Union: Nice, Enlargement and the Future of Europe*. Manchester: Manchester University Press, pp. 94–113.

Costello, Tony, 2014. 'The Fiscal Stability Treaty referendum 2012', *Irish Political Studies* 29:3, pp. 457–70.

Cousins, Mel, 2002. *Social Welfare Law*. Dublin: Roundhall Press

EU, 2016. *Commission Annual Report 2015 on Monitoring the Application of EU Law* 463 final, 15.7.2016. Brussels: EU Commission.

Fisk, Robert, 1983. *In Time of War: Ireland, Ulster and the Price of Neutrality 1939–1945*. London: Andre Deutsch.

Good Friday Agreement, 1998. *The Agreement Reached in the Multi-Party Negotiations 10 April 1998*. Available at: http://peacemaker.un.org (last accessed 1 October 2017).

Hix, Simon, 2016. 'Does the UK have influence in the EU legislative process?', *Political Quarterly* 87:2, pp. 200–8.

Keatinge, Patrick (ed.), 1991. *Ireland and EC Membership Evaluated*. London: Pinter.

Kenealy, Daniel, John Peterson and Richard Corbett (eds), 2015. *The European Union: How Does It Work*? Oxford: Oxford University Press.

Kennedy, Michael J., 2008. *Guarding Neutral Ireland: The Coastwatching Service, Military Intelligence and Ireland's Second World War*. Dublin: Four Courts Press.

Keown, Gerald, 2015. *First of the Small Nations: The Beginnings of Irish Foreign Policy in Inter-War Europe, 1919–1932*. Oxford: Oxford University Press.

Laffan, Brigid, 2001. *Organising for a Changing Europe: Irish Central Government and the European Union*. Dublin: Policy Institute, Trinity College Dublin.

Laffan, Brigid, 2016. 'International actors and agencies', in William K. Roche, Philip J. O'Connell and Andrea Prothero (eds), *Austerity and Recovery in Ireland: Europe's Poster Child and the Great Recession*. Oxford: Oxford University Press, pp. 177–93.

Laffan, Brigid and Jane O'Mahony, 2008. *Ireland in the European Union*. London: Palgrave Macmillan.

Nicolaides, Phedon and Anne-Marie Suren, 2007. 'The rule of law in the EU: what the numbers say', EIPAScope 2007, http://www.eipa.eu/files/repository/eipascope/20070622102127_pniSCOPE 2007-1_internet-7.pdf

O'Halpin, Eunan, 2008. *Spying on Ireland: British Intelligence and Irish Neutrality during the Second World War*. Oxford: Oxford University Press.

O'Mahony, Jane, 2009. 'Ireland's EU referendum experience', *Irish Political Studies* 24:4, pp. 429–46.

Quinlan, Stephen, 2009. 'The Lisbon Treaty referendum 2008', *Irish Political Studies* 24:1, pp. 107–21.

Quinlan, Stephen, 2012. 'The Lisbon experience in Ireland: "No" in 2008 but "Yes" in 2009 – how and why?', *Irish Political Studies* 27:1, pp. 139–53.

Salmon, Trevor, 1989. *Unneutral Ireland: An Ambivalent and Unique Security Policy*. Oxford: Oxford University Press.

Thomas, Martha, 2017. 'The efficiency of ministries in transposing EU directives: evidence from Ireland', *Public Policy and Administration*, doi:10.1177/0952076716687616.

Tonra, Ben, 2007. *Global Citizen, European Republic: Irish Foreign Policy in Transition*. Manchester: Manchester University Press.

Tonra, Ben, Michael Kennedy, John Doyle and Noel Dorr (eds), 2012. *Irish Foreign Policy*. Dublin: Gill and Macmillan.

Wills, Clair, 2007. *That Neutral Island: A Cultural History of Ireland During the Second World War*. Cambridge, MA: Harvard University Press.

Websites

www.dfa.ie/
Department of Foreign Affairs

www.defence.ie
Department of Defence

www.difp.ie/
Documents in Irish Foreign Policy

www.iiea.com/
Institute for International and European Affairs

iicrr.ie/
DCU Institute for International Conflict Resolution and Reconstruction

www.ucd.ie/dei/
UCD Dublin European Institute

www.eufp.eu/
Exploring European Union Foreign Policy

www.oireachtas.ie/parliament/oireachtasbusiness/committees_list/foreign-affairs-trade-defence/
Oireachtas Joint Committee on Foreign Affairs and Trade, and Defence

www.oireachtas.ie/parliament/oireachtasbusiness/committees_list/eu-affairs/Oireachtas Joint Committee
Oireachtas Joint Committee on European Union Affairs

Appendices

John Coakley

Note: The data in these appendices refer to the territory of the Republic of Ireland, except where otherwise stated. Turnout is defined as total votes (valid plus invalid) as a percentage of electorate.

Appendix 1: Demographic data

1a: Population and social indicators, 1841–2016

Year	Population: Total	Urban %	Dublin %	Males in agriculture %	Religion: RC %	Other %	Knowledge of Irish%	Birthplace (%) Other county	Other country
1841	6,528,799	16.7	3.7	74.3	·	·	·	5.0	0.8
1851	5,111,557	22.0	5.8	68.8	·	·	29.1	8.8	1.5
1861	4,402,111	22.2	6.7	64.6	89.3	10.7	24.5	8.1	2.1
1871	4,053,187	22.8	7.4	63.1	89.2	10.8	19.8	9.3	2.8
1881	3,870,020	23.9	8.4	62.6	89.5	10.5	23.9	10.2	3.0
1891	3,468,694	25.3	9.6	61.4	89.3	10.7	19.2	10.8	2.6
1901	3,221,823	28.0	11.2	61.7	89.3	10.7	19.2	11.2	3.7
1911	3,139,688	29.7	12.3	59.5	89.6	10.4	17.6	12.7	4.3
1926	2,971,992	31.8	13.7	58.9	92.6	7.4	19.3	13.4	3.4
1936	2,968,420	35.5	15.9	55.9	93.4	6.6	23.7	14.5	3.4
1946	2,955,107	39.3	17.1	54.1	94.3	5.7	21.2	16.1	3.3
1961	2,818,341	46.4	19.1	43.1	94.9	4.9	27.2	14.1	3.5
1971	2,978,248	52.2	26.9	31.9	93.9	4.3	28.3	14.8	4.6
1981	3,443,405	55.6	29.1	21.7	93.1	3.7	31.6	17.6	6.7
1991	3,525,719	57.0	29.1	19.1	91.6	4.2	32.5	18.1	6.5
1996	3,626,087	58.1	29.2	15.1	–	–	41.1	18.9	7.5
2002	3,917,203	59.6	28.7	8.4	88.4	6.1	41.9	19.7	10.4
2006	4,239,848	60.7	28.0	7.2	86.8	7.1	40.8	20.4	14.7
2011	4,588,252	62.0	27.7	8.7	84.2	8.4	41.4	20.6	16.9
2016	4,761,865	62.7	28.3	–	78.8	8.5	39.8	21.1	17.3

Source: Calculated from *Census of Ireland, Statistical Abstract of Ireland* and *Statistical Yearbook of Ireland*, various dates, and from David Fitzpatrick, 'The disappearance of the Irish agricultural labourer, 1841–1912', *Irish Economic and Social History* 7, 1980, pp. 66–92.

Notes: All data refer to the present area of the Republic of Ireland, except where otherwise stated. Urban areas are defined as those with a population of 1,500 or more, but figures for these and for Dublin are difficult to compare over time due to changes in boundary definition criteria; in 1971, Dublin is defined as including Dun Laoghaire, and from 1981, it has been taken as including all of Dublin county. The data on involvement in agriculture are also difficult to compare over time due to varying classification criteria, and it has been possible to compute comparable data for men only. Data on religion are expressed as percentages of the total population (which includes those refusing to give information on this matter). Data on Irish speakers from 1926 onwards refer to the population aged over three years, but the form of the question changed in 1996, so the data for this and subsequent years are not strictly comparable with the earlier ones. In all cases, knowledge of the language is self-assessed. 'Birthplace other county' refers to those born in Irish counties other than that in which they were resident at the date of the census (for the 1841–1911 period these percentages refer to the whole island). 'Birthplace other country' refers to those born outside the 26 counties.

1b: Emigration and immigration, 1841–2016

Period	Total emigration	Annual average
1841–51	1,132,000	108,000
1852–60	791,648	87,961
1861–70	697,704	69,770
1871–80	446,326	44,633
1881–90	616,894	61,689
1891–00	377,017	37,702
1901–10	266,311	26,631
	Net emigration	
1911–26	405,029	27,002
1926–36	166,751	16,675
1936–46	187,111	18,711
1946–61	531,255	35,417
1961–71	134,511	13,451
1971–81	−103,889	−10,389
1981–91	206,053	20,605
1991–96	−8,302	−1,660
1996–02	−153,881	−25,647
2002–06	−191,331	−47,833
2006–11	−115,800	−23,200
2011–16	97,400	19,500

Source: Computed from W. E. Vaughan and A. J. Fitzpatrick (eds), *Irish Historical Statistics: Population, 1821–1971* (Dublin: Royal Irish Academy, 1989), *Commission on Emigration and Other Population Problems 1948–1954, Reports* (Dublin: Stationery Office, [1956]); *Census 2006: vol. 4: Usual residence, migration, birthplaces and nationalities* (Dublin: Stationery Office, 2007); and *Population and Migration Estimates April 2016* (Cork: Central Statistics Office, 2016).

Note: The data for 1841–51 are estimates based on the assumption that the proportion of Irish emigrants coming from the present territory of the Republic was the same as in the 1852–60 period (the data begin in mid-year 1841). Net emigration refers to out-migration less in-migration, and the negative values in 1971–81 and 1991–2011 indicate a surplus of immigrants over emigrants in these periods.

Appendix 2: Electoral data

2a: Distribution of parliamentary seats by party, 1801–1918

Year	Southern Ireland					All Ireland				
	Tory/ Unionist	Whig/ Liberal	Nat. etc.	Other	Total	Tory/ Unionist	Whig/ Liberal	Nat. etc.	Other	Total
1801	23	16	.	39	78	34	16	.	50	100
1802	27	26	.	25	78	43	28	.	29	100
1806	34	34	.	10	78	50	36	.	14	100
1807	37	32	.	9	78	54	33	.	13	100
1812	43	28	.	7	78	59	30	.	11	100
1818	41	32	.	5	78	61	34	.	5	100
1820	44	29	.	5	78	63	32	.	5	100
1826	38	37	.	3	78	56	41	.	3	100
1830	34	41	.	3	78	49	48	.	3	100
1831	26	48	.	4	78	40	56	.	4	100
1832	14	26	42	.	82	30	33	42	.	105
1835	22	26	34	.	82	37	34	34	.	105
1837	14	38	30	.	82	32	43	30	.	105
1841	23	39	20	.	82	43	42	20	.	105
1847	20	21	36	5	82	31	25	36	13	105
1852	21	11	48	2	82	40	15	48	2	105
1857	26	43	13	.	82	44	48	13	.	105
1859	33	49	.	0	82	55	50	.	0	105
1865	24	58	.	0	82	47	58	.	0	105
1868	19	63	.	0	82	39	66	.	0	105
1874	16	4	60	.	80	33	10	60	.	103
1880	7	10	63	.	80	25	15	63	.	103
1885	2	.	76	.	78	18	.	85	.	103
1886	2	.	76	.	78	19	.	84	.	103
1892	4	.	74	.	78	23	.	80	.	103
1895	4	.	74	.	78	21	1	81	.	103
1900	3	.	75	.	78	21	1	81	.	103
1906	3	.	75	.	78	20	1	82	.	103
1910–1	3	.	75	.	78	21	1	81	.	103
1910–2	2	.	76	.	78	19	1	83	.	103
1918	3	.	2	70	75	26	.	6	73	105

Sources: Calculated from Henry Stooks Smith, *The Parliaments of England from 1715 to 1847*, 2nd ed, edited by F. W. S. Craig (Chichester: Political Reference Publications, 1973), and Brian M. Walker, *Parliamentary Election Results in Ireland, 1801–1922* (Dublin: Royal Irish Academy, 1978).

Notes: 'Southern Ireland' refers to the present territory of the Republic of Ireland. Before 1832, party affiliations are approximate only. 'Tories/Unionists' includes Liberal Unionists; 'Nationalists, etc.' includes the Repeal Party (1832–47), the Independent Irish Party (1852–57) and the Home Rule or Nationalist Party, including breakaway factions and independent nationalists (1874–1918); 'Others' includes non-aligned MPs (1801–32), Peelites (1847–52) and two Irish Confederates in the South (1847); in 1918, it refers to Sinn Féin MPs.

2b: Percentage distribution of first preference votes in Dáil elections, 1922–2016

Year	Fianna Fáil	Fine Gael	Labour Party	Farmers' parties	Republican parties			Others	Turnout
1922	21.7	38.5	21.3	7.8	.			10.6	45.5
1923	27.4	39.0	10.6	12.1	.			10.9	61.2
1927–1	26.1	27.5	12.6	8.9	3.6			21.4	68.1
1927–2	35.2	38.7	9.1	6.4	.			10.7	69.0
1932	44.5	35.3	7.7	3.1	.			9.4	76.5
1933	49.7	30.5	5.7	9.2	.			5.0	81.3
1937	45.2	34.8	10.3	.	.			9.7	76.2
1938	51.9	33.3	10.0	.	.			4.7	76.7
1943	41.9	23.1	15.7	11.3	0.3			7.7	74.2
1944	48.9	20.5	8.8	11.6	.			10.2	67.7
1948	41.9	19.8	8.7	5.6	13.2			10.9	74.2
1951	46.3	25.8	11.4	2.9	4.1			9.6	75.3
1954	43.4	32.0	12.1	3.1	3.9			5.6	76.4
1957	48.3	26.6	9.1	2.4	7.0			6.6	71.3
1961	43.8	32.0	11.6	1.5	4.2			6.8	70.6
1965	47.7	34.1	15.4	.	0.8			2.1	75.1
1969	45.7	34.1	17.0	.	.			3.2	76.9
1973	46.2	35.1	13.7	.	2.0			3.0	76.6
1977	50.6	30.5	11.6	.	1.8			5.5	76.3
1981	45.3	36.5	9.9	.	2.5			5.9	76.2
				PDs	*Sinn Féin*	*Green Party*			
1982–1	47.3	37.3	9.1	.	1.0	.		5.3	73.8
1982–2	45.2	39.2	9.4	.	.	.		6.3	72.9
1987	44.1	27.1	6.4	11.8	1.9	0.4		8.3	73.3
1989	44.1	29.3	9.5	5.5	1.2	1.5		8.9	68.5
1992	39.1	24.5	19.3	4.7	1.6	1.4		9.5	68.5
1997	39.3	27.9	10.4	4.7	2.6	2.8		12.3	65.9
2002	41.5	22.5	10.8	4.0	6.5	3.8		10.9	62.6
2007	41.6	27.3	10.1	2.7	6.9	4.7		6.6	67.0
				*Left**					
2011	17.4	36.1	19.4	2.6	9.9	1.8		13.8	70.0
2016	24.3	25.5	6.6	3.9	13.8	2.7		23.2	65.1

Notes: Fianna Fáil includes Anti-Treaty Sinn Féin (1922–23). Fine Gael includes Pro-Treaty Sinn Féin (1922) and Cumann na nGaedheal (1923–33). 'Farmers' parties' includes the Farmers' Party (1922–32), the National Centre Party (1933) and Clann na Talmhan (1943–61). 'Republican parties' refers to Sinn Féin, including the original party before 1970 (1927–1, 3.6%; 1954, 0.1%; 1957, 5.3%; 1961, 3.1%), 'Official' Sinn Féin in the 1970s (1973, 1.1%; 1977, 1.7%), and the following parties: Córas na Poblachta (1943, 0.3%), Clann na Poblachta (1948, 13.2%; 1951, 4.1%; 1954, 3.8%; 1957, 1.7%; 1961, 1.1%; 1965, 0.8%), Aontacht Éireann (1973, 0.9%), the Irish Republican Socialist Party (1977, 0.1%; 1982–1, 0.2%) and the National H-Block Committee (1981, 2.5%). Left* refers to the United Left Alliance (2011) and to the Anti-Austerity Alliance and People Before Profit (2016). 'Others' includes the National League (1927–1, 7.3%; 1927–2, 1.6%), National Labour (1944, 2.7%; 1948, 2.6%) and the National Progressive Democrats (1961, 1.0%), as well as smaller groups and independents. From 1981, Sinn Féin the Workers' Party and its successor, the Workers' Party, have been grouped with 'others' (1981, 1.7%; 1982–1, 2.3%; 1982–2, 3.3%; 1987, 3.8%; 1989, 5.0%; 1992, 0.7%; 1997, 0.4%; 2002, 0.2%; 2007, 0.1%; 2011, 0.1%; 2016, 0.1%), as has Democratic Left (1992, 2.8%; 1997, 2.5%). Comparable data are not available for 1918 and 1921; see note to Appendix 2c.

Source: Michael Gallagher (ed.), *Irish Elections 1922–44: Results and Analysis* (Limerick: PSAI Press, 1993) and *Irish Elections 1948–77: Results and Analysis* (London: Routledge and PSAI Press, 2009); and official results.

2c: Distribution of seats in the Dáil, 1922–2016

Year	Fianna Fáil	Fine Gael	Labour Party	Farmers' parties	Republican parties			Others	Total
1922	36	58	17	7	.			10	128
1923	44	63	14	15	.			17	153
1927–1	44	47	22	11	5			24	153
1927–2	57	62	13	6	.			15	153
1932	72	57	7	4	.			13	153
1933	77	48	8	11	.			9	153
1937	69	48	13	.	.			8	138
1938	77	45	9	.	.			7	138
1943	67	32	17	14	.			8	138
1944	76	30	8	11	.			13	138
1948	68	31	14	7	10			17	147
1951	69	40	16	6	2			14	147
1954	65	50	19	5	3			5	147
1957	78	40	12	3	5			9	147
1961	70	47	16	2	1			8	144
1965	72	47	22	.	1			2	144
1969	75	50	18	.	.			1	144
1973	69	54	19	.	.			2	144
1977	84	43	17	.	.			4	148
1981	78	65	15	.	2			6	166
1982–1	81	63	15	.	.	.		7	166
				Prog. Dems	*Sinn Féin*	*Green Party*			
1982–2	75	70	16	.	.	.		5	166
1987	81	51	12	14	.	.		8	166
1989	77	55	15	6	.	1		12	166
1992	68	45	33	10	.	1		9	166
1997	77	54	17	4	1	2		11	166
2002	81	31	21	8	5	6		14	166
2007	78	51	20	2	4	6		5	166
				Left*					
2011	20	76	37	4	14	.		15	166
2016	44	50	7	6	23	2		26	158

Notes: Fianna Fáil includes Anti-Treaty Sinn Féin (1922–23). Fine Gael includes Pro-Treaty Sinn Féin (1922) and Cumann na nGaedheal (1923–33). 'Farmers' parties' includes the Farmers' Party (1922–32), the National Centre Party (1933), and Clann na Talmhan (1943–61). 'Republican parties' refers mainly to Clann na Poblachta (1948–65) but includes also Sinn Féin (1927–1, 5 TDs; 1957, 4 TDs) and the National H-Block Committee (1981, 2 TDs). L* refers to the United Left Alliance (2011) and to the Anti-Austerity Alliance and People Before Profit (2016). 'Others' includes the National League (1927–1, 8 TDs; 1927–2, 2 TDs), National Labour (1944, 4 TDs; 1948, 5 TDs), the National Progressive Democrats (1961, 2 TDs), Sinn Féin the Workers' Party and its successor, the Workers' Party (1981, 1 TD; 1982–1, 3 TDs; 1982–2, 2 TDs; 1987, 4 TDs; 1989, 7 TDs), and Democratic Left (1992 and 1997, 4 TDs), as well as smaller groups and independents.

The first Dáil was convened on the basis of the British general election of 1918. At this election, Sinn Féin won 73 seats (all except three of these in the South; two of the northern seats were won by candidates who were also successful in the South, and one candidate was returned for two constituencies in the South, leaving Sinn Féin with 70 MPs), the Unionists 26 (all except three in the North) and the Nationalists six (four in the North and two in the South). The second Dáil was convened on the basis of the elections in 1921 to the proposed Houses of Commons of Southern Ireland and Northern Ireland. At this, Sinn Féin won 130 seats (all except six of these in the South; five of the northern seats were won by candidates who were also successful in the South, leaving Sinn Féin with 125 MPs), the Unionists 40 (all in the North), the Nationalists six (all in the North), and independents won four (all in the South).

Source: As for Appendix 2b.

2d: Distribution of men and women in the Oireachtas, 1922–2016

Dáil Éireann				Seanad Éireann			
Year	Men	Women	Total	Year	Men	Women	Total
1922	126	2	128	-	.	.	.
1923	148	5	153	1922	56	4	60
1927–1	149	4	153	1925	56	4	60
1927–2	152	1	153	1928	55	5	60
1932	151	2	153	1931	55	5	60
1933	150	3	153	1934	57	3	60
1937	136	2	138	1938–1	56	4	60
1938	135	3	138	1938–2	57	3	60
1943	135	3	138	1943	57	3	60
1944	134	4	138	1944	57	3	60
1948	142	5	147	1948	57	3	60
1951	142	5	147	1951	57	3	60
1954	142	5	147	1954	57	3	60
1957	142	5	147	1957	56	4	60
1961	141	3	144	1961	57	3	60
1965	139	5	144	1965	56	4	60
1969	141	3	144	1969	55	5	60
1973	140	4	144	1973	56	4	60
1977	142	6	148	1977	54	6	60
1981	155	11	166	1981	51	9	60
1982–1	158	8	166	1982	52	8	60
1982–2	152	14	166	1983	54	6	60
1987	152	14	166	1987	55	5	60
1989	153	13	166	1989	54	6	60
1992	146	20	166	1993	52	8	60
1997	146	20	166	1997	49	11	60
2002	144	22	166	2002	50	10	60
2007	144	22	166	2007	47	13	60
2011	141	25	166	2011	42	18	60
2016	123	35	158	2016	42	18	60

Notes: The data refer to the position immediately after general elections to Dáil Éireann (1922–2016) and Seanad Éireann (1938–2016). The earlier data on Seanad Éireann refer to the position immediately after the initial installation of the first Seanad under the Free State constitution (1922), and after the triennial elections that renewed a portion of its membership (1925–34).

Only one woman was returned from the 105 Irish seats in the British general election of 1918; of the 73 Sinn Féin seats, 72 were occupied by men (since three of these seats were double returns, the full potential membership of the first Dáil was 69 men and one woman). Eight women were returned from the 180 seats to the Houses of Commons of Southern Ireland and Northern Ireland in 1921, two Unionists in the North and six Sinn Féin members in the South (since the 130 Sinn Féin seats were occupied by only 125 people, due to double returns, the full potential membership of the second Dáil was 119 men and six women).

2e: Percentage distribution of first preference votes in European Parliament elections, 1979–2014

Year	Fianna Fáil	Fine Gael	Labour Party	Workers' Party	Sinn Féin	Green Party	Others	Turnout
1979	34.7	33.1	14.5	3.3	.	.	14.4	63.6
1984	39.2	32.2	8.4	4.3	4.9	.	11.0	47.6
1989	31.5	21.6	9.5	7.5	2.3	3.7	23.9	68.3
1994	35.0	24.3	11.0	1.9	3.0	7.9	16.9	44.0
1999	38.6	24.6	8.7	.	6.3	6.7	15.0	50.2
2004	29.5	27.8	10.6	.	11.1	4.3	16.7	58.6
2009	24.1	29.1	13.9	.	11.2	1.9	19.7	57.6
2014	22.3	22.3	5.3	.	19.5	4.9	25.7	52.4

Source: Computed from *European Parliament Election Results 2014* (Dublin: Department of the Environment, Community and Local Government, n.d.), and corresponding documents for earlier years.

Notes: 'Workers' Party' includes Sinn Féin The Workers' Party; 'Others' includes Democratic Left (1994, 3.5%), the Progressive Democrats (1989, 11.9%; 1994, 6.5%), and independents.

2f: Perccentage distribution of first preference votes in local elections, 1967–2014

Year	Fianna Fáil	Fine Gael	Labour Party	Workers' Party	Sinn Féin	Green Party	Others	Turnout
1967	40.2	32.5	14.8	.	.	.	12.5	69.0
1974	40.1	33.7	12.8	1.5	.	.	11.9	61.1
1979	39.2	34.9	11.8	2.3	2.2	.	9.6	63.6
1985	45.5	29.8	7.7	3.0	3.3	.	10.7	58.2
1991	37.9	26.4	10.6	3.7	1.7	2.0	17.7	55.1
1999	38.9	28.1	10.7	0.5	3.5	2.5	15.8	50.3
2004	31.8	27.6	11.4	0.2	8.1	3.9	17.2	58.6
2009	25.4	32.2	14.7	0.3	7.4	2.3	17.7	57.7
2014	25.3	24.0	7.2	0.2	15.3	1.6	26.4	51.7

Source: Computed from *Local Elections 2014: Results, Transfer of Votes and Statistics* (Dublin: Department of the Environment, Community and Local Government, 2016), and corresponding documents for earlier years.

Notes: These figures relate to the results in county and city council elections only. 'Workers' Party' includes Sinn Féin (1974) and Sinn Féin the Workers' Party (1979); 'Others' includes Progressive Democrats (1991, 5.0%; 1999, 2.9%; 2004, 3.9%), Anti-Austerity Alliance–People Before Profit (2014, 2.9%), and independents.

2g: *Distribution of votes in presidential elections, 1945–2011*

Year	Candidate	Votes	Total	(%)	Comment
1945	**Ó Ceallaigh, Seán T.**	537,965		(49.5)	Elected
	MacEoin, Seán	335,539		(30.9)	Turnout: 63.0%
	McCartan, Patrick	212,834		(19.6)	Eliminated count 1
	Count 2				
	MacEoin, Seán	+117,886	453,425	(44.5)	
	Ó Ceallaigh, Seán T.	+27,200	565,165	(55.5)	Non-transferable: 67,748
1959	**de Valera, Eamon**	538,003		(56.3)	Elected
	MacEoin, Seán	417,536		(43.7)	Turnout: 58.4%
1966	**de Valera, Eamon**	558,861		(50.5)	Elected
	O'Higgins, Thomas F.	548,144		(49.5)	Turnout: 65.3%
1973	**Childers, Erskine**	635,867		(52.0)	Elected
	O'Higgins, Thomas F.	587,771		(48.0)	Turnout: 62.2%
1990	**Robinson, Mary**	612,265		(38.9)	Elected
	Lenihan, Brian	694,484		(44.1)	Turnout: 64.1%
	Currie, Austin	267,902		(17.0)	Eliminated count 1
	Count 2				
	Robinson, Mary	+205,565	817,830	(52.8)	
	Lenihan, Brian	+36,789	731,273	(47.2)	Non-transferable: 25,548
1997	**McAleese, Mary**	574,424		(45.2)	Elected
	Banotti, Mary	372,002		(29.3)	Turnout: 46.7%
	Scallon, Rosemary (Dana)	175,458		(13.8)	Eliminated count 1
	Roche, Adi	88,423		(7.0)	Eliminated count 1
	Nally, Derek	59,529		(4.7)	Eliminated count 1
	Count 2				
	McAleese, Mary	+131,835	706,259	(58.7)	Elected
	Banotti, Mary	+125,514	497,516	(41.3)	Non-transferable: 66,061
2011	**Higgins, Michael D.**	701,101		(39.6)	Elected
	Gallagher, Seán	504,964		(28.5)	Turnout: 56.1%
	McGuinness, Martin	243,030		(13.7)	
	Mitchell, Gay	113,321		(6.4)	
	Norris, David	109,469		(6.2)	
	Scallon, Dana Rosemary	51,220		(2.9)	Eliminated count 1
	Davis, Mary	48,657		(2.7)	Eliminated count 1
	Count 2				
	Higgins, Michael D.	+29,379	730,480	(41.6)	
	Gallagher, Seán	+24,437	529,401	(30.1)	
	McGuinness, Martin	+9,581	252,611	(14.4)	
	Mitchell, Gay	+14,036	127,357	(7.3)	Non-transferable: 15,387
	Norris, David	+7,057	116,526	(6.6)	Eliminated count 2
	Count 3				
	Higgins, Michael D.	+62,648	793,128	(45.5)	
	Gallagher, Seán	+18,972	548,373	(31.5)	Non-transferable: 13,369
	McGuinness, Martin	+12,585	265,196	(15.2)	Eliminated count 3
	Mitchell, Gay	+8,952	136,309	(7.8)	Eliminated count 3
	Count 4				
	Higgins, Michael D.	213,976	1,007,104	(61.6)	
	Gallagher, Seán	79,741	628,114	(38.4)	Non-transferable: 107,788

Source: Adapted from 'Appendix 1: results of presidential elections, 1938–2011', in John Coakley and Kevin Rafter (eds), *The Irish Presidency: Power, Ceremony and Politics* (Dublin: Irish Academic Press, 2014), pp. 210–35.

Note: In 1938, 1952, 1974, 1976, 1983 and 2004, no contests took place as only one candidate was nominated. Ó Ceallaigh, de Valera, Childers, Lenihan and McAleese were nominated by Fianna Fáil members of the Oireachtas; MacEoin, O'Higgins, Currie, Banotti and Mitchell by Fine Gael; Robinson, Roche and Higgins by Labour; McCartan was nominated as an independent with some Labour and Clann na Talmhan support; McGuinness by Sinn Féin and independents; and Nally and Scallon were nominated by county councils in 1997, as were Davis, Gallagher, Norris and Scallon in 2011.

2h: Referendum results, 1937–2015

Date	Subject (article altered)	For %	Against %	Turnout %	Spoiled %
1.7.37	Approve new constitution	56.5	43.5	75.8	10.0
17.6.59	Replace proportional representation with plurality system (*3rd amdt; 16*)	48.2	51.8	58.4	4.0
16.10.68	Permit flexibility in deputy/population ratio (*3rd amdt; 16*)	39.2	60.8	65.8	4.3
16.10.68	Replace proportional representation with plurality system (*4th amdt; 16*)	39.2	60.8	65.8	4.3
10.5.72	Permit EC membership (3rd amdt; 29)	83.1	16.9	70.9	0.8
7.12.72	Lower voting age to 18 (4th amdt; 16)	84.6	15.4	50.7	5.2
7.12.72	Remove 'special position' of Catholic church (5th amdt; 44)	84.4	15.6	50.7	5.5
5.7.79	Protect adoption system (6th amdt; 37)	99.0	1.0	28.6	2.5
5.7.79	Permit alteration of university representation in Senate (7th amdt; 18)	92.4	7.6	28.6	3.9
7.9.83	Prohibit legalisation of abortion (8th amdt; 40)	66.9	33.1	53.7	0.7
14.6.84	Permit extension of voting rights to non-citizens (9th amdt; 16)	75.4	24.6	47.5	3.5
26.6.86	Permit legalisation of divorce (*10th amdt; 41*)	36.5	63.5	60.5	0.6
26.5.87	Permit signing of Single European Act (10th amdt; 29)	69.9	30.1	43.9	0.5
18.6.92	Permit ratification of Maastricht Treaty on European Union (11th amdt; 29)	69.1	30.9	57.3	0.5
25.11.92	Restrict availability of abortion (*12th amdt; 40*)	34.6	65.4	68.2	4.7
25.11.92	Guarantee right to travel (13th amdt; 40)	62.4	37.6	68.2	4.3
25.11.92	Guarantee right to information (14th amdt; 40)	59.9	40.1	68.1	4.3
24.11.95	Permit legalisation of divorce (15th amdt; 41)	50.3	49.7	62.2	0.3
25.11.96	Permit refusal of bail (16th amdt; 40)	74.8	25.2	29.2	0.4
30.10.97	Regulate cabinet confidentiality (17th amdt; 28)	52.5	47.5	47.2	5.2
22.5.98	Permit ratification of Amsterdam Treaty (18th amdt; 29)	61.7	38.3	56.2	2.2
22.5.98	Permit changes agreed to in Good Friday Agreement (19th amdt; 29 and 2, 3)	94.4	5.6	56.3	1.1
11.6.99	Require local elections at least every five years (20th amdt; new 28A)	77.8	22.2	51.1	7.6
7.6.01	Prohibit legislation allowing for death penalty (21st amdt; 13, 15, 28, 40)	62.1	37.9	34.8	1.5
7.6.01	Permit ratification of International Criminal Court statute (23rd amdt; 29)	64.2	35.8	34.8	1.8
7.6.01	Permit ratification of Nice Treaty (*24th amdt; 29*)	46.1	53.9	34.8	1.5
6.3.02	Restrict right to abortion (*25th amdt; 46*)	49.6	50.4	42.9	0.5
20.10.02	Permit ratification of Nice Treaty (26th amdt; 29)	62.9	37.1	48.5	0.4
11.6.04	Permit citizenship change (27th amdt; 9)	79.2	20.8	59.9	1.1
12.6.08	Permit ratification of Lisbon Treaty (*28th amdt; 29*)	46.6	53.4	53.1	0.4
2.10.09	Permit ratification of Lisbon Treaty (28th amdt; 29)	67.1	32.9	59.0	0.4
27.10.11	Permit cut in judges' pay (29th amdt; 35)	79.7	20.3	56.0	2.1
27.10.11	Facilitate parliamentary enquiries (*30th amdt; 15*)	46.7	53.3	55.9	2.5
31.5.12	Permit ratification of European Stability Treaty (30th amdt; 29)	60.3	39.7	50.6	0.5
10.11.12	Secure children's rights (31st amdt; new 42A; 42)	58.0	42.0	33.5	0.4
4.10.13	Abolish Seanad (*32nd amdt; 15, 18, etc.*)	48.3	51.7	39.2	1.2

Date	Subject (article altered)	For %	Against %	Turnout %	Spoiled %
4.10.13	Permit creation of Court of Appeal (33rd amdt; new 34A; 34 etc.)	65.2	34.8	39.2	1.6
22.05.15	Permit same-sex marriage (34th amdt; 41)	62.1	37.9	60.5	0.7
22.05.15	Reduce age limit for presidential candidates to 21 (*35th amdt; 12*)	26.9	73.1	60.5	0.8

Source: *Referendum results 1937–2015* (Dublin: Department of the Environment, Community and Local Government, 2016).

Notes: Amendment numbers in italics refer to constitutional amendment bills rejected at a referendum. The first amendment bill (state of emergency, affecting article 28) and the second amendment bill (emergency provisions and various matters, affecting articles 11–15, 18, 20, 24–28, 34, 40, 47 and 56) were passed by the Oireachtas without a referendum in 1939 and 1941 respectively (see Chapter 3, pp. 62–3). The 22nd amendment bill (dealing with the monitoring of judicial conduct; see Chapter 3, p. 71) lapsed in the Dáil.

2i: Opinion poll support for parties by social group, 1969–2016

Party	Year	All	Middle class	Working class	Large farmers	Small farmers
Fianna Fáil	1969	43	45	42	38	53
	1977	49	46	50	48	48
	1981	44	39	43	42	53
	1985	42	37	45	41	46
	1989	38	35	38	39	47
	1993	36	35	34	40	44
	1997	36	32	37	40	40
	2002	47	47	47	41	61
	2007	41	40	43	44	-
	2011	15	13	15	25	-
	2016	21	20	23	23	-
Fine Gael	1969	25	28	16	46	26
	1977	28	30	21	42	38
	1981	32	41	28	43	32
	1985	28	37	21	38	23
	1989	23	25	17	43	21
	1993	16	14	15	29	15
	1997	23	22	19	36	35
	2002	18	18	15	42	17
	2007	25	26	22	44	–
	2011	36	37	32	49	–
	2016	25	30	18	42	–
Labour Party	1969	18	14	28	2	5
	1977	9	7	15	1	5
	1981	10	4	14	1	4
	1985	5	6	5	0	2
	1989	6	5	9	3	2
	1993	15	16	18	3	8
	1997	9	9	12	1	7
	2002	10	10	11	2	5
	2007	10	11	9	6	–
	2011	21	23	23	2	–
	2016	7	8	6	4	–
Sinn Féin	2011	10	7	14	10	–
	2016	16	10	24	5	–

Notes: The figures relate to the percentage of each occupational group that expressed an intention to vote for the party in question. The occupational groups are defined as follows: middle class, ABC1 (professional, managerial and clerical); working class, C2DE (skilled and unskilled manual workers); large farmers, F1 (farmers with 50 acres or more, except in 1969, when the cutoff was 30 acres); small farmers, F2 (farmers with less than 50 acres, except in 1969, when the cutoff was 30 acres). The data for 2007, 2011 and 2016 refer to all farmers. Poll dates were April 1969 (Gallup), May–June 1977 (IMS), May 1981 (IMS), February 1985 (MRBI), June 1989 (MRBI), July 1993 (MRBI), 28 May 1997 (MRBI), February 2002 (TNS–MRBI), June 2007 (RTÉ–Lansdowne Exit Poll), February 2011 (RTÉ–Millward Brown Lansdowne Exit Poll) and February 2016 (RTÉ–Behaviour and Attitudes Exit Poll). Percentages for a given occupational group will not necessarily total 100 across parties, due to the omission of supporters of other parties or of none. Comparable data are not available for 1973–74.

Appendix 3: Political office holders

3a: Heads of state, 1922–2017

Dates of office	Name
	King
6.12.22–20.1.36	George V
20.1.36–11.12.36	Edward VIII
11.12.36–18.4.49	George VI
	Governor-General
6.12.22–1.2.28	Timothy Healy
1.2.28–1.11.32	James MacNeill
26.11.32–12.12.36	Dónal Ó Buachalla
	President
25.6.38–25.6.45	Douglas Hyde
25.6.45–25.6.59	Seán T. Ó Ceallaigh
25.6.59–25.6.73	Eamon de Valera
25.6.73–17.11.74	Erskine Childers
19.12.74–22.10.76	Cearbhall Ó Dálaigh
3.12.76–3.12.90	Patrick Hillery
3.12.90–12.9.97	Mary Robinson
11.11.97–11.11.2011	Mary McAleese
11.11.2011–	Michael D. Higgins

Note: The King continued to represent the state in external affairs until 1949. The President's role was exclusively domestic until then. The President's functions were filled by the Presidential Commission (the Chief Justice, the Ceann Comhairle and the Cathaoirleach of the Seanad) during those periods when the office was vacant.

3b: Heads and deputy heads of government, 1922–2017

Date	Head of government	Deputy head of government
	President of the Executive Council	*Vice-President of the Executive Council*
6.12.22	William T. Cosgrave	Kevin O'Higgins
		Ernest Blythe (10.7.27)
9.3.32	Eamon de Valera	Seán T. Ó Ceallaigh
	Taoiseach	*Tánaiste*
29.12.37	Eamon de Valera	Seán T. Ó Ceallaigh
		Seán Lemass (14.6.45)
18.2.48	John A. Costello	William Norton
13.6.51	Eamon de Valera	Seán Lemass
2.6.54	John A. Costello	William Norton
20.3.57	Eamon de Valera	Seán Lemass
23.6.59	Seán Lemass	Seán MacEntee
		Frank Aiken (21.4.65)
10.11.66	Jack Lynch	Frank Aiken
		Erskine Childers (2.7.69)
14.3.73	Liam Cosgrave	Brendan Corish
5.7.77	Jack Lynch	George Colley
11.12.79	Charles J. Haughey	George Colley
20.6.81	Garret FitzGerald	Michael O'Leary
9.3.82	Charles J. Haughey	Ray MacSharry
14.12.82	Garret FitzGerald	Dick Spring
		Peter Barry (20.1.87)
10.3.87	Charles J. Haughey	Brian Lenihan
		John Wilson (13.11.90)
11.2.92	Albert Reynolds	John Wilson
		Dick Spring (12.1.93)
15.12.94	John Bruton	Dick Spring
26.6.97	Bertie Ahern	Mary Harney
		Michael McDowell (13.9.06)
		Brian Cowen (14.6.07)
7.5.08	Brian Cowen	Mary Coughlan
9.3.11	Enda Kenny	Eamon Gilmore
		Joan Burton (4.7.14)
		Frances Fitzgerald (6.5.16)
14.6.17	Leo Varadkar	Frances Fitzgerald

3c: Composition of governments, 1922–2017

Date	Government	Initial composition					Dáil support
		Fianna Fáil	Fine Gael	Labour	Other	Total	
14. 1.22	Collins	.	8	.	.	8	-
22. 8.22	Cosgrave 1	.	9	.	.	9	-
9. 9.22	Cosgrave 2	.	11	.	.	11	-
6.12.22	Cosgrave 3	.	10	.	.	10	-
19. 9.23	Cosgrave 4	.	11	.	.	11	-
23. 6.27	Cosgrave 5	.	10	.	.	10	44.4
11.10.27	Cosgrave 6	.	9	.	.	9	49.7
2.4.30	Cosgrave 7	.	9	.	.	9	52.3
9.3.32	de Valera 1	10	.	.	.	10	52.9
8.2.33	de Valera 2	10	.	.	.	10	53.6
21.7.37	de Valera 3	10	.	.	.	10	59.4
30.6.38	de Valera 4	10	.	.	.	10	54.3
1.7.43	de Valera 5	11	.	.	.	11	48.6
9.6.44	de Valera 6	11	.	.	.	11	58.7
18.2.48	Costello 1	.	6	2	5	13	51.0
13.6.51	de Valera 7	12	.	.	.	12	49.0
2.6.54	Costello 2	.	8	4	1	13	53.7
20.3.57	de Valera 8	12	.	.	.	12	53.1
23.6.59	Lemass 1	13	.	.	.	13	51.0
11.10.61	Lemass 2	14	.	.	.	14	50.0
21.4.65	Lemass 3	14	.	.	.	14	50.0
10.11.66	Lynch 1	14	.	.	.	14	49.3
2.7.69	Lynch 2	14	.	.	.	14	51.4
14.3.73	Cosgrave	.	10	5	.	15	50.0
5.7.77	Lynch 3	15	.	.	.	15	55.4
12.12.79	Haughey 1	15	.	.	.	15	55.4
30. 6.81	FitzGerald 1	.	11	4	.	15	48.8
9.3.82	Haughey 2	15	.	.	.	15	51.8
14.12.82	FitzGerald 2	.	11	4	.	15	51.2
10.3.87	Haughey 3	15	.	.	.	15	49.4
12.7.89	Haughey 4	13	.	.	2	15	50.6
11.2.92	Reynolds 1	13	.	.	2	15	50.6
12.1.93	Reynolds 2	9	.	6	.	15	61.4
15.12.94	Bruton	.	8	6	1	15	51.2
26.6.97	Ahern 1	14	.	.	1	15	51.2
6.6.02	Ahern 2	13	.	.	2	15	56.0
14.6.07	Ahern 3	12	.	.	3	15	53.6
7.5.08	Cowen	12	.	.	3	15	53.0
9.3.11	Kenny 1	.	10	5	.	15	70.5
6.5.16	Kenny 2	.	12	.	3	15	37.3
14.6.17	Varadkar	.	12	.	3	15	36.1

Notes: The first three governments were provisional governments. 'Fine Gael' includes also the Pro-Treaty party or Cumann na nGaedheal (1922–33). 'Others' includes two Clann na Poblachta, one Clann na Talmhan, one National Labour and one independent in 1948, one Clann na Talmhan in 1954, two Progressive Democrats in 1989, 1992 and 2002 and one in 1997, 2007 and 2008, one Democratic Left in 1994, two Greens in 2007 and 2008, and one member of the Independent Alliance and two independents in 2016. 'Dáil support' refers to deputies voting for the Taoiseach as a percentage of total Dáil membership. No division took place in the case of the first five appointments.

3d: Ceann Comhairle of Dáil and Cathaoirleach of Seanad, 1922–2017

Date	Ceann Comhairle	Date	Cathaoirleach
9.9.22	Michael Hayes (CnG)	12.12.22	Lord Glenavy (Ind)
9.3.32	Frank Fahy (FF)	12.12.28	Thomas Westropp Bennett (CnG)
		27.4.38	Seán Gibbons (FF)
		8.9.43	Seán Goulding (FF)
		21.4.48	T. J. O'Donovan (FG)
13.6.51	Patrick Hogan (Lab)	14.8.51	Liam Ó Buachalla (FF)
		22.7.54	Patrick Baxter (FG)
		22.5.57	Liam Ó Buachalla (FF)
7.11.67	Cormac Breslin (FF)	5.11.69	Michael Yeats (FF)
		3.1.73	Micheál Cranitch (FF)
14.3.73	Seán Treacy (Lab)	1.6.73	James Dooge (FG)
5.7.77	Joseph Brennan (FF)	27.10.77	Séamus Dolan (FF)
16.10.80	Pádraig Faulkner (FF)	8.10.81	Charlie McDonald (FG)
30.6.81	John O'Connell (Ind)	13.5.82	Tras Honan (FF)
14.12.82	Tom Fitzpatrick (FG)	23.2.83	Pat Joe Reynolds (FG)
10.3.87	Seán Treacy (Ind)	25.4.87	Tras Honan (FF)
		1.11.89	Seán Doherty (FF)
		23.1.92	Seán Fallon (FF)
		12.7.95	Liam Naughten (FG)
		27.11.96	Liam T. Cosgrave (FG)
26.6.97	Séamus Pattison (Lab)	17.9.97	Brian Mullooly (FF)
6.6.02	Rory O'Hanlon (FF)	12.9.02	Rory Kiely (FF)
14.6.07	John O'Donoghue (FF)	13.9.07	Pat Moylan (FF)
13.10.09	Séamus Kirk (FF)		
9.3.11	Seán Barrett (FG)	25.5.11	Paddy Burke (FG)
10.3.16	Seán Ó Fearghaíl (FF)	8.6.16	Denis O'Donovan (FF)

3e: Leaders of major parties, 1922–2017

Fianna Fáil	Fine Gael	Labour Party
Eamon de Valera (1926–59)	William T. Cosgrave (CnaG,1922–33)	Thomas Johnson (1918–27)
Seán Lemass (1959–66)	Eoin O'Duffy (1933–34)	T. J. O'Connell (1927–32)
Jack Lynch (1966–79)	William T. Cosgrave (1935–44)	William Norton (1932–60)
Charles Haughey (1979–92)	Richard Mulcahy (1944–59)	Brendan Corish (1960–77)
Albert Reynolds (1992–94)	James Dillon (1959–65)	Frank Cluskey (1977–81)
Bertie Ahern (1994–2008)	Liam Cosgrave (1965–77)	Michael O'Leary (1981–82)
Brian Cowen (2008–11)	Garret FitzGerald (1977–87)	Dick Spring (1982–97)
Micheál Martin (2011–)	Alan Dukes (1987–90)	Ruairí Quinn (1997–2002)
	John Bruton (1990–2001)	Pat Rabbitte (2002–07)
Sinn Féin	Michael Noonan (2001–02)	Eamon Gilmore (2007–14)
Gerry Adams (1983–)	Enda Kenny (2002–17)	Joan Burton (2014–16)
	Leo Varadkar (2017–)	Brendan Howlin (2016–)

Appendix 4: Government departments

The organisation of Irish government departments was laid out by the Ministers and Secretaries Act (no. 16 of 1924), and modified by subsequent legislation. The Ministers and Secretaries (Amendment) Act (no. 36 of 1939) authorised the government to alter the name of any department, or to transfer functions between departments. The following is a list of departments as they have existed since 1924 (with original and current names in bold, and departments that have disappeared in italics). It should be noted that name changes and transfers of functions sometimes moved the locus of a department far from its original focal point, that functions may have been transferred between departments without name changes, and that in some cases, 'shells' of departments that remained after the loss of all staff and functions were later given entirely new identities.

1. Department of the President of the Executive Council
Established by the Ministers and Secretaries Act, 1924; renamed **Department of the Taoiseach**, 1937, following adoption of new constitution.

2. Department of Finance
Established by the Ministers and Secretaries Act, 1924.

3. Department of Justice
Established by the Ministers and Secretaries Act, 1924; renamed Department of Justice, Equality and Law Reform, 1997; renamed Department of Justice and Law Reform, 2010; renamed **Department of Justice and Equality**, 2011.

4. Department of Local Government and Public Health
Established by the Ministers and Secretaries Act, 1924; renamed Department of Local Government, 1947 on loss of functions to new Department of Health and Department of Social Welfare; renamed Department of the Environment, 1977; renamed Department of the Environment and Local Government, 1997; renamed Department of Environment, Heritage and Local Government, 2003; renamed Department of Environment, Community and Local Government, 2011; renamed Department of Housing, Planning, Community and Local Government, 2016; renamed **Department of Housing, Planning and Local Government**, 2017.

5. Department of Education
Established by the Ministers and Secretaries Act, 1924; renamed Department of Education and Science, 1997; renamed **Department of Education and Skills**, 2010.

6. Department of Lands and Agriculture
Established by the Ministers and Secretaries Act, 1924; renamed Department of Agriculture in 1928 on transfer of Land Commission to Department of Fisheries; renamed Department of Agriculture and Fisheries, 1965; renamed Department of Agriculture, 1977; renamed Department of Agriculture and Food, 1987; renamed Department of Agriculture, Food and Forestry, 1993; renamed Department of Agriculture and Food, 1997; renamed Department of Agriculture, Food and Rural Development, 1999; renamed Department of Agriculture and Food, 2002; renamed Department of Agriculture, Fisheries and Food, 2007; renamed **Department of Agriculture, Food and the Marine**, 2011.

7. Department of Industry and Commerce
Established by the Ministers and Secretaries Act, 1924; renamed Department of Industry, Commerce and Energy, 1977; renamed Department of Industry, Commerce and Tourism,

1980; renamed Department of Trade, Commerce and Tourism, 1981; renamed Department of Industry, Trade, Commerce and Tourism, 1983; renamed Department of Industry and Commerce, 1986; renamed Department of Enterprise and Employment, 1993; renamed Department of Enterprise, Trade and Employment, 1997; renamed Department of Enterprise, Trade and Innovation, 2010; renamed Department of Jobs, Enterprise and Innovation, 2011; renamed **Department of Business, Enterprise and Innovation**, 2017.

8. Department of Fisheries
Established by the Ministers and Secretaries Act, 1924; renamed Department of Lands and Fisheries, 1928, on transfer of Land Commission from Department of Lands and Agriculture; renamed Department of Lands in 1934; renamed Department of Fisheries, 1977; renamed Department of Fisheries and Forestry, 1978; renamed Department of Tourism, Fisheries and Forestry, 1986; renamed Department of the Marine, 1987; renamed Department of the Marine and Natural Resources, 1997; renamed Department of Communications, Marine and Natural Resources, 2002; renamed Department of Communications, Energy and Natural Resources, 2007; renamed **Department of Communications, Climate Action and Environment**, 2016.

9. Department of Posts and Telegraphs
Established by the Ministers and Secretaries Act, 1924; abolished by the Ministers and Secretaries (Amendment) Act, 1983.

10. Department of Defence
Established by the Ministers and Secretaries Act, 1924.

11. Department of External Affairs
Established by the Ministers and Secretaries Act, 1924; renamed Department of Foreign Affairs, 1971; renamed **Department of Foreign Affairs and Trade**, 2011.

12. Department of Supplies
Established by the Ministers and Secretaries (Amendment) Act, 1939; abolished in 1945 and functions transferred to Department of Industry and Commerce by the Minister for Supplies (Transfer of Functions) Act, 1945.

13. Department of Health
Established by the Ministers and Secretaries (Amendment) Act, 1946; renamed Department of Health and Children, 1997; renamed **Department of Health**, 2011.

14. Department of Social Welfare
Established by the Ministers and Secretaries (Amendment) Act, 1946; renamed Department of Social, Community and Family Affairs, 1997; renamed Department of Social and Family Affairs, 2002; renamed Department of Social Protection, 2010; renamed **Department of Employment Affairs and Social Protection**, 2017.

15. Department of the Gaeltacht
Established by the Ministers and Secretaries (Amendment) Act, 1956; renamed Department of Arts, Culture and the Gaeltacht, 1993; renamed Department of Arts, Heritage, Gaeltacht and the Islands, 1997; renamed Department of Community, Rural and Gaeltacht Affairs, 2002; renamed Department of Community, Equality and Gaeltacht Affairs, 2010; renamed **Department of Children and Youth Affairs**, 2011.

16. Department of Transport and Power
Established by the Ministers and Secretaries (Amendment) Act, 1959; renamed Department of Tourism and Transport, 1977; renamed Department of Transport, 1980; abolished by the Ministers and Secretaries (Amendment) Act, 1983.

17. Department of Labour
Established by the Ministers and Secretaries (Amendment) Act, 1966; renamed Department of Equality and Law Reform, 1993; functions transferred to Department of Justice, Equality and Law Reform, 1997 (this department still exists in theory as a 'shell' without any staff or functions).

18. Department of the Public Service
Established by the Ministers and Secretaries (Amendment) Act, 1973; functions transferred to Department of Finance, 1987; renamed Department of Tourism and Transport, 1987; renamed Department of Tourism, Transport and Communications, 1991; renamed Department of Transport, Energy and Communications, 1993; renamed Department of Public Enterprise, 1997; renamed Department of Transport, 2002; renamed **Department of Transport, Tourism and Sport**, 2011.

19. Department of Economic Planning and Development
Established by the Ministers and Secretaries (Amendment) Act, 1977; functions transferred to Department of Finance, 1980; renamed Department of Energy, 1980; renamed Department of Industry and Energy, 1981; renamed Department of Energy, 1983; renamed Department of Tourism and Trade, 1993; renamed Department of Tourism, Sport and Recreation, 1997; renamed Department of Arts, Sport and Tourism, 2002; renamed Department of Tourism, Culture and Sport, 2010; renamed Department of Arts, Heritage and the Gaeltacht, 2011; renamed Department of Arts, Heritage, Regional, Rural and Gaeltacht Affairs, 2016; renamed **Department of Culture, Heritage and the Gaeltacht**, 2017.

20. Department of Communications
Established by the Ministers and Secretaries (Amendment) Act, 1983; functions transferred to Department of Marine and Department of Tourism and Transport, 1987 (this department still exists in theory as a 'shell' without any staff or functions).

21. Department of Public Expenditure and Reform
Established by the Ministers and Secretaries (Amendment) Act, 2011, to assume certain functions of the Department of Finance.

22. Department of Rural and Community Development
Established by the Ministers and Secretaries (Amendment) Act, 2017, to assume certain functions of the Department of Arts, Heritage, Regional, Rural and Gaeltacht Affairs.

Source: Relevant Acts of the Oireachtas and statutory instruments. For additional information, see Niamh Hardiman, Muiris MacCarthaigh and Colin Scott, The Irish State Administration Database, http://www.isad.ie.

Appendix 5: Biographical notes on major political figures

Note: The following notes give basic information on all those who have held the post of Governor-General, President, President of the Executive Council, Taoiseach, Vice-President of the Executive Council or Tánaiste. For short notes on most of these, see Louis McRedmond (ed.), *Modern Irish Lives: Dictionary of 20th-Century Biography* (Dublin: Gill and Macmillan, 1996), Henry Boylan, *A Dictionary of Irish Biography*, 2nd ed. (Dublin: Gill and Macmillan, 1988), Ted Nealon's *Guides* to the Dáil and Seanad, various years, and *Who's Who, What's What* and *Where in Ireland* (London: Geoffrey Chapman, in association with *The Irish Times*, 1973). The definitive source for biographical information on deceased persons is James Maguire and James Quinn (eds), *Dictionary of Irish Biography: From the Earliest Times to the Year 2002*, 9 vols (Cambridge: Cambridge University Press, for the Royal Irish Academy, 2009), with updated online version at dib.cambridge.org; and the definitive source for key information about parliamentarians is Houses of the Oireachtas, Directory of Members, http://www.oireachtas.ie/members/. In a few cases, where sources disagreed or were incomplete (MacEntee, MacNeill and Ó Buachalla), birthdates have been established from the records of the Registrar General's office, available at www.irishgenealogy.ie.

Ahern, Bertie. Born Dublin, 12 September 1951; educated Christian Brothers, Whitehall, Dublin, and College of Commerce, Rathmines; worked as an accountant; Fianna Fáil TD, 1977–2011; leader of Fianna Fáil, 1994–2008; minister of state, 1982; government minister, 1987–94; Taoiseach, 1997–2008. A committed constituency worker, he also developed an outstanding reputation as a negotiator and compromise broker; his skills and commitment were displayed particularly impressively during the negotiation of the Good Friday Agreement of 1998 and during subsequent difficulties in its implementation; resigned as Taoiseach during tribunal hearings into his financial affairs.

Aiken, Frank. Born Camlough, Co Armagh, 13 February 1898; educated Christian Brothers, Newry; worked as a farmer; active in Gaelic League and in Irish Volunteers; leading figure in IRA during War of Independence and civil war; anti-Treaty Sinn Féin and Fianna Fáil TD, 1923–73; government minister, 1932–48, 1951–54, 1957–69; Tánaiste, 1965–69; died 18 May 1983. One of the last IRA divisional commanders to take sides in the civil war, was associated with the pursuit of neutrality also in international affairs; as Minister for External Affairs, guided Ireland along an independent path in the United Nations.

Barry, Peter. Born Cork, 10 August 1928; educated Christian Brothers, Cork; worked as a tea importer and wholesaler; Fine Gael TD, 1969–97; government minister, 1973–77, 1981–82, 1982–87; Tánaiste, 1987; died 26 August 2016. A popular and respected elder statesman in Fine Gael, he built up a positive image as foreign minister; nevertheless, did not succeed to the party leadership in a 1987 contest where youth appeared to take precedence over experience; Tánaiste only for a few weeks after the collapse of the Fine Gael–Labour coalition in 1987.

Blythe, Ernest. Born Lisburn, Co Antrim, 13 April 1889; educated locally; worked as a clerk in the Department of Agriculture; active in the Gaelic League, IRB and Irish Volunteers; Sinn Féin MP/TD, 1918–22; pro-Treaty Sinn Féin and Cumann na nGaedheal TD, 1922–33; lost his seat, 1933; minister in Dáil government, 1919–22; government minister, 1922–32; Vice-President of the Executive Council, 1927–32; died 23 February 1975. A northern Protestant, was strongly associated with the Irish language movement and with Irish cultural activities, going on after his retirement from politics to become managing director of the Abbey Theatre; as Minister for Finance, he won notoriety for reducing the old age pension in 1924 from ten to nine shillings per week (from 63 cent to 57 cent!).

Bruton, John. Born Dublin, 18 May 1947; educated St Dominic's College, Dublin, Clongowes Wood College, Co Kildare, University College Dublin, and King's Inns; qualified as a barrister; Fine Gael TD, 1969–2004; leader of Fine Gael, 1990–2001; parliamentary secretary, 1973–77; government minister, 1981–82, 1982–87; Taoiseach, 1994–97. Noted as a sincere, hard-working politician with an abiding interest in parliamentary reform; his distinctive perspective on Northern Ireland politics placed him close to the unionist position, and made him an object of some suspicion to nationalists; his political skills were challenged when his first budget was defeated in the Dáil in 1982, precipitating a general election; he showed considerable flexibility and skill in heading a 'rainbow coalition' that took over following the collapse of the Reynolds government in 1994; ousted as party leader, 2001; served as EU ambassador to USA, 2004–09.

Burton, Joan. Born Dublin, 1 February 1949; educated Stanhope St, Dublin, and University College Dublin; worked as a lecturer and as a chartered accountant; Labour TD, 1992–97, 2002–; lost her seat, 1997; leader of the Labour Party, 2014–16; minister of state, 1993–97; government minister, 2011–16; Tánaiste, 2014–16. She led the Labour Party through a difficult period when protests against government-imposed austerity measures were mounting, and resigned following Labour's poor performance in the 2016 election.

Childers, Erskine. Born London, 11 December 1905; educated Norfolk and Cambridge University; worked in Paris for an American travel organisation; advertising manager, *Irish Press*; Fianna Fáil TD, 1938–73; government minister, 1951–54, 1957–73; Tánaiste, 1969–73; President of Ireland, 1973–74; died 17 November 1974. His efforts to raise the profile of the presidency were resisted by the government; his father was Robert Erskine Childers (1870–1922), a clerk in the House of Commons who had Irish connections, became involved in the Irish nationalist movement, took the anti-Treaty side during the civil war and was executed in 1922.

Colley, George. Born Dublin, 18 October 1925; educated Christian Brothers, Dublin, and University College Dublin; worked as a solicitor; Fianna Fáil TD, 1961–83; parliamentary secretary, 1964–65; government minister, 1965–73, 1977–81; Tánaiste, 1977–81; died 17 September 1983. Contested the leadership of Fianna Fáil against Jack Lynch in 1966 and against his long-time rival and former school classmate, Charles Haughey, in 1979; intensely suspicious of Haughey since the arms crisis of 1970; insisted during Haughey's first government on being given a veto on appointments to the security ministries (Defence and Justice).

Collins, Michael. Born Clonakilty, Co Cork, 16 October 1890; educated local national school; worked in London as a clerk in the post office and for a firm of stockbrokers; participated in 1916 rising as IRB member; Sinn Féin TD/MP, 1918–22; minister in Dáil government, 1919–22; Chairman of Provisional Government and Commander-in-Chief of the new national army, 1922; killed in an ambush at Béal na mBláth, Co Cork, by anti-Treaty forces during the civil war on 22 August 1922. Was a charismatic leader during the Anglo–Irish war of 1919–21 and a very effective director of intelligence for the IRA; his influence helped to swing the IRB (of whose Supreme Council he was President) and many members of the IRA into support for the Anglo–Irish Treaty, which he had negotiated as one of the representatives of the Irish side.

Corish, Brendan. Born Wexford, 19 November 1918; educated Christian Brothers, Wexford; worked as a local government official; Labour TD, 1945–82; leader of the Labour Party, 1960–77; parliamentary secretary, 1948–51; government minister, 1954–57; Tánaiste,

1973–77; died 17 February 1990. Though a popular party leader, he was relatively unassertive in his later years and allowed strong-willed colleagues considerable latitude when the party was in government, 1973–77.

Cosgrave, Liam. Born Dublin, 13 April 1920; educated Christian Brothers, Castleknock College and King's Inns; called to the bar, 1943; Fine Gael TD, 1943–81; leader of Fine Gael, 1965–77; parliamentary secretary, 1948–51; government minister, 1954–57; Taoiseach 1973–77; died 4 October 2017. A son of William T. Cosgrave; as parliamentary secretary, he functioned as effective minute taker to the cabinet, as the cabinet secretary was excluded from meetings; his period as Taoiseach was marked by a strong emphasis on the maintenance of law and order.

Cosgrave, William T. Born Dublin, 6 June 1880; educated Christian Brothers, Dublin; worked in his father's public house; joined the early Sinn Féin movement and the Irish Volunteers and participated in the 1916 rising; Sinn Féin MP/TD, 1917–22; pro-Treaty Sinn Féin, Cumann na nGaedheal and Fine Gael TD, 1922–44; leader of Cumann na nGaedheal, 1923–33 and of Fine Gael, 1935–44; minister in Dáil government, 1919–22; President of Executive Council, 1922–32; died 16 November 1965. Despite his background as a revolutionary in 1916, he was associated with conservative policies during the first decade of the new state.

Costello, John A. Born Dublin, 20 June 1891; educated Christian Brothers, Dublin, and University College Dublin; called to the bar, 1914; worked in Attorney General's office, 1922–26; Attorney General, 1926–32; Cumann na nGaedheal and Fine Gael TD, 1933–43, 1944–69; head of first and second Inter-Party governments as Taoiseach, 1948–51 and 1954–57; died 5 January 1976. Associated with a striking about-face in Fine Gael when he moved in 1948 to sever Ireland's links with the Commonwealth and declare the state a republic; he did not support his Minister for Health, Noel Browne, whose 'Mother and Child' health care proposals in 1950 were strongly opposed by the Catholic church and led ultimately to the collapse of Costello's first government.

Coughlan, Mary. Born Donegal 28 May 1965; educated Ursuline Convent Sligo and University College Dublin; qualified as a social worker; Fianna Fáil TD, 1987–2011; minister of state, 2001–02; government minister, 2002–11; Tánaiste, 2008–11. Combining the office of Minister for Enterprise and Employment with that of Tánaiste, she encountered strong criticism as the economic position began to deteriorate and unemployment grew in 2008.

Cowen, Brian. Born Clara, 1 January 1960; educated Cistercian College Roscrea and University College Dublin; qualified as a solicitor; Fianna Fáil TD, 1984–2011; government minister, 1992–94 and 1997–2007; Tánaiste, 2007–08; Taoiseach and leader of Fianna Fáil, 2008–11. He established a reputation for himself as an able minister (especially in Foreign Affairs and in Finance), but succeeded as Taoiseach and party leader precisely at the end of Ireland's economic boom and the onset of grave domestic and international threats to the Irish economy got underway; this damaged the reputation of a politician who had been closely associated with the management of economic policy as Minister for Finance, 2004–08; he was forced to resign as leader of Fianna Fáil in January 2011, and retired from politics after the subsequent general election.

de Valera, Eamon. Born New York city, 14 October 1882; brought up Bruree, Co Limerick; educated Christian Brothers, Charleville, Blackrock College, Dublin and Royal University; teacher of mathematics; involved in early Gaelic League and Irish Volunteers and participated in the 1916 rising; senior surviving commandant of the rising; leader of Sinn Féin, 1917–22, of anti-Treaty Sinn Féin, 1922–26 and of Fianna Fáil, which he founded, 1926–59; Sinn Féin TD/MP, 1917–22; anti-Treaty Sinn Féin and Fianna Fáil TD, 1922–59; President of Dáil government, 1919–22, President of Executive Council, 1932–37, Taoiseach, 1937–48, 1951–54 and 1957–59; President of Ireland, 1959–73; died 29 August 1975. An enigmatic figure who played a leading role in Irish politics from 1916 to 1973, and a controversial one at the time of the Treaty negotiations and the subsequent divisions in Sinn Féin in 1921–23; he was largely responsible for leading the bulk of the anti-Treaty side into operating within a constitutional framework in the 1920s; though committed to Irish unity and the Irish language, he made little progress on the former and saw the latter weaken further; he was more successful in the area of foreign relations, where he succeeded in greatly enhancing the state's independence.

Fitzgerald, Frances. Born Croom, Co Limerick, 1 August 1950, as **Frances Ryan**; educated Newbridge, Sion Hill, Dublin, University College Dublin and the London School of Economics; worked as a social worker; Fine Gael TD, 1997–2002 and 2011–; senator, 2007–11; government minister, 2011–; Tánaiste, 2016–. A leading activist in the Irish women's movement; as Minister for Justice and Equality she faced a series of difficult challenges in dealing with management issues in the Garda Síochána at a time when the police force was going through a crisis of leadership.

FitzGerald, Garret. Born Dublin, 9 February 1926; educated Belvedere College, University College Dublin and King's Inns; worked as a research and schedules manager in Aer Lingus and later as lecturer in political economy, University College Dublin; Fine Gael senator, 1965–69 and TD 1969–92; leader of Fine Gael, 1977–87; government minister, 1973–77; Taoiseach, 1981–82 and 1982–87; died 19 May 2011. He led his party to its largest ever share of electoral support in 1982; his liberal agenda was undermined by conservative referendum outcomes on abortion (1983) and divorce (1986), but his Northern Ireland policy was significantly advanced by the signing of the Anglo–Irish Agreement (1985).

Gilmore, Eamon. Born near Mountbellew, Co Galway, 24 April 1955; educated local national school, Garbally College, Ballinasloe, and University College Galway; worked as a trade union official; Workers' Party TD, 1989–92; Democratic Left TD, 1992–99; Labour Party TD, 1999–2016; leader of the Labour Party, 2007–14; minister of state, 1994–97; government minister, 2011–14; Tánaiste, 2011–14. Originally entering public life through student politics, he formed part of a remarkable ideological movement that saw a transition from 'official' Sinn Féin with its nationalist programme, through the Workers' Party with its links to the Communist world, through Democratic Left with its liberal orientation, to unification with the Labour Party, in which he and others who had traversed the same route moved into prominent positions.

Griffith, Arthur. Born Dublin, 31 March 1871; educated Christian Brothers, Dublin; worked as a printer and then as a journalist; editor of a number of nationalist periodicals and pamphlets; founder of Sinn Féin party and member of Irish Volunteers, but did not participate in 1916 rising; Sinn Féin MP/TD, 1918–22; minister in Dáil government, 1919–22; President of Dáil government, 1922; died 12 August 1922. He was responsible for popularising the Sinn Féin policy of economic self-reliance after 1905; this also envisaged following the Hungarian model of 1867, by which an independent Irish state would be established as part of a dual monarchy, linked to Britain only by the crown.

Harney, Mary. Born Ballinasloe, Co Galway, 11 March 1953; educated Convent of Mercy, Goldenbridge, Dublin, Coláiste Bhríde, Dublin, and Trinity College Dublin; employed as research worker; Fianna Fáil senator, 1977–81; Fianna Fáil TD, 1981–85; Progressive Democrat TD, 1985–2009, then independent; leader of the Progressive Democrats, 1993–2006; minister of state, 1989–92; government minister, 1997–2011; Tánaiste, 1997–2006. The first woman leader of a political party with Dáil representation and the first woman Tánaiste, she fought hard to maintain the identity of the Progressive Democrats (of which she was a founding member) in unfavourable circumstances.

Haughey, Charles J. Born Castlebar, Co Mayo, 16 September 1925; educated Christian Brothers, Dublin, University College Dublin, and King's Inns; worked as an accountant; Fianna Fáil TD, 1957–92; leader of Fianna Fáil, 1979–92; parliamentary secretary, 1960–61; government minister, 1961–70 and 1977–79; Taoiseach, 1979–81, 1982, 1987–92; died 13 June 2006. A son-in-law of Seán Lemass; was dismissed as Minister for Finance by Jack Lynch in 1970 in the course of the 'Arms Crisis', but was acquitted in court of all charges; fought his way back to emerge as party leader in 1979 with the support of the party's back-benchers; led his party into its first ever coalition government in 1989; following his retirement his financial affairs were subjected to rigorous examination by tribunals, and these found that over many years he had secretly been in receipt of large sums of money from wealthy individuals of whom some had benefited from decisions made by his governments.

Healy, Timothy. Born Bantry, Co Cork, 17 May 1855; educated local Christian Brothers; worked in England as a railway clerk and later as a nationalist journalist; Nationalist MP, 1880–86, 1887–1910 and 1911–18 (anti-Parnellite, 1890–1900, then an independent Nationalist); Governor-General, 1922–28; died 26 March 1931. Noted as a lively and witty debater, but divisive as a political figure.

Higgins, Michael D. Born Limerick City, 18 April 1941; brought up Newmarket, Co Clare; educated local national school, St Flannan's, Ennis, University College Galway, the University of Manchester and Indiana University; worked as a factory worker, clerk and university lecturer; Labour TD, 1981–82, 1987–2011; lost his seat, 1982; senator, 1973–77, 1983–87; government minister, 1993–97; President of Ireland, 2011–. Noted for his independent mind and egalitarian commitment, his significant achievements include the establishment of an Irish-language television station, now TG4, in 1996, and his active role in developing the profile of the office of President.

Hillery, Patrick. Born Milltown Malbay, Co Clare, 2 May 1923; educated Rockwell College and University College Dublin; practised as a medical doctor; Fianna Fáil TD, 1951–72; government minister, 1959–72; Irish member of EC Commission, 1973–76; President of Ireland, 1976–90, a post for which he was an unopposed nominee; died 12 April 2008. As Minister for External Affairs, he was responsible for handling Irish foreign policy in the difficult period coinciding with the outbreak of the Northern Ireland troubles and with the negotiation of EC membership, and as President was widely respected for his calm discharge of his responsibilities.

Hyde, Douglas. Born Castlerea, Co Roscommon, 17 January 1860; educated Trinity College Dublin; collector of Irish folklore, of which he published many volumes; professor of Modern Irish, University College Dublin; founder member of Gaelic League, of which he was first president (1893–1915); maintained a non-political role, and resigned as president of the League when it began to follow a more political path; independent member in Senate of Irish Free State, 1925, but failed to secure election in 1925 Senate general election; senator (Taoiseach's nominee), 1938; President of Ireland, 1938–45, a post for which he was an all-party choice; died 12 July 1949. Son of a Protestant rector in Co Roscommon, he was much loved by language revivalists for his work for their movement, and was the author of the first play in Irish ever to appear on a professional stage (1901).

Kenny, Enda. Born near Castlebar, Co Mayo, 24 April 1951; educated local national school, St Gerald's, Castlebar, and St Patrick's College of Education, Dublin; worked as a primary school teacher; Fine Gael TD, 1975–; leader of Fine Gael, 2002–17; minister of state, 1986–87; government minister, 1994–97; Taoiseach, 2011–17. Though unassuming in manner, his determination to retain the leadership of his party saw him return in 2016 as the first-ever Fine Gael leader to form a government after two successive elections, even though the second government was a minority one dependent on at least passive independent and Fianna Fáil support.

Lemass, Seán. Born Dublin, 15 July 1899; educated Christian Brothers, Dublin; worked in his father's drapery shop; joined Irish Volunteers and participated in 1916 rising; active in IRA, 1919–23; anti-Treaty Sinn Féin and Fianna Fáil TD, 1924–69; government minister, 1932–48, 1951–54, 1957–59; Tánaiste, 1945–48, 1951–54, 1957–59; Taoiseach 1959–66; died 11 May 1971. Associated with the shift in Fianna Fáil, of which he was a founder member, from traditional nationalist policies to support for rapid economic development, especially in the 1960s, and with normalisation of relations with Britain and Northern Ireland.

Lenihan, Brian. Born Dundalk, Co Louth, 17 November 1930; educated Marist Brothers, Athlone, University College Dublin and King's Inns; worked as a barrister; Fianna Fáil TD, 1961–73 and 1977–95; lost his seat, 1973; Fianna Fáil senator, 1973–77; parliamentary secretary, 1961–64; government minister, 1964–73, 1977–81, 1982, 1987–90; Tánaiste, 1987–90; died 1 November 1995. An enormously popular politician, he was a casualty of an incident during the 1990 presidential election campaign in which he appeared to be giving contradictory versions of an event in 1982 involving an alleged attempt to bring undue pressure to bear on the President; though he sought to explain the incident away as arising from his medical condition (he was seriously ill at the time and under heavy medication), it is believed to have cost him the presidency and it led to his dismissal as Tánaiste.

Lynch, John (Jack). Born Cork, 15 August 1917; educated Christian Brothers, Cork, University College Cork, King's Inns; worked in civil service and later as a barrister; Fianna Fáil TD, 1948–81; parliamentary secretary, 1951–54; government minister, 1957–66; Taoiseach, 1966–73 and 1977–79; died 20 October 1999. His sporting background (in Gaelic football and hurling) and personable character won him immense popularity; his qualities as a leader were severely tested in the early years of the Northern Ireland troubles (1969–70), as his party sought to come to terms with the state's impotence in the face of attacks on nationalists in the North; in 1977, led his party to its greatest ever size in the Dáil and largest share of the vote since 1938, but ironically was forced to step down as leader two years later.

McAleese, Mary. Born Belfast, 27 June 1951, as **Mary Leneghan**; educated Falls Road convent secondary school, Belfast, and Queen's University Belfast; Reid Professor of Law at Trinity College Dublin, 1974–79 and 1981–87; journalist and television presenter, 1979–81; Director, Institute of Professional and Legal Studies, Queen's University Belfast, 1987–97, and Pro Vice-Chancellor, Queen's University Belfast, 1994–97; President of Ireland, 1997–2011. Though associated with Fianna Fáil, she was seen as an outsider within the party; during her election campaign her Northern origins and links were used against her, apparently counter-productively; despite a lukewarm relationship with the media at the beginning of her presidency, her popularity improved quickly following a number of very successful visits abroad; she played an active role as President, bringing a new prominence to the office.

McDowell, Michael. Born Dublin 1 May 1951; educated Gonzaga College, University College Dublin and King's Inns; practised as a barrister; initially associated with Fine Gael, but became a founder member of the Progressive Democrats in 1985; Progressive Democrat TD, 1987–89, 1992–97 and 2002–07, losing his seat in 1989, 1997 and 2007; Attorney General, 1999–2002; government minister, 2002–07; Tánaiste and leader of the Progressive Democrats, 2006–07; announced retirement from politics following his defeat in 2007, but came back as an independent senator in 2016. A forceful politician who does not hesitate to speak his mind, he was an energetic minister and leader.

MacEntee, Seán. Born Belfast, 23 August 1889; educated St Malachy's College, Belfast, and Belfast Municipal College of Technology; worked as a consulting electrical engineer and registered patent agent; active in Irish Volunteers; participated in the 1916 rising, sentenced to death but reprieved; active in IRA; Sinn Féin MP/TD, 1918–22; Fianna Fáil TD, 1927–69; government minister, 1932–48, 1951–54, 1957–65; Tánaiste, 1959–65; died 10 January 1984. Noted as a poet in his early life, later devoted himself fully to politics.

MacNeill, James. Born Glenarm, Co Antrim, 20 March 1869; educated Belvedere College, Dublin, and Cambridge University; worked in Indian civil service; on early retirement joined Sinn Féin; Irish High Commissioner in London, 1923–28; Governor-General, 1928–32; died 12 December 1938. Though with a less political past than his elder brother, Eoin (Professor of History at University College Dublin, leader of the Irish Volunteers and government minister, 1922–25), became fully immersed in political conflict in 1932 following the change of government; de Valera forced his resignation as Governor-General within a few months.

MacSharry, Ray. Born Sligo, 29 April 1938; educated locally and Summerhill College, Sligo; worked as a haulier, auctioneer and farm owner; Fianna Fáil TD, 1969–89; minister of state, 1977–79; government minister, 1979–81, 1982, 1987–89; Tánaiste, 1982. Rated very highly as Minister for Finance; went on to become an extremely successful EC commissioner for agriculture, 1989–92.

Norton, William. Born Dublin, 2 November 1900; educated locally; worked in the post office and as a trade union official; Labour TD, 1926–27, 1932–63; lost his seat, 1927; leader of the Labour Party, 1932–60; Tánaiste 1948–51, 1954–57; died 4 December 1963. Though he built up the support base of his party until 1943 and led it into government for the first time ever in 1948, in his later years he was more preoccupied with trade union affairs and with his own constituency than with the leadership of the party.

Ó Buachalla, Dónal (also known by the English form of his name, **Daniel Buckley**). Born Maynooth, Co Kildare, 3 February 1866; educated Belvedere College and Catholic University School, Dublin; owner of a shop in Maynooth; member of the Gaelic League and IRB; participated in the 1916 rising; Sinn Féin MP/TD, 1918–22; Fianna Fáil TD, 1927–32 (lost his seat in 1922 and again in 1932); Governor-General, 1932–36; died 31 October 1963. Achieved early prominence when prosecuted for painting his name in Irish on his cart; as Governor-General, avoided meeting the King; never left the state and resided in a house in Dún Laoghaire rather than in the Viceregal Lodge in the Phoenix Park.

Ó Ceallaigh, Seán T. (also known by the English form of his name, **Seán T. O'Kelly**). Born Dublin, 25 August 1882; educated Christian Brothers; active in Gaelic League, Celtic Literary Society, IRB and Sinn Féin; participated in the 1916 rising; Sinn Féin MP/TD, 1918–22; anti-Treaty Sinn Féin and Fianna Fáil TD, 1922–45; Ceann Comhairle of first Dáil; government minister, 1932–45; Vice-President of Executive Council, 1932–37; Tánaiste, 1937–45; President of Ireland, 1945–59; died 23 November 1966. Though personally popular, he was in effect 'pushed upstairs' to the presidency in 1945, making way for Seán Lemass, 17 years his junior, to take over as Tánaiste and heir apparent to de Valera.

Ó Dálaigh, Cearbhall. Born Bray, Co Wicklow, 12 February 1911; educated Christian Brothers and University College Dublin; called to the bar, 1944; active in Fianna Fáil; Attorney General, 1946–48, 1951–53; Supreme Court judge, 1953; Chief Justice, 1961; Irish member of European Court of Justice, 1973–4; President of Ireland, 1974–76, a post for which he was an unopposed nominee; died 21 March 1978. A lover of the Irish language; his resignation from the presidency was precipitated by a chain of events that began when the Minister for Defence, speaking at a military function, described him as 'a thundering disgrace' for referring an Emergency Powers Bill to the Supreme Court to test its constitutionality.

O'Higgins, Kevin. Born Stradbally, Co Laois, 7 June 1892; educated Clongowes Wood and University College Dublin; early member of Sinn Féin; Sinn Féin MP/TD, 1918–22; pro-Treaty Sinn Féin and Cumann na nGaedheal TD, 1922–27; government minister, 1922–27; Vice-President of the Executive Council, 1923–27; assassinated on 10 July 1927 while walking to mass by a group of anti-Treaty IRA members of the 1922–23 period who came upon him by accident. As Minister for Home Affairs during the civil war, was associated with the strong measures taken by the government to ensure victory, including the execution of many of the anti-Treaty side; played a central role in suppressing the 'army mutiny' in 1924.

O'Leary, Michael. Born Cork, 8 May 1936; educated Presentation College, Cork and University College Cork; worked as a trade union official; Labour TD, 1965–82; Fine Gael TD, 1982–87; leader of the Labour Party, 1981–82; government minister, 1973–77, 1981–82; Tánaiste, 1981–82; died 11 May 2006. Associated with his party's move to the left in the late 1960s and initially an opponent of coalition, his switch of allegiance to Fine Gael in 1982 was one of the more spectacular somersaults in Irish politics.

Reynolds, Albert. Born Rooskey, Co Roscommon, 1 November 1932; educated Summerhill College, Sligo; worked as director of his own petfood company; Fianna Fáil TD, 1977–2002; government minister, 1979–81, 1982, 1987–91; Taoiseach, 1992–94; died 21 August 2014. Though regarded as one of the more conservative members of his party, negotiated a coalition agreement with Labour following his defeat in the 1992 general election; noted as a risk-taker, he played a crucial role in paving the way for the Good Friday Agreement, 1998, by facilitating Sinn Féin's entry into negotiations.

Robinson, Mary. Born Ballina, Co Mayo, 21 May 1944, as **Mary Bourke**; educated Mount Anville, Paris, Trinity College Dublin and Harvard University; Reid Professor of Law, Trinity College Dublin; independent senator, 1969–76, 1985–89; Labour party senator, 1976–85; President of Ireland, 1990–97. Resigned the Labour whip in 1985 over the party's support for the Anglo–Irish Agreement, but was nominated and supported by Labour in her successful presidential election campaign in 1990; an extremely popular and assertive President, she played a subtle but significant political role; resigned shortly before the expiry of her term of office to assume the position of United Nations High Commissioner for Human Rights, a post she held until 2002.

Spring, Dick. Born Tralee, Co Kerry, 29 August 1950; educated Christian Brothers, Tralee, St Joseph's, Roscrea, Trinity College Dublin and King's Inns; worked as a barrister; Labour TD, 1981–2002; leader of the Labour Party, 1982–97; Tánaiste, 1982–87 and 1993–97. Enjoying an enormously high rating with the voters as leader of his party, his victory in 1992 placed him in a much stronger position than any previous Labour leader in hammering out a coalition deal and in giving Labour a more powerful position in cabinet than ever previously; resigned following the defeat of Adi Roche, the candidate sponsored by his party in the 1997 presidential election.

Varadkar, Leo. Born Dublin, 18 January 1979; educated King's Hospital school and Trinity College Dublin; qualified as a general practitioner; Fine Gael TD, 2007–; leader of Fine Gael, 2017–; government minister, 2011–17; Taoiseach, 2017–. The son of an Indian doctor and an Irish nurse, he was Ireland's first openly gay government minister, and his succession to the office of Taoiseach following Enda Kenny's resignation was seen as symbolising a new, more diverse and more multicultural Ireland.

Wilson, John. Born Kilcogy, Co Cavan, 8 July 1923; educated St Mel's College, Longford, University of London and University College Dublin; worked as a teacher and university lecturer; Fianna Fáil TD, 1973–92; government minister, 1977–81, 1982, 1987–92; Tánaiste, 1990–93; headed the southern Victims' Commission after the Good Friday Agreement, 1998–99; died 9 July 2007. One of the more popular elder statesmen within Fianna Fáil, he took over as Tánaiste when the politically wounded Brian Lenihan was dismissed during the 1990 presidential election campaign; a witty contributor in the Dáil, and a Latin scholar.

Appendix 6: Chronology of main political events

Note: The following lists a selection of the main events in Irish political history. For further information, see *A Chronology of Irish History to 1976: A Companion to Irish History Part 1*, Volume 8 of *A New History of Ireland* (Oxford: Clarendon Press, for the Royal Irish Academy, 1982); J. E. Doherty and D. J. Hickey, *A Chronology of Irish History since 1500* (Dublin: Gill and Macmillan, 1989); Jim O'Donnell (ed.), *Ireland: The Past Twenty Years: An Illustrated Chronology* (Dublin: Institute of Public Administration, 1986); and the annual chronology appearing in *Irish Political Studies,* beginning in Volume 8 (1993).

1169, May	Norman invasion of Ireland begins; most of Ireland subsequently subdued.
1264, June 18	First Irish parliament meets at Casteldermot, Co Kildare.
1541, June 18	King of England declared also to be King of Ireland.
1607, September 4	'Flight of the earls': Earl of Tyrone (Hugh O'Neill), Earl of Tyrconnell (Rory O'Donnell) and others sail from Co Donegal for continental Europe, symbolising the end of the Gaelic social and political order and the near-completion of the English conquest.
1608, July 19	Initiation of 'survey' of ownership of six counties of Ulster (followed by the 'plantation' of these counties with English and Scottish settlers).
1641, October 22	Beginning of rebellion of Catholics (who subsequently organised as the 'Confederation of Kilkenny', but whose rebellion had been largely crushed by Oliver Cromwell by 1650).
1688, November 5	William of Orange lands in Devon to become King of England (war between William and the deposed James II follows in Ireland, 1689–91, with the Irish defeat at the Siege of Derry, which ended on 31 July 1689, the Battle of the Boyne, 1 July 1690 [12 July, old calender] and the Treaty of Limerick, 3 October 1691, as its most noted events).
1798, May 23	Beginning of 'United Irish' rebellion, which was defeated within a few weeks.
1800, August 1	Act of Union passed; came into effect 1 January 1801.
1845, September 9	First report of arrival of potato blight, which led to famine in Ireland over the next four years, with deaths reaching a peak in 1847.
1848, July 29	'Battle of Widow McCormack's cabbage-patch': principal event in short-lived 'rebellion' of the Young Ireland movement.
1858, March 17	Foundation of Irish Republic Brotherhood (IRB) in Dublin (popularly known as the Fenians, it was the principal republican organisation until 1916, and continued to exist for some years after 1922).
1867, February 12	Beginning of Fenian rebellion; skirmishes took place over the following month.
1884, December 6	Representation of the People Act passed; this greatly extended the franchise, permitting the development of mass electoral politics.
1886, April 8	First Home Rule Bill introduced in parliament; defeated in the House of Commons on 8 June.
1893, February 13	Second Home Rule Bill introduced in parliament; passed in House of Commons on 2 September, defeated in House of Lords on 9 September.
1905, November 28	First use of term 'Sinn Féin' by radical nationalists; the Sinn Féin League was formed on 21 April 1907 through an amalgamation of existing organisations
1912, April 11	Third Home Rule Bill introduced in parliament; passed in House of Commons on 16 January 1913; defeated in House of Lords on 30 January 1913; passed in House of Commons a third time, thus overriding the Lords' veto, 25 May 1914; implementation suspended.
1913, January 31	Foundation of Ulster Volunteers.
1913, November 25	Foundation of Irish Volunteers.

1916, April 24	'Easter rising' (IRB-led rebellion in Dublin that ended on 29 April).
1918, December 14	General election, at which Sinn Féin won 73 of the 105 Irish seats, going on to call a meeting of the 'First Dáil' for 21 January 1919.
1919, January 21	Opening shots in War of Independence, which lasted until a truce on 9 July 1921.
1920, February 25	Government of Ireland Bill introduced in parliament; passed 23 December; House of Commons of Northern Ireland meets, 7 June 1921, giving effect to partition; Act largely ineffective in the south.
1921, December 6	Anglo–Irish Treaty signed by representatives of the Dáil and the British government; approved by Dáil, 7 January 1922; formal transfer of power to provisional government on 16 January 1922.
1922, June 16	General election for Dáil; pro-Treaty parties win substantial majority.
1922, June 28	Provisional government attack on Four Courts marks beginning of civil war, which lasts until 27 April 1923.
1922, October 25	Constitution of Irish Free State approved by the Dáil; approved by British parliament, 5 December 1922; in effect 6 December 1922.
1926, March 11	Split in Sinn Féin at *ard-fheis*; de Valera withdraws; Fianna Fáil founded on 16 May.
1927, July 10	Assassination of Kevin O'Higgins, Minister for Justice and for External Affairs; government responds with a legislative package that has the effect of forcing Fianna Fáil deputies to take their seats in the Dáil on 11 August.
1932, February 9	Formation of Army Comrades Association; renamed National Guard on 20 July 1933; commonly known as the Blueshirts.
1932, March 9	Fianna Fáil forms government after becoming largest party in general election.
1933, September 2	Foundation of United Ireland Party through merger of Cumann na nGaedheal, the National Centre Party and the National Guard; in later years, the party became known as Fine Gael.
1936, May 29	Senate abolished by constitutional amendment.
1936, December 11	Abdication of Edward VIII; constitutional amendment to remove remaining references to King and Governor-General; King allowed to retain external functions.
1937, July 1	Referendum approves new constitution; comes into effect 29 December.
1938, April 25	Anglo–Irish agreements covering 'treaty ports', financial relations and trade.
1948, February 4	Fianna Fáil loses power in general election; replaced 18 February by 'Inter-Party' government.
1948, September 7	Taoiseach John A. Costello announces that Ireland is to become a republic; Republic of Ireland Act passed, 21 December; in effect, 18 April 1949.
1958, November 11	Programme for Economic Expansion published; formed basis for shift from 'Sinn Féin' protectionist policies to more open policy on industrial development and trade.
1965, December 14	Anglo–Irish free trade agreement signed; in effect, 1 July 1966.
1968, October 15	Clash between civil rights marchers and police in Derry marks escalation of civil unrest in Northern Ireland.
1970, January 11	Split in Sinn Féin, with secession of supporters of 'Provisional' IRA (who had seceded from the 'Official' IRA in December 1969).
1970, May 6	Dismissal of Charles Haughey and Neil Blaney from government over alleged illegal importation of arms for supply to Northern Ireland; resignation of Kevin Boland.
1972, May 10	Referendum approves Ireland's membership of EEC; in effect, 1 January 1973.
1973, March 14	Coalition government takes office after 16 years of Fianna Fáil rule.
1979, March 13	Republic joins European monetary system; break in parity of Irish currency with sterling follows.
1983, May 30	First meeting of New Ireland Forum, representing Fianna Fáil, Fine Gael, Labour and the SDLP; reports on 2 May 1984 endorsing Irish unity as a solution to the Northern Ireland problem.

1985, November 15	Anglo–Irish Agreement on government of Northern Ireland signed.
1985, December 21	Foundation of Progressive Democrats; voted to wind themselves up, 8 November 2008.
1987, May 26	Referendum on Single European Act.
1989, July 12	Fianna Fáil enters coalition government for the first time, with the Progressive Democrats.
1992, June 18	Referendum endorses Maastricht Agreement on European Union.
1993, January 12	Fianna Fáil and Labour Party form coalition government, breaking the pattern of established interparty relations.
1993, December 15	Downing Street Declaration by British and Irish prime ministers lays down parameters for a Northern Ireland settlement; followed by IRA ceasefire, 31 August 1994.
1994, November 17	Resignation of Albert Reynolds as Taoiseach, following withdrawal of Labour from government; 'rainbow' coalition of Fine Gael, Labour and Democratic Left takes office under John Bruton without an election, 15 December.
1995, November 24	Referendum to permit divorce passed.
1998, April 10	Good Friday Agreement in Belfast; approved by referendum North and South, 22 May.
1998, December 12	Democratic Left agrees to merge with Labour Party; merger in effect, 24 January 1999.
1999, December 2	Good Friday Agreement comes into effect, with devolution to new Belfast institutions; first meetings of North/South Ministerial Council (December 13), British–Irish Council (December 17) and British–Irish Intergovernmental Conference (December 17) follow.
2001, June 7	Irish voters reject Nice Treaty on EU institutional reform; treaty passed in new referendum, 20 October 2002.
2002, January 1	Euro replaces Irish pound as unit of currency.
2005, July 28	IRA announces end of armed campaign; decommissioning commission announces completion of process of putting IRA arms beyond use, 26 September 2005.
2007, May 8	Northern Ireland executive headed by Ian Paisley and Martin McGuinness takes office.
2008, June 12	Irish voters reject Lisbon treaty on European integration; treaty passed in new referendum, 2 October 2009.
2008, September 29	Following sharp deterioration in Ireland's banks, government agrees to underwrite them; it later emerges that the scale of bank losses imposes an unsustainable burden on the state.
2010, November 28	Irish government accepts 'bailout programme' entailing support from, and supervision by, EU Commission, European Central Bank and International Monetary Fund ('troika'), compelling the state to undertake a range of reform measures.
2011, February 25	In context of growing public disillusion, Fianna Fáil slumps to third place in the general election (having consistently been the largest party in the Dáil since 1932); Fine Gael–Labour coalition later takes office.
2012, May 31	Irish voters accept European Stability Treaty in referendum.
2013, December 15	Ireland exits 'bailout programme'.
2015, May 22	Referendum to permit same-sex marriage passed.
2016, February 26	After indecisive election result, a minority Fine Gael government with support from independents and passive support from Fianna Fáil takes office.
2016, June 23	British electorate votes to leave the EU, posing fundamental challenge to Ireland.

Index